ETHICS IN THE WORKPLACE

McGraw-Hill Series in Management

Titles of related interest selected from the McGraw-Hill Series in Management:

ETHICS IN THE WORKPLACE

Edward J. Ottensmeyer

Clark University

Gerald D. McCarthy

Organizational Learning and Values Associates

The McGraw-Hill Companies, Inc.

New York   St. Louis   San Francisco   Auckland   Bogotá   Caracas
Lisbon   London   Madrid   Mexico City   Milan   Montreal   New Delhi
San Juan   Singapore   Sydney   Tokyo   Toronto

McGraw-Hill

A Division of The McGraw·Hill Companies

This book was set in Times Roman by Ruttle, Shaw & Wetherill, Inc.
The editor was Adam Knepper;
the production supervisor was Margaret Boylan.
The cover design and illustration were done by Christopher Brady.
Project supervision was done by Hockett Editorial Service.
Quebecor Printing/Fairfield was printer and binder.

ETHICS IN THE WORKPLACE

This book was printed on acid-free paper.
1 2 3 4 5 6 7 8 9 0   FGR   FGR   9 0 9 8 7 6

ISBN 0-07-048160-1

Library of Congress Catalog Card Number: 95-82014

ABOUT THE AUTHORS

EDWARD J. OTTENSMEYER is a professor in the Graduate School of Management at Clark University where he teaches courses for both MBA and undergraduate students in Business and Society and in Strategic Management. He received the Clark MBA Association Teaching Award in both 1992 and 1995. Prior to joining the Clark faculty in 1986, he taught at The Pennsylvania State University and the University of Denver. Before his doctoral studies, Professor Ottensmeyer worked for seven years in policy analysis and planning in the public sector. His research is published in *The Academy of Management Review, Policy Studies Review, Business Horizons,* and *The Journal of Business Ethics.* An active member of the Academy of Management, he has served as Coordinator of Caucuses, has chaired or co-chaired the research committee and the Faculty Development Workshop of the Social Issues Division, as well as the teaching committee of the Business Policy & Strategy Division. Ottensmeyer has also served as a consultant or advisor to both industrial and public-sector enterprises, including NASA, the U.S. Department of Commerce, Resources for Responsible Management, U.S. West Inc., and the State of Colorado High Technology Council. He received his B.A. from Marian College, and his MBA and Ph.D. from Indiana University.

GERALD D. MCCARTHY has taught Ethics and Religious Studies at a number of schools, including The University of Pennsylvania, Assumption College, The College of the Holy Cross, and Clark University. Among the topics about which he has written and taught are the development of personal values and relationship between religion and ethics. His research has been published by Horizons, The Irish Theological Quarterly, and Scholars Press. At the College of the Holy Cross he served as Acting Director of the Office of Special Studies and organized programs for faculty in areas of professional development and enrichment. Dr. McCarthy has taught in the M.B.A. program at Assumption College and is Managing Director of OLV Associates. He received his A.B. from St. Peter's College, his M.A. from the University of San Francisco, and his Ph.D. from the University of Pennsylvania. In 1983–1984 he did postdoctoral work as a Visiting Scholar at Harvard University.

CONTENTS IN BRIEF

Preface		xv
1.	Introduction to Ethical Reasoning	1
2.	"Sorry, You're Too Old." Senior Workers and Age Discrimination	24
3.	"Fair? To Whom?" Affirmative Action or Reverse Discrimination?	67
4.	"I'm Sick but . . ." Employees with AIDS and the Americans with Disabilities Act	135
5.	"This Makes Me Uncomfortable." Sexual Harassment and Sexual Politics	170
6.	"Whose Job Is It Anyway?" Employee Security and Employer Rights	243
7.	"Good Job—You're Fired." Downsizing and Its Impact	302
8.	"Whose Side Is Big Brother On?" Electronic Monitoring and Employee Privacy	358
9.	"Somebody's Going to Get Hurt." Whistleblowing: Employee Loyalty and Dissent	417
10.	"What's Mine? What's Yours?" Intellectual Property Rights	457

CONTENTS

Preface   xv

**1. INTRODUCTION TO
ETHICAL REASONING**   1

**2. "SORRY, YOU'RE TOO OLD."
SENIOR WORKERS AND
AGE DISCRIMINATION**   24

Introduction   24

Case: Russell Davidson and the
"Dinosaur" Problem   27

READINGS

2-1 The Plight of the Seasoned Worker
(Joseph F. McKenna/
Brian S. Moskal)   30

**2-2 Age Discrimination in Employment:
Case Law and Implications
for Employers**
(Paul N. Keaton/Beth Larson)   35

**2-3 New Developments in
Age Discrimination**
(Bimal Patel/Brian H. Kleiner)   42

2-4 Discrimination
(Janet Radcliffe Richards)   50

**2-5 Managing the Older Worker—Don't
Just Rinse Away the Gray**
(Robert J. Paul/
James B. Townsend)   60

**3. "FAIR? TO WHOM?" AFFIRMATIVE
ACTION OR REVERSE
DISCRIMINATION?**   67

Introduction   67

Case: Olivia Francis   70

READINGS

3-1 White, Male, and Worried
(Michele Galen/
Ann Therese Palmer)   73

**3-2 Affirmative Action: An Assessment
of Its Continuing Role in Employment
Discrimination Policy**
(Michael K. Braswell/ Gary A.
Moore/Stephen L. Poe)   77

**3-3 Affirmative Action: An
Ethical Evaluation**
(Bill Shaw)   103

3-4 The Case Against Affirmative Action
(Terry Eastland)   111

3-5 **From Affirmative Action to Affirming Diversity**
(R. Roosevelt Thomas, Jr.)　　122

4. **"I'M SICK BUT . . ." EMPLOYEES WITH AIDS AND THE AMERICANS WITH DISABILITIES ACT**　**135**
Introduction　　135
Case: Managing AIDS: How One Boss Struggled to Cope　　138

READINGS
4-1 **The Americans With Disabilities Act: An Employer's Perspective**
(C. Richard Scott/Diane M. Baun)　　145
4-2 **Managing AIDS in the Workplace**
(Michael D. Esposito/ Jeffrey E. Myers)　　150
4-3 **Ethical Challenges of HIV Infection in the Workplace**
(Arthur S. Leonard)　　161

5. **"THIS MAKES ME UNCOMFORT-ABLE." SEXUAL HARASSMENT AND SEXUAL POLITICS**　**170**
Introduction　　170
Case: Propmore Corporation　　173

READINGS
5-1 **Perspective Report: Sexual Harassment**
(Mary Ellen Hill Revolt)　　178
5-2 **Sexual Harassment: Rights and Responsibilities**
(Barbara A. Gutek)　　190
5-3 **Justice, Sexual Harassment, and the Reasonable Victim Standard**
(Deborah L. Wells/ Beverly J. Kracher)　　202
5-4 **The Legal, Ethical, and Social Implications of the "Reasonable Woman" Standard in Sexual Harassment Cases**
(Robert S. Adler/Ellen R. Peirce)　　211

5-5 **The Power and Reasons Behind Sexual Harassment: An Employer's Guide to Solutions**
(Donna M. Stringer/Helen Remick/ Jan Salisbury/Angela B. Ginorio)　　236

6. **"WHOSE JOB IS IT ANYWAY?" EMPLOYEE SECURITY AND EMPLOYER RIGHTS**　**243**
Introduction　　243
Case: The Daycare Dilemma　　246

READINGS
6-1 **The Management Termination Trap**
(Clinton O. Longenecker/ Frederick R. Post)　　250
6-2 **Toward a Middle Way in the Polarized Debate over Employment at Will**
(Michael J. Phillips)　　260
6-3 **Wrongful Termination: Balancing Employer and Employee Rights—A Summary with Recommendations**
(Robert J. Paul/ James B. Townsend)　　291

7. **"GOOD JOB—YOU'RE FIRED." DOWNSIZING AND ITS IMPACT**　**302**
Introduction　　302
Case: Layoffs at Alexo Plastics　　305

READINGS
7-1 **R.I.P.: The Good Corporation**
(Robert J. Samuelson)　　309
7-2 **Is the Good Corporation Dead?: A *BSR* Symposium**　　310
7-3 **Sign of the Times: Implementing Reductions in Force**
(Brian W. Bulger/ Carolyn Curtis Gessner)　　318
7-4 **Managing the Effects of Layoffs on Survivors**
(Joel Brockner)　　330
7-5 **Managing Layoffs in the '90s**
(Daniel C. Feldman/ Carrie R. Leana)　　345

8. **"WHOSE SIDE IS BIG BROTHER ON?" ELECTRONIC MONITORING AND EMPLOYEE PRIVACY**   **358**

Introduction   358

Case: Jim Boyd at
Redlow Corporation   361

READINGS

  8-1 **Big Brother or Friendly Coach? Computer Monitoring in the 21st Century**
(Kristen Bell DeTienne)   364

  8-2 **Electronic Monitoring of Employees: Issues & Guidelines**
(Ernest Kallman)   369

  8-3 **Electronic Monitoring of Employees and the Elusive "Right to Privacy"**
(Kenneth A. Jenero/
Lynne D. Mapes-Riordan)   375

  8-4 **Electronic Workplace Surveillance: Sweatshops and Fishbowls**
(Andrew Clement)   396

9. **"SOMEBODY'S GOING TO GET HURT." WHISTLEBLOWING: EMPLOYEE LOYALTY AND DISSENT**   **417**

Introduction   417

Case: Jill LeBlanc and the
Research Grant   420

READINGS

  9-1 **Whistleblowers: Who's the Real Bad Guy?**
(Barbara Ettorre)   424

  9-2 **Whistleblowing: Reaping the Benefits**
(Marcia P. Miceli/Janet P. Near)   430

  9-3 **The Whistleblowing Era: A Management Perspective**
(Kevin M. Smith/John M. Oseth)   437

  9-4 **Whistleblowing: Professionalism, Personal Life, and Shared Responsibility for Safety in Engineering**
(Mike W. Martin)   445

10. **"WHAT'S MINE? WHAT'S YOURS?" INTELLECTUAL PROPERTY RIGHTS**   **457**

Introduction   457

Case: Colin Rhodes at Jansen
Chemical, Inc.   460

READINGS

  10-1 **HR Takes Steps to Protect Trade Secrets**
(Kathleen Murray)   463

  10-2 **Comment: Toward a Clearer Standard of Protectable Information: Trade Secrets and the Employment Relationship**
(Miles J. Feldman)   472

  10-3 **Justifying Intellectual Property**
(Edwin C. Hettinger)   494

  10-4 **Trade Secrets and the Justification of Intellectual Property: A Comment on Hettinger**
(Lynn Sharp Paine)   508

PREFACE

Managers often need to decide among alternative courses of action, some—possibly all—of which cause harm to certain stakeholders. For example, in deciding whether to lay off a group of workers in the face of an economic downturn, a manager must balance the rights of shareholders/owners, who legitimately expect managers to protect and provide a reasonable return on their financial investments, and the workers themselves, who have both legal and ethical rights to fair treatment. How managers and firms deal with these dilemmas shapes their interaction with both internal and external stakeholders.

An effective and fair manager, we believe, will see such "right vs. right" decisions for what they are—multidimensional. That is, because situations can be viewed from a variety of perspectives, many of which are legitimate, managers are called upon to balance these perspectives in their decisions and actions. The ethical dimension comes into play for managers because their decisions and actions have an impact on people, on their rights and dignity, and on the distribution of benefits and harms to them.

Our approach to crafting this book reflects the multidimensional realities that managers face in the contemporary workplace. This collection of readings and cases is designed to provide new managers and managers in training with practical information on, and insight into, some of the ethical issues and dilemmas they are most likely to encounter in the early years of their business careers. Attention has been focused primarily on those issues that are often described as "internal" to a firm's operating environment, even though these may reflect "external" social or legal realities.

The introductory chapter presents several approaches to ethical decision-making and provides a brief theoretical background which can be
used in assessing the issues and dilemmas raised in subsequent chapters
and cases. Short introductions to the other chapters highlight some of the
ethical considerations for each topic as well as providing a brief overview
of that chapter's specific readings.

In each chapter readers can consider the insights of experts in ethics,
law and public policy, and management practice as they analyze and propose solutions for these difficult management problems. The selected
readings reflect our conviction that ethical insights are often found outside
academic ethics, and that ideas from law and management theory can improve, as well as be improved by, ethical reflection. The readings were
carefully chosen—from among hundreds reviewed—to provide students
and managers the highest quality of introductions available, within space
limitations imposed by such a wide-ranging book as this one.

For each topic we have either written or chosen a case that is designed
to give students a challenging decision-making opportunity. In addition,
all of the cases involve situations that junior managers or managers in
training should easily recognize. All require the analyst to develop solutions to very knotty problems.

There are many fine textbooks and anthologies in the fields of business
ethics, human resource management, and organizational behavior. Overall, we believe that this book integrates the insights of those different
fields, and that it reflects our view that the ethical dimension of a manager's decisions—even when that ethical dimension is not explicitly recognized by the manager—intersects with each of the other critical dimensions. Since real decisions are multidimensional, ethics are often involved
even when they are not openly discussed. By recognizing and emphasizing the linkage of ethics to other, more familiar, dimensions, we hope that
we have provided managers and future managers with a sound footing for
bringing ethics and ethical reasoning—explicitly and openly—into the
workplace. We believe that by doing so both the organization and its employees will be the better for it.

We would like to thank the following people for their invaluable assistance during the preparation of this book: Robert Ullrich, Dean of the
Clark University Graduate School of Management, for his encouragement
and financial support; Professor Gary Chaison and Dr. Jean Esposito, for
sharing their expertise in human resource management; Jan Perry and
Betty Naroian, for providing skillful secretarial support; Joy Durand and
Eileen McCarthy, for serving as research assistants and doing much of the
preliminary research (Joy also assisted in the preparation of several of the
case studies); Diane Adams, for doing the proofreading and copyediting
of the first chapter and chapter introductions; the library staffs at Clark
University and Assumption College, particularly Ed McDermott and

Priscilla Berthiaume, for handling our massive interlibrary loan requests and helping us to use other database search services; Dan Alpert, Lynn Richardson, and Adam Knepper of McGraw-Hill, for their encouragement, support, and patient guidance; the external reviewers who gave us countless insightful criticisms and suggestions: Diane Dodd-McCue, McIntire School, University of Virginia; David P. Schmidt, Fairfield University; John Steiner, California State University, Los Angeles; Dennis Wittmer, University of Denver; Kevin C. Wooten, University of Houston, Clear Lake; and, of course, the authors and publishers of the articles and cases who graciously allowed us to use their material.

Finally, we would like to thank our families and friends—especially Anne Donnellon, Jane Ottensmeyer, Diane Adams, Eileen McCarthy, and Michael McCarthy—for their ideas, support, encouragement, and occasional superhuman tolerance. They made the stresses seem endurable and the long hours of work worthwhile.

Edward J. Ottensmeyer
Gerald D. McCarthy

ETHICS IN THE WORKPLACE

Introduction to Ethical Reasoning

VALUES AND ETHICAL DECISION-MAKING

The questions, "Should we embrace ethical values or not?" and "How can we best distinguish right from wrong?," from the Bible to Socrates to the twentieth-century existentialists, have been both hauntingly unavoidable and apparently intractable. These questions are raised not only in our everyday personal lives, but in our professional work lives as well. Consider the following situation.

In November, 1992, Mark Jorgensen, the new manager of a real estate investment fund at Prudential Insurance Company of America, discovered that his boss, a friend who had previously managed the fund and who had hired him into his new job, had arranged for appraisers to inflate the values of certain real estate investments held by the fund. The impact of such an overvaluation was that (1) investors believed, albeit wrongly, that their past investments in the fund were increasing in value, and (2) Prudential's fees for managing the fund increased. When confronted with this information, Jorgensen's friend and boss said that he had taken this action to make the fund's weak performance look better to investors, who might oth-

erwise have moved their money to other investments. Jorgensen faced a difficult dilemma. If he chose to "blow the whistle" on this practice by telling senior managers, his friend's career at the firm might be damaged, his own career opportunities might be hurt, and, should the information become public, Prudential's reputation would surely be injured. If he chose not to act, he would be violating his obligation to the fund's many investors.[1]

What do you think Jorgensen should do?

Individual and Organizational Values

Our values are our most deeply held beliefs, attitudes, and felt reactions about what we think matters most in our lives. They are so important that they shape our lives and our characters. What we value can be (and often is) as concrete as our families or as abstract as an ideal of social justice.

Contemporary management thinkers and organizational theorists have pointed out that values play a similarly important role in organizational life, culture, and motivation. One of the best known observers of contemporary business practices is Tom Peters, who, with his associates Robert Waterman, Jr., and Nancy Austin, has written the best-selling *Excellence* volumes. All the "excellent" companies that they studied were "driven by coherent value systems," which were shaped, promoted, and protected by the organizations' leaders (Peters and Waterman, 1982, pp. 287). Each of the companies they analyze developed its own clearly defined organizational culture, characterized by a set of shared values that shapes its goals and drives its day-to-day operations. Jack Welch sees his transformation of General Electric in just this way.

JACK WELCH'S VALUES

Fortune reports that Jack Welch "has led General Electric through one of the most far-reaching programs of innovation in American business history." Ideas and values are at the heart of his revolution. "My job is to find great ideas, exaggerate them, and spread them like hell around the business with the speed of light." Welch expresses his vision for GE with energetic metaphors like "Stretch," "Boundarylessness," "The $60 billion family grocery business." The heart of his revolution is "boundarylessness"—demolishing hierarchical boundaries separating top management from the front lines and GE from its customers and suppliers. Ideas are GE's capital, and Welch knows that they can come from anywhere. His job is to "get everybody in the game" so that they can contribute theirs.

"Stretch," one of Welch's favorite terms, means "trying for huge gains while having no idea how to get there—but our people figure out ways to get there." As he sees things, it's the big dreams, not bureaucracies, that stretch an organization's imagination and muscle and drive its growth. Loyalty and trust provide the environment in which people can "stretch." "Loyalty means giving people an opportunity. Our job is to provide an atmosphere where they can reach their dreams, where they feel their growth is unlimited. . . . I think that trust in a company is a good word. You can trust that its values and yours are congruent. You can trust it to give you fair treatment."[2]

But the picture is more complex in two ways

than this brief outline indicates. First, values and ethics are not the same. Both persons and businesses can be shaped by and driven by **unethical** as well as ethical values. As we shall see, ethical values have dimensions of fairness, concern for the common good, and respect for persons that distinguish them from values in general. Second, to live is to make choices, and to make choices necessarily involves trade-offs, excluding some possibilities and leaving some values unrealized. In spite of what the advertisers tell us, in our mature moments we know that we really *can't* have it all. Mark Jorgensen, facing his dilemma at Prudential, found it impossible to be loyal to his friend and sponsor and to the many investors in the fund he managed.

As to the first point, consider the following analogy designed to illuminate the values that its author believes to be reflective of business life.

> Poker's own brand of ethics is different from the ethical ideals of civilized human relationships. The game calls for distrust of the other fellow. It ignores the claim of friendship. Cunning, deception and concealment of one's strength and intentions, not kindness and open-heartedness, are vital in poker. No one thinks any the worse of poker on that account. And no one should think any the worse of the game of business because its standards of right and wrong differ from the prevailing traditions of morality in our society. (Carr, 1968, p. 145)

Carr describes a fairly common set of values, but they are not ethical ones. How common they actually are (or ought to be) in business life is a matter of debate.

Respect and Honesty

The Golden Rule ("Do unto others as you would have them do unto you") assumes that normal human beings would like to be treated in certain ways, mainly with a respect that is worthy of their dignity as persons. Note that most of us become **indignant** when we are treated disrespectfully, when our dignity is offended. We suspect that someone who has either failed to develop a

TABLE 1-1

CHARACTERISTICS OF ADMIRED LEADERS

Characteristic	1993 U.S. respondents (percentage of people selecting)	1987 U.S. respondents (percentage of people selecting)
Honest	87	83
Forward-looking	71	62
Inspiring	68	58
Competent	58	67
Fair-minded	49	40
Supportive	46	32
Broad-minded	41	37
Intelligent	38	43
Straightforward	34	34
Courageous	33	27
Dependable	32	32
Cooperative	30	25
Imaginative	28	34
Caring	27	26
Mature	14	23
Determined	13	20
Ambitious	10	21
Loyal	10	11
Self-controlled	5	13
Independent	5	10

Source: James Kouzes and Barry Posner, *Credibility: How Leaders Gain and Lose It, Why People Demand It,* San Francisco: Jossey Bass, 1993, p. 14. Used with permission.

capacity to become indignant or has lost it suffers from a lack of self-worth or of self-esteem.

Much of the research on organizational behavior confirms this intuitive judgment. Perhaps the most explicit work has been done by James M. Kouzes and Barry Z. Posner (1993) in their study, *Credibility: How Leaders Gain and Lose It, Why People Demand It.*

Over the past decade, Kouzes and Posner have investigated the values that people want the leaders of their business organizations to hold. From their extensive research they concluded that honesty was absolutely essential to successful leadership. If people do not believe that a leader is ethical, truthful, and, in general, worthy of their trust, they will not follow him or her (p.

14). (For the results of their most complete survey see Table 1-1.)

Our desire to be led by men and women of honesty and integrity springs, we believe, from the same source as our desire to be treated with respect for our dignity. In another survey, Kouzes and Posner point out that the most admired leaders, the ones who keep to the highest ethical standards, are also the leaders who make their followers feel valued, who raise their sense of self-worth and self-esteem (pp. 30-33.). As we might expect, employees who feel valued and respected are more likely to be loyal, to work harder, and to display more initiative and commitment (pp. 31-33).

Empowerment and Employee Initiative

Over the past few decades, the success of business organizations has come to depend increasingly on the intelligence, responsibility, and involvement of their employees. Reflecting these developments, the concept of employee **empowerment** and the opportunities that empowerment offers both to organizations and their employees have received a lot of attention. Harold L. Sirkin (1993) offers some examples of empowerment that illustrate its connection to an organization's values.

What does empowerment mean? It means giving the most-junior employees the authority to make decisions about customer complaints, so that they can be handled on the spot rather than by working through bureaucratic channels. It means allowing subordinates to solve internal problems without asking permission, so that they are corrected before they have time to get worse. It means giving managers the luxury to think through longer-term issues and assist those empowered to learn and improve, rather than direct each worker's activities. (p. 58)

Obviously this can only work within an organizational culture governed by respect and trust rather than by fear. We cannot overemphasize the importance of the role that an organization's leaders and managers play in creating an environment that supports integrity and initiative. The crucial environmental element is "compassionate leadership," leadership characterized by "openness, receptivity to new ideas, honesty, caring, dignity, and respect for people." (Dobbs, p. 57) Without such leadership, employees will be unwilling (and unable) to experiment with new ways of doing things and to take the appropriate risks that are essential to harvesting empowerment's benefits.

Despite this, Kouzes and Posner also report that many workers are mistrustful of their managers and employers. More than half of the respondents to some surveys indicate that employees do not believe that management is "honest, upright, and ethical," and less than half in other surveys believe that their companies treat them "with dignity and respect." (pp. 34-36) How do we account for this?

Competition and Self-Interest

Most of the organizations people work for are economic entities, operating in competitive environments, whose goal is to make a profit. There is an inescapable emphasis on the bottom line and a corresponding emphasis on finding and utilizing the most efficient means of pursuing the organization's economic goals. There is nothing unethical about this. However, left unchecked, the quest for profit and the search for efficiency can easily become a quest for profit at any cost and expediency. The advantages of expediency are obvious—the results are tangible, measurable, and often quick and handsome.

Just as organizations maneuver within their external environments, employees maneuver within the internal environments of those organizations, and they are constantly reminded that not only is the competition fierce *between* organizations but *within* them as well (for status, salary, opportunities for advancement, and perks). In such a competitive world this cynical old poem often seems too true.

> It rains on the just and the unjust fella
> But more on the just
> Because the unjust's got the just's umbrella.

Rather than get rained on, we would just as soon grab the umbrella. Perhaps we would rather do good and fare well, but, faced with a choice, it may very well appear more reasonable to fare well. Ethical behavior often involves sacrifice; the costs of that sacrifice can sometimes seem prohibitive.

Ethical Values and the Ethical Point of View

Managers must ask themselves, "What sorts of values will guide our decisions?" Theorist Archie Carroll's (1987) analytical chart points out three different kinds of values which managers can use to approach business decisions (immoral, amoral, and moral) and five different areas to which they can be applied (ethical norms, motives, goals, law, and strategy). (See Figure 1-1.)

Business decisions can be approached from a variety of points of view—ethical, economic, legal, political, strategic, and so on; each has its characteristic concerns and values. What values and concerns characterize the ethical point of view? Two have had special prominence in the history of ethical thought: rationality and impartiality. Ideally, an ethical agent employs rational reflection to discover ethical truth and then rationally and impartially applies it. However, this traditional view has been challenged on a number of grounds.

Egoists reject the ideal of impartiality. In their view, some ethical philosophies emphasize impartiality and a commitment to the common good to a degree that the agent's own interests are overlooked. **Ethical egoism** dictates that people are not only *entitled* to take their own interests into account in making ethical decisions, they have a *duty* to choose the course of action that will maximize their long-term interests. This places the egoist in an unusual and, we believe, untenable position. Ordinarily when a person makes an ethical choice, he or she not only believes that others in the same circumstances *should* do the same thing, but also hopes that

FIGURE 1-1

Three approaches to management ethics.

Organizational characteristics	Immoral management	Amoral management	Moral management
Ethical norms	Management decisions, actions, and behavior imply a positive and active opposition to what is moral (ethical).	Management is neither moral nor immoral, but decisions lie outside the sphere to which moral judgments apply.	Management activity conforms to a standard of ethical, or right, behavior.
	Decisions are discordant with accepted ethical principles.	Management activity is outside or beyond the moral order of a particular code.	Conforms to accepted professional standards of conduct.
	An active negation of what is moral is implied.	May imply a lack of ethical perception and moral awareness.	Ethical leadership is commonplace on the part of management.
Motives	Selfish. Management cares only about its or the company's gains.	Well-intentioned but selfish in the sense that impact on others is not considered.	Good. Management wants to succeed but only within the confines of sound ethical precepts (fairness, justice, due process).
Goals	Profitability and organizational success at any price.	Profitability. Other goals are not considered.	Profitability within the confines of legal obedience and ethical standards.
Orientation toward law	Legal standards are barriers that management must overcome to accomplish what it wants.	Law is the ethical guide, preferably the letter of the law. The central question is what we can do legally.	Obedience toward letter and spirit of the law. Law is a minimal ethical behavior. Prefer to operate well above what law mandates.
Strategy	Exploit opportunities for corporate gain. Cut corners when it appears useful.	Give managers free rein. Personal ethics may apply but only if managers choose. Respond to legal mandates if caught and required to do so.	Live by sound ethical standards. Assume leadership position when ethical dilemmas arise. Enlightened self-interest.

(*Source:* Archie B. Carroll, "In Search of the Moral Manager," *Business Horizons,* March/April, 1987, p. 12. Used with permission.)

they will. However, while an egoist might believe that others *should* do the same thing (i.e., pursue their own self-interest), it would be self-defeating for the egoist to *want* them to do so unless their interests happened to coincide with his or hers. Paradoxes like this persuade egoism's critics that, although it is a value-oriented guide to decision-making, it is not a guide to *ethical* decision making.

To **relativists** and **subjectivists,** since ethical beliefs and standards vary from culture to culture and from individual to individual, they are

not "objective" or "rational" like the truths of mathematics or the empirical sciences. Because deep ethical disagreements persist and no absolute ethical truths have been discovered, they conclude that ethical beliefs and standards are like cultural artifacts or subjective preferences, unsuitable for objective assessment or rational criticism.

However, even if people do not believe that there are absolute ethical truths, many criticize or rule out some beliefs as unethical and evaluate some standards as more or less ethically valid than others. Although ethical beliefs and standards cannot be "proven" by rigorous deductive arguments as in mathematics or substantiated by carefully controlled experiments as in the empirical sciences, they are objective in the sense that they can be defended and criticized by arguments that can be rationally appraised; they can also be compared to alternative beliefs and standards in terms of their consistency and adequacy to ethical experience. Both cultures and individuals do so not only with the beliefs and standards of others but also with their own. Such a capacity for criticism, particularly self-criticism, indicates a dimension of objectivity in ethical thought that subjectivists and relativists overlook.

Recent discussions in ethics and other disciplines have been enriched by the contributions of **feminist** scholars who draw attention to features of women's ethical experience which have been, they claim, neglected by ethicists and social scientists (Gilligan, 1982; Held, 1992). In their view, the virtues of an "ethic of care" (empathy, compassion, and a concern for preserving relationships) are as ethically significant, if not more so, than the hallmarks of the traditional "ethic of justice" (rationality and impartiality). Although there is a rough consensus about the features of these ethical styles, there is also considerable debate among feminist philosophers about their relationship to each other. Are they mutually exclusive or complementary? Should one be subordinate to the other (Held, 1995, p. 40)? In a similar vein, some researchers (e.g., Rosener, 1990; Loden, 1995) find a clear difference between the values and leadership styles with which men and women approach business decisions; others (e.g., Eagly and Johnson, 1990; Powell, 1993) do not. Many recommend an androgynous style of values and leadership, one that combines elements of both (e.g., Sargent, 1983).

We agree that feminist thought has uncovered dimensions of ethical experience that have been traditionally overlooked and that the traditional description of the ethical point of view needs to be revised in light of its insights. We also believe that the "ethic of justice" has an important place. Empathy and rationality (or objectivity) need not be viewed as opposites. In a world of diverse views, a rational person must be able to empathize with the perspectives and concerns of people who differ from her or him and evaluate a situation from different points of view. Rationality, particularly in ethics, requires dialogue, and empathy is a necessary condition for successful dialogue. Ethical decisions demand rationality as well as empathy since decision-makers are often required to evaluate objectively and fairly the interests of different persons with whom they empathize equally.

The situation is similar with regard to compassion and impartiality. Impartiality without compassion is cold, but, as any parent who has weighed the conflicting demands of several children knows, compassion *for* each often requires an impartial balancing of the needs and wants *of* each.

Therefore, it seems that objectivity and impartiality, suitably qualified by empathy and compassion, are characteristic concerns of the ethical point of view and shape the values by which ethical decisions are made.

Even managers who commit themselves to using ethical values as the baseline for their decisions may be uncertain about what is ethically the most adequate course of action. Reasonable, fair, and compassionate men and women will honestly disagree not only about the best course of action to take but also about which situations call for ethical consideration.

When Do Situations Have an Ethical Dimension?

The line between situations that legitimately evoke an ethical concern and those that do not is not always clear, and it is important to be able to distinguish between them. People who fail to make the appropriate distinctions (e.g., people who feel guilty *whenever* they assert themselves) often suffer from guilt and shame to a neurotic degree. Consequently, their lives are diminished and unhappy. Others, often more dangerous to others than to themselves, suffer from ethical blindness. They perform what appear to be blatantly immoral actions and yet experience no regret, remorse, or shame. For example, someone who denies that there is any ethical dimension to business decisions will be able to fire a competent and loyal employee without taking any ethical considerations into account or experiencing any ethical regret.

The following characteristics, in our view, mark off those situations in which ethical considerations ought to play an important role. Such a situation involves

- The creation, prevention, or distribution of harms or benefits
- That are of significant importance to human beings
- Who have a right to have their interests taken into account in the creation, prevention, or distribution of those harms or benefits.

Several elements of this description require comment.

1. By "benefits" we simply mean any state of affairs that either is part of or contributes to a person's well-being. By "harms" we mean any state of affairs that diminishes, either directly or indirectly, a person's well-being.
2. Human beings should, in general and unless justified, avoid creating harms. "Do no harm!" is a bedrock ethical principle. We don't necessarily have to *do* anything to obey it. But the prevention of harms and the creation of benefits are different; they require that something be done. As we shall see when we discuss utilitarianism, how far our positive responsibilities extend is a matter of some debate.
3. "Significant importance" means that we must distinguish situations that legitimately evoke ethical concern from those that are

too trivial to do so. For example, the questions of who gets what parking space in the company lot or who gets the corner office are not usually ethical ones. However, a promotion, a layoff, privacy, productivity, safety, and so on are of "significant importance" to merit ethical concern since they involve central human goods (i.e., any good that a reasonable human being would want, such as happiness, pleasure, or freedom).

4. The notion of "a right" is crucial here. Suppose that you are considering buying one of two houses. Both owners are desperate to sell because each has already bought another house and fears that his or her investment will be lost if the original house is not sold. Even though the decision you will make involves the creation and distribution of benefits and harms of significant importance to the homeowners involved, this situation is not one that legitimately evokes ethical concern since neither of the owners *has a right* to have you buy his or her house and you have no *responsibility* to purchase anything at all.

ETHICAL RULES, ETHICAL PRINCIPLES, AND ETHICAL DECISIONS

Some Common Moral Rules

To the best of our knowledge, anthropologists have yet to discover a society that has no ethical rules or code whatsoever, however informal. In our view, this is no accident, nor is it a matter of simple historical fact; a society that lacked rules governing sexual behavior, the protection and disposition of property, the exercise of authority, the rearing of the young, the settling of disputes, appropriate behavior towards common enemies, and so on would be one whose members would be at such odds among themselves that it would be unlikely to endure.

One of the major tasks that any society must perform is to transmit its ethical code, often with modifications, across the generations to its young. The family, various educational institutions and practices, religious teachers and scriptures, and age and occupational associations are among the myriad of institutions entrusted with this job. We learn this common morality in a number of ways: we study rules; we are told stories that illustrate certain values, virtues, and vices; we observe other people's behavior; we are rewarded and punished for certain actions; and so on. Our common morality is, more often than not, simply taken for granted.

Given the social necessity of a common morality, we suspect that most people have not only been exposed to, but have also been taught, a wide variety of ethical rules and ideals. Although one does not have to read extensively or deeply in the newspapers to discover that ours is a society with deep ethical disagreements (e.g., abortion, the death penalty, appropriate sexual behavior, the rights and responsibilities of poor people, etc.), there is also much ethical agreement. Most people believe that they should tend to the welfare of their young, keep their word, be loyal to their friends, repay their debts, refrain from harming innocent people, and so on. The common morality is intended to be a guide to decision-making in these and other important matters.

The philosopher Bernard Gert (1988) has described and analyzed ethical rules in detail and has proposed the following ten as embodying the core of the common morality (pp. 96-159).

1. Don't kill.
2. Don't cause pain.
3. Don't disable.
4. Don't deprive of freedom.
5. Don't deprive of pleasure.
6. Don't deceive.
7. Keep your promise.
8. Don't cheat.
9. Obey the law.
10. Do your duty.

Corresponding to these common rules are common entitlements or rights, for example, the right to life, to be free from hurt, to freedom, to knowledge, to be treated fairly, and so on.

Many corporations have drawn upon common moral rules in formulating their codes of ethics. McDonnell Douglas is one example.

MCDONNELL DOUGLAS CODE OF ETHICS

Integrity and ethics exist in the individual or they do not exist at all. They must be upheld by individuals or they are not upheld at all. In order for integrity and ethics to be characteristics of McDonnell Douglas, we who make up the Corporation must strive to be:

- Honest and trustworthy in all our relationships;
- Reliable in carrying out assignments and responsibilities;
- Truthful and accurate in what we say and write;
- Cooperative and constructive in all work undertaken;
- Fair and considerate in our treatment of fellow employees, customers, and all other persons;
- Law-abiding in all our activities;
- Committed to accomplishing all tasks in a superior way;
- Economical in utilizing company resources;
- Dedicated in service to our company and to improvement of the quality of life in the world in which we live.

Integrity and high standards of ethics require hard work, courage, and difficult choices. Consultation among employees, top management, and the Board of Directors will sometimes be necessary to determine a proper course of action. Integrity and ethics may sometimes require us to forgo business opportunities. In the long run, however, we will be better served by doing what is right than what is expedient.[3]

Although rules are intended to be obeyed, not necessarily analyzed, there is sincere disagreement over the range of situations to which any given rule might apply. For example, while a pacifist will argue that obedience to Rule #1 ought to be absolute, others might believe that it can legitimately be violated in self-defense or in a just war. Perhaps more importantly, it is extremely unlikely that anyone would be able to follow all these rules all the time because situations are common in which different rules point us in different directions. Dentists, in the course of their work, frequently violate Rule #2. A judge, observing Rule #9, may well violate Rule #4. A refusal to violate Rule #6 may occasion a violation of Rule #2. Given the genuine possibility of conflict among different rules, no ethical rule appears absolute.

This tension is exacerbated in complex social systems such as modern workplaces. Various stakeholders, such as stockholders, employees, customers, suppliers, and the general public, are among the many groups of people who have the right to have their interests taken into account in decisions that affect them. But, as any decision-maker knows, often to his or her dismay, the interests of different persons or groups often conflict, and duty often seems to pull in opposite directions. The common morality will not always help us sort out these resulting dilemmas and guide us in our actions. For that, critical, reflective, systematic thinking is required.

Ethical Principles and Ethical Rules

Before we proceed to a discussion of philosophical theories, we need to clarify briefly the difference between an ethical rule and an ethical principle, which is basically one of generality and scope. An ethical principle embraces far more sorts of situations and actions than an ethical rule. Ethical rules typically follow from ethical principles; that is, the ethical principle, together with some relevant factual information, will serve to justify the ethical rule.

Consider Gert's first three ethical rules: Don't kill; Don't cause pain; Don't disable. Now consider an ethical principle: Don't cause harm. Notice that the principle is far wider in scope

than either of the three rules taken individually. In fact, it is wider in scope than the three taken together, since it also covers (among others) Rule #4: Don't deprive of freedom.

If our ethics are to guide our lives, we can easily see how powerful the role of ethical principles can be. Their generality allows them to be applied to novel situations that the more specific rules might not be able to treat. Thus, if in the future we discover that some novel state of affairs, which does not fall under any current ethical rule, causes harm, we can frame a new rule prohibiting that course of action.

Furthermore, if we refine the ethical principle a bit, we can see how it might be of even more use. Let it now read: If in any set of circumstances appropriate for ethical concern a person has several alternative possible courses of action, he or she should choose that course of action which causes the least amount of harm. Suppose now that someone finds himself or herself in a situation where two or more of the rules of the common morality require incompatible courses of action (e.g., not deceiving someone would cause him or her more pain than an act of deception). The ethical principle would then, ideally, advise which rule to follow.

Philosophers who have considered life's ethical questions have been dissatisfied with the common morality's lack of tidiness and simplicity and have hoped to discover *one* underlying ethical principle that would enable them to formulate new ethical rules appropriate to novel situations, to determine when breaking one of the common morality's traditional rules is justified, and to weigh the claims of different ethical rules when they conflict. Though no proposal has won (or seems likely to win) general acceptance, these general principles can help us to decide among the sometimes conflicting demands of the common morality.

Let us return for a minute to our description of a situation that legitimately evokes ethical concern as one that involves the creation, prevention, or distribution of harms or benefits that are of significant importance to human beings, who have a right to have their interests taken into account. The notion of harms and benefits is central to the philosophy of utilitarianism, to which we now turn our attention.

Utilitarianism: The Creation and Prevention of Harms and Benefits

"What good will it do?" and "What harm will it do?" are natural questions to ask when we are contemplating any course of action. We are, after all, usually concerned about the consequences of our actions—to ourselves, to the people we care about, to our communities, and, perhaps, to the world generally. The British philosophers and social reformers Jeremy Bentham (1748-1832) and John Stuart Mill (1806-1873) incorporated these questions into one of the modern age's most influential ethical theories, called variously "consequentialism" or "utilitarianism."

To someone who is morally perplexed about the right course of action to pursue in a given situation, utilitarians offer the following straightforward and easily stated principle as guidance: In any set of circumstances the ethically right course of action is the one that is most expected to produce the greatest **net good** or to prevent the greatest **net harm.** Utilitarianism's central concepts are: good, net, and expected.

1. **Good** (or **Harm**). The advice that utilitarians offer is not of much help until it specifies the sort of good or goods that are to be produced (or harms to be prevented). "Do good and avoid evil" doesn't tell us much. In Bentham's analysis, the *one* good that could serve as the criterion for an ethically correct course of action was pleasure; in Mill's, it was happiness. Since then, philosophers and psychologists have vigorously debated whether the variety of human goods (for example, knowledge, love, freedom, etc.) can be reduced to one (for example, happiness). If they cannot, and if in a given set of circumstances there are alternative goods (for example, free speech and privacy) that are in competition with each other, the utilitarian principle may well point us in different directions and recommend incompatible courses of action, thus depriving us of the very benefit it was intended to provide.

2. **Net.** Almost every choice that we make, ethical or otherwise, involves weighing the benefits and costs of different courses of action and making trade-offs. Utilitarianism recommends that we follow the course of action most likely to produce the greatest **net** good (or prevent the greatest **net** harm). Suppose, for example, that course of action A is likely to produce 20 units of good, while B is likely to produce 13. A utilitarian would recommend A as the ethically correct course of action. However, in addition to producing 20 units of good, perhaps A is also likely to produce 14 units of harm, whereas B is likely to produce only 2 units of harm. Thus A is likely to produce 6 units of net good and B 11. Taking **net** good into account, *B* is now ethically preferable.

3. **Expected.** We have been careful to say that a utilitarian will recommend that course of action which is most *likely* to produce the greatest net good (or prevent the greatest net harm). Because no one can predict the future, we must often make important personal and ethical decisions based on imperfect information. Contrary to our best intentions, events sometimes turn out badly. If we had no way of knowing that events would turn out that way, then we are not usually held responsible. If, however, we knew or should have known (given the information that was available to us) of the unfortunate consequences, then we are blameworthy. Utilitarians therefore insist that our decisions be based upon the net good that a reasonable person (i.e., one who has taken sufficient care in gathering and weighing information relevant to the circumstances under consideration) might **expect.**

To return to our example: Since B promises more net good than A, it is ethically preferable from a utilitarian point of view. However, if it is *very likely* that A will produce the net good it

TABLE 1-2

THE UTILITARIAN METHOD OF REASONING

1. Accurately state the action to be evaluated.

2. Identify all those who are directly and indirectly affected by it.

3. Specify all the pertinent good and bad consequences of the action for all those directly affected—as far into the future as appears appropriate—and imaginatively consider various possible outcomes and the likelihood of their occurrence.

4. Weigh the total good results (the degree of happiness produced) against the total bad results, considering such matters as the quantity and duration of the harms and benefits involved.

5. Carry out a similar analysis, if necessary, for those indirectly affected, and for society as a whole.

6. Sum up all the good and bad consequences. If the action produces more good than bad, the action is morally right; if it produces more bad than good, it is morally wrong.

7. Consider, imaginatively, whether there are various alternatives other than simply performing or not performing the action and carry out a similar analysis for each of the other alternate actions.

8. Compare the results of the various actions. The action that produces the **most good** (or the least bad, if none produces more good than bad) among those available is the morally proper thing to do.

Source: Ronald M. Green, *The Ethical Manager,* New York: Macmillan, 1994, p. 75. Used with permission.

promises and it is *much less likely* that B will do so, then A becomes the ethically correct course of action. (For a step-by-step summary of utilitarian reasoning see Table 1-2.)

Utilitarianism tries to be impartial, humane, and rational. **Impartial,** since it requires that an ethically correct course of action is one that will most likely produce the maximum net good, taking into *equal* account the well-being of *all* involved parties. **Humane,** because it appeals to our deepest human sympathies, indeed to our capacity for the "love of neighbor" demanded by most of the world's great religions, and because it reminds us that the point of ethics is not to follow rules for the sake of tradition or custom, but rather for the enrichment of human life, or at least the diminishment of human suffering. And **rational,** because it promises a clear and consistent method for making ethical decisions, particularly in those situations where the common morality leaves us with conflicting ethical rules. Utilitarianism's rationality and its weighing of the costs and benefits of alternative courses of action often make it attractive to business decision-makers who are familiar with and comfortable with that style of decision-making.

Criticisms of Utilitarianism

Nonetheless critics have argued that utilitarianism is seriously deficient as a method of critical ethical thinking.

The first criticism is that, in spite of its claims, utilitarianism cannot identify *one* good that is both necessary and sufficient for human flourishing. Human flourishing seems to be marked by a *variety* of goods, and reasonable, ethical people may well disagree in their assessment of which goods are more important. Where one person might value liberty more than life itself, another, equally reasonable, person might make the opposite judgment. Thus, utilitarianism is not as complete an ethical guide as it seems at first glance.

A second criticism is that utilitarianism demands too much. A glance at Bernard Gert's rules listed above reveals that the typical ethical rules of ordinary life require us to *refrain* from acting in certain ways, not that we *do* anything.

Utilitarianism, on the other hand, demands that our actions aim at producing the greatest likely net good. Not only must we avoid harming people, we are duty-bound to help them, putting the interests of all parties on a par with our own. For example, a promising young medical researcher whose work holds out the possibility of making a significant contribution to overcoming heart disease suffers from both kidney disease and deteriorating eyesight. According to the utilitarian calculus, a person in excellent health would be *duty-bound* to offer one kidney and one eye to the researcher. He or she, of course, would suffer some loss, but the cost would be small in comparison to the direct benefits to the researcher and the indirect benefits to humanity that could be reasonably expected. But surely this demands too much.

On the other hand, the familiar story of the Good Samaritan severely and justifiably criticizes the two officials who did not stop to help the victim whom bandits left to die. It seems that the demand to avoid evil, if taken as the exclusive ethical demand, requires too little. Perhaps utilitarians have a point after all.

This is not an abstract issue. Social philosophers, legislators, business executives, and ethicists have long discussed the degree to which businesses and corporations have an ethical responsibility to help solve social problems that they did not create. For example, presuming that it is not responsible for creating the problem of hard-core poverty among certain racial and ethnic groups, is it a corporation's ethical duty to try to help relieve the problem through affirmative action programs and other means? Do businesses have an ethical (as opposed to a public relations) responsibility to give to charity? The following extract explores one company's dilemma.

SOCIAL RESPONSIBILITY AND LAYOFFS AT STRIDE RITE

Stride Rite is a corporation with a conscience. Its many good deeds include contributing 5% of its pre-tax profit to a foundation that funds social pro-grams, providing scholarships for disadvantaged youths, and running on-site day- and elder-care facilities. A founding member of Businesses for Social Responsibility, the company has been acclaimed for its community involvement and sense of ethical responsibility.

Yet numbers matter too. As *The Wall Street Journal* points out, "In the past decade, Stride Rite has prospered partly by closing 15 factories, mostly in the Northeast and several in depressed areas and moving most of its production to various low-cost Asian countries." These closings have resulted in layoffs of 3,500 workers. Is this an example of the sort of corporate indifference that business's critics deplore? Or is it a necessary response to economic reality?

Stride Rite acknowledges the criticism but denies that it is acting in a socially irresponsible way. Its management points out that the company must balance the interests of two masters—society and its shareholders. Failing to remain competitive would only result in less money for social programs and perhaps in the failure of the company. Former chairman Arnold Hiatt, well known for his liberal politics and social conscience, expresses the dilemma: "To the extent that you can stay in the city, I think you have to. But if it's at the expense of your business, then you can't forget that your primary responsibility is to your shareholders." Understandably, some former employees see it differently. The *Journal* reports the story of an immigrant worker laid off from Stride Rite's Roxbury, Massachusetts, plant. He owns a home there and has been renting a room to an elderly man and his mentally disabled son. The father died recently, but the immigrant is unwilling to ask the son to leave. "If I did," he explained, "I would be doing to him what my company did to me."[4]

In considering and evaluating courses of action it is possible to distinguish three ethical principles.

1. Do not inflict any ethically unjustifiable harms on anyone.
2. Prevent as much harm as you can.
3. Create as much good as you can.

We believe that the first of these principles is relatively uncontroversial; the third, classically utilitarian, is open to the sort of objection that we proposed. The second is difficult to evaluate. It is the "as you can" clause that raises the problem. Recall the story of the Good Samaritan. What really made the officials' behavior objectionable were the severity of the man's condition and the fact that no risk was involved; it would not have demanded very much of them to help him. We would praise them if they had put their lives at risk, but we would not criticize them for failing to do so.

John Simon, Charles Powers, and Jon Gunnemann (1993) argue that a person or a business has a *positive* responsibility to help prevent (or remedy) a harm for which he, she, or it is not ethically responsible, and they recommend the following guidelines to define that responsibility (pp. 63-65).

1. The greater the need, the greater the responsibility to help. It is the urgent and critical situation of the robbers' victim that gives the Good Samaritan story its ethical punch. Similarly, a whistleblower might be obliged to risk his or her career and livelihood to prevent a great catastrophe, but not to prevent something less threatening.
2. Persons and businesses will generally have a greater responsibility to those close at hand than to those far away.
3. No person or no business has a responsibility to do what he, she, or it cannot do or cannot do without causing a comparable harm to himself, herself, or itself. A person who swims very poorly need not put his or her life at risk to save a drowning child. A corporation need not bankrupt itself trying to avoid layoffs (though sound ethics demand that this step, because of the harms it will inflict, be taken only under severe circumstances).
4. The ethical responsibility to prevent (or remedy) harm increases with the likelihood that no one else can or will help. To the extent that a person, for example a potential whistleblower, knows (or should know) that he or she is the last resort to prevent a significant harm, then his or her responsibility in that situation is increased to that extent.

These four principles may assist us in refining utilitarianism's insistence on "doing good" in such a way that it can meet the objection of being too demanding.

The third criticism of utilitarianism is that its insistence on choosing impartially a course of action that will maximize net good for **everyone** involved overlooks the fact that at times decision-makers have special ties and responsibilities to certain people. A parent, for example, has special ties and duties to his or her children that ought to override utilitarian calculations. To the degree that utilitarianism recommends discounting those ties, it is inadequate ethical advice.

The final objection is that utilitarianism permits far more instances of unethical behavior than a sound ethical principle and method of reasoning should. For example, it would not be hard to produce a utilitarian justification for enslaving perhaps 5 percent of a given population. To be sure, the harm inflicted on that 5 percent would probably be great. But the benefits accumulated by the remaining 95 percent—increased leisure, less drudgery in daily life, greater scientific and artistic development, more time for civic involvement, and so on—would create more net happiness (or some other human good), even with the harms to the slaves subtracted, than would be created in a society without slaves. But, in this instance, utilitarianism justifies what is ethically repugnant because it overlooks crucial features of ethical decision-making.

Consider for a moment the three elements that a situation must have to invoke legitimate ethical concern—the production of humanly significant benefits and harms, the distribution of those benefits and harms, and the entitlements or rights that people possess in that situation. Utilitarianism focuses on the first element and discounts, if not ignores, the other two. If an *unjust* distribution of happiness or some other human good ignores or actively violates the *rights* of some individuals, and by doing so increases the expectable net good, then utilitarians will recommend it as the ethically preferable course of action. This, utilitarianism's critics argue, is ethically absurd. Would a plant manager be justified in permitting a sexually hostile work environment because the pleasure of some people who work there would outweigh the discomfort and psychological pain of some other employees? Was Ford's assessment of the Pinto gas tank design, described below, ethically acceptable?

UTILITARIANISM GONE AWRY?

In the early 1970s, the Ford Motor Company introduced a new subcompact—the Pinto—to the American public. Lee Iacocca, then Ford's president, had initiated the Pinto's development in order to better compete with the smaller cars manufactured by both foreign and domestic rivals. The design of the Pinto called for the placement of the gas tank behind the rear axle, with less than a one-foot gap between the rear axle and the rear bumper. Safety reports generated during the Pinto's development concluded that rear-end collisions could cause fuel spillage from a ruptured gas tank, with the potential for fire. Design improvements to reduce this safety risk were estimated at $11 per car. However, the company, relying in part on an analysis of societal benefits and costs of making these improvements, produced the Pinto with the behind-the-axle placement. Ford estimated that, assuming 180 burn deaths and 180 serious burn injuries, the benefits of improving the safety of the gas tank (and thus of reducing the number of deaths and injuries) would be just over $49 million, while the costs of making the change would equal $137 million. In its calculations, the firm used a value of $200,000 per burn death and $67,000 per serious burn injury.[5]

And yet, of course, if we recall our distinction between creating benefits and preventing harms, we can imagine times when preventing a significant harm might justify violating someone's rights. Even though he believed in the rights of noncombatants in a war, President Truman also believed that the great harm caused to the noncombatant populations of Hiroshima and Nagasaki by the dropping of the atomic bombs

was justified because it averted the far greater loss of life that a full invasion of Japan would have caused. (We are not arguing that Truman was necessarily ethically correct, just that his position is ethically defensible.)

Perhaps we can protect utilitarianism from its critics by insisting that the violation of the rights of innocent people (while compensating those harmed as adequately as possible) can be ethically justified in a genuine emergency, that is, in circumstances when the amount of harm to be prevented is *significantly* greater than the harm to be caused and when a reasonable, ethical person, exercising due care, would be unable to find another, less harmful way of achieving the same end.

These criticisms make clear that it would be wrong to take utilitarianism as the *sole* criterion when making ethical choices. However, we would be equally mistaken if we failed to include it, complemented and qualified by other considerations, as *one* element in our strategy for critical ethical thinking.

Human Rights: Taking an Individual's Interests into Account

Unfortunately, respect for persons and their rights is not universal. Consider the following account of Continental Can's treatment of its employees.

In 1990, after many years of legal wrangling, Continental Can and thousands of its former employees reached a $415 million settlement of a lawsuit brought by the former employees who alleged that the firm devised a specialized information system, termed the liability avoidance plan, to identify and to lay off factory workers who were about to become eligible for pension benefits, and for whom the firm would have to show an unfunded pension liability in its financial records. Speaking on ABC Televison's "20/20" program, after the lawsuit had been settled, one worker stated that he was laid off one day before becoming eligible for pension benefits. In his opinion siding with the laid-off workers, Federal Judge Sarokin wrote: "For a corporation of this magnitude to engage in a complex, secret, and deliberate scheme to deny its workers bargained-for pension benefits raises questions of corporate morality, ethics, and decency which far transcend the legal issues posed by this matter. . . . The plan was shrouded in secrecy and executed company-wide at the specific direction of the highest levels of corporate management. . . . The documents are more than a smoking gun; they are a fusillade."[6]

The employees' rights were clearly violated. But what are rights and why are they so important?

The German philosopher Immanuel Kant (1724-1804) believed that human beings are rational, free agents and, as such, are capable of rationally choosing and freely implementing their own goals. Kant insisted on respect for the value of autonomy and human dignity as a guiding principle of this philosophy. "Act in such a way that you always treat humanity, whether in your own person or in the person of any other, never simply as a means, but always at the same time as an end" (trans. 1964, p. 96).

One way in which we express and implement our respect for a person's autonomy (and for the person) is by acknowledging his or her **rights.** When we say that a person has a moral (or legal) right in a given situation, we mean that it is ethically (or legally) permissible for him or her either to act in a certain way or to insist that he or she be treated in a certain way without obtaining anyone's permission to do so. (For a partial list of what some people view as fundamental human rights, see Table 1-3.)

Drawing some basic distinctions will help us to understand more clearly what's involved when a person claims that he or she has a right in a given situation.

1. Since the western legal and ethical traditions are largely oriented towards a discussion of rights, issues that surface in the workplace are often couched in terms of the rights involved (e.g., privacy, security, ownership and disposition of property, freedom from harm, etc.). Though some rights may be **absolute,** most are **prima-facie,** that is, circumstances may justify their being overridden. Therefore even an exhaustive list of human rights will leave many

TABLE 1-3
SOME FUNDAMENTAL HUMAN RIGHTS

NEGATIVE RIGHTS

    Life

    Physical security

    Autonomy

    Freedom of thought and expression

    Private ownership of property

    Due process

    Privacy

POSITIVE RIGHTS

    Food

    Adequate housing

    Competent medical care

    Employment at a living wage

    Education

ethical issues unsettled, inasmuch as these issues often involve a conflict of rights, and a simple list cannot tell us which rights take precedence over others. Because rights are rooted in the creation and distribution of benefits (enjoying a human good) and harms (avoiding a human evil), justifying a claim to a right or overriding a right may well depend on the evaluation and ranking of the harms and benefits involved. For example, since we usually rank the value of human life higher than the value of property, it is usually ethically permissible to steal in order to survive. But does an employee's right to free speech take precedence over an employer's right to protect trade secrets? Since, as we have seen in our discussion of utilitarianism, reasonable and ethical people can honorably disagree in their evaluation and ranking of harms and benefits, they may well honorably disagree in their evaluation of which rights may be justifiably overridden in which circumstances.

2. Some rights are **negative** while others are **positive.** A negative right is essentially a right to be left alone, to remain undisturbed. A person's right to exercise his or her religious convictions

freely means that everyone else has a duty to refrain from interfering with the exercise of those convictions. It does not, however, mean that anyone has a duty to build him or her a suitable place of worship. A **positive** right, on the other hand, places a moral duty on others to assist a person in exercising it (e.g., the community has the duty to supply an indigent criminal defendant with legal representation so that he or she can exercise the right to a fair trial).

Positive rights are far more controversial than negative rights. While there is virtually universal agreement about the negative right to life (all innocent human beings have at least a **prima-facie** right not to be killed), there is significant disagreement about the positive right to life (and the duty of others to provide food, shelter, health care, employment, and the other necessities of life). This, we believe, is at the heart of much of the current discussion in the United States about "entitlements" (another word for rights), as well as of a business's social responsibility.

3. The rights listed in Table 1-3 are **general** rights. They are often referred to as "human rights," that is, rights that individuals have simply because they are human beings. But many other rights are **particular,** that is, they depend on specific circumstances. A person who is promised something is usually entitled to get it. Other particular rights are role-based. Relationships between parents and children, professionals and their clients, employers and employees, and students and teachers are characterized by interlocking rights and responsibilities. Though there is considerable controversy concerning whether people have **general positive** rights, there is agreement that people have **particular positive** rights, though there is debate as to what those rights are and how they are to be balanced against other rights. For example, in the United States employers have traditionally had the right to terminate "at-will" employees at their discretion. However, recently, some "at-will" employees have argued (and some courts have agreed) that they have a **particular** right, based on an implied promise of fair dealing, not to be fired

without just cause. The readings in this book raise many issues like this one.

Justice—Benefits and Harms Fairly Distributed

In his *Nichomachean Ethics,* the Greek philosopher Aristotle (384-322 B.C.E.) defined justice as treating equals equally and unequals unequally (trans. 1985, V.4). However, in what respects are persons equal or unequal, and what constitutes equal or unequal treatment?

People differ in almost countless ways: size, intelligence, age, temperament, moral qualities, and so on. To some degree, we can compare individuals with respect to those qualities (e.g., some people are more handsome or less courageous than others). Yet not every difference is a relevant inequality requiring or permitting unequal treatment. A teacher who distributes grades based, even in part, on the physical attractiveness of students, acts unfairly. An employer who declines to hire a person because of her or his religious convictions acts unjustly. Why?

Both distribute certain benefits or harms unequally on the basis of *irrelevant* criteria. Physical attractiveness is irrelevant to the mastery of an academic subject that grades are supposed to reflect, and a person's religion is irrelevant to the qualifications that she or he needs to have in order to do a job well.

In Aristotle's view, when one person unjustly harms another, the appropriate distribution of harms and benefits is disturbed. Justice demands "rectification" by restoring appropriate benefits to the injured party, inflicting appropriate harms on the injuring party, or by some combination of both (V.5). "Rectificatory justice" obviously plays a large role in our criminal and civil legal systems and in our ethical thinking as well. For example, much of the contemporary debate concerning the ethical status of affirmative action programs has to do with whether they are ethically justified as "compensation" to women, African-Americans, and other minority groups for past wrongs, or whether they incorporate irrelevant and discriminatory considerations into hiring and promotion decisions, making those decisions unjust.

Though it is often obvious when criteria are *irrelevant,* establishing *relevant* criteria for a fair allocation of benefits and harms can be difficult. Should they be divided equally? According to ability? Effort? Need? Achievement? Much of the current debate in the United States about tax policies and welfare benefits revolves around just these considerations.

These questions are also important to employers, managers, and employees since issues of fairness affect the work environment and the attitudes of the people who work in it. Empirical evidence indicates that employees who believe their workplaces to be fair feel more loyalty and commitment towards their organizations and work more effectively and productively within them (Greenberg, 1993, p. 250; Sheppard et al., 1992, p. 102).

Figure 1-2 represents Minton, Lewicki, and Sheppard's theory of organizational justice (1994, p. 143). In their view, judgments of fairness are based on two general principles of justice, **balance** and **correctness,** which will be differently applied depending on the selection of levels and goals. **Balance** measures the distribu-

tion of goods or harms to different parties against their relative contributions. It is fair that someone who contributes more should receive more in return. Judgments of balance are typically comparative; for example, someone who received a 3 percent raise and discovers that a coworker who performed at roughly the same level of effectiveness received a 10 percent raise is likely to believe that an injustice has been done. **Correctness** refers to the quality which makes a situation or a decision seem "right," that is, compatible with standards of consistency, accuracy, clarity, procedural thoroughness, and the ordinary ethics of the culture (p. 140).

According to Figure 1-2, people make judgments of fairness about the **contents** or **outcomes** of decisions, about the **procedures** by which the decisions were made, and about the larger **systems** in which those decisions and procedures are embedded. Of course, judgments on one level influence judgments made on another; people who believe that a company's termination procedures are generally unjust are unlikely to believe that a particular decision was fair.

People's values and goals also influence their judgments of fairness. If enhanced performance

FIGURE 1-2

Standards of justice.

Level/Goal	Principle	
	Balance	Correctness
Outcome		
Performance effectiveness	Equity	Internal consistency
Community	Equality	Law or policy
Dignity and humaneness	Need	Station in life
Procedure		
Performance effectiveness	Checks and balances	Neutrality
Community	Balance of power	Consistency with procedures
Dignity and humaneness	Balance of inputs	Standing
System		
Performance effectiveness	Control of abuse	Responsiveness to change
Community	Inclusion	Stability
Dignity and humaneness	Opportunity	Legitimates or sustains interest

Source: John W. Minton, Roy J. Lewicki, and Blair H. Sheppard, "Unjust Dismissal in the Context of Organizational Justice, *Annals of the Academy of Political & Social Science, 536* (1994), p. 143. Used with permission.

is important to a person, then he or she may well think that large differences in rewards based on performance are fair. If team spirit or a sense of community is valued, equal rewards to all members of a team might be judged to be in order. Allocations based on need may well be considered fair by someone who emphasizes the dignity and humaneness of each individual.

Minton et al. (1994) identify eighteen standards of justice, not all of which are compatible. Consider the following:

> *Fortune*'s annual survey of CEO pay found that 1993 was an excellent year for the CEOs of 200 of the largest corporations in the United States. Their total compensation averaged $4.1 million, a 28% increase from 1992. The top earners included Sanford Weill (Travelers, Inc.) $45.6 million, George M.C. Fisher (Eastman Kodak) $25.4 million, Gerald M. Levin (Time Warner) $21.1 million, James R. Mellor (General Dynamics) $20.3 million, James E. Cayne (Bear Stearns) $15.9 million. This increases an income gap between CEOs and other wage earners that has been widening dramatically since 1980 and takes place against a background of growing inequality of wealth and incomes in the United States, described in a recent *New York Times* article as the largest in the Western world.[7]

Critics who value community building might object to the "correctness" of the levels of CEO pay, pointing out that such large discrepancies between the salaries of top executives and those of ordinary workers offend the rough standard of equality that is important in our values and culture (Law or policy). They might argue further that the system that generates these discrepancies is itself unfair since the often cozy relationship between top executives and corporate boards of directors fails to prevent abuses of managerial discretion (Control of abuse).

Defenders of the current inequalities, on the other hand, might justify their position by referring to the crucial role that top managers play in an organization's success or failure and by arguing that fairness requires that they should be rewarded (Equity). Or they might point to the fact that the past accomplishments and the station in life of a CEO are such that dignity and humaneness demand that he or she be compensated sufficiently to live a certain style of life (Station in life).

Assessments of justice have a strong subjective component; the biases and self-interest of individuals powerfully influence their judgments (Sheppard et al., pp. 24-25). A union leader and a corporate executive will, in all likelihood, view the issue of executive compensation differently.

Theories of organizational justice describe what people believe about justice; they do not propose that one standard of justice is superior to any other. However, people trying to discover the fairest course of action in a situation need to determine whether one standard of justice is better than another, or at least more appropriate in the particular circumstances. Philosophers, attempting to answer this question, have developed **prescriptive** theories of justice, which evaluate the various standards that people use and propose ones that they think are ethically correct. Two influential modern theories have been advanced by Robert Nozick (1974) and John Rawls (1971).

Because of the premium it places on individual liberty, Nozick's position is described as libertarian. In his view, the sole point of justice is to protest individual entitlements or rights, in particular the right to be free from coercion (pp. 150-155). He traces his opinion to Kant's insistence on individual dignity and autonomy; coercion treats people as means to ends rather than as ends in themselves.

Nozick believes that the total distribution of benefits in a society is just if each individual is entitled to the benefits that he or she has. Some principles propose distributing benefits and burdens according to a preestablished pattern (e.g., equality, merit, need). All of these involve the redistribution of benefits and burdens and inevitably conflict with liberty; they are therefore unjust. Nozick proposes a "historical" principle of justice: a distribution of goods is just to the degree that each individual's holdings are just, and this is determined by the history of how those holdings came about. If the original acquisition and each transfer of a holding involved no coercion or fraud, then the current holding, regardless of whether it conforms to any pattern of distribution, is just. The following parody of the Marxist pattern of distribution ("From each according to his ability, to each according to his need") makes his point.

> From each according to what he chooses to do, to each according to what he makes for himself (perhaps with the contracted aid of others) and what others choose to do for him and choose to give him of what they've been given previously (under this maxim) and haven't yet expended or transferred. (p. 160)

To a libertarian, as long as the owners of a company legitimately own it and freely enter into an agreement to transfer some of its assets or revenues to someone in exchange for his or her services, their actions and the results of their actions are just no matter how they affect the distribution of benefits in the larger society. Since many of the standards people use to object to the "unfairness" of executive salaries (e.g., equity, equality, or need) are "patterned," those objections are simply mistaken. If the process is voluntary, the outcomes are fair.

Libertarian theory fits well with capitalism and the values of individualism prominent in the culture of the United States. Nevertheless, Nozick's critics contend that his theory is one-sided. Although they grant that the negative right to be free from coercion and interference is an important one, they do not believe that it is the only right. As we have seen, some philosophers argue that people also have positive rights. If, for example, we believe that people have the right to an education, then a system of taxation to finance public education is ethically required, even though it interferes with the liberty of peo-

ple to spend their money as they wish. It is very difficult to see how Nozick's theory could accommodate such positive rights.

John Rawls proposes an alternative theory in his influential book, *A Theory of Justice.* His equality-oriented theory differs vastly from Nozick's libertarianism.

> All social primary goods—liberty and opportunity, income and wealth, and the bases of self-respect—are to be distributed equally unless an unequal distribution of any or all of these goods is to the advantage of the least favored. (p. 303)

To compensate for the influence of bias and self-interest, Rawls proposes that deliberations and decisions regarding the selection of principles of justice be conducted in a hypothetical situation, located behind what he calls the "veil of ignorance" (pp. 136-142). Each person behind the "veil" may propose principles of justice for consideration and may either accept or reject the proposals of other participants. No principles are to be adopted without unanimous consent.

Though they understand the general principles of psychology and goal-directed behavior, the deliberators must make decisions ignorant of all the circumstances of their future lives—their race, sex, social standing, psychological makeup, intellectual abilities, and so on. Hence their considerations and judgments will be impartial since none of them will have enough information about himself or herself to argue for principles that will directly benefit him or her.

According to Rawls, the participants will find it rational to adopt a conservative strategy in their selection of principles of justice, which strategy he calls a "maximin" rule (pp. 152-157). The goal of this decision rule is to maximize (make the best of) the minimum (worst) possible outcome of a decision. For example, an investor with $1,000 is considering the purchase of one of two stocks. Stock A is riskier but potentially much more profitable than Stock B. An investment in A could well be lost, though it could also yield a 100 percent return. Stock B's highest potential return is a much lower 20 percent, but there is no risk of loss of principal. A "maximin" strategy would dictate investing in Stock B.

Rawls believes that each hypothetical deliberator will choose a "maximin" strategy in order to protect himself or herself in case she or he winds up in one of the worst positions in society. No one who is ignorant of whether he or she will be a slave is likely to incorporate the right to own slaves into his or her principles of justice.

Employing a "maximin" strategy calls for adopting the following principles of justice (pp. 302-303).

1. Each person is to have an equal right to be the most extensive total system of equal basic liberties compatible with a similar system of liberty for all. (Liberty Principle)
2. Social and economic inequalities are to be arranged so that they are both:
   a. To the greatest benefit of the least advantaged (Difference Principle), and
   b. Attached to offices and positions open to all under conditions of fair equality of opportunity. (Equality of Opportunity Principle)

Rawls prioritizes these principles as follows: (1) Liberty, (2) Equality of Opportunity, and (3) Difference. Thus, for example, basic liberties (political liberty, freedom of speech and assembly, liberty of conscience and freedom of thought, freedom of the personal along with the right to hold personal property, and freedom from arbitrary arrest) may not be abolished in order to eliminate inequality of wealth.

As one might expect, in Rawls' view CEO income inequality is presumed unjust unless everyone has an equal opportunity to obtain the positions to which those salaries are attached and unless the inequalities are so arranged that

the least well-off persons in the system are better off than they would be under any other system. For Nozick, the distribution is just unless there is evidence of coercion or fraud in its history; for Rawls, it is unjust unless it meets his theory's conditions.

Rawls's libertarian and utilitarian critics argue that he has not established that the "maximin" strategy is the only (or the most) rational principle of choice available to the deliberators behind the "veil." Why, for example, would they not gamble a bit and choose the principle of the highest average utility? The resulting principles of justice might be quite different.

A specific criticism concerns the Difference Principle. Libertarian critics argue that it is too restrictive of freedom. In their view, as long as there is fair equality of opportunity, whoever wins the contest and however large the margin of victory, the outcome is fair, regardless of its impact on the least advantaged. Other, more egalitarian critics point out that the Difference Principle is compatible with circumstances in which inequalities of goods are so egregious as to seem obviously unjust.

The difficulty in formulating generally acceptable standards of justice mirrors the difficulties we encountered with the other ethical theories. Ethical decisions, like many others we are confronted with, can be complex. The attempts of various philosophers to formulate *one* ethical principle that would infallibly guide ethical decision-making have not been commonly accepted. Thus, the rules of the common mortality and the principles of critical ethical thinking leave a lot of room for ethical disagreement and doubt.

Nevertheless, some ways are better than others when looking for solutions to ethical problems. The suggestions with which we conclude our introduction draw upon the ethical rules and principles we have discussed. You should keep these concepts in mind as you consider the ethical issues raised in the following chapters.

SOME SUMMARY SUGGESTIONS TO CONSIDER IN MAKING ETHICAL DECISIONS

After obtaining all the facts, both concerning the past (the origins of the situation) and the future (the probable outcomes), determine whether or not the situation and the courses of action under consideration evoke legitimate ethical concern. If so, then, as you weigh alternative courses of action, strive to be:

- Objective

- Describe the situation from the point of view of each person who has an ethically legitimate interest in it. Whenever possible, consult with the individuals involved.
- Determine which facts are agreed upon and which are controversial according to different points of view. Get as clear a picture of the facts as you can.
- Evaluate, as best you can, each course of action and its outcome from the point of view of each legitimately interested party.

- Impartial

- Note whether you or anyone close to you has a special interest in the results of your decision. If so, consider what steps you can take to preserve your impartiality.
- Ask yourself, as you weigh each course of action, what your decision would be if you or someone close to you would suffer as a result of it.
- Evaluate how confident you would be with each proposed course of action if it were to be evaluated by panels of your peers, subordinates, or supervisors.

- Prepared to justify your decision

- Consider whether the benefits of each course of action outweigh the harms.

- Determine whether any proposed course of action violates any elements of the common morality. If it does, identify those elements.
- Consider what principles or rules justify your decision if any ordinary ethical rules are broken or anyone's prima-facie rights are violated.
- If the distribution of harms and benefits that will likely result from your decision appears to be unfair, specify the standard of fairness that is apparently violated, and reflect on how you might defend your decision.
- Describe the strongest ethical objections to your proposed course of action. Determine whether you can effectively respond to them.

THE READING SELECTIONS IN THIS BOOK

We conclude this introduction with a few remarks about the principles that governed our selection of readings. In addition to essays by specialists in ethics, we have selected articles from the fields of organizational behavior, human resource management, and law. This approach reflects our view that the ethical issues that concern the modern workplace are embodied in many areas of management in very practical and concrete ways.

The selections from the field of law are of particular interest. On the one hand, ethical rules and legal rules, while clearly related, are not the same. Some actions are unethical but may not be illegal (e.g., lying to one's spouse about a matter of importance), and others are illegal but not unethical (e.g., the use by African-Americans of a "For Whites Only" restroom under "Jim Crow" laws).

Law makes a substantial contribution to our ethical thinking. Statutory law often represents an ethical consensus that our society has reached on important topics (e.g., racial discrimination), and ongoing case law, at its best, reflects society's reasoned and procedurally sophisticated attempts to resolve ongoing ethical conflicts and concerns.

The converse is also true. The law embodies many ethical concepts (e.g., good faith, fair dealing, reasonable person) that can be best understood and interpreted against an ethical background. The debates that occur in the framing and interpretation of laws (e.g., the various right-to-privacy acts) or in the settling of disputes about the application of laws (e.g., cases involving "wrongful termination" and the limitations of an employer's right to discharge an "employee-at-will") often turn on an appreciation of ethical concepts and procedures for weighing ethical arguments.

NOTES

1. *Source:* Kurt Eichenwald, "He Told, He Suffered, Now He's a Hero," *The New York Times,* May 29, 1994, Business Section (3), p. 1.
2. *Sources:* Charles R. Day, Jr., and Polly LaBarre, "GE: Just Your Average $60 Billion Grocery Store," *Industry Week,* May 2, 1994, pp. 13-18; Noel M. Tichy, "Revolutionize Your Company," *Fortune,* December 13, 1993, pp. 114-118; Marshall Loeb, "Jack Welch Lets Fly on Budgets, Bonuses, and Buddy Boards," *Fortune,* May 29, 1995, pp. 145-147.
3. *Source: Code of Ethics,* McDonnell Douglas Corporation. Used with permission.
4. *Source:* Joseph Pereira, "Social Responsibility and Need for Low Cost Clash at Stride Rite," *The Wall Street Journal,* May 28, 1993, pp. A1, A6.
5. *Source:* Manuel G. Velasquez, *Business Ethics: Concepts and Cases,* 3rd ed., Englewood Cliffs: Prentice Hall, 1992, pp. 110-113.
6. *Sources: McLendon v. Continental Group, Inc. et al.,* 749 Federal Supplement 582 (D. NY 1989), and ABC News, *20/20,* Sept. 20, 1991, transcript by Journal Graphics, Inc.; both as cited in the unpublished case, "Wrongful Termination: The Case of Continental Can Company," by Dr. Michael Benoliel. The authors wish to thank Dr. Benoliel for bringing this case to their attention.
7. *Sources:* Brian Dumaine, "A Knockout Year for CEO Pay," *Fortune,* July 25, 1994, pp. 94–103,26

and Keith Bradsher, "Gap in Wealth Called Widest in the West," *The New York Times,* April 17, 1995, p. A1.

REFERENCES

Aristotle: 1985. *Nichomachean Ethics.* Trans. Terence Irwin. Indianapolis: Hackett Publishing Company.

Bradsher, Keith: 1995. "Gap in Wealth in U.S. Called Widest in West." *The New York Times,* 17 April, p. A1.

Carr, Albert: 1968. "Is Business Bluffing Ethical?" *Harvard Business Review, 46,* 143-153.

Carroll, Archie B.: 1987. "In Search of the Moral Manager," *Business Horizons,* March/April, p. 12.

Dobbs, John H.: 1993. "The Empowerment Environment." *Training and Development, 47* (2), 55-57.

Dumaine, Brian: 1994. "A Knockout Year for CEO Pay." *Fortune, 130* (2) (July 25), 94-103.

Eagly, A.H., and B.T. Johnson: 1990. "Gender and Leadership Style: A Meta-Analysis." *Psychological Bulletin, 108,* 233-256.

Gert, Bernard: 1988. *Morality: A New Justification of the Moral Rules.* New York: Oxford University Press.

Gilligan, Carol: 1982. *In a Different Voice: Psychological Theory and Women's Development.* Cambridge, MA: Harvard University Press.

Greenberg, Jerald: 1987. "A Taxonomy of Organizational Justice Theories." *Academy of Management Review, 12* (1), 9-22.

Greenberg, Jerald: 1993. "Justice and Organizational Citizenship: A Commentary on the State of the *Employee Science." Responsibility and Rights Journal, 6* (3), 249-256.

Held, Virginia: 1992. *Feminist Morality: Transforming Culture, Society and Politics.* Chicago: University of Chicago Press.

Held, Virginia: 1995. "Rights and the Ethic of Care." *APA Newsletter on Feminism and Philosophy, 94* (2) (Spring), 40-42.

Kant, Immanuel: 1964. *Groundwork of the Metaphysics of Morals.* Trans. H. J. Paton. New York: Harper and Row.

Kouzes, James, and Barry Pozner: 1993. *Credibility: How Leaders Gain and Lose It, Why People Demand It.* San Francisco: Jossey-Bass.

Loden, Marilyn: 1985. *Feminine Leadership or How*

to Succeed in Business Without Being One of the Boys. New York: Random House.

Minton, John, et al: 1994. "Unjust Dismissal in the Context of Organizational Justice." *The Annals of the American Academy of Political and Social Science, 536,* 135-148.

Nozick, Robert: 1974. *Anarchy, State and Utopia.* New York: Basic Books.

Peters, Tom, and Nancy Austin: 1985. *A Passion for Excellence.* New York: Random House.

Peters, Tom, and Robert Waterman, Jr.: 1982. *In Search of Excellence.* New York: Harper and Row.

Powell, Gary N.: 1993. *Women and Men in Management.* 2nd ed. London: Sage Publications.

Rawls, John: 1971. *A Theory of Justice.* Cambridge, MA: Harvard University Press.

Rosener, J.B.: 1990. "Ways Women Lead." *Harvard Business Review, 68,* 119-125.

Sargent, Alice: 1983. *The Androgynous Manager.* New York: AMACOM.

Sheppard, Blair H., et al.: 1992. *Organizational Justice: The Search for Fairness in the Workplace.* New York: Lexington Books.

Simon, John G., Charles Powers, and Jon Gunnemann, 1993. "The Responsibilities of Corporations and Their Owners." In Tom L. Beauchamp and Norman E. Bowie, (Eds.), *Ethical Theory and Business* (4th ed., pp. 60-65). Englewood Cliffs: Prentice Hall.

Sirkin, Harold L.: 1993. "The Employee Empowerment Scam." *Industry Week,* 18 October, p. 58.

"Sorry, You're Too Old." Senior Workers and Age Discrimination

INTRODUCTION

"Audrey is a very discriminating person." Are these words of praise or reproach? Until we have some further information, we don't know, because the word "discriminate" is ambiguous. It can mean simply "to distinguish," "to make a distinction" (e.g., to distinguish between truth and falsity). Hence, "She's a discriminating person," referring to Audrey's ability as an attorney to ferret out the truth of a case, puts a positive meaning on the word. On the other hand, "discriminate" can refer to an act of invidiously distinguishing among persons on grounds such as race or gender. We will explore in a moment exactly why and how this sort of discrimination is ethically unjustified.

In the twentieth century the United States has seen some remarkable advances in the efforts to end invidious discrimination, the crowning achievement being the passage of the Civil Rights Act of 1964. It may well be that when the history of the United States in the twentieth century is written, the passage of that Act will stand out as one of its most important moments.

Title VII, Section 703 (a) of that legislation marks clearly the implications for employers and employees of a national commitment to a discrimination-free society.

> It shall be an unlawful employment practice for an employer—(1) to fail to refuse to hire or to discharge any individual with respect to his compensation, terms, conditions, or privileges of employment, because of such individual's race, color, religion, sex, or national origin; or (2) to limit, segregate, or classify his employees or applicants for employment in any way which would deprive or tend to deprive any individual of employment opportunities or otherwise adversely affect his status as an employee, because of such individual's race, color, religion, sex, or national origin. (42 U.S.C. 2000e-2)

In the succeeding decades, the Age Discrimination in Employment Act (1967), the Rehabilitation Act (1973), the Pregnancy Discrimination Act (1978), and the Americans with Disabilities Act (1990) have extended legal protection to other groups of people, most notably older Americans and persons with physical and mental disabilities. The managerial and ethical implications of this legislation for current human resource practices are widely discussed today;

they figure prominently in this and the next three chapters.

Invidious discrimination is a blatant violation of Kant's insistence that respect for human dignity is the pillar of the ethical life. Consider for a moment its close connection with prejudice. Typically, a person who acts in a discriminatory way does so because he or she is prejudiced against a certain group of people. In it most virulent form, prejudice can express itself as raw hatred; in its less virulent form, as stereotyping. Either form *pre*-judges individuals on the basis of their membership in some group and, on the basis of that *pre*-judgment, distinguishes (discriminates) between those individuals and other people. For example, a seventeen-year-old African-American male might be perceived as potentially more violent than another seventeen-year old, just because he is a young African-American. This sort of prejudicial stereotyping is unethical because it disregards the young man's dignity as an individual.

Discrimination is equally objectionable when it is assessed from the vantage point of fairness and justice. Recall, if you will, the brief presentation of Aristotle's thoughts on justice in Chapter 1. In his view, justice required that equals be treated equally and unequals unequally. This is precisely what discrimination fails to do. For example, promoting a man instead of a woman simply on the grounds of gender is discriminatory and is a case of treating equals unequally. Acts of discrimination typically distribute benefits and harms on the basis of *irrelevant* characteristics, like gender or race, and, in doing so, are unfair.

Differences of opinion arise concerning when characteristics such as age, race, or gender *are* ethically relevant (i.e., when they may legitimately be taken into consideration). If it can be shown, for example, that a person's age is relevant to his or her ability to perform the essentials of a given job, then it is ethically and legally permissible to take age into account. Airlines have argued successfully, on grounds of safety, for a mandatory retirement age for pilots. The law calls this a "bona fide occupational qualification." It is worth noting that, except in the *most extraordinary* circumstances, considerations of race, color, ethnic origin, or religion are never ethically or legally permissible.

According to utilitarians, discriminatory actions and practices prevent some members of society from exercising their talents to the full; thus, some of society's potentially most productive and efficient members are prevented from achieving their proper places. Harms are inflicted not only on individuals but on society as well. Businesses fail to realize benefits if they recruit, hire, and develop employees on any basis other than ability and merit; a society loses valuable contributors and suffers harms in terms of the resentments and social distress that discrimination creates.

Age discrimination is one common type of discrimination in our culture. We place great value on youth. We see in young people the epitome of vitality, energy, and attractiveness. This emphasis often overlooks, or even devalues, the strengths that older members of our society have and the contributions that they can make. It is easy to stereotype older people and to discriminate against them on the basis of those stereotypes. Several of this chapter's readings discuss and debunk such stereotypes (e.g., older workers are so set in their ways that they are unwilling or unable to adapt to change; their ideas are outdated; they lack the commitment and enthusiasm of younger workers; they are more prone to accident and have a high rate of absenteeism).

Discrimination against older workers can take place at every stage of the employment process. Recruitment efforts may be directed only at younger people; managers in charge of hiring may disqualify certain applicants on the basis of their age; older workers may be passed over for promotions to jobs for which they are qualified; they may be the first victims of layoffs; and they may be terminated or forced to retire even when they are willing and able to continue working. To combat such discrimination, Congress passed the Age Discrimination in Employment Act (ADEA) of 1967, the stated purpose of which is

> . . . to promote employment of older workers based on their ability rather than age; to prohibit arbitrary age discrimination in employment; and to help employers and workers find ways of meeting problems arising from the impact of age on employment. (29 U.S.C. 621 et seq.)

Discrimination against older workers is not only harmful to the workers themselves and to society at large, it is also detrimental to employers. Discriminatory behavior exposes them to large legal risks (the average jury award in age discrimination cases is in excess of $300,000), and, more importantly, it deprives them of the skills and experience that senior workers have to offer (e.g., their patience, "on-the-job" knowledge, and long-term perspective).

★ ★ ★

In the readings selected for this chapter, "The Plight of the Seasoned Worker" is considered by **Joseph F. McKenna** and **Brian S. Moskal.** They point out that, as companies try to save money, older workers are often the first to be cut, and they discuss several of the erroneous (and self-perpetuating) stereotypes upon which those decisions are frequently based. The articles by **Paul N. Keaton** and **Beth Larson** and by **Bimal Patel** and **Brian H. Kleiner** review the ADEA and other laws protecting the interests of older workers. Keaton and Larson examine their impact on policies and procedures concerning hiring, promotion, discharge, layoffs, and retirement. Patel and Kleiner analyze recent developments in age discrimination law, in particular the Older Workers Benefits Protection Act (1990), which protects older workers from being coerced into retirement. They also explore legal defenses against charges of age discrimination that are available to employers. **Janet Radcliffe Richards,** employing the techniques of philosophical analysis, explores different meanings of "discrimination" and isolates its central features, showing why they are ethically objectionable. **Robert J. Paul** and **James B. Townsend** point out several demographic factors that may contribute to future labor shortages and observe that the effects of those shortages can be lessened for companies who attract and retain older workers. They dispel six myths about older workers which sometimes prevent companies from using their talents, and they offer suggestions for employers wishing to benefit from older workers' skills and experience.

CASE: Russell Davidson and the "Dinosaur" Problem

Russell Davidson had been with Touch and Go Software, Inc., for six years and had rarely faced as tough a decision as the one waiting for him on his desk. Two years ago, he had been promoted to the position of vice president of the new product division at age 34. On this fall afternoon, he pondered the recommendation form for termination on his desk and thought about how to deal with Charlie Shuman, also known as "the Dinosaur." This was a decision that needed to be based on facts and clear logic. His decision could cause an uproar in the firm, possibly even some legal problems. Russ enjoyed a good reputation within the company and wanted to preserve it. But this decision was a tough one. The big questions were: Was age discrimination involved? What signals should he send to the people involved? What was the right thing to do?

BACKGROUND

In his six years at the company, Russ had built a reputation as an effective leader in software design. His subordinates and colleagues saw him as an outgoing friendly man, with an ear open to listen to their problems. Russ was happy to be at Touch and Go and considered himself fortunate to have found a good match for his interests and talents.

Source: This case was prepared by Joy Durand, research assistant, under the supervision of Professor Edward Ottensmeyer as a basis for class discussion rather than to illustrate either effective or ineffective handing of an administrative situation. This case is largely fictional but represents a composite of actual events.

Touch and Go was founded in 1980 by Jason Daniels. Daniels, then a student, had "big dreams" and saw the potential of the newly developing market for networking software. He had formed his company to develop software solutions for more effective networking of personal computers in the workplace. In fifteen years, Jason expanded his 10-person company into a 185-employee corporation with $300 million in annual revenues. The networking industry was booming, and Touch and Go was viewed as a major player in the market.

BOB WANTROSS AND THE PRODUCT TEAM

Two weeks earlier, Bob Wantross had sent Russ a recommendation to terminate Charlie Shuman, 49, a member of Bob's team. Bob was team leader of the group in charge of developing the next-generation networking product for smaller business systems. As Russ read the recommendation, he noticed Bob had provided much detail to support his request. Russ respected Bob as an aggressive and skillful software designer, but Bob was new to the team leader role, and occasionally needed to be "toned down." Russ wanted to hear more from Bob and to analyze his point of view carefully.

Wantross had come to work for Touch and Go three years earlier, fresh out of college. He was a "young tiger," as they called these young hot-shots in the software industry. He graduated near the top of his class at a well-known engineering school and knew software. Bob, now 26 years old, had a cool, somewhat distant personality, Russ thought. However, Russ saw that Bob's team worked well with him because they were mostly young programmers with an eye to technical challenge and future advancement. Bob had been assigned a team of extraordinary professionals, most of whom were very young and one or two years out of top colleges. Bob was respected by his team (they sometimes referred to him by his log-on code "TopGun"), but it had been mentioned by his coworkers that his drive sometimes got in the way of personal relations within the team. In his quest for top quality work, he could be abrasive.

Bob's team, working from a lab on the third floor of Touch and Go headquarters, was, irreverent but very hard working. At 26, Bob was an old-timer in this group! The lab was open all hours of the day and night. Music could be heard coming from behind the lab doors, and pizza deliverers asked receptionists directions to the third floor lab at all hours of the day. These kids, with their top-notch technical skills, Russ thought, were exactly what Touch and Go needed to stay on top of this fast-paced and rapidly changing market.

In considering the recommendation for termination, Russ thought back to his recent meeting with Bob Wantross. Bob had many reasons for wanting to fire Charlie Shuman. He was a lot older than the others, and he wasn't "at the cutting edge." He wasn't a fast learner and seemed uncooperative and "crotchety." He also did not seem enthusiastic about the product development process Bob had constructed for the team and did not "fit in" well with the group's work style, rarely staying past 7 p.m. because of family obligations. Bob worried that his team of twelve was not doing its best work because one of its members was "over the hill." Charlie had been assigned to the team without his approval, Bob was fast to point out, and served in a client liaison role. Bob wanted him out of the way of his creative team, since he affected the team's spirit and effectiveness in a negative way. Bob thought that Charlie could not be relied on to tell customers about new products

since he did not know the "inside scoop" well enough. Bob also felt that Charlie was set in his ways and not prepared or willing to follow Bob's lead. He might be glad to get out now, he added, possibly even to take early retirement.

Bob reported that talking to Charlie about new products was like trying to teach his mother about rap music when all she understood was big band. It was nothing personal, just that he didn't fit into the team and, more importantly, might hurt the team by dealing ineffectively with major users or customers.

Bob knew that Charlie was one of the original employees when Touch and Go opened its doors in 1980. Bob believed that Charlie's "time was up" in this industry, his "prime had passed." Even the founder had stepped aside a few years back, Bob pointed out, making way for more professional managers. Why shouldn't Charlie?

Bob thought it important that Touch and Go's client base was also part of this younger generation. The team had one piece of the new product ready for beta testing. Bob recalled speaking to one major client, who had asked about Bob's team. They were eager to know who they would be working with. Could a fax be sent to him about the Touch and Go people who would be coming to work with him? How was it going to look, Russ asked Bob, if he sent the profile of a late-40-something?

CHARLIE SHUMAN

Charlie had started his career at Touch and Go as an applications programmer. Before coming to Touch and Go, he had been a high school math teacher who decided that there were more attractive opportunities in the computer industry of the early 1980s. He approached Jason Daniels, a personal friend, and asked if he could have a shot at being a programmer. He wanted to leave teaching; at 33, he was ready for a change. Charlie had taken a few classes in computer programming in college. Jason saw Charlie as an asset to his new company, able to contribute his skills and hard work. He was a "people person" and adjusted well to the environment in the start-up firm. He encouraged coworkers and was an unselfish team player.

Charlie developed his skills further by taking night classes at a local community college. He focused on programming and software courses to upgrade his skills. He was creative and was able to apply these new skills quickly to his work assignments.

Charlie made it known to his managers that he was happy to work at Touch and Go. In recent years, he often stated that he was enthusiastic about working with a younger group of people—"It keeps me young," he would say.

Russ thought that older workers could make good role models at Touch and Go. They brought experience, perspective, and a sense of responsibility that might rub off on younger employees.

RUSS'S DILEMMA

Russ wanted to handle this matter in a fair way. He didn't want to lose either employee. Charlie had been a loyal and effective employee at Touch and Go for fifteen years. Bob was a rising star in his field and in the firm. Russ thought that Touch and Go was fortunate to have hired Bob. He was young and energetic; any other software company would hire him in a minute. He would become an increasingly visible player in the industry and had a bright future. Russ wanted to make sure that that future was at Touch and Go. He also recognized that Bob was untested as a manager. What sort of coaching might Russ need from Bob, in this instance? What message did Russ need to send Bob and others like him on this issue of age? Similarly, what message did he want to send Charlie and others like him? What was best for the firm in the long run?

Russ tried to clear his mind and began to write a few notes about the situation. He knew it would be a long afternoon. His next meeting with Bob was tomorrow morning.

The Plight of the Seasoned Worker

Joseph F. McKenna
Brian S. Moskal

They've been battered by downsizing like everyone else, maybe worse. They know how intense the competition for each promotion has become and have seen younger, more inexperienced co-workers get the promotions they themselves feel they have earned. And they understand the dystrophy of talents that don't get enough use. They are the mid-to-late-career whitecollar professionals in the 45-to-65-year age group. Increasingly they're being asked to retire early, whether or not they are pension-eligible. Many of them are accepting what they know will be their last promotion at a time when, in fact, they are still vibrant and vigorous and ready for more growth in authority and responsibility. Some of them, fearful of the push of younger colleagues, simply opt to bail out. Consider the story of this manager, who finally walked away from his job at a major corporation's aerospace division.

"People who have seniority need to be reinforced about being valued," he tells INDUSTRY-WEEK. "Nothing works more as a demotivator than feeling you have been shoved aside and that your ideas don't count. That's what made me leave the company at the age of 44. As the company was making cuts, I was hearing guys 39 and 42 saying, 'We've got to get rid of old Sam in HR because he's no good anymore.'

"It occurred to me that I could be one of those guys," he adds. "Maybe not fired, but just set over on the side and not paid attention to. That scared the hell out of me."

He searched for a company "with a CEO who was at least a year older" than himself. In a short time, another major corporation latched on to

him, recognizing his abilities as a motivator of employees and a disciple of worker empowerment. Ironically, his former company, itself having grown older and wiser in the interim, ultimately tried to lure him back—but to no avail.

And so go the winners and losers who function and malfunction respectively amid the myths and the realities about seasoned workers—a vulnerable but competent human-resource component of business organizations.

One myth is that these "older" workers are set in their ways, that they can't adapt to new work situations, and that they rely on stale information to make business decisions. Yet, even if they carry a knowledge base with some outdated parts, that doesn't mean they can't accept new information and apply it.

"The workplace expectations of our management seem to decrease as we mature workers age. Our assignments start to get stale and less challenging and it almost ensures that management will perceive our job-performance skills as being on the decline. This can become a deadly self-fulfilling prophecy," says a member of the 45-plus age group, who adds, "If you want to stay vital during the aging process you have to take charge of yourself and your work life. You can't become a victim of the system."

Another myth: Only the younger workers need developmental programs to help them grow on the job. The truth is that mature professionals need job- and skill-growth programs to keep them fired up and to bolster their self-esteem on the job—and most welcome such growth opportunities.

"It's a sad commentary when so many companies are in a downsizing mode. There is a myth that the 45-plus-year-old workers don't contribute and can't wait to get out the door—and that only young people are full of energy. People in their prime are put in this category," asserts Robert L. Faulkner, superintendent, Reliability Dept., Packard Electric Div. of General Motors Corp., Warren, Ohio. Echoing that sentiment are Drs. Denise Tanguay Hoyer and Bar-

Source: Reprinted with permission *Industry Week* (June 7, 1993). Copyright Penton Publishing Inc. Cleveland, Ohio.

bara Hirshorn, researchers who have extensively studied how retirees in particular fit into the contemporary American economy. Mature workers bring a much more quality-oriented work ethic to the job as compared with their younger counterparts, reports Dr. Tanquay Hoyer, professor of management at Eastern Michigan University's College of Business, Yipsilanti.

Moreover, she says, "they tend to have job experience that exceeds the level of the current job." Dr. Hirshorn, an associate professor for research at Wayne State University's Institute of Gerontology, Detroit, adds that some companies are particularly interested in seasoned workers' ability to transfer their workplace knowledge to younger workers. "We've found this in workplaces of all sizes," she says. *"Nobody knows this area like Charlie.'"*

Mature professionals are "the backbone of American commerce and industry. As a group, they are more sensitive to superiors who might think their workplace skills are on the decline. Sometimes senior management makes cuts to save dollars and, as a result, workers in this age group feel more threatened or endangered [than their younger co-workers]," says Dr. Jack Thompson, president and CEO, RHR International Co., Wood Dale, Ill., a consulting firm that applied the behavioral sciences to business management issues.

"Eventually you get past the demons of wanting to get ahead and making more and more money. You start taking a broader view of what is important to yourself and to society as a whole. You ask yourself how you can contribute to society as a whole," says James A. Lenarz, at age 69 a partner in Exploration Inventories, Eden Prairie, Minn. His firm creates assessment tools that help managers explore their strengths and weaknesses in order to develop a road map for future job growth and development.

Despite such realities, though, myths continue. One concerns whether the 45-plus whitecollar worker should be or deserves to be promoted, say mature professionals. "Compa-

nies are reluctant to 'waste' promotions on people in the 40-to-45-plus age group. Nowadays, companies start encouraging people to leave at age 50 to 55 or so, and management feels it is wasting a promotion on someone with only seven to 10 years left," says one professional middle manager who is 45-plus and thinks he'll be lucky to get another promotion with his current employer.

"My boss actually *told* me I would not receive another promotion and informed me who my 'replacement' is when he promoted him," says another manager, 48. "Am I supposed to care anymore?"

"I know what will and won't work," says Mr. Lenarz who retired from Honeywell Inc. in 1982 at age 58 after 30 years as a line manager in engineering, quality, and professional development of scientists and engineers. Well before his retirement, he says his work life was "getting a little dull. Even the crises were getting predictable. I felt stymied and I didn't have much energy to go to work every day." Mr. Lenarz then took more control of his work life and reinvigorated himself with a succession of new positions, including quality manager at Honeywell's Golden Valley plant and manager of development for technical and engineering professionals. As a result of working as corporate manager of professional development of engineers, scientists, and technicians in the late '70s and early '80s, his workplace philosophy now says the ideal mixture in business is the older worker teamed with younger workers. It can be a mutual admiration society. "These days I don't think the wisdom of the elders is revered in our society. There is a lot of information and experience that older people have to share but it usually doesn't dawn on people to ask us for it," he adds.

Consider David L. Schiska, who accepted early retirement at 55 from his position as manager in the regulatory department of Ohio Bell, a unit of Ameritech. "I've managed up to 100 people at one time and it's hard for early career people to have these work-related skills," says Mr.

Schiska of Lakewood, Ohio. He now wants to embark on a second career because "55 is too young to stop working and because I have a lot of productivity left in me."

A slightly different perspective comes from Mr. Faulkner, who just completed his college degree requirements on weekends while working full-time for Packard Electric. He not only offers 20 years of experience after starting at the bottom as a first-line supervisor at Packard Electric but also an education that is as up-to-date as those received by recent college graduates. Mr. Faulkner completed his final 2.5 years of college courses in business management and sociology during four years of weekend classroom instruction.

"Professionally, I offer the experience of having a number of assignments in manufacturing, quality control, and engineering. I haven't just focused on one area and I can put together all the experiences from various jobs that a younger professional would find hard to match," says Mr. Faulkner, who studied weekends at Hiram College, Hiram, Ohio, in a program tailor-made to retool seasoned workers for today's marketplace challenges. "Because of my experience, I can get to people and cut through the red tape in order to get done quickly a job that a younger professional wouldn't be able to do. It takes time to acquire that kind of knowledge and expertise," says the 47-year-old Mr. Faulkner, who is also president of the local school board in Warren—7,000 students in grades one through 12—and serves as the local president of the United Negro College Fund.

"I interface with adults and young people, get a chance to talk to them about careers, I'm a mentor in the community and a very positive reflection on Packard Electric. Not many younger professionals can say the same," stresses Mr. Faulkner.

In addition to experience, mature workers also have "more patience to roll with the punches than do their younger counterparts," thinks Dr. Thompson of RHR International.

The advantages offered by seasoned workers are becoming more obvious. The question is, will management better use the inherent wisdom, savvy, knowledge, and experience of the 45-plus professional?

If the answer ultimately is yes, management must change its level of expectations for the group. "One of the most deadly things is if top management has a low level of expectation for the 45-plus whitecollar professional. If managements want to tap into the power of older professionals they need to reinvest in the training of these workers. They should help create a learning organization for all, including mature and late-career professionals," says Exploration Inventories' Mr. Lenarz.

Eastern Michigan's Dr. Tanguay Hoyer and her colleague found that workplace experience helps flatten the learning curve for employees who were never trained in a particular skill. "Because of their other work characteristics," she says, "they were given training and were successful at responding to that training."

Organizations should, in addition, apply continuous quality-improvement techniques to workers and the workplace. "Otherwise you send a silent message to people over 40 that they should stop improving. When management doesn't ask members of this age group to improve their workplace skills, it sends a message that top management believes their productivity will fall off, regardless," says Mr. Lenarz.

If there is concern that being in a position too long will cripple performance, argues Wayne State's Dr. Hirshorn, companies should consider intentional reassignment—matching certain experience-related characteristics to positions. That, she says, shows an unquestionable interest in retaining seasoned workers.

But, at the very core of managing people, there's no real difference between a young union worker on the production line and a senior accounting manager who's been around the company for ages, says Paul J. Giddens, corporate director of organizational effectiveness at Georgia-Pacific Corp., Atlanta. "I had expected major differences between the young, the mid-

Rating Older Workers

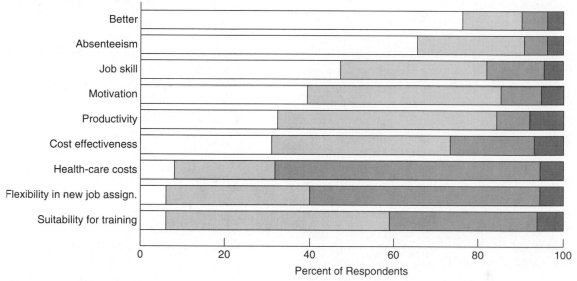

Percent of Respondents

Source: The Conference Board. Based on interviews with 406 human-resource executives; older workers in this case are 55 and over.

dle-aged, and the older person," he says, "but I've found that everybody is just working out of their own comfort zone."

The real managerial skill, then, lies in navigating through those zones. As Mr. Giddens sees it, "the comfort zone for young folks is *'There's more to life than work.'* The middle-aged employees are concerned about their jobs and being able to send their kids to school. And the older employees are reluctant to change because they're comfortable. They don't want to give up what they perceive to be their power, and they're afraid of having to relearn anything."

For Mr. Giddens, a Former HR "Wizard" at General Electric Co., managing the most seasoned of workers translates into "having their managers create an empowering environment where they discover the needs of both the team and the individual employees and then serve as a positive resource to getting them what they need to do their jobs, rather than getting them to leap out of their comfort zones." (See "Workforce

Wizardry: How Empowerment Transforms Scarecrows," IW, July 16, 1990, Page 8.)

One case in point is the reworking of accounting processes at Georgia-Pacific. This makeover is more than a new way of bean-counting; it requires the use of a team, a contemporary business term that still raises eyebrows among veterans. "Older employees are less into teams than younger ones—unless you do it right," notes Mr. Giddens. "If people don't like the word team, don't call it a team. Call it a banana. Let's say we have 150 accountants across the board and we're saying, 'Your role is changing. The green eyeshade is gone. You all are going to be business partners. You're going to have to access data, work with your partners, extract appropriate data, and then turn that data into some type of meaningful information for others.' Now strangely enough, the older employees are looking at this as an opportunity to do something they always thought they were doing and not getting recognized for." So, insists Mr. Giddens, managing older workers isn't really much different from managing their younger counterparts. "It's the way you color the banana," he says.

Ah, but what if the banana, be it bright green or golden yellow, gets sliced? Downsizing is quickly becoming a constant in the economy of the '90s. But if companies want to wipe out older workers and go only with younger employees, they will be losing experience and knowledge gained over decades. A better solution is to blend old and new ideas together.

In its 1992 report "The Availability of a Quality Work Force," The Conference Board notes that "the current focus on downsizing and cost reductions may be obscuring the potential for skills loss represented by the growing number of early retirees. The aging of the labor force, combined with the trend toward early retirement, represents a potentially large loss of experienced workers from the labor force. Employers are faced with the ironic possibility that they will be remediating large numbers of unqualified job entrants while simultaneously encouraging the early exit of many highly trained employees."

Adds Mr. Schiska, "If you wipe the slate clean and end up with only younger workers without much experience, you run a risk. It's much better to have a blend of age groups and ideas." On the bright side, he sees a natural, though still largely untapped, landing pad for mid- and late-career professionals: small business.

"It would be very productive for small businesses to use those people who have been removed from the payrolls due to downsizing. Their experience could be vital to such companies. But I don't even know if small businesses are thinking about hiring the displaced of corporate America."

He cites himself as an example: "I could come in and train people two to three days a week and I wouldn't mind working for less money and having my weekends free after having worked long hours for most of my career. Small companies and mature workers can complement each other with a very mature working

relationship but I don't know if small companies recognize the potential yet."

Meanwhile, other pre-baby boom professionals think they need to be shown more patience and tolerance. They should be given the chance to do the next-level-up job. Eastern Michigan's Dr. Tanquay Hoyer advises, fit them into positions where their current characteristics—both physical and experiential—fit. And if they need mentoring, mentor them.

Otherwise, the productivity of this age group will live up to the expectations of management—it will decline significantly.

An "attitude adjustment" on the part of top management should be threefold: training, investment, and mentoring.

"The real message I would like people to take home is that the leader in business has the obligation to value the unique contributions of their employees," says Georgia-Pacific's Mr. Giddens. "This is the real meaning of diversity. Diversity is not just some government number to meet in terms of race, sex, etc. It's more than a competitive edge. It is the key to innovative survival in the years to come.

"Diversity means creating a business culture that encourages and reinforces honest and candid input from a wide variety of people, ages, and races. Diversity means a greater source of ideas."

There is, says Mr. Giddens, no difference in the basic approach of managing the seasoned employee and the rest of the workforce. However, "it takes a gutsy leader to actually know his people well enough to uncover individual 'hot buttons,' and to be a unique resource to the team members," he says.

Mr. Giddens reaches back some 20 odd years for a lesson he learned from his Army Master Sergeant—"all I'll ever need to know about leadership, or young, middle-aged, and older people," he says. "Addressing me in private, he said, 'Sir, do you want to be some kind of cowboy hero, or do you want to live? It ain't complicated. You don't need anyone's permission to be a good leader—not your mommy's, not your daddy's, not your Colonel's, not even mine.

"'Just be a resource to your team. All you have to do is 1. Know your people. 2. Look out for their welfare. 3. Keep them informed. 4. Let them take part in the decisions that affect them. You don't need to be a hero. Wear your medals on *their* chests.'

"If," says Mr. Giddens, "we in management would simply lead and follow this simple, yet profound, advice, we would see that people are people regardless of age.

"We all have unique differences in perception, apprehension, and approach. But we are more alike than we are different in how we approach our work: We want to be valued, respected, and listened to."

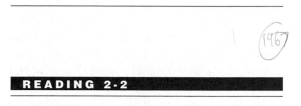

READING 2-2

Age Discrimination in Employment: Case Law and Implications for Employers

Paul N. Keaton
Beth Larson

The Age Discrimination in Employment Act[1] was enacted in 1967, and amended in 1978 and 1986, to promote employment of older persons based on ability rather than age. Age discrimination does not take individual characteristics into account, but rather only the qualities derived from group membership.[2]

The purposes of this article are to discuss some of the special characteristics of the aged employee, to look at the laws providing protec-

Source: Reproduced with permission from the September 1989 *Labor Law Journal,* published and copyrighted by CCH Incorporated, 2700 Lake Cook Road, Riverwoods, Illinois 60015.

tion and the case law, and finally to examine the implications for employers.

As individuals age, hearing and vision tend to decline. The speed of reaction time also decreases, although this can be compensated for to some degree. For example, a middle-aged driver may start slowing the car before a young driver would. Problem-solving, recent memory, and abstract reasoning tend to be less acute with age.[3] However, individual differences do exist.

Age-related differences at work include positive differences in job attitudes. Older employees tend to have higher job satisfaction, and age and job involvement appear to be positively correlated. Lower turnover suggests the older worker is more committed to the organization.[4]

Some studies indicate that the aged worker, although slower, is more accurate. Empirical evidence suggests that the older employee differs in performance from the younger in the areas of speed, accuracy of movement, problem-solving, perception, and hearing and vision.[5]

The older worker tends to have a lower rate of avoidable absence than does the younger worker. The two groups also differ in the seriousness of the work accidents in which they are involved. The younger workers' accidents are less severe and are related to lack of caution and inexperience, whereas the older group is likely to have accidents due to sensory-motor skill decline.[6]

With all of these differences, it is not surprising that some need for protection of the older employee is needed. Legislation attempts to see that employees are not discriminated against on the basis of age, but rather considered on an individual basis. A large group of employees is affected; currently, about 21 percent of the U.S. labor force is between the ages of 40 and 70.[7]

THE LEGISLATION

The Age Discrimination in Employment Act and its subsequent amendments cover all employers with 20 or more employees who work for at least 20 weeks yearly, as well as labor unions with 25 or more members, and employment agencies. As of October, 1984, U.S. citizens working in a foreign country for an American employer are covered, unless compliance would violate the laws of the host country.

Originally only employees from age 40 to age 65 were protected by the ADEA. In 1978, an amendment was passed which stated that an individual could not be retired solely on the basis of age until age 70, except for executives meeting specific criteria (see Mandatory Retirement below). An individual could be retired if unable to meet the physical, mental, or other demands of the job. The 1986 amendment removed the age 70 cap for most private sector employees.

The law includes a bona fide occupational qualification (BFOQ) clause. A BFOQ may exist if there is reason to believe that all individuals over a certain age cannot perform the job safely, or if it is highly impractical to deal with all members of the protected group individually. The easier defense for employers is the "reasonable factor other than age," in which it is asserted that the reason for the action was not solely the employee's age.

Originally administered by the U. S. Department of Labor, the ADEA is now enforced by the Equal Employment Opportunity Commission (EEOC). Both individuals and the EEOC may file a suit. Relief may include court-ordered reinstatement, promotion, liquidated damages (double back pay), and attorney's fees.

AGE CEILING FOR HIRING

One of the most widespread forms of discrimination has been the age ceiling for hiring. At one time, most civil service agencies enforced this. This is a clear case of treating the aging as a group, rather than considering individual characteristics involved.

The age ceiling is legal only if age is a BFOQ. The most obvious BFOQ is for reasons of safety. In *Hodgson v. Greyhound Lines,*[8] the court upheld the validity of the company's refusal to hire bus drivers over the age of 40, as there was some slight probability of increased safety risk. The court allowed that the suppositions connecting age and safety were sufficient to allow this age limit to be a BFOQ. However, three years later, in *Houghton v. McDonnell Douglas,*[9] this approach was rejected. To justify the BFOQ, the defendant employer needed to prove that it was impractical to deal with the older employee on an individual basis in terms of determining the safety risk for hiring.

Courts have upheld the age ceiling as a BFOQ for reasons of safety. The burden of proof must be met by the employer, and courts have differed as to what constitutes evidence in these cases.

In another case, a college's practice of restricting new campus security officers to individuals under the age of 45 was upheld because "older individuals lack the acute physical and mental ability and stamina required to serve effectively as rookie campus police officers . . . younger officers . . . 'relate' better to college-age students."[10]

Courts have generally upheld both maximum hiring ages and mandatory retirement ages for police officers, where the broad issues of public safety and employee fitness are crucial.[11]

DISPARATE TREATMENT

There are two theories about using the ADEA to prove allegations of age discrimination. It is clear that the intent of the law was to eliminate disparate treatment of the aged employee. Treatment would include such actions as decisions involving promotion and discharge, compensation, and other terms and conditions affecting the protected group member.[12]

However, it is not as clear that the intent of the law was also to reduce employment practices that have a disparate *impact* on the aged. Disparate impact occurs when the employment practice has a differential effect between older and younger employees, regardless of employer motivation.[13]

Stacy points out that the legislative history of the ADEA differs from that of Title VII. Those over age 40 have not experienced a history of unequal treatment, as in race discrimination.

Administrative guidelines of the EEOC published in 1981 support the possibility of disparate impact claims. The use of statistics by the plaintiff may support this type of claim. However, as those seeking employment tend to be younger than those already employed, a very wide statistical discrepancy is required.[14]

Issues under the disparate treatment theory include those of promotions, discharges, layoffs, and retirement. In the case of the first three, specific behavior-oriented performance evaluations may assist the employer to prevail in the ADEA case.

Courts have not been receptive to trait-oriented evaluations. A job analysis, if done correctly, can be of great assistance. It is also viewed positively if feedback is given to the employee and if presentation of written instructions is provided to the evaluator.[15] Holley and Field[16] state that the legal aspects of a performance evaluation system are reflected in the EEOC's Guidelines on Employee Selection Procedures.[17] Selection procedures, as well as evaluation procedures must be specific, unbiased, and job-related.

PROMOTION

In the case of promotion, the ADEA plantiffs' performance in the present job is not the main issue involved. This has been misunderstood. The principal issue involves the plaintiff's potential performance relative to the other candidates for promotion.[18] In *Zell v. United States,*[19] written performance evaluations were of assistance in asserting the employer's claim that Zell's performance relative to the promoted candidate was inferior. In *Braswell v. Kobelinski,*[20]

comparison of the performance of the plaintiff and the promoted candidate was not made until the case came to trial. However, the employer prevailed in the absence of a formal evaluation procedure.

In *Mistretta v. Sandia Corporation,*[21] the plaintiff received liquidated damages. Fewer wage increases and promotions were available for older workers. The employer had attempted to justify this on the basis of lower performance evaluations of the older workers.

DISCHARGE

Discharges present another issue. In the case of a discharge, the criteria are different. If the plaintiff has been performing adequately, s/he is expected to win the case. The issue is not relative ability, but minimal ability.[22]

The formulation for a *prima facie* case of this type can be seen in the elements of *McDonnell Douglas v. Green.*[23] The criteria are as follows: the employee's membership in the protected group; his or her discharge; his or her replacement with a person outside the protected group; the discharged employee's ability to do the job. Sometimes all the elements of this formulation do not exist; the essence of the formulation in a case is what is important. *McCorstin v. U.S. steel Corporation*[24] held that "discrimination, unfortunately, exists in forms as myriad as the creative perverseness of human beings can provide."

In discharge cases, performance evaluations have been helpful to the employer. In *Sherrod v. Sears, Roebuck & Company,*[25] a retail collection manager of 40 years was found to be legally terminated after receiving written negative performance evaluations from five supervisors. Employers have also prevailed in discharge cases upon the credible testimonies of supervisors and management, as in *Cova v. Coca-Cola Bottling Co. of St. Louis.*[26] The cases in which there are no formal evaluations and where management testimony is not credible are won by the employee.

Another example of a discharge case is that of *Wadeson v. American Family Mutual Insurance Company.*[27] In this case, despite youth-oriented personnel policies, there was no evidence that the 51 year old district manager was discharged for any reason other than an inability to get along with his superiors. *Gladys Horn v. Bibb County Commission*[28] utilized all elements of the *McDonnel Dougalas* formulation, including the replacement of Horn by a younger worker; Horn prevailed.

LAYOFFS

In layoff circumstances, the employer must prove that there is a business necessity for this action, as well as defend the decision to lay off or involuntarily retire the plaintiff rather than another employee. This will involve the defense of "good cause" or "reasonable factors other than age."[29]

An example of a layoff case is *Mastie v. Great Lakes Steel Corporation.*[30] Two members of the protected age group were laid off when the steel mill operations were reduced. The employer, in deciding which employees to lay off, had utilized a thorough evaluation process. The two employees who were terminated were ranked the lowest. The employer was victorious in this case; although the terminated employees were minimally capable of doing the job, others were more capable.[31]

In *McCorstin v. U.S. Steel Corporation,*[32] the claimant prevailed. The employer was charged with laying off employees in such a way that there was "a biased reduction in force."

MANDATORY RETIREMENT

A major issue in age discrimination cases has been that of mandatory retirement. This was made illegal (in most situations) by the 1978 amendment to the ADEA. Many factors encouraged this change. A special committee of the American Medical Association reported in 1966 that forced retirement was unhealthy. Changes

in demographics and pressure from the media also influenced the rethinking of this policy.[33]

In 1890, seventy percent of those over 65 held jobs; there was little choice in the matter. Later the Social Security Act encouraged retirement and pension fund development, and collective bargaining agreements covering retirement were more common. By 1977, the situation had changed so much that 11 million workers faced involuntary retirement at age 65.[34] However, the possibility (and attractiveness) of early retirement appears to have great appeal for the American worker; the average age of retirement is now 63 and has been declining slowly for the past 25 years.[35]

Executives in "high policy-making" positions may be mandatorily retired at age 65 if they will receive a nonforfeitable pension of at least $44,000 annually and if they have been in a policy-making position for at least two years prior to retirement.[36]

If age is a BFOQ, mandatory retirement may be legal, as in a few instances of public safety. In *Johnson v. Mayor of Baltimore,*[37] the court held that only when the individual employee is incapable of adequate job performance is forced retirement legal in the case of fire fighters.

The airline industry has provided numerous test cases of mandatory retirement. Under Federal Aviation Administration regulations, commercial airline and corporate pilots must retire at age 60. Several court decisions have upheld this policy.[38] In a related case,[39] a helicopter manufacturer's rule retiring experimental test pilots at age 55 was upheld.

When an employee needs to be terminated and is offered either retirement or termination, the employer must be careful to document that the employee voluntarily chose retirement. The employee must be fully aware of the options and should be given time to think about the decision and given the right to consult an attorney, if desired.[40]

A signed statement should be obtained from retiring employees stating that the decision to retire was voluntary and that the employees understood what they were doing. Sometimes formal waivers or releases are obtained, which state that the retiree waives the right to an ADEA claim. In order for this to be legal, some extra inducement or enhanced benefits must be offered.[41]

The waivers are a grey area as evidenced in the case of *Runyan v. NCR Corporation*.[42] In this case, the 6th Circuit Court of Appeals held that in order for a waiver of rights to be valid, it must be supervised by the Equal Employment Opportunity Commission. Following this, the EEOC issued regulations for the voluntary release of ADEA claims, and the *Runyan* opinion was withdrawn.

Offering large-scale, voluntary retirement plans is another issue. This may occur when the employer desires to reduce staff, and each eligible employee makes a decision whether or not to retire. This type of plan need not be offered company-wide; it can focus on a single department, and the employer may place limits on the number of employees retired. In *Coburn v. Pan American World Airways*,[43] the court stated that offering enhanced benefits to a portion of the workforce was a humane way to reduce the workforce, and that those not offered enhanced retirement benefits do not have a valid ADEA claim. It is still necessary to consider the employees' feelings about the equity of the plan, and it is advisable to document the reasons for offering the enhanced benefits to only a part of the workforce.

For a voluntary plan to be successful, it may be wise to state in the retirement release that the retiree is not eligible to return to work. An EEOC opinion letter states that retired employees must be considered for future openings if they apply. Also, the rules of a plan must be enforced consistently. Employee counseling and management training are advisable to ensure that the plan remains voluntary.[44]

In the event of workforce reduction, as in a factory closing, all employees must receive layoffs benefits. In *EEOC v. Westinghouse Corpo-*

ration,[45] it was determined that regardless of the status of previously earned retirement benefits, it was discriminatory not to offer layoff benefits to those of retirement age.

IMPLICATIONS FOR EMPLOYERS

ADEA cases are on the rise. In 1979, approximately 5,000 cases were filed. By 1983, the number had grown to over 19,000.[46] During the 1980s, each year on average has seen a 17 percent increase in cases filed.[47] The bulk of the complaints come from plaintiff employees in their fifties. Individuals file about 75 percent of these cases, and the EEOC files the remainder. Sixty-seven percent of the cases filed are discharge cases.[48]

ADEA case law is still being developed, and there is uncertainty in some areas of law interpretation. Employers who wish to protect themselves from ADEA suits would be wise to adopt a policy of consistent, job-related, behavior-oriented evaluations. Reasons for making employment decisions should be thoroughly documented. Employment policies and retirement plans need to be followed consistently.

In addition, employers need to be careful of loose language, including age-biased comments. There is nothing about the word old that automatically implies discrimination. However, referring to an employee as old and tired or a sleepy, droopy kind of guy could lead to a finding against the employer as in *Meschino v. ITT Corporation*.[49] Youth movement statements, such as telling an employee that there will be no future for men his age in the company, are damaging as well.[50]

Internal memoranda can also be injurious. Writing that younger people are needed in the department is certain ADEA evidence. In *Bernstein v. Consolidated Foods*,[51] an organizational chart listing the incumbents and their ages was deemed evidence as well.

It has been determined that an employer's efforts to save money are age discrimination if the actions taken stem directly from the protected employee's length of service.[52] Thus, saving money by eliminating the older employees with longer service and therefore higher pay cannot be justified generally by a business necessity defense. Making employment decisions based on the anticipated future service of an employee is also not a justifiable defense.

The timing of employment actions is very important. Firing an individual before retirement or before a pension fund is vested can be found to be indicative of age discrimination.[53]

Dube[54] stresses the need to train supervisors and other managerial personnel about the provisions of the ADEA, as well as the relevant state laws concerning age discrimination. However, managers also need to be educated, he urges, about "the type of conduct that has been held to evidence age discrimination." Periodic updating of this aspect of supervisory training should go a long way toward preventing actionable conduct by the employer's representatives.

In addition to protecting themselves against ADEA claims, employers can go the extra mile. Some suggest that accommodating the effects of aging may avert the filing of age discrimination claims.[55] Such activities as modified work hours, job reassignment, and increased lighting may enable the effects of aging to be overcome and may enable the further service of valuable employees.

NOTES

1. Age Discrimination in Employment Act, 29 U.S.C. 621 as amended.
2. G. Boglietti, "Discriminating Against Older Workers and the Promotion of Equality of Opportunity," 110 *International Labor Review* 351 (1974).
3. S. R. Rhodes, "Age-Related Differences in Work Attitudes and Behavior: A Review and Conceptual Analysis," 93 *Psychological Bulletin* 328 (1983).
4. *Ibid.*
5. *Ibid.*
6. *Ibid.*
7. J. Ivancevich and W. Gluek, *Foundations of Personnel/Human Resource Management,* 4th ed. (Homewood, Illinois: BPI/Irwin, 1989).
8. 5 EPD ¶ 8445 (DC Ill, 1973), rev'd 7 EPD ¶ 9286 (CA-7, 1974). Cited in E. Howard, N. Peavy, & L. Selder, "Age Discrimination and Mandatory Retirement," in M.H. Morrison, Ed., *Economics of Aging: The Future of Retirement* (New York: NY: Van Nostrand Reinhold Company, 1982), pp. 217–261.
9. EPD ¶ 10,200 (CA-8, 1975), 12 EPD ¶ 10,984 (DC Mo, 1976), rev'd & rem'd 13 EPD ¶ 11,623 (CA-8, 1977), cert. denied 15 EPD ¶ 7946 (S Ct, 1977), 21 EPD ¶ 30,338 (DC Mo, 1979), aff'd, rev'd, & rem'd 23 EPD ¶ 31,180 (CA-8, 1980), denial of cost rev'd & rem'd 32 EPD ¶ 33,793 (CA-8, 1983). Cited in Howard at note 8 above.
10. *EEOC v. University of Texas Health Science Center at San Antonio,* 32 EPD ¶ 33,751 (CA-5, 1983). Cited in T. Leap and M. Crino, *Personnel/Human Resource Management* (New York, NY: Macmillan Publishing Co., 1989), p. 90.
11. *EEOC v. Missouri Highway Patrol,* 30 EPD ¶ 33,293 (DC Mo, 1982), rev'd and aff'd 35 EPD ¶ 34,778 (CA-8, 1984); *EEOC v. City of Providence,* 41 FEP Cases 906 (1986). Cited in Leap and Crino at note 10 above, page 90.
12. D. R. Stacy, "A Case Against Extending the Adverse Impact Doctrine to ADEA," 10 *Employee Relations Law Journal* 437 (1984).
13. R. H. Faley, L. S. Kleiman, and M. L. Lengnick-Hall, "Age Discrimination and Personnel Psychology: A Review and Synthesis of the Legal Literature with Implications for Future Research," 37 *Personnel Psychology* 327 (1984).
14. Stacy above at note 12. See also *Wards Cove Packing v. Atonio,* 50 EPD ¶ 39,021 (SCt, 1989) regarding disparate impact.
15. H. S. Field and W. H. Holley, "The Relationship of Performance Appraisal System Characteristics to Verdicts in Selected Employment Discrimination Cases," 25 *Academy of Management* 392 (1982).
16. W. H. Holley and H. S. Field, "Performance Appraisal and the Law," LABOR LAW JOURNAL, Vol. 26, No. 6, June, 1975, p. 423.
17. CCH Employment Practices Guide ¶ 4010, 29 CFR 1607, 41 CFR 60-3, 28 CFR 50.14.

18. M. H. Schuster and C. S. Miller, "Performance Appraisal and the Age Discrimination in Employment Act," 29 *Personnel Administrator* 48 (1984).
19. 21 EPD ¶ 30,469 (DC Pa, 1979), cited in Schuster at note 18 above.
20. Cited in Schuster above at note 18.
21. 10 EPD ¶ 10,279 (DC NM, 1975), decision on liability 15 EPD ¶ 7902 (DC NM, 1977), aff'd 23 EPD ¶ 31,175 (CA-10, 1980), decision on individual claims 18 EPD ¶ 8852 (DC NM, 1978), aff'd 24 EPD ¶ 31,304 (CA-10, 1980), reconsidered in part 24 EPD ¶ 31,379 (CA-10, 1980), 26 EPD ¶ 31,864 (CA-10, 1981).
22. M. H. Schuster and C. S. Miller, "Performance Evaluation as Evidence in ADEA Cases," 6 *Employee Relations Law Journal* 561 (1981).
23. 2 EPD ¶ 10,009 (DC Mo, 1969), dism'd on merits 3 EPD ¶ 8014 (DC Mo, 1970), rev'd and rem'd 4 EPD ¶ 7742 (CA-8, 1972), mod. on petition for reh'g 5 EPD ¶ 8102 (CA-8, 1972), rem'd 5 EPD ¶ 8607 (CA-8, 1973), decision on remand 9 EPD ¶ 10,087 (DC Mo, 1975), aff'd 11 EPD ¶ 10,663 (CA-8, 1976). Cited in Faley at note 13 above.
24. 23 EPD ¶ 31,112 (CA-5, 1980). Cited in Faley at note 13 above.
25. 36 EPD ¶ 36,073 (CA-5, 1986).
26. 16 EPD ¶ 8272 (CA-8, 1978), amended opinion 34 EPD ¶ 34,380 (CA-8, 1978). Cited in Schuster above at note 18.
27. 34 EPD ¶ 34,459 (ND SCt, 1984).
28. 32 EPD ¶ 33,799 (CA-11, 1983).
29. Cited in Schuster at note 22 above.
30. 14 EPD ¶ 7707 (DC Mich, 1976).
31. Cited in Schuster at note 18 above.
32. Cited at note 24 above.
33. Howard cited at note 8 above.
34. *Ibid.*
35. W. Cascio, *Managing Human Resources,* 2nd ed. (New York, NY: McGraw-Hill Book Co., 1989), p. 94, citing S. Cabot, "Living with the New Amendments to the Age Discrimination in Employment Act," 32 *Personnel Administrator* 53 (1987).
36. B. A. Brown, "Voluntary Versus Mandatory Retirement: What is the Line?" 13 *Employment Relations Today* 39 (1986).
37. 29 EPD ¶ 32,784 (DC Md, 1981), rev'd and rem'd 34 EPD ¶ 34,298 (CA-4, 1984), rev'd and rem'd 37 EPD ¶ 35,292 (SCt, 1985). Cited in Brown at note 36 above.
38. *Johnson v. American Airlines,* 35 EPD ¶ 34,781 (CA-5, 1984); *EEOC v. Boeing,* 37 EPD ¶ 35,436 (DC Wash, 1985), rev'd and rem'd 46 EPD ¶ 37,907 (CA-9, 1988), cert denied 48 EPD ¶ 38,455 (SCt, 1988); *EEOC v. El Paso Natural Gas Co.,* 35 EPD ¶ 34,875 (DC Tex, 1985), 39 EPD ¶ 35,930 (DC Tex, 1985), 40 EPD ¶ 36,399 (CA-5, 1988). Cited in Leap at note 10 above.
39. *Williams v. Hughes Helicopter,* 42 EPD ¶ 36,768 (CA-9, 1986). Cited in Leap at note 10 above.
40. Brown at note 36 above.
41. *Ibid.*
42. 39 EPD ¶ 36,000 (CA-6, 1986), cert. denied 41 EPD ¶ 36,473 (SCt, 1986). Cited in W. L. Kandel, "Waiving ADEA Rights After *Runyan v. NCR,*" 10 *Employee Relations Law Journal* 524 (1985).
43. 32 EPD ¶ 33,723 (CA-DC, 1983), cert. denied 32 EPD ¶ 33,926 (SCt, 1983). Cited in Brown at note 36 above, p. 42.
44. Brown at note 36 above.
45. 33 EPD ¶ 34,035 (CA-3, 1983), cert. denied 35 EPD ¶ 34,663 (SCt, 1984). Cited in W. L. Kandel, "ADEA Caseload Rises: Recession Issues Dominate," 10 *Employee Relations Law Journal* 524 (1984).
46. Ivancevich at note 7 above, p. 120.
47. L. Dube, "Removing the Cap—Eliminating Mandatory Retirement under the ADEA," 15 *Employment Relations Today* 199 (1988), citing "Older Americans in the Workforce: Challenges and Solutions" (BNA 124, 1987).
48. Schuster above at note 18.
49. 35 EPD ¶ 34,926 (DC NY, 1983). Cited in M.K. Denis, "The Roots of Age Discrimination Claims," 12 *Employment Relations Today* 257 (1985).
50. *Rose v. NCR Corp.,* 31 EPD ¶ 33,485 (CA-6, 1983), cert. denied 32 EPD ¶ 33,867 (SCt, 1983). Cited in Denis at note 49 above.
51. 36 EPD ¶ 34,975 (DC Ill, 1984). Cited in Denis at note 49 above.
52. *Dace v. ACF Industries,* 32 EPD ¶ 33,949 (CA-8, 1983), supplemented 33 EPD ¶ 34,210 (CA-8, 1984). Cited in Denis at note 49 above.
53. Denis at note 49 above.
54. Dube cited at note 47 above.
55. Faley cited at note 13 above.

READING 2-3

New Developments in Age Discrimination

Bimal Patel
Brian H. Kleiner

During the course of history, one of the most frequently used methods in teaching a younger worker a new skill was to match him or her with a veteran worker who was quite competent in that skill. The young worker learned by observing, assisting, and practicing the skill. The "student" spent many hours with the "master" for little or no pay. In time the student learned to become as capable as his teacher. In some societies, the passing along of such skills from mentor to student was considered a noble tradition. The actions of corporate America within the past few years are often contrary to such traditional teaching methods. The restructuring of companies has led to an increasing perception that older workers are less necessary to corporate success. This trend began in the late 1980s and has continued through the present.

Almost on a daily basis the workplace is becoming more competitive as corporations face competition not only on a domestic level but internationally as well. When an organization faces stiff competition, many times the result means cutting costs wherever possible. One of the easiest ways to cut costs is to eliminate human resources. The question that must be answered is: "Who should be laid off?" One of the answers is older workers, about whom there exist many stereotypes. "Too many companies today assume that workers over 50 are less flexible and productive, more expensive, and just not as 'with it' as their younger colleagues."[1] Other generalizations about older workers (those over 40) include "they are stubborn, they do not

learn, they are lazy, thick, resist change and are slow thinkers and doers."[2]

When such perceptions abound, it is not difficult to see why older workers quickly become the prime targets of corporate downsizing. In addition to dealing with these stereotypes, older workers must also deal with the fact that they command higher salaries than younger workers. Many times a younger worker is paid about half of what his senior counterpart earns. The wide gap in compensation leaves the door open for management to justify the hiring of two young workers for the price of one older worker.

The fallacy that older workers possess less capability than their younger counterparts results in a sort of vicious cycle. This can be seen in job assignments. When an older worker is no longer assigned the newest and most challenging assignments, his skills become dated as he continues to work on older technology or methodology. The result is that younger workers who receive such assignments display the most desired skills in the organization. Thus, they are perceived as the "movers and shakers" while the older workers are seen as "has beens." A sort of self-fulfilling prophecy is born when younger workers are favored over seniors. Older workers cannot get new assignments which would increase their skill; and because they cannot increase their skills in this manner, they are perceived as less creative. Ultimately, even if they are not laid off, the older workers find that this form of age discrimination results in a distinct lack of interest in their jobs. This further results in being relegated to slower tasks and less important responsibilities. Although not explicit, more and more psychological discrimination results as older and younger workers interact less with each other and more with coworkers their own age. When management allows and encourages such behavior, it becomes almost inevitable that one group suffers from both explicit and subtle forms of prejudice.[3]

With youth comes the perception of strength and vitality. By laying off older workers and replacing them with younger ones, corporations

Source: Reproduced with permission from the November 1994 *Labor Law Journal* published and copyrighted by CCH Incorporated, 2700 Lake Cook Road, Riverwoods, Illinois 60015.

may feel that, along with getting the most for their salary expense, they are receiving the contributions of a fresh and eager group of employees. Employers see young workers as able, motivated, and very trainable. That is, they do not hold preconceived notions on how tasks and ideas should be implemented, so they can be encouraged to do things as management thinks best. These factors along with the stereotypes discussed above have helped to fuel the fire of age discrimination in recent years.

DEALING WITH DISCRIMINATION AND UNEMPLOYMENT

Are companies acting wisely in letting go older talent? By looking only at the short term bottom line, talented resources might be going to waste. Although there is much to be said for the enthusiasm that youth may bring to an organization, there are also points which maturity brings to an organization that should be considered. Various pieces of research show that stereotypes of older workers just are not true. Older workers consistently receive high ratings on key job skills, loyalty, reliability, and lack of turnover and absenteeism according to a recently completed five-year study by the Commonwealth Fund in New York, as well as other research.[4]

Peter Naylor suggests that even when the negative stereotypes discussed previously apply to a worker, other favorable factors must also be considered, particularly, a stable work record, fewer on-the-job accidents, and higher job satisfaction resulting in less likelihood to leave. Additionally, some jobs require a large amount of knowledge which can only be acquired over time.[5] Finally, companies need to consider the costs savings in laying off an older employee versus the value he brings through experience.

John Lawrie, contributing editor in *Personnel Journal,* sees the trend toward change and faster performance leading companies to what is called the "Detroit syndrome." With regard to older workers, this means, "devalue them, discount them, and dump them."[6] On the other

hand, some companies are beginning to realize that older workers have much to contribute to their organizations. They are responding not only to past mistakes in perceptions but to increasing state and federal legislation as well as litigation brought on by workers who have been victims of age discrimination.

There are policies and programs that companies can implement in order to change attitudes about older workers throughout the organization as well as change older workers' attitudes about themselves. In retraining older workers, companies can allow longer lead times for workers to acquire new skills and adopt new policies. Older workers supposedly resist change, but they have lived through vast amounts of social and technical change in their lifetimes; thus, they are indeed capable of adjustments. Perhaps allotting them a little extra time is all that is necessary to combat their reluctance to try something new.[7]

Two factors work well with all employees, praise and guidance. By giving praise to older workers, they find that new jobs pose less of a threat, resulting in a greater tendency to accommodate changes. Also, providing older workers with direction gives them support during periods of change.[8]

Another very important use for older workers is simply one of their traditional roles as mentioned above: mentor and coach. By allowing older workers to interact with younger employees, the stereotypes which cripple productivity can be lifted. The transfer of skill and knowledge may result in negative stereotypes being dissipated. Younger workers may see that they have much to learn from senior members of the organization. Conversely, older employees may find more purpose and meaning in their positions when they see that they can positively influence workers who previously were their detractors. Such interaction may result in higher productivity and enthusiasm from both groups of employees; thus, on the whole, the organization's attitude about all its employees becomes more positive.

While some organizations are discovering that the changing of attitudes is beneficial for all concerned, there are still many older workers who are unemployed. Finding jobs in the 90s has been difficult for all levels of employees, but older workers still seem to have an especially difficult time. "They have had to fight society's preoccupation with youth, not to mention outright age discrimination. And their high salaries have made them prime targets for layoffs."[9] From 1989 to 1992, the number of people over 50 becoming unemployed increased by 68.1% compared to a 40.6% increase for those under 50.

For those who have been laid off and do not perceive legal recourse as a solution, there are some things that can be done to increase the chances of finding employment. Basically, the suggestions follow those methods used by younger workers. Older workers need to increase their skills by taking courses. They need to look at smaller or high growth companies to find employment. In marketing themselves they need to show flexibility and energy. Finally, they must realize that their salaries may be based on market rates, not what they were earning previously.

LAWSUITS AND WAIVERS

As we have seen, older workers are prime targets for layoffs, especially in the corporate downsizing that has been ongoing over the past several years. Companies need to realize that the penalties of engaging in age discrimination can be quite severe. A recent survey of 515 verdicts in wrongful-termination lawsuits found that the average age discrimination award was $302,914. That average is higher than those found for race, sex, and disability discrimination. According to Brian Shenker, research director at Jury Verdict Research, juries are more sympathetic toward older workers because they're basically unemployable at this point and they're probably never going to be able to earn

that kind of money again. Other victims of discrimination usually can move on to other jobs at comparable pay.[10]

Two related trends in the area of age discrimination have developed over the past few years. First, there have been an increasing number of age discrimination claims. "Age discrimination claims filed with the Equal Employment Opportunity Commission jumped 34 percent to 19,884 in 1993 from 14,789 in 1989."[11] When a plant closes and a large number of people are laid off at the same time, it is almost guaranteed that age bias suits will be filed. The second trend has been the use of generous early retirement packages offered by companies to older workers; in accepting these packages employees have been required to waive their rights under various labor laws including the Age Discrimination in Employment Act (ADEA) of 1967.

HISTORY OF LABOR LAW

The ADEA was passed by Congress in 1967. Its purposes are: "to promote employment of older persons based on their ability rather than age; to prohibit arbitrary age discrimination in employment; to help employers and workers find ways of meeting problems arising from the impact of age on employment."[12] The law makes it illegal for an employer to discriminate against persons 40 years of age or older with regard to "compensation, terms, conditions or privileges of employment because of such individual's age."[13] Thus, the ADEA requires that employers not implement policies and procedures which discriminate against an employee simply because of his age. The law requires that employees are evaluated on their performance as opposed to age.

The ADEA also provides for some exemptions. Businesses with less than 20 employees are not subject to the act. The act allows age to be used as a qualification where it is a bona fide occupational qualification (BFOQ). The act is administered by the Equal Employment Opportunity Commission (EEOC).[14]

When the ADEA was passed it placed an upper limit of age 65 on those who were protected. Thus, employers could force retirement on employees who reached 65. In 1978, Congress lifted the limit to 70 because it was concerned about older people losing income because of forced retirement. Additionally, Congress was concerned that society on the whole would suffer when productive people were no longer allowed to contribute to a productive society and became a burden on the government through their use of social security and other programs. Finally in 1986, Congress removed the upper age limit altogether.[15]

In order to persuade employees who need to be laid off to leave the company, many employers now offer benefits which are well in excess of that which an employee would have received if he was laid off involuntarily. For example, additional severance pay, increased length of health benefit coverage, and job-placement assistance are some of the benefits being offered to such employees. In return for these benefits, the employee signs a waiver that says he will not sue the company for age discrimination at a later date. The concept behind such an arrangement is to "head off" claims of age discrimination filed by workers who are laid off.[16]

The waiver has been used for many years and has been increasingly used over the past several years. With respect to use of waivers, the U.S. General Accounting Office (GAO) has found that "data indicate a steady increase in the use of waivers as an exit incentive practice of corporate America during the period from 1979 through 1988."[17] The concern of Congress has been whether such agreements have been entered into by the employee on a voluntary basis or under duress. That is, the employee was told that if he did not sign such a waiver and leave the company he would suffer the loss of his job because of its elimination through company reorganization effort; after signing the release, the employee would then find it extremely difficult to find work of similar position and pay when the additional severance benefits ran out. In particular, Congress was concerned that older employees were being forced into signing such waivers without the oversight of any government agency.

Congress saw the tactics described above as a means of circumventing the ADEA, especially when the signing of releases was not monitored. In order to better protect the interests of older workers, Congress passed the Older Workers Benefits Protection Act (OWBPA) in 1990. Provisions with regard to waivers were added to the Act to "ensure that older workers are not coerced or manipulated into waiving their rights to seek legal relief under the Age Discrimination in Employment Act."[18] The Act essentially outlines requirements that must be followed in order to ensure that when an employee waives his rights under the ADEA, it is done so on a "knowing and voluntary basis."

The OWBPA "establishes eight minimum conditions that must be met before a release can be deemed to be knowing and voluntary." Specifically, the requirements of the act are: (1) the waiver is part of an agreement between the employer and employee, and as such it must be written in plain English; (2) the agreement refers to rights the employee has under the ADEA as opposed to the generic release of "any and all claims"; (3) the waiver does not waive rights and claims that arise after the date of the agreement; (4) in exchange for signing the waiver, the employee is entitled to compensation that is in addition to what he would already receive; (5) the employee is advised in writing to consult with an attorney prior to signing the agreement; (6) the employee is given a reasonable time period to review the agreement; (7) a seven day time period is allowed in which the employee may revoke the agreement; (8) when a group or class of employees are being terminated, the employees must be given 45 days to consider the release agreement.[19]

Thus, the conditions listed above give workers protection when considering a release. The individual is given relief with respect to time pressures. He cannot be threatened into signing a waiver because he feels that the deal he is being offered will disappear in a few days, and he will procure no additional benefits. The individual can now consult the opinion of an attorney of his choosing. In doing so he will be advised by counsel who has only his best interest in mind. Also of consideration is the fact that the individual has not been forced to give up the right to claims that have not yet arisen.

Prior to the passage of the OWBPA, most courts accepted waivers as a legal method of terminating relations between employee and employer as long as it could be shown that the agreement was entered into voluntarily. In determining whether such conditions existed at the time of signing, courts looked at the "totality-of-circumstance test." That is, in general, noting the educational level of the individual, the time allotted for consideration, whether a private attorney was consulted, the simplicity of the language of the agreement, and the additional considerations that were offered the individual. Also, it should be noted that the courts viewed the acceptance of considerations after agreement as a ratification of the contract. That is, an individual could not make a claim of discrimination after the continued acceptance of termination benefits.[20]

HOW EMPLOYERS CAN HANDLE DISCRIMINATION CLAIMS

To an employer it might appear that the laws discussed above are inherently biased against businesses. That is a debatable point. What is certain is that continued layoffs will bring more age discrimination lawsuits as cited previously. In order to better position themselves against lawsuits filed for ADEA violations, it would be in the best interest of employers to fully understand and abide by the laws. In doing so, they are abiding by guidelines that allow them to lay off older workers legally.

To ensure that older workers are not discriminated against, businesses can take specific steps. Companies should make sure that layoffs are for "legitimate business purposes" as opposed to getting rid of just one person. When a whole department is being eliminated rather than an overall reduction in workforce, it is easier to defend against claims of age discrimination. Companies should be clear about the manner in which a reduction in human resources will take place. Guidelines for evaluating who will be kept and who will be laid off must be adhered to strictly. Charges of discrimination can be brought up when someone is terminated who does not fit the overall criteria for the layoff.

The goal should be to keep the best qualified people, not try to sneak in the termination of an employee simply because of his age. Companies which disseminate information with regard to possible layoffs may find it easier to defend against claims of discrimination brought up later. The layoff process should be perceived by employees as being as fair as possible. When downsizing needs to occur, the possibility of transfers should also be mentioned to employees. Thus, careful communication of potential layoffs may serve as a deterrent to litigation.

For those employees who have been laid off, the employer may consider setting up an "appeals" process whereby the human resources department or some neutral party will listen to employees who have been let go and feel that they've been treated unfairly. Again, the cost of such an action may be considerably less than involvement in a lawsuit.[21] Even if the employer is successful in defending against a discrimination claim, he must also consider the non-monetary loss to the reputation of his business as well the loss of morale of current employees.

From a purely legal standpoint, employers may be able to defend against claims of age discrimination if they can show that age is a BFOQ. The ADEA explicitly allows for BFOQ age discrimination. There are two guidelines an employer can follow in order to show BFOQ: "(1)

The age limit is reasonably necessary to the essence of the business, and (2) all or substantially all individuals over that age are unable to perform adequately, or some of the individuals over that age possess a disqualifying trait that cannot be ascertained except by reference to age."[22] Thus, if the above generalization is found to be true, a BFOQ can be established. Discrimination against older people has been allowed particularly when safety is a chief concern.

Obviously, the best way for an employer to protect himself from claims under the OWBPA is simply to make sure that the release agreement satisfies the eight minimum requirements. Essentially, ADEA release agreements are contracts and thus, even with the OWBPA considerations, follow standard contract principles. One of those principles is ratification of contract. It is based on the principle of equity: one party cannot be allowed to enjoy the benefits of a contract and not maintain his or her end of the bargain. When employers are threatened with a lawsuit that claims that the OWBPA was violated they may use the argument that ratification of a contract (in this case, the considerations given to the employees) requires that such considerations be returned prior to bringing a lawsuit.

In a court of law, the employer can argue that precedence has been set showing the acceptance of compensation is adequate to ratify the release and that the only way the plaintiff may continue the suit is to return all considerations that were part of the agreement. If the plaintiff reconsiders and decides that the OWBPA was not violated by his former employer, he will simply keep the considerations and drop the lawsuit. The above concept of ratification of contract may be very useful to employers who face claims after waivers have been signed.[23]

The waiver is a tool which allows employees and employers to sever relations in a manner which is beneficial to both. The increasing use of waivers makes it necessary for both parties to carefully consider the legal implications in following through with the agreement. The ADEA and OWBPA provide the rules which must be followed in order to ensure that age discrimination in the workplace does not occur. The proper use of release agreements will continue to safeguard the rights of older workers as well as employers.

THE DISCONTENT OF YOUTH

A third recent development in age discrimination has been what is known as the baby boomer generation versus the post-boomer generation. The baby boomers were born in the twenty years following World War II. As such, they are now in their 40s. The post-boomer generation, born during the mid to late 1960s, are now in their 20s. This generation has also recently been designated Generation X. With the influx of these younger workers into the business world over the past few years, there has been an increasing tension in corporate America between older and younger workers.

Perhaps what we see is not blatant age discrimination but a spin-off of discrimination known as "ageism." Ageism, broadly defined, is the disregard for the contributions of older employees. Many older workers today are finding that their bosses are younger than they are, much younger in some cases. The workplace has become one of the arenas where Generation X, for better or worse, is making its presence felt.

The "forty something" generation sees the younger workers as immature, arrogant, and unwilling to "pay their dues" in the corporate world. The older workers see Generation X as unwilling to work hard for lower pay as they move up the corporate ladder. They want control, power, and money at the beginning of their careers. In many cases younger workers have just those things and they continue to devalue the contributions that older workers can make and have made in the past. The forty-somethings see the "twenty-somethings" as a generation that only wants to work with its contemporaries and is not compelled to work long and hard hours as the "workaholic" boomers have done. They are unwilling to show respect for authority and the traditional hierarchical structure of most companies. One summation about the younger generation: "They aren't loyal or committed to work, detractors say, changing jobs more casually than sex partners and refusing to go that extra mile to do things right."[24]

The twenty-something workers see the modern workplace full of corporate politics and bickering. They don't see progress but merely people trying to "get ahead" of each other. They claim that strict hierarchies in corporations only contribute to political problems. That being the case they find the people in control (the forty-somethings) are the very cause of their grief and frustrations. The younger workers say they want to make a contribution in the place they work, not deal with unnecessary "make-work." The perception of Generation X is that they need to make things happen for themselves in order to feel that their contributions are worthwhile.

For older workers, the Eighties were a time to make money; and that's just what they did, whether they produced something of substance or not. Most of those in their mid to late twenties were not in a position to catch the "wave of wealth" that they perceive took place during the Eighties. As such, the twenty-somethings bear some animosity toward the previous generation that, on the whole, did fairly well for itself only ten years previously.

Generation X wants a piece of the pie, but they don't see much left for them. They blame forty-somethings for using resources that they never got to touch. Thus, with today's lower salaries and tighter job market, there is no room for "silliness." As one 29 year old put it: "Today, with wage stagnation the way it is, people's patience for nonsense has hit the floor."[25] As far as Generation X is concerned, the forty-somethings had life easy from childhood through the corporate workplace and has left the younger workers with no opportunity in the workplace.

Job security has become a thing of the past, and the twenty-something crowd has seen it firsthand. Not only have they seen their parents laid off, many of them have experienced job loss through no fault of their own. The older generation sees the younger as being disloyal, while the younger sees the older as unwilling to change. The twenty-somethings don't see loyalty and working for people who are not open to their ideas as particularly strong selling points of corporate America. Thus, they are prone to resent their superiors. The younger workers feel that companies need to be loyal to them in order to receive reciprocation. The older management is particulary guilty of espousing "participatory management" but then adhering to the old way of making decisions. Twenty-somethings feel this is especially true in the case of finances.

As the U.S. workforce ages and more people step into retirement, the younger generation of workers will be responsible for keeping more senior citizens well. "In 1960, less than 10 percent of the U.S. population was over 60, but that's expected to double by 2020. So a growing tax burden will fall on a smaller fraction of young workers."[26] Not only will Generation X have to deal with more taxes, it also perceives that it will not be able to enjoy the same standard of living that previous generations have enjoyed. The people they blame are the very people they work for or, many times, the people they are now supervising.

To create a better working environment between older and younger workers, some steps need to be taken. One solution is to create an environment that is more open to the ideas of not only young workers, but all workers: an entrepreneurial environment. Along with such an environment there needs to be real implementation of the concepts of empowerment and teamwork. In any organization, large or small, the input of all employees should carry some degree of importance in order to create an atmosphere where people can thrive. The younger generation wants recognition for its accomplishments and achievements in the workplace. The older generation, within management and external to management, needs to realize and act on this in order to decrease tensions that may exist between younger and older employees.

By the same token, the twenty-something workers would be wise to see that recognition for contributions, both past and present, is a two-way street and that they need to acknowledge older workers to whom they are subordinate and superior in position. Whether they realize it or not, each group of employees needs the other to some degree. Accommodating the needs of both in corporate America will benefit organizations as a whole.

CONCLUSIONS

We have observed that age discrimination can take on many forms in the workplace. Many times it is the result of inaccurate perceptions of society as a whole. It appears that within the past few years, as competition throughout America and the world has increased dramatically, age discrimination has been on the rise. Within organizations there has been a great need to cut costs and justify existing costs. In doing so, many times the most expensive employees in salary terms are the first to be terminated. Whether or not this is done legally is a question that has prompted legislation on both the federal and state level. The recent increase in termination of all employees has increased age discrimination lawsuits. Businesses need to be aware that age discrimination is not being tolerated in the same way it might have been in the past.

Corporate belt tightening and the perception that opportunities are few in corporate America has also resulted in a new generation of workers who find no pleasure in politics and feel they are being ignored by the older management. Some of these younger workers are creating tensions and disrespect toward older employees which lowers the overall effectiveness of companies.

In order for American businesses to stay competitive, they need to realize that older workers can contribute many things to an organization which are not simply represented in salary paid. If businesses fail to recognize that age discrimination cannot continue, the legal system may well be sending stronger messages. In recognizing older workers, corporate America must endeavor to create environments where all employees can work together. This can be done by the mutual giving of respect and recognition when achievements are made by any employee regardless of his position.

NOTES

1. Galen, M., "Myths About Older Workers Cost Business Plenty," *Business Week,* 155.3351, Dec. 20, 1993, p. 83.
2. Naylor, P., "In Praise of Older Workers," *Personnel Management,* Nov 1987, pp. 44–48.
3. Lawrie, J., "Subtle Discrimination Pervades Corporate America (Age Discrimination)," *Personnel Journal,* Vol. 69, Jan 1990, pp. 53–55.
4. Galen, supra.
5. Naylor, supra.
6. Lawrie, supra, at 53.
7. Ibid., at 11.
8. Ibid.
9. Bongiorno, L., "Jobless at 50? It's Not Hopeless," *Business Week,* Iss. 3351, Dec. 20, 1993, pp. 82–83.
10. *Small Business Reports.* "Age Before . . . ," Vol. 19 No. 3, Mar 1994, p. 19. Marley, S., "Age-Related Suits Increase," *Business Insurance,* Vol. 28, No. 3, Jan 17, 1994, pp. 1, 29.
11. Marley S., "Age-Related Suits Increase," *Business Insurance,* Vol. 28, No. 3, Jan. 17, 1994, pp. 1, 29.
12. Cavaliere, F. J., "Derogatory Remarks as Evidence of Discrimination Under the Age Discrimination in Employment Act of 1967," *Labor Law Journal,* Vol. 44 Nov. 1993, pp. 664–672.
13. Ibid., at 665.
14. Ibid.
15. Ledvinka, J., and Scarpello, V. G., *Federal Regulation of Personnel and Human Resource Man-*

agement (2nd ed.), Wadsworth Publishing Co., Belmont, California.

16. Caldwell, V., "Fear of Firing," *Incentive,* Vol. 167 No. 7, Jul. 1993, pp. 68–69.
17. Mitchell, C. E., "Waiver of Rights Under the Age Discrimination in Employment Act: Implications of the Older Workers Benefit Protection Act of 1990," *Labor Law Journal,* Vol. 43, Nov 1992, pp. 735–744.
18. Ibid.
19. Nager, G.D. and Catlett, S.T., "Employees Can't Have Their Cake and Eat It Too: Estopping Age Discrimination Complainants Who Have Signed Releases," *Employee Relations Law Journal,* Vol. 19 No. 2, Autumn 1993, pp. 295–305. Mitchell, supra, at 736–737.
20. Mitchell, supra, at 743.
21. Marley, supra.
22. Ledvinka, supra, at 102.
23. Nager, supra.
24. Ratan, S., "General Tension in the Office: Why Busters Hate Boomers," *Fortune* Vol. 125 No. 8 Oct. 4, 1993, pp. 56–70.
25. Ibid. at 64.
26. Becker, G.S.: "Cut the Graybeards a Smaller Slice of the Pie," *Business Week,* Iss. 3364, Mar 28, 1994, p. 20.

READING 2-4

Discrimination

Janet Radcliffe Richards

A few years ago, when the EEC was as usual sinking beneath lakes of this and mountains of that, someone had the bright idea that if we removed the duty from wine we should be able to mop up that particular surplus in no time at all. However, the plan ran into problems straight

---

Source: Janet Radcliffe Richards, "Discrimination," PASS Vol. LIX, 1985. Reprinted by courtesy of the Editor of the Aristotelian Society © 1985.

away. Any such policy, it was claimed, would discriminate against the working man, who drank beer. At about the same time, when VAT was about to be imposed on sweets, irate parents appeared on radio programmes protesting about 'discrimination against the kiddies'. If taxes are spread evenly, that apparently discriminates against the poor (or perhaps more commonly, the family man); if they are slanted to the higher incomes, they discriminate against the rich. When duty on petrol or tobacco goes up, the government is discriminating against the motorist or the smoker. And in general, the word tends to be invoked the moment any group finds that some policy or action is making it worse off than it would like to be.

It is easy to see why this happens. 'Discrimination', in its recent, political sense, comes trailing connotations of arbitrariness and injustice, so that to label a disadvantage 'discrimination' is implicitly to claim that it is unjustified, and should be eliminated on grounds of justice to the disadvantaged group. To this extent the meaning of the word seems fixed: anyone who disagrees that some disadvantage is unjust is more likely to express this by saying that the case is not one of discrimination, rather than that it really is discrimination but nevertheless justified. The rest of the meaning, on the other hand, is very far from clear, and there are no well-entrenched criteria for distinguishing disadvantages which are cases of discrimination from ones which are not. This means, in turn, that if a group does call its disadvantage discrimination—thereby implying that it is unjustly treated—it is not at all obvious how anyone wanting to dispute the label's appropriateness could set about doing so. In practice, therefore, 'discrimination' allows a transition from *disadvantage* to *injustice* which may be far too rapid, and has become an invaluable tool for the fudger of political arguments.

My intention in this paper is to embark on the process of making such conjuring tricks more difficult, by trying to sort out not so much the meaning of the word (although a definition will be suggested) as the terrain which tends to be its habitat.

The paper is in two parts. The first deals with the question of when a social rule or convention which differentiates between two groups actually discriminates between them, and argues that discrimination is quite distinct from other things which may reasonably be objected to in such rules. The second part turns to the subject of discrimination in the actions of individuals, and argues that what is normally seen as discrimination by individuals is really either dependent on discriminatory rules, or something so different in kind that it should probably not be called discrimination at all. If discrimination does reside essentially in rules rather than malevolent or misguided individuals there are considerable consequences for campaigns to eliminate discrimination, and the final section suggests what some of these may be.

The argument is illustrated mainly by discussions of questions about sex discrimination, but the conclusions are relevant—though in rather complicated ways which there is no space to discuss here—to other kinds of discrimination. And it should be stressed that I am intending only to discuss what discrimination is, and not to prove that discrimination against women or anyone else actually exists. In one or two places discrimination is referred to in ways which suggest that some group really is discriminated against, but nothing I shall say here either proves or depends on the justifiability of such claims. It is compatible with the limited thesis of this paper that no discrimination exists, or ever has existed.

I

1. By way of a promising-looking case history, which has the slight merit that it concerns neither the appointment of university teachers nor admission to medical schools, but still raises questions of public policy, consider the position of London Transport in 1969.[1] Plans were going ahead to increase the number of single-operator buses, and as people gradually came to recognize the full implications of the part of the scheme which involved keeping the former conductors employed by training them as drivers, murmurs of discontent began to be heard. The idea would not do at all, according to the existing drivers, because quite a lot of the conductors were women, and women were just not strong enough to cope with buses. The little buses, they eventually conceded, might perhaps just be manageable, but certainly not the big ones. And for a while they succeeded in having the exclusion of women from driving established as a policy.

Whether or not the details are accurate, such a case is typical of innumerable actual and proposed policies which specify that two groups are to be treated differently, and where the group which finds itself worse off as a result is likely to complain—or have it complained on its behalf by others—that it is discriminated against. The example is limited in various ways, since woman-excluding rules and rules which concern suitability to occupy particular positions are by no means the only ones which may be thought discriminatory. However, the bus case raises questions which are relevant to all, and the ensuing arguments are meant to apply to all cases of differential treatment of different groups, even though transposing the discussion to such other contexts would in places be tricky.

For now, for reasons which will be more obvious later, I shall consider questions about discrimination only as they arise in contexts like this one, where what is at issue are the policies and institutions which form the basis of organization of a society. Some of these actually determine what it is possible for different groups to do; others make it inadvisable for individuals to trespass on the wrong territory by penalizing offenders. The rules and institutions may be formal, as in the case of laws, or informal, as when social convention decrees that people are to act or be treated in a certain kind of way, and inappropriate behaviour incurs social disapproval of varying degrees of severity.[2] All such social devices I shall for the sake of convenience, since there is no well-entrenched term to catch them all, call rules.

The problem is to decide when a rule which draws a distinction between two groups should be regarded as discriminating between them, where it is at least a necessary condition of its counting as discriminatory that the less well off group should have legitimate grounds for complaint about its treatment. Women are undoubtedly disadvantaged by the bus-driving rule, but are they actually discriminated against? And if they are, what is it about the rule which makes it discriminatory?

One way to set about sorting the matter out is through a consideration of the drivers' own defence of their position. To provide an adequate justification of a rule is to show that the rule is not objectionable. If the drivers' arguments are good, therefore, those arguments must show that the proposed woman-excluding rule is acceptable and therefore, a fortiori, not discriminatory. Conversely, if a rule is objectionable in any way, it should be possible to show where any attempted justification of it falls short.

The drivers' defence was elliptical, but it is easy enough to imagine how it might have looked if spelt out in full. Buses must be driven competently, for the efficiency of the service and the safety of passengers and other road users, and this calls for drivers with enough strength to handle the bus properly. Women, however, are not strong enough, and therefore must not be allowed to drive buses.

There are all kinds of ways in which this argument might be attacked. Perhaps to start with, however, it is best to keep it at a slight distance (from where, as is so often the case with works of art, it appears at its best), resisting any temptation to pursue the remarkable empirical claim about the relative toughness of women and

buses, and to consider first only the general *form* of the justification.

This is of a perfectly ordinary and easily recognized kind: something is to be achieved, and in order to achieve it some things must be used rather than others. To make a cake sweet it is necessary to use sugar rather than salt. If a car is to function properly, what goes in the tank must be petrol and not water. If buses are to be driven the way they should be driven, it is necessary to distinguish between people who are capable of doing the job properly and those who are not. Some things or people are used in preference to others *because* of the need to achieve a particular end. The justification of the choice is expressed in terms of the end.

In the case of cakes and the like, of course, we say 'explain' more readily than 'justify' because there is no moral issue: no question of discriminating against salt in specifying sugar. The question of possible discrimination, and therefore of justification, arises when the excluded group is not only animate, but actually wants the thing it is excluded from—or at least, when that thing is regarded by others as something it ought to have.

This need not happen in all cases of selection: sometimes it makes no difference to people whether they are selected for some particular purpose or not. But what of the cases when this does arise? Is the group excluded from the advantage unfairly treated in any way?

If it were, the only way to avoid unfairness in selection would be to distinguish between people only when there was nothing to choose between being selected or not. This would often mean either refusing to select at all, or doing so only after making sure that circumstances had been so adjusted as to make the non-selected as well off as the selected. There may indeed be certain kinds of egalitarian who incline to ideas of justice which have this sort of consequence (though I think there are problems even in expressing them coherently). Nevertheless, even though according to such a theory a group left worse off by a selection may have some kind of injustice to complain of, that still seems to have nothing to do with what is at issue when people complain about discrimination.

To start with, allegations of discrimination can be, and frequently are, made by people with no such egalitarian ideas at all. Furthermore, whatever anyone's general views about equality, it is simply not the case that whenever someone is appointed to a desirable position, the appointment is said to discriminate against everyone who did not get it on the grounds that they would have been better off if they had done. If discrimination consisted of this, *everyone* disqualified from bus driving (including the blind, the perpetually drunk and all the rest) could claim discrimination with as much plausibility as the excluded women. Clearly, however, it is not the case that everyone excluded from bus driving is discriminated against.

A complaint about discrimination is not about a selection's being made, or about the relative advantages of being selected or not, but about *who* is selected. It is not, therefore, a sufficient condition of women's being discrimination against by the bus driving rule that it makes them worse off than the men who are allowed to drive. There must be more to discrimination than that.

2. If there is more to discrimination against a group than simply its being disadvantaged by differential treatment, perhaps it has something to do with the purposes the differentiation is intended to achieve. Suppose, for instance, that the reason for the drivers' thinking strength necessary to their profession had nothing whatever to do with the competent handling of buses for the good of all. Suppose that in fact they were motivated by fantasies about a fleet of buses which would dominate the road and put terror into the hearts of Londoners, with drivers who would mow down motorists who got in the way and roar away from bus stops when old ladies with heavy bags were scurrying in their direction. It would certainly be an advantage for such drivers to be strong, so that they could deal efficiently with anyone who might be moved to protest about this kind of behaviour, but if that were indeed the reason for demanding strength in bus drivers most people would think it a pretty bad one. In such a case, then, could we reasonably say that the policy did discriminate against women, on the grounds that if transport policies had been as they should have been, with no need for aggressiveness and strength in drivers, women would have been suitable for the work?[3]

Certainly if the ends achieved by a rule are bad, there are grounds on which the rule can be objected to. It must also often be true that when bad purposes are to be achieved, different qualities will be needed than would have been the case if the purposes had been good ones, and that therefore people who would have been selected by a good policy are made worse off, because of the bad one, than they ought to be. However, it does not follow from the fact that discrimination is bad that everything bad is some kind of discrimination, and it does seem to me that it would involve an intolerable stretching of even so ill-defined a word to say that in a case such as this one women would be discriminated against.

In a case of discrimination, what is wrong is that the discriminated-against group has grounds for complaining that it is badly treated. In this imaginary case, however, if the bus company's purpose is bad it is not bad *because* women are not selected, even though their exclusion may be one consequence of the policy. The purpose is bad for reasons having nothing to do with women, and would be equally bad whoever was selected to fulfill it. Another way of putting this is to say that in order to know that women were discriminated against, you would have to know that women were badly treated in some way, but in order to decide whether the bus company's ideas about what constituted a well-driven bus were good or bad it would be quite unnecessary to know which groups of people would be excluded from bus driving as a result, or anything about women at all.

A rule's having an objectionable purpose, therefore, seems by no means the same as its being discriminatory, even when it is bad for some non-selected group as well as being just generally bad. Anyone who did want to insist that this was indeed a kind of discrimination, however, would still have to concede that it could not be the only kind, since it would otherwise be impossible for there to be discrimination in cases where the purposes were good. In the case in hand, for instance, we have no reason to believe that London Transport had any intention of running a fleet of killer buses, but the rule excluding women, even if the background ideas of bus driving are entirely respectable, does still look as though it may be discriminatory.

3. The bus drivers' woman-excluding policy cannot be said to discriminate against women simply on the grounds that women are disadvantaged by it, and could not be said to discriminate against them even if their exclusion had been in consequence of bus-driving purposes which left a lot to be desired. If the rule is indeed discriminatory, therefore, it must be for some other reason, and the drivers' justification of it needs closer scrutiny.

The claim is that women must be excluded because this is a necessary means to a desirable end: a certain amount of strength is needed for competent driving, and women have not got it. Even if the empirical claim about women's weakness were true, however, (a matter which can still be left to one side for a while), a woman-excluding rule would certainly not be sufficient to achieve the end of having buses well driven. Even though strength might be deemed a necessary requirement for the ideal bus driver, there would not be much point in excluding women on the grounds of their inadequacy if the specifications were not tight enough to keep out substandard men as well.

However, if a certain level of strength is indeed needed for adequate driving, the ordinary rules of driver selection must include a strength requirement. This in turn means that if the men are right about women's not being strong enough, the rule excluding women must exclude only people *already* excluded by the existing specifications. And it is hardly an argument in favour of having a particular rule, that whatever it is supposed to achieve would have been achieved anyway, without it. If the men are right about women's weakness, their woman-excluding rule can have no purpose at all.

A rule or policy can only be justified in terms of its bringing about something which would not have been achieved without it. If this policy achieves anything which would not have been brought about by the ordinary criteria of driver selection, that must necessarily be the exclusion of people *not* excluded by the other rules. Those rules themselves exclude all people unsuitable to drive. The only people who are additionally excluded by the rule saying that there should be no women, therefore, are ones who *are* suitable; women who are competent to drive buses, in strength as in other respects. The rule which was defended in terms of producing good drivers turns out to have no other effect than to exclude some good drivers.

Although the drivers claimed that women should be excluded *because they were incompetent,* then, their rule only makes sure that they are to be excluded *in spite of the fact that they may be competent.* And this does seem to catch the most fundamental connotations of 'discrimination': the exclusion of people from some position not because of their unsuitability to achieve a particular purpose, but in spite of their suitability.

A different, and slightly more accurate, way of putting the matter is this. The bus drivers tried to justify the exclusion of women in terms of an end they claimed they wanted to achieve. However, as their argument in terms of that end could not justify the exclusion of women, they failed to show that their wish to treat women differently from men was anything other than an end in itself. It is in this that the discrimination against women seems to consist. A social rule or convention discriminates between two groups when it treats them differently not as a means to some other end, but as an end in itself. If, on the other hand, the differential treatment is a means to some end which can be expressed in quite general terms, even if that end is a dubious one, there is no discrimination.

4. There is still more to be said, however. The original problem was to find out whether the woman-excluding rule (and so others of the kind) was in fact, as it appeared, discriminatory. But the account of discrimination just given applies only to the purposes to be achieved by a rule, rather than to the rule itself, and these are two very different matters. So far all that has been shown of the bus drivers is that they have *failed to explain* their rule in terms of a non-discriminatory purpose. But that is not enough to show that the rule itself is discriminatory: perhaps someone else could make a better job of justifying it. Any given rule might in principle be justified in various different ways, and be capable of explanation in both discriminatory and non-discriminatory terms. This looks like a serious matter, if the reason for trying to find a definition of discrimination is to be able to say when a rule really is discriminatory, and therefore to be objected to.

However, although I think there is no escaping the conclusion that discrimination must be understood in terms of ends to be achieved by rules, that does not mean that rules themselves cannot be objected to on the basis of arguments about discrimination.

In the first place, it is important that the onus of proof lies with anyone who wants to show that a potentially discriminatory rule is not in fact so. Whenever a rule specifies that two

groups shall be treated differently, we know that one thing the rule must achieve is that differential treatment, and until someone shows that it is a means to some other end, that is *all* we know it achieves. In other words, discrimination is the default value: the onus of proof lies with anyone who wants to maintain that any differentiation is a means to something else rather than an end in itself. Any rule which specifies different treatment for different groups must therefore be regarded as discriminatory until proved otherwise.

Second, although there may be no objective question about whether a rule is discriminatory or not, there certainly are objective questions about whether any particular attempt at justification actually works. As I hope I have already shown, the bus drivers' attempt to justify their woman-excluding policy in terms of a commendable concern that buses should not run amok through having weaklings at their wheels failed, quite objectively, on grounds of logic. And if after their recognition of this setback they were to pick themselves up and try another argument to their conclusion it would not be enough just to get the logic right. Other things are necessary too.

Obviously, a successful justification must also be empirically plausible. The failure of the bus drivers' argument was in fact over-determined, since the most superficial attempt to investigate the matter would have shown—as has since appeared—that women can cope with buses perfectly well. And people who do try to salvage conclusions like the drivers' by devising arguments which escape the logical trap frequently do so only at the cost of slipping further into empirical absurdity.

In this particular case, for instance, the next move is (invariably, the natural history of argument in this area seems to suggest) to shift to some form of efficiency argument. 'Maybe *some* women are strong enough', it is said, 'but *most* are not, and if we waste our time looking at floods of unsuitable applicants the service will suffer and that will be bad for everyone . . .' Or, in other words, since there is a correlation between sex and strength, and sex is easier to spot than strength, it is more efficient to select by sex instead. However, although this kind of argument does indeed succeed in avoiding logical trouble (there are a great many cases in which it is perfectly reasonable to produce an argument of such a form), all the versions I have yet come across in this context depend on pretty silly empirical premises. Is it plausible that most women are too weak to drive buses? If they are, is it really likely that they will clog up the system by applying in droves? Even if they would, why is it not most efficient simply to insist that all applicants, of either sex, come to interview carrying the hundredweight sack of coke which is kept at the depot gates?

Finally, if someone did manage to pass through all the logical and empirical hoops unscathed, and succeeded in justifying a differentiating rule in terms of some non-discriminatory end, that would still not be much use if the chosen non-discriminatory end were itself unacceptable. There is no point in producing a nondiscriminatory defense of a particular rule if that defence is equally objectionable on other grounds. It would be possible, for instance, to argue that women of childbearing age should be excluded from all other activities on the grounds that they should be producing endless supplies of children to enable the state to fight indefinitely many wars. This would be a nondiscriminatory justification, but how many people would be willing to defend the bus drivers' conclusion by an argument like that? And how many people would they persuade if they tried?

If of course someone does succeed in defending some differentiating rule in terms of a non-discriminatory and otherwise acceptable end (and nothing in this paper rules out the possibility that this might happen in the case of rules separating men and women), then, whatever was thought about the motives of the defender, there would no longer be any basis on which the rule could be objected to. But that means only that there would no longer be any reason to oppose the rule in question. Something originally thought to be objectionable would simply have been shown not to be so at all, and all would be well.

So although discrimination has been defined in terms of ends, we can say of any differentiating rule that it is objectionable on grounds of being discriminatory unless proved otherwise. For such rules whose real purpose is the achieving of some acceptable end, of course, such a proof will not be difficult to provide. It is only for the rationalizer of discriminatory intentions in non-discriminatory terms that the way is hard.

5. The account given so far has dealt only with discrimination *between* two groups, whereas the kind of discrimination needed to give a group grounds for complaint about a rule seemed to be discrimination *against* it. Discrimination against a group, therefore, must be seen as the different treatment of two groups as an end in itself which involves advantage to one at the expense of the other.

It certainly does seem that where the fundamental rules which organize a society differentiate between two groups in this way, there is a clear case of injustice. If anyone were to disagree with this I am not sure what arguments could be brought to prove the point, but in fact that problem does not seem to arise. That everyone implicitly accepts that discriminatory rules which advantage one group at the expense of another are unjust appears from the efforts everyone seems to go to explain their recommendations of differential treatment in terms of some non-discriminatory end. The bus drivers, for instance, could easily have said that they wanted women kept out just so that they could keep what they wanted to themselves, but they were obviously unwilling to do that, and so tried to explain their purpose in terms of the non-discriminatory end of well-driven buses. And as this seems to be the kind of thing which people who want to defend apparently discriminatory rules always try to do, I propose to take it as settled that when rules really do discriminate in this way they are unjust to the discriminated-against group, which is therefore entitled to demand that they should be changed.

What, however, should be said about any rules which discriminate between two groups without advantaging either? Or about discriminatory sets of rules which, taken individually, disadvantage one group against another, but on balance seem to give equal advantage and disadvantage to both sides? It is often claimed that the rules which distinguish men and women are like this: that in the case of many of these neither side is worse off than the other (convention may decree that men wash cars and women wash dishes, but neither activity seems to have any edge over the other), and that although all kinds of rules do give advantage to men, there are just as many others (such as the ones which dictate that men should serve in armies, or be chivalrous to women) which make matters equal. If there are discriminatory rules or sets of rules of this kind, they presumably cannot be objected to on the grounds of being unjust to either side.

Nevertheless, what can certainly be said about such rules is that they must (at best) be unjustifiable in the negative sense of being pointless. A genuinely discriminatory rule, according to my account, is by definition one which treats two groups differently as an end in itself, so that if some other justification could be produced (such as in some way ordering society for the good of all, even at the cost of overriding a good many individual interests) it would not be discriminatory. The only possible purpose of discrimination, therefore, is giving an advantage to one of the groups discriminated between. In fact, however, equal discrimination would be worse than pointless, since any discriminatory rules must

have bad effects for a good many individuals, and it is no consolation to women who want to be bus drivers if men are equally arbitrarily excluded from something else. All that does is double the number of people disadvantaged. Even though equal discrimination would not be open to quite the same objections as discrimination which gave advantage to one group, therefore, it would still be objectionable, and there is no reasonable defence of discrimination on the grounds that it may treat two groups equally.

However, it is perhaps worth adding that when it is claimed that discriminating[4] rules make two groups equal in their difference (and perhaps therefore may be in less urgent need of change than if they discriminated against one of the groups), the claim should be looked at with some care. It is reasonable to be suspicious in such cases, because, as has been said, there could be no possible purpose for such sets of rules; discriminatory rules could have as their purpose only the advantaging of one group over the other. This is not enough to prove that any discriminatory set of rules must actually do that, since presumably rules could appear, or remain, in a society, for no particularly good reason. Still, there is a sufficient reason for suspicion.

And in fact I think it can be shown (though there is no space to do this here) that in most cases where rules which discriminate between two groups do so apparently sometimes to the advantage of one, sometimes the other, and sometimes neither, what is really going on is that the rules taken together define the situation the two groups are to hold in relation to each other. The rules separating men and women define the traditional separate spheres to be occupied by the sexes, and I suspect that this is true of all cases of discrimination between two groups. Discriminatory rules probably rarely if ever take the form of a simple specification that all members of one group are to be treated better than any member of the other. Questions of advantage or disadvantage—and, indeed, of whether there is discrimination at all—should therefore usually be considered in the context of sets of rules defining relative position, rather than one rule at a time.

Probably when the situation of two groups is viewed as a whole in this way, it will generally (though perhaps not invariably) be found that one is better off than the other. I certainly take this to be the case with the rules separating men and women, irrespective of whether those rules can be shown to be discriminatory or not. However, that is another matter, and beside the point of this paper.

6. There is one final point which has been implied in the previous discussion, but needs making explicit. Discrimination as it has been defined here is logically quite distinct from all other things which may be wrong with the rules of a society, and is irreducible to them.

The rules which order a society may be open to objection in a number of ways. They may reward and penalize the wrong kinds of thing, or may do so to the wrong extent. They may provide too little compensation for misfortune, or too few rectifying mechanisms to improve the situation of people who are not in a position to get the rewards a society has to offer. However, discrimination is different from all such matters.

It has already been argued that the question of whether a society's values are good is separate from the question of whether women are discriminated against: whether the bus-driving rule discriminates against women has nothing to do with questions about whether London Transport has acceptable ideas of how buses should be driven. We could reform bus driving in general while continuing to discriminate against women, or end discrimination against women without changing ideas about how buses should be driven. What is perhaps even more important to stress is that discrimination is also a different issue from others concerning distributive justice. A society might have impressive systems of compensation and redistribution which made

sure that no one fell below a certain level of well being, and still discriminate against women or other groups. Or, conversely, it might end all kinds of discrimination entirely, but still contain massive inequalities of wealth and status.

Whenever anything at all is wrong with a society's rules, groups which are worse off than they would have been if the rules had been good may reasonably claim that they are unjustifiably disadvantaged. However, none of these disadvantages is the same as what I have called discrimination.

Perhaps there is some inclination to call some of these other unjustified disadvantages discrimination as well. However, there can surely be no doubt that 'discrimination' is paradigmatically applied to cases such as the ones I have described, and if I am right in arguing that these are totally distinct from other cases of unjustified disadvantage, it would be useful to limit the use of the term in the way I have suggested. As far as I can see the only advantage of resisting this restriction would be to retain a useful aid to political sleight of hand. In the cases which I have called discriminatory a legitimate inference can be made from a particular kind of disadvantage to injustice. If, however, the meaning of the word is kept imprecise enough, it is easier to get away with making the same inference illicitly, and to convey the impression of any disadvantage which is unwelcome that it is also unjust, without the need to argue the case.

Whatever word is used, however, the distinction I have drawn makes a great deal of difference to the *kind of argument* a disadvantaged group needs to use to defend any claim for better treatment.

For instance, women may be able to show that all the rules, formal and informal, which push them towards a special female sphere are discriminatory and therefore should be brought to an end. But if it still happened *after the ending* of all such rules and pressures that women were still disadvantaged by various aspects of femaleness (such as having their attention taken from other things by children they had chosen to have, or not being as physically strong as they might like to be) because these things made them *genuinely* unsuitable for certain sorts of work, this would no more involve discrimination than when people were unsuitable for work for any other reason. If women wanted to argue for special concessions while they were bringing up children, therefore, it would not be enough to point out their own disadvantage. They would have to argue from *general* principles about what society ought to be like that these concessions should be given. For instance, they might argue that too many valuable skills were being wasted, or that so many women were made unhappy by the present arrangements that there would be a far higher general level of happiness in society as a whole if things were changed. Neither of these arguments has to do with women's advantage as such: they depend on general principles about how best to arrange a society. And if, for instance, it could be shown that special concessions for mothers would in fact lower the general well being of society, the argument for those concessions (on that basis) would fail.

The same kinds of consideration apply in other contexts. It would be discriminatory to have a general law or social convention that blacks were always to be subordinate to whites. If, however, the members of a particular racial groups were disadvantaged by (for instance) the demands of employers for high standards of written English, those demands could not be objected to just on the grounds that the particular group was disadvantaged. They would have to be shown to be undesirable for some *general* reason. Nearly any test will disadvantage somebody, and the argument for disadvantaging a new lot of people by the introduction of a new set of requirements must therefore be quite a complicated one, not just referring to the existence of a disadvantaged group.[5]

These very different kinds of arguments for social change need to be kept completely unconfused. Limiting the use of 'discrimination' would make this a great deal easier. . . .

NOTES

1. Sheila Rowbotham, *Woman's Consciousness, Man's World* (Penguin) p. 95.
2. It is important for my purposes to distinguish between genuine conventions which determine that certain kinds of activity are unacceptable, and people's own inherent likes and dislikes which mean that they respond in negative ways to kinds of behaviour they dislike. This is a difficult distinction to make adequately, and it is a shortcoming of the argument of this paper that it is not properly developed here. The general idea is that conventions, like laws and institutions, could be other than they are while people's inherent likes and dislikes remained the same. Conventions decree that certain kinds of behaviour should be censured irrespective of whether the person doing the censuring actually would have condemned the behaviour if the convention had not existed—in rather the same way that a law decrees that certain kinds of conduct should be punished, irrespective of what any particular judge's personal feelings about the matter may be. A simple illustration is the convention of queueing. A group of people in a society which has a queueing convention acts quite differently from the way the same group would have acted without the convention. In contrast, the fact that unpleasant people get shunned and pleasant ones sought out has nothing to do with convention. However, the distinction is tricky to spell out even in theory, and how to establish where the line should be drawn in practice is an even more complicated issue.
3. Strictly speaking the people who can claim to be unjustifiably disadvantaged in this case are not women, but all people who would have been selected if the policy had been as it should have been, including non-killer men. This inaccuracy (and one or two others of the same kind later on in the paper) does not affect my arguments here, but failure to make this kind of distinction does seriously undermine a great many arguments about disadvantaged groups.

4. For the sake of avoiding unduly convoluted sentences I imply in some places that the rules which differentiate the sexes are genuinely discriminatory. As I have already said, this has not been proved in this paper. And, indeed, according to this account, there could be no *general* proof that any particular set of rules was discriminatory; a positive, as opposed to negative, proof of discrimination could only be relative to a specific set of ends to be achieved by the rules.

5. One important subject for which there has been no space in this paper is indirect discrimination: the issue of policies stated in terms which do not explicitly pick out women or blacks, but are thought to discriminate against them nevertheless. I believe, however, that they can be dealt with within the framework I have presented.

READING 2-5

Managing the Older Worker—Don't Just Rinse Away the Gray

Robert J. Paul
James B. Townsend

. . . Could it be true? Are the Beatles really now middle-aged? Is former President Nixon actually eighty? Is the "Pepsi generation" fast becoming the "Geritol generation"? As a population that has tended to shelve its elders, our massive march toward senior citizenry is alarming. According to the Census Bureau, there are now more Americans over thirty than under thirty. America is graying—a social phenomenon without precedent or parallel in this country.

Our proclivity toward youthfulness, of debatable wisdom in the first place, must be reexamined. Many have forgotten, or never knew, that George Bernard Shaw won the Nobel Prize at

Source: Academy of Management Executive, 7 (3) (1993), 67–74. Used with permission.

age sixty-nine; that Arturo Toscanini at seventy assumed the baton of the New York Symphony; that at eighty Jessica Tandy won an Oscar for "Driving Miss Daisy." Picasso's largest work was created when he was eighty-eight. The London Palladium has booked George Burns to appear when he reaches 100.

HOW OLD IS OLD?

When Dean Acheson, at the age of fifty-seven, was tapped by Harry Truman to be Secretary of State, he remarked that he was "in the middle of middle age." We, however, define an older worker as someone who is between fifty and eighty years old. Our definition includes employees at all levels—from the shipping dock worker to the salaried executive.

Employing older workers presents problems, both real and imaginary. Problems stem from societal values in general and common beliefs about employing older workers.[1] Value systems are changing as a result of social, economic, and legal pressure, but old beliefs fade slowly.

Dramatic new findings are emerging, however, about the millions of older workers between the ages of fifty and sixty-four.

- They are in very good health—more than three-fourths rate their health as good or excellent.
- Most already have health insurance through former employers, a spouse, or by an individual policy.
- Three out of four are willing to work without additional employer health insurance.
- They are willing to improve their skills through additional training. In fact, more than fifty percent would have accepted such training if their former employer had offered it.
- Terms of employment are flexible with this group. More than one-third would have accepted reduced pay, status, and hours to stay with their former employer.
- The primary reason for going back to work is money. Nearly half need money for essentials,

including thirteen percent who need money to meet medical expenses.

- Finding work could improve the life satisfaction of many. Only twenty-nine percent of this group rated their lives as "very satisfied" compared to sixty-three percent of their counterparts who are working.
- Most wanted to continue working full-time when they left their last job. Only twenty percent stopped working to pursue other activities.[2]

IMPENDING LABOR SHORTAGE

As the active workforce ages and diminishes, it must be replenished. This, however, does not appear to be happening. Shortages of skilled and talented workers rather than surpluses may dominate the 1990s.[3] In the past, women and baby boomers helped fill the gaps in the expanding workforce. This source of workers has diminished in number. Fewer new entrants, early retirements, and immigration restrictions may also contribute to a future labor shortage.

Paradoxically, while labor needs are growing, takeovers, restructuring, and the recession have caused many companies to ease out senior employees. Lifetime employees at such companies as AT&T, Citicorp, General Motors, and IBM have taken advantage of early retirement packages, greatly adding to the numbers of retired workers.

To exacerbate the problem, the high school dropout rate is increasing while business technology advances. Basic mathematics and communication skills are missing in a large part of the entry level workforce. Employers are already complaining of their inability to hire high-tech workers. Providing training is an option but it is not without its problems.

The managerial ranks will also be affected. As a company responds to short-term problems by thinning out its older and usually more expensive employees, it is creating a shortage of experienced executives to run the company.

A GOLDEN LIGHT AT THE END OF THE TUNNEL

Forty million Americans, sixty years of age and older, have more than one billion years of cumulative work experience.[4] How about those qualifications on a résumé! In addition, three out of five do not have a disability which would preclude their employment.

We maintain that any impending labor shortage can be lessened by attracting and retaining older workers. In fact, many companies are already doing just that. Combustion Engineering, for example, is now bringing back skilled workers who went into early retirement.[5] More than thirty percent of Days Inn's Knoxville and Atlanta reservationists are older workers. McDonald's McMasters program is geared specifically toward retired people. Texas Refinery Corporation has recruited nationally for older sales personnel for the past twenty years; sixty percent of its sellers are fifty-five or older, fifty are in their eighties, and several are past ninety!

Many common myths surround the older worker, however. Since these common beliefs still exert some influence on hiring decisions, we will attempt to dispel them here.[6]

Myth I—Work Capacity and Ability to Perform Decline with Age

Research indicates that workers aged sixty-five to seventy-five generally perform as well as younger workers when jobs do not require heavy physical labor. Most of the "handicaps" of older workers are social, conventional, and imaginary.

Functional age drew attention prior to World War II when older workers were employed for defense production. A study performed during that time, *The Older Worker in Industry,* found that older workers performed very effectively if properly placed in the firm. Age was no longer a justification for judging workers.

Technological advances and the changes to a service economy are removing many of the physical stresses of work. Jobs that require significant physical activity, such as heavy lifting, can be assigned to younger employees, while the older workers perform duties more suited to their capacities.

While motor performance, especially speed, begins to decline around the age of twenty-seven to thirty, older workers can compensate by using a steady work pace and by their experience and knowledge. Declines in motor skills will only be a problem if older workers are not permitted to use their other strengths to compensate for these limitations.

Recent research has provided some new definitions of physical abilities. Respondents were asked whether they could perform at least five or six tasks which related to their ability to perform in a job. They were quizzed on whether they could walk a mile, polish a car, read a phone book, use a calculator, do their own shopping. More than a million were physically able to do these key job tasks.[7]

Myth II–Older Workers Lack Learning and Retraining Abilities, as well as Motivation to Learn

Psychologists have sought for years to disprove the widespread belief that older people are unable to learn new skills. Their capacity to learn new things is not much less than that of younger people. Not only do they have the ability but they also have the desire to learn.

The Manpower Development and Training Act (MDTA) of 1962 established training programs for workers of all ages. Tabulations of program results showed that older workers improve their employment experience, job status after training, and employment opportunities. The completion rate of older participants was higher than that of the younger people, and once older workers had completed their training, sixty percent of them were employed in training-related fields. One year after completion of MDTA training, eighty-one percent of the older trainees were employed.[8]

It has been established that older people can be retrained as readily as young people, provided the training methods are suitable to them and that intelligence, a factor in retraining, does not decline with age.[9]

Based on research on learning, training, and the older worker in general, there is no truth to the cliché "You can't teach an old dog new tricks." However, it is also worth retaining the senior worker's knowledge of "old tricks." During the Gulf War, for instance, ninety-five percent of the material transported to the Gulf went by ship. The Navy called up its Ready Reserve, referred to by some as "the Rustbucket Fleet." Some of the ships' engines hadn't been started for twenty years. Where did they find the skills to operate these old carriers? Not from the active Navy. It was already heavily committed and probably not knowledgeable about operating the older systems. Merchant Marine veterans of World War II, men in their sixties and seventies, responded to the Navy's call. They had the skills and they successfully operated the fleet. One watch officer on a container ship was reported to be in his eighties!

Myth III—Sixty-five Is the Right Age to Retire

Sixty-five as the age of retirement has been attributed to Chancellor Bismarck of Germany, who, in the late 1800s, instituted compulsory retirement to rid the German Army of old generals judged to be incompetent. His scheme worked, and sixty-five has been the "right age" for retirement ever since. The U.S. Social Security Act, passed in 1935, lent further credence to this age as the proper one at which to retire.

This age is arbitrary and meaningless—especially in light of the many deviations from it. For instance, Social Security permits retirement at sixty-two. Even the Federal Government, which sanctioned sixty-five as the right age, has departed from its original plan. The U.S. military services, many private businesses, and several European countries also have flexible retirement ages. W. Withers, in his article, "Some Irrational Beliefs about Retirement in the United States," assesses the "right age" idea as follows:

> Fixing retirement universally at a given age is irrational because it: (1) bears no strict relationship to work capacity; (2) is not adapted to the conditions or practices of different industries or occupations; (3) limits older peoples' potential earnings even though security benefits fail to supply them with enough income; (4) creates an artificial reason for the premature discharge of older workers; and (5) if the pension system is based strictly on an actual basis, the number of years worked and contributions made, not the retirement age, should determine the eligibility of an employee to receive a pension.[10]

Myth IV—Compulsory Retirement Is Necessary; Older Workers Won't Retire Voluntarily; They Should Make Room for Younger Workers

Retirement is socially acceptable and it provides a way to move older workers out so that younger workers may be promoted.[11] It is convenient to specify a retirement age as a normal company operating procedure. This way older workers can be dismissed gracefully and keep their self-respect. No person is singled out since everyone in that age group is removed from the workforce.

Employers may also point to the high cost of pension plans, lack of current skills and experience, limited work life expectancy, unmet educational or training requirements, low adaptability, inferior quality of work, slowness in becoming proficient in a job, undesirable personal characteristics, and costly health and life insurance as reasons for dismissing its senior members. While any one of these characteristics could be true for a given individual (young or old!), current research certainly does not support any of these assumptions for a group.

Many employees do retire voluntarily. A nationwide survey conducted by the University of Oregon revealed that the majority of hourly and salaried workers who retired early did so voluntarily. These volunteers did not regret their decision and claimed that they would do the same thing again.

Given predicted labor shortages, however, emphasis should switch to the retention of older workers, rather than encouragement for them to leave.

It is also worth noting that the Age Discrimination in Employment Act (ADEA), enacted in 1967, prohibits mandatory retirement in most occupations. What this means is that older workers may be both physically and legally able to remain on the job after 65.

Myth V—People Should Retire so that They Can Relax and Enjoy Their Golden Years

This myth makes two major assumptions—that retirement is good for everybody, and that everyone has the resources to enjoy a comfortable retirement.

In our society, work provides quite a bit more than a source of income. Individual advancement is enhanced both economically and socially by the type of job one performs. It is a source of self-respect, identity, and a means of achieving recognition. It also provides social contacts and new experiences and opportunities for creativity. Retirement may deprive workers of meaningful economic and psychological support. Little wonder that many people do not look forward to being without it!

Most retirement families must spend less as their income has decreased. It has been argued that retirees spend less because they need less. In fact, the opposite may be true. A worker receives certain amenities from the job, fringe benefits, recreation and social opportunities, and other psychological rewards which are free. To obtain equivalent benefits and services during retirement, the individual has to pay. Economically, retirement may not be as comfortable.

Older Americans often consider themselves victims rather than beneficiaries of retirement.

These psychological implications are important.[12] In fact, a study commissioned by the Commonwealth Fund[13] found that a significant number of older workers would still like to work. Their study determined that:

- Eighty-three percent of available older workers who are qualified, able, and willing to work would take seasonal work
- Seventy-three percent would work alone
- Sixty percent would work standing up
- Sixty percent would commute more than thirty minutes
- Fifty-four percent would work weekends and evenings
- Sixty-six percent were willing to work full-time and eighty-six percent part-time

Many older workers are ready, willing, and able to stay employed. The negative view of aging, particularly during the retirement period, marked by feelings of uselessness, is not shared by all.

Myth VI—Older People Have More Absences Due to Illness and Injury, and They Aren't Worth Hiring Because They Have Such a Short Work Life Left; There Will also Be Increased Insurance Costs

At sixty-five people generally can look forward to fifteen more years of life and at least ten years of good health.[14] Most people reach sixty-five without having their health pose major employment problems. In fact, a recent study concluded that attendance records of older workers equaled those of younger workers. Absentee rates were lower for the fifty to sixty-five age group than for the thirty-three to forty-four group. In addition, workers fifty-five and older who compose 13.6 percent of the workforce have only 9.7 percent of workplace injuries.[15]

Recent statistics from the Department of Labor Statistics also cast skepticism on the belief that older workers won't be on the job as long as younger ones. In fact, the Department found that workers forty-five and older had median job tenures of 10.4 years. In contrast, people between the ages of twenty-five and forty had a median job tenure of 4.2 years. As Goddard stated in the article *How to Harness America's Gray Power,* "Older workers show greater stability and have a better record of continued acceptance by the employer once they are hired."[16]

Group insurance costs may be affected if there are enough older employees to increase the average age. It has been found, however, that insurance costs are not appreciably affected by hiring older workers. McNaught, Barth, and Henderson learned that seventy-five percent of available workers had health insurance and were willing to work without additional coverage. Seventy-two percent of those without insurance were also willing to work without health insurance!

SUGGESTIONS FOR EMPLOYING OLDER WORKERS

- *Talk with general counsel.* Relevant portions of legislation should be discussed. Topics should include the ADEA and its subsequent amendments, the Senior Community Service Employment Program of 1973, the Employee Retirement Income Security Act (ERISA), the Job Training Partnership Act of 1982, the Social Security Act and its 1983 amendments, and the Tax Reform and Budget Reconciliation Acts of 1986.
- *Review the strategic plan.* In particular, the human resources section should be examined. The HRM officer can forecast personnel needs which will indicate whether the policies related to recruitment, orientation, retention, and retirement are adequate.
- *Reconsider human resource policies.* Accommodating older workers by using flexible benefits, part-time work, flexible work schedules and incentives for continued employment is desirable. Other options such as consulting, seasonal work, reduced hours with reduced pay, job sharing, compressed work weeks, ex-

panded or reduced shifts, voluntary demotions, and job rotation may suggest themselves.[17]

- *Give thought to job redesign.* Individual job preferences should be considered rather than strictly job enrichment. Older workers excel at teaching, counseling, consulting, research, long-range planning, security, arbitration, crafts, child care, working with young people, and managing judicial and administrative roles. Jobs that require certainty, accuracy, judgment and reason are more appropriate than those requiring speed, innovation, and creativity.

- *Provide for career-long training.* Training for older workers involves a program that builds confidence for learning new skills and is adapted to their needs. A non-threatening environment that does not emphasize speed or compare older workers to younger is best. Verbal assurances, adequate learning time, and privacy are important.[18]

- *Examine benefit plans.* Having a choice is important so that employees may match their specific needs. Insurance, pension credits, vacation days, extended leaves, voluntary demotions, and flexible benefits are alternatives.

- *Reconsider incentives.* Incentives that appeal to younger workers, such as promotions, opportunity to demonstrate abilities, and desire for more responsibilities, may not motivate older workers. Recognition of accomplishments, financial rewards, recognition by peers, and being consulted by management are more appropriate.

- *Ensure that performance appraisal programs are current.* This step is often forgotten. Performance appraisal data does form the basis for many personnel decisions.

CONCLUSION

We are going to need more workers. Our economy, demography, the nature of work, and legal changes all support this idea.

Several million older workers form an easily accessible, highly skilled, capable, and well-motivated pool of employees. Most beliefs concerning this group of workers are myths and little more. They can perform very well if placed in jobs that utilize their unique strengths and accommodate their relative limitations. They have the ability and the motivation to learn new skills and work under difficult conditions.

The task of the manager is to recruit, retain, assign, and motivate older workers. The experience and wealth of knowledge of this group is invaluable.

NOTES

We gratefully acknowledge the advice and assistance of Shirley Ahlgren. AARP Research Librarian; Sally Dunaway, Denise Loftus and Lorene Ulrich with AARP's Washington, D.C. Office; and Penny Duckham and Mollie McKaughan of the Commonwealth Fund.

1. R. Goddard, "How to Harness America's Gray Power," *Personnel Journal,* May 1987, 33–40.
2. W. McNaught and M. Barth, "Americans Over 55 at Work Program," *Research Report #1,* The Commonwealth Fund, January 1990, 1–7.
3. A. Ramirez, "Making Better Use of Older Workers," *Fortune,* January 30, 1989, 179 187.
4. J. McCain, Senatorial remarks, *Uniformed Services Journal,* October/November 1992, 30.
5. "The 'Young Old' Forget the Rocking Chairs," *Business Week,* September 25, 1989, 145.
6. Our myths are drawn from: D. Waldman and B. Avolio, "A Meta-Analysis of Age Differences and Job Performance," *Journal of Applied Psychology,* 71, 1986, 33–38; S. Rhodes, "Age Related Differences in Work Attitudes and Behavior—A Review and Conceptual Analysis," *Psychological Bulletin,* 93, 1983, 328–367; G. McEvoy and W. Cascio, "Cumulative Evidence of the Relationship Between Employee Age and Job Performance," *Journal of Applied Psychology,* 74, 1989, 11–17.
7. W. McNaught, M. Barth, and P. Henderson, "The Human Resource Potential of Americans Over 50," *Human Resource Management,* Winter 1989, 455–473.

8. H. Shapiro, "Do Not Go Gently," *New York Times Magazine,* February 6, 1977, 3–4.

9. H. Sterns and D. Doverspike, in Dennis (Ed.), *Fourteen Steps in Managing an Aging Workforce* (Lexington, MA: D.C. Heath and Company, 1988), 97–107.

10. W. Withers, "Some Irrational Beliefs about Retirement in the United States," *Industrial Gerontology,* 1, Winter 1974.

11. *Ibid.*

12. D. Machan, "Cultivating the Gray," *Forbes,* September 4, 1989, 126–128.

13. Commonwealth Fund is a national philanthropic foundation founded in 1918 by Anna M. Harkness. The Fund has been actively concerned with issues affecting the elderly. Address: Harkness House, One East 75th Street. New York, NY 10021–2692.

14. R. Benson and T. Jerdee, "Investing in the Older Worker," *Personnel Administrator,* April 1989, 70–74.

15. R. Nader and K. Blackwell, "The Older American Worker," Report of the Secretary of Labor, June 1965, 10.

16. Goddard, *op. cit.,* 39.

17. Benson and Jerdee, *op. cit.,* 74.

18. Goddard, *op. cit.,* 39.

CHAPTER 3

"Fair? To Whom?" Affirmative Action or Reverse Discrimination?

INTRODUCTION

Programs of affirmative action are under increasing scrutiny and pressure. Conservative Supreme Court justices are anxious to test the legal foundations of affirmative action programs, and politicians of both political parties have called for their reexamination. Race, ethnicity, and gender have always been volatile issues in our national life, and they are close to the heart of the debate about affirmative action, which touches upon the values of equality and individual achievement that have been traditionally treasured in the United States.

Three decades ago, in the excitement of the Civil Rights Movement, the questions seemed less complex. In 1964, Congress passed the most sweeping antidiscrimination legislation in the history of the United States. The next year, in a speech at Howard University, President Johnson argued that simple antidiscrimination measures were insufficient to enable groups of people who had traditionally been discriminated against to enter the mainstream of the nation's economic, social, and political life.

> You do not take a person who, for years, has been hobbled by chains and liberate him, bring him up to the starting line of a race and then say, "You are free to compete with all the others," and still justly believe that you have been completely fair. . . . Men and women of all races are born with the same range of abilities. But ability is not just the product of birth. Ability is stretched or stunted by the family that you live with, and the neighborhood you live in—by the school you go to and the poverty or the richness of your surroundings. It is the product of a hundred unseen forces playing upon the little infant, the child, and finally the man. (quoted in Lipset, 1992, p. 56)

As a remedy, Johnson proposed a variety of programs designed to counteract the effects of past discrimination. Among these was a program of employment outreach to members of disadvantaged groups—affirmative action. Subsequent administrative and court decisions furthered affirmative action (its critics would say, distorted it) and required employers, if their work forces were found to be "imbalanced," to take race and gender into account in their hiring and promotion decisions until they had achieved the required degree of racial and sexual balance.

Myrl L. Duncan (1982) defines affirmative action as "a public or private program designed to equalize hiring and admissions opportunities for historically disadvantaged groups by taking into consideration those very characteristics which have been used to deny them equal treatment" (p. 503). Though this definition states clearly the purpose of affirmative action, it leaves open the question of how that purpose might be achieved. Since different programs are open to different ethical and legal assessments, it is important to specify the types under consideration.

Professor Laura Purdy (1994) distinguishes between procedural programs, designed to increase the probability of successfully recruiting qualified individuals in historically disadvantaged groups, and substantive programs (both "weak" and "strong"), designed to benefit those individuals directly. In its "weak" form, affirmative action is essentially a tie-breaker; that is, it recommends that, in a personnel decision among equally qualified candidates, preference be given to the member of the traditionally disadvantaged group. The "strong" form recommends that preference be given to members of that group even when they are somewhat less qualified than other candidates. Affirmative action's critics find the "strong" form the most ethically objectionable, claiming that it replaces a legitimate interest in equality of opportunity with an impermissible concern with obtaining equality of results.

The following brief classification of ethical arguments on both sides of this controversial issue should help you sort out the different types of considerations to which these arguments frequently appeal.

Supporters of affirmative action often justify their position on grounds of fairness, social utility, and the rights of individuals to equal opportunity. For example:

1. For centuries, the white community has oppressed and discriminated against blacks, women, and different ethnic minorities and still reaps the benefits of its discrimination. Affirmative action is simply just restitution

to members of those communities.
2. The riots that erupt periodically in urban areas are but one indication of a deep and persistent social and economic unrest that is the direct result of past and present discrimination. Programs of affirmative action are designed to better the social and economic lives of disadvantaged people and, by alleviating the causes of that unrest, improve the life of society in general.
3. Both the legacy of past discrimination *and* current discrimination prevent members of disadvantaged groups from exercising their rights to an equal opportunity to use their talents to the fullest and to reap the benefits of their successes. Affirmative action will help guarantee that each citizen enjoys the equal opportunity to which he or she is entitled.

Critics of affirmative action not only reject these arguments but, appealing to the same ethical standards (fairness, utility, and rights), propose counterarguments to warrant their position.

1. Affirmative action is not fair compensation since, more often than not, it takes from people who have committed no wrong and gives to those who have suffered no injustice. How is it fair that a white male who may have discriminated against no one be passed over for a promotion in favor of a black woman who may never have suffered from any discrimination?
2. Affirmative action may have noble goals but it is incapable of achieving them, and, even if it were capable, its social costs are too high. Rather than alleviating the sources of social unrest, it only exacerbates them by generating social resentment. It undermines the efficiency of businesses and schools alike by allowing less qualified people to take the places that should go to better qualified individuals. Finally, it diminishes the self-esteem of blacks, women, and ethic mi-

noritics by casting a pall of doubt over their achievements. People will always wonder whether a female black professor received tenure because she deserved it or because she was black and a woman.

3. Affirmative action is not equality of opportunity; rather it is reverse discrimination and, as such, violates the equal opportunity rights of white males in the same way that the rights of blacks, ethnic minorities, and women have been violated in the past. Reverse discrimination is still discrimination.

Defenders of affirmative action reject these arguments, insisting, for example, that all (or virtually all) members of disadvantaged groups have suffered from past and current discrimination and are thus entitled to compensation. They question the value of the qualifications on which affirmative action's critics insist, and they deny the similarity between affirmative action and previous invidious discrimination.

However this discussion proceeds and whatever decisions are reached in the political and legal arenas, the larger issues of the relationships among whites, blacks, and ethnic minorities, and between men and women, both in our workplaces and in society at large, will persist. For example, sheer demographics and social mobility guarantee that the work force in the United States will become racially, ethnically, and sexually more diverse, whether or not there are programs of affirmative action, and managers will need to work effectively within that context. How reasonably and ethically we live with that diversity may well be shaped, at least in part, by how we conduct our present debate about the ethics and legality of affirmative action.

★ ★ ★

In the readings selected for this chapter, **Michael Galen** and **Ann Therese Palmer** describe some of the dilemmas that the growing diversification of the work force raises for employers, among which are finding ways to cope with changing demographics and to capitalize on diversity's potential without alienating white males, and implementing plans to undo the effects of past discrimination without creating new forms of it. **Michael K. Braswell, Gary A. Moore,** and **Stephen L. Poe** trace in detail the historical and legal development of affirmative action, examine the most significant Supreme Court decisions concerning its permissible scope and limits, and review ethical and legal arguments for and against it. The articles by **Bill Shaw** and **Terry Eastland** continue the discussion of the ethical arguments criticizing and defending affirmative action. **R. Roosevelt Thomas, Jr.** analyzes the assumptions upon which affirmative action programs have been based and concludes that they are no longer adequate. He contrasts programs of affirmative action with strategies for managing diversity, which recognize racial, ethnic, and gender differences and create an environment in which employees' contributions reflect their talents and backgrounds.

REFERENCES

Duncan, Myrl L. (1982) "The Future of Affirmative Action: A Jurisprudential Critique." *17 Harvard Civil Rights—Civil Liberties Law Review* (Summer), 503–553.

Lipset, Seymour Martin. (1992) "Affirmative Action and the American Creed." *Wilson Quarterly, 16* (1) (Winter), 52–62.

Purdy, Laura M. (1994) "Why Do We Need Affirmative Action?" *Journal of Social Philosophy, 25* (1) (Spring), 133–143.

CASE: Olivia Francis

Jim Markham did not know what to do. The more he tried to analyze the problem, the murkier it became. Normally, Jim felt confident in counseling his students—both past and present—but this time it was different. Olivia Francis had been one of the best students he had ever taught in the MBA program. She was bright and curious, one of those rare students whose thirst for knowledge was uppermost in her reasons for being in the program.

She had never disclosed much about her family or her past to him, but he knew from her student file and information sheet, and from bits and pieces of conversations with her, that she had come from a poor, somewhat impoverished neighborhood in St. Louis and had earned her way through college on academic scholarship and part-time jobs. Upon graduation from the MBA program she left the Midwest, taking a job with a prestigious consulting firm in Los Angeles, and at the time he had felt sure she would travel far in her career. Perhaps that is why her phone call earlier that morning troubled him so.

Awaiting him on his arrival at the office was a message on his answering machine from Olivia. He returned her call and wound up talking to her for an hour. The salient portions of their conversation began to run through his mind again. What had struck him the most initially was the range and the depth of her emotions. He had never spoken to anyone in his life who had so much rage seething within them. After she had

Source: This case was written by Mark Mendenhall, University of Tennessee, Chattanooga, and is used here with his permission.

vented the rage, like air slowly being discharged from a balloon, she became almost apathetic, and her resignation to her situation almost frightened him—her only way out, as far as she could see it, was to find another job. Jim could not recall ever being in a situation where he felt he had absolutely no control over what happened to him, where his input was meaningless to the resolution of a problem he faced.

Olivia had stated that her first performance appraisal had been below average, and two weeks ago, her second appraisal was only average. She felt that she had worked hard on her part of the team's projects and believed her work was first rate. The only reason for the appraisals, as far as she could see, was that she was black. She was the only black on the team—in the whole office for that matter. Jim believed her when she said that her work was excellent, for her work had always been excellent as a graduate student and as a research assistant. He had attempted to get her to analyze the situation further, but it was like pulling teeth; she seemed emotionally worn out and just wanted out.

"Surely they gave you more feedback about your performance than that it was below average?" he remembered saying. All she would say is that they mentioned something about her attitude, not being a team player, that her work was technically exemplary, but that she was part of a team and that working with others was as critical as the nature of the work she did by herself. Olivia felt that this was a smokescreen for the fact that she had been dumped on the office by a corporate recruiter with an EEO quota to fill, and that they were trying to get rid of her by using subjective criteria that she couldn't really defend herself against. The frustration came back to Jim as he remembered probing her for more information.

"What was the tone of your manager in the feedback session?"

"Condescending, false sincerity; there was a lot of talk on his part of 'my potential.' It was humiliating, actually."

"How do the other people in your team act towards you? Are they friendly, aloof, or what?"

"Oh, they're friendly on the surface—especially the project leader—but that's about as far as it goes."

"Is the project manager the person who gave you this feedback?"

"No, she is under the group manager. He is a long-time company guy. But obviously she gives him her evaluation and impressions of me, so I'm sure that they both pretty much see issues regarding me eye-to-eye."

"Tell me more about the group manager."

"Mr. Bresnan? I don't know much about him to tell you the truth. He oversees five project teams, and each project manager reports to him. He comes in and gives a pep talk from time to time to us. Other than that I've never had occasion to really interact with him. He's always cracking jokes, putting people at ease. Kind of a 'Theory Y' type—at least on the surface."

"Do you ever go to lunch as a group?"

"Yes, they go to lunch a lot and they invite me along, but all they talk about are things I don't find very interesting—they're kind of a shallow bunch."

"What do you mean, shallow?"

"They could care less about real issues—their discussions range from restaurants to social events around town to recent movies they've seen."

"Does the project manager go to these lunches?"

"Yes, she comes and even plans parties after work too. Her husband is in the entertainment industry, a movie producer. Nothing big, docu-

mentaries and that type of thing, but they put on airs, if you know what I mean. She is really gregarious and always wants to be of help to people, but she strikes me as putting on a front, a mask—obviously she isn't really sincere in wanting to help everyone 'be the best that they can be'; that's one of her little slogans by the way; after all, look what happened to me."

"Why do you think they're prejudiced against you?"

"Well, the poor appraisals for one thing—those are completely unfounded. They do other less obvious things too. Twice I've overheard some of them from behind cubicles relaxing and telling racist jokes about 'wetbacks.'"

"Is it just a few of them that do this? I can't believe all of them are racist."

"I don't know; I don't enter the cubicle and say, 'Hi guys, tell some more jokes!' But it isn't just one or two of them. Look, I obviously don't fit in, do I? It's lily-white in the office, and I'm not."

"What do they do that's work related that bothers you?"

"Well, when project deadlines get closer, their anxiety level increases. They run around the office, yell at secretaries . . . it's like a volcano building up power to explode. They worry and agonize over the presentation to the client and have two or three trial 'presentation runs' that everyone is required to go to. It's all so stupid."

"Why is that?"

"The clients always like what we produce, and with a few relatively small adjustments, our work is acceptable to the clients. So, it's like all that wasted energy was needless. We could accomplish so much more if they would just settle down and trust their abilities."

"How do you act when they are like this?"

"I do my work. I respond to them rationally. I turn my part of the project in on time, and it is *good* work, Professor Markham. I guess I try to be the stabilizing force in the team by not acting like they do—I guess I just don't find the work pressures to be all that stressful."

"Why not?"

"Oh, I don't know really. Well, maybe I do a little bit. I don't know if you know this or not, but my mother was a single parent with four kids. I was the oldest. She worked and I looked after the kids when I came home from school. She worked two jobs to provide for us, so I would be in charge of the smaller kids sometimes upwards of nine o'clock at night. Doing your homework while taking care of a sick kid with the others listening to the television—that's stressful! These people at work, they don't know what stress is. Most of them are single or if they are married, they don't have any kids. They all seem very self-centered, like the universe revolves around them and their careers."

"What kind of behavior at work seems to get rewarded?"

"I guess doing good work doesn't. What seems to get rewarded is being white, being more or less competent, and being interested in insipid topics. Professor Markham, don't you know of any firms that are more enlightened I can send my resume to? I'm looking for a firm that will reward me for the work I do and not for who I am or am not."

Jim leaned back in his chair pondering what to do next. He had promised Olivia that he would call her back in a day or two with some advice. He sensed that he didn't quite understand her problem, that there was more to it than what appeared on the surface. But he just felt like he didn't have good enough data to analyze it properly. He decided to go for a walk around the neighborhood to clear his mind. As he opened the front door and gazed down his street, he suddenly realized for the first time that his neighborhood was lily-white.

READING 3-1

White, Male, and Worried

Michele Galen
Ann Therese Palmer

Last April, Doug Tennant lost his job as a long-term contract employee for Pacific Gas & Electric Co. in Tracy, Calif. He says he was the first one in his three-person unit to be laid off. He claims the others—a black woman and a man of Indian descent—were kept on even though he was more qualified. Tennant, who is white, blames PG&E's push for a more diverse workplace. "I feel like I'm losing out," he says. PG&E says his race and sex had nothing to do with his departure.

Marilyn Moats Kennedy, a Chicago-based career counselor, recently got a plaintive letter from a white male who wanted a job hauling baggage for United Airlines Co. It seemed that all the candidates who were having any luck were women and minorities. "How am I going to get on with the airlines?" the man wrote. "Wrong pigment, wrong plumbing."

He hasn't selected any colleges yet, but Curt Harms is concerned about the impact of diversity on his chances for acceptance. "I'm worried," says Harms, a 15-year-old sophomore from Lake Bluff, Ill. who is white. "If there's a candidate who has grades and credentials exactly the same as mine, these days it's more likely they'll take that person over me, if the person is a minority or a woman. There's nothing I can do."

Peek inside any corporate boardroom, or take a look at the senior managers of most top corporations, and it's hard to see what Harms, Tennant, and others like them are complaining about: It's still a white man's world.

Source: Reprinted from January 31, 1994 issue of *Business Week* by special permission, copyright © 1994 by McGraw-Hill, Inc.

But in a growing minority of companies—especially those aggressively pushing diversity programs—some white males are coming to a different conclusion. They're feeling frustrated, resentful, and most of all, afraid. There's a sense that, be it on the job or at home, the rules are changing faster than they can keep up. "Race and gender have become factors for white men, much the way they have been for other groups." says Thomas Kochman, a professor at the University of Illinois-Chicago who consults with companies on white male issues. "The worm is turning, and they don't like it."

The phenomenon Kochman and others are talking about is far from universal in Corporate America. In fact, most white males don't feel particularly threatened or haven't noticed such changes where they work. But then, the impact of diversity programs, even in the companies that have them, is still limited. "Sadly, we find a lot of these diversity programs hang out there by themselves and don't loop back into a coherent management development program," says Jeffrey A. Sonnenfeld, director of the Center for Leadership & Career Studies at Emory University. "The programs often are window-dressing."

OPEN SEASON

But in such companies as AT&T, DuPont, and Motorola, where diversity is becoming more than just a buzzword, the emotional landscape for white males is changing. There, white men must compete against people they may not have taken all that seriously as rivals—mainly women, blacks, Hispanics, and Asians. White males also say that the diversity programs often make them feel threatened or attacked. "In the diversity group I was in, there were some understandable reprisals against white males and, implicitly, the company," says John L. Mason, vice-president for recruiting and equal employment at Monsanto Co. The reprisals "discounted all the good things white males have done."

Even in companies where diversity programs are new or haven't made much impact, white males are feeling pressure. Often for the first time in their lives, they're worrying about their future opportunities because of widespread layoffs and corporate restructurings. Outside the corporation, white men are feeling threatened because of racial and gender tensions that have been intensifying in recent years. "'White male' is what I call the newest swear word in America," says Harris Sussman, president of Workways, a strategic consulting firm in Cambridge, Mass. "We all know that's not a compliment."

No matter what company they're in, white males must face a sobering new reality: With a more diverse population entering the work force, white men are slowly becoming a minority. From 1983 to 1993, the percentage of white, male professionals and managers in the work force dropped from 55% to 47%, while the same group of white women jumped from 37% to 42%. The diversification of the workplace will only pick up. Through the year 2005 the Labor Dept. estimates that half of all labor force entrants will be women, and more than one-third will be Hispanics, African Americans, and those of other races.

All this is driving what some diversity experts and executives call a white, male backlash. So far, it has occurred mostly in companies experiencing the greatest flux, where some men blame their stalled careers on racial or gender differences. "When everybody is working and happy, diversity is just talk over the water cooler," says one laid-off, white, male executive who attributes his 18-month job hunt to employers who "earmark" jobs for female and minority candidates. "But when it impacts you directly, you become kind of angry."

QUANDARY

At the heart of the issue for many white males is the question of merit—that in the rush for a more diverse workplace, they will lose out to less qualified workers. Most white men claim they have no problem with promoting or hiring women and minorities if they are the best people for the job. It's another story when two candidates are of equal merit. In that case, if the company picks a woman or minority, some white men are quick to cry reverse discrimination—even though the law lets companies take race into account in employment decisions to remedy past discrimination.

The shifting dynamics of the work force have placed managers, many of whom are white males themselves, in a moral quandary. In their efforts to make their companies more diverse, they are certain to hire or promote women and minorities over other white males. That is sure to lead to anger from those who are passed over. In the extreme, productivity could suffer as white males flee to more old-line competitors. Yet if these managers fail to embrace diversity, they not only perpetuate past injustices but risk leaving their companies less globally competitive.

Many white, male managers say that those pressures become even harder to bear when they, rather than senior executives, are blamed for a litany of past wrongs committed by white men. "I'm certainly not part of the power structure," says James Gault, a systems engineer with American Telephone & Telegraph Co. in New Jersey, "But compared to blacks and women, I am."

Complicating such issues is the split between what many white men say they believe and what they actually feel: They recognize intellectually that they're still calling the shots and getting most of the promotions. But that does little to assuage fears that the pendulum will swing too far. "White males are like the firstborn in the family, the ones who have had the best love of both parents and never quite forgave the second child for being born," says Kochman, the University of Illinois professor. "We're dealing here with a sense of entitlements."

For companies committed to a corporate culture that embraces groups besides white males, all this raises two dilemmas: First, how to ensure a diverse work force without antagonizing either white males, whose support is critical for change, or women and minorities, who may resent efforts to win over white males; and second, how to reverse historical discrimination without creating new forms of it.

The experience at Rochester Telephone Corp. shows how tough those tasks can be. Until recently, white males criticized the company's diversity efforts as affirmative action under a different name—something they say doesn't affect them. The predominately white unions refused to support the initiative. "It was very divisive," says Robert Flavin, president of Local 11709 of the Communications Workers of America. "The minorities had an open door to the president."

Now, Michael O. Thomas, who is black, is trying to change all that. Hired last summer as Rochester's corporate director of staffing and diversity, Thomas expanded the definition of diversity to cover job sharing, career planning, and other employee concerns as well as race and gender. To oversee those efforts, he and members of an internal Diversity Council, already comprising a cross section of the company, hired a diversity manager—who happened to be a white female—and eliminated the minority-run diversity department. He also refocused the council's mission to make it more inclusive and help set an agenda. Thomas says his efforts have drawn mixed reactions from minorities, some of whom worry he's ignoring their problems. Thomas is determined to prove them wrong. His approach is already winning over labor. "The old program didn't have anything to do with our members. Now it does," says Flavin.

TOKENISM CHARGES

While Rochester's diversity program isn't focusing on white males, some of the most aggressive employers on the diversity front are realizing that winning over white male employees requires special efforts—and is crucial to their

programs' success. AT&T and Motorola Inc. are hiring consultants to lead seminars that help white males handle anxieties over their changing status. CoreStates Financial Corp. is forming a white men's support group similar to those in place for people of color as well as gays, lesbians, and bisexuals. For all male employees, DuPont Co. is creating a "Men's Forum." "White males are feeling left out," says Bernard Scales, DuPont's manager of diversity, who is black. "They are questioning from the sidelines: What is going on? What is the company doing? What is it that women and people of color are trying to tell them?"

Managers who ignore such issues risk inflaming dissension and hurting morale and productivity. At some companies, white middle managers are filing internal complaints about unfair treatment. At NutraSweet Co., CEO Robert E. Flynn says evidence of white, male resistance surfaced in two similar incidents in recent months: White men picked white males for key positions—without posting the jobs for females, minorities, and others. Both jobs were reopened so that a broad range of candidates could apply. In one case, the initial candidate got the job, but some of the women and minorities who were interviewed got promoted as well. The other case is pending. "There is a backlash," Flynn says. "There is some uneasiness about how aggressive we are in terms of diversity."

All too often, say many women and minorities, that uneasiness is expressed in the kind of behavior they have long had to put up with from white men. Women complain that some white, male managers try to undermine their credibility by doing such things as attributing their rise to tokenism. "When a female or minority or some combination is appointed to a particularly prestigious job, there's always the comment that the reason they were selected is that they were a woman or minority. That's one of the statements white males still aren't afraid to make in public," says Sara Kelsey, vice-president and assistant general counsel at Chemical Bank in New York.

"I find those remarks very irritating because the men make it sound like that's the only reason."

ORGY OF BLAME

Rather than address such behavior, white males say too many diversity programs just encourage women and minorities to vent their anger. Ken E. Richardson, a white male, attended a week-long diversity program in the spring of 1992. An administrator with the Licking County (Ohio) Sheriff's office, he was one of five white males in a racially and sexually diverse group of 30. Having lived in a mixed neighborhood and abroad, Richardson says he has always respected cultural and racial differences. But in the training session, he says he was blamed "for everything from slavery to the glass ceiling." The instructors—a white female and two black males—seemed to "feed into the white-male-bashing," he says. "I became bitter and remain so."

Despite the risk that some programs will alienate men like Richardson, even such white, male bastions as the oil industry are pushing diversity initiatives. For Amoco CEO H. Laurance Fuller, managing diversity is a "business imperative." He says women and minorities account for 40% of his work force, though they remain disproportionately in lower-ranked jobs; one of every six employees is not a U.S. citizen. Last fall, Fuller established a Diversity Advisory Council, which he chairs. Its mission is to create an environment in which Amoco Corp.'s increasingly diverse work force can reach its full potential.

The council is finalizing a long-term action plan, but some white, male middle managers are already worried. From time to time, they've questioned Fuller—himself white—about the consequences of diversity on their careers. "I reply that they have nothing to fear but more and better competition, which can only enhance Amoco's prosperity and their own," Fuller says.

For now, such reassurance is all the attention some white males at Amoco seem to want. Last summer, the company accepted a consultant's suggestion to hold a focus group solely for white, male middle managers. It was intended to get them to express their concerns, says Jim Fair, Amoco's director of media relations who attended the workshop. But some men didn't think they needed the seminar. "Are you trying to get me to be upset?" Fair reports one manager asked the moderator. Others objected to being singled out. Fair said the men agreed that a more valuable experience would be sessions with different people together.

SURPRISING CONCLUSIONS

AT&T has embraced just such an approach, partly through a course called "White Males: The Label, the Dilemma." Led by consultant Sussman, the course presents the future work force, then asks white men how they feel about being labeled a minority. The women and minorities in the class react to the white males' views or challenge their conclusions. Beate Sykes, an AT&T diversity counselor, sought out the course in response to requests by white men "to do something for them."

The intensity of the one-day seminar surprised some of the white men who attended. "I didn't realize how much other white men felt attacked and how oblivious" they were to the benefits that their race and gender bestowed, says James Gault, the systems engineer. "They felt everything was equal now." Other attendees say the seminar changed their self-image. "I never thought of myself as a white male," says Lee Arpin, a development manager. "In a lot of cases, we have privileges we don't appreciate."

Minorities left the seminar with insights into white men. David Clanton, a software designer who is black, says the class made him "more empathetic" to white males because it showed how deeply felt their concerns were, just like other groups. He learned that white men don't like being lumped together or blamed for "something their fathers and grandfathers might have done." The class also helped him feel more comfortable with white male colleagues who seemed to be "more to my way of thinking than I would have expected."

Not all AT&T employees view the company's attention to white men favorably. On Nov. 5, Sussman was the key speaker at a mandatory, all-day conference sponsored by an affirmative action committee at an AT&T division in northern New Jersey. The occasion drew some complaints from women and minorities, who wanted to know why an affirmative action workshop should devote any time at all to white men. One minority employee was so incensed that the worker didn't attend.

Other companies with diversity programs are reaching out to white males. Corning Inc. has made a big diversity push since 1987 and, among other things, now requires all employees to attend race and gender sensitivity training. The result, says Gail O. Baity, manager of strategic corporate education, is that "white males are asking questions like, 'The demographics show there will be fewer white males entering the work force. Will we be in the minority?' Or they're asking about parity. 'You have all these programs focused on women and color. What about me?'"

CORE REQUIREMENTS

In response, Corning has made a special effort to share employment statistics to correct a misperception of trends. "White males still predominate within the company and still hold the predominant positions of authority," Baity says. Corning also is trying to make the advancement process more objective by identifying core competencies for various jobs. When an employee gets a certain post, Corning can then point to the fulfillment of the core competencies as a valid reason why he or she deserved it. Ultimately, Corning expects managers to assemble a diverse talent pool for any opening, then select the best person.

That's an approach more companies are likely to take as women and minorities continue to make strides. Companies will also find that

diversity programs to encourage those trends are in their interest. The programs are in their customers' interests as well: They help to promote employees who, given their rich backgrounds, are not only qualified but more sensitive to the diverse cultures of the markets they serve. "There's not too many white faces in Indonesia," says NutraSweet's Flynn, who is pushing to raise the company's foreign revenues.

But companies must walk a fine line: If they pay only lip service to diversity, they risk losing or alienating women and minorities, an increasingly important sector of the talent pool. If they push diversity too hard without taking stock of the fears of their white, male employees, they risk losing white males or their backing. To be sure, the transition from a corporate culture dominated by white males to one that embraces all employees equally will not take place without a degree of tension. But if companies are to compete in the changing marketplace, and if they are to treat all employees with equal respect, diversity is essential. And so, too, is the proper training for all involved.

READING 3-2

Affirmative Action: An Assessment of Its Continuing Role in Employment Discrimination Policy

Michael K. Braswell
Gary A. Moore
Stephen L. Poe

Affirmative action continues to be a source of controversy for many Americans.[1] With the passage of the Civil Rights Act of 1991, Congress failed once again to address the problems asso-

Source: Excerpted from *Albany Law Review, 57* (1993), 365–440. Used with permission.

ciated with quotas and other forms of affirmative action under Title VII. Meanwhile, the current conservative majority of the U.S. Supreme Court appears to be on a course to limit affirmative action as a component of antidiscrimination policy. More than thirty years after the introduction of the concept of affirmative action as a tool of U.S. policy in the fight against employment discrimination, questions persist about the validity and the necessity of its use. The purpose of this Article, accordingly, is to evaluate and assess the use of affirmative action and to consider whether it should remain a cornerstone of U.S. civil rights policy. After a discussion of the historical and legal development of affirmative action, the arguments supporting and then those challenging affirmative action will be reviewed, and the effect of the Civil Rights Act of 1991 on affirmative action will be analyzed. An economic framework will then be proposed as a tool to evaluate affirmative action as policy, and empirical evidence on the effects of affirmative action programs will be presented. Finally, an assessment will be made as to whether affirmative action should continue to play an important role in civil rights policy.

I. INTRODUCTION

The term "affirmative action," although embodying a variety of concepts,[2] generally can be used to describe any plan or program designed to redress past unlawful discrimination, or its present effects, against women or racial and ethnic minorities by considering such characteristics in allocating "public or private economic and other resources or opportunities in our society,"[3] particularly by increasing participation of these groups in the work force and in government programs.[4] Although the concept of assuring equal opportunity for minority group members can be traced back to the constitutional amendments and federal statutes passed during the Reconstruction era,[5] the more modern concept of affirmative action originated with Execu-

tive Order No. 10,925, issued by President Kennedy in 1961.[6] The Order stated that the policy of the United States government was to "promote and ensure equal opportunity for all qualified persons, without regard to race, creed, color, or national origin, employed or seeking employment with the Federal Government and on government contracts"; the Order required federal contractors to engage in "affirmative action" to implement this policy.[7] The President's Committee on Equal Employment Opportunity ("PCEEO") was established by the Order to enforce this requirement by sanctioning noncomplying contractors, either by cancelling their contracts or by barring them from receiving further government contracts.[8]

Three years later, Congress extended the concept of affirmative action to private employment by passing Title VII of the Civil Rights Act of 1964.[9] Title VII specifically prohibited private employers from discriminating on the basis of race, color, religion, sex, or national origin with regard to employment decisions.[10] The statute also established the Equal Employment Opportunity Commission ("EEOC"), authorized to investigate and conciliate complaints of discrimination filed by individuals.[11] In the event the parties were unable to reach a conciliation, the statute provided that complainants could file a civil suit and seek a judicial resolution of their claim. If the employer was found to have intentionally engaged in discriminatory practices, the courts were permitted to award an appropriate affirmative action remedy, including hiring, reinstatement, and back pay.[12] Thus, affirmative action was first introduced into the private sector as a means of remedying proven intentional discrimination.

Congressional acquiescence to the policy of equal employment opportunity, as evidenced by its passage of Title VII of the Civil Rights Act of 1964, laid the basis for a stronger approach to enforcement of the nondiscrimination prohibitions and the affirmative action obligations articulated in Executive Order No. 10,925.[13] Accordingly, President Johnson in 1965 issued Executive Order No. 11,246, which restated these objectives and sought to implement them in several ways.[14] First, the Order abolished the PCEEO and transferred enforcement authority to the Secretary of Labor.[15] Second, it required every agency and department in the executive branch to establish and maintain an affirmative action program in order to realize the goal of equal employment opportunity.[16] Third, the Order again required businesses that contracted with the federal government to refrain from engaging in employment discrimination and to take affirmative action to ensure that employees and applicants were treated without regard to race, creed, color, or national origin.[17]

Four years later,[18] the federal government began to implement the policies and objectives expressed in these orders with a series of measures designed to define more specifically the affirmative action obligation and to ensure the compliance of federal contractors. For example, the Department of Labor, both directly[19] and through the Office of Federal Contract Compliance ("OFCC"),[20] initiated enforcement programs advocating the use of numerical goals and timetables to achieve these objectives. The Department of Justice also began to seek affirmative-type relief in the form of back pay, numerical goals, and timetables both in consent orders and judgments obtained in employment discrimination litigation.[21] The implementation of these programs, and the willingness of the government to seek and of the courts to award such relief, effectively institutionalized among federal contractors and subcontractors employment practices that gave preferential treatment to women and minorities.[22]

In 1971, the Supreme Court decided *Griggs v. Duke Power Co.,*[23] a case which had a marked effect on the adoption of affirmative action plans by private employers. In *Griggs,* the first case that reached the Supreme Court under Title VII of the Civil Rights Act of 1964, the Court recog-

nized the disparate impact cause of action under Title VII.[24] Under the disparate impact theory, employers may be liable for damages and other relief to employees and job applicants for engaging in employment practices that disproportionately affect woman and minorities, unless such practices can be justified by "business necessity."[25] As a result of *Griggs,* and subsequent Court rulings which reaffirmed and refined its holding,[26] many private employers implemented affirmative action programs to avoid liability for disparate impact discrimination and the cost of litigating such actions.[27] Many of these employers looked to the goals and timetable requirements of OFCC Order No. 4 for guidance in formulating their own affirmative action programs.[28]

In 1972, Congress amended Title VII by enacting the Equal Employment Opportunity Act.[29] The Act empowered the EEOC to bring its own employment discrimination cases in federal court,[30] extended the applicability of Title VII to state and local governments,[31] and gave federal courts additional remedial authority under Title VII.[32] The adoption of these amendments, which appeared to indicate congressional approval of the policy of preferential treatment currently being implemented by the administrative and judicial branches,[33] paved the way for extensive litigation subsequently brought by the EEOC and the Department of Justice against businesses in the telephone, steel, and trucking industries in the mid-1970s. This litigation led to consent decrees and other court orders imposing back pay, numerical goals, timetables, and related affirmative relief affecting two million employees.[34]

In 1978, authority over all employment discrimination matters was centralized in the EEOC.[35] Pursuant to this authority the EEOC, in 1979, issued a series of guidelines designed to assist private employers in developing their own affirmative action programs; the guidelines expressly allowed the use of plans that contained goals and timetables for achieving a balanced work force.[36] Employers who complied with such guidelines in good faith were protected from liability for discrimination suits under Title VII.[37] Given the disincentive provided by the threats of agency enforcement actions[38] and private suits for disparate impact discrimination,[39] and the protection from liability afforded to businesses adopting affirmative action programs pursuant to the EEOC guidelines,[40] employers during this period had every reason to adopt affirmative action programs containing goals and timetables.[41]

The advent of public[42] and private affirmative action programs implemented pursuant to these various policies and guidelines has generated a number of claims of "reverse discrimination" by males and nonminorities excluded from the preferential treatment provided to members of the protected groups. These claims typically allege discrimination on the basis of race or gender as a result of such exclusion and challenge the validity of the programs on statutory and constitutional grounds. In resolving such claims, the Supreme Court has been called upon to determine in each case the particular program's validity in view of a host of often conflicting public policy goals, such as ensuring equal employment opportunity for all, remedying prior discrimination against women and minority groups, and protecting the legitimate expectations of excluded males and nonminorities. A wide variety of programs has been challenged, including affirmative action plans adopted voluntarily or pursuant to consent decrees by private and public employers, court-ordered affirmative action relief under Title VII, and minority preference policies mandated or approved by federal, state, or local governmental entities. In the following Section, each of the significant Supreme Court affirmative action cases will be discussed.[43j82]

★ ★ ★

V. ARGUMENTS SUPPORTING AFFIRMATIVE ACTION

The original goal of affirmative action was to establish an affirmative commitment to avoid discrimination.[202] The idea was to increase awareness of discrimination and how it was manifested so that it could be avoided. For the employer this meant a self-examination of the practices used in the workplace, particularly those used for hiring and promotion, to determine if the practices were, in effect, discriminatory (and, later, whether the practices constituted violations of Title VII). Affirmative action also meant taking conscious steps to avoid discrimination, such as making a commitment to establish practices and policies ensuring that recruitment efforts of the business would extend to the protected groups. This original understanding of affirmative action caused little controversy. However, affirmative action defined as the "benign" use of race- or gender-conscious preferences has caused unending controversy. The arguments for and against this type of affirmative action have been the focus of concern since the hearings before the adoption of the Civil Rights Act of 1964. The debate over "quotas" continues today even after the passage of the Civil Rights Act of 1991 because Congress failed to address the issue in the legislation and a divided Supreme Court has sent so many mixed signals.

Many arguments have been used to support the use of race- or gender-conscious affirmative action. The most widely accepted reason, but most limited in effect, is affirmative action as a remedy for identifiable discrimination. Other arguments have supported the use of affirmative action as a remedy for societal discrimination usually evidenced by a statistical underrepresentation of the protected group. The underlying rationale for this argument is that true equal opportunity requires hastening the removal of the vestiges of past discrimination. Race-conscious affirmative action has also been supported as a reparation for slavery and the associated years of preferential treatment granted to whites. Some arguments defending affirmative action have been "forward-looking," seeking beneficial social objectives, such as racial harmony or improved productivity, through the use of role models and diversity. Finally, affirmative action has been defended as a legal necessity to counter the potential liability, created by *Griggs,* for disparate impact discrimination.

A. Affirmative Action as a Remedy for Identifiable Discrimination

One of the primary areas of disagreement concerning affirmative action in the Supreme Court opinions from *Bakke* to *Metro Broadcasting* is its use as a remedy. The Court has dealt with court-ordered affirmative action, consent decrees, congressionally mandated programs, executive orders with set-aside programs in the construction industry, municipal set-aside programs for minority business enterprises, and other voluntary affirmative action plans in both the public and private sector. The more liberal coalitions in the Supreme Court have favored an expansive use, while the more conservative coalitions have endeavored to limit the availability of affirmative action as a remedy. Prior to *Metro Broadcasting,* it was believed that with respect to affirmative action plans adopted by state and local governments—as well as, under *Fullilove,* the federal government—the compelling governmental interest necessary to satisfy the strict scrutiny standard required by *Croson* and the Equal Protection Clause was predicated on identifiable past discrimination. In contrast, the standard for private, voluntary affirmative action plans, established by *Weber* and *Johnson,* was a broader "manifest racial imbalance in traditionally segregated job categories."[203] The present members of the Supreme Court are likely to reverse this standard and adopt one which is more closely related to the

predicate of past discrimination required of governmental bodies.

The use of affirmative action as a remedy for identified discrimination is supported by many of the Supreme Court decisions. In *Bakke,* Justice Powell said, "[W]e have never approved preferential classifications in the absence of proved constitutional or statutory violations."[204] He stated further that "there has been no determination by the legislature or a responsible administrative agency that the University engaged in a discriminatory practice requiring remedial efforts."[205] In *Wygant,* Justice Powell noted that "the Court has insisted upon some showing of prior discrimination by the governmental unit involved before allowing limited use of racial classifications in order to remedy such discrimination."[206] In *Croson,* a majority indicated that "a generalized assertion that there has been past discrimination in an entire industry provides no guidance for a legislative body to determine the precise scope of the injury it seeks to remedy."[207] Because there was no evidence of "any identified discrimination in the Richmond construction industry,"[208] the Court held "that the city has failed to demonstrate a compelling interest in apportioning public contracting opportunities on the basis of race."[209] In *Metro Broadcasting,* Justice O'Connor said, *"Fullilove* applies at most only to congressional measures that seek to remedy identified past discrimination."[210] Moreover, O'Connor continued, the "Court upheld the challenged measures in *Fullilove* only because Congress had identified discrimination that had particularly affected the construction industry and had carefully constructed corresponding remedial measures."[211]

B. Affirmative Action as a Remedy for Societal Discrimination

There has always been considerable support for affirmative action as a more aggressive remedy in overcoming the effects of past discrimination. The argument is based on the premise that merely ending identifiable discrimination or remedying its particular effects will not provide true equal opportunity.[212] Affirmative action is considered to be a method to hasten the elimination of the vestiges of discrimination.[213]

In *Bakke,* Justices Brennan, Marshall, Blackmun, and White seemed prepared to accept benign race preferences by the state government to remedy societal discrimination.[214] "Government may take race into account when it acts not to demean or insult any racial group, but to remedy disadvantages cast on minorities by past racial prejudice, at least when appropriate findings have been made by judicial, legislative, or administrative bodies."[215] The four Justices accepted past societal discrimination, under an intermediate scrutiny standard, as a sufficient predicate for a state government to adopt race-conscious programs to remove the disparate racial impact produced by such past discrimination.[216] Justice Blackmun, in a separate opinion, said that his "earnest hope [is] that the time will come when an 'affirmative action' program is unnecessary and is, in truth, only a relic of the past . . . [but] to get beyond racism, we must first take account of race."[217]

In *Weber,* the Supreme Court provided more latitude for private employers to correct the effects of prior societal discrimination. Unions and private employers were given the right to take race-conscious steps "to eliminate manifest racial imbalance in traditionally segregated job categories"[218] so long as certain safeguards were followed. In a concurring opinion, Justice Blackmun described the definition of "traditionally segregated" as used by the majority:

> The sources cited suggest that the Court considers a job category to be "traditionally segregated" when there has been a societal history of purposeful exclusion of blacks from the job category, resulting in a persistent disparity between the proportion of blacks in the labor force and the proportion of blacks among those who hold jobs within the category.[219]

It is clear from Justice Blackmun's opinion that he believed private affirmative action could go where Title VII did not reach: to a statistical disparity, even without present or pre-Act discrimination.[220]

In *Wygant,* the Supreme Court disallowed "societal discrimination" as a sufficient predicate for race-conscious affirmative action by a state. The district court had allowed the racial preferences, even though not grounded on a finding of prior discrimination, as an attempt to remedy societal discrimination by providing "role models."[221] Justice Powell, writing for a plurality of the Court, stated, "This Court never has held that societal discrimination alone is sufficient to justify a racial classification."[222] He went on to indicate that a "showing of prior discrimination by the governmental unit involved."[223] has been required: "[S]ocietal discrimination, without more, is too amorphous a basis for imposing a racially classified remedy."[224]

C. Affirmative Action as a "Forward-Looking Paradigm"

In *Johnson v. Transportation Agency,*[225] Justice Stevens, in a concurring opinion, adopted a "forward-looking" rationale which had been suggested in an article by Kathleen M. Sullivan.[226] After a discussion of how the *Bakke* and *Weber* cases had changed the pre-1978 construction of the Civil Rights Act of 1964, which has provided a blanket prohibition against discrimination, Justice Stevens made the following argument:

> The logic of antidiscrimination legislation requires that judicial constructions of Title VII leave "breathing room" for employer initiatives to benefit members of minority groups. If Title VII had never been enacted, a private employer would be free to hire members of minority groups for any reason that might seem sensible from a business or a social point of view. . . .
>
> As construed in *Weber* and in *Firefighters,* the statute does not absolutely prohibit preferential

hiring in favor of minorities; it was merely intended to protect historically disadvantaged groups *against* discrimination and not to hamper managerial efforts to benefit members of disadvantaged groups that are consistent with that paramount purpose. . . .

I see no reason why the employer has any duty, prior to granting a preference to a qualified minority employee, to determine whether his past conduct might constitute an arguable violation of Title VII. Indeed, in some instances the employer may find it more helpful to focus on the future.[227]

Sullivan had suggested that by allowing affirmative action only as a remedy for past discrimination, the Supreme Court had been looking backward for a justification instead of forward for a paradigm "justifying affirmative action as the architecture of a racially integrated future."[228] Such a paradigm would include affirmative action to accomplish any worthwhile business or social purpose such as establishing workplace peace, providing role models and cultural diversity in the workplace, as well as many other business benefits.[229] One commentator has argued that the following benefits could be derived: increased productivity, a competitive advantage, diversity of ideas, an enlarged talent pool, improved labor relations, a public relations image boost, increased sales, better ideas, improved recruiting, and higher profits.[230]

D. Affirmative Action as Reparation for Slavery

Somewhere in the background of discussions and attitudes concerning race-conscious affirmative action in the United States lurks the specter of slavery. Although usually not mentioned in the debates, a collective "white guilt"[231] lies at the foundation of the dispute. Justice Marshall raised the argument publicly in *Bakke:* "Three hundred and fifty years ago, the Negro was dragged to this country in chains to be sold into slavery."[232] After discussing the legal history of "[t]he status of the Negro as property"[233] up to the point of the Court's decisions invalidating

the Jim Crow laws, Marshall said, "Those decisions, however, did not automatically end segregation, nor did they move Negroes from a position of legal inferiority to one of equality. The legacy of years of slavery and of years of second-class citizenship in the wake of emancipation could not be so easily eliminated."[234] Justice Marshall then described the plight of the black family in America in 1978, concluding:

The relationship between those figures and the history of unequal treatment afforded to the Negro cannot be denied. At every point from birth to death the impact of the past is reflected in the still disfavored position of the Negro.

In light of the sorry history of discrimination and its devastating impact on the lives of Negroes, bringing the Negro into the mainstream of American life should be a state interest of the highest order. To fail to do so is to ensure that America will forever remain a divided society.[235]

Other proponents of affirmative action argue that whites have been the beneficiaries of centuries of preferences including exclusive access to information, education, and experience, and that affirmative action is only fair as a method to partially account for it.[236] Finally, Justice Marshall, in chastising the Court for failing to recognize a class-based remedy for black America, stated:

In declining to so hold, today's judgment ignores the fact that for several hundred years Negroes have been discriminated against, not as individuals, but rather solely because of the color of their skins. It is unnecessary in 20th-century America to have individual Negroes demonstrate that they have been victims of racial discrimination; the racism of our society has been so pervasive that none, regardless of wealth or position, has managed to escape its impact. The experience of Negroes in America has been different in kind, not just in degree, from that of other ethnic groups. It is not merely the history of slavery alone but also that a whole people were marked as inferior by the law. And that mark has endured. The dream of America as the great melting pot has not been realized for the Negro; because of his skin color he never even made it into the pot.

These differences in the experience of the Negro make it difficult for me to accept that Negroes cannot be afforded greater protection under the Fourteenth Amendment where it is necessary to remedy the effects of past discrimination. . . .

It is because of a legacy of unequal treatment that we now must permit the institutions of this society to give consideration to race in making decisions about who will hold the positions of influence, affluence, and prestige in America. For far too long, the doors to those positions have been shut to Negroes. . . . I do not believe that anyone can truly look into America's past and still find that a remedy for the effects of that past is impermissible.[237]

E. Affirmative Action as a Necessary Tool to Defend Against Disparate Impact Discrimination Claims

In *Weber,* the private employer argued that the affirmative action plan was "justified because they feared that black employees would bring suit under Title VII if they did not adopt an affirmative action plan."[238] This fear was based on potential liability for disparate impact discrimination that had been recognized in *Griggs v. Duke Power Co.,*[239] a liability that was not based on intentional discrimination but on discriminatory effects of neutral employment practices.[240] Justice Blackmun agreed with the characterization of this dilemma as a " 'high tightrope without a net.' "[241] The concern that disparate impact liability would lead to the use of quotas in the workplace was a continuing concern to the Supreme Court in *Watson* and *Wards Cove* and to President Bush and Congress in considering amendments to the Civil Rights Act in 1990 and 1991.[242] The matter remains unresolved. With respect to the issue of affirmative action, *Griggs* shifted the focus in discrimination cases from the individual to the group.[243]

After *Griggs,* an employee could establish a prima facie case of disparate impact discrimination with statistics demonstrating that the em-

ployer's practices excluded a disproportionate percentage of a protected group or that the employer's work force composition was disproportionate relative to the composition of the local community. The employer's defense was to establish the business necessity or job-relatedness of the practice in question. The EEOC Guidelines required that business necessity or job-relatedness be proven by professionally developed validation studies. In an article critical of *Griggs,* one commentator said:

> There is a straight line from *Griggs* to *Weber.* Once the Supreme Court adopted the adverse impact definition of discrimination, employers had to keep their numbers in order. Validation of tests is too costly. Indeed, because a test may turn out to lack job relatedness or differential validity, the money spent on validation can be completely wasted. . . . Therefore, so long as the Court remained committed to *Griggs,* the result in *Weber* was the most efficient way to mold legal doctrine. Employers must be allowed to discriminate in favor of blacks in order to dispel the appearance of adverse impact.[244]

Wards Cove changed the burden of proof under *Griggs,* making the employer's fear of losing a disparate impact case a matter of history. *Wards Cove* has been described as a "back-door approach to limiting the use of, and the perceived need for, voluntary affirmative action."[245] The Civil Rights Act of 1991, however, restored the burden of proof required by *Griggs,* but left in issue the proof requirements to establish the defense of business necessity which is at the core of the problem.[246]

VI. ARGUMENTS AGAINST AFFIRMATIVE ACTION

The arguments against affirmative action will be presented in four parts. The first part presents the argument that affirmative action constitutes reverse discrimination. The second addresses the argument that affirmative action has too many harmful side effects. The third includes arguments that have been made to counter the arguments supporting affirmative action based on the goals of diversity, role models, reparations for slavery, and avoiding liability for disparate impact discrimination. The fourth part presents the argument that affirmative action is not the best, nor even a good, remedy for discrimination. It also discusses a closely associated argument that, with respect to minorities, the current problem is not discrimination but economic disadvantage caused by poor education, training, and motivation; therefore, a discrimination remedy like affirmative action makes the majority feel good and is easy to apply, but avoids the real problems.

A. Affirmative Action as Reverse Discrimination

The debate over reverse discrimination has been extensive.[247] One commentator has said, "*Any discrimination based solely on race or sex is inherently wrong and destructive to society, even if dressed in the euphemistic clothing of affirmative action.*"[248] In *Weber,* the respondent argued that affirmative action plans violated Title VII because Congress had made it unlawful to discriminate on the basis of race in hiring and training[249] and because the Supreme Court in *McDonald v. Santa Fe Trail Transportation Co.*[250] had held that Title VII protects whites as well as blacks.[251] The majority decided against the absolute language of the statute by looking at the "legislative history of Title VII and the historical context."[252] Justice Rehnquist strongly objected, contending that the Court was rewriting the statute: "[B]y a *tour de force* reminiscent . . . of escape artists such as Houdini, the Court eludes clear statutory language, 'uncontradicted' legislative history, and uniform precedent in concluding that employers are, after all, permitted to consider race in making employment decisions."[253] Justice Blackmun also indicated that he shared some of the misgivings of Justice Rehnquist "concerning the extent to which the legislative history of Title VII clearly supports

the result the Court reaches today."[254] Chief Justice Burger, in his dissent, said, "Under the guise of statutory 'construction,' the Court effectively rewrites Title VII to achieve what it regards as a desirable result. It 'amends' the statute to do precisely what both its sponsors and its opponents agreed the statute was *not* intended to do."[255]

B. The Harmful Side Effects of Affirmative Action

In *United Steelworkers v. Weber,* Justice Rehnquist took a strong position against affirmative action, predicting harmful social repercussions:

> Whether described as "benign discrimination" or "affirmative action," the racial quota is nonetheless a creator of castes, a two-edged sword that must demean one in order to prefer another. In passing Title VII, Congress outlawed *all* racial discrimination, recognizing that no discrimination based on race is benign, that no action disadvantaging a person because of his color is affirmative. With today's holding, the Court introduces into Title VII a tolerance for the very evil that the law was intended to eradicate, without offering even a clue as to what the limits on that tolerance may be. . . . By going not merely *beyond,* but directly *against* Title VII's language and legislative history, the Court has sown the wind. Later courts will face the impossible task of reaping the whirlwind.[256]

In *City of Richmond v. J.A. Croson Co.,* Justice O'Connor argued that racial classification carried the "danger of stigmatic harm . . . [and may] promote notions of racial inferiority and lead to a politics of racial hostility."[257] In *Metro Broadcasting, Inc. v. FCC,* Justice O'Connor, joined in dissent by Chief Justice Rehnquist, Justice Scalia, and Justice Kennedy, stated that racial classifications contribute to racial hostility, embody stereotypes, and "may stigmatize those groups singled out for different treatment. . . ."[258]

Other authors have denounced the stigma caused by affirmative action. Stephen L. Carter has called the stigma a "badge of shame" and labeled it one of the principal costs of affirmative action programs.[259] Glenn C. Loury has said that the stigma, the unintended consequence of racial preferences, is the assumption that the person is less qualified, an assumption that carries over into the post-selection environment.[260] Thomas Sowell has cited resentment and the undermining of minority and female self-confidence and pride of achievement as harmful side effects of preferential treatment.[261] Some studies have shown that affirmative action leads to negative self-regard and makes its intended beneficiaries victims.[262]

Resentment, together with the hostility and polarization it causes, has been cited as another side effect of affirmative action. One frequently cited reason for resentment is the "innocent white victim" argument.[263] Adding to the resentment is the fact that the beneficiaries of the affirmative action programs are often middle-class women and minorities who could hardly be described as disadvantaged.[264]

Shelby Steele, in his book *The Content of Our Character,* states that blacks "have a hidden investment in victimization and poverty"[265] as a source of power. Entitlements such as affirmative action are derived from past injustice, but lead to an avoidance of personal responsibility.[266] The victimization syndrome also leads to self-doubt, a feeling of inferiority, and what Steele calls "opportunity aversion,"[267] the fear of failure or the racial anxiety that leads to an avoidance of real opportunity and a withdrawal of effort. Steele believes that affirmative action has done more harm than good for blacks because it stands in the way of development and does not teach skills or motivation.[268]

Perhaps one of the most harmful side effects of race- and gender-conscious affirmative action is that race and gender will continue to be relevant factors in decision making.[269] The ideal of a meritocratic society, a society in which opportunities and rewards are based on an individual's qualifications, will not be realized as long as race and gender remain part of the decision-making process.

C. Responses to the Role Model, Diversity, Reparations, and Disparate Impact/Reverse Discrimination Tightrope Arguments

1. Role Model   In *Wygant v. Jackson Board of Education,* the Court refused to accept the role model argument as a justification for race-conscious government affirmative action. Justice Powell said that "the role model theory does not necessarily bear a relationship to the harm caused by prior discriminatory hiring practices."[270] Justice O'Connor also opined that the role model justification does not support a legitimate remedial purpose.[271]

One author, a member of a minority group, has asked the question, "Do you really want to be a role model?"[272] Answering the question in the negative, the author takes the position that the minority person is hired not because of merit, but for what others think he or she will do for the next generation.[273] The one occupying the position of the role model is in an awkward position and is caught in a lie.[274] The author states that affirmative action is soothing and therapeutic for whites but "psychologically and materially injurious to populations of color."[275] He concludes, "The program was designed by others to promote their purposes, not ours."[276]

2. Diversity   In *Metro Broadcasting, Inc. v. FCC,* Justice O'Connor, in her dissent, strongly disagreed with the concept of "diversity" as a predicate for affirmative action:

> The interest is certainly amorphous: The FCC and the majority of this Court understandably do not suggest how one would define or measure a particular viewpoint that might be associated with race, or even how one would assess the diversity of broadcast viewpoints. Like the vague assertion of societal discrimination, a claim of insufficiently diverse broadcasting viewpoints might be used to justify equally unconstrained racial preferences, linked to nothing other than proportional representation of various races.[277]

Stephen L. Carter, in his book *Reflections of an Affirmative Action Baby,* describes "diversity" as the new conception of affirmative action.[278] He takes offense to its use because it adopts the stereotype that all blacks think alike. He also argues that "if the views of people who are not white turn out to be just the same as the views of people who are, the case for using race as a proxy for viewpoint diversity collapses."[279] He also argues that those who are using the diversity argument for affirmative action are trying to get around the arguments of unfairness, stigma, and underqualification.[280] The diversity argument, based upon adding quality, seems to solve the above problems unless you are troubled by stereotypes, and Carter is bothered by the stereotypes which he calls durable and demeaning, citing race-norming, set-asides, and quotas.[281]

3. Reparations for Slavery   Glenn C. Loury, in his article *Why Should We Care About Group Inequality?,* has criticized the use of affirmative action as a "just recompense"[282] for slavery as a matter of right. He argues that the reparations-for-slavery rationale does not explain why "a middle-class black should be offered an educational opportunity which is being denied to a lower-class white."[283] He also argues that many Americans are descended from groups that were discriminated against, such as the Japanese and Jews. The suffering of these groups is devalued if blacks receive special treatment.[284] He also states that the slavery rationale is an attempt to place guilt on everyone and is a request for pity. He indicates that you cannot get to dignity and equality through guilt and pity.[285] In conclusion, Loury states that the rationale produces resentment, contempt, and disdain:

> Why should others—the vast majority of whom have ancestors who arrived here after the emancipation, or who fought against the institution of slavery, or who endured profound discriminations of their own—permit themselves to be morally blackmailed with such rhetoric? How long can the

failures of the present among black Americans be excused and explained by reference to the wrongs of the past?[286]

4. The Argument Against Proportional Representation   The rationale or theoretical basis for disparate impact discrimination, first recognized in *Griggs,* was never carefully articulated by the Court. The disparate impact concept, not originally contemplated by Congress, may be justified because the neutral criteria are a pretext for intentional discrimination. The doctrine may have been designed to protect against the unintended discriminatory effects of neutral employment criteria or other institutional factors.[287] It may also have been a surreptitious effort to correct societal discrimination.[288] In any case, the Court accepted without question that significant underrepresentation was evidence of discrimination. Many do not agree.

In *Johnson v. Transportation Agency,* Justice Scalia said that the goal of a discrimination-free society has been replaced with the incompatible goal of proportionate representation.[289] He also stated that proportional representation in all job categories would be a "statistical oddity."[290] One author posed the question "Why should the mere existence of group disparities evidence the oppressive treatment of individuals?"[291] The argument is that laissez-faire will not lead to equality of result because too many other factors influence the outcome, and that too much intrusive governmental interference would be necessary to eliminate all "socially and economically relevant discriminatory behavior."[292]

D. Affirmative Action Is Not the Best Remedy and Discrimination Is Not the Only Problem

1. Not the Best Remedy   Clarence Thomas, while Chairman of the EEOC, wrote an article on affirmative action as a remedy.[293] Thomas contended that one weakness of affirmative action is that it allows the employer to avoid paying victims back pay.[294] He also argued that affirmative action allows the employer to shift the costs of remedying past discrimination to its actual victims.[295] In addition, Thomas wrote that affirmative action, "far from eliminating consideration of race in the workplace, actually seems to have encouraged the treatment of blacks as fungible and fundamentally unlike non-blacks."[296] Finally, Thomas argued that if the problem is poor training and education, the remedy should not be affirmative action, but better training and education, i.e., the remedy should be based on the problem.[297]

Recognizing that artificial barriers which inhibit minority participation in the labor market still exist, Stephen Carter nevertheless argues that racial preferences "are not the most constructive method for overcoming the barriers. . . ."[298] He argues that the benefits of affirmative action fall to those that least require them, and fail to reach those truly in need.[299] "The structure of affirmative action programs in admission . . . offers a simple explanation: *The most disadvantaged black people are not in a position to benefit from preferential admission.*"[300] He argues that elite colleges and professional schools make race a proxy for disadvantage, and then, ignoring other aspects of background, admit the nonwhite applicants most likely to succeed.[301] Affirmative action, Carter asserts, is an inexpensive method to obtain racial justice. The real needs, such as housing, medical care, and education, are expensive and go unmet.[302]

2. Discrimination Is Not the Only Problem

One prominent writer, Glenn C. Loury, has said:

> Many, if not most, people now concede that not all problems of blacks are due to discrimination, and that they cannot be remedied through civil rights strategies or racial politics. I would go even further: using civil rights strategies to address problems to which they are ill-suited thwarts more direct and effective action. Indeed, the broad application of these strategies . . . threatens to make it impossible for blacks to achieve full equality in American society.[303]

Loury argues that "[a]ll sorts of voluntary associations . . . are the result of choices often influenced by racial criteria, but which lie beyond the reach of civil rights laws . . . [and] the elimination of racial discrimination in the economic sphere—but not in patterns of social attachment—will probably not be enough to make up the difference."[304] The argument is that the current civil rights strategy will not reach these issues, and that the judicial and legislative bodies cannot grant what must be won through "outstanding achievements of individual black persons."[305] Shelby Steele has argued that "[i]f conditions have worsened for most of us as racism had receded, then much of the problem must be our own making."[306] He believes that "black Americans are today more oppressed by doubt than racism. . . "[307] As a result, Steele concludes advancement will come only from individual effort and personal responsibility.[308]

3. Politics and Affirmative Action

It is becoming increasingly obvious that the consensus forged by the civil rights community in the 1960s is fragmenting, and that affirmative action is a measure of that division. One author, an advocate of civil rights since the 1950s, describes the current civil rights leadership as a political interest group seeking a piece of the pie.

> A large segment of the civil rights lobby has turned from the struggle for equality in civil and political rights to the advocacy of redistribution of economic and social rights. And it has made support for the redistribution of these rights a precondition for being part of the movement; anyone whose does not support this redistribution is labeled a racist, a bigot, or even a klansman.[309]

The civil rights leadership is losing the support of moderate Americans, both black and white.[310] In a recent poll, "77% of black leaders believed affirmative action should be the most important factor in hiring and education decisions," while the same percentage of their constituency believed "ability rather than race should be the determining factor."[311]

★ ★ ★

IX. FINAL ASSESSMENTS AND CONCLUSIONS

Affirmative action has been regarded both judicially and administratively as a cornerstone of civil rights policy. To the extent that employers have been required or otherwise influenced by governmental institutions to adopt these programs, either "voluntarily" to receive federal contracts or to avoid Title VII liability or pursuant to court decree, affirmative action has been used actively as a tool of government policy in both public and private employment as a means of achieving equality of opportunity for protected minority groups and women. Prior to evaluating this policy tool and assessing whether its use should be continued, a summary and comparison of the relevant costs and benefits is in order.

Certain types of non-preference-based affirmative action, such as employer self-examination plans, outreach plans, and affirmative commitments not to discriminate, are relatively cost-free from a social standpoint. However, the social costs imposed by the continuing use of absolute preferences, quota-based programs, and other preference-based plans are numerous. Governmental sanctioning of such affirmative action programs clearly may be said to violate the letter, if not the spirit, of Title VII and the Equal Protection Clauses of the Fifth and Fourteenth Amendments, that employers should not discriminate on the basis of race, ethnicity, or sex, and that all citizens should receive equal treatment under the law. Such government-sponsored favoritism, which perpetuates differential treatment of individuals based on the color of their skin or on their gender, creates resentment and enforces stereotypical beliefs among nonminorities. It also stigmatizes members of the groups receiving preferential treatment, and may contribute to feelings of victimization, self-doubt, anxiety, and opportunity aversion among the members of such groups.

Among the benefits realized by all types of affirmative action is that employers are required, as part of the process, to evaluate their employment practices and to modify or eliminate those that they perceive as having a discriminatory effect.[397] Also, implementation of an affirmative action program can be an effective way to quickly eradicate intentional, statistical, or institutionalized discrimination in the workplace. Other benefits, such as increased racial harmony, more role models for protected groups, and greater diversity, are also often attributed to affirmative action. These, however, usually flow not from the process of affirmative action but from its intended result, enhanced integration of the workplace.

Given these costs and benefits, non-preference-based affirmative action plans should continue to be encouraged and, where necessary, mandated, as they effectively complement the liability scheme of Title VII and are relatively cost-free. Continued use of preference-based affirmative action as a remedy only for identifiable discrimination, together with other remedies available under Title VII, also appears to be appropriate, since the costs associated with such plans are then limited only to situations where the benefits are likely to be greatest. Indeed, this restricted use of such affirmative action is the use that receives the most support from the current members of the Supreme Court[398] and the limited empirical evidence available.[399]

When preference-based affirmative action is justified for other purposes—for example, as a remedy for societal discrimination or as a reparation for slavery—the benefits are not as clear or as direct, however, though the costs imposed remain constant. In fact, continued use of such affirmative action may not so much remedy societal discrimination as inflame it, given the resentment caused and the stereotypes reinforced among nonminorities, and the stigma branded on the intended beneficiaries of such plans. As a result, it seems that any remedial benefits realized from the continued use of preference-based plans that emphasize differences among the races and genders are likely to be directly offset by the costs. Perhaps a better remedy for societal discrimination, as well as a better reparation for slavery, is not the continued use of such a socially cost-imposing mechanism but rather the realization of the objectives that affirmative action was originally intended to achieve: equal employment opportunity and integration of the workplace.

Although preference-based affirmative action has been somewhat effective in creating more equal employment (in terms of proportionate representation), it has been far less effective in achieving its original goal, equal employment opportunity. Such affirmative action may have been a useful and effective tool for accomplishing this objective when it was initially implemented during the early 1970s. It no doubt hastened the integration of blacks and other minority members into the nation's work force by mandating employers to abandon the racist policies deliberately created and imposed to deny employment to blacks and other minorities. Two questions arise, however, as to whether such affirmative action can continue to be justified for use today: (1) is preference-based affirmative action still necessary to maintain and foster integration of the workplace, and (2) is it an effective means of removing the barriers to true equal employment opportunity?

As to the first question, there is considerable evidence indicating that integration of the workplace will continue with or without preference-based affirmative action. Evidence that the employment shares of minorities and women increased throughout most of the 1980s despite the lack of aggressive affirmative action policy intervention during the period suggests that such intervention may have become less necessary to ensure integration of the workplace. At least part of the reason for this growth can be explained by changing demographics, which also indicate that participation by women and minorities in the nation's work force will continue to grow during the next ten to fifteen years.[401] If these trends continue, governmental mandating of affirmative action as a necessary means to ensure integration of the workforce becomes increasingly more questionable.

Put simply, what appears to be emerging is a widespread "diversity-based" voluntary affirmative action that is not driven by legal requirements or even a sense of social obligation, but rather by demographic realities. Moreover, this diversity-based affirmative action is not the "viewpoint diversity" that Stephen Carter and others have condemned,[402] in fact, it is not rigidly race- or gender-based at all, but rather "disadvantaged-based." To the extent that certain racial or gender groups are disproportionately disadvantaged, they will benefit as groups. But the real focus is on enhancing employment, training, and promotion opportunities for disadvantaged *individuals,* because there are or will be an insufficient number of appropriately "advantaged" employees to meet employers' increasingly technical needs.

The answer to the second question, whether preference-based affirmative action is an effective means of removing barriers, is yes if widespread racism and sexism by employers in the hiring and promotion process are still the primary obstacles to equal employment opportunity. If so, then perhaps preference-based affirmative action should continue to be the primary tool used to achieve equal employment opportunity. If, however, the process of mitigating the effects of racism and sexism in the workplace has advanced far enough so that other factors have begun to overshadow them in creating obstacles to equal employment opportunity, then continuing reliance on preference-based affirmative action again appears misplaced.

Perhaps the primary barriers to achieving true equal employment opportunity today are not so much racist and sexist employment policies but the unequal access to resources encountered by a disproportionate percentage of minority groups as the result of years of societal discrimination.[403] This unequal access, which can be linked to disparities in education, training, and motivation among many members of these groups, perpetuates itself in a continuing pattern of unequal earnings and employment outcomes.[404] Affirmative action, which primarily addresses discrimination in the workplace, is simply not an effective means to deal with these problems, as they affect the prospects of these individuals before they even enter the labor force. In fact, continuing emphasis on affirmative action as a means of achieving equal employment opportunity detracts from measures that might be more effective and appropriate to addressing these disparities and to help those disadvantaged individuals who need it most.[405]

Although preference-based affirmative action may soothe the conscience of nonminorities, promote the political agenda of certain groups interested in the redistribution of economic and social rights, cost less than resolving the true problems, and be easy to apply, it does not address many of the most fundamental reasons for unequal employment opportunity today. The objective then, from a policy point of view, should instead be to change the focus of affirmative action policy; rather than rely so heavily on programs designed to achieve proportionate representation in various job categories, emphasis should be placed on measures designed to enhance individual effort and productivity, such as improved education programs, additional government training programs, and loan and grant programs for human-capital investment purposes.[406] Such an allocation of public resources would be less discriminatory, and less controversial, as it would be aimed at attaining equal employment opportunity for all economically disadvantaged individuals, rather than members of a particular race, ethnic group, or gender. Such a policy would also be more consistent with the original vision of affirmative action policy.

As society evolves, so must affirmative action policy. Perhaps the time has finally come to take race and gender explicitly out of the decision-making process by shifting the focus of affirmative action toward measures aimed at resolving the disparities in education and training that afflict disadvantaged individuals regardless of race or gender and result from unequal access to resources.[407] These obstacles may be extremely difficult to overcome, but such an effort is a far worthier use of public resources than the perpetuation of the current system if equal opportunity for all, rather than redistribution of resources to a select few, is the true objective of U.S. civil rights policy.

NOTES

1. A sample of stories from the popular media gives some indication of both the nature and the scope of the affirmative action debate. *See, e.g.,* Don Aucoin, *Affirmative Action: Perception Policy,* BOSTON GLOBE, Apr. 2, 1992, at 1; Peter Brimelow & Leslie Spencer, *When Quotas Replace Merit, Everybody Suffers,* FORBES, Feb. 15, 1993, at 80; Stephen L. Carter, *Sometimes, Color-Blindness Needs Correction,* N.J. L.J., Jan. 6, 1992, at 15; *Controversial Civil Rights Directive Short-Lived in Wake of Fire Storm of Criticism,* BNA WASH, INSIDER, Nov. 22, 1991, at 1; John C. Cook, *Continuing Confusion Over the Civil Rights Compromise,* RECORDER, Mar. 18, 1992, at 8; Jeanne Cummings, *Mixed White House Signals on Civil Rights Raise Distrust,* ATLANTA J. & CONST., Nov. 23, 1991, at A10; Robert D. Davila & Deb Kollars, *City, County, RT Accused of Bias in Awarding Contracts,* SACRAMENTO BEE, Dec. 16, 1992, at B1; Ann Devroy & Sharon LaFraniere, *U.S. Moves to End Hiring Preferences; Affirmative Action Policies Targeted,* WASH. POST, Nov. 21, 1991, at A1; David R. Francis, *A Black Economist Critiques Old-Style Affirmative Action,* CHRISTIAN SCI. MONITOR, Apr. 3, 1992, at 8; Patrick A. Hall, *Against Our Best Interests: An Ambivalent View of Affirmative Action,* 22 AM. LIBR. 898 (1991); Dennis Hayashi & Dale Shimasaki, *When Racial Preferences Are Permissible,* WASH. POST, Oct. 26, 1992, at A21; William A. Henry III, *What Price Preference?,* TIME, Sept. 30, 1991, at 30; Sharon LaFraniere & Kenneth

J. Cooper, *U.S. May Ban Scholarships Based Exclusively on Race,* WASH. POST, Dec. 3, 1991, at A1; Leon F. Litwack, *America Is Reaping Two Centuries of Law Treating Blacks Lawlessly,* L.A. TIMES, May 5, 1992, at B7; Eva J. Paterson, *Benefits of Boalt Hall's Affirmative Action Program,* S.F. CHRON., Oct. 7, 1992, at A19; Jay Romano, *Bias Charged in Promotions of Firefighters,* N.Y. TIMES, Mar. 14, 1993, at 13NJ1; *Shoney's, Ex-CEO in Bias-Charge Flap,* USA TODAY, Dec. 22, 1992, at 2B.

2. Oppenheimer has suggested that affirmative action plans can be categorized and grouped into five "models" of affirmative action:

> [S]trict quotas favoring women or minorities (Model I); preference systems in which women or minorities are given some preference over white men (Model II); self-examination plans in which the failure to reach expected goals within expected periods of time triggers self-study, to determine whether discrimination is interfering with a decisionmaking process (Model III); outreach plans in which attempts are made to include more women and minorities within the pool of persons from which selections are made (Model IV); and, affirmative commitments not to discriminate (Model V).

David B. Oppenheimer, *Distinguishing Five Models of Affirmative Action,* 4 BERKELEY WOMEN'S L.J. 42, 42 (1988–89).

3. Robert Belton, *Reflections on Affirmative Action After* Paradise *and* Johnson, 23 HARV. C.R.-C.L. L. REV. 115, 116 (1988).

4. See *id.* at 115–16 n.1; Fullilove v. Klutznick, 448 U.S. 448 U.S. 448, 506–07 n.8 (1980) (Powell, J., concurring). Employers might use a variety of measures to implement this concept in the workplace. Examples of such measures include:

> A recruitment program designed to attract qualified members of the group in question; A systematic effort to organize work and redesign jobs in ways that provide opportunities for persons lacking "journeyman" level knowledge or skills to enter and, with appropriate training, to progress in a career field; Revamping selection instruments or procedures which have not yet been validated in order to reduce or eliminate exclusionary effects on particular groups in particular job classifications; The initiation of measures designed to assure that members of the affected group who are qualified to perform the job are included within the pool of persons from which the selecting official makes the selection; and a systematic effort to provide career advancement training, both classroom and on-the-job, to employees locked into dead end jobs.

J. Clay Smith, Jr., *Review: Affirmative Action,* 27 HOW. L.J. 495, 496 (1984) (quoting Equal Employment Opportunity Coordinating Council, Policy Statement on Affirmative Action Programs for State and Local Government Agencies, 41 Fed. Reg. 38,814 (1976), *quoted in* Interpretative Guidelines on Affirmative Action, 44 Fed. Reg. 4422, 4427 (1979)).

5. *See* U.S. CONST. amends. XIII (abolishing slavery) (effective 1865), XIV (guaranteeing former slaves citizenship status, due process, equal protection, and other rights) (effective 1868), and XV (guaranteeing former slaves the right to vote) (effective 1870). For examples of legislation passed during Reconstruction that provided special benefits to former slaves, see the Freedmen's Bureau Act of 1866, ch. 200, 14 Stat. 173; the Civil Rights Act of 1866, ch. 31, 14 Stat. 27 (current version at 42 U.S.C. §§ 1981, 1982 (1988)); and the Civil Rights Act of 1871, ch. 22, § 2, 17 Stat. 18 (current version at 42 U.S.C. § 1985(3) (1988)). *See* Eric Schnapper, *Affirmative Action and the Legislative History of the Fourteenth Amendment,* 71 VA. L. REV. 753 (1985).

One commentator has traced the "basic concept of affirmative action" back to the writs issues by the old English courts of equity. James E. Jones, Jr., *The Genesis and Present Status of Affirmative Action in Employment: Economic, Legal, and Political Realities,* 70 IOWA L. REV. 901, 902 (1985).

6. Exec. Order No. 10,925, 26 Fed. Reg. 1977 (1961). Although the Order is often credited as the origin of modern affirmative action, neither

the concept of federal mandating of equal opportunity in the workplace nor use of the phrase "affirmative action" in the employment discrimination context were particularly new in 1961. The former has been traced to certain New Deal programs that barred racial discrimination in the selection of individuals for the training and employment opportunities of these programs, and to an executive order issued by President Roosevelt in 1941 that prohibited defense contractors from discriminating on the basis of race and that charged both employers and unions with a duty "to provide for the full and equitable participation of all workers in defense industries without discrimination." *See* Jones, *supra* note 5, at 907 (emphasis omitted). Presidents Truman and Eisenhower also issued executive orders involving equal employment opportunity in the context of government contracting. *See* David L. Rose, *Twenty-Five Years Later: Where Do We Stand on Equal Employment Opportunity Law Enforcement?*, 42 VAND. L. REV. 1121, 1124–25 (1989). Affirmative action in its original form, however, as evidenced by these early executive orders, was merely a duty to make sure that minority workers were treated equally and not discriminated against. Thus, these early executive orders fit within Oppenheimer's Model V (affirmative commitments not to discriminate). *See supra* note 2.

Use of the phrase "affirmative action" in the employment discrimination context also first occurred in the New Deal era. *See* National Labor Relations Act, Pub. L. No. 74-198, 49 Stat. 449 (1935) (codified at 29 U.S.C. § 160(c) (1988)) (authorizing National Labor Relations Board to order employers who commit discriminatory labor practices "to take such affirmative action including reinstatement of employees with or without back pay" as is necessary to enforce the Act).

7. Exec. Order No. 10,925, 26 Fed. Reg. at 1977. Under the Order, however, federal contractors were required, as part of their contract with the government, to acknowledge this duty and to take "affirmative action to ensure that applicants are employed, and that employees are treated during employment, without regard to their race, creed, color, or national origin." *Id.*

As part of such affirmative action, contractors were required to advertise and publish notices of their commitment not to discriminate, and to furnish reports and other information to the government that would evidence their compliance with the Executive Order and any related governmental orders or regulations, *Id.* at 1977–78.

8. *Id.* at 1978. The PCEEO was the first executive committee granted the authority to enforce the government's affirmative action policy for employees of federal contractors. *See* Rose, *supra* note 6, at 1125. Despite this power, it appears the PCEEO was reluctant to use it. For a discussion of the actions taken by the PCEEO to enforce Executive Order No. 10,925 in the early 1960s, *see* James E. Jones, Jr., *Twenty-One Years of Affirmative Action: The Maturation of the Administrative Enforcement Process Under the Executive Order 11,246 as Amended,* 59 CHI. KENT L. REV. 67, 71–72 (1982).

9. Pub. L. No. 88-352, § 701, 78 Stat. 253 (codified as amended at 42 U.S.C. §§ 2000e to 2000e-17 (1988)).

10. 42 U.S.C. § 2000e-2 (1988). Initially, Title VII applied to employers and unions with 25 or more employees or members. The Equal Opportunity Act of 1972 amended Title VII to apply to private employers and unions with 15 or more employees or members. *See id.* § 2000e (1988).

11. *Id.* § 2000e-4 (1988).

12. *Id.* § 2000e-5 (1988).

13. *See* Jones, *supra* note 8, at 71.

14. Exec. Order No. 11,246, 30 Fed. Reg. 12,319 (1965), *reprinted as amended in* 42 U.S.C. § 2000e (1988). For a comprehensive discussion of both this Order and its implementing regulations, *see* Note, *Voluntary Affirmative Action After* United Steelworkers of America v. Weber: *Constructing A Peaceful Coexistence Between Title VII and Executive Order 11,246,* 27 U.C.L.A. L. REV. 1159 (1980).

15. Exec. Order No. 11,246, 30 Fed. Reg. at 12,325. The Secretary of Labor subsequently established the Office of Contract Compliance to administer this program. The Office of Federal Contract Compliance was renamed the Office of Federal Contract Compliance Programs ("OFCCP") in 1975 and in 1978 assumed con-

trol of the federal contracting program for all federal agencies. *See* Exec. Order No. 12,086, 43 Fed. Reg. 46,501 (1978), *reprinted in* 42 U.S.C. § 2000e (1988).

16. 30 Fed. Reg. at 12,319. The Order directed the Civil Service Commission to guide and assist executive departments and agencies with the development of their affirmative action programs. *Id.* This directive was later reinforced by Executive Order 11,478, issued by President Nixon in 1969, and supplemented by affirmative action requirements contained in the Civil Service Reform Act of 1978. *See* Exec. Order No. 11,478, 34 Fed. Reg. 12,985 (1969), *reprinted as amended in* 42 U.S.C. § 2000e (1988); Pub. L. No. 95-454, § 310, 92 Stat. 1111, 1152 (1978) (codified at 5 U.S.C. § 7201 (1988)).

17. Exec. Order No. 11,246, 30 Fed Reg. at 12,320. Such treatment was to cover all aspects of employment, including, without limitation, "upgrading, demotion, or transfer; recruitment or recruitment advertising; layoff or termination; rates of pay or other forms of compensation; and slection for training, including apprenticeship." *Id.*

President Johnson later expanded the list of groups protected under Executive Order 11,246 to include women. Exec. Order No. 11,375, 32 Fed. Reg. 14,303 (1967).

18. For a discusson of the reasons underlying the lack of government enforcement action from 1965 to 1969, *see* Rose, *supra* note 6, at 1135–39.

19. On June 27, 1969, the Department of Labor issued the Philadelphia Plan pursuant to Executive Order 11,246. The plan required businesses that bid on federally assisted construction contracts in the Philadelphia area to establish and satisfy numerical goals and timetables for using minority workers in local building trades. For a discussion of the plan and its history, see Contractors Ass'n v. Secretary of Labor, 442 F.2d 159 (3d Cir.), *cert. denied,* 404 U.S. 854 (1971) (upholding the validity of the plan). The Philadelphia Plan was adopted in response to the traditional exclusion of minorities from local building trade unions, with whom the federal government had no direct contractual relationship. *See* Jones, *supra* note 5, at 921; Rose,

supra note 6, at 1141–42. The plan served as a blueprint for subsequent plans adopted by the Department of Labor for federally assisted construction contracts in other cities and for OFCC Order No. 4, a regulation promulgated in 1970, which imposed numerical goals and timetable requirements on nonconstruction contractors and subcontractors, 41 C.F.R. § 60-2 (1971). *See* Robert P. Schuwerk, Comment, *The Philadelphia Plan: A Study in the Dynamics of Executive Power,* 39. U. CHI. L. REV. 723 (1972).

20. In 1970, the OFCC issued Order No. 4, which directed nonconstruction contractors to satisfy certain guidelines relating to the employment of minorities, and allowed employees who were victims of past discrimination to obtain relief from their employers. *See* 41 C.F.R. § 60-2 (1971). Although the OFCC had begun in 1968 to require federal contractors to prepare and submit written affirmative action plans, it had not indicated precisely what was required to be included in such plans. *See* 41 C.F.R. § 60-1.40 (1969). In OFCC Order No. 4, however, the agency required for the first time that contractors analyze their past and present employment practices and evaluate their work forces in order to determine whether any minority employment "problem areas" existed and, if so, to develop goals and timetables for achieving a balanced work force. Specifically, Order No. 4 stated that each plan must include an

> analysis of areas within which the contractor is deficient in the utilization of minority groups and, further, goals and timetables to which the contractor's good faith efforts must be directed to correct the deficiencies and, thus to increase materially the utilization of minorities at all levels and in all segments of his work force where deficiencies exist. 41 C.F.R. § 60-2.10 (1971).

> Possibly to appease critics of affirmative action, the Order cautioned that "[g]oals may not be rigid and inflexible quotas which must be met, but must be targets reasonably attainable by means of applying every good faith effort to make all aspects of the entire affirmative action program work." 41 C.F.R. § 60-2.24(e) (1971).

The self-examination requirement fits within Oppenheimer's Model III. *See* Oppenheimer, *supra* note 2, at 42. As a means of correcting past or current discrimination and its effects, the contractor might adopt a quota system (Model I), a preference system (Model II), or an outreach plan (Model IV).

In December 1971, the OFCC issued Revised Order No. 4, which provided that such plans must benefit women as well as minority groups. 41 C.F.R. § 60-2.10 (1972).

21. *See* United States v. N.L. Indus., 479 F.2d 354 (8th Cir. 1973) (back pay); United States v. Hayes Int'l Corp., 456 F.2d 112 (5th Cir. 1972) (back pay); United States v. Ironworkers Local 86, 443 F.2d 544 (9th Cir.), *cert. denied,* 404 U.S. 984 (1971) (numerical goals and timetables).

22. *See* HERMAN BELZ, EQUALITY TRANSFORMED: A QUARTER-CENTURY OF AFFIRMATIVE ACTION 94, 135 (1991).

23. 401 U.S. 424 (1971).

24. *Id.* at 429–31.

25. *Id.* at 431.

26. (. . .)

27. *See* Charles Fried, *Affirmative Action After* City of Richmond v. J.A. Croson Co.: *A Response to the Scholars' Statement,* 99 YALE L.J. 155, 161 n.47 (1989).

28. *See supra* note 20 for a discussion of Order No. 4; *see also* BELZ, *supra* note 22, at 135. In a subsequent decision, Albemarle Paper Co. v. Moody, 422 U.S. 405 (1975), the Supreme Court ruled that tests or employment selection devices that had a disparate impact were unlawful under Title VII, despite their job-relatedness, unless they had been validated under the EEOC's Guidelines on Employment Selection Procedures, 29 C.F.R. pt. 1607 (1971). Validation in accordance with these guidelines was a difficult and expensive process, requiring the employer to prepare a graphical and statistical analysis comparing the selection device with the desired criteria, in order to demonstrate the device's "utility" in making predictions about an applicant's future work behavior. 29 C.F.R. § 1607.5(c), .6 (1971). As an alternative to testing, many employers found it cheaper and easier to adopt affirmative action plans using goals and timetables as a means of balancing their work force and avoiding the risk of liability for disparate impact discrimination. Although in a later decision, Washington v. Davis, 426 U.S. 229 (1976), the Court indicated that employment selection devices that had a disparate impact but had not been validated under the EEOC guidelines did not necessarily violate Title VII, employers continued to prefer to adopt affirmative action programs to combat potential disparate impact suits rather than use validated tests and selection devices.

In 1978, the EEOC issued guidelines similar to its 1970 Guidelines on Employment Selection Procedures for adoption by all federal agencies. Uniform Guidelines on Employee Selection Procedures, 29 C.F.R. pt. 1607 (1992).

29. Pub. L. No. 92-261, 86 Stat. 103 (1972) (amending 42 U.S.C. §§ 2000e to 2000e-17 (1972)) (codified as amended at 42 U.S.C. §§ 2000e, 2000e -1 to -b 2000e-8 to -9, 2000e-13 to -17 (1988)).

30. Pub. L. No. 92-261, § 4(a), 86 Stat. 104 (1972) (codified at 42 U.S.C. § 2000e5(a) (1988)). The EEOC had not been granted any power to enforce Title VII in the Civil Rights Act of 1964. Prior to 1972, its principal role had been restricted to issuing regulations on record-keeping and reporting matters and adopting guidelines interpreting various aspects of Title VII. *See, e.g.,* Guidelines on Discrimination Because of Sex, 29 C.F.R. pt. 1604 (1966); Guidelines on Religious Discrimination, 29 C.F.R. pt. 1605 (1967); Uniform Guidelines on Employment Selection Procedures, 29 C.F.R. pt. 1607 (1971).

31. Pub. L. No. 92-261, § 2(1), 86 Stat. 103 (1972) (codified at 42 U.S.C. § 2000e(a) (1988)). The Act also extended the applicability of Title VII to private employers and unions with 15 or more employees or members. Pub. L. No. 92-261, § 2(2), 86 Stat. 103 (1972) (codified at 42 U.S.C. § 2000e(b) (1988)).

32. *See* Pub. L. No. 92-261, § 4(a), 86 Stat. 103 (1972) (codified at 42 U.S.C. § 2000e-5(g) (1988)). Specifically, the Act authorized federal courts to order, in addition to affirmative action, "any other equitable relief as the court deems appropriate." *Id; see* Local 28, Sheet Metal

Workers' Int'l Ass'n v. EEOC, 478 U.S. 421, 466-70 (1986).

33. *See* BELZ, *supra* note 22, at 77.

34. Rose, *supra* note 6, at 1145-46; *see, e.g.,* EEOC v. American Tel. & Tel. Co., 556 F.2d 167 (3d Cir. 1977), *cert. denied,* 438 U.S. 915 (1978); United States v. Allegheny-Ludlum Indus., 517 F.2d 826 (5th Cir. 1975), *cert. denied,* 425 U.S. 944 (1976); United States v. Bethlehem Steel Corp., 446 F.2d 652 (2d Cir. 1971); *In re* Trucking Indus. Employment Practices Litig., 384 F. Supp. 614 (J.P.M.L. 1974).

35. *See* Reorg. Plan No. 1 of 1978, 3 C.F.R. pt. 321 (1979), *reprinted in* 42 U.S.C. § 2000e-4 (1988). As part of this reorganization, a subsequent executive order issued by President Carter consolidated enforcement of Executive Order 11,246 for all federal contracting agencies with the Department of Labor, which subsequently delegated this authority of the OFCCP. *See* Exec. Order No. 12,086, 43 Fed. Reg. 46,501 (1978), *reprinted in* 42 U.S.C. § 2000e (1988).

36. 29 C.F.R. §§ 1608. 1-.12 (1993). To be consistent with these guidelines, an affirmative action plan must consist of a reasonable self-analysis, determining whether existing employment practices adversely affect members of protected groups or continue the effects of prior discrimination; a reasonable basis for concluding action is appropriate, which exists if such adverse treatment or continuation is present; and reasonable action, which must be rationally related to the problems revealed by the self-analysis. *Id.* § 1608.4. Such reasonable action may consist of "goals and timetables or other appropriate employment tools which recognize the race, sex, or national origin of applicants or employees." *Id.* Thus, the EEOC guidelines largely follow the standards set by the OFCC in Revised Order No. 4 for affirmative action plans adopted by federal contractors.

37. Under § 713 of Title VII, an employer who has relied in good faith upon a written interpretation or opinion of the EEOC has a defense for at least monetary liability. *See* 42 U.S.C. § 2000e-12(b)(1) (1988).

38. *See supra* note 30 and accompanying text.

39. Potential liability under Title VII for disparate impact discrimination has been a "'spur or catalyst which causes employers and unions to self-examine and to self-evaluate their employment practices and to endeavor to eliminate, so far as possible, the last vestiges of an unfortunate and ignominious page in this country's history.'" Albemarle Paper Co. v. Moody, 422 U.S. 405, 417-18 (1975) (quoting United States v. N.L. Indus., 479 F.2d 354, 379 (8th Cir. 1973)). *See infra* notes 141-59 and accompanying text. As Herman Belz has noted:

> Under disparate impact theory, good-faith efforts, intention, and relative improvement in minority hiring were irrelevant in determining unlawful discrimination. If anything, equal employment progress was rewarded by the imposition of more systematic racial hiring requirements. The only way to remain in compliance, corporate equal employment opportunity advisors concluded, was to have the company work force reflect the minority population of the local community. BELZ, *supra* note 22, at 85-86.

40. Federal contractors who adopt an affirmative action program consistent with OFCC Revised Order No. 4 are given additional protection under Title VII. Section 718 of Title VII prohibits the denial, termination, or suspension of a federal contract for employment discrimination reasons without a full hearing if the employer has implemented a government-approved affirmative action plan. 42 U.S.C. § 2000e-17 (1988).

41. The incentive to adopt such programs was further strengthened by the Supreme Court's decision in United Steelworkers v. Weber, 443 U.S. 193 (1979), which protected employers from liability under Title VII to nonminority workers adversely impacted by the adoption of an affirmative action plan. (. . .)

Support for quotas, numerical goals, and timetables as remedial measures began to wane in this executive branch during the years of the Reagan and Bush Administrations. For example, after the Supreme Court's decision in Firefighters Local Union No. 1784 v. Stotts, 467 U.S. 561 (1984), the Department of Justice began to actively espouse a more conservative approach to enforcement of employment discrimination laws and to civil rights in general. *See* Neal Devins, *Affirmative Action After Reagan,* 68 TEX. L. REV. 353, 355-56 (1989); Rose, *supra* note 6, at 1155. The EEOC and the OFCCP also played far less active roles in the enforcement of these laws during this period. *See* Devins, *supra,* at 355 n.16; Rose, *supra* note 6, at 1155, 1157–62. In fact, the OFCCP issued proposed regulations that would have undermined the enforcement of the affirmative action requirements of Executive Order No. 11,246. *See* 46 Fed. Reg. 42,979-43,017 (1981); Arthur F. Silbergeld, *New Affirmative Action Regulations for Government Contractors,* 33 LAB. L.J. 230 (1982).

Even during this period, however, legislation was enacted that was consistent with the affirmative action policies of Executive Order No. 11,246. Jones, *supra* note 5, at 940-41. In the aftermath, very few of the guidelines or other regulations issued by the EEOC and the OFCCP relating to affirmative action were changed by the Reagan Revolution. Devins, *supra,* at 355.

42. At the federal level, Congress has adopted a variety of public affirmative action programs. *See, e.g.,* Surface Transportation Assistance Act of 1982, Pub. L. No. 97-424, § 105(f), 96 Stat. 2097, 2100 (1983) (codified at 23 U.S.C. § 101 (1988)); Job Training Partnership Act, Pub. L. No. 97-300, § 481, 96 Stat. 1322, 1390 (1982) (codified at 29 U.S.C. §§ 1501, 1781 (1988)); Amendments to the Small Business Act, Pub. L. No. 95-507, § 211, 92 Stat. 1757, 1767 (1978) (current version at 15 U.S.C. § 637(d) (1988)); Public Works Employment Act of 1977, Pub. L. No. 95-28, § 103 (f)(2), 91 Stat. 116, 117 (codified at 42 U.S.C. § 6705(f)(2) (1988)) (upheld by the Supreme Court in Fullilove v. Klutznick, 448 U.S. 448 (1980)). As a result of the Equal Opportunity Act of 1972, which amended Title VII to protect state and local government workers, almost all states and many local governments have adopted affirmative action plans with regard to the hiring and promotion of minorities and women. For examples of such programs, see Mary C. Daly, *Affirmative Action, Equal Access and the Supreme Court's 1988 Term: The Rehnquist Court Takes a Sharp Turn*

to the Right, 18 HOFSTRA L. REV. 1057, 1074–75 (1990).

43. The cases discussed in the next Section were decided by the Supreme Court in the following order: In the 1978 case of Regenta of the University of California v. Bakke, 438 U.S. 265 (1978), the Court applied a strict scrutiny test to hold that an affirmative action admissions program adopted by a university medical school was invalid under the Fourteenth Amendment's Equal Protection Clause, but refused to enjoin the school from considering the race of applicants as a factor in future admission decisions. The next year, in United Steelworkers v. Weber, 443 U.S. 193 (1979), the Court ruled that an affirmative action plan contained in a master collective-bargaining agreement between a corporation and a labor union was lawful under Title VII of the 1964 Civil Rights Act in light of the legislative history of the statute and the historical context from which it arose. Next, in the 1980 case of Fullilove v. Klutznick, 448 U.S. 448 (1980), the Court upheld the validity of a federal program requiring that a percentage of federal funds awarded for local public works projects be set aside to purchase services or supplies from minority-owned businesses. The Court found that Congress did not violate the equal protection component of the Fifth Amendment's Due Process Clause by establishing this program.

Four years later, in the case of Firefighters Local Union No. 1784 v. Stotts, 467 U.S. 561 (1984), the Court invalidated a district court injunction that required a city fire department to comply with a layoff plan that resulted in the laying off of several nonminority firefighters who had more seniority than some recently hired black firefighters. The injunction was held to exceed the limited authority that courts have under Title VII to enter orders that override existing seniority systems in pattern or practice cases. In 1986, in the case of Wygant v. Jackson Board of Education, 476 U.S. 267 (1986), the Court applied a strict scrutiny standard to hold unlawful on equal protection grounds a provision in a collective-bargaining agreement that resulted in minority teachers being retained while nonminority teachers with greater seniority were dismissed. That same year, in the case of Local No. 93, International Ass'n of Firefighters v. City of Cleveland, 478 U.S. 501 (1986), the Court addressed whether a district court had authority under Title VII to enter a consent decree that required a specified number of promotions to be given to minority firefighters over the following four-year period. The Court upheld the consent order, holding that a consent decree awarding relief that benefits minority members who were not actual victims of the employer's discrimination does not violate Title VII regardless of whether § 706(g) of the Act prohibits a court from imposing race-conscious relief after trial. In Local 28, Sheet Metal Workers' International Ass'n v. EEOC, 478 U.S. 421 (1986), the companion case to *Local No. 93,* the Court also upheld a district court order that required a labor union to set up a fund that would be used to increase minority membership in the union and its apprenticeship program, to meet a specified minority membership goal by a specified date, and to implement an affirmative action program to achieve this goal under the guidance of a court-appointed administrator. Again the Court found that the order did not violate Title VII, noting that § 706(g) did not prohibit federal courts from ordering affirmative race-conscious relief to remedy past discrimination in appropriate circumstances.

In the 1987 case of United States v. Paradise, 480 U.S. 149 (1987), the validity of a federal court order was again the subject of dispute. In this case, the district court had required a state agency to promote to the next higher rank one minority employee for every nonminority employee promoted, if qualified minority employees were available. The Court, applying a strict scrutiny test, upheld the district court's order, concluding that the one-for-one promotional requirement did not violate equal protection, in view of the agency's long history not only of excluding minorities from employment and promotions but also of failing to comply with court orders to remedy such discriminatory practices. Also in 1987, in Johnson v. Transportation Agency, 480 U.S. 616 (1987),

the Court upheld a voluntary affirmative action plan adopted by a county agency which allowed it to consider the gender of employees as one factor in making promotions to job categories where women had been underrepresented, and pursuant to which a woman was promoted who had scored slightly lower than a male candidate on a promotion qualification examination that both had passed. The plan was upheld under Title VII since the agency had shown that it was necessary to correct a conspicuous imbalance that still existed in what traditionally had been segregated job categories and that it satisfied the *Weber* criteria for voluntary affirmative action plans.

★ ★ ★

202. *See supra* notes 6–7 and accompanying text; Oppenheimer, *supra* note 2, at 42, 46–50 (concerning Models III, IV, and V).

203. United Steelworkers v. Weber, 443 U.S. 193, 197 (1979).

204. Regents of the Univ. of Cal. v. Bakke, 438 U.S. 265, 302 (1978) (plurality opinion).

205. *Id.* at 305 (plurality opinion).

206. Wygant v. Jackson Bd. of Educ. 476 U.S. 267, 274 (1986) (plurality opinion).

207. City of Richmond v. J.A. Croson Co., 488 U.S. 469, 498 (1989).

208. *Id.* at 505.

209. *Id.*

210. Metro Broadcasting, Inc. v. FCC, 497 U.S. 547, 607 (1990) (O'Connor, J., dissenting).

211. *Id.* (citations omitted).

212. *See* Harry T. Edwards, *The Future of Affirmative Action in Employment,* 44 WASH. & LEE L. REV. 763, 765 (1987) (concluding the cycle of discrimination can be broken only by "reversing the preference").

213. United Steelworkers v. Weber, 443 U.S. 193, 204 (1979).

214. Regents of the Univ. of Cal. v. Bakke, 438 U.S. 265, 325 (1978) (Brennan, White, Marshall, and Blackman, JJ., concurring in judgment in part and dissenting in part).

215. *Id.* at 325.

216. *Id.* at 369. But see City of Richmond v. J.A. Croson Co., 488 U.S. 469 (1989), where a ma-

jority of the Court, for the first time, accepted a strict scrutiny standard for state and local programs granting race preferences, and Wygant v. Jackson Board of Education, 476 U.S. 267 (1986), where the Court refused to accept societal discrimination as a sufficient predicate for state and local race preferences.

217. *Bakke,* 438 U.S. at 403, 407 (Blackmun, J.).
218. United Steelworkers v. Weber, 443 U.S. 193, 197 (1979).
219. *Id.* at 212 (Blackmun, J. concurring).
220. *See id.* at 214 (Blackmun, J., concurring).
221. Wygant v. Jackson Bd. of Educ., 476 U.S. 267, 272 (1986) (plurality opinion).
222. *Id.* at 274 (plurality opinion).
223. *Id.* (plurality opinion).
224. *Id.* at 276 (plurality opinion).
225. 480 U.S. 616 (1987).
226. Kathleen M. Sullivan, *Sins of Discrimination: Last Term's Affirmative Action Cases,* 100 HARV. L. REV. 78 (1986).
227. *Johnson,* 480 U.S. at 645-46 (Stevens J., concurring).
228. Sullivan, *supra* note 226, at 80.
229. *Id.* at 81.
230. Note, *Rethinking* Weber: *The Business Response to Affirmative Action,* 102 HARV. L. REV. 658, 668-69 (1989).
231. *See* SHELBY STEELE, THE CONTENT OF OUR CHARACTER 89 (1990).
232. Regents of the Univ. of Cal. v. Bakke, 438 U.S. 265, 387 (1978) (Marshall, J.).
233. *Id.* at 390.
234. *Id.* at 394.
235. *Id.* at 396.
236. *See, e.g.,* STEPHEN L. CARTER, REFLECTIONS OF AN AFFIRMATIVE ACTION BABY 19 (1991).
237. *Bakke,* 438 U.S. at 400-02 (Marshall, J.).
238. United Steelworkers v. Weber, 443 U.S. 193, 209 n.9 (1979).
239. 401 U.S. 424, 431 (1971).
240. (. . .)
241. *Weber,* 443 U.S. at 210 (Blackmun, J., concurring) (quoting Weber v. Kaiser Aluminum & Chem. Corp., 563 F.2d 216, 230 (5th Cir. 1977) (Wisdom J., dissenting)).
242. *See supra* (. . .); notes 169–178 and accompanying text; Moore & Braswell, *supra* note 169.

. . . of disparate impact has been made, the effect of disparate impact analysis upon quotas and affirmative action, and other related issues, however, will need to be determined by future Supreme Court decisions.[169]

Many employers, spurred by the rulings in *Griggs, Albemarle,* and other early disparate impact cases, adopted affirmative action programs to avoid liability for disparate impact discrimination.[170] To the extent that the obstacles created for plaintiffs in disparate impact cases by *Watson* and *Wards Cove* have not been resolved by the Civil Rights Act of 1991, however, the bringing of such actions probably will be discouraged, and an important legal motivation for voluntary affirmative action will be lost.[171] As some commentators have noted:

> When [the loss of this incentive] is coupled with a heightened prospect of being sued for reverse discrimination because of implementing an affirmative action plan, there is little doubt but that many employers will eschew voluntary affirmative action altogether. Since it will be more difficult for plaintiffs to prove liability and easier for employers to defend against it, fewer employers will see the predicate of a "manifest imbalance" as a justification for affirmative action.[172]

IV. THE EFFECT OF THE CIVIL RIGHTS ACT OF 1991 ON AFFIRMATIVE ACTION

The primary area of disagreement and controversy surrounding the Civil Rights Act of 1990[173] and the Civil Rights Act of 1991[174] concerned quotas and affirmative action.[175] The 1990 Act was vetoed by President Bush because it allegedly would induce the use of employment quotas.[176] The same concerns existed for the 1991 legislation,[177] but a sudden compromise late in October 1991 ended the two-year stalemate.[178]

169. *See* Gary A. Moore & Michael K. Braswell, *"Quotas" and the Codification of the Disparate Impact Theory: What Did*

Griggs Really Say and Not Say?, 55 ALB. L. REV. 459, 484, 492-93 (1991).

170. *See* Fried, *supra* note 27, at 161 n.47.

171. Braswell et al., *supra* note 163, at 33 (citing Fried, *supra* note 27).

172. *Id.* at 33–34 (citations omitted).

173. Bills were introduced in both the Senate and House of Representatives. *See* S. 2104, 101st Cong., 2d Sess., 136 CONG. REC. S1018-25 (daily ed. Feb. 7, 1990); H.R. 4000. 101st Cong., 2d Sess., 136 CONG. REC. H364 (daily ed. Feb. 7, 1990). A Conference Report, H.R. CONF. REP. No. 856, 101st Cong., 2d Sess., 136 CONG. REC. H9552-59 (daily ed. Oct. 12, 1990) was subsequently agreed to by both houses. *See* 136 CONG. REC. S15407 (daily ed. Oct. 16, 1990); 136 CONG. REC. H9994-95 (daily ed. Oct. 17, 1990).

174. Pub. L. No. 102-66, 105 Stat. 1071 (1991).

175. *See* Moore & Braswell, *supra* note 169, at 459-62.

176. *See* 136 CONG. REC. S16457-58 (daily ed. Oct. 22, 1990) (veto message of President Bush on S. 2104).

177. *See* Moore & Braswell, *supra* note 169, at 475–76.

178. The best explanation for the sudden agreement was to save face after the Clarence Thomas/Anita Hill debacle in the Senate.

★ ★ ★

243. For discussions of group versus individual rights, *see* Alfred W. Blumrosen, *The Group Interest Concept, Employment Discrimination, and Legislative Intent; The Fallacy of* Connecticut v. Teal, 20 HARV. J. ON LEGIS. 99 (1983); Glenn C. Loury, *Why Should We Care About Group Inequality?* 5 SOC. PHIL. & POL'Y 249 (1987); William B. Reynolds, *Individualism v.*

Group Rights; The Legacy of Brown, 93 YALE L.J. 995 (1984).

244. Michael E. Gold, Griggs' *Folly: An Essay on the Theory, Problems, and Origin of the Adverse Impact Definition of Employment Discrimination and a Recommendation for Reform,* 7 INDUS. REL. L.J. 429, 509 (1985).

245. Braswell et al., *supra* note 163, at 34. multicomponent selection process as one employment practice for purposes of showing disparate impact).

246. (. . .)

247. *See, e.g.,* Ken Feagins, *Affirmative Action or the Same Sin?,* 67 DENV. U.L. REV. 421 (1990).

248. *Id.* at 421 n.2.

249. 42 U.S.C. § 2000e-2(a), (d) (1988).

250. 427 U.S. 273, 287 (1976).

251. *Weber,* 443 U.S. at 201.

252. *Id.*

253. *Id.* at 222 (Rehnquist, J., dissenting).

254. *Id.* at 209 (Blackmun, J., concurring).

255. *Id.* at 216 (Burger, C.J., dissenting).

256. 443 U.S. at 254-55 (Rehnquist, J., dissenting).

257. 488 U.S. 469, 493 (1989) (plurality opinion).

258. 497 U.S. 547, 603-04 (1990) (O'Connor, J., dissenting); *see* Rocco Potenza, *Affirmative Action: Will Justice O'Connor Author Its End?,* 22 TOLEDO L. REV. 805, 823 (1991).

259. *See* CARTER, *supra* note 236, at 12.

260. Loury, *supra* note 243, at 263–64; *see* Morris B. Abram, *Affirmative Action: Fair Shakers and Social Engineers,* 99 HARV. L. REV. 1312, 1319 (1986) (declining occupational and professional standards are cited as a possible consequence of affirmative action).

261. THOMAS SOWELL, CIVIL RIGHTS: RHETORIC OR REALITY? 118 (1984).

262. *See* Madeline E. Heilman et al., *Intentionally Favored. Unintentionally Harmed? Impact of Sex-Based Preferential Selection on Self-Perceptions and Self-Evaluations,* 72 J. APPLIED PSYCHOL. 62, 67–68 (1987); Rupert W. Nacoste & Darrin Lehman, *Procedural Stigma,* 17 REPRESENTATIVE RES. SOC. PSYCHOL. 25 (1987). In a recent newspaper article, one woman was quoted as saying, "I almost felt that I was a product of reverse discrimination . . . [and] when I applied to Harvard Business School, I got in and a lot of my peers did not. . . . I can't say that I was much more qualified. It tarnishes the joy

of that achievement for me because I'm not sure I deserved it more than somebody else." Kathy Swindle, *Comparing Notes of Classroom Bias,* DALLAS MORNING NEWS, Aug. 5, 1992, at C1.

263. *See* David A. Strauss, *The Myth of Colorblindness,* 1986 SUP. CT. REV. 99, 103.
264. *See* STEELE, *supra* note 231, at 124.
265. *Id.* at 15.
266. *Id.* at 14, 33.
267. *Id.* at 39, 50.
268. *Id.* at 113, 121.
269. *See* City of Richmond v. J.A. Croson Co., 488 U.S. 469, 495 (1989) (plurality opinion).
270. 476 U.S. 267, 276 (1986) (plurality opinion).
271. *Id.* at 288 (O'Connor, J., concurring).
272. Richard Delgado, *Affirmative Action as a Majoritarian Device: or, Do You Really Want to Be a Role Model?,* 89 MICH. L. REV. 1222 (1991).
273. *Id.* at 1226.
274. *Id.* at 1228. The author estimates that out of 35,000 blacks starting school in California in one year, only one will become a law professor. *Id.* at 1229.
275. *Id.* at 1226 n.20.
276. *Id.* at 1226.
277. 497 U. S. 547, 614 (1990) (O'Connor, J., dissenting).
278. CARTER, *supra* note 236, at 34.
279. *Id.* at 35.
280. *Id.* at 44.
281. *Id.* at 44-45, 50.
282. Loury, *supra* note 243, at 260.
283. *Id.*
284. *Id.* at 260–61.
285. *Id.* at 262.
286. *Id.* at 263.
287. *See* Pamela L. Perry, *Two Faces of Disparate Impact Discrimination,* 59 FORDHAM L. REV. 523 (1991).
288. *See* Griggs v. Duke Power Co., 401 U.S. 424, 432 (1971).
289. 480 U.S. 616, 658 (1987) (Scalia, J., dissenting).
290. *Id.* at 659.
291. Loury, *supra* note 243, at 249.
292. *Id.* at 258.
293. Thomas, *supra* note 65, at 402.

I continue to believe that distributing opportunities on the basis of race or gender, whoever the beneficiaries, turns the law against employment discrimination on its head. Class preferences are an affront to the rights and dignity of individuals—both those individuals who are directly disadvantaged by them, and those who are their supposed beneficiaries. I think that preferential hiring on the basis of race or gender will increase racial divisiveness, disempower women and minorities by fostering the notion that they are permanently disabled and in need of handouts, and delay the day when skin color and gender are truly the least important things about a person in the employment context.

Id. at 403 n.3.

65. *See* the majority opinion in City of Richmond v. J.A. Croson Co., 488 U.S. 469 (1989), discussed *infra* at text accompanying notes 88–98, which was joined by Justice Kennedy. Prior to joining the Court, while Chairman of the EEOC, Clarence Thomas expressed his discomfort with affirmative action plans that offer preferential treatment on the basis of race or gender. *See* Clarence Thomas, "Affirmative Action Goals and Timetables: Too Tough? Not Tough Enough!," 5 YALE L. & POL'Y REV. 402, 403 n.3 (1987).

294. *Id.* at 405–06. The Civil Rights Act of 1991, however, does allow successful plaintiffs to recover compensatory damages for intentional employment discrimination. *See* Pub. L. No. 102-166, § 102, 105 Stat. 1072 (1991) (codified at 42 U.S.C. § 1981(a) (1992)).
295. Thomas, *supra* note 293 at 406.
296. *Id.* at 408.
297. *Id.* at 410–11.
298. CARTER, *supra* note 236, at 67.
299. *Id.* at 71. Carter says, "I have never been denied a promotion, a job, an education, shelter or food." *Id.* at 77.
300. *Id.* at 80.
301. *Id.*
302. *Id.* at 82–83.
303. Glenn C. Loury, *Beyond Civil Rights,* NEW REPUBLIC, Oct. 7, 1985, at 22.

304. *Id.*
305. *Id.* at 25.
306. STEELE, *supra* note 231, at 15.
307. *Id.* at 54.
308. *Id.* at 16, 33, 68, 80.
309. Abram, *supra* note 260, at 1325.
310. Clint Bolick, *Blacks and Whites on Common Ground,* WALL ST. J., Aug. 5, 1992, at A14.
311. *Id.*

★ ★ ★

397. This benefit is also achieved, perhaps even more effectively by threatening employers with potential liability for back pay or other make-whole relief for disparate impact discrimination under Title VII.
398. There seems to be no clear consensus of support for preference-based affirmative action among the current membership of the Supreme Court except when narrowly tailored plans are adopted as a remedy for identifiable past discrimination. Insofar as private, voluntary affirmative action is concerned, it is likely that the present Court will overrule United Steelworkers v. Weber, 443 U.S. 193 (1979), or at least significantly modify the decision to allow such plans only if the imbalance to be redressed by the plan consists of a statistical disparity that is so great that a prima facie violation of Title VII exists . . . In the area of state-adopted affirmative action plans, it looks as though the Court will continue to apply a strict scrutiny test, making such programs highly questionable unless they have been adopted to remedy demonstrated acts of racial, ethnic, or gender discrimination committed either by the govermental unit adopting the plan or by other entities subject to the governmental unit's jurisdiction. Even then, such plans must employ a narrowly tailored means such as a preference to benefit the group discriminated against, rather than adopting a strict quota, numerical requirement, or other rigid requirement that might unduly burden nonminorities. . . .

    District courts have some authority under Title VII to order employers to implement race- or gender-conscious affirmative action programs, especially if the employer has previously demonstrated reluctance to redress such discriminatory acts. The type of relief contained in the program is again important, as the court-approved plan must not unduly burden the interests of nonminority employees. . . . Congressionally mandated programs appear to have the strongest backing by the Court, as such plans are usually accorded deference by the Court and are subjected to a more relaxed standard of scrutiny for purposes of satisfying equal protection concerns. Like *Weber,* however, support for much plans among members of the Court is apparently receding, and it is questionable whether a majority can be composed in the future that will continue to grant such favorable treatment to federal affirmative action programs that mandate disparate treatment on the basis of race, national origin, or gender. . . .

399. There is no strong empirical evidence supporting the effectiveness of affirmative action in substantially lessening societal discrimination. *See supra* text accompanying notes 395-96. Economic theories of discrimination and human capital theory also do not generally suggest a need for such affirmative action, as Title VII suits are typically sufficient. . . .
400. (. . .)
401. According to labor force projections prepared by the Bureau of Labor Statistics and the Hudson Institute, the work force in the United States is projected to become much more diverse in terms of race, gender, and ethnicity by the end of this decade. *See* BUREAU OF LABOR STATISTICS, U.S. DEP'T OF LABOR, BULLETIN NO. 2352, OUTLOOK 2000, at 1-10 (1990); HUDSON INST., WORKFORCE 2000: WORK AND WORKERS FOR THE TWENTY-FIRST CENTURY 75, 76 (1987). According to the most recent report released by the Bureau of Labor Statistics almost 75% of the nation's work force is expected to be comprised of women and racial and ethnic minority group members by the year 2005 (47.4% women; 11.6% Blacks; 11.1% Hispanics; 4.3% Asian and other minorities). BUREAU OF LABOR STATISTICS, U.S. DEP'T OF LABOR, BULLETIN NO. 3402. OUTLOOK, 1990–2005, at 4, 29–42 (1992). This report also indicates that protected group members will continue to enter the job market at a far higher rate, and leave the work force at a far lower rate, than white males. *Id.* at 8. These projections suggest that employers may have little choice but to fully integrate their labor force in order to continue to meet the demands of business.

402. *See supra* text accompanying notes 277–81.

403. *See supra* text accompanying notes 297-302. De-emphasizing affirmative action as a means of achieving equal employment opportunity would not give employers carte blanche to revert to racist and sexist employment policies in the workplace, as employers would still be subject to Title VII liability in such cases.

404. Recent statistical studies of the labor force indicate that a growing barrier to future employment for all prospective workers will be the lack of education, skills, and technical proficiencies necessary to perform even entry level jobs, especially those in the industries expected to grow most rapidly in the next 15 years. *See e.g.,* BUREAU OF LABOR STATISTICS, U.S. DEP'T OF LABOR, BULLETIN NO. 2402, OUTLOOK, 1990-2005, at 82–92 (1992). As of 1990, for example, the unemployment rate for 25–34 year olds without a high school degree was almost double that of those with a high school degree, and this gap is expected to increase. *Id.* at 9, BUREAU OF LABOR STATISTICS, U.S. DEP'T OF LABOR, BULLETIN NO. 2352, OUTLOOK 2000, at 9 (1990). This barrier is especially significant for minorities since the high school dropout rate for these groups has been significantly higher than that of nonminorities. *Id.* at 9–10.

405. As several commentators have noted, many of the jobs that affirmative action programs reserve for minorities go more to upper-class and middle-class minority members rather than the truly disadvantaged, who often are not in a position to benefit from such programs. *See supra* text accompanying notes 264, 298–302.

406. Following the release of its Workforce 2000 study, the Hudson Institute proposed a number of initiatives that private businesses could employ as a means of investing in human capital, including direct and cooperative basic skills training programs, literacy training, internships, work-study programs, partnerships with public schools, and corporate philanthropy. *See* HUDSON INST., OPPORTUNITY 2000; CREATIVE AFFIRMATIVE ACTION STRATEGIES FOR A CHANGING WORKFORCE 69–84 (1988).

407. Any action to lessen governmental endorsement of race- or gender-conscious affirmative action, to be effective, must also reduce the primary incentive for private employers to adopt such programs, namely, the difficulty of defending against charges of disparate impact discrimination. As a result of the Civil Rights Act of 1991, the Supreme Court has the opportunity in future cases to make it less burdensome (from an evidentiary and a cost plan of view) for employers to justify employment practices that have a disparate impact under the business necessity defense. This objective might be accomplished, for example, by eliminating the pre-*Ward's Cove* requirement of validated testing to show job-relatedness. *See supra* and accompanying notes . . . To the extent that this burden is eased, the necessity to adopt affirmative action programs as a panacea for disparate impact liability should be reduced.

READING 3-3

Affirmative Action: An Ethical Evaluation

Bill Shaw

1. INTRODUCTION

Affirmative action has been defined as "a public or private program designed to equalize hiring and admissions opportunities for historically disadvantaged groups by taking into consideration those very characteristics which have been used to deny them equal treatment."[1] As comprehensive as this definition may be, it is obvious that, in the employment area, affirmative action plans often encompass more than equalized hiring opportunities. Such programs often seek to increase the number of minorities and women in higher level/higher paying jobs by equalizing their promotion opportunities and protecting them from being laid off under the "last hired,

Source: Journal of Business Ethics, 7 (1988), 763–770. Reprinted by permission of Kluwer Academic Publishers.

first fired" rule of seniority. In all three of these situations—hiring, promotion and layoff—the effect is to deprive some individual, normally white males, of a "potential benefit, or opportunity, in order to enhance the opportunities of others," i.e., minorities and females.[2]

While one would think that this "redistribution of potentials"[3] would be less controversial than a redistribution of actual wealth, this is simply not the case. Unlike social welfare programs, affirmative action has given rise to rigorous debate.[4] In truth, even the coalition responsible for Civil Rights legislation is in disagreement over how the U.S. should remedy the effects of past discrimination.

Opponents of affirmative action adhere to a policy of strict colorblindness. They believe that all governmental distinctions based on race should be presumed illegal unless the distinctions pass the stringent requirements of "strict scrutiny".[5] Proponents of affirmative action contend that only malign distinctions based on race should be abolished; benign distinctions that favor minorities and women should be allowed. This is because, "in order to get beyond racism, we must first take race into account," and "in order to treat some people equally, we must treat them differently."[6]

Initially, the affirmative action debate was not aided by the Supreme Court's seemingly contradictory rulings.[7] And the controversy intensified when Reagan Administration officials, most notably Attorney General Edwin Meese and Assistant Attorney General for Civil Rights William Bradford Reynolds, voiced their opposition to affirmative action programs. Mr. Reynolds attempted to persuade fifty-one localities to abandon their affirmative action hiring and promotion programs, and announced his intention to ask the Supreme Court to overturn *United States Steelworkers v. Weber,*[8] which authorized companies and unions to adopt voluntary affirmative action programs. Pitted against the Administration's position are various civil rights and women's groups who view affirmative action as an appropriate remedy for redressing past dis-

crimination, and as a way to open the doors for blacks and women to professions which have historically excluded them.

The Supreme Court re-addressed the issue of affirmative action and, in recent major decisions,[9] reaffirmed race- and gender-conscious hiring and promotion preferences in the workplace. These pronouncements signal a rejection of the Reagan Administration's stance on affirmative action. However, despite the Supreme Court's rulings, it is apparent that the controversy over affirmative action continues, and there are strong arguments to be met on both sides. Rather than examining the affirmative action debate from a purely legal viewpoint, this paper will look at it from an ethical perspective. The question this paper will address is, how can affirmative action be ethically justified?

II. THE PROBLEM OF DISCRIMINATION

Affirmative action seeks to remedy the problem of the strong, persistent, and irrational discriminations made by large portions of society.[10] Irrational discrimination is taken to mean the use of such irrelevant characteristics as color or gender to judge an individual's human worth or capability.

In the past, women and minorities have been blatantly excluded from the process of attaining jobs sought by white males, and the effects of this discrimination continue today. For example, because blacks have historically been relegated to lower paying jobs, today's seniority systems, which effectively lock blacks into these jobs, perpetuate past discrimination against the entire group.[11] Affirmative action seeks to remedy the effects of this irrational discrimination by "alter[ing] our environment so as to weaken or extinguish such discriminations, or at least to break up the stratifications."[12]

III. AFFIRMATIVE ACTION MECHANISMS

There are two mechanisms by which affirmative action programs have been implemented.[13] One applies a fairly rigid formula or quota to determine how many minority group members should be granted a benefit.[14] For example, under the quota system, a given number of minority workers will be hired until the proportion of minority employees reaches the minimum percentage within the overall labor pool. Because a quota system precludes nonminority employees from consideration, this mechanism is viewed as inequitable and has been highly criticized; legally it is permissible only as a last resort effort to remedy egregious discrimination.[15]

Hiring goals, the second mechanism for affirmative action, does not designate positions for minorities only; in contrast to a quota system, a system utilizing hiring goals only requires that employers make every effort to hire minorities, but nonminorities are not barred from competition.[16] Quite understandably, hiring goals are less controversial, and more equitable, than quotas. The mechanism for affirmative action that this paper will be referring to is a hiring goal system.

IV. ETHICAL ARGUMENTS FOR AND AGAINST AFFIRMATIVE ACTION[17]

A. Colorblind v. Race-Conscious Plans

As stated earlier, affirmative action seeks to remedy the problem of irrational discriminations. However, as opponents of affirmative action argue, if race/gender is morally irrelevant, it should never be a consideration in hiring, promotions and other job related situations because to prefer one employee over another on this basis cannot be morally justified. The law, they argue, should be "colorblind" and totally neutral.

There are several responses to this argument. First, it is obvious that our culture has never considered race or gender irrelevant to employment decisions. A cursory reading of American history bears out this contention.[18] Thus opponents of affirmative action, by stripping the historical context from our employment practices with the demand for race- and gender-blind laws, favor a policy that will tolerate the effects of past discrimination for years to come. To suggest otherwise is simply to ignore a social reality.[19]

Second, if the social order which subjected groups on the basis of race or sex was unjust, why is it unjust to redefine that social order to fashion group remedies for group injuries? "To ignore the fact that a person is [black] would be to ignore the fact that there had been a social practice in which unjust actions were directed toward [black] persons as such."[20] It is obvious that our earlier social practices worked to the benefit of white males who attained and maintain an unfair advantage of the expense of blacks and women. To disregard collective injury, then, would be "morally speaking . . . the most hideous aspect of the injustices of human history: those carried out systematically and directed toward whole groups of men and women as groups."[21]

Third, in examining the historical income distribution in the United States, it becomes apparent that the disparity between races cannot be correlated to such morally relevant characteristics as "rights, deserts, merits, contributions and needs of recipients."[22] Under a distributive justice theory of affirmative action, group members are entitled to preferential treatment, not because society is admitting and paying for past errors, but because those persons deserve a greater "shot" at the limited resources available simply in virtue of being members of the human community.[23] Distributive theories require no admission of social or collective guilt; they merely require the acknowledgement that, from this time forward, society's resources be distributed on the basis of morally relevant factors.

Given this concept of justice, considering an applicant's race as part of the bundle of traits that constitute "merit" is entirely consistent with the understanding of merit as a unique combination of factors that best meets society's needs.[24] This understanding is buttressed by the observation that getting ahead in American society has often turned on quite obviously nonmeritocratic factors.[25]

Where does it end, and when? It ends when the proportion of women and minorities in unskilled positions approximates that of the population generally, and when their proportion in the ranks of skilled and professional positions approximates their appearance in the pool of qualified applicants. Affirmative action is not committed to maintain those targets. Once they are reached, it becomes a matter of personal choice for group members to decide whether they will seek these positions. If they do not, that is an issue that can be addressed (or not addressed) when it arises, and on a basis that will have no necessary connection with the reasons here advanced in support of affirmative action.

B. Individual v. Group Protection

If affirmative action is supposed to remedy the effects of past discrimination, opponents of such programs often ask, what of the fact that many of the victims of discrimination are dead? Further, are not many nonvictims receiving undeserved compensation for injuries they never experienced?

First, it is apparent that historical injuries cannot be separated from the present effects of history.[26] The classic example involves seniority systems: in the past, black employees were relegated to the lowest paying positions in a company with no chance of elevating themselves: The higher paying jobs were restricted to "whites only." After civil rights legislation prohibited such segregation in the work place, blacks were allowed to compete for and attain higher level positions. However, when it came to receiving employment benefits and avoiding layoffs, black employees suffered by virtue of past segregation. Due to their lack of seniority, black employees were denied employment benefits and fell victim to the "last hired, first fired rule of seniority."[27] Then, as the "badges of slavery" continue, it becomes irrelevant whether affirmative action redresses past discrimination or the present effects of past discrimination.[28]

Second, it is also apparent that racial discrimination is "all encompassing". An examination of early American attitudes toward blacks documents the fact that race discrimination is directed not at individuals, but blacks as a group.[29] By way of illustration, note the language from *Scott v. Sandford*[30] referring to negroes as a "race fit for slavery." Further, Jim Crow laws stamped all blacks as the inferior race. The all encompassing nature of discrimination was further documented by the Supreme Court in *Brown v. Board of Education*.[31] Thus, it is almost inconceivable that individual group members did not suffer humiliation and injury.[32]

Next, the argument that affirmative action frequently aids those who need it least ignores the extent affirmative action has opened up opportunities for blue collar workers.[33] It also assumes that affirmative action should be provided only to the most deprived strata of the black community, or those who can best document their victimization. To the contrary, however, affirmative action operates at its most effective level in assisting the efforts of those with threshold ability to integrate the trades and professions. After all, if it cannot be utilized to assist those on the verge of breaking through, i.e., those who will serve as role models for the remainder of the community, this may mean that additional social intervention to address unmet needs may be required for those left untouched by affirmative action.[34]

Finally, even if some individual group members managed to escape injury, affirmative action can be justified on the ground of administrative convenience.[35] The correlation between race or sex and relative inequality of opportunity is sufficiently high that it justifies use of such traits for the efficient administration of this policy.[36]

C. Unfair Burden on Present Generation of White Workers

Opponents of affirmative action also argue that, even if blacks and women deserve compensation, it is unfair to extract that compensation through the imposition of harm on innocent white males. Or, to phrase the issue in terms of utility rather than fairness, affirmative action causes unqualified persons to be placed in jobs that would otherwise be held by those of greater skills and abilities, and this is socially harmful because our resources are not producing "the greatest good for the greatest number."

In addressing both the unfairness and inefficiency claims of affirmative action opponents, note first that whatever injury white males incur does not give rise to a constitutional claim because the damage "does not derive from a scheme animated by racial prejudice."[37] The lessened opportunity that white males face is simply an incidental consequence of addressing a compelling societal need. If white males are deprived of anything, it is the expectation of unearned position. Only because they stand to gain so much from past discrimination do they stand to lose from affirmative action. But white males are not excluded on the basis of racial prejudice, they are excluded "because of a rational calculation about the socially most beneficial use of limited resources. . . ."[38]

This paper does not undertake an analysis of the constitutionality of affirmative action plans, but recent observations of the Supreme Court in the context are supportive of a fairness evaluation. Justice Brennan, writing for the Court in *U.S.A. Paradise,*[39] related that governmental bodies, including courts, "may constitutionally employ racial classifications essential to remedy unlawful treatment of racial . . . groups subject to discrimination."[40] The following criteria will be employed to assess the constitutionality of racial classifications:

1. The necessity for relief and the efficacy of alternative remedies,
2. The flexibility and duration of relief including the availability of waiver provisions to be utilized in the event there are no qualified minority candidates,
3. The relationship of the numerical goals to the relevant labor market,
4. The impact of the relief on non-minority applicants.[41]

With regard to the issue of burdening white males who did not discriminate, it should be noted that, while these individuals may not have discriminated, they have received the benefits of a society that has discriminated and has supplied them better education and better economic conditions. Under these circumstances, a white male, aware of the discrimination against women and blacks, who insisted on being hired, would essentially endorse and condone prior discrimination. Even if a white male was ignorant of past discrimination against women and minorities, given our historical record, the assumption should be that these groups were discriminated against.

One way of analyzing the situation is by way of a hypothetical. Imagine two runners at the starting line. If one runner is somehow weighted-down but the other runner is not, it is obvious that, once the race begins, the first runner is at a severe disadvantage. Even if that runner is released halfway through the race, he or she is still far behind. In order to equalize the first runner's position with that of the second, the second needs to be handicapped in some way. The opportunity to catch up and to become competitive is only fair under the circumstances.

However, even upon applying this reasoning in support of affirmative action, opponents may argue that it results in the advancement of incompetent workers. This argument can be addressed by setting up certain minimum standards of competence that every applicant must meet, i.e., applicants must demonstrate some basic degree of proficiency in order to qualify for the labor pool.[42] Affirmative action does not require employers to hire unqualified individuals, nor does it require the discharge of white employees, i.e. white employees do not lose their entitlements.[43]

It should be noted that by opening up opportunities for women and minorities, affirmative action broadens the talent base of business and leads to a recognition of the potential of these groups. A utilitarian argument would demonstrate that a refusal to employ these talents to their best use is "wasteful", and further that affirmative action would benefit the general welfare by (1) promoting minority role models, and (2) improve services for minority communities. For example, blacks who become doctors and lawyers are more likely to meet minority needs than white doctors and lawyers.[44]

> Suppose for example that there is a need for a great increase in the number of black doctors, because the health needs of the black community are unlikely to be met otherwise. And suppose that at the present average level of premedical qualifications among black applicants, it would require a huge expansion of total medical school enrollment to supply the desirable absolute number of black doctors without adopting differential admissions standards. Such an expansion may be unacceptable either because of its cost or because it would produce a total supply of doctors, black and white, much greater than the society requires. This is a strong argument for accepting reverse discrimination, not on grounds of justice but on grounds of social utility. (In addition, there is the salutary effect on the aspirations and expectations of other blacks, from the visibility of exemplars in formerly inaccessible positions.)[45]

Further, the virtual absence of black policemen helped spark the ghetto rebellions of the 1960s. However, after the police force became integrated through strong affirmative action, relations between the minority communities and the police improved.[46]

D. Preference Cheapens Real Achievement of Women and Minorities

Finally, there is always the argument that affirmative action stigmatizes the preferred group and causes others to denigrate their achievements. Although affirmative action probably causes some whites to denigrate black achievements, it is unrealistic to argue that these programs cause most white disparagement of black abilities. Such disparagement was around long before affirmative action.[47] Given this inevitable

resistance, one must be wary of the fear of backlash to limit necessary reforms. Further, it is apparent that affirmative action can help combat disparagement of these achievements by breaking down stereotypes and changing people's attitudes. Thus, the uncertain extent to which affirmative action diminishes the accomplishments of women and minorities in the eyes of some people must be balanced against the stigmatization that occurs when they are virtually absent from important societal institutions.

Opponents of affirmative action argue that such programs sap the internal morale of blacks, i.e. their not truly earned positions cause them to lower their expectations of themselves. Again, although this might be true in some cases, it is incorrect to say that affirmative action undermines the morale of the black community. Most black beneficiaries view affirmative action programs as "rather modest compensation" for the many years of racial subordination; for them, affirmative action is a form of social justice.[48]

It is also apparent that many blacks view claims of meritocracy, as it applies to attaining employment, dubiously. The over-exclusion of blacks from public and private educational and employment institutions is an indictment of the concept of meritocracy. It is clear that many non-objective, non-meritocratic factors influence the distribution of opportunity. Most people realize the thoroughly political nature of merit, i.e., that is a malleable concept determined by the perceived needs of society.[49]

Lastly, most blacks and women are aware that, in the absence of affirmative action, they would not receive equal consideration with white males. Racism and sexism continue, and the "rules" are not impartial. For example, many women are socialized to seek marriage and motherhood from birth. Additionally, as human beings identify most easily with members of their own race and sex, a white male employer may be unable to judge a black or female applicant objectively. Affirmative action forces employers to consider the qualifications and potentialities of these individuals.

V. CONCLUSION

This paper has examined four major arguments advanced by opponents of affirmative action and attempted to rebut them on the basis of moral considerations. It is clear that the problem of past racial/gender discrimination has not disappeared; its effects linger, resulting in a wide disparity in opportunities and attainments between blacks/women and white males. Affirmative action, although not the "perfect solution", is by far the most viable method of redressing the effects of past discrimination. Thus it cannot be dismissed lightly by way of arguing for mere colorblindness.

NOTES

1. Duncan, 'The Future of Affirmative Action: A Jurisprudential/legal Critique', 17 HARV. C.R.–C.L. L. REV. 503 (1982).
2. Barton, 'Affirmative Action: Making Decisions', 83 W. VA. L. REV. 47 (1980).
3. *Id.*
4. *Id.* at 60–61. As Barton notes, social welfare programs guarantee that, henceforth, no person shall suffer the consequences of any discrimination based on race, color, sex, age, ethnicity, or creed. Social welfare programs do not seek to correct existing inequities or to prevent the making of discrimination. Affirmative action, on the other hand, seeks compensate for past harm by redistributing certain opportunities. Affirmative action seeks to prevent the effects and the making of unjust discrimination by, inter alia, changing the way people think.
5. Kennedy, 'Persuasion and Distrust: A Comment on the Affirmative Action Debate', 99 HARV. L. REV. 1327, 1334 (1986).
6. Regents of the University of California v. Bakke, 438 U.S. 265, 407 (1978) (Blackmun, J., plurality opinion).
7. Cf. United Steelworkers v. Weber, 443 U.S. 193 (1979) (5–2) holding that Title VII does not pro-

hibit all private, voluntary race conscious affirmative action plans, and Fullilove v. Klutznick, 448 US 448 (1980) (6–3), approving a 10% set aside for minority contractors under federal law, with Regents of University of California v. Bakke, 438 U.S. 265, 407 (1978) (5–4), holding that the admissions program of the University of California (Davis) which set aside 16 class positions for minority students to be unlawful, and Memphis Firefighters Local #1784 v. Stotts, 467 U.S. 561 (1984) (6–3), holding that the Civil Rights Act bars a federal judge from ordering that recently hired blacks can keep their jobs while whites with more seniority were being laid off except on evidence that the blacks were actual victims of illegal discrimination.
8. Robinson, 'A Record of Hostility', 71 ABAJ 39, 40 (Oct 1985); 'Justice Official Terms Court's ruling a Disappointment and Unfortunate', NEW YORK TIMES, Thurs. July 3, 1986, page 13, col. 3.
9. Local 93, International Association of Firefighters v. Cin of Cleveland, 106 S. Ct. 3063 (1986) (6–3), held that lower federal courts have broad discretion to approve consent decrees in which employers, over the objections of white employees, settle discrimination suits by agreeing to preferential hiring or promotion of minority group members. The Court upheld a decree where Cleveland agreed to settle a job discrimination suit by temporarily promoting black and Hispanic workers ahead of whites who had more seniority and higher test scores. In Local 28, Sheet Metal Workers v. EEOC, 106 S. Ct. 3019 (1986) (5–4), the court approved a lower court order requiring NYC sheet metal workers union to meet a 20% minority membership goal by 1987. The Court also held, 6–3, that judges may order racial preferences in union membership and other contexts if necessary to rectify especially "egregious" discrimination. During its next session, the court held, in U.S. v. Paradise, 107 S. Ct. 1053 (1987) (5–4), that because of the Alabama State Police's long history of egregious discrimination coupled with a strong federal interest in supporting prior judicial decrees, the enforcement of numerical quotas (one black promotion for every white), for as long as the upper ranks of the department had a smaller percentage

of blacks than the lower ranks, was appropriate. In a companion case involving gender-based discrimination, Johnson v. Santa Clara County Transportation Agency, 55 U.S.L. W. 4379 (daily ed., Mat. 25, 1987), the court upheld a voluntary affirmative action plan that promoted a female instead of a male, though both were qualified for the job. The plan was based on a comparison of the county's work force with the level of women and minorities qualified for higher level positions rather than general population statistics.

10. Barton, *supra* n. 2 at 50.

11. E.g., Local 189 United Papermakers and Paperworkers v. United States, 416 F.2d 980 (5th Cir. 1969); Teamsters v. United States, 431 U.S. 324 (1977) (relying on § 703(h) of Title VII, 42 U.S.C. § 2000e-2(h), the Court held that absent their having been entered into and maintained with a discriminatory purpose, such systems, regardless of their impact, do not violate Title VII. Individual claimants may, however, obtain relief in the form of back pay or retroactive seniority).

12. Barton, *supra* n. 2 at 51. In Barton's view, there are 4 ways society can respond to discrimination: (1) institutionalize it by legislation, (2) ignore it, (3) articulate principles prohibiting people from acting on their discrimination, yet take affirmative steps to extinguish discrimination (4) adopt affirmative measures to end existing stratification and extinguish the discrimination which strengthened the stratification. *Id.* at 49, n. 6.

13. Specific methods often suggested to remedy the effects of historical discrimination in the workplace include: (1) retroactive seniority, (2) front pay, (3) inverse seniority, (4) work sharing, (5) plantwide seniority, (6) governmental intervention. This paper will not examine specific mechanisms in implementing affirmative action, but will concentrate on the broader concepts of quotas and goals.

14. Ducan, *supra* n. 1 at 507–508.

15. *Id.* at 508; Local 28, Sheet Metal Workers v. EEOC, 106 S. Ct. 3019 (1986); U.S. v. Paradise, 107 S. Ct. 1053 (1987).

16. Duncan, *supra* n. 1 at 508.

17. Throughout this paper the followng ethical concepts will be advanced to evaluate the worth of targets or goals as they are required by affirmative action programs: compensatory and distributive justice, and utility or utilitarianism. See Nickel,

Preferential Policies in Hiring and Admissions: Jurisprudential Approach, 75 COLUM. L. REV. 534 (1975). Although these three theories will be referred to throughout this paper, the format is designed to set out the ethical arguments levelled at affirmative action, and to rebut them.

18. M. Wasserstrom, *Philosophy and Social Issues* (1980), p. 14.

19. *Id.* at 12.

20. Taylor, 'Reverse Discrimination and Compensatory Justice' *Analysis* 33 (1973), p. 179.

21. *Id.* at 181–182.

22. R. K. Greenawalt, Discrimination and Reverse Discrimination—Essay and Materials in Philosophy and Law (1979), pp. 65–67. Statistics do not conclusively establish distributive injustice however, because careers are a function of individual priorities. Greenawalt, Judicial Scrutiny of 'Benign' Racial Preferences in Law School Admissions, 75 COLUM 1 REV. 559, 589 n. 129 (1975).

23. This is the distributive justice theory of affirmative action. It looks to the future, not to the past as compensatory justice does. Benefits and burdens are distributed in accordance with such relevant considerations as the rights, merits, contributions, needs and deserts of recipients. Nickel, *supra* n. 17 at 539. Duncan, *supra* n. 1 at 521.

24. For the most part, with regard to hiring or admission policy, the institution will develop a benchmark/minimally qualified score consisting of aptitude test, admission score, grade point average, interview (subjective evaluaton) and the like. If sex or race will enable a person to do a job better in the judgment of the hiring authority/admission committee, i.e., bring better medical care to the black community or break down the stereotypic image of women in the construction industry, then race or sex may well qualify as a meritocratic quality. The fact that race or sex may be a socially useful trait in particular circumstances should not be confused "with the very different and despicable idea that one race [or sex] may be inherently more worthy than another." Dworkin, The Rights of Alan Bakke, *The New York Review of Books* (1977), in J. DesJardins and J. McCall, *Contemporary Issues in Business Ethics* (1985), pp. 407, 411.

25. After all, "Would anyone claim that Henry Ford II was head of the Ford Motor Company because he was the most qualified person for the job?"

Wasserstrom, Rascism, Sexism, and Preferential Treatment: An Approach to the Topics, 24 U.C.L.A. L. REV. 581, 619 (1977).

26. Duncan, *supra* n. 1 at 510. Present day discrimination in hiring is a "but for" result of historical practices. It contributes to housing patterns which in turn result in *de facto* school segregation. U.S. Commission on Civil Rights, Affirmative Action in the 1980's: Dismantling the Process of Discrimination 11 (1981).

27. Teamsters v. United States, 431 U.S. 324 (1977); Firefighters Local Union No. 1784 v. Stotts, 467 U.S. 561 (1984); Wygant v. Jackson Board of Education, 106 S. Ct. 1842 (1986).

28. *See* City of Memphis v. Greene, 101 S. Ct. 1584, 1610–13 (1981) (Marshall, J., dissenting); Sullivan v. Little Hunting Park, 396 U.S. 229 (1969); Jones v. Alfred H. Mayer Co., 391 U.S. 409 (1968).

29. Duncan, *supra* n. 1 at 516.

30. 60 U.S. 393, 407 (1856).

31. 347 U.S. 483 (1954).

32. Even on the argument that some blacks have overcome losses and humiliation through their own efforts and are not deserving of compensation, affirmative action can still be justified on a group basis for reasons of administrative convenience. Nickel, Discrimination and Morally Relevant Characteristics, *Analysis* 32 (1972), pp. 113, 114; Dworkin, *supra* n. 24 at 411.

33. *See,* e.g., Firefighters Local Union No. 1784 v. Stotts, 467 U.S. 561 (1984) (affirmative action for firefighters); United Steelworkers v. Weber, 443 U.S. 193 (1979) (affirmative action for craft workers).

34. Kennedy, *supra* n. 5 at 1333.

35. Nickel, *supra* n. 17 at 538.

36. Although 11.2% of the U.S. population is black, blacks (and other minorities) comprise only 4.2% of the legal profession and account for only 5.9% of engineers. Only 5.2% of the nation's managers and administrators and 5.1% of its sales workers are nonwhite. 27.5% of cleaning workers, 25.3% of taxi drives and chauffeurs and 43.1% of garbage collectors are black. Similarly, 99.1% of secretaries and 80.1% of clerical workers in general are women. Domestic cleaners and servants are 96.9% women, 53.4% black. Statistical Abstract of the U.S. (1981) at 402–404.

37. Kennedy, *supra* n. 5 at 1336.

38. R. Dworkin, *A Matter of Principle* (1985), p. 301.

39. 107 S. Ct. 1053 (1987).

40. *Id.* at 1065.

41. *Id.* This framework is similar, though not identical, to that applicable to private sector, voluntary affirmative action plans such as the one approved in United Steelworkers v. Weber, 443 U.S. 193 (1979).

42. *Supra* n. 9.

43. Wygant v. Jackson Board of Education. 106 S. Ct. 1842 (1986).

44. Nickel, *supra* n. 17 at 545.

45. Nagel, 'Equal Treatment and Compensatory Discrimination', *Philosophy and Public Affairs* 2 (1973), p. 348.

46. Kennedy, *supra* n. 5 at 1329.

47. *Id.* at 1331–1332.

48. *Id.*

49. *Supra* n. 24.

READING 3·4

The Case Against Affirmative Action

Terry Eastland

I. INTRODUCTION

Thirty-one years have passed since President John F. Kennedy began the modern era of affirmative action by issuing Executive Order 10,925[1] in response to the concerns of civil rights leaders. In addition to forbidding government contractors from discriminating on account of "race, creed, color, or national origin,"[2] the order required them to "take affirmative action to ensure that applicants are employed, and that employees are treated during employment,

Source: William and Mary Law Review, 34 (33) (1992), 33–51. Used with permission.

without regard to their race, creed, color, or national origin."[3] In due course, lawmakers stitched affirmative action into a series of federal laws and regulations affecting all public employers and all but the smallest private employers.[4] Affirmative action, however, was not limited to the employment context. Most notably, it extended to the admissions offices of colleges, universities, and professional and graduate schools.[5]

Those whom affirmative action was intended to benefit came to include not only blacks, the original focus of Executive Order 10,925, but also, in most cases, Hispanics, Asian-Pacific Americans, and Native Americans.[6] By the early 1970s, affirmative action had come to mean for most people most of the time, treating, as opposed to *not* treating, those belonging to the designated or protected groups *with* regard to their race, creed, color, or national origin. Indeed, it meant treating members of protected groups in such a way as to hire, promote, or admit the designated minorities in enough instances that the total numbers of those so advanced were not trivial.

However its supporters propose to justify affirmative action, treating people *with* regard to their minority status is what affirmative action means in practice today. It has become a way of life throughout the public sector and in many parts of the private sector. It is a way of life that many institutions, especially those of higher education, are proud of.[7] Even affirmative action's most severe critics must concede that it has done some good. It has helped employers and other gatekeepers of opportunity understand that the United States is indeed a nation of many peoples and races—potentially as many as are found on the globe itself. It has forced an often useful rethinking of employment and academic standards and practices.[8] Schools, businesses, and government, chief among other bodies, have in some important ways become fairer and more egalitarian.[9] Also, many people who but for their race would not have been given an opportunity have made the most of the chances affirmative action afforded them; their achievements are truly of the first rank. Although affirmative action is not the only reason for these results, it is surely an important one.

Merely touting the successes of affirmative action, of course, is to glance at only one side of the ledger. On the other side are substantial costs. When examined in terms of both theory and practice, affirmative action deserves a negative judgment. Affirmative action cannot remain a way of life unless we wish to change for the worse the very essence of what it means to be an American.

II. PROBLEMS OF AFFIRMATIVE ACTION

Affirmative action arose as a response to the special case of blacks in America, and indeed that *is* a special case. No other racial or ethnic group endured centuries of slavery and Jim Crow laws. Past wrongs, it is said, must be corrected today. Here, however, there is a set of problems for affirmative action. Even if past wrongs and compensation for those wrongs can be inherited across decades and centuries, how can blacks living today who are not the descendants of the victims of past racial discrimination[10] be "owed" the compensation of affirmative action? Similarly, how can whites living today who are not the descendants of slave owners or segregationists be morally obligated to pay for affirmative action by losing out on a promotion or a place in medical school? Even if we could identify all the descendants of those wronged in ages past and all the descendants of those who committed the wrongs, and then limit affirmative action to transactions between these groups, the question would remain whether past wrongs and the duty to compensate them can indeed be inherited. Unless we wish to live our lives through our parents, grandparents, great-grandparents, and beyond, the answer is obvious: they cannot be.

None of this discussion is to deny the special experience of blacks in America. However, the best we can humanly do today, in a nation that changes daily through death, birth, and immigration, is to turn our face to the present and treat each one of those around us honestly and honorably. As Thomas Sowell has observed, this is more than enough moral challenge.[11]

As Sowell notes, some have made the argument in a more sociological way, to wit, that blacks and other minorities living today are suffering from the ill effects of past wrongs inflicted on their forbears, and that it is these effects that affirmative action must overcome.[12] One obvious problem with this argument is that, even if past discrimination against minorities has caused present disabling effects in their descendants, it does not follow that affirmative action is the best response. More than one way exists to improve the prospects for equality. Unlike preferential affirmative action, other means such as Head Start are more compatible with the best in the American political tradition, and they enjoy the majority support of the American people.[13]

A. The Case Against "Underrepresentation"

The arguments from history and sociology are sometimes made in shorthand fashion in terms of "underrepresentation." Commentators label a certain minority group as "underrepresented" for reasons of historical discrimination or its present-day disabling effects in a given job or profession, and use percentages to make the point. The American Society of Newspaper Editors (ASNE), for example, believes minorities are "underrepresented" by about one third in the nation's newsrooms (because roughly twenty-five percent of the general population is black, Hispanic, Asian-American or Native American, and yet not quite nine percent of all newspaper journalists are members of these minority groups.[14] ASNE wants to correct this "underrepresentation" by hiring enough minorities by the year 2000 so that twenty-five percent of newspaper journalists will be minorities.[15] The problem with arguments (conceding that they are argu-

ments) based on "underrepresentation" of this most general kind is that the term is practically meaningless. No one can say to what degree racial and ethic groups should be "represented" in various jobs and pursuits, and social science has challenged powerfully the idea that they should be proportionately "represented."[16] Nonetheless, concepts of "underrepresentation" and their like, such as "underutilization" and "disparity," have crept into our language and law in such ways as to place a heavy burden of proof on institutions whose work forces do not divide into percentages reflecting approximate proportional representation based on race and ethnicity. Such institutions are under social pressure, if not also legal pressure, to justify the "underrepresentation" and correct their "deficiencies," or face correction by relevant authorities, including the courts.[17]

Because the differences among racial groups in income levels and jobs can be explained to some degree by such variables as age, education, and work experience, advocates of affirmative action sometimes try to determine just how much "underrepresentation" is a result of these factors. Once they determine that amount, they make the problematic move of attributing the remaining amount to past discrimination or its disabling effects, maintaining that this irreducible underrepresentation must be "corrected" through affirmative action. Thus, in discussions about minority underrepresentation on a university faculty, the more sophisticated argument for affirmative action will point to any "disparity" between the number of minority professors hired in a particular academic discipline and the number of minorities nationwide with the requisite credentials to be hired. The problem with this facially more plausible comparison is that it errs in treating all credentials as though they were alike. Not every credential, such as a Ph.D. is created equal, and mere statistical comparisons cannot tell us the quality of each PhD, or of the other merits an applicant might possess. To speak of underrepresentation even in this way is still dubious. Inevitably, we must focus on individual cases if we are to have any hope of knowing who might be best qualified for a job, unless, of course, we wish merely to congratulate ourselves for having achieved a faculty that is demonstrably racially and ethnically diverse, even if at the expense of turning away more highly qualified candidates.

B. The Exclusionary Effect

In addition to the usual arguments for affirmative action, the actual practice of affirmative action also deserves review. One impact of affirmative action is visible in the line of Supreme Court cases initiated by plaintiffs named Marco DeFunis,[18] Allan Bakke,[19] and Brian Weber.[20] These cases show that affirmative action is a barrier to those who otherwise, because of their superior qualifications, would have advanced had they been members of the necessary racial group. This denial of opportunity is a very real cost for those who lose out on account of affirmative action, considering especially that these individuals are innocent of discriminatory conduct. Advocates of affirmative action take different views of this cost, some even dismissing it,[21] but there is no getting around the fact that affirmative action is unfair action when it unambiguously deprives nondiscriminatory actors of their opportunities.

Whites have been the primary victims of affirmative action, and it may well be, as William Van Alstyne of Duke University Law School has observed, that among whites, it is *working-class* whites—or, in the case of educational opportunities, their offspring who have been the largest class of affirmative action victims.[22] If Van Alstyne is right, the elites in business, government, or academe, have had to "pay" little, if any, of the exclusionary cost of affirmative action.

Whites, though, are not the only victims of affirmative action. Bear in mind that to benefit from affirmative action, one must be a member of one of the minority groups covered by the program at issue. Affirmative action, therefore, necessarily has an exclusionary effect upon members of all noncovered groups. For this reason, not all alleged victims of affirmative action are white. For example, in early 1992, the United States Court of Appeals for the Fourth Circuit struck down a blacks-only scholarship fund at the University of Maryland at College Park.[23] The plaintiff in that case, Dennis J. Podberesky, had been admitted to Maryland. He had scored 1340 on the Scholastic Aptitude Test (SAT) and possessed a 3.56 high school grade point average.[24] The minimum academic requirements for the scholarship he sought were a 900 SAT score and a 3.0 grade point average.[25] The unchangeable racial requirement for the scholarship, however, was that the applicant be black,[26] and Dennis J. Podberesky was and is Hispanic.[27]

Because affirmative action excludes all those whom it does not include, it creates incentives for those excluded to acquire the credentials necessary for inclusion. Stories are not uncommon of individuals who have attempted to give themselves the kind of surnames that might entitle them to affirmative action treatment.[28] Business set-aside programs[29] have attracted companies fraudulently representing themselves as being owned by minorities.[30] Thus, although affirmative action has performed a useful function by reminding employers and admissions officers that ours is a nation of all peoples, it has also encouraged what the public choice theorists[31] could have foretold—rent-seeking behavior. The correction of this behavior requires a vigilant enforcement apparatus that is able and willing to inquire into matters of race and ethnicity.

C. The Devaluation of Testing

Affirmative action has led to more careful consideration of qualification tests to determine their fairness, what they are testing for, and, in the employment context, their relevance to the job to be done. It has also led to an indefensible devaluing of testing. An example of such devaluation is the "race-norming" of what was until recently the most widely used job test in the country, the General Aptitude Test Battery (GATB).[32] The Labor Department conceived the practice of race-norming GATB scores in the late stages of the Carter administration and pursued it during the Reagan and Bush administrations until its revelation in 1990 led to its proscription under the Civil Rights Act of 1991.[33] In 1981, the United States Employment Service, a division within the Labor Department, recommended that state Employment Service agencies should stop reporting job candidates' scores on the GATB in relation to all other test takers and report them only in relation to those of the same race.[34] So it happened: the testers ranked black applicants relative only to other blacks, Hispanics only to other Hispanics, and "others" to all but blacks and Hispanics.[35] Test officials converted raw scores on the tests to percentile scores according to the standing of the test takers within their own comparison group. Before presenting the results to a prospective employer, the officials combined the percentile scores from the several comparison groups without reference to the race of the test takers and then listed the scores as though they had graded everyone by the same nonracial norms.[36] The fiftieth percentile score of a black, therefore, was not necessarily the same as the fiftieth percentile score of a white, even though both names were listed together without reference to race in the final ordering.

Neither employers nor jobseekers were aware of this practice, which no fewer than forty states adopted.[37] Once the media publicized race-norming in 1990 and 1991[38] it could not survive. Although the Civil Rights Act of 1991 bans score adjustment of a test,[39] the Bush Labor Department has warned, in announcing an end to race-norming, that raw GATB scores should be "only one factor in in the selection and referral process, with appropriate weight given to other factors."[40] Thus, the devaluing of a particular test has stopped, but the general devaluing of objective testing measures in "the selection and referral process" has not necessarily ceased. Those "other factors" will intrude as long as affirmative action persists.

On this point, *Regents of the University of California v. Bakke*[41] is instructive. Allan Bakke challenged the admissions program of the Medical School at the University of California at Davis (UC-Davis), which set aside sixteen of one hundred places in each class for members of the preferred minority groups.[42] The Supreme Court struck down this "rigid" program,[43] but Justice Powell's pivotal opinion said that race may be a "plus" in the admissions process.[44] On this basis, after *Bakke,* UC-Davis proceeded automatically to award each minority applicant five points on account of race.[45] Because an applicant needed a total of only fifteen points before being grouped among those to be given first consideration for admission, the award of five points made the Medical College Admissions Test and undergraduate grade point average less important for the preferred minorities, and even more important for all others.[46]

D. The Stigma of Affirmative Action

Perhaps the most damning judgment against affirmative action, as it is typically practiced today, comes in the form of objections that could only be expressed by blacks and members of other minority groups typically included in affirmative action programs. Their criticisms concern the costs borne by the ostensible beneficiaries of affirmative action. For example, an Hispanic officer for the Bank of America asks: "Sometimes I wonder: Did I get this job because of my abilities, or because they needed to fill a quota?"[47] Glenn Loury of Boston University has said that affirmative action can undermine "the ability of people to confidently assert, if only to themselves, that they are as good as their achievements would seem to suggest."[48] In *The Content of Our Character,* Shelby Steele examines the "enlargement of self-doubt" caused by affirmative action.[49] "Under affirmative action the quality that earns us preferential treatment is an implied inferiority. However this inferiority is explained . . . it is still inferiority."[50] So long as affirmative action governs an institution in which such concerns are expressed, objections of this nature can be expected to continue.

What is especially perverse about affirmative action is its suggestion that all protected minorities are alike, that for each minority group member, race has been an equal factor in his or her achievement. This suggestion, of course, is not true, but it will be surpassingly hard to know as long as affirmative action exists. In 1987, three black students at the University of Virginia Law School made law review just after the adoption of an affirmative action plan for selecting law review members.[51] They were confident, however, that they could have made law review under the previous selection procedures and evidently wished they had.[52] One of them told William Raspberry of the *Washington Post,* "Affirmative action was a way to dilute our personal victory. It took the victory out of our hands."[53]

The practical problems of affirmative action that I have surveyed stem from its central focus on race and ethnicity. To state the obvious, affirmative action is not race-neutral. Advocates, nevertheless, tout affirmative action as an instrument of equality. Affirmative action raises the question of how true equality can be achieved when ostensible equals know that there are different rules for different racial groups. Surely members of minority groups who have rejected the putative benefits of programs for which they are eligible have asked and answered this question in a telling way. The story of Freddie Hernandez, a Hispanic who serves in the Miami fire department, serves as an example. In 1983 Hernandez rejected an affirmative action promotion to lieutenant.[54] Instead, he waited three years until he had the necessary seniority and had scored high enough to qualify for the promotion under procedures that applied to all non-minorities.[55] This decision cost Hernandez $4,500 a year in extra pay and forced him to study 900 additional hours to attain the required test results.[56] Hernandez told the *Wall Street Journal,* "I knew I could make it on my own."[57]

III. A RETURN TO RACE-NEUTRAL PRINCIPLES

Inevitably, affirmative action forces us to attend to the basic question of whether race should be a deciding factor in the allocation of society's benefits and opportunities. The best in the American political tradition answered that question negatively, at least until the early 1960s. Drawing on this tradition, for example, Thurgood Marshall argued in the 1948 case of *Sipuel v. Board of Regents,*[58] a forerunner to *Brown v. Board of Education,*[59] that "[c]lassifications and distinctions based on race or color have no moral or legal validity in our society."[60] Embedded in this statement was the moral truth that the mere race of a person tells us nothing morally important about him or her that should compel either negative or positive treatment. In his book, *First Things,* Hadley Arkes elaborates: "Merely by knowing a person's race we cannot . . . know that he has done a wrong and deserves punishment; neither can we know that he has suffered an injury and deserves compensation."[61] This discussion is not to deny what social science reports about Americans when examined in terms of their racial and ethnic groups. However, social science by its own terms is interested in groups, not individuals, and it is to individuals that we owe just treatment.

Race-neutral principles informed our greatest civil rights legislation, the Civil Rights Act of 1964.[62] This statute created a federal right of equal employment opportunity for every individual.[63] Congress rejected the idea of race-based affirmative action, including in the new law a provision stating that nothing in Title VII is to be interpreted as requiring an employer to grant preferential treatment to any individual or group on account of racial imbalance.[64] In *Equality Transformed,* Herman Belz writes that Title VII "constitutes a clear rejection of the demand for preferential treatment"[65] and "requires equal opportunity based on individual rights and is intended to prohibit race-conscious employment practices."[66]

Until at least 1964, equal opportunity was central to the definition of America. Whereas traditional hierarchical societies had organized themselves on the basis of race, religion, social rank, or family, the United States, in its origins and development, aspired to an equality of opportunity for individuals in which these characteristics would not control. Toward this end, and in regard to race in particular, nondiscrimination laws became necessary to ensure that these inherited traits truly did not matter and that each individual was judged according to what he had done. "Equality of opportunity," Belz observes, "is the social philosophy of modern industrial societies. It is individual-regarding and presupposes a single class based on common citizenship."[67]

A. The Primacy of Race-Consciousness in Affirmative Action

Affirmative action not only contradicts the principle that race should be irrelevant in the allocation of society's goods and opportunities, but also proposes to displace the philosophy of equal opportunity, of which the race-neutral principle is a key element. In the 1960s, and to some degree in the 1970s, affirmative action did not propose to undermine equal opportunity. Indeed, most initial advocates of race preferences implicitly recognized the moral superiority of the principle of colorblindness, arguing that race-conscious measures would be only "temporary."[68] Most supporters of affirmative action said they envisioned a day when race would not be a basis for employment or admissions decisions. Most also appeared to keep faith with the philosophy of equal opportunity, maintaining that someday each person would be allowed to rise to whatever level he could, on the strength of his own abilities and talents.[69]

Today, however, most advocates of affirmative action have accommodated their once-liberal principles to the practices they now endorse. Some supporters have come to embrace a new social philosophy. In *Bakke,* Justice Black-

mun said that we must take race into account in order to get beyond racism.[70] Now, we take race into account because race itself has become a basis for evaluation. For some advocates of affirmative action, the notion has transpired that race *is* morally interesting after all, and it is part of any respectable definition of individual merit.[71] These advocates would decide the allocation of society's goods and opportunities on the very basis that the old liberalism once so firmly rejected. It bears emphasis that affirmative action, so conceived, cannot be temporary but must be permanent. This is because once race, or "diversity," as some now camouflage it, is admitted to be meritorious in and of itself, and thus relevant to the distribution of a society's opportunities, then race must be taken into account for its own sake in perpetuity.[72] Equal results for racial and ethnic groups, rather than equal opportunity for individuals, is the essence of today's affirmative action. Indeed, the *individual* disappears from the new philosophy of affirmative action.

If race should be the basis for the allocation of society's goods and opportunities, and if racial groups matter more than individuals, then we must accept affirmative action as it has evolved, even if such acceptance requires us to jettison the best in the American tradition. Race cannot serve this purpose, however, because the mere fact of a person's race is morally uninteresting.

The danger of affirmative action lies in the kind of society it proposes to create. When conceived as a permanent feature of American life, affirmative action requires permanent attention to race and, therefore, permanent social engineering of a kind necessary to overcome problems of "underrepresentation," "disparity," and the like.[73] In such a society, race and ethnicity necessarily will become more and more important. Affirmative action that takes us in this direction must be considered disharmonious when judged against the best in the American political tradition.

B. Genuine Equality

Herman Belz observes that the federal government has never really tried race-neutral equal opportunity, at least not for long.[74] Soon after Congress codified that idea in law in 1964,[75] the federal bureaucracy and the courts began enforcing color-conscious equal results.[76] The time has come, however, to consider trying what we once proposed to try. Now is as good a time as any to do so, because affirmative action has yielded a few, although only a few, useful benefits. Affirmative action has made almost all employers and universities think about recruiting truly far and wide. R. Roosevelt Thomas, Jr., has remarked that "[t]here are very few places in the United States today where you could dip a recruitment net and come up with nothing but white males."[77] Racial and ethnic diversity exists in almost every line queuing up for some opportunity or other.

Under race-neutral equal opportunity that does not compromise standards—or that holds *everyone* to the same standards—most minorities in the various queues would be hired or admitted, if not by the employer or institution of choice, then by someone somewhere. The difference, therefore, would be in the distribution, for minorities covered by affirmative action programs would find opportunities commensurate with their qualifications. Yet their qualifications would be the same as all those of nonminorities in the same positions. Genuine equality thus would be possible. In a universe explicitly without affirmative action, no one could doubt the basis for advancement, and no minority could doubt his own achievements. Furthermore, the exclusionary effects of affirmative action would not exist, nor would incentives that promote rent-seeking behavior and efforts by new or old immigrant groups seeking to establish themselves as a new protected group.[78]

Phasing out affirmative action would require patience. It was impatience with the potential achievement of race-neutral equal opportunity that motivated many well-intentioned Americans to embark upon the experiment in preferential treatment. Indeed, the best argument for implementing affirmative action was not one that drew on history or sociology, or some combination. Rather the better argument was the practical one which maintained that having a much larger black middle class was in the public interest, and that the jump start of affirmative action, although requiring a temporary suspension of our best principles, might in a few years be able to achieve that end. The economic studies of affirmative action in employment are inconclusive,[79] and affirmative action simply may have reshuffled middle class minorities into government jobs or jobs regulated by the government.[80]

Whatever the economic impact of affirmative action, those who made this practical argument in the past must now reflect, as columnist Charles Krauthammer has, on the various costs of affirmative action.[81] Whether one agrees that protected minorities would have been better off had the nation been more patient from the late 1960s onward, many good reasons support adopting race-neutral principles and fashioning policy accordingly. Such an approach would not foreclose affirmative action programs that focus on disadvantage rather than race. Affirmative action that takes into account individual circumstances such as racial discrimination, economic hardship, or family disintegration, which the applicant has worked hard to overcome, asks the right question—a question about the individual. This brand of affirmative action is a far cry from the program that simply awards points on the basis of race.[82]

C. Transcending the Current Political Structure

Inevitably the important question of political leadership remains. Through the end of 1991, neither political party has given reason to believe that it can provide the kind of leadership necessary to take us beyond affirmative action, as it has developed, toward the kind of public policies that are race-neutral and promise to enhance opportunity for more of our citizens. The Republican Party rails against racial quotas even as it accepts other forms of racial preference.[83] Its opposition to quotas is merely a tactical ploy designed to wedge white Democratic voters into Republican columns. No prominent Republican has made the best case against today's affirmative action—the inclusive case, which points out that any race-based affirmative action program is necessarily exclusive of whites and noncovered minorities, and that such programs inevitably divide us all. Instead, as occurred in North Carolina in the 1990 Senate race, we see ads pitting whites against blacks.[84] Republicans should look to their own heritage and to Lincoln in particular. Lincoln demonstrated unsurpassed statesmanship guided by the great truth of the Declaration of Independence that all men are created equal.[85]

Republicans are not the only ones who need to be tutored by Lincoln. The Democratic Party has allowed itself to become, as the title of a recent book calls it, the "minority party";[86] a party defined by its commitment to certain minority groups. Manifestly untrue of the party in the 1960s, the Democratic Party today has no national figure willing to raise the standard of race neutrality and invite his party to take the lead in recovering the best in the American political tradition as the basis for a new pursuit of equality.

Given the current state of the two parties with respect to this fundamental issue, one can expect more of the same: Republican rhetoric against quotas, Democratic agreement that quotas are bad, but that affirmative action grounded in race is nonetheless good, and policy stasis that allows affirmative action more or less to continue in its current, racially exclusionary form. The tragedy is that meanwhile, a great complex of issues lies untreated beyond affirmative action. Although these issues bear on life's prospects and the nature of opportunity in America, our leaders will not address them as directly as they should. These issues concern health, safety in the streets, and education, both academic and vocational. More attention must focus on, among other things, improving the quality of education in all schools. Especially deserving of improvements are those schools in which minorities are predominant, particularly the elementary grades, kindergarten, pre-kindergarten, and apprentice programs in which those without adequate job skills can learn them.

Curiously, polling data suggests that the American people might be receptive to principled, prudent leadership that proposes going beyond affirmative action and rebuilding the national consensus on civil rights and equal opportunity.[87] For years now, large majorities of Americans have expressed opposition to preferential treatment on the basis of race.[88] At the same time, Americans remain strongly opposed to racial discrimination and are willing to help minorities at the wholesale level through race-neutral programs such as Head Start.[89]

IV. CONCLUSION

Another reason exists for principled, prudent leadership of the kind I have described. With the end of the Cold War, as Seymour Martin Lipset has observed, undoubtedly "much of the world will see a new emphasis on competitive meritocracy and individualism."[90] In the world context, it would be ironic if the first new nation built not upon race, ethnicity, or religion, but upon the idea that all persons are created equal, continued policies whose focus on race may well make it less competitive in international markets.

One can only wish that some national politician of correct principle, who understands the case against the present regime of affirmative action, will map a prudent strategy for the American future that seeks to leave behind this affirmative action regime as the "interim" measure it was once vouchsafed to be. The alternative is a body politic increasingly embittered by measures that count by race but do not, and cannot, forge genuine equality.

NOTES

1. Exec. Order No. 10,925, 3 C.F.R. 448 (1959–1968).
2. *Id.* at 449–50.
3. *Id.*
4. *See e.g.,* 42 U.S.C. § 2000e to 2000e-17 (1988) (establishing equal employment opportunities).
5. *See e.g.,* Regents of the Univ. of Cal. v. Bakke, 438 U.S. 265, 272–77 (1978) (describing preferential admissions policy for minorities at the Medical School of the University of California at Davis in 1973 and 1974).
6. Affirmative action for women raises different issues and for that reason is not addressed in this paper.
7. *See* Judith Areen, *Affirmative Action: The Benefits of Diversity,* WASH. POST, May 26, 1991, at D7 (defending Georgetown Law Center's affirmative action program after a student newspaper reported that black students were admitted to the school despite lower grade point averages and Law School Admission Test scores).
8. *See e.g., id.* (commenting on the value of diversity in the classroom which results from affirmative action admissions policies).
9. Through the success of minority group members in its ranks, the military serves as a prime example of a government body that has moved beyond its discriminatory past.
10. West Indian immigrants are an example of blacks whose ancestors did not endure past racial discrimination in this country.
11. THOMAS SOWELL, CIVIL RIGHTS: RHETORIC OR REALITY 120–21 (1984).
12. Thomas Sowell, *"Affirmative Action": A Worldwide Disaster,* COMMENTARY, Dec. 1989, at 21, 30.
13. *See* William Schneider, *Public Against Social Issues Activism,* 1955 NAT'L J. 2502, 2503.
14. Howard Kurtz, *At Newspapers, A Clash of Perceptions About Push to Recruit Minority Staff,* WASH. POST, Apr. 14, 1991, at A4.
15. Alex Jonos, *Of Hiring of Minorities and Newsroom Ethics,* N.Y. TIMES, Apr. 15, 1989, § 1, at 50.

16. Sowell, *supra* note 12, at 21 (noting that throughout the world it is extremely rare to find racial and ethical groups proportionally represented in various occupations).
17. *See* Civil Rights Act of 1991, Pub. L. No. 102–166, § 105, 106 Stat. 1071, 1074–75 (to be codified at 42 U.S.C. § 2000e-2) (expanding the use of underrepresentation percentages to prove discrimination).
18. DeFunis v. Odegaard, 416 U.S. 312 (1974). Thirty-six out of 37 minority applicants admitted to the University of Washington Law School had lower admisison "Averages" than DeFunis based on grade point averages and Law School Admission Test scores. *Id.* at 324.
19. Regents of the Univ. of Cal. v. Bakke, 438 U.S. 265 (1978). In both years Bakke applied to the Medical School at the University of California at Davis, minority applicants were admitted with lower "benchmark scores." *Id.* at 277.
20. United Steelworkers v. Weber, 443 U.S. 193 (1979). Weber had more seniority than seven black coworkers who received promotions for which Weber had been passed over. *Id.* at 199.
21. *See e.g.,* Joint Statement, *Constitutional Scholar's Statement on Affirmative Action After City of Richmond v. J.A. Croson Co.,* 98 YALE L.J. 1711, 1712 (1989).
22. TERRY EASTLAND & WILLIAM J. BENNETT, COUNTING BY RACE 170 (1979).
23. Podberesky v. Kirwan 956 F.2d 52 (4th Cir. 1992).
24. *Id.* at 53.
25. *Id.* at 54.
26. *Id.*
27. *Id.*
28. In 1975 two whites applying for jobs as Boston firefighters failed the applicable civil service exam. In 1977 they reapplied to take the test, saying they were black. They both scored below the standard minimum acceptable for white applicants but were hired apparently on the basis of their "race." Both were dismissed in 1988 after a Department of Personnel Administration hearing on their case. Susan Dissenhouse, *Boston Case Raises Questions on Misuse of Affirmative Action,* N.Y. TIMES, Oct. 9, 1988, § 1, at 54.
29. Set-aside programs typically involve a government body "setting aside" a specific portion of

government contracts or grants for minority group access only. *See, e.g.,* Alan Finder, *Daunting New Task: Helping Minority Companies,* N.Y. TIMES, Feb. 16, 1992, § 1, pt. 1, at 46 (reporting New York City's Mayor David Dinkins' plan to set aside more than five billion dollars a year in city contracts for companies owned by minorities and women).

30. *Id.* (revealing that companies will often set up fronts, such as declaring a minority employee a 51% owner, in order to qualify for the preferential government treatment).
31. For an overview of public choice theory, *see* Robert D. Tollison, *Public Choice and Legislation,* 74 VA. L. REV. 339 (1988).
32. *Race-Norming, Finis,* RICHMOND TIMES-DISPATCH, Dec. 14, 1991, at A12.
33. Civil Rights Act of 1991 § 106.
34. Stuart Taylor, Jr., *Rigging Test Scores by Race,* LEGAL TIMES, May 13, 1991, at 21.
35. *Id.*
36. *Id.*
37. *Id.*
38. *The Richmond Times-Dispatch* led the way. *See Race-Norming, Finis, supra* note 32, at A12.
39. Civil Rights Act of 1991 § 106.
40. *Race-Norming, Finis, supra* note 32, at A12.
41. 438 U.S. 265 (1978).
42. *Id.* at 279. The preferred minority groups included blacks, Chicanos, Asians and American Indians. *Id.* at 274.
43. *Id.* at 271.
44. *Id.* at 317.
45. EASTLAND & BENNETT *supra* note 22, at 194.
46. *Id.*
47. Sonia L. Nazario, *Many Minorities Feel Torn by Experience of Affirmative Action,* WALL ST. J., June 27, 1989, at A1.
48. Glen Loury, Crisis in Black America, Address at the National Press Club (Dec. 17, 1985).
49. SHELBY STEELE, THE CONTENT OF OUR CHARACTER 116 (1990).
50. *Id.*
51. William Raspberry, *Affirmative Action That Hurts Blacks,* WASH. POST, Feb. 23, 1987, at A11.
52. *Id.*
53. *Id.*
54. Nazario, *supra* note 47, at A10.
55. *Id.*

56. *Id.*
57. *Id.*
58. 332 U.S. 631 (1948) (per curiam).
59. 347 U.S. 483 (1959).
60. Petitioner's Brief, *Sipuel* (No. 369), *quoted in* RICHARD KLUGER, SIMPLE JUSTICE 259 (1976).
61. HADLEY ARKES, FIRST THINGS 98 (1986).
62. 42 U.S.C. § 2000e to 2000e-17 (1988).
63. *Id.* § 2000e.
64. *Id.* § 2000e-2(J).
65. HERMAN BELZ, EQUALITY TRANSFORMED: A QUARTER CENTURY OF AFFIRMATIVE ACTION 26 (1991).
66. *Id.*
67. *Id.* at 10.
68. Thus, in 1984, Father Robert F. Drinan described affirmative action as having been adopted as "an interim strategy for a period during which sex-based and race-rooted discrimination will gradually fade away." Robert F. Drinan, *Affirmative Action Under Attack, in* RACIAL PREFERENCE AND RACIAL JUSTICE 117, 124 (Russell Nieli ed., 1991).
69. A Gallup survey in 1977 supports the idea of "ability as the main consideration." Among non-southern Democrats and nonwhite respondents, traditional supporters of affirmative action, 81% and 64% respectively stated that ability, not membership in a minority group, should be the main consideration in getting jobs and places in college. RACIAL PREFERENCE AND RACIAL JUSTICE, *supra* note 68, app. C at 513.
70. Regents of the Univ. of Cal. v. Bakke, 438 U.S. 285, 407 (1978) (Blackmun, J., concurring in part and dissenting in part).
71. *See, e.g.,* Areen, *supra* note 7, at D7 (discussing the value of diversity in the classroom as a justification for preferential admission policies).
72. In 1983, the city of Richmond, Virginia, held a hearing on whether to adopt an ordinance requiring that 30% of all public-works contracts be subcontracted to businesses owned by blacks or members of other officially designated minority groups. Terry Eastland, *Racial Preference in Court (Again),* COMMENTARY, Jan. 1989, at 32, 33. The ordinance's expiration date of 1988 drew a response from the Mayor, who said he believed "we were going to perpetuity with" the ordinance *Id.* at 36. The city did not change the ordinance

although the Supreme Court ruled it unconstitutional in City of Richmond v. J.A. Croson Co., 488 U.S. 469 (1989). My point here is that the Mayor spoke the new language of affirmative action, which now sees the policy not as an interim, but a perpetual measure.

73. *See supra* part II. A. (discussing underrepresentation and disparity).

74. BELZ *supra* note 65, at 235–39.

75. Civil Rights Act of 1964, Pub. L. No. 88–352, 78 Stat. 241 (codified as amended at 42 U.S.C. § 2000e (1988).

76. *See* BELZ, *supra* note 65, at 43–68.

77. R. Roosevelt Thomas, Jr., *From Affirmative Action to Affirming Diversity,* HARV. BUS. REV., Mar-Apr. 1990, at 107, 108.

78. *See supra* part II. B (discussing these effects of affirmative action).

79. *See, e.g.,* NATHAN GLAZER, AFFIRMATIVE DISCRIMINATION: ETHNIC INEQUALITY AND PUBLIC POLICY 63 (1987) (noting the difficulty of qualifying the many factors that contribute to the distribution of jobs in the labor force); Richard A. Posner, *The Defunis Case and the Constitutionality of Preferential Treatment of Racial Minorities,* 1974 SUP. CT. REV. 1, 17 (noting lack of evidence concerning the root causes of minority choice in employment); Thomas Sowell, Weber *and* Bakke, *and the Presuppositions of Affirmative Action,* 26 WAYNE I. REV. 1309, 1314–16 (1980) (assessing empirical presuppositions of affirmative action).

80. *See* BELZ, *supra* note 65, at 235–39.

81. *See* Charles Krauthammer, *Quota by Threat,* WASH. POST, May 18, 1990, at A19 (noting the danger of "implied inferiority" that results from affirmative action, which not only demoralizes blacks, but also incites white racism).

82. I first argued this positon in 1979. *See* EASTLAND & BENNETT, *supra* note 22, at 164.

83. Despite their rhetoric, neither the Reagan nor the Bush administration made coherent efforts to eliminate quotas and other race preferences.

84. *See* Alan McConagha, *Helms' Victory Follows Pattern; Floors Pundits, Pollsters Who Thought Race Was Over,* WASH. TIMES, Nov. 8, 1990, at B7 (discussing a Helms campaign advertisement depicting a white worker crumbling a job-rejection letter while the narrator says the position went to a less qualified applicant who was a member of a minority group).

85. THE DECLARATION OF INDEPENDENCE para. 2 (U.S. 1776).

86. PETER BROWN, MINORITY PARTY (1991).

87. *See supra* note 69.

88. Mass opinion remains invariably opposed to preferential treatment for deprived groups. The Gallup Organization repeated the same question five times between 1977 and 1989; Some people say that to make up for past discrimination, women and minorities should be given preferential treatment in getting jobs and places in college. Others say that ability, as determined by test scores, should be the main consideration. Which point of view comes closest to how you feel on the subject? In each survey, 10 or 11 percent said that minorities should be given preferential treatment, while 81, 83, or 84 percent replied that ability should be the determining factor.

Seymour M. Lipset, *Affirmative Action and the American Creed,* WILSON Q., Winter 1992, at 52, 58.

89. *Id.* at 53.

90. *Id.* at 62.

From Affirmative Action to Affirming Diversity

R. Roosevelt Thomas, Jr.

Sooner or later, affirmative action will die a natural death. Its achievements have been stupendous, but if we look at the premises that underlie it, we find assumptions and priorities that look

---

increasingly shopworn. Thirty years ago, affirmative action was invented on the basis of these five appropriate premises:

1. Adult, white males make up something called the U.S. business mainstream.
2. The U.S. economic edifice is a solid, unchanging institution with more than enough space for everyone.
3. Women, blacks, immigrants, and other minorities should be allowed in as a matter of public policy and common decency.
4. Widespread racial, ethnic, and sexual prejudice keeps them out.
5. Legal and social coercion are necessary to bring about the change.

Today all five of these premises need revising. Over the past six years, I have tried to help some 15 companies learn how to achieve and manage diversity, and I have seen that the realities facing us are no longer the realities affirmative action was designed to fix.

To begin with, more than half the U.S. work force now consists of minorities, immigrants, and women, so white, native-born males, though undoubtedly still dominant, are themselves a statistical minority. In addition, white males will make up only 15% of the increase in the workforce over the next ten years. The so-called mainstream is now almost as diverse as the society at large.

Second, while the edifice is still big enough for all, it no longer seems stable, massive, and invulnerable. In fact, American corporations are scrambling, doing their best to become more adaptable, to compete more successfully for markets and labor, foreign and domestic, and to attract all the talent they can find. (See the inserts for what a number of U.S. companies are doing to manage diversity.)

Third, women and minorities no longer need a boarding pass, they need an upgrade. The problem is not getting them in at the entry level; the problem is making better use of their potential at every level, especially in middle-management and leadership positions. This is no longer simply a question of common decency, it is a question of business survival.

Fourth, although prejudice is hardly dead, it has suffered some wounds that may eventually prove fatal. In the meantime, American businesses are now filled with progressive people— many of them minorities and women themselves—whose prejudices, where they still exist, are much too deeply suppressed to interfere with recruitment. The reason many companies are still wary of minorities and women has much more to do with education and perceived qualifications than with color or gender. Companies are worried about productivity and well aware that minorities and women represent a disproportionate share of the undertrained and undereducated.

Fifth, coercion is rarely needed at the recruitment stage. There are very few places in the United States today where you could dip a recruitment net and come up with nothing but white males. Getting hired is not the problem—women and blacks who are seen as having the necessary skills and energy can get *into* the work force relatively easily. It's later on that many of them plateau and lose their drive and quit or get fired. It's later on that their managers' inability to manage diversity hobbles them and the companies they work for.

In creating these changes, affirmative action had an essential role to play and played it very well. In many companies and communities it still plays that role. But affirmative action is an artificial, transitional intervention intended to give managers a chance to correct an imbalance, an injustice, a mistake. Once the numbers mistake has been corrected, I don't think affirmative action alone can cope with the remaining long-term task of creating a work setting geared to the upward mobility of *all* kinds of people, including white males. It is difficult for affirmative action to influence upward mobility even in the short run, primarily because it is perceived to conflict

---

Out of the Numbers Game and Into Decision Making

Like many other companies, Avon practiced affirmative action in the 1970s and was not pleased with the results. The company worked with employment agencies that specialized in finding qualified minority hires, and it cultivated contacts with black and minority organizations on college campuses. Avon wanted to see its customer base reflected in its work force, especially at the decision-making level. But while women moved up the corporate ladder fairly brisky—not so surprising in a company whose work force is mostly female—minorities did not. So in 1984, the company began to change its policies and practices.

"We really wanted to get out of the numbers game," says Marcia Worthing, the corporate vice president for human resources. "We felt it was more important to have five minority people tied into the decision-making process than ten who were just heads to count."

First, Avon initiated awareness training at all levels. "The key to recruiting, retaining, and promoting minorities is not the human resource department," says Worthing. "It's getting line management to buy into the idea. We had to do more than change behavior. We had to change attitudes."

Second, the company formed a Multicultural Participation Council that meets regularly to oversee the process of managing diversity. The group includes Avon's CEO and high-level employees from throughout the company.

Third, in conjunction with the American Institute for Managing Diversity, Avon developed a diversity training program. For several years, the company has sent racially and ethnically diverse groups of 25 managers at a time to Institute headquarters at Morehouse College in Atlanta, where they spend three weeks confronting their differences and learning to hear and avail themselves of viewpoints they initially disagree with. "We came away disciples of diversity," says one company executive.

Fourth, the company helped three minority groups—blacks, Hispanics, and Asians—form networks that crisscrossed the corporation in all 50 states. Each network elects its own leaders and has an adviser from senior management. In addition, the networks have representatives on the Multicultural Participation Council, where they serve as a conduit for employee views on diversity issues facing management.

---

with the meritocracy we favor. For this reason, affirmative action is a red flag to every individual who feels unfairly passed over and a stigma for those who appear to be its beneficiaries.

Moreover, I doubt very much that individuals who reach top positions through affirmative action are effective models for younger members of their race or sex. What, after all, do they model? A black vice president who got her job through affirmative action is not necessarily a model of how to rise through the corporate meritocracy. She may be a model of how affirmative action can work for the people who find or put themselves in the right place at the right time.

If affirmative action in upward mobility meant that no person's competence and character would ever be overlooked or undervalued on account of race, sex, ethnicity, origins, or physical disability, then affirmative action would be the very thing we need to let every corporate talent find its niche. But what affirmative action

means in practice is an unnatural focus on one group, and what it means too often to too many employees is that someone is playing fast and loose with standards in order to favor that group. Unless we are to compromise our standards, a thing no competitive company can even contemplate, upward mobility for minorities and women should always be a question of pure competence and character unmuddled by accidents of birth.

And that is precisely why we have to learn to manage diversity—to move beyond affirmative action, not to repudiate it. Some of what I have to say may strike some readers—mostly those with an ax to grind—as directed at the majority white males who hold most of the decision-making posts in our economy. But I am speaking to all managers, not just white males, and I certainly don't mean to suggest that white males somehow stand outside diversity. White males are as odd and as normal as anyone else.

THE AFFIRMATIVE ACTION CYCLE

If you are managing diverse employees, you should ask yourself this question: Am I fully tapping the potential capacities of everyone in my department? If the answer is no, you should ask yourself this follow-up: Is this failure hampering my ability to meet performance standards? The answer to this question will undoubtedly be yes.

Think of corporate management for a moment as an engine burning pure gasoline. What's now going into the tank is no longer just gas, it has an increasing percentage of, let's say, methanol. In the beginning, the engine will still work pretty well, but by and by it will start to sputter, and eventually it will stall. Unless we rebuild the engine, it will no longer burn the fuel we're feeding it. As the work force grows more and more diverse at the intake level, the talent pool we have to draw on for supervision and management will also grow increasingly diverse. So the question is: Can we burn this fuel? Can we get maximum corporate power from the diverse work force we're now drawing into the system?

Affirmative action gets blamed for failing to do things it never could do. Affirmative action gets the new fuel into the tank, the new people through the front door. Something else will have to get them into the driver's seat. That something else consists of enabling people, in this case minorities and women, to perform to their potential. This is what we now call managing diversity. Not appreciating or leveraging diversity, not even necessarily understanding it. Just managing diversity in such a way as to get from a heterogeneous work force the same productivity, commitment, quality, and profit that we got from the old homogeneous work force.

The correct question today is not "How are we doing on race relations?" or "Are we promoting enough minority people and women?" but rather "Given the diverse work force I've got, am I getting the productivity, does it work as smoothly, is morale as high, as if every person in the company was the same sex and race and nationality?" Most answers will be, "Well no, of course not!" But why shouldn't the answer be, "You bet!"?

When we ask how we're doing on race relations, we inadvertently put our finger on what's wrong with the question and with the attitude that underlies affirmative action. So long as racial and gender equality is something we grant to minorities and women, there will be no racial and gender equality. What we must do is create an environment where no one is advantaged or disadvantaged, an environment where "we" is everyone. What the traditional approach to diversity did was to create a cycle of crisis, action, relaxation, and disappointment that companies repeated over and over again without ever achieving more than the barest particle of what they were after.

Affirmative action pictures the work force as a pipeline and reasons as follows: "If we can fill the pipeline with *qualified* minorities and women, we can solve our upward mobility problem. Once recruited, they will perform in accordance with our promotional criteria and move naturally up our regular developmental ladder. In the past, where minorities and women have failed to progress, they were simply unable to meet our performance standards. Recruiting qualified people will enable us to avoid special programs and reverse discrimination."

This pipeline perspective generates a self-perpetuating, self-defeating, recruitment-oriented cycle with six stages:

1. *Problem Recognition.* The first time through the cycle, the problem takes this form—We need more minorities and women in the pipeline. In later iterations, the problem is more likely to be defined as a need to retain and promote minorities and women.

2. *Intervention.* Management puts the company into what we may call an Affirmative Action Recruitment Mode. During the first cycle, the goal is to recruit minorities and women. Later, when the cycle is repeated a second or third time and the challenge has shifted to

"It Simply Makes Good Business Sense."

Corning characterizes its 1970s affirmative action program as a form of legal compliance. The law dictated affirmative action and morality required it, so the company did its best to hire minorities and women.

The ensuing cycle was classic: recruitment, confidence, disappointment, embarrassment, crisis, more recruitment. Talented women and blacks joined the company only to plateau or resign. Few reached upper management levels, and no one could say exactly why.

Then James R. Houghton took over as CEO in 1983 and made the diverse work force one of Corning's three top priorities, alongside Total Quality and a higher return on equity. His logic was twofold:

First of all, the company had higher attrition rates for minorities and women than for white males, which meant that investments in training and development were being wasted. Second, he believed that the Corning work force should more closely mirror the Corning customer base.

In order to break the cycle of recruitment and subsequent frustration, the company established two quality improvement teams headed by senior executives, one for black progress and one for women's progress. Mandatory awareness training was introduced for some 7,000 salaried employees—a day and a half for gender awareness, two-and-a-half days for racial awareness. One goal of the training is to identify unconscious company values that work against minorities and women. For example, a number of awareness groups reached the conclusion that working late had so much symbolic value that managers tended to look more at the quantity than at the quality of time spent on the job, with predictably negative effects on employees with dependent-care responsibilities.

The company also made an effort to improve communications by printing regular stories and articles about the diverse work force in its in-house newspaper and by publicizing employee success stories that emphasize diversity. It worked hard to identify and publicize promotion criteria. Career planning systems were introduced for all employees.

With regard to recruitment, Corning set up a nationwide scholarship program that provides renewable grants of $5,000 per year of college in exchange for a summer of paid work at some Corning installation. A majority of program participants have come to work for Corning full-time after graduation, and very few have left the company so far, though the program has been in place only four years.

The company also expanded its summer intern program, with an emphasis on minorities and women, and established formal recruiting contacts with campus groups like the Society of Women Engineers and the National Black MBA Association.

Corning sees its efforts to manage diversity not only as a social and moral issue but also as a question of efficiency and competitiveness. In the words of Mr. Houghton, "It simply makes good business sense."

retention, development, and promotion, the goal is to recruit *qualified* minorities and women. Sometimes, managers indifferent or blind to possible accusations of reverse discrimination will institute special training, tracking, incentive, mentoring, or sponsoring programs for minorities and women.

3. *Great Expectations.* Large numbers of minorities and women have been recruited, and a select group has been promoted or recruited at a higher level to serve as highly visible role models for the newly recruited masses. The stage seems set for the natural progression of minorities and women up through the pipeline. Management leans back to enjoy the fruits of its labor.

4. *Frustration.* The anticipated natural progression fails to occur. Minorities and women see themselves plateauing prematurely. Management is upset (and embarrassed) by the failure of its affirmative action initiative and begins to resent the impatience of the new recruits and their unwillingness to give the company credit for trying to do the right thing. Depending on how high in the hierarchy they have plateaued, alienated minorities and women either leave the company or stagnate.

5. *Dormancy.* All remaining participants conspire tacitly to present a silent front to the outside world. Executives say nothing because they have no solutions. As for

those women and minorities who stayed on, calling attention to affirmative action's failures might raise doubts about their qualifications. Do they deserve their jobs, or did they just happen to be in the right place at the time of an affirmative action push? So no one complains, and if the company has a good public relations department, it may even wind up with a reputation as a good place for women and minorities to work.

If questioned publicly, management will say things like "Frankly, affirmative action is not currently an issue," or "Our numbers are okay," or "With respect to minority representation at the upper levels, management is aware of this remaining challenge."

In private and off the record, however, people say things like "Premature plateauing is a problem, and we don't know what to do," and "Our top people don't seem to be interested in finding a solution," and "There's plenty of racism and sexism around this place—whatever you may hear."

6. *Crisis.* Dormancy can continue indefinitely, but it is usually broken by a crisis of competitive pressure, governmental intervention, external pressure from a special interest group, or internal unrest. One company found that its pursuit of a Total Quality program was hampered by the alienation of minorities and women. Senior management at another corporation saw the growing importance of minorities in their customer base

Turning Social Pressures into Competitive Advantage

Like most other companies trying to respond to the federal legislation of the 1970s, Digital started off by focusing on numbers. By the early 1980s, however, company leaders could see it would take more than recruitment to make Digital the diverse workplace they wanted it to be. Equal Employment Opportunity (EEO) and affirmative action seemed too exclusive—too much "white males doing good deeds for minorities and women." The company wanted to move beyond these programs to the kind of environment where every employee could realize his or her potential, and Digital decided that meant an environment where individual differences were not tolerated but valued, even celebrated.

The resulting program and philosophy, called Valuing Differences, has two components:

First, the company helps people get in touch with their stereotypes and false assumptions through what Digital calls Core Groups. These voluntary groupings of eight to ten people work with company-trained facilitators whose job is to encourage discussion and self-development and, in the company's words, "to keep people safe" as they struggle with their prejudices. Digital also runs a voluntary two-day training program called "Understanding the Dynamics of Diversity," which thousands of Digital employees have now taken.

Second, the company has named a number of senior managers to various Cultural Boards of Directors and Valuing Differences Boards of Directors. These bodies promote openness to individual differences, encourage younger managers committed to the goal of diversity, and sponsor frequent celebrations of racial, gender, and ethnic differences such as Hispanic Heritage Week and Black History Month.

In addition to the Valuing Differences program, the company preserved its EEO and affirmative action functions. Valuing Differences focuses on personal and group development, EEO on legal issues, and affirmative action on systemic change. According to Alan Zimmerle, head of the Valuing Differences program, EEO and Valuing Differences are like two circles that touch but don't overlap—the first representing the legal need for diversity, the second the corporate desire for diversity. Affirmative action is a third circle that overlaps the other two and holds them together with policies and procedures.

Together, these three circles can transform legal and social pressures into the competitive advantage of a more effective work force, higher morale, and the reputation of being a better place to work. As Zimmerle puts it, "Digital wants to be the employer of choice. We want our pick of the talent that's out there."

and decided they needed minority participation in their managerial ranks. In another case, growing expressions of discontent forced a break in the conspiracy of silence even after the company had received national recognition as a good place for minorities and women to work.

Whatever its cause, the crisis fosters a return to the Problem Recognition phase, and the cycle begins again. This time, management seeks to explain the shortcomings of the previous affirmative action push and usually concludes that the problem is recruitment. This assessment by a top executive is typical: "The managers I know are decent people. While they give priority to performance, I do not believe any of them deliberately block minorities or women who are qualified for promotion. On the contrary, I suspect they bend over backward to promote women and minorities who give some indication of being qualified.

"However, they believe we simply do not have the necessary talent within those groups, but because of the constant complaints they have heard about their deficiencies in affirmative action, they feel they face a no-win situation. If they do not promote, they are obstructionists. But if they promote people who are unqualified, they hurt performance and deny promotion to other employees unfairly. They can't win. The answer, in my mind, must be an ambitious new recruitment effort to bring in quality people."

And so the cycle repeats. Once again blacks, Hispanics, women, and immigrants are dropped into a previously homogeneous, all-white, all-Anglo, all-male, all native-born environment, and the burden of cultural change is placed on the newcomers. There will be new expectations and a new round of frustration, dormancy, crisis, and recruitment.

TEN GUIDELINES FOR LEARNING TO MANAGE DIVERSITY

The traditional American image of diversity has been assimilation: the melting pot, where ethnic and racial differences were standardized into a kind of American puree. Of course, the melting pot is only a metaphor. In real life, many ethnic and most racial groups retain their individuality and express it energetically. What we have is perhaps some kind of American mulligan stew; it is certainly no puree.

At the workplace, however, the melting pot has been more than a metaphor. Corporate success has demanded a good deal of conformity, and employees have voluntarily abandoned most of their ethnic distinctions at the company door.

Now those days are over. Today the melting pot is the wrong metaphor even in business, for three good reasons. First, if it ever was possible to melt down Scotsmen and Dutchmen and Frenchmen into an indistinguishable broth, you can't do the same with blacks, Asians, and women. Their differences don't melt so easily. Second, most people are no longer willing to be melted down, not even for eight hours a day—and it's a seller's market for skills. Third, the thrust of today's nonhierarchical, flexible, collaborative management requires a ten- and twentyfold increase in our tolerance for individuality.

So companies are faced with the problem of surviving in a fiercely competitive world with a work force that consists and will continue to consist of *unassimilated diversity*. And the engine will take a great deal of tinkering to burn that fuel.

What managers fear from diversity is a lowering of standards, a sense that "anything goes." Of course, standards must not suffer. In fact, competence counts more than ever. The goal is to manage diversity in such a way as to get from a diverse work force the same productivity we once got from a homogeneous work force, and to do it without artificial programs, standards—or barriers.

Managing diversity does not mean controlling or containing diversity, it means enabling every member of your work force to perform to his or her potential. It means getting from employees, first, everything we have a right to expect, and, second—if we do it well—everything they have to give. If the old homogeneous work force performed dependably at 80% of its capacity, then the first result means getting 80% from the new heterogeneous work force too. But the second result, the icing on the cake, the unexpected upside that diversity can perhaps give as a bonus, means 85% to 90% from everyone in the organization.

For the moment, however, let's concentrate on the basics of how to get satisfactory performance from the new diverse work force. There are few adequate models. So far, no large company I know of has succeeded in managing diversity to its own satisfaction. But any number have begun to try.

On the basis of their experience, here are my ten guidelines:

1. *Clarify Your Motivation.* A lot of executives are not sure why they should want to learn to manage diversity. Legal compliance seems like a good reason. So does community rela-tions. Many executives believe they have a social and moral responsibility to employ minorities and women. Others want to placate an internal group or pacify an outside organization. None of these are bad reasons, but none of them are business reasons, and given the nature and scope of today's competitive challenges, I believe only business reasons will supply the necessary long-term motivation. In any case, it is the business reasons I want to focus on here.

In business terms, a diverse work force is not something your company ought to have; it's something your company does have, or soon will have. Learning to manage that diversity will make you more competitive.

2. *Clarify Your Vision.* When managers think about a diverse work force, what do they picture? Not publicly, but in the privacy of their minds?

One popular image is of minorities and women clustering on a relatively low plateau,

Discovering Complexity and Value in P&G's Diversity

Because Procter & Gamble fills its upper level management positions only from within the company, it places a premium on recruiting the best available entry-level employees. Campus recruiting is pursued nationwide and year-round by line managers from all levels of the company. Among other things, the company has made a concerted—and successful—effort to find and hire talented minorities and women.

Finding first-rate hires is only one piece of the effort, however. There is still the challenge of moving diversity upward. As one top executive put it, "We know that we can only succeed as a company if we have an environment that makes it easy for all of us, not just some of us, to work to our potential."

In May 1988, P&G formed a Corporate Diversity Strategy Task Force to clarify the concept of diversity, define its importance for the company, and identify strategies for making progress toward successfully managing a diverse work force.

The task force, composed of men and women from every corner of the company, made two discoveries: First, diversity at P&G was far more complex than most people had supposed. In addition to race and gender, it included factors such as cultural heritage, personal background, and functional experience. Second, the company needed to expand its view of the value of differences.

The task force helped the company to see that learning to manage diversity would be a long-term process of organizational change. For example, P&G has offered voluntary diversity training at all levels since the 1970s, but the program has gradually broadened its emphasis on race and gender awareness to include the value of self-realization in a diverse environment. As retiring board chairman John Smale put it, "If we can tap the total contribution that everybody in our company has to offer, we will be better and more competitive in everything we do."

P&G is now conducting a thorough, continuing evaluation of all management programs to be sure that systems are working well for everyone. It has also carried out a corporate survey to get a better picture of the problems facing P&G employees who are balancing work and family responsibilities and to improve company programs in such areas as dependent care.

with a few of them trickling up as they become assimilated into the prevailing culture. Of course, they enjoy good salaries and benefits, and most of them accept their status, appreciate the fact that they are doing better than they could do somewhere else, and are proud of the achievements of their race or sex. This is reactionary thinking, but it's a lot more common than you might suppose.

Another image is what we might call "heightened sensitivity." Members of the majority culture are sensitive to the demands of minorities and women for upward mobility and recognize the advantages of fully utilizing them. Minorities and women work at all levels of the corporation, but they are the recipients of generosity and know it. A few years of this second-class status drives most of them away and compromises the effectiveness of those that remain. Turnover is high.

Then there is the coexistence-compromise image. In the interests of corporate viability, white males agree to recognize minorities and women as equals. They bargain and negotiate their differences. But the win-lose aspect of the relationship preserves tensions, and the compromises reached are not always to the company's competitive advantage.

"Diversity and equal opportunity" is a big step up. It presupposes that the white male culture has given way to one that respects difference and individuality. The problem is that minorities and women will accept it readily as their operating image, but many white males, consciously or unconsciously, are likely to cling to a vision that leaves them in the driver's seat. A vision gap of this kind can be a difficulty.

In my view, the vision to hold in your own imagination and to try to communicate to all your managers and employees is an image of fully tapping the human resource potential of every member of the work force. This vision sidesteps the question of equality, ignores the tensions of coexistence, plays down the uncomfortable realities of difference, and focuses in-

stead on individual enablement. It doesn't say, "Let *us* give *them* a chance." It assumes a diverse work force that includes us and them. It says, "Let's create an environment where everyone will do their best work."

Several years ago, an industrial plant in Atlanta with a highly diverse work force was threatened with closing unless productivity improved. To save their jobs, everyone put their shoulders to the wheel and achieved the results they needed to stay open. The senior operating manager was amazed.

For years he had seen minorities and women plateauing disproportionately at the lower levels of the organization, and he explained that fact away with two rationalizations. "They haven't been here that long," he told himself. And "This is the price we pay for being in compliance with the law."

When the threat of closure energized this whole group of people into a level of performance he had not imagined possible, he got one fleeting glimpse of people working up to their capacity. Once the crisis was over, everyone went back to the earlier status quo—white males driving and everyone else sitting back, looking on—but now there was a difference. Now, as he put it himself, he had been to the mountaintop. He knew that what he was getting from minorities and women was nowhere near what they were capable of giving. And he wanted it, crisis or no crisis, all the time.

3. *Expand Your Focus.* Managers usually see affirmative action and equal employment opportunity as centering on minorities and women, with very little to offer white males. The diversity I'm talking about includes not only race, gender, creed, and ethnicity but also age, background, education, function, and personality differences. The objective is not to assimilate minorities and women into a dominant white male culture but to create a dominant heterogeneous culture.

The culture that dominates the United States socially and politically is heterogeneous, and it works by giving its citizens the liberty to achieve their potential. Channeling that potential, once achieved, is an individual right but still a national concern. Something similar applies in the workplace, where the keys to success are individual ability and a corporate destination. Managing disparate talents to achieve common goals is what companies learned to do when they set their sights on, say, Total Quality. The secrets of managing diversity are much the same.

4. *Audit Your Corporate Culture.* If the goal is not to assimilate diversity into the dominant culture but rather to build a culture that can digest unassimilated diversity, then you had better start by figuring out what your present culture looks like. Since what we're talking about here is the body of unspoken and unexamined assumptions, values, and mythologies that make your world go round, this kind of cultural audit is impossible to conduct without outside help. It's a research activity, done mostly with indepth interviews and a lot of listening at the water cooler.

The operative corporation assumptions you have to identify and deal with are often inherited from the company's founder. "If we treat everyone as a member of the family, we will be successful" is not uncommon. Nor is its corollary "Father Knows Best."

Another widespread assumption, probably absorbed from American culture in general, is that "cream will rise to the top." In most companies, what passes for cream rising to the top is actually cream being pulled or pushed to the top by an informal system of mentoring and sponsorship.

Corporate culture is a kind of tree. Its roots are assumptions about the company and about the world. Its branches, leaves, and seeds are behavior. You can't change the leaves without changing the roots, and you can't grow peaches on an oak. Or rather, with the proper grafting, you *can* grow peaches on an oak, but they come out an awful lot like acorns—small and hard and

not much fun to eat. So if you want to grow peaches, you have to make sure the tree's roots are peach friendly.

5. *Modify Your Assumptions.* The real problem with this corporate culture tree is that every time you go to make changes in the roots, you run into terrible opposition. Every culture, including corporate culture, has root guards that turn out in force every time you threaten a basic assumption.

Take the family assumption as an example. Viewing the corporation as a family suggests not only that father knows best; it also suggests that sons will inherit the business, that daughters should stick to doing the company dishes, and that if Uncle Deadwood doesn't perform, we'll put him in the chimney corner and feed him for another 30 years regardless. Each assumption has its constituency and its defenders. If we say to Uncle Deadwood, "Yes, you did good work for 10 years, but years 11 and 12 look pretty bleak; we think it's time we helped you find another chimney," shock waves will travel through the company as every family-oriented employee draws a sword to defend the sacred concept of guaranteed jobs.

But you have to try. A corporation that wants to create an environment with no advantages or disadvantages for any group cannot allow the family assumption to remain in place. It must be labeled dishonest mythology.

Sometimes the dishonesties are more blatant. When I asked a white male middle manager how promotions were handled in his company, he said, "You need leadership capability, bottom-line results, the ability to work with people, and compassion." Then he paused and smiled. "That's what they say. But down the hall there's a guy we call Captain Kickass. He's ruthless, mean-spirited, and he steps on people. That's the behavior they really value. Forget what they say."

In addition to the obvious issue of hypocrisy, this example also raises a question of equal opportunity. When I asked this young middle manager if he thought minorities and women could meet the Captain Kickass standard, he said he thought they probably could. But the opposite argument can certainly be made. Whether we're talking about blacks in an environment that is predominantly white, whites in one predominantly black, or women in one predominantly male, the majority culture will not readily condone such tactics from a member of a minority. So the corporation with the unspoken kickass performance standard has at least one criterion that will hamper the upward mobility of minorities and women.

Another destructive assumption is the melting pot I referred to earlier. The organization I'm arguing for respects differences rather than seeking to smooth them out. It is multicultural rather than culture blind, which has an important consequence: When we no longer force people to "belong" to a common ethnicity or culture, then the organization's leaders must work all the harder to define belonging in terms of a set of values and a sense of purpose that transcend the interests, desires, and preferences of any one group.

6. *Modify Your Systems.* The first purpose of examining and modifying assumptions is to modify systems. Promotion, mentoring, and sponsorship comprise one such system, and the unexamined cream-to-the-top assumption I mentioned earlier can tend to keep minorities and women from climbing the corporate ladder. After all, in many companies it is difficult to secure a promotion above a certain level without a personal advocate or sponsor. In the context of managing diversity, the question is not whether this system is maximally efficient but whether it works for all employees. Executives who only sponsor people like themselves are not making much of a contribution to the cause of getting the best from every employee.

Performance appraisal is another system where unexamined practices and patterns can have pernicious effects. For example, there are companies where official performance appraisals differ substantially from what is said informally, with the result that employees get their most accurate performance feedback through the grapevine. So if the grapevine is closed to minorities and women, they are left at a severe disadvantage. As one white manager observed, "If the blacks around here knew how they were really perceived, there would be a revolt." Maybe so. More important to your business, however, is the fact that without an accurate appraisal of performance, minority and women employees will find it difficult to correct or defend their alleged shortcomings.

7. *Modify Your Models.* The second purpose of modifying assumptions is to modify models of managerial and employee behavior. My own personal hobgoblin is one I call the Doer Model, often an outgrowth of the family assumption and of unchallenged paternalism. I have found the Doer Model alive and thriving in a dozen companies. It works like this:

Since father knows best, managers seek subordinates who will follow their lead and do as they do. If they can't find people exactly like themselves, they try to find people who aspire to be exactly like themselves. The goal is predictability and immediate responsiveness because the doer manager is not there to manage people but to do the business. In accounting departments, for example, doer managers do accounting, and subordinates are simply extensions of their hands and minds, sensitive to every signal and suggestion of managerial intent.

Doer managers take pride in this identity of purpose. "I wouldn't ask my people to do anything I wouldn't do myself," they say. "I roll up my sleeves and get in the trenches." Doer managers love to be in the trenches. It keeps them out of the line of fire.

But managers aren't supposed to be in the trenches, and accounting managers aren't supposed to do accounting. What they are supposed to do is create systems and a climate that allow accountants to do accounting, a climate that enables people to do what they've been charged to do. The right goal is doer subordinates, supported and empowered by managers who manage.

The Daily Experience of Genuine Workplace Diversity

Chairman David T. Kearns believes that a firm and resolute commitment to affirmative action is the first and most important step to work force diversity. "Xerox is committed to affirmative action," he says. "It is a corporate value, a management priority, and a formal business objective."

Xerox began recruiting minorities and women systematically as far back as the mid-1960s, and it pioneered such concepts as pivotal jobs (described later). The company's approach emphasizes behavior expectations as opposed to formal consciousness-raising programs because, as one Xerox executive put it, "It's just not realistic to think that a day and a half of training will change a person's thinking after 30 or 40 years."

On the assumption that attitude changes will grow from the daily experience of genuine workplace-diversity, the Xerox Balanced Work Force Strategy sets goals for the number of minorities and women in each division and at every level. (For example, the goal for the top 300 executive-level jobs in one large division is 35% women by 1995, compared with 15% today.) "You *must* have a laboratory to work in," says Ted Payne, head of Xerox's Office of Affirmative Action and Equal Opportunity.

Minority and women's employee support groups have grown up in more than a dozen locations with the company's encouragement. But Xerox depends mainly on the three pieces of its balanced strategy to make diversity work.

First are the goals. Xerox sets recruitment and representation goals in accordance with federal guidelines and reviews them constantly to make sure they reflect work force demographics. Any company with a federal contract is required to make this effort. But Xerox then extends the guidelines by setting diversity goals for its upper level jobs and holding division and group managers accountable for reaching them.

The second piece is a focus on pivotal jobs, a policy Xerox adopted in the 1970s when it first noticed that minorities and women did not have the upward mobility the company wanted to see. By examining the backgrounds of top executives, Xerox was able to identify the key positions that all successful managers had held at lower levels and to set goals for getting minorities and women assigned to such jobs.

The third piece is an effort to concentrate managerial training not so much on managing diversity as on just plain managing people. What the company discovered when it began looking at managerial behavior toward minorities and women was that all too many managers didn't know enough about how to manage anyone, let alone people quite different from themselves.

8. *Help Your People Pioneer.* Learning to manage diversity is a change process, and the managers involved are change agents. There is no single tried and tested "solution" to diversity and no fixed right way to manage it. Assuming the existence of a single or even a dominant barrier undervalues the importance of all the other barriers that face any company, including, potentially, prejudice, personality, community dynamics, culture, and the ups and downs of business itself.

While top executives articulate the new company policy and their commitment to it, middle managers—most or all of them still white males, remember—are placed in the tough position of having to cope with a forest of problems and simultaneously develop the minorities and women who represent their own competition for an increasingly limited number of promotions. What's more, every time they stumble they will themselves be labeled the major barriers to progress. These managers need help, they need a certain amount of sympathy, and, most of all, perhaps, they need to be told that they are pioneers and judged accordingly.

In one case, an ambitious young black woman was assigned to a white male manager, at his request, on the basis of her excellent company record. They looked forward to working together, and for the first three months, everything went well. But then their relationship began to deteriorate, and the harder they worked at patching it up, the worse it got. Both of them, along with their superiors, were surprised by the conflict and seemed puzzled as to its causes.

Eventually, the black woman requested and obtained reassignment. But even though they escaped each other, both suffered a sense of failure severe enough to threaten their careers.

What could have been done to assist them? Well, empathy would not have hurt. But perspective would have been better yet. In their particular company and situation, these two people had placed themselves at the cutting edge of race and gender relations. They needed to know that mistakes at the cutting edge are different— and potentially more valuable—than mistakes elsewhere. Maybe they needed some kind of pioneer training. But at the very least they needed to be told that they were pioneers, that conflicts and failures came with the territory, and that they would be judged accordingly.

9. *Apply the Special Consideration Test.* I said earlier that affirmative action was an artificial, transitional, but necessary stage on the road to a truly diverse work force. Because of its artificial nature, affirmative action requires constant attention and drive to make it work. The point of learning once and for all how to manage diversity is that all that energy can be focused somewhere else.

There is a simple test to help you spot the diversity programs that are going to eat up enormous quantities of time and effort. Surprisingly, perhaps, it is the same test you might use to identify the programs and policies that created your problem in the first place. The test consists of one question: Does this program, policy, or principle give special consideration to one group? Will it contribute to everyone's success, or will it only produce an advantage for blacks or whites or women or men? Is it designed for *them* as opposed to *us?* Whenever the answer is yes, you're not yet on the road to managing diversity.

This does not rule out the possibility of addressing issues that relate to a single group. It only underlines the importance of determining that the issue you're addressing does not relate to other groups as well. For example, management in one company noticed that blacks were not moving up in the organization. Before instituting a special program to bring them along, managers conducted interviews to see if they could find the reason for the impasse. What blacks themselves reported was a problem with the quality of supervision. Further interviews showed that other employees too—including white males—were concerned about the quality of supervision and felt that little was being done to foster professional development. Correcting the situation eliminated a problem that affected everyone. In this case, a solution that focused only on blacks would have been out of place.

Had the problem consisted of prejudice, on the other hand, or some other barrier to blacks or minorities alone, a solution based on affirmative action would have been perfectly appropriate.

10. *Continue Affirmative Action.* Let me come full circle. The ability to manage diversity is the ability to manage your company without unnatural advantage or disadvantage for any member of your diverse work force. The fact remains that you must first have a work force that is diverse at every level, and if you don't, you're going to need affirmative action to get from here to there.

The reason you then want to move beyond affirmative action to managing diversity is because affirmative action fails to deal with the root causes of prejudice and inequality and does little to develop the full potential of every man and woman in the company. In a country seeking competitive advantage in a global economy, the goal of managing diversity is to develop our capacity to accept, incorporate, and empower the diverse human talents of the most diverse nation on earth. It's our reality. We need to make it our strength.

"I'm Sick But . . ." Employees with AIDS and the Americans with Disabilities Act

INTRODUCTION

There are more than 40 million persons in the United States with various disabilities. To combat widespread discrimination, Congress passed the Americans with Disabilities Act (ADA) in 1990 in order to

> provide a clear and comprehensive national mandate to end discrimination against individuals with disabilities and to bring persons with disabilities into the economic and social mainstream of American life; to provide enforceable standards addressing discrimination against individuals with disabilities, and to ensure that the Federal government plays a central role in enforcing these standards on behalf of individuals with disabilities. (42 USC 12101 (b)(4))

The ADA does not protect every individual with a disability; it protects only "qualified individuals with a disability," that is, individuals who "with or without reasonable accommodation" can perform the "essential functions" of a job.

The "reasonable accommodation" clause of the ADA, however, marks a legal and ethical shift from other antidiscrimination rules and laws. The ADA requires not only that employers refrain from discriminatory behavior but also that they take *positive* action to accommodate qualified employees' physical or mental limitations (e.g., altering existing facilities to make them more accessible, adopting modified work schedules to meet worker needs, and acquiring equipment and devices to assist workers in doing their jobs).

As we observed in Chapter 1, the positive duty to help is more controversial than the negative duty to refrain from inflicting harm, and this positive duty can be interpreted in such an expansive way that it becomes too burdensome. Congress recognized this when it acknowledged that employers are not obliged to make accommodations that would impose undue hardship on them or their businesses.

The ADA's critics argue that, because it fails to identify its protected class clearly (the class of persons who are over 40 years old is clear in a way that the class of persons who are disabled is not) and fails to define crucial terms such as "*reasonable* accommodation," "*essential* job function," and "*undue* hardship" with any precision, the Act opens up a Pandora's box of potential illegitimate employee complaints and exposes employers to unfair liabilities and expenses, making its costs far exceed its benefits.

By contrast, its defenders maintain that the Act creates a winning situation for everyone involved. Persons with disabilities win because their dignity and rights are affirmed and their lives made more satisfying. Society at large wins because billions of dollars in lost productivity and dependency costs are saved. Businesses win because the pool of available labor is significantly expanded by the introduction of many talented individuals.

This chapter will focus on persons with HIV/AIDS who fall under the protection of the ADA. Frequently regarded with the fear and apprehension that is often the burden of people with contagious and fatal diseases, many people with HIV/AIDS belong to two other stigmatized groups, homosexuals and intravenous drug users. As such, they are frequently the objects of contempt, often based on negative moral judgments. Most of the "win-win" aspects that the ADA's defenders point to seem conspicuously and painfully absent here.

In an article relating his personal experiences as a manager, Gary Banas (1992) describes the human issue poignantly.

> Don't let anyone kid you, when you confront AIDS in the workplace, you will face untenable choices that seem to pit your obligation to humanity against your obligation to your organization. Contrary to popular opinion, you will almost certainly fall short in both areas. (26)
>
> One of the most difficult dilemmas a manager faces in this situation is how to weigh the obvious, painful needs of the dying person against the less dramatic but clearly compelling needs of the organization. I have no ready answers. I only know that managers will be plunged into moral and professional choices at the most mundane, specific level, that there will be little precedent for many of these choices and that almost all will cause injury to someone. Fatal disease permits no win-win solutions, only lose-lose ones. A manager's task is to minimize the losses—to people and to organizations. (30)

When someone in an organization has HIV/AIDS, the organization and its members are confronted with substantial practical, ethical, and legal questions. Can the person perform his or her job? For how long? Who determines when he or she no longer can? What risk, if any, is there to his or her coworkers? Should the organization's insurance and/or disability plans cover HIV/AIDS victims? For how long? What are the proper standards of confidentiality and privacy to be observed? What accommodations should be made to meet the victim's needs? What are the victim's responsibilities to his or her employer and coworkers? How should the organization deal with the concerns and fears of coworkers or customers?

Kant's emphasis on the dignity and autonomy of individual persons extends to the HIV/AIDS victim, just as it would to the victim of any terminal illness. His or her capacity to make effective choices should be respected, and unjustified discrimination against the victim is not only illegal but ethically prohibited as well. Gary Banas' experience reminds us that we cannot realistically speak of maximizing good in this situation, only of minimizing net harm—harm to the victim, to his or her associates, and to the organization and its stakeholders. The ethically sensitive organization will search out strategies and policies for doing this. Finally, there is the challenge of finding ways that the inevitable harms and difficulties can be distributed fairly. Often, significant burdens fall to the victim's coworkers, and the difficult question will arise concerning how much they are ethically obligated to bear.

★ ★ ★

In the readings selected for this chapter, **C. Richard Scott** and **Diane M. Baun** use a question-and-answer format to provide managers with a basic understanding of the ADA, including definitions, requirements, gray areas, and proactive measures to insure compliance. **Michael D. Esposito** and **Jeffrey E. Myers** discuss legal considerations relating to the issues of

HIV/AIDS in the workplace and analyze in detail the steps that employers must take both to comply with the ADA and the relevant OSHA regulations and to manage effectively the problems associated with HIV/AIDS. **Arthur S. Leonard** argues that ethical concerns for victims of HIV/AIDS must go beyond the requirements of the law. In his opinion, ethical decisions and policies in this area should conform to the ethical principles of respect for persons, avoidance of harm, beneficence, and justice, and he advances several concrete proposals how they might do so.

REFERENCES

Banas, Gary E. (1992) "Nothing Prepared Me To Manage AIDS." *Harvard Business Review, 70,* 26–33.

CASE: Managing AIDS: How One Boss Struggled to Cope

Even today, Jean Langone Smith can't talk about that December morning in 1991 without stumbling, second-guessing, searching the air around her for just the right words. The truth is, she's never really gotten over the way she felt when Frank Daloisio walked into her office and tried to tell her he was slowly dying of AIDS.

Jean thought she knew Frank pretty well—about as well as most bosses know their employees, anyway. Off and on, they had worked together at Digital Equipment Corp. for nearly a decade. For the past two years, Frank had worked happily for Jean as a sales representative in DEC's Blue Bell (Pa.) office. Lately, though, a spate of illnesses had left Frank moody and despondent. His chronic absences were disrupting the entire office.

Frank's first attempt to break the news to Jean ended with the revelation that he was terminally ill. But that was all he said. Then, on an icy Monday morning a few weeks later, he sat down in Jean's office and rambled on about a friend who had died of AIDS. Both of them knew what he was trying to say, but neither knew how to express it. Finally, Frank stopped and asked: "You know what it is, don't you?" "Yes, I do," she said. "It's a terrible thing in our society." Jean still stings from the shame she felt. "What a dumb, impersonal thing to say," she chided herself. "The man is dying, for God's sake!"

This is the story of how one American middle manager struggled with AIDS at the office. It is a tale of fear and compassion, denial and hope, anger and humanity. In one way or another, it is a story being played out in nearly every U.S. corporation. The federal Centers for Disease Control estimate that 1 in every 250 Americans has been infected by HIV, the virus that causes acquired immune deficiency syndrome. Most are 25 to 44—the core age group of the U.S. work force.

Despite the spread of the epidemic, Corporate America's response has come in fits and starts. Many companies have thrown a policy at the problem and left it at that. Experts, however, agree it demands more: an ongoing educational effort, sanctioned from the chief executive on down, to dispel the destructive attitudes that swirl around HIV. As Jean discovered during her yearlong ordeal with Frank, managing AIDS is much too complicated for policy manuals.

Even DEC's much-lauded AIDS-education program was overwhelmed by the issues surrounding the disease. Unlike cancer and other terminal illnesses, AIDS provokes some of our worst fears and most insidious impulses. Had Frank, 40, and Jean, 39, felt comfortable talking about his illness early on, they could have avoided a lot of the problems they encountered. But candor comes hard with AIDS, and experts agree confidentiality is an essential element of any policy.

Lee Smith, a former executive of Levi Strauss & Co. and now chairman of the National Leadership Coalition on AIDS, echoes many managers when he laments: "I was not trained to

Source: Ron Stodghill II, *Business Week,* February 1, 1993, 48–52. Reprinted from February 1, 1993 issue of *Business Week* by special permission, copyright © 1993 by McGraw-Hill, Inc.

manage fear, discrimination, and dying in the workplace." Unfortunately, resources for educating managers in how to cope with such thorny issues are often scarce and ineffective. Managing AIDS successfully distills into patience, empathy, and flexibility. And for managers such as Jean who are focused on profits, that involves an awkward—if humanizing—shift in perspective.

For Jean, that shift began on a balmy May evening in 1991. That's when she threw a cookout for her six-member sales team in the backyard of her suburban Philadelphia home. Things couldn't have gone more smoothly. As the aroma of chicken, hamburgers, and hot dogs drifted up from a grill on the wooden deck, Jean's guests laughed and chatted. The friendly atmosphere gave her plenty of reassurance that her sales team was having a good time.

She needed it. Jean knew her reputation wasn't the best among her employees. Tough, serious, and demanding were among the nicer labels. Even her husband, Alan, sometimes chided her about her hard-driving management style ("Jean, you've gotta get your people to like you more"). He encouraged her, whenever possible, to show a softer side. The cookout was a way of loosening up a little, while also saying thank you for a strong sales performance over the winter.

It wasn't that Jean was incapable of opening up to coworkers. It had just never been a priority. She had worked hard to rise up the corporate ladder and wasn't given to coddling. Born in Woburn, Mass., in 1953, she was the second-oldest child in a hardworking Irish-Italian family. Her father was a carpenter, her mother a homemaker. Both parents instilled in their eight children a strong work ethic.

After graduating from high school, Jean tried college and a job at a law firm before joining DEC as a secretary in the company's Maynard (Mass.) headquarters in 1976. Ambitious and strong-willed, she was never content in her support-staff role. By 1979, she had persuaded her superiors to send her to DEC's Washington (D.C.) office as a sales representative. Within six years, she rose to sales manager, and in 1987, Jean transferred to DEC's Blue Bell office, just outside Philadelphia.

She may not have been a touchy-feely manager, but Jean was certain her people knew they could count on her to be fair. In her eyes, that's all that really mattered. The Blue Bell office had only one customer: Shared Medical Systems Corp., a large health-care-services company based in Malvern, Pa. Jean's mission was to sell the company more computers while providing technical support, and training. DEC set ambitious targets for the office, and Jean demanded that her reps be self-starters. "I expect my people to think on their feet," she says. "They're getting paid as professionals and should manager their own destinies."

Despite a good winter, however, office morale in the spring of 1991 had been dismal. Beyond the normal pressures of selling in a rotten economy, a series of crises—both personal and professional—had put the team on edge. One of Jean's sales reps was struggling with the death of a newborn child. Another was on maternity leave. Jean, meantime, had a problem of her own: She and Alan were trying to adopt a child, and the on-again, off-again adoption process had been a study in frustration.

The most recent crisis, the one that involved Frank Daloisio, was about to pass, or so she had hoped. For the past month, Frank had been out of the office sick; a doctor's excuse described his illness as shingles. Energetic, personable, and seasoned, Frank handled the technical end of the department's sales efforts—advising the customer on using DEC's machines. Jean didn't know exactly what shingles was, but she did know Frank's absence had really thrown a monkey wrench into operations.

Her sales reps were busy enough without carrying Frank's load. They were an understanding lot, but Jean knew they wouldn't tolerate the extra work forever. Frank, too, must have figured sympathy for him was wearing thin. Earlier that week, he had phoned with terrific news. Not only was he planning to attend Jean's party, but the team could expect to see him back at work the following Monday. Jean breathed a great sigh of relief.

Until she saw him. The moment Frank walked through the backyard gate to join the picnic, Jean was overwhelmed by the stark change in his appearance. "My God, he looks terrible," she thought. That had taken some doing. At 40, Frank was a handsome man— olive-skinned, with silky, jet-black hair and a chiseled face. Yet he had lost 30 pounds since Jean had last seen him. Dark rings circled his eyes, and his cheeks were sunken. His tall frame seemed unsteady as he leaned on a cane.

Frank's broad smile was enough to reassure Jean. But in fact, he was at an all-time low in what had been an eight-year battle against HIV. While he had suffered many bouts of sickness since having tested positive for the virus in 1983, nothing had been as debilitating as this case of shingles. An affliction related to chicken pox, shingles had wreaked havoc on his body, infecting a major nerve running through his right leg, causing it to go numb. The illness had also caused unsightly skin eruptions and irritation on his legs and lower back. A steady dose of painkillers helped, but they also kept him up all night.

Until that point, Frank was certain he could keep his condition private—and he was determined to do just that. Having grown up in the small town of Phoenixville, Pa., the only son in a household of five children, he was well aware of how swiftly secrets travel once uncorked. Even today, he is quick to put in their place anyone probing the cause of his illness. "How I got it is nobody's business," he says. "Whether I'm homosexual, a straight man, an IV drug user. That's not the issue."

Frank always spoke his mind. He inherited both the unflinching candor and the free spirit of his dad, an Italian immigrant who at 13 saw America by hopping trains and hoboing across the country. While his sisters endured the strictures of their Catholic upbringing, Frank was a feisty teen, smoking cigarettes openly at home. His father tried coaxing him into the family beer-and-soda distributorship. But Frank politely declined. Too boring, he said.

Instead, Frank attended Pennsylvania State University, graduating in 1976 with a bachelor's degree in liberal arts. Unable to find a job, he supplemented his education with computer science courses at a community college. By 1979, he landed a job in DEC's Landover Hills (Md.) office, providing computer training to customers. He moved to the company's Washington office in 1984.

Just a year earlier, Frank had learned that he was HIV-positive. "The last thing on my mind was getting up and going to work," he recalls. "But the reality was, I needed my benefits." At the time, AIDS was even more baffling to the medical community than it is today. Frank had been told he could expect to live two more years, at best. He began seeing a psychiatrist to help battle depression.

It was during this time that he first met Jean. As part of the Washington division's sales-support staff, Frank's job was to show her customers how to operate the computers she sold them. During their brief yet critical exchanges, Jean always impressed Frank as "a woman who was totally about business." He enjoyed working with her.

By 1987, however, rumors about Frank had begun swirling wildly in the office. Not long before, he had offered himself up as a "guinea pig" to a group of scientists searching for an AIDS cure at George Washington University. The study demanded Frank leave the office once a week to get blood drawn. "Why are you always going to the doctor?" his co-workers began asking. The inquiries so worried Frank that within months, he fled D.C. for DEC's office in Dallas.

For Frank, maintaining his privacy was worth the inconvenience of relocating. "I've always been paranoid about presenting my illness," he says. "I've seen people lose jobs, life insurance, health insurance, you name it. Plus, I had been told that if you're healthy, there is no reason to disclose to anyone."

But after six months in Dallas, Frank became severely ill with pneumonia. He spent the next six months at home on temporary disability. His oldest sister, Antoinette—the only person besides his lover whom Frank had told about his condition—flew in from Philadelphia to be at his bedside. They decided it might be better, all things considered, for Frank to move back East, preferably to Philadelphia, where he would be closer to his family. Frank concealed the truth from DEC's executives, saying a family illness required him to relocate.

The best DEC could offer him was a transfer back to the Washington office. But a year later, on Nov. 6, 1989, Jean hired him to work for her in Blue Bell. Frank considered it an ideal situation. "I had heard good and bad stories about Jean as a manager," he says. "She was tough on her people, but she was not nosy, which was very important to me."

Things worked out fine during Frank's first 18 months on the job. His health didn't seem an issue, though Jean recalls Frank spending a lot of time puffing Winstons in the designated smoking area. A couple of times, when she heard him hacking, she would walk over to him, concerned. "Frank, you really need to start taking better care of yourself," she'd tell him. He always took her remarks in good spirit, and a couple of times he even tried to quit.

By now, though, he had bigger worries. His illness had begun to accelerate. His T-cell count—a measurement of white blood cells, which fight infectious disease—had plummeted from 529 in 1982 to a hazardous 338. A healthy person has a T-cell count that ranges around 1,200. With his immune system faltering, he became easy prey for a host of illnesses—the most serious being the bout of shingles. After his month off work, Frank had only warily attended Jean's party. "I really started to get paranoid be-

cause people my age just don't get shingles," he says. "I was hoping nobody would question me, and luckily nobody did. But I was scared for my life. When T-cells drop, I know the inevitable outcome. And I knew that eventually my illness had to come out."

Increasingly worried about his job, Frank took his first big step: In late July, he showed up at the office of Nona Robinson, a personnel consultant in DEC's human-resources department. "It broke my heart," recalls Nona of Frank's disclosure. "Here was this poor employee who was gravely ill, but he was afraid to tell me. He was scared to death."

ΔDigital is widely recognized as having one of the nation's most progressive aids programs. Not only does it have a strong policy, but since 1988 it has had an HIV/AIDS Program office, which holds employee seminars, acts as an information clearinghouse, and provides confidential counseling to any employee. Frank would receive full benefits, and his condition would be kept confidential as long as he wished. Moreover, he would be assured that his job status would not change until the time came that he was unable to complete his duties effectively. Then, he and dec would adjust his job or design another that took into account his failing health. The confidentiality appealed most to Frank. In due time, he would begin telling others in the company, he said, but until then he asked Nona to keep his secret. She agreed.

Experts concur that there's no way around confidentiality when it comes to AIDS policy. An employee has a right to privacy. But the secrecy that attends the disease also creates many of the problems involved in managing an employee who has it. The sicker Frank got, the more puzzling his behavior became—and the less Jean understood what was happening.

Within a week of returning to work after the picnic, Frank walked into Jean's office and firmly told her he wanted to use some vacation time, starting with a two-week trip to Thailand and Hong Kong. The request startled Jean. "I was thinking he was very assertive about what he wants. He's entitled to a vacation. But, frankly, I was a little annoyed." That wasn't all, either. Frank then declared he was planning another trip in December—this one to St. Barts in the Caribbean. "Up to that point, I had known Frank as dedicated and committed," Jean says. "Something just wasn't adding up."

Frank had become consumed by the thought of his own mortality. "I was like, I want to see the world. I pass through this place only once, and I want to see as much of it as I can." Jean decided not to challenge him. She knew Frank as a man who didn't bend easily. And confronting him on something like this might cause unnecessary stress between them. "I gave some time to Frank's issue, and then it was time to worry about other people and other business issues," she says.

But over the next few months, Frank's sick days kept racking up. He was still a heavy smoker, and a common cold often wound up as acute bronchitis. There were also side effects from his various medications that kept him out of work for two and three days at a time. Jean started to lose her patience—as did the rest of the sales team.

One teammate was Betty Ann McMichael. Although fond of Frank, she admits she and the others began resenting his being off work so often. "There was a feeling of inequality," she says. "We had team sales goals, and even though Frank was sick and others were carrying his load, he was still getting credit for helping meet those goals."

Disruptive rumors also began to fly. Frank's illness often became the topic of lunchtime conversations, sometimes focusing on his sexuality and the possibility he had AIDS. It's a testament to educational efforts about the disease that Frank's co-workers weren't particularly afraid of contracting AIDS. But at least one sales rep was so incensed that Frank appeared to be getting an easy ride that he badgered one of the secretaries—a friend of Frank's—to find out why

Frank missed so much work. Others inquired directly if he was gay. "It got to the point where I was avoiding certain people," the friend says.

Jean ran some interference for Frank, but she, too, was under pressure. A consultant from headquarters had recently been assigned to help boost her team's productivity, and Frank's chronic absence was hurting. "It was beginning to be a real juggling act," she recalls.

In late November, things finally blew open. With emotions running high because of yearend sales goals and general holiday-season anxiety, Jean and Frank collided during a staff meeting. The team was just coming off a bad quarter, and Jean believed part of the reason was that the reps were acting more as individuals than as a cohesive unit. At the meeting, she was trying to motivate her staff and create a stronger sense of teamwork. She was also divvying up various roles that each of the members would play.

She started with Frank, but couldn't get his attention. Despondent, he just sat in his seat, staring out the window. "It looked like he was totally tuning me out," Jean recalls.

"I expect you to respond," Jean shouted. But Frank wouldn't budge. He remembers being in great physical pain at the time and not caring what she thought. Jean, who was already upset by the team's lack of enthusiasm, became furious. "Well, you all figure it out," she said, storming out of the conference room. "I'm leaving."

When she returned to her office later that afternoon, there was a message on her voice mail. It was from Frank: "Jean, I did not like the way you confronted me at the meeting. I would like for us to have a meeting with human resources." Jean was baffled. Human resources? Her first reaction was paranoia. "I'm thinking: 'I'm about to lose my job. What did I do? What did I do? We know each other, why can't we talk? How thin-skinned can somebody be? This *is* a business.'"

That night, Jean took her frustration home to her husband. Distraught, she didn't know what to do. After talking it over with Alan and tossing through a sleepless night, she decided to talk to

Frank again. "I admit that I was a little uptight," Jean says of the incident. "It was the end of the year, and we were all uptight." She figured their troubles would blow over.

Frank's disclosure of the real problem stretched over several weeks and two more meetings. In the first, Jean finally confronted Frank. "Like I said," he answered, "I think we need to have human resources here."

"But Frank, I felt we could trust each other," she said. Something about the way she said it, Frank explains, finally shook him up. He saw the concern on her face, and "she became a person for me then." But he still wasn't ready to tell her everything. "All I could think was: 'I don't know how she's going to react. I don't know how my co-workers are going to react, how my customers are going to react.' There were just so many unknowns." He decided to hedge.

"I have a terminal illness," he said.

Jean thought AIDS immediately but didn't say so. "I really felt incompetent and unprepared hearing that from somebody," she remembers. "I felt guilty, like 'Geez, I've been putting all this pressure on this person.' But I didn't say I'm sorry he was sick, and I didn't know that's what he wanted to hear. You just say as little as possible."

Jean vaguely recalled that DEC had an AIDS policy and program. In fact, she could remember taking time out to read a pamphlet on the subject. The AIDS office at DEC headquarters near Boston had some exemplary seminars that would have helped both Jean and her sales team cope with the situation. Unfortunately, the seminars hadn't made it to Blue Bell yet.

Jean had absorbed enough company literature to know at least one basic fact: DEC would take full care of an employee with HIV. And Frank's admission—however inadequate—began to explain his behavior. But Jean was still in a fix. Frank immediately took several days off to sit by the bedside of a friend in the final stages of AIDS. The friend, who had been ostracized by his family, was dying alone. Jean tried to be

sympathetic, but she ended up furious. "I had other people trying to hold his work load," she says. "I was calling customers. They were saying, 'Where's Frank? He's normally right on the ball.' I felt like I was holding the bag."

Frank and Jean finally came to an understanding on that cold December morning after Frank returned—even though the word "AIDS" never passed their lips. To this day, they can't remember the first time they discussed his disease openly. Eventually, they were able to—and it helped enormously. Jean tapped into the resources of DEC's HIV/AIDS Program Office. And she turned to Nona Robinson in human resources for guidance in creating a new job for Frank.

Even that wasn't easy. "We came up with some suggestions that Frank didn't like," Jean says, noting several options that included lots of sales work on the phone. Retorts Frank: "They didn't take advantage of the skills I have. I've been working here 18 years. Calling up people on the telephone, I felt like they were saying, 'O.K., let's put him in the corner over there.'" In the end, Frank wound up in a newly created position, which played to his technical strengths while limiting his visits to clients. The job required Frank to draw up computer-system configurations, perform sales quotations, as well as do paperwork that bogs down other sales representatives.

After Frank disclosed his illness to Jean, he took each of his co-workers aside and told them he had AIDS. He had agreed to talk about his illness during a DEC-sponsored AIDS-awareness workshop, and he wanted to prepare them. At the workshop, Frank choked back tears as he revealed to the entire sales force his condition. "When it came out at the presentation, everybody just sat there and cried," recalls Betty Ann, Frank's co-worker. Jean attended the workshop and even stood up to share a few of the experiences she had with Frank.

That was last summer. In October, Frank went on short-term disability. The medication he takes is causing serious side effects. He has a swollen spleen, which doctors are considering removing. Shingles has also returned. Frank is living at his parents' home, where he has a computer linking him to the office. He goes in when he can and sometimes has lunch with a favorite customer or co-worker.

At the office, life is almost back to normal. Jean credits DEC's AIDS policy for helping sort out the details. But she also points out that she and her staff bore most of the trauma of managing AIDS. "The AIDS office didn't come in and run my business for me," she says. "I had to solve the organizational problems. I had to make the decisions that would impact Frank, his co-workers, and his customers."

It's not exactly Jean's style to psychoanalyze herself. "As a manager, it raised the bar for what I need to be," she says flatly. Others think she's changed a lot. "In the past, people didn't feel comfortable going in and saying what was on their mind, or just shooting the breeze," says Betty Ann. "But after Frank's ordeal, Jean seemed to become more agreeable to hearing your thoughts and just letting you talk to her."

Jean opened up, and that was crucial. DEC's policy on AIDS, and others like it, represent an enlightened effort to institutionalize compassion. Rules, though, are merely rules. For Jean and her co-workers, managing AIDS came down to discovering a greater humanity within themselves. For Frank, it meant marshaling the courage to confront his problem openly. Offices aren't typically the crucible for a mixture so personal and emotional. But there's nothing typical about AIDS.

READING 4·1

The Americans With Disabilities Act: An Employer's Perspective

C. Richard Scott
Diane M. Baun

People differ in terms of the opportunities they have for acquiring wealth, status, and power. An individual's opportunities for success may depend, in part, on talent, luck, timing, experience, and training. Unfortunately, individuals may also be limited by an employer's preconceived notions as to their abilities and worth if they are disabled. Thus, although a person may have all the qualifications for a certain job, an incumbent employee or applicant may be denied an opportunity simply because he or she has a physical or mental impairment.

The patchwork quilt of American society is replete with examples of disabled individuals who in one way or another made significant contributions to society. One only has to remember the image of four-time elected, polio-stricken President Franklin Roosevelt, confined to a wheelchair or walking with braces. No one would argue that his physical limitation prevented him from making major contributions— he led America out of the Great Depression and to victory in World War II. Yet, American society has tended to look on successful disabled people as special cases, and not as representative of a sizable minority population whose less conspicuous members' capabilities have gone largely unappreciated.

Not only are disabled workers unappreciated, they have been discriminated against in employment practices and isolated from job opportunities. The disabled account for 43 million Americans and are the nation's largest minority group.

Source: Reprinted by permission. *SAM Advanced Management Journal,* Spring, 1992, Society for Advancement of Management, Vinton, VA 24179.

Yet, a Harris poll reveals that 67% of this minority are unemployed. And, in terms of salaries, the employed disabled earn only 64% of what their nondisabled co-workers make. While the federal government spends approximately $170 billion on programs and benefits for the disabled, the Harris survey found that 82% of all disabled people would give up their government benefits in favor of full-time employment (Harris, 1987).

Contrary to common belief, no federal law prevented private employers from discriminating against disabled persons prior to 1990. The oft-cited Rehabilitation Act of 1973 requires only *federal* contractors to take affirmative action to hire or promote qualified disabled individuals. While approximately 41 states had antidiscrimination laws that supplement or fill the void of federal law for disabled workers (Sovereign, 1989), their protections differed greatly and uniformity was needed. Consequently, Congress passed the Americans With Disabilities Act of 1990 (ADA), and President Bush signed the legislation into law on July 26, 1990.

PURPOSE AND SCOPE OF THE ACT

The legislative purpose of the ADA is fourfold: (1) to provide a clear and comprehensive national mandate for the elimination of discrimination against individuals with disabilities; (2) to provide clear, strong, consistent, enforceable standards regarding discrimination against individuals with disabilities; (3) to ensure that the federal government plays a central role in enforcing the standards established in the Act on behalf of disabled individuals and, (4) to invoke the sweep of congressional authority to address the major areas of discrimination faced by people with disabilities (Kelly and Aalberts, 1990).

The Act bars discrimination against the disabled in a variety of contexts, including access to public facilities and employment. The ADA's employment discrimination provisions are phased in beginning in July 1992 and reach their full scope in 1994.

PROVISIONS OF THE ACT

• What Employers Are Covered by the Act?

For two years following the effective date of the Act (i.e., from July, 1992, to 1994), only employees are covered. Thereafter, employers with 15 or more employees are also covered. The only exemptions are U.S. wholly-owned government corporations and *bona fide* tax-exempt private membership clubs.

• How Does the ADA Define "Disability"?

Disability is defined in three ways: (1) a physical or mental impairment that substantially limits one or more of the major life activities of the individual; or, (2) a record of such an impairment; or, (3) being regarded as having such an impairment. Common, but not exhaustive, examples of disabilities include individuals with mental retardation, paraplegia, schizophrenia, cancer, AIDS or the HIV virus. Homosexuality and bisexuality are not disabilities. Similarly, *current* drug use is not a disability. Rehabilitated drug users, drug users in treatment who no longer use illegal drugs, and individuals erroneously regarded as drug users are considered disabled for purposes of the employment discrimination provisions of the Act.

• Who Does the Act Protect?

The ADA prohibits discrimination against any "qualified individual with a disability because of his or her disability." A "qualified individual with a disability" is defined as a person who can perform the "essential functions" of the job that person holds or desires with or without "reasonable accommodation." For example, many employers require driver's licenses for a variety of positions which do not require driving or where driving is incidental to the job. A driver's license is often required because it is presumed that

people who drive to work are more likely to arrive at work on time or because a driver can do an occasional errand. The "essential functions" requirement assures that people who cannot drive because of their disabilities are not disqualified for these reasons if they can do the actual duties of the job.

Notwithstanding the use of the term "Americans," the Act protects all individuals with disabilities who are in this country—regardless of their ethnic origin and immigration status. Additionally, it protects qualified individuals who are discriminated against because they associate with disabled persons.

• What Constitutes Discrimination under the Act?

The goal of the statute is to achieve a work environment where discrimination against the disabled is not present. To accomplish this, the ADA mandates that the disabled should not be discriminated against in organizational decisions. These include:

1. Recruitment advertising and the processing of applications for employment.
2. Hiring, updating, promotion, award of tenure, demotion, transfer, layoff, termination, right of return from layoff and rehiring.
3. Rates of pay or any other form of compensation and changes in compensation.
4. Job assignments, job classifications, organizational structures, position descriptions, lines of progression, and seniority lists.
5. Leaves of absence, sick leave, or any other leave.
6. Fringe benefits available by virtue of employment, whether or not administered by the employer.
7. Selection and financial support for training, including apprenticeship, professional meetings, conferences, and other related activities, and selection for leave of absence to pursue training.
8. Employer sponsored activities, including social or recreational programs.

Discrimination also includes a wide spectrum of activities such as limiting, segregating, or classifying disabled job applicants in a way that adversely affects their opportunities or status because of their disabilities.

Moreover, discrimination under the ADA also embraces the concept of "reasonable accommodation." That is, an employer must make reasonable accommodations to the known physical or mental limitations of an otherwise qualified individual with a disability who is an applicant or employee, unless the employer can demonstrate that the accommodation would impose an undue hardship on the operation of the business. Failure to make reasonable accommodations is a violation of the Act.

• What Is a "Reasonable Accommodation"?

The employer must notify applicants and employees of its obligation under the Act to make reasonable accommodation. But, employers are obligated to make reasonable accommodations only to "known" physical or mental limitations of a qualified individual with a disability. Thus, the duty to accommodate is generally triggered by a request from an employee or job applicant. In the absence of a request, it would be inappropriate for the employer to provide an accommodation, especially where it could impact adversely on the individual. Of course, if a person with a known disability is having difficulty performing his or her job, it would be permissible for the employer to discuss the possibility of a reasonable accommodation with the employee.

A precise definition of reasonable accommodation is not provided in the ADA. Instead, the Act offers examples of what reasonable accommodation may encompass. The following is a non-exhaustive list of typical accommodations which employers may make to their disabled employees.

1. Make existing facilities used by employees readily accessible to and usable by individuals with disabilities.

2. Adopt part-time or modified work schedules.

3. Reassign to a vacant position; however, reassignment may not be used to accommodate applicants for employment (i.e., efforts should be made to accommodate an employee in the position that he or she was hired to fill before reassignment should be considered).

4. Acquire or modify facilities, equipment, or devices.

5. Adjust or modify examinations, training materials, or policies.

6. Provide qualified readers, interpreters, or similar accommodations.

While this list presents some conspicuous examples of reasonable accommodation, employers should first consult with the disabled individual in deciding on the appropriate accommodation. Disabled people may have a lifetime of experience identifying ways to accomplish tasks differently in different circumstances. Frequently, therefore, the disabled person will know exactly what accommodation is needed to enable them to successfully perform a particular job.

It is important to note, however, that the employee cannot *dictate* the accommodation decision. For example, in situations where there are two effective accommodations, the employer may choose the accommodation that is least expensive or easiest to implement as long as the selected accommodation provides meaningful equal employment opportunity.

• When Are Employers Not Required to Accommodate?

The employer's legal obligation to provide an accommodation depends on whether the accommodation would impose an undue hardship on the employer's business operation. An employer does not need to make any accommodation that would be too expensive, substantial, or disruptive, or that would fundamentally alter the nature of the job. Importantly, the employer has the burden of showing that a given accommodation constitutes an undue hardship.

Even if an accommodation would constitute an undue hardship, receipt or eligibility to receive financial support from an external source (e.g., a government agency or the employee) mitigates an employer's claim of financial hardship to the extent that the employer receives such support. However, the lack of outside funding does not obviate the need to provide a reasonable accommodation.

• What Criteria May an Employer Use to Screen Applicants?

As with most other antidiscrimination statutes, job criteria must actually measure skills required for the job and must be consistent with business necessity. If disabled applicants meet all of the selection criteria except one, that criterion must concern an essential, not marginal, aspect of the job. Otherwise, the employer will likely face a discrimination claim.

• What Questions Can an Employer Ask a Disabled Applicant?

To help assure that bias does not enter into the selection process, the Act sharply limits the questions an employer can ask an applicant concerning disabilities. An employer may inquire into an applicant's ability to perform job-related functions, but may not inquire into the nature or extent of an applicant's disability. For example, if driving is an essential job function, the employer may ask whether the applicant has a driver's license, but may not ask whether the employee has a visual disability.

The limitations on questions during preemployment interviews does not hamper an employer's ability to request that the applicant voluntarily disclose disabilities when (and only when) the employer is 1) taking remedial action to correct the effects of past discrimination against the disabled, 2) is taking voluntary action to overcome the effects of conditions that have resulted in limited employment opportunities for the disabled, and 3) is taking affirmative action.

When requesting voluntary disclosure, the employer must clearly state:

1. That the information requested is intended only for remedial, voluntary, or affirmative action.
2. That the information is requested on a voluntary basis, and that applicants are not subject to adverse treatment if they refuse to provide it.
3. That the information will be kept confidential.
4. That the information will be used only in accordance with the provisions of the ADA.

• What Is the Role of the EEOC in Implementing the Act?

The enforcement of the ADA falls under the administration of the EEOC. The EEOC will issue regulations soon, and by the summer of 1991 technical assistance plans should be available. The EEOC will use means other than litigation to the extent possible to resolve complaints filed under the Act. This includes negotiations, conciliation, facilitation, mediation, fact-finding, mini-trials, and arbitration. However, the ADA incorporates Title VII's enforcement procedures, and employees should expect most claims under the ADA to follow those familiar enforcement procedures. Relief for ADA claims will include injunctions, reinstatement, hiring, backpay, and attorneys' fees.

WHERE CAN EMPLOYERS FIND OUT MORE ABOUT THE ACT?

Further information on the Act can be obtained from any one of the EEOC's 21 district and 27 area offices, or by calling 1-800-USA-EEOC. District offices are full-service units, handling all charge processing and all compliance and litigation enforcement functions. Area offices generally handle charge intake and initial investigations, with some of them also performing various compliance and litigation activities. The EEOC has offices in the following cities:

Albuquerque, NM
*Atlanta, GA
*Baltimore, MD
*Birmingham, AL
Boston, MA
Buffalo, NY
*Charlotte, NC
*Chicago, IL
Cincinnati, OH
*Cleveland, OH
*Dallas, TX
*Denver, CO
*Detroit, MI
El Paso, TX
Fresno, CA
Greensboro, NC
Greenville, SC
*Houston, TX
*Indianapolis, IN
Jackson, MS
Kansas City, MO
Little Rock, AR
*Los Angeles, CA
Louisville, KY

*Memphis, TN
*Miami, FL
Milwaukee, WI
Minneapolis, MN
Nashville, TN
Newark, NJ
*New Orleans, LA
*New York, NY
Norfolk, VA
Oakland, CA
Oklahoma City, OK
*Philadelphia, PA
*Phoenix, AZ
Pittsburgh, PA
Raleigh, NC
Richmond, VA
San Antonio, TX
San Diego, CA
*San Francisco, CA
San Jose, CA
*Seattle, WA
*St. Louis, MO
Tampa, FL
Washington, DC

*District Offices

WHAT SHOULD EMPLOYERS DO NOW?

While the Act does not affect any employers until July 1992, employers should begin now to carefully assess their employment practices to assure that they are doing their statutory duty to avoid discrimination against the disabled and to accommodate the needs of their incumbent or future disabled employees. In most cases, this duty already exists under most state laws which protect the equal employment rights of disabled workers. However, to avoid exposure to ADA litigation, employers should consider the following proactive measures.

1. *Educate supervisory staff.* Inform each supervisor of the requirements of the Act. The line supervisor is generally the one who has frequent contact with disabled employees and is probably best suited to assist in rea-

sonably accommodating their needs. Supervisors need to know the law.

2. *Outreach and Positive Recruitment.* Review employment practices to ensure that human resource programs are consistent with the provisions of the Act in terms of the employment and advancement of qualified disabled applicants and current employees.

3. *Proper Consideration of Qualifications.* Look at employment procedures to ensure careful, thorough, and systematic consideration of the job qualifications of known disabled individuals for job vacancies filled either by hiring or promotion and for all training opportunities offered or available.

4. *Physical and Mental Qualifications.* Review all physical and mental job qualification requirements with line management to ensure that, to the extent qualification requirements tend to screen out qualified individuals with disabilities, those requirements are job-related and consistent with business necessity and the safe performance of the job.

5. *Reasonable Accommodations.* Develop policies to make reasonable accommodations to the physical and mental limitations of employees or applicants to the extent that such accommodation does not impose an undue hardship on the conduct of the business.

6. *Compensation.* Insure that the compensation package is equitable between the disabled employee and others who are doing the same or similar jobs. In offering employment or promotions to the disabled, certainly do not reduce the amount of compensation offered because of any disability income, pension, or other benefits the applicant or employee receives from other sources.

CONCLUSION

The Americans With Disabilities Act arms the disabled with a powerful mechanism to maximize their job opportunities and employment potentials. The largest minority group (43 million) now has a private basis for action against employment discrimination. Therefore, the law is predicted to be a major source of litigation in the next 15 years; in fact, it will likely rival Title VII in terms of claims. Prudent employers will anticipate this rush of litigation and begin preparations to ensure compliance with the law when it becomes effective.

REFERENCES

Harris, Louis and Associates. *The ICD Survey of Disabled Americans,* cited in: The President's Committee on Employment of the Handicapped, "Out of the Job Market: a National Crisis," Washington, D.C., 1987: p. 16.

Kelly, Eileen P. and Aalberts, Robert J. "Americans with Disabilities Act: Undue Hardship for Private Sector Employers?" *Labor Law Journal,* Vol. 10, No. 10, October 1990: pp. 675–684.

Sovereign, Kenneth L. *Personnel Law* (Englewood Cliffs, New Jersey: Prentice-Hall, Inc., 1989, 2nd Edition).

READING 4-2

Managing AIDS in the Workplace

Michael D. Esposito
Jeffrey E. Myers

With the advent of the Americans with Disabilities Act of 1990 (ADA) and the new OSHA regulations promulgated in 1991, employers are faced with a variety of requirements they must satisfy when dealing with Acquired Immunodeficiency Syndrome (AIDS) and Human Immun-

Source: "Managing AIDS in the Workplace," Michael Esposito and Jeffrey Myers, *Employee Relations Law Journal,* copyright © 1993 John Wiley & Sons, Inc. Reprinted by permission of John Wiley & Sons, Inc.

odeficiency Virus (HIV) in the workplace. The purpose of this article is to explore the steps employers should consider taking to ensure compliance under applicable law, to reduce exposure to employee claims, and to efficiently manage issues associated with AIDS in the workplace.

AIDS/HIV AND THE ADA

An employee's recent "spate of illnesses" has left him "moody and despondent." The entire office has been disrupted by his "chronic absences." There is "a feeling of inequity" among his coworkers, since they have been carrying his load to reach their sales goal yet he is "still getting credit for helping to meet those goals."[1] Before discussing how to manage this real-life scenario, it is important to understand some key terms and to appreciate the full scope of the AIDS epidemic in the United States.

The Nature and Extent of AIDS/HIV

Americans first began to hear about AIDS and HIV in the early 1980s. HIV is the virus that causes AIDS. If an individual is infected with HIV, he or she does not necessarily have AIDS. Rather, HIV is an infection that can weaken the body's natural ability to fight diseases. Someone who is infected with HIV is called "HIV-positive." A person who is HIV-positive cannot always fight infections that someone with a healthy immune system could resist.[2]

HIV infection progresses in stages. Over time, the body may become more vulnerable to illness, including severe pneumonia, cancer, damage to the nervous system, extreme weight loss, and blindness.

AIDS is the most serious stage of HIV infection. To have AIDS, a person must be HIV-positive *and* meet certain specific medical standards. A patient may also have infections or diseases such as those noted above. If a person is HIV-positive, he or she can generally delay the onset of AIDS with medication.

Despite all the publicity surrounding AIDS, the trends are not encouraging. The number of deaths is growing and HIV infection is spreading throughout the country. Consider a few facts provided by the National Leadership Coalition on AIDS, a not-for-profit corporation that works with the private sector to address AIDS-related workplace issues.

- One in 250 or over 1 million Americans are infected with HIV.
- AIDS strikes adults in their most productive years (ages eighteen to forty-five).
- The total cost associated with the AIDS epidemic in the United States was over $55 billion in 1991.
- By 1993, it is estimated that there will be between 150,000 and 225,000 people living with AIDS.
- HIV infection and AIDS are rising among women, racial and ethnic minorities, and young people.
- AIDS is a leading cause of death among young adults in the United States.

Although significant progress has been made in the medical battle against AIDS, no cure or vaccine is yet available, and thus the epidemic continues to spread. Individuals who have been infected with HIV fall into the following four categories.[3]

1. *Those who have been exposed to the virus but display no physical symptoms*—The AIDS antibody tests are the primary means of identifying members of this group. A positive test result does not mean, however, that an individual has AIDS or will automatically develop AIDS. A positive test result simply means that the person has been infected by the AIDS virus and can transmit it to others.
2. *Those who experience so-called warning symptoms that AIDS may develop*—These symptoms might include swollen lymph nodes, weight loss, abnormal fatigue, night sweats, fever, and diarrhea. This condition is often referred to as AIDS-Related Complex (ARC). Many persons with these symptoms are physically capable of working, while other individuals may be seriously ill, so much so that their job performance can be adversely affected.
3. *Those who have developed opportunistic infections but do not require hospitalization and are physically unable to work*—Opportunistic infections do not normally develop in healthy individuals; instead, they attack those whose immune systems are not functioning properly.[4]
4. *Those who have multiple infections*—This condition is often referred to as full-blown AIDS, and extended hospitalization is often necessary. Those inflicted are so weakened by secondary infections and HIV that they are relatively immobile, and most are unable to continue working.

AIDS-related problems primarily arise in the workplace because many employers are "in a total vacuum on how to deal with AIDS; they are unaware of the potential legal and benefits issues and are simply uninformed about the medical picture—like most Americans," according to the San Francisco AIDS Foundation.[5] Such employer ignorance is like a time bomb waiting to explode. First, having a single employee with AIDS can cause significant increases in health care premiums for employer medical plans. Also, small businesses in particular take significant financial risks if they are self-insured for health care or have their premium determined by their own experience. The latter is particularly true for businesses that pay large premiums for (or do not have) insurance that covers catastrophic illnesses.

Although difficult to quantify, AIDS or the perception that an employee has AIDS can wreak havoc in the workplace. Morale may plummet. Coworkers may refuse to work with an employee. Customers may be frightened away. The extent to which a workplace can be disrupted is only limited by one's imagination.

The Requirements of the ADA

According to a recent Wyatt survey of 536 mid- and large-size U.S. employers, only 36 percent have developed companywide policies for dealing with AIDS. The developing enforcement of the Americans with Disabilities Act may change that. Title I of the ADA, which became effective for most employers on July 26, 1992, may provide the impetus to alter the way most employers respond to individuals with disabilities in general and to AIDS in particular. Businesses not currently covered by the ADA face similar obligations under the fair employment practices laws of most states.

Prior to the passage of the ADA, "handicap"[6] discrimination protection under federal law was provided by the Rehabilitation Act of 1973 and extended only to federal employees, grantees, and contractors. The ADA's protections are far broader and potentially more demanding than those of the Rehabilitation Act.

Before discussing various strategies for managing AIDS in the workplace, a brief review of the interplay of the ADA's employment provisions and AIDS is appropriate. Title I of the ADA,[7] which pertains exclusively to employment, prohibits covered employers from discriminating against a "qualified individual with a disability" in regard to job applications, hiring, advancement, discharge, compensation, training, or other terms, conditions, or privileges of employment. The ADA requires that individuals with disabilities receive employment opportunities equal to those provided to nondisabled employees and job applicants. In addition, as will be discussed below, the ADA mandates that employers *reasonably accommodate* individuals with disabilities who request assistance.

The primary goal of the ADA is to eliminate discrimination against individuals with disabilities. An underlying goal is to increase employ-ment opportunities for individuals with disabilities. Only "qualified" individuals with disabilities are protected. To be qualified, an individual must satisfy the requisite skill, experience, education, and other job-related requirements of a position held or desired and must be able to perform the essential functions of the job with or without reasonable accommodation.

Essential functions are primary tasks critical to the successful performance of a job. An employer does not have to hire or retain individuals whose disabilities prevent them from performing such essential job functions.

The ADA's Application to AIDS

Congress adopted a three-part definition of disability for the ADA from the Rehabilitation Act definition of the term "individual with handicaps." Accordingly, the relevant case law developed under the Rehabilitation Act will generally apply to the term "disability" as used in the ADA. Disabilities covered by the ADA include

- A physical or mental impairment that substantially limits one or more of an individual's major life activities; or
- A record of such an impairment; or
- Treating an individual as having such an impairment.[8]

Section 1630.2(j) of the Interpretive Guidelines for Title I of the ADA expressly provides that "HIV infection" is "inherently substantially limiting," and thus would be covered by the ACT.[9] It stands to reason that, if HIV infection is covered under the first prong of the definition of disability, an infected individual would certainly have a record of the impairment under the second prong of the definition, because according to current medical literature, an individual has HIV infection for life.

Moreover, the third prong of the definition would protect an individual who is HIV-negative if such individual were perceived or regarded by others as having AIDS. As set forth in Section 1630.2(1) of the Interpretive Guidelines:

The rationale for the "regarded as" part of the definition of disability was articulated by the Supreme Court in the context of the Rehabilitation Act of 1973 in *School Board of Nassau County v. Arline*, 480 U.S. 273 (1987). The Court noted that, although an individual may have an impairment that does not in fact substantially limit a major life activity, the reaction of others may prove just as disabling.

Section 1630.2(1) further provides an instructive discussion of the "regarded as" analysis by using HIV as an example:

> An individual satisfies the third part of the "regarded as" definition of "disability" if the employer or other covered entity erroneously believes the individual has a substantially limiting impairment that the individual actually does not have. This situation could occur, for example, if an employer discharged an employee in response to a rumor that the employee is infected with Human Immunodeficiency Virus (HIV). Even though the rumor is totally unfounded and the individual has no impairment at all, the individual is considered an individual with a disability because the employer perceived of this individual as being disabled.

Even though an individual may not satisfy any of the above prongs of the disability definition, he or she may still be covered by the ADA. Section 1630.8 of the regulations provides that

> It is unlawful for a covered entity to exclude or deny equal jobs or benefits to, or otherwise discriminate against, a qualified individual because of the known disability of an individual with whom the qualified individual is known to have a family, business, social or other relationship or association.

Section 1630.8 of the Interpretive Guidelines expressly extends such coverage to persons with AIDS: "This provision would prohibit an employer from discharging an employee because the employee does volunteer work with people who have AIDS, and the employer feels that the employee may contract the disease."

Employer Defenses under the ADA

An employer's defenses to an allegation that it has discriminated against an individual who is HIV-positive or who has AIDS are (1) that the individual is unable to perform the essential functions of the job, with or without an accommodation; (2) that he or she cannot reasonably be accommodated; or (3) that he or she represents a *direct threat* to the health or safety of himself or herself or others.

The first defense turns on the issue of whether the individual is "qualified" to do the job. If an individual with a disability cannot satisfy the job's prerequisites or is unable to perform the essential functions of a job, with or without reasonable accommodation, that person is not considered to be qualified and thus is not protected by the ADA. Accordingly, if an individual who is HIV-positive or who has AIDS does not satisfy the position's eligibility requirements or is unable to perform one or more of the essential job functions, with or without a reasonable accommodation, that individual would be unqualified for the position and would not be covered.

Moreover, if a needed accommodation would cause an employer an "undue hardship" (i.e., "significant difficulty or expense"), the employer would be relieved of the duty to provide an accommodation. An employer would typically attempt to demonstrate undue hardship by establishing that the available accommodations would either be excessively expensive or unduly disruptive to operations.

For example, a sales manager with AIDS may be responsible for visiting each of his twenty-five salespersons each month so that he may accompany them on their calls and monitor their performance. Thus, making personal visits would represent an essential function of his job. Assume because of his weakened condition that the sales manager is unable to travel and therefore is not able to perform an essential function of his job. His employer should explore whether the sales manager could be accommodated so that he would be able to satisfy this essential function. After engaging in a reasonable accommodation discussion with the sales manager, the employer may conclude that it would be impossible for the sales manager to monitor the performance of his subordinates without personally supervising their work at least once a month and, thus, conclude that the individual is not capable of fulfilling the requirements of his job. It would represent an undue hardship on the employer to eliminate the need of the sales manager to personally accompany his sales people once a month.

The "direct threat" defense reaffirms an employer's right to deny a position to an individual with a disability if he or she would pose "a significant risk of substantial harm to the health or safety of [himself or herself] or others that cannot be eliminated or reduced by reasonable accommodation."[10] An employer's determination that an individual represents a direct threat must be based on a *personalized assessment* of the person's present ability to safely perform the essential job functions. This assessment must be based on reasonable medical judgment that relies on the most current medical knowledge and/or on the best available objective evidence.

The direct threat defense is difficult to apply. A showing of a "significant risk of substantial harm" must be based on an assessment of the *particular* individual and the *specific nature* of the job to be performed. Because experts agree that AIDS is not readily transmittable in most workplace settings, it will be very difficult for an employer to successfully argue that an individual with AIDS poses a direct threat to the health or safety of others, particularly as the employer would be under a duty to attempt to reasonably accommodate the person to *reduce* or *eliminate* the risk.

The bottom line is an individual just can't "catch" AIDS like a cold or the flu. Rather, medical experts agree that people are at risk of becoming infected if they have sexual intercourse or oral-genital contact without protection with an infected person, use any unsterile drug injec-

tion device that may have been used by an infected person, or use unsterile needles in other situations, such as tattooing or ear piercing. Because one cannot contract the AIDS virus through typical workplace activities, it will be very difficult for employers to successfully use the direct threat defense as the basis for taking a negative employment action against an infected individual.

Finally, an employer's concern about the reaction of customers and/or coworkers to the disclosure that an individual has AIDS does not provide employers with a lawful basis on which to take a negative employment action.[11]

Reasonable Accommodations

Perhaps the most challenging aspect of managing AIDS or HIV-related physical problems under the ADA will be dealing with and implementing accommodations for affected individuals. The ADA provides that an employer must make reasonable accommodations for the known limitations of a qualified individual with a disability *unless* the employer can show that the accommodation would pose an "undue hardship" on its operations. The terms "reasonable accommodation" and "undue hardship" are intended to be linked—i.e., reasonable accommodation *will not* be required if it imposes an undue hardship on the employer.

Under the Rehabilitation Act, the meaning of reasonable accommodation depended on the specific individual, the specific nature of the disability, and the specific job. The ADA, however, is more precise and expressly defines a reasonable accommodation as certain possible actions that an employer may take to accommodate a qualified individual with a disability. Section 1630.2(o) of the regulations provides that the term "reasonable accommodation" refers to

- Modifications or adjustments to a job application process to enable a qualified applicant with a disability to be considered for the position he or she desires; or

- Modifications or adjustments to the work environment or the manner of circumstances under which the position held or desired is customarily performed to enable a qualified individual with a disability to perform the essential job functions; or
- Modifications of adjustments that enable the employee with a disability to enjoy equal benefits and privileges of employment as are enjoyed by the employer's other similarly situated employees without disabilities.

The appropriate reasonable accommodation should be determined on a case-by-case basis and "is best determined through a flexible, interactive process that involves both the employer and the qualified individual with a disability." In cases where there are two possible accommodations, the employer may choose the one that is less expensive or easier to implement so long as it gives the individual a meaningful employment opportunity.

The Job Accommodation Network (JAN), an information and consulting service providing individualized accommodation solutions, states that the typical accommodations for individuals with AIDS fall into four general categories. First, employers purchase computer equipment to enable individuals to work at home. Second, individuals are provided with flexible hours that enable them to perform the essential functions of their jobs. Third, they are transferred to positions that are either less physically demanding or provide them with better hours of work. Fourth, they are provided with the assistance of coworkers to help them to perform their jobs.

The steps taken by Digital Equipment Corporation to accommodate Frank, the sales representative profiled in the *Business Week* article discussed earlier, are instructive on how to accommodate an individual with AIDS. Frank's manager initially asked DEC's Human Resources Department to help her create a new job for Frank:

Even that wasn't easy. "We came up with some suggestions that Frank didn't like," Jean says, not-

ing several options that included lots of sales work on the phone. Reports Frank: "They didn't take advantage of the skills I have. I have been working here 18 years. Calling up people on the telephone, I felt like they were saying, 'O.K., let's put him in a corner over there!'" In the end, Frank wound up in a newly created position, which played to his technical strengths while limiting his visits to clients. The job required Frank to draw up computer-system configurations, perform sales quotations, as well as do paperwork that bogs down other sales representatives.

Thus, a rule of thumb when exploring accommodations for individuals with AIDS is to look for ways to maximize their strength while at the same time maintaining their dignity. . . .

PRACTICAL POINTERS

Despite the problems associated with a misinformed or uninformed workforce, most employers have yet to aggressively address AIDS issues. Indeed, as noted in the February 1 issue of *Business Week,* many corporate officials responded to questions about their respective companies' AIDS policies as follows: "We don't discriminate in any way. We treat HIV-positive employees in the same manner as victims of other terminal illnesses."[13]

This generally means that a company will provide its HIV-positive employees with a full range of medical benefits, will respect their privacy, will not isolate them, and will tailor their workloads to accommodate the restrictions imposed on them by their illness. If the individual becomes too ill to work, long-term disability assistance may be available. However, although this may be recognized as a great start, the article points out that AIDS should be treated differently from other diseases:

Because it is both deadly and transmittable (though not through casual contact), fear about catching HIV can run rampant. The virus' association with homosexuals and drug users can inspire scorn and prejudice other diseases don't. "No matter how sophisticated or educated you are, AIDS can trigger irrational things in people." . . . "There is big potential for disruption." . . . "It could close a plant down."[14]

Thus, although general workplace environments pose virtually no risk for the transmission of HIV, there are a number of measures that can be taken to minimize the risks and to reassure the workforce. The following guidelines apply to the *general* workplace, not settings identified as "high risk" by the Centers for Disease Control and Prevention (e.g., health care facilities, correctional institutions, long-term care facilities, drug treatment centers, and homeless centers).

1. Assign Responsibility   Each employer should identify someone in the company to be responsible for developing an AIDS policy and education program. In larger companies, the responsible individual may even chair a committee that should include representatives from human resources, as well as medical, safety, labor relations, union officials, and any other key individuals who interact with the workforce. Committee members should have access to up-to-date medical, social, and legal information about AIDS. To obtain this knowledge, consultation with local health officials, legal counsel, and outside resources is strongly recommended. The committee should evaluate AIDS' potential impact on the company and suggest changes to top management.

2. Ensure High-Level Support   The highest level of management and union leadership should actively support appropriate education programs about HIV and offer these programs to all employees. Providing the workforce with sound information that has the imprimatur of top management is essential to overcoming employee anxiety and emphasizing that all employees are expected to work toward achieving their company's goals.

3. Review the Company Benefits Package   Management should review the catastrophic ill-

nesses covered by its employee health insurance program to determine if the coverage meets management's goals and objectives. Any reductions or limitations should have a sound actuarial basis and should be reviewed with counsel before implementation.[15] Indeed, there is growing confusion concerning the ADA's impact on employee benefit plans. Section 1630.5 of the Interpretive Guidelines states that limitations on coverage for certain procedures/treatments are lawful as long as they are uniformly applied to all insured individuals, regardless of disability, and as long as an individual with a disability is not denied coverage for other procedures.

Despite EEOC assurances to the contrary, employers are perplexed over their liability under the ADA if they restrict coverage for certain procedures or treatments or limit reimbursements under the company's health insurance plans. Their anxiety results from a potentially conflicting provision in the Interpretive Guidelines. Section 1630.16(f) of the guidelines forbids benefit changes that are a "subterfuge" to avoid ADA obligations. Unfortunately, neither the regulations nor the guidelines provide examples of circumstances that would constitute a subterfuge, and it is difficult to say with certainty to what extent employer changes to health insurance plans—and the timing of those changes—will be challenged successfully as being subterfuges for noncompliance with the ADA.

To minimize the likelihood of being charged with discrimination when modifying insurance plans, employers should ensure that any changes are in accordance with accepted principles of risk assessment and/or risk classification. They also should take great pains to thoroughly communicate the basis for such changes to their employees in easy-to-understand language.

4. Understand Legal Responsibilities   An employer's responsibilities extend to employees with and without AIDS. Those with AIDS are protected against discrimination under federal, state, and local statutes, while employees without AIDS have the right to a safe workplace. Therefore, adverse employment decisions about employees with AIDS should be made only if they are unable to perform the essential functions of the job with or without a reasonable accommodation and/or represent a direct threat to the health or safety of themselves or others.

5. Develop an AIDS Policy A written AIDS policy should present factual information that explains the employer's commitment to adhere to and enforce its obligations under the ADA and other laws and to ensure that such protections are extended to employees who are HIV-positive. To guard against discrimination, employers should ensure that the following points are covered in their AIDS policy:

- Discrimination or harassment will not be tolerated.
- The company will attempt to reasonably accommodate employees.
- Medical information will remain confidential, and all policies, including sick leave and other benefits, will be applied uniformly.
- HIV-positive employees should be allowed to continue working as long as they can safely and effectively perform the essential functions of their jobs.
- HIV-positive employees who demonstrate no clinical symptoms will be treated in the same manner as other employees, and those who demonstrate clinical symptoms will be treated in the same manner as employees who suffer from other illnesses of comparable severity.
- There is no medical basis for employees to refuse to work with fellow employees or customers who are HIV-positive.
- The concerns of employees or customers who fear HIV-positive coworkers and customers should be taken seriously and should be addressed with appropriate information and counseling. Where such measures are unsuccessful, management should take appropriate corrective or disciplinary action against an employee who threatens or actually refuses to work with HIV-positive employees or customers. Under no circumstances should action be taken against the HIV-positive employee because of the attitude or actions of other employees.
- All supervisors and employees are expected to implement the employer's goals.

In conjunction with developing a written AIDS policy, employers should take the following steps:

- Create a system for job applicants and employees to file complaints internally, rather than filing them with a government agency or in court, if they feel they have been discriminated against on the basis of their disability. This might be similar to the mechanism created to handle the company's sexual harassment complaints. If applicable, existing Employee Assistance Programs may be used to work with persons with AIDS-related problems.
- Review existing policies that provide that formerly injured or ill employees can only return to work if they are certified 100 percent fit to do so. Reasonable accommodation obligations under the ADA and state law require that employers consider accommodating employees who may not be able to completely assume their former duties.[16]
- Evaluate policies regarding transfers and reassignments to ensure they are uniformly administered and do not contravene the ADA or state law. For example, an employer may lawfully reassign an individual with a disability to a lower-graded position if there are no accommodations that would enable him or her to remain in the current position and there are no vacant equivalent positions for which such employee is qualified, with or without reasonable accommodation. Furthermore, an employer is not required to maintain the individual's salary at that of the higher-graded

position if it does not maintain the salaries of reassigned employees who are not disabled.

- Handle the information that an applicant or an employee is HIV-positive or has AIDS with extreme caution, because unwarranted disclosure could result in potential liability for invasion of privacy or for violation of federal and state laws regulating disclosure of medical information.[17]

6. Reconsider and Revise Personnel Policies
Among the policies employers should address are

- *Attendance*—Draft neutral policies concerning absenteeism and lateness and ensure they are distributed to all employees, understood, and consistently enforced. An employee with AIDS may be disciplined if his or her violation (e.g., repeated absences or lateness) exceeds the employer's attempts at reasonable accommodation (e.g., flextime, unpaid leave, job restructuring, transfer). In addition, an employee who violates a neutral policy may be disciplined even if the reason for the violation was excessive absenteeism to care for his or her disabled spouse.
- *Leave of absence*—Employers should review their leave-of-absence policies, particularly with respect to leaves *with pay*. Employees with disabilities are not entitled to more paid leave time than nondisabled employees. Employers may wish to provide employees with disabilities with more leave *without pay* to accommodate them but are *not* required to pay them for such additional time.

  Further, uniformly applied leave policies do not violate the ADA simply because they do not address the special needs of every individual with a disability. If reductions in paid leave or sick leave or other modifications are made to such policies and plans for legitimate, nondiscriminatory reasons (e.g., to reduce costs, control abuse, etc.), such reductions are probably lawful. Similarly, employers may

limit dependent coverage so long as it is not done to discriminate against the disabled dependents of otherwise nondisabled individuals. Remember, in addition to protecting qualified individuals with disabilities, the ADA also protects individuals who are related to or associated with individuals with known disabilities.

- *Work schedules*—Consider developing part-time or modified work schedules to help accommodate *all* employees, not only those with disabilities. Such schedules are often inexpensive and can serve as a valuable recruitment tool.
- *Interview and discipline forms*—Prepare objective interview and discipline forms. The forms should indicate why one applicant was chosen over another applicant and why an individual was disciplined or demoted. Such contemporaneously prepared forms provide a nondiscriminatory record should an individual bring a claim alleging discrimination based on disability—or on some other protected basis such as age, race, sex, national origin, age, marital status, or veteran status.

7. Train Personnel Identify key personnel to become familiar with and knowledgeable about AIDS. This could include human resources staff, interviewers, supervisors, labor relations staff, union representatives, and others who have a "need to know." Local health officials and other external representatives (see resource list below) are often available to provide education programs or train in-house personnel. Presentations made jointly by external representatives and in-house employees are preferable to presentations done exclusively by external or in-house personnel.

8. Educate Employees Employees at all levels must be sensitive to working with people with disabilities, including AIDS. It can be a very disconcerting experience for someone interacting with an individual with AIDS for the first time. In order to promote compliance with the ADA and to avoid singling out employees who are HIV-positive, a single program could be developed to cover *all* disabilities. Such training may help to create productive internal partnerships and minimize workplace disruptions and costly litigation.

An additional goal may be to create an atmosphere that encourages HIV-positive employees to disclose their illnesses, thereby better enabling companies to address the issues head-on. Ignorance and secrecy are often identified as being the most disruptive factors when it comes to AIDS in the workplace:

> As soon as someone shows signs of illness or starts to miss work, rumor-mongering among co-workers can fan irrational responses. Managers, meantime, have no context within which to evaluate a sick employee's lagging performance. The result can be bitterness, frustration, and fear all around. The person with AIDS—afraid of losing health benefits, being harassed, or even being fired—may put off disclosing the illness as long as possible. That only compounds management's problem.[18]

An employee education program can take many forms and can include videos, seminars, and literature. The goal is to dispel myths, present the company's policy, and discuss ways to prevent the spread of the disease.

Part of the company's strategy should be to develop a "blueprint" for introducing the topic and then advancing it over a specific period of time. A regular communication vehicle, such as the company newsletter or bulletin board, can be used to familiarize employees with the AIDS issue.

Part of the training for employees should be to emphasize that AIDS *is not transmitted by casual contact,* particularly the type of contact that occurs in the vast majority of workplaces. Training should inform employees about the disease and answer their questions but should not provide a forum for publicly castigating individuals who may offer a contrary point of view.

Training might best be done in small groups. Employees might be asked to submit their questions to the group leader who would then discuss the issues with the entire audience. An AIDS question box or "hotline" could be established to which employees could direct questions to be addressed in the company newsletter. By permitting employees to submit anonymous questions, the company will avoid directly linking employees to specific questions and thereby will create a more open environment.

9. Keep Employees Informed Because information and statistics about AIDS change quickly and regularly, the company should stay abreast of new developments and disseminate up-to-date information as it becomes available. Continual education and reenforcement is the best weapon for combating employee fears about AIDS.

10. Evaluate the Program The program should be evaluated for its overall effectiveness. This process should begin by asking whether the task force members have sufficient knowledge about all aspects of the disease and its ramifications. Managers' and supervisors' understanding of their employees' concerns, as well as the importance of confidentiality, should be carefully assessed. In addition, the evaluation should examine whether the workforce understands important facts and myths about AIDS and related company policies.

11. Document Accommodation Efforts Always document the company's efforts to reasonably accommodate applicants and employees with disabilities, including AIDS. Such a paper trail is valuable in the event legal action is commenced. Consider developing a "reasonable accommodation worksheet" to ensure that uniform and consistent efforts are made to accommodate individuals with AIDS. Incorporate an internal procedure so that all documents are reviewed carefully to ensure that each document is nondiscriminatory and records the employer's reasonable accommodation efforts.

12. Take Stock of Resources Evaluate resources in both the public and private sectors that can be contacted for guidance. Develop contacts now to avoid chaos later. Ensure that contacts are available at all company locations and ascertain if the consultants/resources will be available to testify if litigation arises. Consider the following resources:[19]

- *The Centers for Disease Control's National AIDS Hotline*—The CDC offers twenty-four-hour service seven days a week to respond to any questions about HIV infection and AIDS (800-342-AIDS).
- *State and local health departments*—The National AIDS Hotline can tell you how to reach your state or local health department. You can also find the number listed under "Health Department" in the local and state government section of your telephone book.
- *Community organizations*—Thousands of local organizations, such as the March of Dimes, National Urban League, American Red Cross, and Boys Clubs and Girls Clubs, are working to stop the spread of HIV infection. Look for them in the telephone book or call your local health department.
- *Schools*—Talk to your local school board, superintendent, principal, teachers, or guidance counselors to find out about the HIV and AIDS education programs offered and how you can help to make them work.
- *Equal Employment Opportunity Commission*—The EEOC provides copies of its Technical Assistance Manual, Resource Directory, and other ADA informational materials (800-669-EEOC).
- *National AIDS Clearing House*—This organization provides information and materials for employers on national, state, and local resources related to HIV/AIDS in the workplace. Its reference specialists can assist employers in identifying appropriate materials, resources, and programs for its employees. A variety of educational materials (e.g., posters, brochures, guidelines, and videos) are available. The Clearing House also offers information on other organizations that can present workplace programs in local communities (800-458-5231).
- *National Leadership Coalition on AIDS*—This group focuses on the impact of AIDS on the business and labor communities. It is a membership organization serving business, labor, and volunteer groups in establishing sound policies, ongoing education, and civic support and leadership (202-429-0930).

CONCLUSION

Managing AIDS in the workplace requires a significant and ongoing commitment, particularly for small companies. Furthermore, efforts to restructure jobs, educate employees, and provide benefits can be difficult whether small or large companies are involved. AIDS is also extremely expensive, despite estimates by the Centers for Disease Control that it is no more costly than other terminal illnesses that are also insured against. However, the difference between AIDS and many other terminal illnesses is that AIDS is preventable through education, which is affordable.

Unfortunately, most companies seem inclined to roll the dice and take their chances that AIDS will not affect them. Now is the time for employers to step up their efforts to implement an AIDS policy and education program or risk the costly and disruptive consequences of their inaction.

NOTES

1. "Managing AIDS," *Business Week,* February 1, 1993, pp. 48, 51.
2. For purposes of simplicity, we will refer to AIDS throughout this article and will only refer to HIV when that specific condition is at issue.

3. Leonard, Arthur, "Employment Discrimination Against Persons with AIDS," 10 *U. Dayton L. Rev.* 681 (1985).

4. Opportunistic infections include pneumocystic carinii pneumonia (PCP) and Kaposi's sarcoma (KS), a rare form of cancer. In or about 1981, the medical community discovered the highly unusual occurrence of PCP and KS in several dozen individuals. These infections, which occur only in immunodeficient individuals, focused medical attention on the condition now known as AIDS.

5. Franklin, McClure, Gresham, Fontenot, "AIDS in the Workplace," *Journal of Small Business Management,* April 1992, vol. 30, p. 61.

6. The term "handicapped" derived from the English phrase "cap in hand" and was a negative reference to beggars. The current term of choice when dealing with disabled applicants and employees is "individual with a disability."

7. In addition to Title I, the ADA contains four other Titles: Public Services (II); Public Accommodations, Commercial Facilities, and Private Transportation (III); Telecommunications (IV); and Miscellaneous Provisions (V).

8. See 42 USC §12102(2); Interpretive Guidelines §1630.2(g).

9. See also, EEOC Technical Assistance Manual §2.1(a)(iii) (1992), which reiterates that HIV infection and AIDS "are by their nature substantially limiting."

10. Regulations §1630.2(r).

11. Interpretive Guidelines §1630.2(r); see also EEOC Technical Assistance Manual, §4.5 (1992) for a discussion regarding the "very specific and stringent requirements" an employer must satisfy under the ADA to establish the existence of a direct threat.

12. . . .

13. "Managing AIDS," *Business Week,* February 1, 1993, p. 53.

14. Id.

15. In *McGann v. H&H Music Company,* 946 F.2d 401 (5th Cir. 1991), cert. defined, 61 U.S.L.W. 3355 (Nov. 9, 1992), the Supreme Court declined to review an unsuccessful challenge brought by an AIDS-afflicted employee under the Employee Retirement Income Security Act of 1974 after the employer unilaterally reduced its medical benefits for AIDS treatment from $1,000,000 to $5,000. A case with similar facts brought under the ADA might have a different result.

16. The absence of an AIDS policy—or at least the company's failure to adhere to a policy—might have led to a recent lawsuit brought in U.S. District Court for the Eastern District of Pennsylvania. In *Doe v. Mercy Health Corp. of Southeastern Pennsylvania,* D.C. E.D. Pa., No. 92-6711, 11/23/92, a hospital allegedly failed to offer reasonable accommodation to an HIV-infected physician after its board of directors rejected a unanimous recommendation of its own medical review board to reinstate the physician to full privileges without restrictions.

17. The ADA sets forth stringent requirements for maintaining the confidentiality of medical records. See Interpretive Guidelines §1630.14(b); EEOC Technical Assistance Manual §6.5 (1992). Also, when developing this policy, be advised that in several states there are very strict limitations on the disclosure of AIDS testing.

18. "Managing AIDS," *Business Week,* February 1, 1993, p. 54.

19. See also EEOC Resource Directory (1992).

READING 4-3

Ethical Challenges of HIV Infection in the Workplace

Arthur S. Leonard

INTRODUCTION

Infection with the Human Immunodeficiency Virus (HIV) associated with Acquired Immune Deficiency Syndrome (AIDS)[1] poses significant ethical challenges for employers and employees

Source: Excerpted from *Notre Dame Journal of Law, Ethics & Public Policy, 5* (1990), 53–73. Used with permission.

in America's workplaces. As new medications make it physically possible for persons infected by HIV to participate in normal workplace activities for longer periods of time in greater numbers,[2] and as more workers respond to the urgings of public health officials to be tested and submit to prophylactic treatment to prevent the development of physical symptoms,[3] many more known HIV-infected persons[4] than heretofore will be asserting their legal rights to continue working. Employment of persons with life-threatening medical conditions will predictably have a significant impact on workplaces, affecting morale and productivity, as well as imposing direct financial burdens both due to claims on employee benefit systems and to necessary accommodations for impaired persons.[5] Employers will have to make decisions that respond to these impacts.

While the issue of legal workplace rights of HIV-infected persons is by no means finally settled,[6] there is an emerging trend in administrative, judicial and legislative forums toward protection of HIV-infected persons from unjustified employment discrimination.[7] However, the slow pace of administrative and judicial processes, the emphasis on monetary settlements of claims by administrative agencies, and the reluctance of HIV-infected people to expose themselves to publicity and stress by asserting their legal rights, combine to make it possible for many employers to eliminate known HIV-infected persons from their workplaces if they are willing to bear the costs involved.[8] Thus, an ethical dilemma is posed for employers, who must decide whether to take the possibly unlawful but practical course of termination of employment or forced exclusion from the workplace, or to retain the employee, with the attendant problems that retention will entail, and if the employee is retained, the employer must further decide how to proceed to accommodate the employee.[9]

Neither is the issue of workplace confidentiality settled. While some states have legislated specific confidentiality requirements regarding

information about HIV infection to supplement existing provisions in some jurisdictions which generally protect the confidentiality of medical records[10] and some courts have held that government agencies will be constitutionally liable for damages for unjustified disclosure of such information,[11] many persons injured by breaches of confidentiality may decide not to assert claims, and monetary damages will not in most instances suffice to repair the emotional and reputational damage imposed by such breaches. The employer may imagine conflicting imperatives with regard to confidentiality, including concerns about protecting co-workers and customers from danger (whether real or perceived). The infected employee may even present a different confidentiality issue: by not desiring confidentiality, the employee may create circumstances which prove disruptive of normal workplace routine. Thus, both employers and employees face serious ethical issues about confidentiality.

Costs of employee benefits constitute one of the most significant workplace expenses associated with HIV infection. Drugs now in common use for prophylaxis against development of symptoms are expensive, and hospitalization for serious opportunistic infections is also quite expensive. Most employees rely on job-based group health programs to pay for their health care expenses. HIV-infected persons encounter great difficulty obtaining individual insurance coverage outside of employment-based groups. Existing gaps in federal and state law may make it possible for employers to avoid major costs of covering HIV-related illness while inflicting considerable injury on their affected employees, including a shortened lifespan of inferior quality when lack of insurance coverage results in denial of access to acceptable health care. Once again, the employer is faced with an ethical dilemma, balancing economic and human issues.

In this article, I propose to discuss these ethical issues using principles described by medical ethicists Carol Levine and Ronald Bayer in their analysis of HIV screen policies.[12] They identify four "widely accepted ethical principles . . . derived from secular, religious, and constitutional traditions" which are "commonly applied to medicine, research, and public health":[13]

1. the principle of respect for persons (an autonomy principle);
2. the harm principle (acknowledging that limits may be placed on individual rights when others will be harmed by the exercise of those rights);
3. the beneficence principle (the requirements that individuals act on behalf of the interests and welfare of others, taking into account a realistic risk/benefit analysis); and
4. the justice principle (requiring equitable distribution of benefits and burdens and forbidding invidious discrimination).[14]

These principles may come into conflict in considering each of the ethical dilemmas posed above. The justice principle may present the most difficulties, since the negative impact, both psychological and economic, of employing a person with HIV-infection in a society which has refused to take collective responsibility for health care costs may be considerable. I will suggest how I would resolve these conflicts in proposing an ethical solution of the challenges of HIV infection in the workplace.

I begin with the premise that ethical obligations of individuals and businesses exist independently from minimal legal requirements, but that such requirements are a starting point for analyzing the appropriate response to HIV-related problems, since they are one representation of society's consensus regarding minimally acceptable conduct. Serious inefficiencies in civil rights enforcement enhance the ethical dilemmas, since employers may coldly calculate that violation of the law is justified by cost/benefit analysis. A conscious decision to violate the law based on cost/benefit analysis (rather than, for example, on a sincerely held belief that a law is unconstitutional or otherwise invalid or inap-

plicable) does not constitute ethical conduct. I will also make some arguments about the ethical obligations of society, transcending those of individual employers or employees.

★ ★ ★

II. ETHICAL ISSUES

The ethical issues raised by the HIV epidemic and the realities of existing workplace law can be dealt with at several levels. I will first discuss the ethical issues for individual employers, and then briefly consider the broader ethical issues facing society.

Employers confronting the reality or perception of HIV infection can select from an array of responses. The ideal response from the point of view of a person infected with HIV would be for the employer to undertake an objective evaluation of the individual's ability to work, taking into account a realistic assessment of the risk of infection to others; to base employment decisions upon the results of such evaluation, taking into account the expressed desires of the affected employee, without regard to the possible reactions of managers and supervisors, co-workers, customers or members of the public or to costs which might be incurred as a result of employing an HIV-infected person. This response would exclude a commitment to maintain confidentiality to the extent requested by the employee and consistent with the company's actual needs, a commitment to maintain full employee benefits to the extent consistent with the continued economic viability of the business, and appropriate workplace educational programs to deal with employee fears. This approach would constitute a plausible means of compliance with existing handicap discrimination law and ERISA principles applicable to most workplaces.

The employer might widen the range of consideration, taking greater account of reactions of others or financial implications. One would be surprised to find an employer making such decisions without considering the wider impact, because an employer has responsibilities to a variety of constituencies. Part of that impact will be psychological: the effect on the workplace of having an employee whose physical and mental condition may deteriorate alarmingly if available medications prove unable to contain the impairing effects of opportunistic infections, and the impact on co-workers, clients or customers, or other members of the public of knowing that an HIV-infected person will be dealing with them, should such information become known.[64] Such an evaluation would require a realistic assessment of the current level of knowledge in the workplace and the community, and the ability and willingness of the employer to commit resources to increase that level of knowledge. Such an evaluation might also consider the possibility of accommodating the special needs of an HIV-infected person, and how the employer's handling of such issues as confidentiality and employee benefits administration might affect the reactions of others.

Having considered these factors, how might an ethical employer proceed?

One response would be to determine the employer's legal obligations in the situation and to proceed strictly in accordance with those obligations, doing no more and no less than the employer's legal counsel advises is required, but the equation of ethical behavior with mere obedience of the law is unsatisfactory in this context, for the law provides at best a floor of minimally acceptable behavior. Furthermore, strict compliance without a more affirmative response is likely to have a negative effect on the employer's business, since some of the negative impact of AIDS on the atmosphere and productivity of a workplace can be avoided through a more active, positive response.

An ethical employer will be concerned with respecting the autonomy of the individual and with preventing harm to the individual and others with whom the individual will come into contact in the workplace. This requires a realistic assessment of workplace transmission risk as well as workplace risk of exposures for the HIV-infected employee with a weakened immune system, especially in a health care institution (where the employee's job could require exposure to contagious conditions) or a manufacturing job with heightened exposure to toxic substances. There may seem to be a significant clash between the principle of respect for persons and the principle of beneficence, as the former would dictate letting the HIV-infected employee decide whether to expose himself to work-place risks, given full knowledge of those risks, while the latter might justify a more paternalistic approach of the employer deciding to "do what is right" for the HIV-infected employee against the employee's wishes. An employer desiring to pursue the paternalistic course would have a duty to base such a course on knowledge rather than speculation. The ethical employer will want to surmount negative or fearful emotional reactions in accordance with the beneficence principle, which would require a rational response based on a careful weighing of benefits and risks. Finally, an ethical employer will seek a fair distribution of benefits and burdens in line with the justice principle.

How might this play out in a workplace where an ethical approach is affirmatively sought? First, the employer would resolve to make decisions which will not exacerbate the problems the HIV-infected individual confronts, to the extent this can be done without endangering the viability of the business. Second, the employer would resolve to involve the HIV-infected person in the decisionmaking process to the extent this is feasible, since the principle of respect for persons requires that individuals be accorded the right to participate in determinations about their status and opportunities. Effectuating the harm and beneficence principles, the employer would undertake appropriate educational programs in the workplace about HIV infection, employee benefits and personnel policies, so that employees will know their rights and obligations and make decisions in light of such information.[65] Respect for individual autonomy would require the employer to safe-guard the confidentiality of HIV-related information, restricting knowledge about an employee's HIV status consistent with the employee's wishes, except to the extent that such knowledge is necessary for others to do their jobs properly. (For example, the reasonable accommodation requirements of disability discrimination law may not be implemented effectively if a supervisor does not know about the need to accommodate and the reasons for it.) The justice principle will require the ethical employer to undertake a realistic assessment of the costs dictated by the other principles, and to attempt a fair allocation of costs.

The justice principle poses difficult issues. How much expense may an employer fairly be expected to assume to accommodate an HIV-infected employee? The concept of reasonable accommodation found in most handicap discrimination laws has not received extensive caselaw development. In the *Arline* case, the Supreme Court commented that accommodation responsibilities do not include changes in the basic function or mission of the operation, or even job redesign or transfers not normally available under the employer's personnel policies.[66] Regulations suggest that the accommodation duty will vary depending upon the size and scope of the employer's operation.[67] But beyond what the law may require, which may really be quite minimal, what is the right thing for an employer to do? Incurring a major expense to accommodate an employee with symptomatic HIV infection may present undue financial hardship to a small employer, but for many employers the real expenses of accommodation may, upon sober consideration, be over-balanced by the continued productive participation of an individual in whom the employer has a significant training investment. The accommodation requirements under existing disability laws seems to strike an appropriate balance between the beneficence principle, respect for persons, and the justice principle, by recognizing that people with disabilities should be integrated into the workforce,

but only to the extent that is consistent with the legitimate interests of employers and fellow employees in the practical ability to get the job done, safety concerns, and the economic health of the business.

Ethical questions are more starkly drawn in the current economic climate surrounding employee benefits. Premiums for health insurance have been escalating, and conversion to self-insurance will undoubtedly grow as a cost saving measure. Such conversions may provide an escape route from state insurance regulations forbidding caps or benefit limits for particular diseases, but an ethical employer will surely resist the temptation to take advantage of this opportunity to discriminate against HIV-infected employees. Health benefit expenses related to HIV infection are not necessarily greater than those related to other life-threatening illnesses normally covered without question by health plans, so singling out HIV infection but not other conditions for exclusions or caps does not have an objective justification.

Those employers who have justified HIV exclusions as a "self-inflicted problem" because of its association with IV drug use or promiscuous sexual behavior[68] are displaying ignorance about the spectrum of behaviors in which viral transmission may take place, or the state of knowledge of individuals at the time of their infection. It seems likely, given the long period which may elapse between infection and symptoms, that the overwhelming majority of HIV-infected employees became infected when the danger of HIV was unknown to them an information about safer sex practices was unavailable. Also, some portion of HIV-infected employees will have acquired their infection through other behaviors, such as use of tainted medications or receipt of tainted blood transfusions. Even if one were to grant employers the right to allocate health care benefits based on their normative evaluation of the conduct which led to infection, one would question why HIV-related claims should be excluded while illnesses arising from other behaviors, such as smoking, drinking, or poor dietary habits, were not similarly treated. Exclusion of some "lifestyle" claims but not others seems based arbitrarily on employer dislike or disapproval of the people involved, and violates the justice principle by discriminating in compensation, since some employees would be covered for their "lifestyle" illnesses and others would not, regardless of their contribution to workplace productivity.

HIV infection raises ethical issues beyond the individual workplace. The epidemic, together with the phenomenon of rising health insurance premium rates, refusals by insurance companies to sell group policies to employers in particular industries, and the significant number of Americans who are individually considered uninsurable, raises ethical problems for our whole society. Is it consistent with the principles of beneficence and justice for our nation, alone among the great Western democracies, to relegate a large portion of our population to the inferior quality of health care available to the uninsurable? Is it consistent with the principle of respect for persons to tolerate a system in which access to health care turns on the decisions of individual employers about how to allocate their assets, or in which access to health care for uninsurable persons may require them to deplete their assets to qualify for public assistance programs which carry stigmatizing connotations?

The substitution of a system which cuts health care access free from any workplace tie would seem a more appropriate approach for a society which embraces an equitable distribution of benefits and burdens as suggested by the justice principle. Halfway proposals to supplement or perpetuate the current employment-based system do not achieve this equitable distribution, since they still leave a significant portion of the burden on individual employers. A full discussion of the arguments for and against a national health insurance program are beyond the scope of this article, but it is certainly relevant to note that a substantial portion of the ethical issues raised by HIV and the workplace just does not occur in other countries which have chosen to deal with access to health care as primarily a public sector concern.

Another ethical issue for society is raised by our employment at will system, under which employers have no obligation to maintain the employment relationship with employees who are unable to work due to illness or other long-term disabilities. Disability laws only provide protection for those who are able to work. So long as quality health care access is closely tied to employment status, a system which affords no protection to that status once an employee is too disabled to perform falls down on the obligation of beneficence. Without contending that employers should be required to continue compensating employees who can no longer work, our society must address the ethical problem raised by the severance of workplace ties.

The continuation coverage provisions of ERISA are a half-hearted step in this direction, and a further step is the action being taken by some states to authorize their Medicaid systems to help former employees pay the premiums to maintain their health coverage under the ERISA continuation entitlement.[69] Because HIV infection has proven to be an unpredictable phenomenon in terms of the long-term outlook for individual physical well-being, the maintenance of some workplace tie might be useful in assisting HIV-infected persons to have gainful employment upon recovery from significant opportunistic infections, and might help provide a psychological lift that would be helpful in the recovery process. In addition, governmental assistance to employers in meeting the expenses of maintaining regular health insurance coverage for temporarily disabled HIV-infected employees might deter unnecessary terminations of employee status.

CONCLUSION

Many American employers have responded ethically to the epidemic of HIV disease with compassion and understanding. Others have placed regard for the bottom line over the ethical principles of respect for persons, beneficence, justice and avoidance of harm, or, with disregard for basic principles of individual autonomy, have made decisions, albeit well-intentioned, without consulting the involved employee.

The developing law of HIV and the workplace suggests minimum standards of an ethical approach, but our society needs to reach beyond the notion of compliance with minimal legal standards if people affected by the epidemic are to be treated in a way consistent with our collective sense of ethical behavior. The ethical approach may also be the most rational approach, since appropriate health education for workforces and compassionate assistance for HIV-infected employees and their family members may result in the least workplace disruption while enabling the employer to continue tapping the skills and experience of infected employees.

More significantly, employers can help form the vanguard of those arguing that our society should radically restructure our health care financing system to more equitably distribute the benefits and burdens of providing quality health care to employees and the unemployed alike. Such a fundamental restructuring could more equitably spread the burdens of a new epidemic while preserving that respect for individual human dignity which lies at the heart of ethical concerns.

NOTES

1. As the AIDS epidemic completes its first observable decade in the United States, it becomes increasingly clear that discussions of law and policy which focus on AIDS as defined by the Centers for Disease Control (CDC) in the first years of the epidemic are misleading and incomplete. CDC clings to a surveillance definition so that comparative statistics will have some meaning, but the reality is HIV infection and its numerous symptomatic manifestations, including CDC-defined Acquired Immune Deficiency Syndrome, AIDS-Related Complex or Conditions, immune deficiency related tuberculosis, lymphatic cancers, and other conditions, all of which have an impact in the workplace. Indeed, "asymptomatic" HIV infection and the mere perception that one is infected with HIV have workplace implications, such that an appropriate discussion of ethical implications must cover all these areas. For that reason, this article will have little mention of AIDS as such, and will normally refer to the phenomenon under discussion as HIV infection.

2. Dr. Ruth Berkelman, Chief of AIDS Surveillance for the U.S. Centers for Disease Control, has speculated that "the introduction of some effective therapies" has delayed the onset of AIDS among infected persons. *See AIDS Cases in U.S. Rose 9% in 1989,* N.Y. Times, Feb. 11, 1990, at 43.

3. In 1990, the Food and Drug Administration responded to research showing the efficacy of AZT as a prophylaxis against the development of symptoms of HIV infection by relabelling the drug for use by asymptomatic persons, thus lending encouragement to increased testing. *See Wider Use of AZT Is Urged for Adults With AIDS Virus,* N.Y. Times, Mar. 3, 1990, at 10.

4. Public health officials have urged persons who may be at risk for AIDS to undergo testing for HIV antibodies. While there is no national count of HIV-infected persons, the U.S. Centers for Disease Control reported that 117,781 cases of AIDS, as tightly defined by the CDC, were counted by the end of 1989. *AIDS Cases in U.S. Rose 9% in 1989, supra* note 2.

5. It is hard to obtain reliable data on the per patient costs of AIDS treatment, because the nature of available treatments is changing rapidly but careful studies of costs take time. Thus, by the time a careful study is published, its conclusions, to the extent valid, are only valid for an earlier period when different treatment modes and survival rates existed.

6. *Compare* Chalk v. United States Dist. Court, 840 F.2d 701 (9th Cir. 1988) (ordering reinstatement to classroom of schoolteacher with AIDS) *with* Leckelt v. Board of Commissioners, 714 F. Supp. 1377 (E.D. La. 1989) (refusing to order reinstatement of licensed practical nurse who declined to

reveal antibody status after roommate died from AIDS). The Supreme Court has reserved judgment on whether seropositive persons are protected from discrimination by Section 504 of the Rehabilitation Act of 1973, School Bd. v. Arline, 480 U.S. 273, 282 n.7 (1987).

7. A cursory check of state laws compiled in BNA's Individual Employment Rights Manual revealed more than a dozen states with AIDS or HIV-specific laws affecting the workplace, virtually all seeking to protect HIV-infected persons from discrimination or breaches of confidentiality. In addition, several state and federal courts have concluded that discrimination against HIV-infected persons violates laws on handicap or disability discrimination. The federal Office of Personnel Management has issued guidelines forbidding HIV-related discrimination in federal workplaces.

8. In this context, "costs" refers to the lost investment in training and expertise when employees are discharged, the costs of defending discrimination claims when those are asserted, and the costs of settlement in such cases. Although federal law requires most employers to allow discharged employees to continue to participate in group health benefit programs, the former employee can be required to bear the cost of such participation. . . .

9. Handicap discrimination law applicable to most workplaces requires employers to make "reasonable accommodations" to enable persons with impairments to continue to work. *See infra* text accompanying notes 66-67.

10. *E.g.,* N.Y. Pub. Health Law § 2781 (McKinney Supp. 1990); Calif. Health & Safety Code § 199.21 (West Supp. 1990); Hawaii Rev. Stat. § 325-101(a) (1989 Supp.); Mass. Gen. Laws Ann., ch. 111, § 70F (West Supp. 1990); Mo. Ann. Stat. § 191.653 (Vernon Supp. 1990); Tex. Health & Safety Code Ann. § 81.103 (Vernon Supp. 1990). *See also* U.S. Office of Personnel Management, AIDS Guidelines, Bulletin No. 792-42 (1988).

11. Woods v. White, 689 F. Supp. 874 (W.D. Wis. 1988) (disclosure of prisoner's HIV status to non-medical personnel actionable under 42 U.S.C. § 1983); *accord* Doe v. Borough of Barrington, 729 F. Supp. 376 (D.N.J. 1990). *See also*

Zinda v. Louisiana Pac. Corp., 149 Wis. 2d 913, 440 N.W.2d 548 (1989).

12. Carol Levine is Executive Director of the Citizens Commission on AIDS for the New York City Metropolitan Area. Ronald Bayer is a professor at the Columbia University School of Public Health. *See* Levine & Bayer, *The Ethics of Screening for Early Intervention in HIV Disease,* 79 Am. J. Pub. Health 1661 (1989).

13. *Id.* at 1663.

14. *Id.*

★ ★ ★

64. Such reactions were described in a BNA interview with David M. Herold, Director of Georgia Tech's Center on Work Performance Problems, who had conducted a study on attitudes of workers:

> He said that workers say, "I know, I've read, I understand I can't get it this way"— but there is an infinitesimal probability of getting a horrible disease and they don't want to chance it. Other experts said that, given the certain fatal outcome of the disease, the reaction is understandable, meaning that employers must help employees overcome their fears so they can get on with business. The best way to do this, they agreed, is to educate workers.
>
> Daily Lab. Rep. (BNA) No. 45, at C-2–C-3 (Mar. 7, 1990).

65. To date, workplace education programs have proven the most effective way to reduce employee fears and facilitate smooth operation of a workplace where an employee is known to have AIDS. *See More Workplaces Dealing With AIDS as Cases, New Treatments Increase,* Daily Lab. Rep. (BNA) No. 45, at C-1 (Mar. 7, 1990).

66. School Bd. v. Arline, 480 U.S. 273, 289 n.19 (1987).

67. 45 C.F.R. § 84.12(a) (1989).

68. A prime example of this kind of thinking is U.S. Representative William Dannemeyer, a Republican who represents Orange County, California. During consideration of the Americans With Disabilities Act by the House Committee on Energy and Commerce, of which he is a member, Dannemeyer proposed amendments to eliminate protection for people with infectious diseases. Dan-

nemeyer stated that he had no problem with extending protection against discrimination to "innocent acquires" of AIDS but that he would "have trouble extending that protection to the 93 percent who acquire AIDS through homosexual activity or drug abuse." Daily Lab. Rep. (BNA) No. 50, at A-7 (Mar. 14, 1990).

69. New York Governor Mario Cuomo has proposed such an approach for New York State. 4 AIDS Pol'y & Law (BNA) No. 24, at 3 (Jan. 10, 1990). Michigan has already adopted such a program. 4 AIDS Pol'y & Law (BNA) No. 21, at 8-9 (Nov. 15, 1989).

CHAPTER 5

"This Makes Me Uncomfortable." Sexual Harassment and Sexual Politics

INTRODUCTION

As the numbers of women entering the work force in the 1970s and 1980s increased, attitudes and patterns of behavior that had been traditional in many (predominantly male) business, political, and social environments were challenged. Perhaps more than any other event, the confrontation between Anita Hill and Clarence Thomas during the latter's Senate confirmation hearings focused attention on the nature and extent of sexual harassment in the workplace. More recently, Paula Jones accused President Clinton of sexual harassment, and Senator Robert Packwood resigned after an investigation into his conduct by the Senate Ethics Committee. Sexual harassment will be a significant issue for years to come.

The United States Equal Employment Opportunity Commission (EEOC) distinguishes two types of sexual harassment. "Quid pro quo" harassment occurs when submission to "unwelcome sexual conduct is made either explicitly or implicitly a term or condition of an individual's employment." "Hostile environment" harassment involves unwelcome sexual conduct that "unreasonably interferes with an individual's job performance or creates an intimidating, hostile, or offensive working environment (6681–6682)."

Both types of sexual harassment are ethically objectionable because psychological (and sometimes physical) harms are inflicted on innocent people for no ethically valid reason, and because victims are treated without respect for their dignity as persons. Both are abuses of power and are often egregious examples of gender discrimination.

Sexual harassment is ethically inexcusable. It is, for example, worth noting that the controversy surrounding Justice Thomas' confirmation did not concern the definition of sexual harassment or its ethical rightness or wrongness. The question was whether he had, in fact, behaved as Professor Hill alleged. Had she been able to prove her allegations, Justice Thomas would have found few defenders and would, in all likelihood, today be Mr. Thomas.

But while "Quid pro quo" harassment is easy to recognize, recognizing a "hostile environment" is more difficult. When is an environment so sexually charged that it is "hostile," and by whose standards is that judgment made? Traditionally, to qualify as harassment, the unwelcome sexual conduct must be of such a nature that "the work environment of a reasonable person would be substantially affected." Until recently many courts held that, in order to have a valid legal claim, a person alleging sexual harassment must show that she (or he) suffered significant psychological harm as a result of the offensive behavior. However, in 1993, the Supreme Court decided in *Harris v. Forklift Systems, Inc.* [62 USLW 4004 (November 9, 1993)] that such a requirement was too stringent, and thus made it easier for many victims of harassment to pursue their claims.

Some legal scholars and some courts have disagreed with the "reasonable person" standard, arguing that the standards of judgment should be those of a "reasonable victim," who, far more often than not, is a woman. What, from a male point of view, is office banter might, from a female perspective, constitute a "hostile environment." Some feminists argue that the "reasonable person" standard overlooks a female perspective and betrays a male bias.

It seems clear that the pervasive use of obscene language, displays of pornography, crass sexual jokes and observations, and unwelcome touching of private areas of the body are all examples of behavior that is legally and ethically objectionable. Milder forms of behavior, however, prove more difficult to assess. Differences in background, experience, and work situations might make sexual joking and flirting appear humorous to reasonable men and, at the same time, threatening to reasonable women. If a male supervisor invites a female subordinate to dinner to discuss her work performance and career options, is that harassment or mentoring?

These are not insignificant issues. Victims, alleged harassers, and organizations all have rights, responsibilities, and liabilities in these matters, the nature and scope of which will be determined by how the significance of the situation is described and assessed. Recall, for example, that we defined a situation evoking legitimate ethical concern as one which involves the creation and distribution of *significant* harms and benefits to persons who have a right to have their interests taken into account. What or whose standard will be used to determine if the alleged harms are significant enough to warrant an adverse ethical or legal judgment? This is a crucial question because, particularly since the passage of the Civil Rights Act of 1991, the penalties for violations can be severe. The answer will in all likelihood shape an organization's efforts to establish policies and programs designed to prevent, investigate and remedy (alleged) instances of sexual harassment. These in turn will impact the organization's culture and the ethical norms which govern the social and professional interaction of the people who work for it.

★ ★ ★

This chapter's readings explore the topic of sexual harassment from a variety of perspectives. **May Ellen Hill Revolt** outlines the historical and legal background of sexual harassment issues and briefly discusses some recent important Supreme Court decisions. **Barbara A. Gutek** examines sexual harassment in the context of organizational behavior and describes the ethical and legal rights and responsibilities of different groups affected by it (harassers, victims, and employing organizations). The next two articles discuss what is the best perspective from which to evaluate claims of sexual harassment. **Deborah L. Wells** and **Beverly J. Kracher** use John Rawls' concept of justice to support the view that questionable behavior is best evaluated from the perspective of a "reasonable woman" rather than that of a "reasonable person." **Robert S. Adler** and **Ellen R. Peirce** disagree. Their article traces the legal development of the "reasonable woman" standard and finds it deficient on both legal and ethical grounds. **Donna M. Stringer** and her coauthors, noting that sexual harassment is frequently an abuse of power rather than of sex, analyze the different kinds of power abused by harassers and suggest various strategies for managing different types of offenders.

REFERENCES

Equal Employment Opportunity Commission. (1995) Policy Guidance on Sexual Harassment. *Fair Employment Practice Manual* (The Bureau of National Affairs, Inc: Washington, D.C., 1995): 405:6681–6701

CASE: Propmore Corporation

OVERVIEW

Don Bradford was on the fast track at the Propmore Corporation. But he wished he could slow things down a bit, given several hard choices he had to make.

Propmore Corporation was a good place to work. It had sales of about $500 million per year, a net profit margin of 5 percent, and a return on equity of 15 percent. Propmore made several key components used by the aerospace industry and consumer goods market. It was a leader in its field. The company was organized by product divisions, each reporting to the executive vice-president. Its operations were decentralized, with broad decision-making capability at the divisional level. However, at the corporate level, functional departments (Purchasing, R&D, Personnel, and Marketing) set company policy and coordinated divisional activities in these areas. Propmore was financially successful, and it treated its people well, as Don Bradford's experience showed.

After earning his M.B.A. four years ago from a respected state university, Don quickly rose through the ranks in Purchasing. At age 31, he holds the prestigious position of manager. Before joining Propmore, Don earned a B.S. in engineering and worked for three years in the aerospace industry as a design engineer. During his first three years at Propmore, Don was a buyer and received "excellent" ratings in all his performance appraisals.

As purchasing manager, Don enjoyed good working relationships with superiors and subordinates. He was accountable directly to the division general manager and, functionally, to the corporate vice-president of procurement, Mr. Stewart. His dealings with these people were always amiable, and he came to count upon them for technical guidance, as he learned the role of divisional purchasing manager. Don had several staff assistants who knew the business of buying and were loyal employees. He had done a good job of handling the resentment of those passed over by his promotion to manager, and he had developed a good deal of trust with the buying staff. At least he thought he had—until Jane Thompson presented him with the first in a series of dilemmas.

Jane Thompson, age 34, had been with Propmore for ten years. She had a B.A. in English literature and two years' experience as a material expediter before coming to Propmore. Initially hired as a purchasing assistant, Jane became a buyer after two years. She enjoyed her job and the people she worked with at Propmore. In four years of working with Don, Jane had come to admire and respect his approach to management. She appreciated his sensitive yet strong leadership and saw him as an honest person who could be trusted to look after the interests of his subordinates.

Source: This case was developed by Peter Madsen and John Fleming for the Arthur Andersen & Co. SC Business Ethics Program. "Propmore Corporation Case" developed by the Arthur Andersen & Co., SC Business Ethics Program. Copyright © 1991. Printed with permission of Arthur Andersen & Co., SC.

But the dilemma with which Jane now presented Don made him wonder whether he had the skill to be a manager in a major division.

A LUNCHEON HARASSMENT

After a two-hour purchasing meeting in the morning, Bill Smith, an Airgoods Corporation sales representative, had invited Jane Thompson to lunch. They left at noon. An hour and a half later, Jane stormed into Don Bradford's office, obviously upset. When Don asked what was wrong, Jane told him in very strong terms that Bill Smith had sexually harassed her during and after the luncheon.

According to Jane, Bill made some sexual comments and suggestions toward the end of the meal. She considered this to be offensive and unwelcome. Jane, however, told Bill to take her back to the office. He attempted to make light of the situation and said he was only joking, but on the way back he made some further comments and several casual physical contacts to which she objected. When they arrived at the company, Bill was embarrassed and tried to apologize. But Jane entered the office before he could finish.

Jane demanded that the Airgoods Corporation be taken off the bidder list for the raw material contract and that Airgoods' president be informed of the unseemly and illegal behavior of one of his salesmen. She would also consider taking legal action against Bill Smith through the Equal Employment Opportunity Commission for sexual harassment. Also, Jane stated she would investigate suing the Propmore Corporation for failure to protect her from this form of discrimination while she was performing her duties as an employee of the company. At the end of this outburst, Jane abruptly left Don's office.

Don was significantly troubled. Jane played a critical role in getting bids for the raw material contract. He needed her. Yet he knew that if he kept Airgoods on the bidder list, it might be difficult for her to view this vendor objectively.

Don was somewhat concerned about Jane's threat to sue Propmore but doubted that she had a very good case. Still, such an action would be costly in legal fees, management time, and damage to the company's image.

Don wasn't sure what to do about the bidder list. Airgoods had an excellent record as a reliable vendor for similar contracts. Propmore might be at a disadvantage if Airgoods were to be eliminated. On the other hand, Don firmly believed in standing behind his subordinates.

At this point, he needed more information on what constitutes sexual harassment and what policy guidelines his company had established. He examined two documents: the EEOC Definition of Sexual Harassment (Exhibit 1) and the Propmore Corporation's Policy HR-13, on Sexual Harassment (Exhibit 2).

GATHERING MORE INFORMATION

Don Bradford had met Bill Smith, the Airgoods Corporation salesman, on several occasions but did not feel he really knew him. To learn more about Bill, Don talked with his other key buyer, Bob Peters. Bob had dealt with Bill on many contracts in the past. After Don finished recounting the incident concerning Jane, Bob smiled. In his opinion, it was just a "boys will be boys" situation that got blown out of proportion. It may have been more than a joke, but Bob did not think Bill would do something "too far out." He pointed out that Bill had been selling for ten years and knew how to treat a customer.

Don's next step was a visit to the division personnel office. In addition to going through Jane's file, he wanted to discuss the matter with Ann Perkins, the division's human resource manager. Fortunately, Ann was in her office and had time to see him immediately.

Don went over the whole situation with Ann. When he had finished his account, Ann was silent for a minute. Then she pointed out that this was a strange sexual harassment situation: it

EXHIBIT 1

Equal Employment Opportunity Commission Definition of Sexual Harassment

Unwelcome sexual advances, requests for sexual favors and other verbal or physical contact of a sexual nature constitute sexual harassment when (1) submission to such conduct is made either explicitly or implicitly a term or condition of an individual's employment, (2) submission to or rejection of such conduct by an individual is used as the basis for employment decisions affecting such individual, or (3) such conduct has the purpose or effect of unreasonably interfering with an individual's work performance or creating an intimidating, hostile or offensive working environment.

Applying general Title VII principles, an employer, employment agency, joint apprenticeship committee or labor organization (hereinafter collectively referred to as "employer") is responsible for its acts and those of its agents and supervisory employees with respect to sexual harassment regardless of whether the employer knew or should have known of their occurrence.

_____

EEOC guideline based on the Civil Rights Act of 1964, Title VII

did not happen at the company, and the alleged harasser was not a member of the Propmore organization. The extent of the company's responsibility was not clear.

She had heard of cases where employees held their companies responsible for protecting them from sexual harassment by employees of other organizations. But the harassment had taken place on company premises, where some degree of direct supervision and protection could have been expected.

Ann filled out a slip authorizing Don to see Jane's personnel file. He took the file to an empty office and went through its contents. There were the expected hiring and annual evaluation forms, which revealed nothing unusual and only confirmed his own high opinion of Jane.

Then Don came to an informal note at the back of the file. It summarized a telephone reference check with the personnel manager of Jane's former employer. The note indicated that

EXHIBIT 2

The Propmore Corporation Policy HR-13

POLICY AREA: Sexual Harassment

PURPOSE: The purpose of Policy HR-13 is to inform employees of the company that The Propmore Corporation forbids practices of sexual harassment on the job and that disciplinary action may be taken against those who violate this policy.

POLICY STATEMENT: In keeping with its long-standing tradition of abiding by pertinent laws and regulations, The Propmore Corporation forbids practices of sexual harassment on the job which violate Title VII of the Civil Rights Act of 1964. Sexual harassment on the job, regardless of its intent, is against the law. Em-

ployees who nevertheless engage in sexual harassment practices face possible disciplinary action, which includes dismissal from the company.

POLICY IMPLEMENTATION: Those who wish to report violations of Policy HR-13 shall file a written grievance with their immediate supervisors within two weeks of the alleged violation. In conjunction with the Legal Department, the supervisor will investigate the alleged violation and issue his or her decision based upon the findings of this investigation within 30 days of receiving the written grievance.

Jane had complained of being sexually harassed by her supervisor. The personnel manager had "checked it out" with the supervisor, who claimed "there was nothing to it." The note also indicated that Jane was terminated two months after this incident for "unsatisfactory work."

Don returned to his office and called his functional superior, Mr. Stewart, to inform him of the situation. Mr. Stewart was the corporate vice president of procurement. He had known Bill Smith personally for a number of years. He told Don that Bill's wife had abandoned him and their three children several years ago. Although Bill had a reputation for occasional odd behavior, he was known in the industry as a hard-working salesperson who provided excellent service and follow-through on his accounts.

A TELEPHONE CALL

Don felt he needed even more informaton to make a thorough investigation. He contemplated calling Bill Smith. In fairness to Bill, he should hear his version of what happened during the luncheon. But he knew he was not responsible for the actions of a nonemployee. Furthermore, he wondered if talking to Bill would upset Jane even more if she found out? And would it be a proper part of an investigation mandated by company policy?

As Don considered his options, the phone rang. It was Bill Smith's boss, Joe Maxwell. He and Bill had talked about the luncheon, he said, and wanted to know if Jane had reported anything.

"Don, I don't know what you know about that meeting," said Joe, "but Bill has told me all the facts, and I thought we could put our heads together and nip this thing in the bud."

Don wasn't sure if this call was going to help or hinder him in his decision making. At first, he felt Joe was trying to unduly influence him. Also, he wasn't sure if the call was a violation of Jane's right to confidentiality. "Joe, I'm not sure we should be discussing this matter at all," said

Don. "We might be jumping the gun. And what if Jane—"

"Wait, wait," Joe interrupted. "This thing can be put to rest if you just hear what really happened. We've been a good supplier for some time now. Give us the benefit of the doubt. We can talk 'off the record' if you want. But don't close the door on us."

"Okay," said Don, "let's talk off the record. I'll hear Bill's version, but I won't reach a conclusion over the phone. Our policy requires an investigation, and when that's complete, I'll let you know our position."

"Gee, Don," said Joe, "I don't think you even need an investigation. Bill says the only thing that went on at lunch was some innocent flirtation. Jane was giving him the old 'come on,' you know. She was more than friendly to him, smiling a lot and laughing at his jokes. Bill saw all the signals and just responded like a full-blooded male."

"You mean Jane was the cause of his harassing her?" Don asked.

"No, he didn't harass her," Joe said with urgency in his voice. "He only flirted with her because he thought she was flirting with him. It was all very innocent. These things happen every day. He didn't mean any harm. Just the opposite. He thought there was a chance for a nice relationship. He likes her very much and thought the feeling was mutual. No need to make a federal case out of it. These things happen—that's all. Remember when you asked out one of my saleswomen, Don? She said 'no,' but she didn't suggest sexual harassment. Isn't this the same thing?"

'I don't know. Jane was really upset when she came to me. She didn't see it as just flirting that went on," said Don.

"Come on, Don," insisted Joe. "Give her some time to calm down. You know how women can be sometimes. Maybe she has PMS. Why don't you let things just settle down before you do anything rash and start that unnecessary investigation? I bet in a couple days, you can talk to Jane and convince her it was just a misunderstanding. I'll put someone else on this contract, and we'll forget the whole thing ever happened. We've got to think about business first, right?"

Joe Maxwell's phone call put things in a new light for Don. If it was only innocent flirtation, why should good relations between Propmore and Airgoods be damaged? Yet he knew he had an obligation to Jane. He just wasn't sure how far that obligation went.

READING 5-1

Perspective Report: Sexual Harassment

Mary Ellen Hill Revolt

Life in the 1990s can be hectic and complicated. One more challenge for business people today is to be aware of potential workplace problems and to be ready to handle negative situations when they arise.

One battleground that has become a prominent concern in the '90s is sexual harassment. Would you recognize sexual harassment if it happened at your business? Would you know what to do? Do you know how to try to prevent it? Do you know how to handle complaints within your workplace? Though sexual harassment is a complex legal issue, as well as a potentially emotionally devastating ordeal, the key to preventing it and to knowing how to stop it quickly if it occurs is said to be simple.

The key is education, say local attorneys and others who have studied the issue.

This special section addresses many aspects of sexual harassment: legal issues, the importance education can play in preventing it, and important past cases and judicial decisions.

HARASSMENT IS CONTINUALLY EVOLVING LEGAL ISSUE

Sexual harassment is a very complex and continually evolving legal issue. Legal protection against sexual harassment has grown out of Title VII of the Civil Rights Act of 1964, which states that: "It shall be an unlawful employment practice for an employer to fail or refuse to hire or to discharge any individual, or otherwise to dis-criminate against any individual, with respect to his compensation, terms, conditions, or privileges of employment, because of such individual's race, color, religion, sex, or national origin."

Title VII was designed originally to protect people from such occurrences as being fired or not hired at all, or overlooked for promotions, or paid less simply because of their race, color, religion, sex or national origin.

Then in the late 1970s and early 1980s, complaints of a different type of unfair treatment or sex discrimination in the workplace began to surface.

"People began bringing claims of sex discrimination, saying they were being treated differently because of their sex by being subjected to dirty jokes, comments, whatever. They weren't necessarily being fired, but they weren't being treated fairly," said Ruby Fenton, an attorney with Rogers, Fuller & Pitt in Louisville.

In 1964, Title VII had established the Equal Employment Opportunity Commission, the federal agency responsible for receiving and investigating all types of employment discrimination charges.

In 1980, the EEOC issued guidelines on sexual harassment, declaring it a type of discrimination prohibited by Title VII. The guidelines were important in "establishing criteria for determining when unwelcome conduct of a sexual nature constitutes sexual harassment, defining the circumstances under which an employer may be held liable, and suggesting affirmative steps an employer should take to prevent sexual harassment," according to a 1990 EEOC document, "Policy Guidance on Sexual Harassment."

Although the EEOC guidelines do not have the force of law, courts study and consider the guidelines when making decisions in sexual-harassment cases, said Fenton.

Eventually in 1986, with its decision in the Meritor Savings Bank vs. Vinson case, the

Source: Business First, October 3, 1994, 23–27.

Supreme Court recognized sexual harassment as a form of sex discrimination, and thus a violation of Title VII.

Since the Meritor decision, many subsequent cases and decisions have further expanded the repertoire of information and documentation on sexual harassment. "Sexual harassment is one of the most rapidly expanding areas of law we have," said Louisville attorney Thomas Clay.

Many issues need to be considered when dealing with sexual harassment. For example, in its guidelines, the EEOC outlined two forms of

Employers Can Follow Steps to Avoid Liability

According to "Considerations in Defending Sexual Harassment Cases," a paper prepared for the Labor and Employment Law Institute in 1991 by Ruby Fenton, an attorney with Rogers, Fuller & Pitt in Louisville, employers should consider taking the following steps to prevent sexual harassment in the workplace and to minimize liability. The steps are based on the EEOC's guidelines and judicial decisions.

1. Specifically include sexual harassment as prohibited activity in the employer's written nondiscrimination policy.
2. Conduct training programs for supervisors and management to advise them of the law, their responsibility, and the consequences to the employer and the manager should sexual harassment occur.
3. Designate one individual, preferably a respected member of management, to receive complaints of sexual harassment. Employees should not be required to take their sexual-harassment complaints to their supervisors because the harasser may be the supervisor.

   (But note: It is generally a good idea to designate an alternate in the event that the primary designee is the alleged harasser.)
4. Establish a procedure for the handling of sexual-harassment complaints that includes documentation and thorough investigation. Avoid making the procedure unduly complicated or burdensome, and once it is established, be sure that it is followed in each case.
5. Take each complaint seriously. Resist the temptation to treat complaints as frivolous. The embarrassment and stress involved in complaining of sexual harassment may affect the complainant's ability to articulate the problem. Advise the complainant that an immediate investigation will be conducted.
6. When a complaint of sexual harassment is raised by an employee, be careful to avoid retaliatory actions against the complainant.
7. In conducting an investigation and determining what action should be taken, employers must attempt to be fair to both the complainant and the accused.
8. If the investigation reveals that a supervisor or other employee is guilty of sexual harassment, appropriate action should be taken immediately, including disciplinary action against the harasser. Keep a written record of the discipline taken and why, and let the victimized employee know what has been done to protect that victim's rights and personal dignity.
9. Be discreet in conducting the investigation and do not reveal the complaint or other information gathered during the investigation to anyone in the company who does not need to know.
10. When credibility of the complainant and the accused becomes an issue, the investigator should inquire as to whether witnesses are available to substantiate the employee's sexual-harassment complaint. If no substantiating witnesses are available, the investigator should look for other evidence that would support either parties' version of what happened. This may require the investigator to talk with people who are familiar with both parties' professional conduct.
11. Establish written guidelines to be used in making employment decisions, especially promotion and compensation decisions, and make sure they are followed.
12. Keep written records showing the reasons for employment actions.
13. Establish some form of review for hiring and firing decisions to avoid discriminatory action being taken by an individual supervisor.
14. Do not permit sexual jokes, teasing and innuendoes to become a routine part of the work environment.

sexual harassment, commonly referred to as quid pro quo and hostile environment.

Quid pro quo harassment occurs in a "this for that" situation. For example, if a supervisor tells an employee, "you will be promoted if you sleep with me," that's quid pro quo harassment, said Fenton.

Likewise, if an employee loses a raise or promotion as a result of denying a supervisor's sexual advances, that can also be quid pro quo sexual harassment.

"Quid pro quo harassment occurs when submission to unwelcome sexual advances of supervisory personnel is an express or implied condition for receiving job benefits or where there is a loss of job benefits as a result of an employee's failure to submit to a supervisor's sexual demands," wrote Dorothy M. Pitt, a partner in Rogers, Fuller & Pitt, and Fenton in an article published in Louisville Lawyer in 1987.

Sources said various types of conduct, including telling sexual jokes, making suggestive or derogatory sexual remarks, displaying sexual photos, showing sexual videos or making sexual physical contact, could constitute hostile environment sexual harassment if they are unwanted activities and if they do indeed create a hostile environment and prevent others from performing their duties.

The Fair Employment Practices Manual issued by The Bureau of National Affairs Inc., which publishes materials on government-related subjects, states: "The EEOC's guidelines also recognize that unwelcome sexual conduct that 'unreasonably interferes with an individual's job performance' or creates an 'intimidating, hostile, or offensive working environment' can constitute sex discrimination, even if it leads to no tangible or economic job consequences."

"Hostile environment sexual harassment results from harassing conduct, based on sex, by either a co-worker or supervisor which has the effect of unreasonably interfering with the employee's work performance and creating an in-

timidating, hostile and offensive work environment," wrote Pitt and Fenton in their article.

To constitute hostile environment sexual harassment, such behavior must be "sufficiently severe or pervasive to alter the victim's conditions of employment and to create an abrasive working environment," wrote Pitt and Fenton.

"Moreover, the circumstances must be viewed from the perspective of a reasonable person's reaction to a similar environment under similar or like circumstances. In addition, the employee must be able to show he or she was actually offended by the alleged harassment."

At one time, the U.S. Supreme Court required that plaintiffs prove they suffered severe psychological injury that made it impossible for them to do their jobs. In its decision in Harris vs. Forklift Systems Inc., the Supreme court said that requirement was too strong, and that, "so long as the environment would reasonably be perceived, and is perceived, as hostile or abusive, there is no need for it also to be psychologically injurious."

Most sexual-harassment cases involve women being harassed by men. Cecilee Tangel, project coordinator for the Jefferson County Office for Women estimates, "90 percent of cases are males harassing females."

But the law covers sexual harassment in all forms. "The victim may be a woman or man. The victim does not have to be of the opposite sex," states an EEOC document, "Questions and Answers about Sexual Harassment."

In cases of either hostile environment or quid pro quo sexual harassment, the key is whether the sexual advances were "unwelcome." The nature of the victim's conduct can determine whether the advances were unwelcome.

"Sexual conduct becomes unlawful only when it is unwelcome," states the EEOC's "Questions and Answers about Sexual Harassment." "The challenged conduct must be unwelcome in the sense that the employee did not solicit or incite it, and in the sense that the employee regarded the conduct as undesirable or offensive."

To determine whether the conduct in question was unwelcome, the EEOC studies the circumstances of each situation individually.

Sexual harassment can take many forms. Quid pro quo and hostile environment harassment can occur simultaneously. In an organization, only one individual might be guilty and one victim harassed, or harassment could be a rampant part of that organization's culture.

"It can be one person, or it can permeate the whole organization. It can be fleeting, or it can be pervasive and ongoing," said Clay.

Determining who is liable is another aspect of the sexual-harassment issue. Depending on the facts of the case, either the individual accused of the acts of harassment or the company, or both, might be liable.

In quid pro quo cases, employers can be held liable for sexual harassment by supervisors who are responsible for hiring, promoting and firing decisions.

According to Pitt and Fenton, hostile environment cases are different in that many factors can determine whether the employer is liable. Factors can include when and where the events in question occurred, and whether the acts took place in the scope of the accused's employment.

Prior to 1991, victims of sexual harassment were permitted to be compensated only if they had suffered some form of economic loss, such as termination or loss of promotion, and then they could recover only back pay and/or be reinstated to their former positions, said Fenton.

But the Civil Rights Act of 1991 made it possible for victims to be awarded punitive damages and compensatory damages, including those for emotional distress.

This change has been significant for many victims who did not actually lose wages but who did suffer psychological distress and humiliation.

The act outlines limits for punitive damages based on the number of employees an employer has. For example, for a company with 201 to 500 employees, the limit is $200,000, and for a company with over 500 employees, the limit is $300,000.

These limits are applicable to individuals as well as to employers, although it is fairly uncommon for an individual to be held solely liable in a sexual-harassment suit, said Fenton.

An individual might be held liable along with the employer, but most often the employer is held liable even though it might try to push the liability onto an individual.

In addition to punitive damages, victims also might be entitled to back pay, attorneys' fees, and damages for inconvenience and future pecuniary losses.

Juries often sympathize with plaintiffs and award big damages, Clay said.

In a number of cases, victims have received substantial settlements, and the possibility of large monetary settlements has helped send a "loud and clear message to employers" that sexual harassment can hit them hard, said Clay.

Such large settlements also have set the stage for some people to bring weaker claims because of the possibility of getting big bucks, Clay said.

The state of Kentucky also offers legal protection from sexual harassment, as do all states. The Kentucky Civil Rights Act of 1966 includes Title VII of the federal Civil Rights Act and prohibits discrimination in the workplace under Kentucky law. "The state act was modeled after the federal act. It contains the same proscriptions," said Fenton.

One difference is that no limit has been placed on damages that can be awarded in a suit filed under the state act. This difference was more significant, however, before the Civil Rights Act of 1991 allowed punitive damages under federal law.

A victim has two options for filing a claim at the state level in Kentucky, she said. A victim

Harassment Can Take Many Forms

Sources agree that sexual harassment can take many forms:

- Making sexual body movements or hand gestures;
- Making suggestive facial expressions, such as winking or staring, or looking someone up and down;
- Making kissing or howling noises;
- Whistling at a person;
- Displaying suggestive visuals, such as posters containing nudity;
- Standing too close or brushing up against a person;
- Touching oneself sexually in the presence of another person;
- Kissing, hugging, patting, or touching a person's clothing, hair, or body;

- Giving inappropriate personal gifts;
- Spreading rumors about someone's private sex life;
- Asking personal questions about social life, sexual preferences, or fantasies;
- Telling stories or jokes with sexual content;
- Making sexual remarks about someone's clothing or looks;
- Calling an adult a name such as doll, babe, girl, hunk, or stud;
- Pressuring someone for a date;
- Pressuring someone for sexual favors;
- Assaulting sexually or raping someone.

can file a suit directly with state court within five years of the alleged harassment. Or, within 180 days of the alleged harassment, a victim can file a complaint with the Kentucky Commission on Human Rights.

The commission is a state agency that "has authority to investigate and hear these cases and award damages," said Fenton. A victim choosing this option agrees to abide by the findings of the commission and cannot then go to court.

To file a suit at the federal level, a victim first must file a complaint with the EEOC within 300 days of the discriminatory act, said Fenton. The

EEOC "investigates and conciliates, but has no authority to award damages," she said.

If the EEOC is not able to resolve a complaint, the case then can go to federal court.

Cases can take as long as a year to get to the courts after a suit has been filed, but Clay said most cases are settled out of court.

Employers can try to protect themselves from potential sexual-harassment occurrences and liability. Fenton and Clay agreed that to do so, employers must have in place clear and effective policies and procedures regarding sexual harassment.

Q & A

Question: Aren't women too sensitive, making a big deal out of nothing?

Answer: No. Sexual harassment is a clear and direct threat. It can affect everything about a woman's job, which she needs, wants and enjoys.

Question: I work in a respected professional organization. Can sexual harassment happen here?

Answer: Yes. Sexual harassment is an abuse of power that happens in all types of jobs and all types of companies.

Questions: Can men be victims of sexual harassment?

Answer: Yes. And they have equal protection under the law.

Adapted from "How to Recognize and Prevent Sexual Harassment in the Workplace" with permission of the publisher.
© 1992 Business & Legal Reports Inc., 39 Academy Street, Madison, Conn., 06443

According to Mike O'Loughlin, vice president of HR Enterprise Inc., a human-resource consulting firm, these policies should define sexual harassment and should establish clear and effective guidelines for employees to follow in the event of sexual harassment.

Professionals agree that training should go hand in hand with establishing policies. "It is important for management to develop policies and to make sure their managers are well-trained," said Fenton.

"The company could be on the hook, depending on the circumstances, so the company had better be sure that employees are trained in this area," she added.

The EEOC's guidelines on prevention state: "Prevention is the best tool for the elimination of sexual harassment. An employer should take all steps necessary to prevent sexual harassment from occurring."

A company has to disseminate the policy to everyone, she said. "The key is effectiveness. You could have a great policy, but people have to be aware of it, and it has to work," said Fenton.

DECISIVE CASES HELP DEFINE SEXUAL HARASSMENT LAW

While sexual-harassment cases often are settled out of court, many cases have reached the courts through the years. Decisions in some of these cases have further defined sexual-harassment law.

Here are brief summaries of four cases and the resulting decisions. Court decisions may be reversed or altered by rulings in later decisions.

Meritor Savings Bank vs. Vinson

Michelle Vinson worked at the same branch of Meritor Savings Bank for about four years after being hired by vice president Sidney Taylor, the branch manager. Through the years she was promoted from teller-trainee to teller to head teller to assistant branch manager.

After Vinson took extensive sick leave in the fall of 1978, the bank discharged her. Then Vinson brought the claim against Taylor and the bank that she had been sexually harassed by Taylor throughout her four years of employment.

Vinson claimed that after her period as teller-trainee, Taylor asked her to dinner, where he suggested they have sexual relations. She agreed because she was afraid of losing her job, and voluntary sexual relations continued over the next several years.

Vinson also claimed that Taylor had followed her into the restrooms at the bank, exposed himself, and raped her on several occasions. Vinson said that, out of fear, she never reported the harassment to Taylor's supervisors.

Taylor denied these charges. The bank also denied the charges, saying that it was not aware of any sexual harassment by Taylor, and that if it did occur, it was without the approval or consent of the bank.

A federal district court ruled in favor of the bank, saying the relationship between Vinson and Taylor was voluntary, and that Vinson was not a victim of sexual harassment. The court also found that since Vinson had never filed a complaint according to the bank's policy against discrimination, the bank could not be held liable for Taylor's actions.

In 1985, the Court of Appeals for the District of Columbia Circuit reversed this decision, however, reinforcing the Equal Employment Commission guidelines that define hostile environment sexual harassment as a violation of Title VII of the Civil Rights Act of 1964.

The court reinforced the EEOC guidelines by agreeing that sex discrimination that creates a "hostile or abusive" work environment does constitute a violation of Title VII. The court rejected the idea that Title VII prohibits only discrimination that causes economic or tangible injury.

The court held that the voluntary nature of Vinson's actions was immaterial if her toleration of Taylor's sexual actions was in any way a condition of her employment.

The court also found that regardless of whether an employer is aware of sexual harassment by its supervisory personnel, the employer can be held liable for such action.

The court also stated that although a supervisor might not have the real authority to hire, fire or promote, the mere fact of holding a supervisory position gives the appearance of influence over job decisions, and places the supervisor in a position to take advantage of employees.

In 1986 the Supreme Court affirmed the court of appeals' reversal of the district court's judgment. The Supreme Court's opinions included the ruling that hostile environment sexual harassment is actionable under Title VII, and that Vinson's complaint could constitute such harassment.

The Supreme Court added, however, that it believed the court of appeals was wrong to rule that employers are always liable for the acts of their supervisory employees regardless of the circumstances of individual cases.

Rabidue vs. Osceola Refining

Vivienne Rabidue worked for Osceola Refining Co. from December of 1970 to January of 1977. During that time, she was promoted from executive secretary to administrative assistant, credit manager, and office manager.

The company acknowledged that Rabidue was a capable and ambitious employee, but also considered her argumentative, uncooperative and rude. The company claimed that she flagrantly disregarded supervisory direction and company policy any time they conflicted with her own ideas.

On occasion Rabidue had to work closely with Douglas Henry, an employee of a different department who was on an equal level with Rabidue. Many Osceola employees considered Henry a vulgar person who regularly made obscene comments about women. Sometimes Henry directed these remarks at Rabidue.

The company had been unsuccessful in changing Henry's behavior, and Henry and Rabidue were constantly in conflict. Other female employees also were annoyed with Henry's behavior.

In addition, other male employees sometimes displayed photos of partially or totally naked women, to which the female employees were subjected.

After heated arguments over business dealings with Osceola's vice president and the vice president of a company which was one of Osceola's customers, Rabidue was discharged in 1977. She then filed discrimination charges against Osceola.

Q & A

Question: Can sexy calendars and pinups on the walls of a warehouse or office be considered sexual harassment?

Answer: Yes, they can. They may contribute to a hostile work environment.

Question: One of our co-workers wears very short skirts. Isn't she asking for trouble?

Answer: No. Everyone has the right to do his or her job in a harassment-free workplace. What someone chooses to wear doesn't change that.

Question: How can sexual harassment be a problem in our workplace? No one's complaining.

Answer: That may be because people are too afraid to complain.

Adapted from "How to Recognize and Prevent Sexual Harassment in the Workplace" with permission of the publisher. © 1992 Business & Legal Reports Inc., 30 Academy Street, Madison, Conn. 06443

In this case, a federal district court and court of appeals supported the idea that an offensive work environment could constitute a violation of Title VII.

The court concluded in its ruling that to show hostile environment sexual harassment under Title VII, it must be proven that ". . . the employee was subjected to unwelcome sexual harassment in the form of sexual advances, requests for sexual favors, or other verbal or physical conduct of a sexual nature; the harassment complained of was based upon sex; the charged sexual harassment had the effect of unreasonably interfering with the plaintiff's work performance and creating an intimidating, hostile or offensive working environment that affected seriously the psychological well-being of the plaintiff."

The court ruled, however, that in this case, Rabidue failed to prove that the vulgar comments and sexual posters displayed by co-workers were severe enough to create an abusive, offensive or hostile environment.

Ellison vs. Brady

Kerry Ellison and Sterling Gray were revenue agents for the Internal Revenue Service in San Mateo, Calif. They were not friends and did not work closely together, although their desks were only 20 feet apart.

Ellison claimed that after she went to lunch with Gray once, in June of 1986, Gray asked her repeatedly out for lunch or for drinks after work. Ellison never accepted.

In October 1986, Gray wrote Ellison a love note that shocked and scared her, causing her to leave the room. When Gray followed her, demanding that she speak to him, she left the building. Ellison reported this to her supervisor, but asked her supervisor not to intervene, even though the supervisor recognized this as sexual harassment.

The following week, Ellison began a four-week training period in St. Louis. Gray sent her a three-page typed letter that Ellison regarded as strange and frightening. She called her supervisor and said she would be uncomfortable working in the same office with Gray again.

In November 1986, Gray transferred to the San Francisco office, and Ellison returned to San Mateo from St. Louis.

Gray filed union grievances requesting return to the San Mateo office, and the IRS and the union agreed to let him return to San Mateo after six months had passed.

Ellison found out that Gray was returning through a letter from her supervisor. Her supervisor said the decision had been made to solve Ellison's problem with a six-month separation period, and that further action would be taken if the problem resurfaced.

Then, in January of 1987, Ellison filed a formal complaint with the IRS alleging sexual harassment, and she requested a temporary transfer to San Francisco.

The IRS representative investigating the allegation agreed that Gray's conduct constituted sexual harassment. But in its final decision, the Treasury Department rejected Ellison's complaint, saying that it did not constitute sexual harassment covered by EEOC regulations. After an appeal, the EEOC agreed with the Treasury Department, saying the IRS took sufficient action to prevent a recurrence of Gray's conduct.

In September 1987, Ellison filed a complaint in federal district court. The court found that Ellison had failed to prove that hostile environment sexual harassment had occurred. It described Gray's conduct as "isolated and genuinely trivial."

Ellison appealed. A federal appeals court then reversed the previous decision, stating that harassment should be analyzed from the victim's perspective.

The court explained that because women are more often the victims of rape and other types of sexual assault, women are more likely to be concerned with offensive sexual behavior. It is understandable that women who are victims of rather mild sexual harassment might worry if that harassment is a preview of more violent attacks in the future, the court said.

Therefore, the court adopted the idea that to prove hostile environment sexual harassment, a female plaintiff must show that a reasonable woman would consider the circumstances severe or pervasive enough to create an abusive working environment or to alter the conditions of employment.

The court then found that a reasonable woman would have found Gray's alleged conduct severe and pervasive enough to create a hostile environment.

Another important outcome of this case is that the court set a standard for determining the effectiveness of an employer's attempt to put an end to alleged sexual harassment. The court said that an employer's remedy for harassment should be assessed in relation to the seriousness of the offense and in terms of its ability to stop the harassment.

Harris vs. Forklift Systems

Teresa Harris was a manager for Forklift Systems Inc., an equipment rental company, from April 1985 until October 1987. Charles Hardy was president of the company.

Harris claimed that Hardy repeatedly insulted her on the basis of her gender and often directed sexual comments torwards her and other female employees. For example, in the presence of others, he asked Harris to go with him to a hotel to negotiate her raise.

Harris also alleged that Hardy also sometimes asked her and others to retrieve coins from the front pockets of his trousers, and he sometimes threw things on the ground and asked female employees to pick them up, according to Harris.

In August 1987, Harris complained to Hardy. He apologized and promised to stop, saying he did not realize his behavior was offensive. But by September, Harris said, Hardy was behaving unacceptably again.

Harris quit in October and sued Forklift.

A federal district court originally held that Hardy's conduct did not constitute an abusive environment. The court said it believed that his actions would be offensive to a reasonable person, but that they were not so severe as to seriously affect the plaintiff's psychological well-being or to interfere with her job performance.

After Harris appealed, a federal appeals court affirmed the decision. Eventually, the Supreme Court reversed the previous decision, saying that Title VII comes into play before the harassment causes severe psychological injury or nervous breakdown.

The court said: "So long as the environment would reasonably be perceived, and is perceived, as hostile or abusive, there is no need for it also to be psychologically injurious."

EDUCATION CAN BE KEY IN PREVENTING HARASSMENT

The more you know, the better off you'll be. That statement rings true for many topics, including sexual harassment. Education can be the key to preventing sexual harassment and to preparing employees to recognize it and deal with it.

Although sexual harassment has received a great deal of publicity through media-hyped cases, it seems some people still have not learned that this issue is taken seriously, and harassment continues to occur.

Although he does not often handle such cases, Louisville attorney Bruce Boldt Jr. said that when he hears about instances of sexual harassment, "it's like someone dropped a bomb. I want to say to the harasser, 'Where have you been for the last 20 years? Have you been in a cave?'

"I'm constantly amazed that there are still men who don't seem to get it," said Boldt.

To help everyone, men and women alike, eventually "get it," said Ruby Fenton, an attorney with Rogers, Fuller, & Pitt in Louisville, "education is the key. The way to eradicate sexual harassment is not to file lawsuits. It's education."

Many professionals and agencies in the Louisville area work to educate people about sexual harassment. For example, professional human resources managers and consultants develop company policies and train employees on related issues and preventing sexual harassment.

Mike O'Loughlin, vice president of HR Enterprise Inc., a human resources consulting firm, has helped many clients develop sexual-harassment policies. Policies should outline what constitutes sexual harassment and what employees should do if it occurs, he said. "A policy states that these acts and behaviors are not acceptable, and that the organization won't tolerate them."

The Equal Employment Opportunity Commission has guidelines, said O'Loughlin. "They're the same for everyone, so it's not a fielder's choice kind of thing. In essence, policies are the same, altered slightly for different employers. You can usually commit a policy to a page or two."

Developing the policy is not the hard part, he said. "The challenge is getting the company exposed to the policy and getting the management team to understand it."

To familiarize employees with the company's policy and sexual-harassment issues, a company may have training sessions devoted to the subject of sexual harassment. These can be conducted either by the company's human resources manager or by a professional consultant like O'Loughlin.

"Training sessions can be a lot of fun. You can generate interesting discussions," said O'Loughlin. "People ask provocative questions to get reactions."

For example, at one particular training session, a salesman asked O'Loughlin the definition of leering. "He knew, but he was testing me," O'Loughlin said. The salesman's female partner asked if she could answer the question, "so she and he came up to the front of the room. She leered at him, and then there was no question about the definition of leering."

Training sessions might consist simply of an explanation of the policy, and an opportunity for questions and answers. Or, training can be fairly sophisticated, involving activities such as role playing or videos. "There are lots of ways to really drive the point home," said O'Loughlin.

Sources agree that the important thing is to ensure that everyone in an organization understands sexual harassment and the company's policy. "Training can be fun, but it also can get some issues out that might not be asked otherwise," said O'Loughlin.

One employer that educates its employees about sexual harassment and has a policy is the U.S. Small Business Administration's Kentucky District Office in Louisville.

"The policy was developed with a strong statement about what it should accomplish," said Sam Harris, assistant director for business development for the SBA office. "It was developed at the highest levels of SBA and was disseminated down through the regional offices to the district offices."

The office also has an annual staff meeting that all employees are required to attend. Sexual harassment is one of the topics covered at this meeting.

"In this particular office, there's no excuse for people not to understand what constitutes sexual harassment," said Harris.

In addition to training programs in the workplace, a number of agencies in the Louisville area are working to educate women on sexual harassment. One example is the Jefferson County Office for Women, a county agency founded in 1991 to serve as "a voice for women in Jefferson County," said Cecilee Tangel, project coordinator. "It's an advocacy office to improve the status of women in the county."

This agency works on various topics, including domestic violence, child support, day care, small-business issues, legal issues and sexual harassment. Representatives of the agency hold speaking engagements on these topics as well.

The agency explains the types of sexual harassment as defined by the law, and also provides down-to-earth advice on understanding and identifying sexual harassment. For instance, Tangel said one piece of advice agency reps offer is, "If in doubt, ask yourself if you would want your sister or mother subjected to that."

The agency also teaches that sexually harassing behavior "has no place at work, even if everyone chuckles. You always run the risk of offending someone. It's best to keep your remarks to yourself," said Tangel. "It's not how you intend them, it's how the receiver interprets them."

The agency advises women on how to respond if they are subjected to sexual harassment. The agency suggests that victims "initially should respond by saying to the person, the harasser, that the behavior is offensive. This can be hard, especially if the person is their supervisor," said Tangel. "We tell people to record times and places and to report the harassment within their company's guidelines. We encourage people to handle it as close to the source as possible."

Another local agency that is helping people deal with sexual harassment is the Jefferson County chapter of the National Organization for Women. "One significant thing we've done is we've had support groups for women who have filed suit against companies and need support," said Jean Murphy-Jacob, president of the Jefferson County chapter.

The process of suing an employer for sexual harassment can be emotionally draining. "There's a psychological cycle a woman goes through when she's a victim," said Louisville attorney Thomas Clay.

Clay said a victim usually is repelled by the harasser's conduct but also is intimidated and scared of being fired if she reports it. Since there usually are not witnesses, a victim often feels isolated and trapped, and even afraid to tell her spouse.

Eventually, "she gets mad, and she wants revenge. She wants to expose him (the harasser) to the public eye," said Clay. "Once she decides to go public, she's relieved, but then others might think she's blown the whistle and is causing problems."

Empathy can help. "Mostly in the support group, women shared what it was like going through the process," said Murphy-Jacob.

To be most effective, education on sexual harassment should be an ongoing process, said Clay. For example, developing a good policy and having a training session does not ensure that sexual harassment will never occur within an organization.

"It's not a one-shot deal. You can't have a seminar one day and think that'll do it. It's a mistake to think that if we put on a seminar today, everything will be fine," he said.

METHOD OF HANDLING COMPLAINTS CAN AFFECT OUTCOME

Employers' responses to employees' complaints of sexual harassment will affect the outcome of sexual-harassment charges filed down the road.

Right: Prompt, Effective Action

Anytime an employer becomes aware that sexual harassment has occurred, the "burden is on the employer to act promptly and efficiently," said Ruby Fenton, an attorney with Rogers, Fuller & Pitt in Louisville.

Even if an employee reports an incident but asks the employer not to act, the employer is wise to take some type of action to protect itself from liability, she said. In such a case, an employer might try to deal with the situation subtly, without revealing the identity of the person who complained.

When an investigation shows that a victim has been sexually harassed, the employer is responsible for "terminating the possibility of it happening again," said Fenton. Appropriate actions might include firing the offender, or transferring the offender or victim to another plant or city.

Whatever the solution, it must remove the possibility of a recurrence of the harassment.

Prompt and effective action can help reduce the chances that a company will be found liable for sexual harassment.

In a 1992 case, Kauffman vs. Allied Signal, the U.S. 6th District Court stated that taking prompt remedial action can protect an employer from liability in a sexual-harassment case.

In this case, a woman who had returned to work after having breast implants alleged that her male supervisor made inappropriate remarks about her chest. After being subjected to his comments for several days, she complained to a union representative, and the company quickly fired the offender.

Despite the supervisor's dismissal, the employee sued the company, alleging sexual harassment.

The court ruled in favor of the defendant, saying the employer had a good policy in place and acted promptly and effectively.

This case shows that "if an employer has a policy, and it's effective, it goes a long way towards insulating the employer against liability for sexual harassment," said Fenton.

Wrong: Retaliation

Retaliation is another crucial issue for employers to consider when dealing with complaints of sexual harassment, said Fenton. Retaliation occurs when an employer treats unfairly or takes adverse action against an employee who has complained of sexual harassment.

"Retaliatory action against an employee for complaining of sexual harassment is very dangerous for an employer," said Louisville attorney Thomas Clay.

Whenever an employee complains of sexual harassment, that employee is protected from retaliation under the same acts that provide protection from sexual harassment, namely Title VII of the Civil Rights Act of 1974 at the federal level, and in Kentucky, the Kentucky Civil Rights Act of 1966.

An employee can file a charge of retaliation, which is an entirely separate legal violation and proceeding, regardless of the outcome of the sexual-harassment charge, and regardless of whether the employee filed the sexual-harassment charge with the Equal Employment Opportunity Commission, the Kentucky Commission on Human Rights, or the courts, or filed a sexual-harassment complaint directly with the employer.

To prove retaliation, the employee must show a causal connection between the sexual-harassment claim and the act in questions. The employee must prove that "the retaliatory act was related to the sexual-harassment charge or complaint," said Fenton.

If for any reason an employer takes action against an employee who previously complained of sexual harassment, the employer should be able to prove that the action is not related to the harassment charge, she said.

"An employer should make sure that any action they're going to take can be supported by legitimate business reasons," she said.

For example, if an employee who has complained of sexual harassment is then repeatedly late or absent, the employer should document the tardiness and absenteeism as reasons for any disciplinary action.

Once an employee informs the employer of sexual harassment or files a charge at any level, "the employer has to be certain that they don't retaliate," said Fenton.

Employers should note that often "it's easier (for the victim) to win a claim of retaliation than it is to win a claim of sexual harassment," said Fenton.

READING 5-2

Sexual Harassment: Rights and Responsibilities

Barbara A. Gutek

INTRODUCTION

In the past 15 years, there has been a profound shift in thinking about sexual behavior in the workplace. Although employees and managers might have thought about sex when they encountered an attractive person in the workplace, researchers did not study it or write about it. In the mid-1970s, sexual behavior at work suddenly received considerable attention through the discovery of sexual harassment which appeared to be relatively widespread and to have long-lasting effects on a significant number of working women. The discovery of sexual harassment was somewhat counterintuitive, since, if people were pressed for their knowledge of sexual behavior at work, they might well have believed that some women benefited from seductive behavior at work, acquiring perks and privileges in exchange for sexual favors or the promise of them (Lipman-Blumen, 1976; 1984; Quinn, 1977). The first accounts of sexual harassment were journalistic reports and case studies (Bernstein, 1976; Fleming, 1979; Lindsey, 1977; Pogrebin, 1977; Rivers, 1978; Safran, 1976) and included a book by Lyn Farley, who said she coined the term "sexual harassment" (Farley, 1978).

Sexual harassment moved from a social issue to a legal offense largely through the efforts of MacKinnon, a lawyer, whose book, *Sexual Harassment of Working Women* (1979), sought a legal mechanism for handling sexual harassment

and compensating its victims. In a strong and compelling argument, MacKinnon contended that sexual harassment was primarily a problem for women, that it rarely happened to men, and therefore that it should be viewed as a form of sex discrimination. Viewing sexual harassment as a form of sex discrimination would make available to victims the same legal protection available to victims of sex discrimination. In 1980, the Equal Employment Opportunity Commission (EEOC) established guidelines consistent with MacKinnon's position, and numerous cases of sexual harassment have reached the courts in the U.S. (see Livingston, 1982). Since 1980, several states have passed their own increasingly strong laws aimed at eliminating sexual harassment (see, for example, Pearman & Lebrato, 1984). Thus, within one year of the publication of a book that first used the term "sexual harassment" (Farley's book), there was a legalistic rationale for handling cases of harassment (MacKinnon's book), and within two years, there were legal guidelines in place (EEOC).

The EEOC guidelines contain a very broad definition of sexual harassment. They (1980) state that "unwelcome sexual advances, requests for sexual favors, and other verbal or physical conduct of a sexual nature constitute sexual harassment when (1) submission to such conduct is made either explicitly or implicitly a term or condition of an individual's employment, (2) submission to or rejection of such conduct by an individual is used as the basis for employment decisions affecting such individual, or (3) such conduct has the purpose or effect of reasonably interfering with an individual's work performance or creating an intimidating, hostile, or offensive working environment."

By the time most managers and most researchers heard the term "sexual harassment," there was a legal definition of sexual harassment as well as a legalistic rationale for handling

Source: Employee Responsibilities and Rights Journal, 6 (4) (1993), 325–340. Used with permission.

cases of harassment and compensating victims of harassment. [In 1980, the year the legal guidelines were issued, a stratified, random sample of working men and women in Los Angeles County was asked whether or not they had heard of sexual harassment; 85% responded in the affirmative (Gutek, 1985).]

The rapid development of a legal rationale and guidelines for sexual harassment had an attendant effect: a rapid rise in formal charges of sexual harassment, resulting in court cases. For example, the EEOC reported that the number of complaints filed rose from 4,272 in 1981 to 7,273 in 1985. These figures do not include complaints made to other relevant agencies or cases where a complainant sought the services of a private attorney (*New York Times,* 1986). Since the Clarence Thomas confirmation hearings in fall, 1991, sexual harassment complaints have risen even more. In the first nine months of 1992, the EEOC received more complaints than it did for all of 1991 (*U.S.A. Today,* Oct. 2, 1992).

How and why did sexual harassment move from concept to law so quickly? First, like rape, it is a rare issue over which both liberals and conservatives can agree—albeit for different reasons. Like rape, conservatives usually view sexual harassment as a moral issue; a person should not be subjected to immoral acts and the perpetrator ought to be punished. Liberals are less likely to focus on sexual harassment as a moral issue, but instead as a feminist or a power issue. In any event, professing to be against sexual harassment is hardly a controversial stance (unlike being in favor of abortion, for example, or the death penalty.) Second, as mentioned above, MacKinnon (1979) successfully argued that sexual harassment could be treated as sex discrimination so that the lengthy process of putting a law in place was short-circuited. The EEOC guidelines were developed by a task force within the EEOC (Lipman-Blumen, personal communication, 1986). Employing organizations were not involved in the discovery of sexual harassment or in the formulation of policy and law. For many managers, their first encounter with the term sexual harassment might well have been a sexual harassment complaint.

SEXUAL HARASSMENT AS A FORM OF ORGANIZATIONAL BEHAVIOR

One of the guiding principles of modern organizations is the meritocracy (Katz and Kahn, 1978). In general, people are hired and promoted on the basis of their performance and contribution to the organization; similarly, they are demoted or terminated on the basis of their performance and the business needs of the organization. Sexual harassment violates the principle of meritocracy and thus violates people's sense of fairness and justice in an organization. It also interferes with the efficient functioning of the organization.

Sexual harassment is a form of organizational behavior in that it occurs in the context of work, and has effects upon workers, their careers, and the organization itself. In fact, the context may occasionally determine whether or not an incident is harassment, depending on whether it creates a hostile or intimidating work environment for some workers. When one person makes a sexual remark to another at a party or on the beach, it has different implications and effects than if the identical interchange took place at work. In the former case, the person making the remark occupies some role within the organization, a role that is associated with various obligations, resources, and decision-making ability. If the person who makes the remark is one's supervisor, the recipient responds differently than if the same remark came from a passerby on the sidewalk or an acquaintance at a party. In the workplace, a woman who is target of a man's sexual remarks, even ones not severe enough to be sexual harassment, is generally insulted, not flattered (Gutek, 1985, Chap. 6), although she may be less insulted (or more flattered) by the same remark made by someone else in another setting. To the extent that the sexual remarks at work come from a person who has some influence on her career opportunities, the woman is likely to feel threatened and harassed: "Why is he making that comment? What kind of a response does he expect from me? Is he noticing my work or just me? What happens next? Is he going to make sexual demands?"

While most women are not unduly concerned about one or two sexual remarks and they are unlikely to consider them harassment, there is some reason for apprehension because cases of sexual harassment often start with seemingly innocent sexual remarks. Although the range of sexually harassing experiences is very broad and thus difficult to typify, a "typical" severe case of harassment involves a male supervisor who has a history of harassment, sometimes unknown to many people in the organization except perhaps to the female employees' through an informal grapevine.[2] His target is probably younger and is subject to repeated, increasingly severe sexual demands, which may begin with his self-disclosing personal information and suggestions of working on weekends or having lunch together. As she evades or rebuffs his advances, he escalates his demands. For example, he may demand that she accompany him on business or quasi-business trips, make sexual comments in front of other workers, and make job threats that eventually lead to his firing her or her quitting her job. She is unlikely to tell anyone about the harassment except perhaps a close friend. She is reluctant to tell anyone or complain for several reasons: she fears that she will be labeled a troublemaker, that a complaint will be a wasted effort because no one will do anything, and that by making a complaint she will be subject to retaliation when she applies for other jobs. Sometimes, too, the victim feels embarrassed for the harassment and blames herself for not being able to handle the situation better (Jensen &

Gutek, 1982). Unless the harassment is extremely severe or prolonged, women also do not want to hurt the harasser's career or family life. Being charged with harassment is a serious step which many women are reluctant to initiate. Of the women who were harassed in a representative survey of working people in Los Angeles, 60% of the victims who did not report the harassment to anyone in their organization said one of the reasons for failure to report was not wanting to hurt the harasser (Gutek, 1985, Chap. 4).

As the above "typical" case shows, sexual harassment is organizational behavior in that the harasser uses his position within the organization and sometimes the organization's resources (e.g., business trips) to further his sexual wishes. The organization is affected when harassers hire the wrong women for the wrong reasons, fire women who personally reject them but who may be good organizational performers, and squander the organization's resources in pursuit of personal sexual exploits. Finally, of course, the victim is also affected, not only as a person, but also as an organizational actor. She may leave a good job or even a promising career in order to avoid the harassment, or may see her career prospects stymied, as well as face all the repercussions of being terminated if she is.

It is worth noting that sexual harassment is not always viewed as a form of organizational behavior. Sexual harassment and less severe social-sexual behavior at work are often viewed as resulting from a personality flaw in some men, or as an interpersonal phenomenon that has no organizational consequences. This view is illustrated with the following examples I have encountered:

> When a secretary complained to a vice-president that her boss was sexually harassing her, the vice-president told her that she was probably being too sensitive, and besides, she ought to be able to outrun her boss who was 20 years her senior. The alleged harasser was a valuable organizational contributor and the vice-president said that he didn't

feel comfortable telling the man how he should do his job.

A manager of a real estate firm said he had heard that some of his sales people "used sex" to facilitate sales but the organization did not condone their actions.

While the first example is likely to be viewed sexual harassment today by the courts, the second one is usually not in so far as the behavior was presumably not "unwelcome." (It is interesting to note, however, that in the second case other employees who felt they did not have the opportunity to exchange sex for a sale might be able to make a charge of harassment based on discriminatory treatment.)

In both examples, management views potential harassment as a personal proclivity and therefore not the organization's business. The respondents apparently see no or little organizational consequences to the use of sex to make sales or the use of a position in the organization to sexually exploit a subordinate. In short, they see it as personal behavior, not a form of organizational behavior. In the latter example, the vice-president apparently took into account the relative value of the two persons to the organization. The secretary, as the more expendable employee, would have to adjust to the personal proclivities of the man, the person occupying the more valuable organization position.

These examples, both the "typical" case of harassment noted above as well as the two short scenarios above, suggest that there are a number of separable constituent groups involved in any instance of alleged harassment: victims of harassment; harassers; and employing organizations and their representatives, i.e., managers. Each of the constituent groups has a different set of interests, rights, and responsibilities. Each has a stake in the issue and has somewhat different goals for a sexual harassment policy and legal and organizational mechanisms for dealing with it.

In the remainder of this article I will first elucidate three different perspectives on sexual harassment and then review the rights and responsibilities of each of the constituent groups. In particular, I will focus on the extent to which the introduction of government regulation and attendant legal liability experienced by organizations for sexual harassment has shifted the right and responsibilities of the parties involved: the target of harassment, the alleged harasser, and the employing organization.

PERSPECTIVES ON SEXUALITY AT WORK

The major players in defining and interpreting sexual behavior at work are three: feminists, lawyers, and organizations. These "major players" overlap with, but are not the same set of, constituents involved in actual cases of alleged harassment. The main premises of the three major players are shown in Table 1. These points of view are neither independent nor mutually exclusive. Each perspective is presented in Table 1 in its purest form; not all feminists, lawyers, or managers would agree with them exactly as they are presented here. This presentation is intended to underscore the divergence in thinking and to show how the introduction of laws about sexual harassment has shifted the "center" of thought as well as the rights and responsibilities of people involved in any allegation of harassment: the recipient, the initiator, and the employing organization.

The Feminist Perspective

This wide-ranging perspective sees sexual harassment as a logical consequence of sexism in society. It is both a cause and an effect. Sexual harassment exists because women are considered the inferior sex. Men can exploit women with impunity, in the workplace and outside it. Sexual harassment is also a cause; its occurrence helps to maintain gender stratification. Feminists may view sexual harassment as analogous to rape. Rivers (1978) expressed this viewpoint

| **TABLE 1** |

THREE PERSPECTIVES ON SEXUAL HARASSMENT

Feminist Perspective
  Reflects a power relationship, men over women
  Constitutes economic coercion
  Threatens women's economic livelihood
  Reflects the status of women in society
  Asserts a woman's sex role over her work role
  Parallels rape

Legal perspective
  Reflects unequal power relationship that is exploitative
  Involves both implicit and explicit terms of employment
  Is used as a basis for employment decisions
  Produces consequences from submission to, or refusal of, advances
  Promotes an intimidating, hostile, or offensive work environment

Managerial perspective: Older view
  Reflects personal proclivities
  Consists of misperception or misunderstandings of a person's intentions
  Is a result of "a love affair gone sour"
  May be considered normal behavior at work
  Can hurt the reputation of the accused

Managerial perspective: Newer view
  Is improper use of power to extort sexual gratification
  Treats women as sex objects, asserts sex role over work role
  Is coercive, exploitative, improper, unprofessional
  Is aberrant behavior

---

in her article, "Sexual harassment: The executive's alternative to rape."

One of the ways gender stratification is maintained is by emphasizing sex role expectations. Being a sex object is part of the female sex role. Sexual harassment is a reminder to women of their status as sex objects; even at work, women are sex objects.

Because sexual harassment is an outgrowth of societal gender stratification, its occurrence in organizations might be viewed as normal or expectable by nonfeminists. At the very least, handling sexual harassment would be viewed by nonfeminists as women's responsibility. If a woman wishes to venture into the world of work, she should expect overtures from men and be able to handle them. This is the general attitude of managers who responded to a survey sent to readers of the *Harvard Business Review* in the late 1970s: Women should be able to handle whatever comes their way (Collins & Blodgell, 1981). Thus, feminists would contend that sexual harassment is difficult to treat because it is not always veiwed as a problem. Accordingly, they committed themselves to documenting the existence of harassment and exposing it as a form of male domination over women.

Because in the feminist perspective, sexual harassment is an outgrowth of sexism in society, it has relatively little to say about the workplace itself. The workplace is just another sphere of male domination and another arena—like marriage—where men can assert their power over women.

The Legal Perspective

The legal perspective on sexual harassment currently parallels the legal approach to sex discrimination. Sexual harassment occurs when compliance with sexual requests serves as a basis for employment decisions, such as employee selection, performance appraisal, merit increases, promotions, or tenure. Sexual harassment occurs when the offending behavior affects an employee's job performance, mental health, or physical health. Any particular behavior is harassment when it leads to negative consequences for the worker or when it puts members of that worker's group—in this case, women—at a disadvantage relative to other groups, that is men.

While the legal perspective recognizes the contribution of societal influences to sexual harassment, it focuses on behavior in the work environment. Thus, complying with the legal requirements necessitates some changes in regulations and actions in the workplace. The employing organization must try to create an environment free of harassment and to respond vigorously to complaints of sexual harassment.

The Organizational Perspective

The organizational perspective comes in two variants, one old and the other relatively new. In the older organizational perspective, sexual harassment was not taken very seriously. Like the two short scenarios shown above, sexual interactions were viewed as personal matters that occasionally got out of hand. For example, perhaps a woman could not handle the local office "Don Juan" or perhaps he became too aggressive with too many female employees. An allegation of sexual harassment might also be an outgrowth of a lovers' quarrel or a result of misunderstandings or misperceptions. A woman might be insulted by a remark meant to be a compliment. Women's accusations of sexual harassment might also arise from their own (1) inability to handle men who are a "little too friendly," (2) sensitivity or modesty about sexuality, or (3) rejection by the man they have accused. This last viewpoint is reflected in the saying, "Hell hath no fury like a woman scorned."

Under this point of view, protecting the reputation of the high-status person—almost always a man—from unwarranted accusations that could damage his career might be the organization's prime responsibility. Allegations of harassment would be handled informally since they are viewed as personal, not organizational matters. The accuser may be transferred or fired, even when the accuser is acknowledged as having a legitimate case, as in the first scenario presented earlier. A senior manager might prefer to transfer a secretary or assistant who complains of harassment and replace her with someone who either will not be harassed (like a much older woman or a man) or with someone who "can handle the situation better," rather than directly confront the alleged harasser.

The second, newer organizational point of view takes sexual harassment more seriously, giving more rights to the recipient of unwanted overtures, and more responsibilities to both the perpetrator or initiator of those overtures, and the management of the firm. Here, sexual harassment is usually viewed as an organizational phenomenon that is the organization's business because the harasser has misused the power associated with his or her organizational position. Sexual harassment is viewed as an expression of personal proclivities in an exploitative, unprofessional, and inappropriate way.

The shift from the old to the new organizational position has been facilitated by the journalistic efforts of early feminists (e.g., Farley, 1978), the research conducted by feminists and others on sexual harassment (e.g., MacKinnon, 1979; Gutek et al., 1980; Brewer, 1982; Benson & Thomson, 1982), and, especially, the introduction of federal and state regulations. The manager who earlier may have felt it inappropriate to impinge on what he thought of as the personal (harassing) style of an employee now faces legal liability for that employee's behavior. Thus, both feminist thinking and legal requirements have influenced the shift from the old to the new organizational perspective.

RIGHTS AND RESPONSIBILITIES

In the remainder of the article, I will focus on the rights and responsibilities of three constituent groups: the harassed, the harassers, and the employing organization.

Victims of Harassment: Rights and Responsibilities

Before the 1970s, little was known about sexual harassment and sexual harassment victims had very few rights. Organizations relied on the employees' sense of morals and organizational norms to prevent sexual exploitation of employees. The "discovery" of sexual harassment led people to recognize that organizational norms and individuals morals were insufficient to prevent sexual harassment. Correspondingly, once the phenomenon was labeled, a variety of researchers and advocates sought to gather information about sexual harassment to find out if it was more likely to occur in some organizations or in some kinds of situations than in others. This information could be used to establish some rights and responsibilities based on knowledge of the phenomenon.

Farley's (1978) book, for example, showed that sexual harassment is not limited to some subset of employed women; it can happen to any working woman. Her book was replete with examples of sexual harassment victims varying from a minority janitor who is a single parent to single waitresses to married lawyers, etc. Gutek's research (1985; Gutek, Cohen, & Konrad, 1990) provided some baseline information about the frequency and type of harassment and also illuminated some of the workplace factors that affect sexual harassment.

The passage of the EEOC guidelines provided victims of harassment with some rights for the first time. The existence of government regulations has led many organizations to set up their own policies and sets of procedures for handling complaints of sexual harassment. Thus, for about the last 5 to 10 years, a significant number of employees have now had the right to work in an harassment-free work environment with those rights backed up by organizational policies and procedures, federal guidelines, and in many cases, state guidelines.[3]

Victims of sexual harassment also have some responsibilities. They must make the harassment known before the organization can respond. But survey data suggest that few do, contrary to many people's expectations. When a random sample survey of a division of California state workers were asked what they would do if they were harassed, most said they would tell the harasser to stop (Dunwoody-Miller & Gutek,

1985). However, actual victims rarely asked the harasser to stop (Gutek, 1985; Grauerholz, 1990). Their organizational position vis-à-vis the harasser usually makes them feel uncomfortable telling the person to stop because they are powerless to enforce their demands and may suffer retaliation for their complaints (Crull, 1982; Dunwoody-Miller & Gutek, 1985; Schneider, 1984). In fact, in at least one situation, those women who did tell harassers to stop generally found their efforts only moderately successful (Grauerholz, 1990).

Alleged Harassers: Rights and Responsibilities

While sexual harassment can happen to almost any employed woman, an extremely small percentage of men and an even smaller percentage of women are sexual harassers. Demographic characteristics do not differentiate sexual harassers from non-harassers; they are no more likely to be unmarried than the average employed man and they are not clustered into only a few occupations (Gutek, 1985, Chap. 4). In his research, Pryor (1987; 1990) has developed and provided validation for a measure of propensity to harass. In laboratory studies, Pryor found that men who scored high on his measure of propensity to harass were more likely than other men to use an ambiguous experimental situation to touch women and make comments to them. Naive women subjects were more likely to say that they were uncomfortable with the men who scored high on the sexual harassment proclivity scale than with men who scored low on it. Thus, willingness or propensity to sexually harass may be a personality trait, and in extreme cases, a pathological disorder. Most employed men probably have no more direct contact with sexual harassment than they do with rape. They hear about it through the media but it is foreign to their own experience. In an early pilot study conducted on sexual harassment in the late 1970s, respondents were asked first if they knew of anyone who had been sexually harassed. Our reasoning was that such a question was less embarrassing or threatening than asking about their own experiences. As it turned out, many more people were sexually harassed than knew about someone else being harassed. Almost no one knew of someone else having been harassed. Since harassment is much more of a problem for women than it is for men, and very few men are harassers, it is understandable that most male managers have no experience with it. Thus, it would probably not occur to them to set up formal rules to deal with sexual harassment.

In the absence of guidelines or regulations in the past, harassers had very little beyond their own consciences to keep them from harassing. Sex was a "freebie" for the men who chose to cajole, seduce, pressure, or harass women at work into sexual relationships with them. There were no sanctions against men who used work to find willing or unwilling sexual partners. Some of their harassment appeared to be intentionally hostile and was an attempt to intimidate women and force them out of certain jobs. Some harassment is a display of power, of "showing who's boss." In some cases of harassment, the harasser may not realize the extent of his effects on the victim. Some harassment may not be harassment in some other situation, as when a man's repeated comments about a woman's sexual attractiveness make her uncomfortable because they are not appropriate at work. And some harassment is a response to a work environment that encourages sexual overtures.

Sexual harassment is no longer a freebie. Both the initiator and the management of his/her organization are responsible for it. Thus, people who are inclined to overstep the bounds in this area—for whatever reason—now have some responsibility to curtail their behavior. In order to monitor and control their behavior, they need to know what is illegal; thus, they also have a responsibility to understand the legal guidelines on sexual harassment. To fail to do so could re-

sult in a variety of sanctions including termination.

People who are accused of sexual harassment also have some rights. In order to build a successful case against a harasser, a victim needs plausible evidence, written documentation and/or eye witnesses. A situation of the word of the complainant against the word of the alleged harasser is not a good "case," although the harassment may be real. In an organization where the legal guidelines are understood, employees need not be afraid that they will be unjustly sanctioned for sexual harassment if they are accused by a vindictive or unhappy subordinate. The available evidence (Gutek, 1985; USMSPB, 1981) suggests that few people make these unjust charges. However, in case someone does, the accused has some rights. In the event that he/she believes that treatment is unjust, he/she also has a right to sue the organization, and such cases of unlawful termination, for example, have been tried.

Employing Organizations: Rights and Responsibilities

Sexual harassment occurs more in some organizations than others. While the data on the incidence of harassment by industry sector are rare, they can be inferred from other studies which focus on individuals', not organizations, experiences with harassment. Harassment seems to be somewhat more likely in traditionally male industries where men are unaccustomed to working with women (O'Farrell & Harlan, 1982). Within organizations, harassment is also more common in departments and situations in which women work with many men rather than mostly with women (Gutek, 1985, Chap. 8). Finally, sexual harassment seems to be more common in sexualized environments, i.e., where people, especially women, are expected to dress in a sexually attractive or seductive manner and sexual comments, jokes, and innuendoes abound (Gutek, Cohen, & Konrad, 1990).

In the past, organizations had no legal responsibilities with respect to sexual harassment. According to the feminist perspective on sexual harassment reviewed above, being products of a male-dominated culture, both male and female managers in organizations may interpret reports of sexual harassment in a way that is advantageous to men and disadvantageous to women. For example, a complaint of harassment by a woman might lead a manager to (a) note that in the absence of prior complaints by other women, (b) this particular woman is probably just a troublemaker, (c) who may have a personal reason for disliking the man she is accusing, and besides (d) the man holds a position of importance in the organization, whereas (e) the woman is easily replaceable. The manager's decision, therefore, to dismiss or transfer the complaining woman appears sensible and just to him/her. Although any (or all) of the above suppositions made by the manager might be correct, they can also be interpreted as an outgrowth of sexist assumptions. Such a line of thinking used in the past went unchallenged, whereas today that manager may find himself/herself faced with a sexual harassment lawsuit in which he/she as well as the offending individual is listed as a defendant.

Organizations today not only have the responsibility to provide a harassment-free environment for their employees, but they are also required to know about sexual harassment, to know when and where it exists in their organization, and to eliminate it as soon as possible. The requirement of doing something about sexual harassment when it becomes known has, strangely enough, led some organizations to decline to collect any information on sexual harassment if they feel that it probably is not a problem, do not anticipate any lawsuits, and are not prepared to deal with harassment if it emerges as a problem.[4]

Other things being equal, harassment harms an organization as it harms the individual victim. An organization in which some employees use the organization's resources to satisfy their own sexual wishes is not operating efficiently and alienates their female employees, who increasingly make up larger proportions of many companies' payroll.

There is much the organization can do, of course, to meet its responsibilities without violating its general goals or operating procedures—unless their procedures condone or promote harassment. Many steps need not be unduly costly in time or money. Organizations can meet their responsibilities by using a variety of good management practices, for example, including sexual harassment or inappropriate, nonprofessional treatment of employees in the performance appraisal process, making a statement about sexual harassment in all new-hire orientations, and setting up a policy and set of procedures for handling allegations of sexual harassment. Perhaps more important than any particular step is the support of top management. Various policies and procedures will be perceived as serious steps, not just window dressing, only if top management provides clear support for them and acts in a manner consistent with them, for example, not promoting men who sexually harass women. Employees understand the difference between policies that are important to top management and the policies that exist merely to comply with government regulation.

Top management support makes all steps used to combat harassment more effective. For example, more victims of harassment may be willing to tell their harassers to stop when the organization has a real policy against it. As mentioned above, most women do not complain to anyone, and a recent study in academia showed that those women professors who told a harasser to stop thought the measure was only moderately effective (Grauerholz, 1990). It is likely to be much more effective when the harasser knows that the organization is serious about harassment than when he/she feels that no one but the victim is concerned about such behavior.

DISCUSSION

Journalistic accounts, analyses of male-female relations, research on the frequency and antecedents of sexual harassment, and the various policies, procedures, legal guidelines, and regulations have had the effect of granting more rights to victims of harassment and more responsibilities to perpetrators and their organizations. It is quite appropriate to ask if we now have a fairer system than we had in the past and whether there are abuses in the current system. While I know of no systematic research on the topic, it would appear that the answer is probably yes to both questions.

Organizations do not rely exclusively on people's consciences to keep them from stealing from the organization, nor do they rely completely on an employee's word to be sure that he/she is honest. Today, organizations no longer rely on people's consciences to prevent sexual harassment. A person who continues to harass an organization's employees is as legitimately subject to a variety of sanctions as is the person who steals, embezzles, or perjures him/herself.

Problems still arise. Some are similar to the problems of the past; a woman may be harassed but be unable to provide sufficient evidence of the harassment to warrant any redress. It is the victim's responsibility to provide the evidence that harassment occurred, not the perpetrator's responsibility to prove that it did not occur. Many cases of harassment do not have witnesses or other "sufficient evidence," and thus, many victims have no "case." In other instances, women may still be reluctant to come forward even if they do have a good case for many of the same reasons that prevented them from speaking out before there were organizational policies and legal guidelines about harassment. Many women are still embarrassed by the experience.

Some will feel guilty for not anticipating and somehow preventing it from happening; some fear they will be labeled troublemakers for their whisteblowing and will experience retaliation (see Parmalee, Near, & Jensen, 1982). Complaints take time; lawsuits take even more time—and money.

But there are also some new problems. An organization may respond quickly by firing the alleged harasser and then face another lawsuit for unlawful termination. In other cases, the organization decides to back up the employee who is charged with harassment and engages in a protracted and costly law suit. In these lawsuits, some employees are afraid to back the victim for fear that they too will experience retaliation. Others feel obligated to support their employer. Sometimes people who file law suits after receiving assurances that certain people will serve as witnesses find that their potential witnesses abandon them after they more carefully consider their own position vis-à-vis the organization.

A commonly recommended way to deal with an allegation of sexual harassment is to do a careful investigation (Rowe, 1981; Gutek, 1985, Chap. 9). Even an internal investigation, however, is disruptive of productivity and morale. As various people are questioned, rumors fly. Investigations and interviews tend to divide and polarize employees. It is no wonder that most managers are not at all pleased to learn that an employee feels she/he has been sexually harassed. It is quite understandable that the manager is reluctant to do anything, because "anything" is going to be disruptive. The mistake is to believe that there was no disruption before the complaint; the harassment, after all, is also disruptive to the victim and perhaps to others as well. But, of course, it did not disrupt the manager.

Sometimes male managers turn against women for bearing bad news. After having to face two cases of clear harassment in one year, a manager told me that "it is getting hard to find a man to supervise a group of women because you never know when one of them will pull a number on you." He did not seem to understand that his attitude may have been part of the problem.

Victims of sexual harassment want a law that will both prevent harassment from occurring and will provide some relief and compensation for them when it occurs. They want regulations that are comprehensive enough to cover all possible instances of sexual harassment. And they want a set of procedures that handle allegations of harassment swiftly and with no cost to them, no financial cost, and no career cost.

Potential harassers probably want legal requirements that are explicit and clear if there are going to be any laws at all. Employing organizations, too, want legal requirements that are explicit and clear. Some would prefer to go back to "the good old days" when there was one less government regulation, but others may even be somewhat grateful that there are legal guidelines to back up their attempts to provide a harassment-free environment for all. On the other hand, they are unlikely to be enthusiastic about guidelines that are difficult to define and enforce.

As far as the EEOC guidelines are concerned, the third clause, often called "the polluted work environment" clause, is the most nebulous and difficult to define. In addition, there is an abundance of research showing that whether or not ambiguous instances of potential harassment are, in fact, defined as harassment depends on many factors including the evaluator's gender, age, education, religiosity, attitude toward women, and experience with harassment, among others (Baker, Terpstra, & Larntz, 1990; Gutek, Morasch, & Cohen, 1983; Konrad & Gutek, 1986; Powell, 1983; Terpstra & Baker, 1985, 1989). This clause, which literally "covers a multitude of sins," may also constitute a nightmare for an employer. From the employer's standpoint, he/she may be unsure whether or not the environment is intimidating or hostile to some workers. Employers may also be con-

cerned that if it is too easy to sue, many "undeserving" people will do so. Easy and renumerative legal recourse may encourage people to engage lawyers when they have not been harassed on the grounds that large organizations will settle a case (meaning that the claimant and her/his lawyer will receive enough money to make the allegation worthwhile to them) rather than engage in a costly lawsuit. Under the current system, legal recourse is not easy, nor is renumeration guaranteed. The *perception* that suing is both easy and profitable, however, can be as potent as the reality that it is never easy and rarely profitable.

Nevertheless, despite the shortcomings of the current guidelines, they are unlikely to disappear, at least not before something better than no guidelines can replace them. They provide, albeit imperfectly, some measure of much-needed relief for those employees who become victims of sexual harassment.

NOTES

1. University of Arizona. Department of Management and Policy, McClelland Hall, Tucson, Arizona 85721.
2. Similarly, although often unknown to other faculty, faculty members who regularly harass female students are often known to women students, who warn each other about taking classes from the offending professors. I learned of this phenomenon when I began studying sexual harassment in the late 1970s and undergraduate women began telling me about their experiences. Many of them had heard in advance that certain faculty had a reputation as an harasser, but the course was required or not taught by anyone else. In all cases, as a faculty member, I had heard no such rumors about any of the alleged harassers.
3. As more cases of sexual harassment have passed through the legal system, clever and enterprising lawyers have been able to find a number of other statutes and laws that they can use on behalf of sexual harassment victims. For example, if phys-

ical contact is involved, the alleged harasser may be charged with assault.

4. In several cases, where I have conducted clinical surveys for large organizations, they have declined to include any questions on sexual harassment because they did not want the legal liability associated with that knowledge. They said if they were charged with a lawsuit, they would deal with it then.

REFERENCES

Baker, D. D., Terpstra, D. E., & Larnitz, K. (1990). The influence of individual characteristics and severity of harassing behavior on reactions to sexual harassment. *Sex Roles, 22*(576), 305–326.

Benson, D. J., & Thomson, G. E. (1982). Sexual harassment on a university campus: The confluence of authority, relations, sexual interest, and gender stratification. *Social Problems, 29*(3), 236–251.

Bernstein, P. (1976, August). Sexual harassment on the job. *Harper's Bazaar,* p. 33.

Brewer, M. (1982). Further beyond nine to five: An integration and future directions. *Journal of Social Issues, 38*(4), 149–158.

Collins, E. G. C., & Blodgett, T. B. (1981). Sexual harassment: Some see it . . . some won't. *Harvard Business Review, 59*(2), 76–95.

Crull, P. (1982). Stress effects of sexual harassment on the job: Implications for counseling. *American Journal of Orthopsychiatry, 52*(3), 539–594.

Dunwoody-Miller, V., & Gutek, B. A. (1985). *S.H.E. Project Report: Sexual Harassment in the State Workforce: Results of a Survey.* Sacramento: Sexual harassment in employment project of the California Commission on the Status of Women.

Equal Employment Opportunity Commission (1980). Guidelines on discrimination on the basis of sex (29 CFR Part 1604). *Federal Register, 45*(219).

Farley, L. (1978). *Sexual Breakdown: The Sexual Harassment of Women on the Job.* New York: McGraw-Hill.

Fleming, J. D. (1979, July). Shoptalk about shop sex. *Working Woman,* pp. 31–34.

Grauerholz, E. (1990). Sexual harassment of women professors by students: Exploring the dynamics of power, authority, and gender in a university setting. *Sex Roles, 21*(11/12), 789–802.

Gutek, B. A. (1985). *Sex and the Workplace: Impact of Sexual Behavior and Harassment on Women, Men, and Organizations.* San Francisco: Jossey-Bass.

Gutek, B. A., Cohen, A. G., & Konrad, A. (1990). Predicting social-sexual behavior at work: A contact hypothesis. *Academy of Management Journal, 33*(3), 560–577.

Gutek, B. A., Morasch, B., & Cohen, A. G. (1983). Interpreting social sexual behavior in the work setting. *Journal of Vocational Behavior, 22*(1), 30–48.

Gutek, B. A., Nakamura, C., Gabart, M., Handschumacher, I. J., & Russell, D. (1980). Sexuality in the workplace. *Basic and Applied Social Psychology, 7*(3), 355–365.

Jensen, I., & Gutek, B. A. (1982). Attributions and assignment of responsibility in sexual harassment. *Journal of Social Issues, 38*(4), 121–136.

Katz, D., & Kahn, R. L. (1978). *The Social Psychology of Organizations.* New York: Wiley.

Konrad, A. M., & Gutek, B. A. (1986). Impact of work experiences on attitudes towards sexual harassment. *Administrative Science Quarterly, 31*(4), 422–438.

Lindsey, K. (1977, November). Sexual harassment on the job. *Ms.,* 47–51, 74–78.

Lipman-Blumen, J. (1976). Toward a homosocial theory of sex roles: An explanation of the sex segregation of social interaction. In Blaxall, M. and Reagan, B. (eds.) *Women and the Workplace.* Chicago: University of Chicago Press.

Lipman-Blumen, J. (1984). *Gender Roles and Power.* Englewood Cliffs, NJ: Prentice-Hall.

Lipman-Blumen, J. (1986). *Personal Communication.*

Livingston, J. A. (1982). Responses to sexual harassment on the job. Legal, organizational, and individual actions. *Journal of Social Issues, 38*(4), 5–22.

MacKinnon, C. (1979). *The Sexual Harassment of Working Women.* New Haven: Yale University Press.

New York Times (1986). A grueling struggle for equality, *November* 9: 12–13.

O'Farrell, B., & Harlan, S. L. (1982). Craftworkers and clerks: The effects of male co-worker hostility on women's satisfaction with nontraditional jobs. *Social Problems: 29*(3), 252–264.

Parmalee, M., Near, J., & Jensen, T. (1982). Correlates of whistleblowers concerns about retaliation. *Administrative Science Quarterly, 27,* 17–34.

Pearman, M. I., & Lebrato, M. (1984). *Sexual Harassment in Employment: Investigator's Guidebook.* State Women's Program of the California State Personnel Board and Sexual Harassment in Employment Project of the California Commission on the Status of Women.

Pogrebin, L. (1977, June). Sex harassment: The working woman. *Ladies Home Journal,* 24.

Powell, G. N. (1983). Sexual harassment: Confronting the issue of definition. *Business Horizons, July/August* (83405), 24–25.

Pryor, J. B. (1987). Sexual harassment proclivities in men. *Sex Roles, 13,* 273–286.

Pryor, J. B. (1990, August). *Presentation at American Psychological Association,* Boston, MA.

Quinn, R. (1977). Coping with cupid: The formation, impact, and management of romantic relationships in organizations. *Administrative Science Quarterly, 22*(1), 30–45.

Rivers, C. (1978). Sexual harassment: The executive's alternative to rape. *Mother Jones, 3*(5), 21–22, 24, 28–29.

Rowe, M. (1981). Dealing with sexual harassment. *Harvard Business Review, 59*(5/6), 42–46.

Safran, C. (1976, November). What men do to women on the job: A shocking look at sexual harassment. *Redbook, 149,* 217–223.

Schneider, B. E. (1984). The office affair: Myth and reality for heterosexual and lesbian women workers. *Sociological Perspectives, 27*(4), 443–464.

Terpstra, D. E., & Baker, D. D. (1985). Reactions to Sexual Harassment. Presented at the 45th Annual Meeting of the Academy of Management, Boston.

Terpstra, D. E., & Baker, D. D. (1989). The identification and classification of reactions to sexual harassment. *Journal of Organizational Behavior, 10*(1), 1–14.

U.S.A. Today (1992, October 2). Sexual Harassment Charges Rise, p. 6A.

U.S. Merit Systems Protection Board, (1981). *Sexual harassment in the federal workforce: Is it a problem?* Washington, DC: U.S. Government Printing Office.

READING 5-3

Justice, Sexual Harassment, and the Reasonable Victim Standard

Deborah L. Wells
Beverly J. Kracher

INTRODUCTION

The Senate judiciary committee hearings confirming the appointment of Justice Clarence Thomas to the United States Supreme Court provided dramatic testimony that sexual harassment remains a formidable workplace problem. Although the practical impact in the workplace of the Thomas-Hill controversy is difficult to judge, two recent lower court decisions related to sexual harassment should cause managers to take stock of the treatment of sexual harassment within their companies. The impact of these decisions on employers who permit sexually hostile work environments to exist is dubious at this time. This paper presents a compelling moral argument that explains why employers must identify sexually hostile work environments from the perspective of the victim, most often a woman.

FORMS OF SEXUAL HARASSMENT

There are two generally recognized forms of sexual harassment (EEOC Guidelines, 1980). In *quid pro quo* sexual harassment, the victim is promised an employment benefit or advantage in return for a sexual favor or is denied continued employment or some advantage for refusing to participate in sex (*Arbitration Journal,* 1988). The victim is implicitly or explicitly told that he or she will be selected to fill a position,

Source: Journal of Business Ethics, 12, (1993), 423–431. Reprinted by permission of Kluwer Academic Publishers.

receive a pay increase, a promotion, or a favorable performance rating, for example, in return for performing a sexual act. Or, the victim is implicitly or explicitly told that he or she will lose his or her job, or receive a low performance rating, for example, if he or she does not perform sexually.

The second widely recognized form of sexual harassment, hostile environment sexual harassment, occurs when an employee's work performance suffers because sex-related behaviors in the work place create an intolerable work environment (EEOC Guidelines, 1980). Co-workers, supervisors, or even customers or clients who continuously ask employees for dates, or make lewd remarks or gestures to employees, can create a hostile working environment. So can the posting of suggestive calendars, posters, or centerfolds or the display of lewd magazines.

SEXUAL HARASSMENT AND THE LAW: RULINGS PRIOR TO ELLISON AND JACKSONVILLE SHIPYARDS

Section 703 (a) (1) of Title VII of the 1964 Civil Rights Act prohibits employment discrimination on the basis of sex. For more than ten years after the passage of the Civil Rights Act, however, the judicial system did not recognize sexual harassment as employment discrimination. Reasoning that sexual attraction would naturally play a role in employment decisions and that perpetrators were acting on their own when they harassed others, courts declined to view sexual harassment as deprivation of employment opportunities to victims, chiefly women (Koen, 1990; Morlacci, 1987). This "boys will be boys" reasoning prevailed until the mid-1970s, when lower courts at last allowed that the most invidious type of sexual harassment, *quid pro quo,* was indeed a form of discrimination. Even so, courts found sexual harassment to be discriminatory only if the victim suffered a tangible economic loss, such as denial of a promotion or pay

increase, by refusing the harasser's sexual demands. If the impact of harassment was psychological or otherwise intangible, no discrimination was found to have occurred (Morlacci, 1987).

In 1986, the United States Supreme Court heard its first case dealing with sexual harassment. The high court's ruling in Meritor Savings Bank v. Vinson was particularly important because it recognized hostile environment sexual harassment as a form of employment discrimination that could be as potentially harmful as *quid pro quo* sexual harassment. Although this Supreme Court decision regarding hostile environment sexual harassment was viewed by feminists and interested others as a triumph, the text of the ruling itself leaves much interpretation for the lower courts (Hauck and Pearce, 1987; Hukill, 1991). Specifically missing is a test or decision rule for when a work environment is so contaminated by sexual behavior that it can be considered truly hostile (Koen, 1990).

HOSTILE ENVIRONMENT SEXUAL HARASSMENT AND THE LAW: REASONABLE VICTIM STANDARDS IN ELLISON AND JACKSONVILLE SHIPYARDS

A contemporary and controversial legal development in hostile environment sexual harassment employment discrimination litigation is the product of lower court rulings in two states. A California appellate court, in Ellison v. Brady, demanded that hostile environments be judged from the viewpoint of a reasonable victim, not a reasonable person. In Jacksonville Shipyards, a Florida court ruled that the impact of sexually suggestive calendars and other photographs prominently displayed in a workplace be judged from the viewpoint of those negatively affected: women (Murphy *et al.,* 1991; Simon, 1991).

ELLISON V. BRADY AND JACKSONVILLE SHIPYARDS: BRIEF DESCRIPTION AND IMPLICATIONS

Ellison v. Brady

After accompanying colleague Gray to lunch on one occasion, IRS employee Kerry Ellison received a number of letters, in addition to subsequent social invitations, from Gray. Ellison reported Gray's behavior to her supervisor, but attempted to further discourage Gray with the assistance of a coworker who asked Gray to leave Ellison alone. Subsequently, the supervisor, too, asked Gray to stop, but he continued to write letters to Ellison. Although, as the court later acknowledged, many of these letters were innocuous in nature, in one letter Gray stated that he could not stand to feel Ellison's hatred of him, and he continued to write even after she was temporarily relocated in another city for training. When Ellison returned following the completion of her training, Gray agreed to be transferred to a different office, but later changed his mind and successfully protested the transfer through his union's grievance procedure. Upon his return to the office in which Ellison worked, she filed a complaint with the California EEOC (Simon, 1991).

The judge in the federal court that first heard Ellison's case declared that love letters did not constitute sexual harassment, according to any reasonable person. But the decision in Ellison v. Brady rendered by the appeals court overturned the original decision, saying that what does or does not constitute sexual harassment can only be determined by viewing the alleged harassing acts from the perspective of a reasonable victim. This appellate court decision achieved notoriety because it overturned the reasonable person test for judging the impact of one individual's behavior on another.

Jacksonville Shipyards

The Ninth Circuit Court of Appeals, in Ellison v. Brady, was not the only court to recognize the merits of the reasonable victim standard. A federal court in Jacksonville, Florida, recognized that by allowing male welders latitude in posting printed materials depicting women in sexually submissive positions, the Jacksonville Shipyards perpetuated a work atmosphere that was degrading to female welders (Hayes, 1991; Murphy *et al.*, 1991). This court, too, declared that the impact of posting sexually demeaning materials should be judged from the perspective of the victim; in this case from the perspective of the female employees.

REACTIONS TO ELLISON AND JACKSONVILLE SHIPYARDS

Some members of the legal community have labeled the courts in Ellison v. Brady and Jacksonville Shipyards "maverick." These critics discount the impact of the reasonable victim standard, saying that such a standard will not be widely adopted (Larsen, 1991; Epping, 1992). These attorneys narrowly define the reasonable victim standard to mean that only a person who is exactly like the victim (same race, same gender, same age, and so on) is able to judge a situation from that victim's perspective. But it is not necessary to understand the reasonable victim standard in this sense. The reasonable victim standard only requires that a person is able to put himself or herself in the position of the victim in order to judge a situation from that victim's perspective, and it is in this latter sense that we will use the reasonable victim standard in this paper. As of today, there is no agreement within the legal community to use the reasonable victim standard in either sense to identify hostile environment sexual harassment.

REASONABLE VICTIM STANDARD: FROM THE LAW TO MORALITY

The fact that there is no single set of legally accepted criteria for identifying hostile work environments created by sexual harassment is problematic for business since accepted legal standards often function as adequate guides for constructing policies for the workplace. But this has been overcome with past problems. Many policies, for example smoking policies, have been made without the benefit of legal precedent. That policies must be set without benefit of legal precedent is not surprising, since it often takes years before court edicts, especially Supreme Court edicts, are issued in response to problems arising in day-to-day work life. Given this legal vacuum, it is imperative that businesses look to other sources of standards for conducting their activities. One such source has been, and will be, morality.

Morality is a relevant source of standards for business since, other than legal precedent, it is the only other criterion for determining what is just or fair. Thus, in the case of hostile environment sexual harassment we can look to morality in order to construct a policy that fairly identifies sexually hostile environments. The thesis of this paper is that fair workplace policies regarding sexually hostile environments identify sexually hostile environments from the perspective of the reasonable victim. We use the modern moral theory of John Rawls to defend this thesis.

RAWLS' MORAL THEORY

Heralded as the most ambitious and influential work in social philosophy in the late twentieth century, John Rawls' *A Theory of Justice* (1971) establishes a fair method for arriving of fundamental principles of justice for individuals as well as for the basic institutions of society. Rawls' central idea is that just principles are those principles people, when in a certain fair situation, would unanimously accept. Rawls calls the situation of fairness "the original position" and describes it as a hypothetical situation where free, self-interested, impartial, and rational people agree to principles of conduct they must live by once outside of the original position.

Anyone who has ever tried to get a group of self-interested people to unanimously agree to anything will immediately recognize a problem Rawls faced when constructing his theory. Self-interested people pursue private agendas and thus it is difficult if not impossible to achieve consensus among them. Furthermore, it is difficult to maintain impartiality in self-interested people. Rawls responds to these problems by requiring that we drop all knowledge of our private agendas and, like justice herself, become more or less blindfolded to the qualities that bias our agreements. Thus, in the original position individuals know nothing about who they will be once outside of the original position. That is, in the original position individuals know nothing about what race they will be, their intellectual ability, social status, religion, or class. Rawls calls imposition of the blindfold "the veil of ignorance." This veil of ignorance ensures impartiality and promotes unanimity.

Rawls argues that rationality in the original position dictates use of the maximum strategy. This means that an individual will choose principles where the worst outcome for him or her is the least bad. In *A Theory of Justice* Rawls argues for and systematically explores two social principles of justice he believes would be agreed to in the original position, namely, the equal liberty principle and the difference principle (p. 302).

In particular, the difference principle is the assertion that social and economic inequalities are to be arranged so that they are both:

(A) to the greatest benefit of the least advantaged . . . and,

(B) attached to offices and positions open to all under conditions of fair equality of opportunity (Rawls, 1971, p. 302).

Rawls also argues that in the original position individuals would consent to at least five principles of justice for individuals and individual arrangements (which he calls natural duties). These principles are the duty to uphold just institutions, the duty to give mutual aid, the duty of mutual respect of persons, the duty not to harm the innocent, and the duty not to injure.

Rawls' principles pertain to hostile environment sexual harassment in two important ways. First, there must be equal opportunity to hold offices and positions in a just society, according to the second part of the difference principle. Since hostile environment sexual harassment violates this principle by closing off to victims the offices and positions they would otherwise hold, hostile environment sexual harassment is shown to be unjust. Second, an understanding of the duty to show respect to persons and the duty not to harm the innocent provides a framework from which we can devise fair workplace policies regarding hostile environment sexual harassment, as we shall show in the following section.

NATURAL DUTIES AND HOSTILE ENVIRONMENTS

The duty not to harm the innocent and the duty to show mutual respect to persons provide an excellent moral framework for constructing a standard from which to judge whether or not a sexually hostile work environment exists. The rest of this section shows how the duties to show respect to persons and not to harm the innocent provide an identification of sexually hostile environments from the perspective of the victim.

Both duties, namely, to show respect to persons and not harm the innocent, would be agreed to in the original position and thus are important moral constraints. Regarding the duty not to harm the innocent, we can assume that the innocent are persons who are unwilling recipients of harm done to them.

Regarding the duty to show mutual respect Rawls states:

Mutual respect is shown in several ways: in our willingness to see the situation of others from their point of view, from the perspective of their conception of their good; and in our being prepared to give reasons for our actions whenever the interests of others are materially affected . . . Further, . . . to respect another as a moral person is to try to understand his aims and interests from his standpoint and to present him with considerations that enable him to accept the constraints on his conduct . . . Also respect is shown in a willingness to do small favors and courtesies . . . because they are an appropriate expression of our awareness of another person's feelings and aspirations . . . parties in the original positions know that in society they need to be assured by the esteem of their associates. Their self-respect and their confidence in the value of their own system of ends cannot withstand the indifference much less the contempt of others. Everyone benefits from living in a society where the duty of mutual respect is honored (Rawls, 1971, pp. 337–338).

Rawls tells us that respect for persons involves being willing to see things from another's point of view. We need not agree with this other person's perspective, but in order to show respect we must be willing to recognize the other person's perspective and act appropriately. This respect, Rawls tells us, must be mutual and not one-sided. For example, I must be willing to see your perspective and you must be willing to see mine.

Prima facie, there are four ways to identify sexually hostile work environments. First, sexually hostile environments could be identified from the perspective of the reasonable harasser. Second, sexually hostile environments could be identified from the perspective of the reasonable harasser and the reasonable victim (assuming that these perspectives are different from one another). Third, sexually hostile environments could be identified from the perspective of the reasonable person, that is, from the perspective of the reasonable harasser or the reasonable victim (where these perspectives are ultimately the same). Fourth, sexually hostile environments could be identified from the perspective of the reasonable victim. While there are these four possibilities, we assert that only by identifying sexually hostile environments from the perspective of the reasonable victim will a workplace policy be practical and just. Our reasons for not choosing the first three alternatives are the following.

If sexually hostile environments are identified from the perspective of the reasonable harasser, then the duty not to harm the innocent is not fulfilled. For the innocents in this case are the employees being subjected to unwelcome sex-related behavior. They are innocent since they are unwilling participants in the sexually harassing environment in which they find themselves. Innocents are harmed when hostile environments are defined only from the perspective of the harasser since that environment, unproblematic to the harasser who created it, is demeaning to the target or victim and undermines his or her sense of self-esteem. If sexually hostile environments are identified only from the perspective of the harasser, then people are not required to consider the perspective of the victim. This allows harm to occur to the victim, which is morally unacceptable on the grounds of our natural duty not to harm the innocent.

While the duty to show mutual respect may lead us to think that we must identify sexually hostile environments from both perspectives, identifying hostile environments from the perspectives of both the reasonable harasser and the reasonable victim is practically worthless. For while persistent jokes, remarks, and gestures may be perceived as innocuous from the viewpoint of the employee or employer making them, they are threatening or abusive from the viewpoint of the target employee. The duty of mutual respect does require us to take into account another's perspective. But when the perspectives involved are irreconcilable, as in the case of sexually hostile environments, no constructive practical policy can be devised which identifies sexually hostile environments from both perspectives.

If sexually hostile environments are identified from the perspective of the reasonable person, then it does not matter whether the reasonable person assumes the role of the harasser or the victim. For if sexually hostile environments are identified from the perspective of the reasonable person, then there is only one perspective in hostile environment issues, namely, the reasonable person. If there is only one perspective, then as a reasonable person, that individual is able to extrapolate from the particulars of any role assumed and judge whether or not a sexually hostile environment exists in a situation. However, there is more than one perspective in hostile environment issues. As we show in a later section of the paper, men and women generally have different perspectives regarding sexual behavior at work. Since, generally, men are sexual harassers and women are the victims of sexual harassment, then generally harassers have a different perspective than victims. Thus, sexually hostile environments cannot be identified from the reasonable person perspective since there is no *one* reasonable person standard regarding sexually hostile environments.

Since there are reasons for not using the first three alternatives to identify sexually hostile environments, we are left with the alternative of identifying sexually hostile environments from the fourth perspective, namely, through the perspective of the reasonable victim. This alternative is acceptable for the same reasons the others were not. First, it is practically workable since it provides us with a real way to discern instances of sexually hostile environments. For we need only ask reasonable victims if they see a sexual situation as unwelcome and abusive in order to identify sexually hostile environments. Second, it promotes an individual's duty not to harm the innocent because it requires that people identify sexually hostile environments from the perspective of the innocents. Third, it is consistent with current studies which evidence the differences in perspectives between harassers and victims.

Determining the exact qualifications for being a reasonable victim takes us outside the scope of this paper. Nevertheless, assuming that Rawls is correct in arguing that persons in the original position would consent to the duty to show respect to persons, we can say that a reasonable victim's perspective is restricted by the duty to show respect to persons. This is as it should be. The reasonable victim must show respect to others in as much as others must respect the victim. Thus, on the one hand, the reasonable victim must allow some sexual behavior that she finds merely annoying for the sake of the person with a more highly sexual orientation. On the other hand, the reasonable victim can restrict some sexual behavior in the workplace, namely, that sexual behavior that creates an abusive and thus harmful environment. Thus, adhering to the duty to show respect to persons allows us to distinguish between harmful sexual environments and sexual environments which are offensive yet not harmful and to assert that the reasonable victim identifies hostile environments as only those sexual situations that are abusive or harmful.

In summary, we argue that we should identify sexually hostile environments from the perspective of the reasonable victim. This identification standard is practical, and fulfills the duty not to harm the innocent. In keeping with Rawls, we affirm that a reasonable victim is a person who accepts a duty to show respect to persons. We argue that accepting this duty restricts the reasonable victim's perspective. And this is how it should be. On account of the duty to show respect to persons who are more highly sexually oriented, the reasonable victim allows sexual environments in the workplace that are merely annoying. Yet on account of the duty to show respect to persons with less sexual orientations,

the reasonable victim is permitted to restrict sexual environments which are abusive and harmful, that is, which are sexually hostile environments.

EMPLOYER RESPONSES TO SEXUAL HARASSMENT

Practitioner-oriented literature is filled with advice on how to avoid sexual harassment claims and costly subsequent litigation. The basic advice, followed by many employers, is to treat sexual harassment in much the same way other serious employee-reported problems are treated: Draft a policy forbidding the behavior, make workers and supervisors aware of the prohibition, establish a reporting procedure, and subject violators to progressive discipline. The persistence of workplace sexual harassment complaints and litigation, however, suggests that employer responses have been inadequate in the past and a revised approach should be taken.

SEXUAL HARASSMENT TRAINING AND THE REASONABLE VICTIM STANDARD

We have used the duty not to harm the innocent and the duty to show respect to persons as a framework from which we arrived at an identification standard for sexually hostile environments. Our thesis is that sexually hostile environments should be identified from the perspective of the reasonable victim. But consideration of the duty to show respect to persons and the duty not to harm the innocent also leads us to say that sexually hostile environments can be curtailed in the workplace through two types of training programs: consciousness-raising, aimed at promoting understanding of the different perspectives men and women hold on sexual behavior in the workplace, and assertiveness training, geared toward teaching potential victims how to respond more forcefully to harassment so that harassers clearly understand there is a perspective other than their own.

Training to Promote Consciousness Raising

Hostile environment sexual harassment training programs must promote mutual respect of persons by changing men's and women's understanding and behaviors so that they can perceive, tolerate, and respect their divergent perceptions of the workplace environment. Research shows that men and women experience workplace sexuality quite differently. Men, in general, report a more sexualized work atmosphere than do women (Gutek *et al.,* 1990), in that conversations among men at work are more likely to contain sex-related jokes, comments, and stories of sexual conquests than are conversations among women. Increased contact between the genders, an inevitable consequence of increasing labor force participation rates for women, promotes a more sexualized work environment for women, too, (Gutek *et al.,* 1990) thus increasing the likelihood that sexual harassment will occur. When men and women do encounter sexual behavior at work, they view it very differently. One survey uncovered a stunning dichotomy between men and women: 75 percent of male respondents would be flattered by sexual advances in the workplace; 75 percent of females would be offended (Hayes, 1991).

Sex-related conduct, statements, acts, or events that may not be offensive or harmful to men are offensive and even frightening to women. Women simply have learned to see more of the sexual conduct in the workplace as threatening because they are much more often than men the victims of sexual assault and rape (Simon, 1991). Likewise, men have learned, through sex role socialization, that they should initiate social and sexual activities with women. Men may not turn off this role expectation when they come to work, and so "role spillover" undoubtedly accounts for some sexually harassing behavior (Gutek *et al.,* 1990). Because both of these sets of responses, male and female, are learned, it makes sense that training can help employees "unlearn" them.

Segal (1990) has developed a training exercise designed to sensitize employees to interpersonal differences in perception of sexual behaviors. He advocates preparing ". . . a list of 20 to 30 examples of conduct which, either alone or in conjunction with other conduct, arguably might give rise to a hostile work environment" (Segal, 1990, p. 176). Participants individually rate the degree to which they believe the conduct gives rise to a hostile work environment. Discussion within mixed gender groups then ensues. In Segal's experience, three patterns have emerged. First, there are wide differences in what women do and do not view as harassing. Second, women are more likely than men to see any given sex-related behavior as giving rise to a hostile environment, and third, when sexual conduct is aimed at women, rather than men, both genders are more likely to see its hostile potential. Participants in this training come away with a heightened awareness of differences between male and female perceptions of workplace sexuality and are more likely to understand the consequences of their sex-related speech and behavior. We recommend this kind of approach to enable employees to see that there are other viewpoints on sexuality and to help them develop a sense of duty to show respect to others.

Assertiveness Training

Workplace training programs must enable individuals to fulfill their duty not to harm the innocent and their duty to show respect to persons. They must reinforce those abilities in individual employees that allow them clearly and forcefully to show how unwelcome particular acts of sexual behavior are, while understanding that the behavior may arise not from malice, but from having a different perspective. Reinforcement of these abilities is necessary since it is questionable whether we can hold a harasser at fault for his or her actions if there is no response from the victim to indicate to the harasser that his or her actions are unwelcome and harmful. That is, the harasser must reasonably be able to know that this or her actions are creating a hostile environment in order to be able to hold the harasser responsible for his or her actions. And since it is sufficient for the harasser's knowledge that his or her actions are creating a hostile environment that the victim clearly states or shows that the actions are unwelcome and harmful, it is beneficial to reinforce the abilities of the victim to make this known.

We recommend that potential victims learn to clearly show their disfavor with particular sexual behaviors through assertiveness training programs. These training programs must accomplish two goals. First, they must determine participants' current levels of assertiveness. The Rathus Assertiveness Schedule, for example, is a diagnostic instrument that has been successfully used for this purpose (Dawley and Wenrich, 1976).

The second goal that must be achieved by training programs is to impart techniques individuals can use to be more assertive when needed. One valuable technique is role playing. Role playing allows individuals to practice being assertive. Role playing may include rehearsing what to say to a harasser. For example, it is valuable to rehearse using "I" statements (e.g., "I am uncomfortable with how you are acting") rather than "you" statements (e.g., "You are making me uncomfortable"). "I" statements are more valuable than "you" statements since they arouse less defensiveness from the listener, evoke feelings of power within the speaker, and encourage discussion of differences of opinion (Drury, 1984).

Teaching a technique called DESC (Bower and Bower, 1976) is also worthwhile in assertiveness training courses. DESC is an acronym for describe the situation, express how you feel, specify what can be done (by both parties) to change the situation, and state rewarding consequences from the change. A DESC script can be used to formulate a letter to a harasser or as the basis of a verbal response to harassment to get a harasser to recognize and change offensive behaviors.

The training we have advocated above is designed to bring about changes in perceptions, attitudes, and behaviors on the part of both potential sexual harassers and their victims. We harbor no illusions regarding the difficulty of producing such changes. In fact, in other contexts, institutionalizing major attitude and behavioral change takes, on the average, eight years (Murray, 1976). Because this is true, the training will have to be offered regularly and be reinforced by strong management support that includes much of the traditional approach to dealing with sexual harassment: clearly written policies, good reporting procedures, and discipline for offenders who resist change even after participation in training.

CONCLUSION

Although there is no legal consensus on reasonable victim standards, we have shown that employers should adopt this reasonable victim perspective in order to identify sexually hostile work environments. Widespread adoption of the reasonable victim perspective has the potential to curb sexually hostile environments in the workplace as employees seek to fulfill two important moral duties: the duty to show mutual respect and the duty not to harm the innocent.

The most efficacious manner for bringing about this change is to widely sensitize employees to individual perceptual differences on sex-related behaviors through consciousness raising sessions and to increase the assertiveness of potential victims in order to further emphasize that there are two perspectives on sexual harassment in action, not one. Training programs geared to achieve these results must be seriously undertaken and reinforced by repetition and strong management support.

REFERENCES

Bower, S. A. and Bower, G. H.: 1976, *Asserting Yourself A Practical Guide for Positive Change* (Addison-Wesley, Reading, MA).

Dawley, H. H. and Wenrich, W. W.: 1976, *Achieving Assertive Behavior* (Brooks/Cole, Monterey, CA).

Drury, S. S.: 1984, *Assertive Supervision: Building Involved Teamwork* (Research Press, Champaign, IL).

Epping, A. R.: 1992 (January 16), 'Everything You've Always Wanted to Know About Sexual Harassment but Were Afraid to Ask', *Speech to The Association of Government Accountants Omaha Metro Area Chapter.*

Guidelines on Discrimination on the Basis of Sex: 1980, (Equal Employment Opportunity Commission, Washington, DC).

Gutek, B. A., Cohen, A. G., and Konrad, A. M.: 1990, 'Predicting Social-Sexual Behavior at Work: A Contact Hypothesis', *Academy of Management Journal 33,* pp. 560–577.

Hauck, V. E. and Pearce, T. G.: 1987, 'Vinson: Sexual Harassment and Employer Response', *Labor Law Journal 38,* pp. 770–775.

Hayes, A. S.: 1991 (May 28), 'Courts Concede the Sexes Think in Unlike Ways', *Wall Street Journal 217,* pp. B1 and B5.

Hukill, C.: 1991 (May), 'Significant decisions in labor cases', *Monthly Labor Review 114,* pp. 32–40.

Larsen, D. A.: 1991, Personal communication.

Morlacci, M.: 1987, 'Sexual Harassment Law and the Impact of Vinson', *Employee Relations Law Journal 13,* pp. 501–512.

Murphy, B. S., Barlow, W. E. and Hatch, D. C.: 1991 (May), '"Reasonable Woman" is New Standard for Sexual Harassment', *Personnel Journal 67,* pp. 34–36.

Murray, E. A.: 1976, (July) "The Social Response Process in Commercial Banks: An Empirical Investigation', *Academy of Management Review 1,* pp. 5–15.

Nowlin, W. A.: 1988 (December), "Sexual Harassment in the Workplace', *The Arbitration Journal 43,* pp. 32–40.

Rawls, J.: 1971, *A Theory of Justice* (Harvard University Press, Cambridge, MA).

Segal, J. A.: 1990 (June), 'Safe Sex: A Workplace Oxymoron?', *HRMagazne 35,* pp. 175-176, 178, 180.

Simon, H. A.: 1991, 'Ellison v. Brady: A "Reasonable Woman" Standard for Sexual Harassment', *Employee Relations Law Journal 17,* pp. 71–80.

READING 5-4

The Legal, Ethical, and Social Implications of the "Reasonable Woman" Standard in Sexual Harassment Cases

Robert S. Adler
Ellen R. Peirce

INTRODUCTION

Much controversy and confusion surround the appropriate standard of review for evaluating "hostile environment"[1] sexual harassment cases.[2] In a 1986 decision, the Supreme Court directed lower courts to assess, in examining allegedly harassing conduct, whether the conduct was both unwelcome and so severe or pervasive that it altered the plaintiff's working environment.[3] This directive, however, leaves open the question of whose perspective—that of the particular victim, a reasonable person undifferentiated by sex, or a reasonable woman[4]—the fact finder should use to assess the seriousness of the offense. Herein lies the dilemma: When sexual

Source: Reprinted by permission of the *Fordham Law Review, 61* (1993), 773–827.

harassment is at issue, "[s]ome see it . . . some won't."[5]

Recently, the Equal Employment Opportunity Commission (EEOC) addressed this problem in a publication titled *Policy Guidance on Current Issues of Sexual Harassment.*[6] In that document, the EEOC recommended that "[i]n determining whether harassment is sufficiently severe or pervasive to create a hostile environment, the harasser's conduct should be evaluated from the objective standpoint of a 'reasonable person.'"[7] The EEOC further stated that Title VII should not serve as a "vehicle for vindicating the petty slights suffered by the hypersensitive."[8] That is, unless the challenged conduct substantially affects the work environment *of a reasonable person,* no Title VII violation will be found.[9] The EEOC did, however, temper this position by pointing out that such an objective standard should take into consideration "the victim's perspective and not stereotyped notions of acceptable behavior."[10]

Although the "reasonable person"[11] standard has long been accepted by most courts as the correct measure for evaluating allegedly culpable conduct, most notably in negligence cases,[12] a number of commentators[13] and courts[14] have recently challenged its applicability in cases of sexual harassment. At the heart of this debate, as we shall discuss, is a body of research[15] suggesting that men and women differ in their judgments of what particular behaviors and comments constitute sexual harassment. This issue was summed up succinctly in a recent case:

> A male supervisor might believe, for example, that it is legitimate for him to tell a female subordinate that she has a "great figure" or "nice legs." The female subordinate, however, may find such comments offensive. Such a situation presents a dilemma for both the man and the woman: the man may not realize that his comments are offensive, and the woman may be fearful of criticizing her supervisor.[16]

One study that examined whether women perceive sexual overtures in a different light than men found that men see such comments from women as flattering while women find similar comments from men as insulting.[17] Another study indicates that men view milder forms of behavior such as "suggestive looks, repeated requests for dates and sexist jokes, as harmless social interactions to which only overly-sensitive women would object."[18] Women, however, are more likely to see this behavior as overt harassment.[19]

As suggested above, courts differ on which standard should be used to judge allegedly harassing conduct. While a number of courts adhere to the traditional "reasonable person"[20] standard, others modify the reasonable person standard through a two-step "subjective/objective" approach that explicitly considers the perspective both of the victim and of a reasonable person.[21] Along similar lines, one court has indicated that the fact finder should apply both male and female perspectives in evaluating the conduct at issue.[22] In addition, and most important for our present discussion, a growing number of courts have concluded that the differing social experiences of men and women warrant a new standard in sexual harassment cases—that of the "reasonable woman."[23] In 1991, the Ninth Circuit expressly adopted this standard in *Ellison v. Brady,*[24] a case that received widespread publicity.[25] In that case, the Ninth Circuit justified its rejection of the "reasonable person" standard in favor of the "reasonable woman" approach by explaining that "a sex-blind reasonable person standard tends to be male-biased and tends to systematically ignore the experiences of women."[26]

The adoption of a "sex-specific" standard raises a host of questions, not the least of which is the issue of whether it is fair to hold males to a standard that, because they are males, they may be unable to appreciate or understand fully. In this Article, we examine the development of the "reasonable woman" standard and consider the legal, ethical and social issues raised by the implementation of such a standard. Section I reviews the general history of sexual harassment causes of action and the leading cases in this area.[27] Section II identifies the different standards of review applied in harassment cases, culminating in a discussion of the reasonable woman standard.[28] Finally, Section III explores the legal, ethical, and social questions that warrant consideration prior to the widespread adoption of the reasonable woman standard as the appropriate gauge for measuring culpable conduct in sexual harassment cases.[29] . . .

★ ★ ★

III. IMPLICATIONS OF ADOPTING A "REASONABLE WOMAN" STANDARD

Applying a "reasonable woman" standard in Title VII cases raises numerous legal, ethical, and social questions. Undoubtedly, the most troubling question is whether it is proper or fair to impose liability, including potential liability for substantial money damages[181] on men (and on their employers) for well-intentioned behavior that they do not realize is illegal or offensive.

A. Sexual Harassment: Facts and Figures

Practical experience and a substantial body of research data suggest that the behavior of many men in the workplace annoys and offends many women. Estimates of the number of women who feel they have been sexually harassed in the workplace range from forty percent,[182] to fifty percent,[183] to sixty percent.[184] In fact, one report estimates the true figure to be as high as ninety percent.[185] Studies show that most incidents involve men over 35 years old harassing women under the age of 34.[186] In over eighty percent of the cases, according to one study, the harasser occupies a more powerful position in the organi-

zation than the victim.[187] Relatively few of the victims are men—only about fifteen percent.[188]

Although women have historically considered it "career suicide" to take formal action against their harassers,[189] a growing number of women have begun breaking their silence.[190] For example, since 1980, over 38,500 persons, the vast majority of whom are women, have filed sexual harassment complaints with the EEOC.[191] Moreover, the number is on the rise. In 1986, the Commission received 4,504 complaints.[192] In 1991, that number rose to 6,675.[193] Based on the reported rate of increase, the EEOC seemed likely to receive over 9,000 complaints in 1992.[194]

B. Men's Intentions and Motives

One of the most controversial aspects of the sexual harassment debate centers on the reasons for men's harassing behavior. On the one hand, some would agree with the reader responding to a survey conducted by *Working Woman* magazine who asserted that harassing behavior is motivated by men's desire to control women rather than by sexual desire. According to this view, " '[t]he harasser wants a victim, not a playmate, and a woman with modest dress, makeup and comportment is just as likely—maybe even more likely—to be harassed.' "[195] On the other hand, a number of courts[196] and commentators[197] have concluded that a great deal of what women consider to be sexual harassment constitutes innocent, well-intentioned behavior by men. To say that this behavior is innocent and well-intentioned, however, is not to say that those who analyze it think it should be ignored or excused. To the contrary, critics of male behavior assert that, despite men's benign intentions, behavior that offends women should be prohibited and punished. As Professor Nancy Ehrenreich writes:

> I . . . believe that some men who engage in (what I would call) harassing behavior do so with neither conscious hostility towards women nor an aware-

ness of the effect of their conduct, and I have no doubt that such men would feel personally wronged by judgments declaring their conduct harassment. (Other men, of course, are perfectly aware of what they are doing.) Nevertheless, I am convinced . . . that while the elimination of inequality in society inevitably makes some people feel wronged—entailing, as it does, a reduction in the social status and privilege of those on the top of the hierarchy, regardless of whether they harbor personal hostility toward those beneath them—that fact does not justify its perpetuation.[198]

The recent passage of the Civil Rights Act of 1991[199] makes it even more important for men and their employers to address this issue, since intentional sexual harassment under Title VII now carries the potential for substantial compensatory and punitive damages.[200]

C. Differences Between the Sexes

To conclude that male behavior, however innocent and well-intentioned from the man's point of view, can offend many women indicates the existence of fundamental differences in attitudes and approaches between the sexes. Such a view challenges the notion that women and men are virtually interchangeable in the workplace. Although this realization may trouble proponents of absolute equality in employment, the fact is that recent research strongly suggests major differences between the sexes on a number of dimensions not previously recognized.[201] For example, Professor Deborah Tannen's research has focused on the differences between men's and women's conversational styles. Despite her misgivings about the differences between the sexes, she insists they are real and significant:

> The desire to affirm that women are equal has made some scholars reluctant to show they are different, because differences can be used to justify unequal treatment and opportunity. Much as I understand and am in sympathy with those who wish there were no differences between women and men—only reparable social injustice—my research, others' research, and my own and others'

experience tell me that it simply isn't so. There *are* gender differences in ways of speaking, and we need to identify and understand them. Without such understanding, we are doomed to blame others or ourselves—or the relationship—for the otherwise mystifying and damaging effects of our contrasting conversational styles.[202]

Why do men and women have such different perspectives? Professor Tannen suggests that, in the case of conversational styles, the sexes differ because they grow up in different worlds:

> Even if they grow up in the same neighborhood, on the same block, or in the same house, girls and boys grow up in different worlds of words. Others talk of them differently and expect and accept different ways of talking from them. Most importantly, children learn how to talk, how to have conversations, not only from their parents but from their peers.[203]

If such differences exist in conversational styles, one should not be surprised to find even greater differences in attitudes toward sex. Presumably the gender differences cited by Professor Tannen with respect to conversational styles produce dramatically different views between men and women regarding what constitutes sexual harassment.

On this point, Professor Kathryn Abrams argues that women are more sensitive to sexual matters, offering several reasons why this is so: women often feel their positions in the work force are precarious, and therefore "are likely to construe disturbing personal interactions, stereotypical views of women, or other affronts to their competence as workers as serious judgments about their ability to succeed in the work environment."[204] Moreover, their greater physical and social vulnerability to sexual coercion makes many women wary of sexual encounters. Accordingly, "the appearance of sexuality in an unexpected context or a setting of ostensible equality can be an anguishing experience."[205]

Although studies such as these strongly suggest that substantial differences exist between the sexes, other data challenge this view. A recent poll by the Roper Organization[206] based on interviews with 1,026 employed men and women found that:

Despite the uproar following the Clarence Thomas hearings, sexual harassment [sic] in the workplace is not common, and the vast majority of Americans are satisfied with the way their employers are treating the problems . . . . Moreover, the survey finds no great difference between men and women in their perceptions of the relative severity of the problem and on the definitions of what constitutes sexual harassment.[207]

Whatever the reason for the differences—if they exist—with respect to the extent of sexual harassment, courts have expressed concern that applying the traditional "reasonable man's" or "reasonable person's" standard in sexual harassment cases may excuse behavior that most men find acceptable but that irritates and offends many reasonable women.[208] Yet as we discuss below, applying a "reasonable woman's" standard raises other important concerns.

D. Competing Standards

The term "reasonable man" is burdened by an enormous amount of historical baggage. Dating back at least two hundred years,[209] the term undeniably evolved from extremely male-oriented legal and cultural roots. As A.P. Herbert noted in a 1928 commentary, "[i]n all [the] mass of authorities which [bear] upon this branch of the law there is no single mention of a reasonable woman."[210] To the contrary, early American jurisprudence equated the degree of diligence required of women with that which the law expected of children or incompetents.[211]

Although we have not undertaken an empirical study on this point, we believe that most courts and scholars have in recent years abandoned the term "reasonable man" in favor of the term "reasonable person."[212] Presumably, this alternative term encompasses both sexes and is gender-neutral. The more traditional "reason-

able man" or "reasonable person" standard was applied in many areas of law.[213] In their conventional application, these terms generally carried two meanings: (i) an ideal, albeit not perfect, person whose behavior served as an objective measure against which to judge our actions and (ii) an average or typical person possessing all of the shortcomings and weaknesses tolerated by the community.[214]

In the context of the Title VII debate, the latter meaning is key.[215] That is, those courts that have moved to the "reasonable woman" standard intend it to describe average or typical women—women who react differently to situations than do most men but who, at the same time, are neither hypersensitive to[216] nor unoffended by[217] men's workplace behavior.

E. Models of Sexual Harassment Views

In reviewing the approaches that courts have adopted to date in distinguishing between the reasonable man and reasonable woman perspectives, we find it helpful to consider the various views that courts *could* take on this issue. We identify five general possibilities, each of which is reviewed below.

First, it is conceivable that what reasonable men and reasonable women consider sexual harassment might not overlap at all. If such a model accurately described the state of attitudes in the American workplace, any attempt to develop a "reasonable person" test would create a null set (unless, of course, one were simply to choose one sex as reasonable and reject the other as unreasonable).[218] In such a case, behavior considered harassing by one sex would not be considered so by the other. Common sense suggests that this model is inaccurate, since both reasonable men and reasonable women regard certain male conduct toward women (e.g., rape and other physical attacks, lewd sexual overtures, and the sending of obscene letters) with disgust or distaste. Reasonable members of both sexes, we suggest, would find these actions to constitute sexual harassment [Figure 1]. Even male perpetrators of these extremely coercive acts, except perhaps those lost to insanity, would concede their impropriety.

Figure 2 illustrates the equally unlikely possibility that reasonable men and women might view behavior with respect to sexual harassment from precisely identical perspectives. If this model reflected the true state of affairs, there would be no need for a "reasonable woman" standard. Instead, court could simply apply the "reasonable person" standard, since this standard would by definition fully reflect the views of both reasonable men and reasonable women. It is this model, however, that a number of courts and scholars have strongly challenged in recent years.[219] According to these critics, men and women may see some behavior similarly, but they see other behavior quite differently. Of course, whether broad, meaningful differences exist between the perspectives of the sexes remains a question that is subject to ongoing research and debate.[220]

The next three models illustrate possibilities in which some, but not all, of men's and women's views toward sexual harassment overlap. Figure 3 depicts the possibility that reasonable men and reasonable women share some views, but that men view some behavior as harassment that women do not and that, conversely, women view some behavior as harassment that men do not. Assuming that Figure 3 presented a realistic picture of the sexes' attitudes toward harassment (an assumption that seems highly improbable), the task of deciding which conduct violates Title VII and which does not would be daunting. Obviously, courts would reject a test that implicates only the behavior that one sex or the other considers to be harassment, since that would exclude acts such as rape and sexually-oriented physical abuse that reasonable members of both sexes see as harassing. Choosing only the area on which both sexes agree (the intersection of the two circles in Fig-

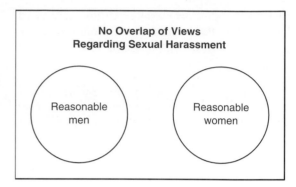

FIGURE 1

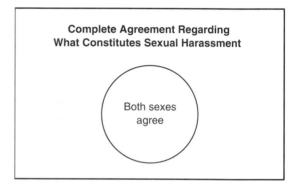

FIGURE 2

ure 3) would permit a form of "reasonable person" test, but would fail to consider the serious additional concerns on which the sexes disagree. Perhaps the more realistic approach would be to include offensive conduct that falls into the circle representing *either* sex plus any behavior included in the area of overlap. Thus, the definition of a "reasonable person" under this model would be offensive conduct that reasonable members of either or both sexes consider sexual harassment.

Although theoretically possible, this model implies a reality not suggested in any research or court rulings of which we are aware. Most researchers would undoubtedly agree that many women take offense at certain behavior of men that men think acceptable. The reverse, however, seems questionable—i.e., that many men con-

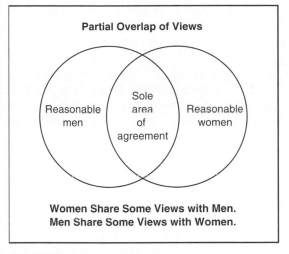

FIGURE 3

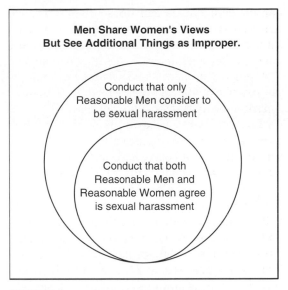

FIGURE 4

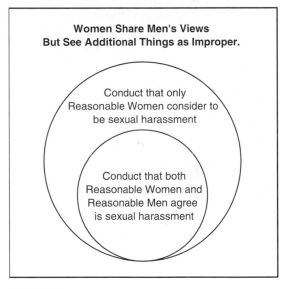

FIGURE 5

sider certain conduct to be sexual harassment that women do not also consider improper. Of course, one can conjure up situations in which, for example, some men might take umbrage at a female superior's insistence on calling them "sensitive" or "considerate" in violation of the "macho" image that they prefer to project. But such situations would seem rare, if they exist at all. For the most part, we find it difficult to imagine harassing behavior that men find offensive that would not also be offensive to women.

Along similar lines, Figure 4 illustrates the possibility that reasonable men completely share women's views regarding sexual harassment, but that reasonable men see *additional* behavior as harassment that reasonable women do not. To say the least, this model flies in the face of current research and recent court rulings.[221] For the same reasons that we questioned the practical application of the previous model, we also find this model unrealistic.

Figure 5 describes a world in which reasonable women completely share men's views regarding sexual harassment, but in which women consider *additional* behavior as harassment that reasonable men do not. As we have noted, although by no means a unanimous view,[222] this model comports with the current research and commentary of many scholars in this area and with the thinking of a growing number of courts.[223] Under this model, courts that wish to extend Title VII to include behavior that falls within both circles can do so in one of two ways: they can define all conduct within either of the circles as offensive to a "reasonable persons," or they can indicate that they will apply a "reasonable woman" standard that encompasses all behavior falling into either circle. The trend seems to be toward the latter approach.[224]

Precisely what behavior is it that troubles women, yet appears innocent to men? Unfortunately, as several courts have indicated, there is no clear answer under Title VII. The problem is compounded by the fact that "[c]onduct considered harmless by many today may be considered discriminatory in the future."[225] For those courts that apply a "reasonable victim's" or a "reasonable woman's" standard, then, the standard for what constitutes sexual harassment will change as the views and attitudes of women change.[226]

To say that the standard is a fluid one is not to say that the question of what constitutes offensive conduct remains a complete mystery. A review of recent sexual harassment cases reveals at least some broad patterns and trends. These cases indicate that, among the types of behavior not generally viewed as offensive by male workers but objected to by female employees are the pervasive use of obscene language by co-workers,[227] displays of pornography in common areas and in the plaintiff's personal work space,[228] and the conduct of male supervisors who tell female subordinates that they have a " 'great figure' " or " 'nice legs' "[229] or who write repeated unwelcome love letters.[230]

As we have noted, a number of writers and researchers have suggested an expanded view with respect to other conduct that fits into the "men see nothing wrong; women find it offensive" category. Professor Ehrenreich would include "milder" forms of harassment, such as "suggestive looks, repeated requests for dates, and sexist jokes."[231] Professor Abrams would include "verb224

al sexual abuse, casual touching, and dissemination or display of pornography."[232] Professor

Riger adds that "more subtle forms of behavior such as sexual jokes or comments" offend many women and should be considered sexual harassment.[233] Above all, Riger believes that "policymakers and others need to learn to 'think like a woman' to define which behaviors constitute harassment."[234] Whether behavior of this type troubles working women as much as these authors assert remains unclear, however.[235]

F. Legal Liability for Innocent Reasonable Acts

To the extent that courts impose liability on men's conduct that stems from innocent and reasonable motives, courts apply a form of strict liability. To analogize to section 402A of the Restatement of Torts, liability would attach to men's behavior despite the fact that they have exercised "all possible care"[236] in their conduct toward women.

Casting a wide liability net under Title VII is not a new approach. The EEOC has long interpreted Title VII as forbidding conduct that "has the purpose *or effect of* . . . creating an intimidating, hostile, or offensive working environment,"[237] and the *Ellison* Court noted the "no fault" nature of Title VII in explaining its adoption of the reasonable woman standard:

> We note that the reasonable victim standard we adopt today classifies conduct as unlawful . . . even when harassers do not realize that their conduct creates a hostile working environment . . . . That is because Title VII is not a fault-based tort scheme. "Title VII is aimed at the consequences or effects of an employment practice and not at the . . . motivation" of co-workers or employers.[238]

Further, courts have historically been willing, in certain types of cases, to hold an actor liable for harmful behavior despite the actor's good intentions.[239] For example, courts have for many years applied liability without fault to the owners of animals that inflict physical harm or property damage, to those individuals who engage in abnormally dangerous activities, and to the producers of manufactured products.[240]

Of course, saying that ample precedent exists for applying strict liability generally does not answer the question of whether strict liability should be applied in Title VII cases specifically. Despite the fact the Professor Prosser and his co-authors seem comfortable with the concept of no-fault tort liability,[241] most people sense a substantial moral difference between offenses committed deliberately and those done unwittingly, and the question of intent figures prominently in many civil and most criminal cases.[242] Moreover, as discussed in the section that follows, the 1991 amendments to the Civil Rights Act have upped the ante considerably. Previously, Title VII violations carried only relatively mild sanctions: back pay and injunctive relief.[243] Under the new amendments, however, intentional violations are now subject to punitive and expanded compensatory damages.[244]

G. Damages for Intentional Violations Under the Civil Rights Act of 1991

Historically, the primary federal statute for recovering damages for employment discrimination has been section 1981 of the Civil Rights Act of 1866.[245] In the past, however, damages under section 1981 were available only in intentional discrimination cases in which the discrimination was based on the race of the victim.[246] This changed with the Civil Rights Act of 1991, under which victims of intentional discrimination on the basis of sex, religion, or disability are now entitled to recover compensatory and punitive damages,[247] albeit with some limitations.[248] If, as seems likely, courts continue to adopt a "reasonable woman" standard and to expand the types of conduct that constitute a "hostile environment" under Title VII, the 1991 Civil Rights Act will become a battleground of major proportions, especially with respect to what constitutes "intentional" discrimination. Specifically, those courts that have adopted a "reason-

able woman" standard that encompasses conduct that "harassers do not realize . . . creates a hostile working environment"[249] will have to decide whether such conduct falls within the intent requirement of the 1991 amendments.

The most directly analogous precedents for determining the meaning of "intent" in this context are the so-called "disparate treatment" cases under section 1981 and Title VII of the Civil Rights Act—cases that require a showing of discriminatory intent for a plaintiff to recover.[250] Presumably, the courts will look to this established case law for guidance regarding what constitutes "intentional" discrimination under the 1991 amendments.

In "disparate treatment" cases, courts generally follow the guidelines set for by the U.S. Supreme Court in *Texas Department of Community Affairs v. Burdine*.[251] First, a plaintiff must establish a "prima facie" case in which she shows that (1) she is a member of a protected class, (2) she is otherwise situated similarly to members of the unprotected class, and (3) she was treated differently from members of the unprotected class.[252] Once the plaintiff has established this prima facie case, the burden then shifts to the employer to produce evidence that the reason for treating the plaintiff differently was not an "invidious" one (i.e., the employer must show that its treatment of the employee was not motivated by a discriminatory intent).[253] The employer must further produce a legitimate nondiscriminatory reason for treating the plaintiff differently from members of the unprotected class. The burden then shifts back to the plaintiff, who must prove by a preponderance of the evidence that the employer's articulated reason was merely a "pretext" for discrimination.[254]

Whether the courts will adopt this model to address cases in which a reasonable man innocently creates a hostile working environment remains to be seen. These cases are difficult because the offensive conduct is clearly intentional in the sense that the defendant will have committed a volitional, voluntary act. The defendant will not, however, have intended—either from his perspective or that of a "reasonable man"—anything improper. Yet, his behavior would have offended a "reasonable female" employee, thereby qualifying the plaintiff's claim as a Title VII cause of action in those courts that have adopted the reasonable woman standard.

Based on our review of current law, we question whether the courts will impose damages for intentional sexual harassment in these cases. In analogous "disparate treatment" cases, many courts look for a discriminatory "animus" indicating that the defendant was in fact motivated by ill will or meanspiritedness.[255] Simply using bad judgment, as in cases involving employment favoritism towards relatives that effectively denies opportunities to members of a protected class, has been found not to rise to the level of discriminatory intent.[256] Moreover, several courts have held that acts committed in good faith, even if the acts are in fact discriminatory or otherwise improper, do not demonstrate discriminatory intent.[257]

Traditional tort principles place the concept of intent on a sliding scale[258] demarcated by at least five possible categories of intentional or quasi-intentional behavior: (i) mere inadvertence, (ii) acts in disregard of consequences likely to follow, (iii) acts that invade the rights of another under a mistaken belief of committing no wrong,[259] and (iv) acts where the motive is a malevolent desire to do harm.[260] Our reading of the "disparate treatment" cases convinces us that the courts tend to find intentional violations only with respect to the last category. If this is true, one would imagine that the "reasonable man who innocently creates a hostile working environment" cases will not trigger damages under the 1991 amendments to the Civil Rights Act. It is entirely possible, however, that those courts willing to apply a "reasonable woman" standard will adopt an extremely expansive view of what constitutes

intentional discrimination under the 1991 Amendments.

H. Concerns About the "Reasonable Woman" Standard

As Professor Ehrenreich has noted, no substantial change in social policies is pain-free.[261] The move toward a "reasonable woman" standard certainly qualifies as a substantial change in policy, the implementation of which will create a number of potential problems that warrant discussion. The analysis that follows should not be read as indicating that we either reject or endorse the new standard. We do, however, see several potential trouble spots that should be considered by the courts and by advocates of an expansive "reasonable woman" standard under Title VII.

1. Overreaction The adoption of the reasonable woman standard carries a strong potential for overreaction by corporate officials who find that their companies are subject to a standard that presents such a moving and unclear target. As previously noted,[262] courts that have adopted the "reasonable woman" standard have indicated that, as women's views change, workplace behavior that is acceptable today may violate Title VII tomorrow. With this in mind, risk-averse personnel managers and other corporate supervisors may well adopt rules that go well beyond the law to ensure that their companies will not face Title VII liability.[263] For example, some companies might adopt rules that threaten employees with immediate dismissal for any physical contact, other than perhaps a simple handshake, with fellow employees on the job.[264] Or companies might bar any display of nudity in the workplace, including in works of art, on the assumption that nudity, however aesthetically portrayed, may offend someone.[265] Similarly, to deal with concerns about "suggestive looks" in the office,[266] companies might adopt complex rules that prohibit "sexual staring" or "offensive watching" by their employees.[267] Further, in an effort to combat both dirty jokes and jokes that demean women, companies might flatly prohibit the telling of jokes in the workplace.[268] We could go on, but we trust the point is clear: companies faced with potential liability under rapidly evolving and vague standards[269] may feel the need to protect themselves by adopting intrusive and, ultimately, unfair, workplace restrictions. In particular, many harried corporate executives may simply decide that they have neither the time nor the resources to conduct workplace polls on a regular basis to determine with precision which types of conduct currently offend their female employees. As a result, they will tend to operate with a meat axe rather than a scalpel, putting in place broad, prophylactic rules in an attempt to reduce the risk of Title VII litigation and liability.

2. Fewer Women Hired   Under the "doctrine of unintended consequences," which states that attempts at reform sometimes produce effects opposite to those intended, it is possible that some employers in jurisdictions that adopt the "reasonable woman" standard will become wary of hiring women. For example, when a company hires women to fill traditionally male jobs, it may feel the need to implement immediate and, perhaps, costly changes in the workplace to ensure that nothing in the environment offends the new women workers. The unclear and evolving rules regarding what offends "reasonable women" will also create concerns that, despite its best efforts, a company will be found to have tolerated behavior and conditions later determined to constitute harassing conduct or a hostile environment. Faced with these prospects, the company may simply adopt an explicit strategy to structure jobs in the "sex is a bona-fide occupational qualification" mold[270] or, more likely, continue its unenthusiastic approach to hiring women. In other words, companies in reasonable woman jurisdictions may be reluctant to hire women if every one hired carries a heightened threat of a lawsuit.

3. Freedom of Speech   Although we tend not to see an increased push for "politically correct" speech in the workplace, a trend that we deplore, as an imminent danger, there are legitimate freedom of speech concerns associated with the widespread adoption of a "reasonable woman" standard. At the outset, we note that the recent Supreme Court ruling in *R.A.V. v. City of St. Paul*[271] clearly raises more questions than it answers regarding permissible restrictions of free speech. In that case, the Court invalidated, by a 5-4 vote, a city ordinance banning certain types of "hate speech" on the ground that the ordinance improperly imposed "content discrimination" on otherwise proscribable speech. Writing for the Court, Justice Scalia stated that the city could not ban hate speech if the only categories covered by the ordinance were speech directed at race, color, creed, religion, or gender. In the Court's opinion, the ordinance must ban either all such speech or none of it. For the city to do otherwise would, in effect, "license one side of the debate to fight freestyle, while requiring the other to follow Marquis of Queensbury Rules."[272]

In an apparent effort to assuage the concerns of those who might conclude that, like the hate speech ordinance, hostile environment rules promulgated under Title VII are also unconstitutional because they prohibit only certain offensive words,[273] the majority specifically stated that under the so-called "secondary effects" doctrine, the incidental regulation of speech under Title VII would not be considered unconstitutional under the Court's reasoning in *R.A.V.*[274] But this attempt to distinguish regulation under Title VII from the St. Paul ordinance drew a skeptical response from Justice White and the other dissenting justices. To them, "hostile environment" rules directly address the impact of speech on the victimized worker in same manner that the majority's opinion prohibited.[275] In making this point, however, neither Justice White nor any of the other dissenters suggested that they viewed Title VII regulation as constitutionally suspect. Instead, they simply pointed out the inconsistency in the majority's opinion. Whatever the merits of either side's argument, it seems clear that none of the nine justices saw *R.A.V.* as a real threat to Title VII.

Despite the implicit assurance in *R.A.V.* that Title VII rules appear consistent with the First Amendment, we share some of the concerns of Professor Kinsley Browne, who argues that the courts and commentators too quickly dismiss First Amendment concerns arising from hostile environment cases.[276] Addressing this issue, Professor Browne raises a number of fairly compelling points:

> Far from having an "incidental effect" on the right of speech, regulation of offensive speech has as its primary purpose the limitation of "offensive" expression, often in the form of "offensive" ideas, that has no relation to any threat of future action. Although advocates of such regulation may argue that there is no desire to censor ideas, only to guarantee equal participation of women or blacks in the workplace the fact remains that the purpose of the regulation is to prohibit expression because of the ideology expressed.[277]

Browne particularly takes issue with what he terms the "thought-control" rationale of restricting expression that runs through the reasoning of judges and academics. Criticizing this reasoning, he reiterates Justice Brandeis' celebration of the First Amendment's "freedom to think as you will and to speak as you think,"[278] as "a duty to think as you are told and to speak as you are told to think."[279]

We see considerable merit in Browne's argument. If, in the workplace, we permit only speech that "reasonable women" consider acceptable, we run a very real risk of suppressing basic First Amendment freedoms. We continue

to subscribe to the proposition that, with the possible exception of speech that constitutes insubordination or a clear violation of legitimate work rules, the best antidote to hateful or harassing speech in the workplace is not suppression, but debate and refutation.

4. A Multitude of "Reasonable Victim" Standards Title VII bars discriminatory behavior based not only on sex, but also based on race, color, religion, or national origin. If the courts are to apply a "reasonable woman" standard in sexual harassment cases, does this suggest that a "reasonable victim" standard will apply in other hostile environment cases? We see no basis for refusing to extend the reasoning in *Ellison* and similar sexual discrimination cases to causes of action involving other classes protected under Title VII.

One court has already extended the reasoning of *Ellison* to racial discrimination cases. In *Harris v. International Paper Co.*,[280] the district court judge explicitly adopted the standard of the "reasonable black person" in determining whether a work setting constituted a hostile environment, stating that "[t]the appropriate standard to be applied in hostile environment harassment cases is that of a reasonable person from the protected group of which the alleged victim is a member."[281]

Further, at least one judge, inspired by the *Ellison* case, would apply a "reasonable nonadherent" test in matters involving religious rights. In *Murray v. City of Austin*,[282] the plaintiff, an atheist, challenged the City of Austin's right to use a Christian cross in its insignia. Although the Fifth Circuit rejected the plaintiff's freedom of religion claims,[283] Judge Goldberg's dissent challenged the majority's view that the city had acted properly, raising the same arguments used by the court in *Ellison*.[284] Had this case been brought under Title VII by a city employee offended by having to wear such an insignia, the majority would have found it more difficult to dismiss the plantiff's claims, at least if it followed the *Ellison* rationale.

If consistency rules in those courts that adopt the "reasonable woman" standard, we see no way for them to avoid adopting similar standards in cases involving race, color, religion, or national origin. To say the least, this presents serious concerns for corporate officials who must comply with Title VII in future years as increasing numbers of women and racial, ethnic, and religious minorities enter the job market.[285] Tailoring the workplace to avoid offending "reasonable Haitians," "reasonable blacks," "reasonable Asians," "reasonable Rastafarians," "reasonable Muslims," as well as "reasonable women," may prove to be an insuperable task.

5. Rights in Conflict   Closely related to, but conceptually distinct from, the issue of accommodating the rights of a multitude of "reasonable victims" protected under Title VII is the problem of resolving conflicts among the protected groups. How, for example, is an employer to deal with the claims of Muslim women that the relatively skimpy attire worn by other female employees offends their more restrictive dress code? Similarly, how should a supervisor respond to a Jewish employee who claims to be deeply pained by office Christmas parties or pictures of Jesus displayed by her Christian co-workers?

Virtually none of the courts or commentators who have addressed the "reasonable victim" or "reasonable woman" issue in harassment cases has explicitly discussed how to resolve such conflicts between protected groups.[286] Following the principles adopted in the "reasonable woman" cases and the authors cited in those cases, the most likely approach would be to resolve conflicts by accommodating the concerns of "reasonable victims" in whichever group the court determined to be less powerful. Presumably one would not search for a middle-ground "reasonable person" solution because that would

diminish the less powerful group's ability to participate on an equal footing[287] with the relatively more powerful group.[288]

There are some obvious practical problems with this approach. For example, do we really expect employers to order female employees to wear veils at work or to stop wearing lipstick because doing so deeply offends female employees from other disadvantaged groups? Must women who have fought for the right to wear slacks on the job give up that right because a newly hired immigrant finds it painful, as a "reasonable immigrant," to work in an atmosphere where such modes of dress are permitted?

We cannot necessarily resolve these conflicts by saying that members of protected minority groups in the workforce must simply accept existing majority practices that deeply offend them. The point of "hostile environment" cases is that members of the majority must alter behavior, including acts that they consider innocent, reasonable and well-intentioned, that disturbs protected minorities.[289] The majority may disregard the feelings of the protected minority member only if she is hypersensitive for her group.

6. Fairness   To us, one of the most ethically difficult problems raised by current interpretations of Title VII is that behavior considered to be innocent by reasonable men may in fact be found illegal in a court of law. As we have documented, however, a growing number of courts find no significant problem in requiring men to take on this burden. Many commentators, including Professor Stone, agree:

> Are men supposed to be mind-readers, you ask? Well, yes. Parents, who exercise inordinate physical and psychological control over children, are morally and legally obliged to understand their children's needs, even when their children can't talk. They are not free to abuse children because the children don't protest. In any situation of power, the powerful have a moral obligation to see

the world from the point of view of those they govern or control, and to exercise power in the interests of the governed. Just consent is what makes power legitimate instead of tyrannical. . . . As long as men are in positions of power, the burden is on them to anticipate how their actions affect weaker people. This is the burden that goes with the privilege of power.[290]

It is obviously true that, as Professor Stone argues, the powerful should not simply run roughshod over the weak. But this does not automatically translate into imposing legal liability whenever the powerful unintentionally offend the weak. We do not, for example, bar the rich from wearing expensive clothes or eating elegant meals simply because this conduct may distress the poor. Professor Stone's parent-child analogy also overlooks the intimacy of family life, which is very different from the atmosphere of the workplace. In the family context, society places enormous, albeit not unbridled, discretion in the hands of parents with respect to their children's punishment, education, and life-styles, however unhappy that may make children on occasion. In modern society, we would never provide this much discretion to employers.

One finds it hard to avoid the conclusion that Professor Stone and others would impose liability under Title VII whenever men in powerful positions unintentionally engage in behavior that pains relatively less powerful women. But the all-encompassing nature of this approach troubles us. In our opinion, the right to sue and collect damages should derive from a stronger moral base than a worker's discomfort at well-intentioned behavior of questionable offensiveness. Further, until society reaches a stronger consensus on the proper response to "mild" forms of sexual harassment such as a male employee making comments about a female coworker's appearance, staring at a woman's figure, or touching a female coworker in a non-sexual manner, it seems premature to permit employees offended by this conduct to sue in pursuit of large money damages.[291]

As with many interesting and important social and legal questions, the dividing line between what is acceptable and unacceptable is not clear. At some point, however, the commendable effort by women to restructure the workplace environment can take on oppressive tones of its own. If we are to avoid excessive "political correctness" or "sexual correctness" in the workplace, we must promote a spirit of tolerance that forgives well-intentioned slights from above and below.

On this point, we return to Professor Tannen's discussion regarding the different conversational styles between men and women. In that discussion, she strikes a strong note for tolerance on the part of both sexes:

> Many experts tell us we are doing things wrong and should change our behavior—which usually sounds easier than it turns out to be. Sensitivity training judges men by women's standards, trying to get them to talk more like women. Assertiveness training judges women by men's standards and tries to get them to talk more like men. No doubt, many people can be helped by learning to be more sensitive or more assertive. But few people are helped by being told they are doing everything all wrong. . . . The biggest mistake is believing there is one right way to listen, to talk, to have a conversation—or a relationship. Nothing hurts more than being told your intentions are bad when you know they are good, or being told you are doing something wrong when you know you're just doing it your way.[292]

We recommend that courts apply Professor Tannen's perspective to sexual harassment cases, balancing the very real need to provide appropriate relief to the victims of sexual harassment with understanding and tolerance toward well-meaning companies and individuals who are at least trying to do the right thing.

CONCLUSION

Efforts to eradicate social evils such as sexual discrimination inevitably raise substantial legal and ethical issues. This Article has addressed one such issue: whether the benefits of applying the reasonable woman standard in sexual discrimination cases brought under Title VII will outweigh the questions and risks raised by the standard. As with any new legal norm, it will be difficult to assess the true impact of the reasonable woman standard until several years of application have elapsed. Our discussion has not been intended to reject or condemn the new standard so much as it has been to point out that trying to protect the rights of one group unavoidably results in some restriction of the rights of other groups. In some cases, this is justifiable. In others, it is not. We will watch with great interest to see how the benefits and risks balance out in the great "reasonable woman" debate.

NOTES

1. The term "hostile environment" in sexual harassment cases refers to employment contexts in which unwelcome sexual conduct unreasonably interferes with an individual's job performance or creates an intimidating, hostile or offensive work environment. . . .
2. *See, e.g.,* Ellison v. Brady, 924 F.2d 872, 879 (9th Cir. 1991) (holding that "a female plaintiff states a prima facie case of hostile environment sexual harassment when she alleges conduct which a *reasonable woman* would consider sufficiently severe or pervasive to alter the conditions of employment and create an abusive working environment") (emphasis added); Rabidue v. Osceola Refining Co., 805 F.2d 611, 620 (6th Cir. 1986) (asserting that "the trier of fact, when judging the totality of the circumstances impacting upon the asserted abusive and hostile environment . . . must adopt the perspective of a reasonable person's reaction to a similar environment under essentially like or similar circumstances"), *cert. denied,* 481 U.S. 1041 (1987); Robinson v. Jacksonsville Shipyards, Inc., 760 F. Supp. 1486, 1524 (M.D. Fla. 1991) (stating that both a subjective and an objective standard need to be applied in evaluating allegedly harassing conduct).

Within the First Circuit, confusion abounds regarding the appropriate perspective to apply in evaluating harassing conduct. One Court has applied a "two perspective standard." *See* Lipsett v. University of Puerto Rico, 864 F.2d 881, 898 (1st Cir. 1988) (stating that the trier of fact should consider both the man's and the woman's perspectives). Another has adopted a "reasonable person" standard. *See* Morgan v. Massachusetts Gen. Hosp. 901 F.2d 186, 193 (1st Cir. 1990). And yet a third has addressed harassing behavior from the standpoint of the particular plaintiff. *See* Chamberlain v. 101 Realty, Inc., 915 F.2d 777, 784 (1st Cir. 1990); *see also* Nancy S. Ehrenreich, *Pluralistic Myths and Powerless Men: The Ideology of Reasonableness in Sexual Harassment Law,* 99 Yale L. J. 1177 (1990) (criticizing both the "reasonable person" and "reasonable woman" standards); Georgia A. Staton & Angela K. Sinner, *Sexual Harassment: the 'Reasonable Woman' Standard,* 33 For The Defense 6 (Dec. 1991) (analyzing implications of adopting the reasonable woman standard); Note, *Sexual Harassment Claims of Abusive Work Environment Under Title VII,* 97 Harv. L. Rev, 1449, 1459 (1984) (advocating adoption of a "reasonable woman" standard).

3. *See* Meritor Sav. Bank v. Vinson, 477 U.S. 57, 67–68 (1986).
4. Or, alternatively, from the perspective of a reasonable man in those cases in which the plaintiff is male.
5. Eliza G. C. Collins & Timothy B. Blodgett, *Sexual Harassment . . . Some See It . . . Some Won't,* Harv. Bus. Rev., Mar.-Apr. 1981, at 76, 92 (finding little recognition of sexual harassment by upper level management). As discussed in a recent article, conduct that women perceive as sexual harassment will not necessarily be perceived as such by men. *See* Stephanie Riger, *Gender Dilemmas in Sexual Harassment Policies and Procedures,* 46 Am. Psychol., 497, 499 (1991); *see also* Lipsett v. University of Puerto Rico, 864 F.2d 881, 898 n. 19 (1st Cir. 1991) (discussing and citing report concerning the different perceptions of men and women toward sexual harassment).
6. Equal Employment Opportunity Comm'n, Policy Guidance on Current Issues of Sexual Ha-

rassment, N-915-050 (BNA) 89 (March 19, 1990) [hereinafter Policy Guidance on Current Issues].

7. *Id.*

8. *Id.* (quoting Zablowicz v. West Bend Co., 589 F. Supp. 780, 784 (E.D. Wis. 1984)).

9. *See id.*

10. *Id.* at 103.

11. We presume that the reasonable man standard has been almost universally set aside in favor of the "reasonable person" standard, thereby incorporating, in theory at least, the feminine as well as masculine standard. *See infra* note 212 and accompanying text. One of the earliest reported uses of the reasonable man standard occurred in a 19th century British case, Vaughan v. Menlove, 132 Eng. Rep. 490 (1837). In that case, the court stated that "[i]nstead . . . of saying that the liability for negligence should be coextensive with the judgment of each individual . . . we ought rather to adhere to the rule which requires in all cases a regard to caution such as a *man of ordinary prejudice* would observe." *Id.* at 493 (emphasis added). The reasonableness test, as it has developed, is intended to reflect changing social mores as well as to present an objective standard that imposes the name behavior on everyone, thereby limiting arbitrary or politically based decision-making by judges. *See* W. Page Keeton et al., Prosser & Keeton on the Law of Torts 173–75 (5th ed. 1984); Ronald K. L. Collins, *Language, History and The Legal Process: A Profile of the 'Reasonable Man,'* 8 Rut.-Cam. L. J. 311 (1977).

12. *See* Keeton et al., *supra* note 11, at 175.

13. *See, e.g.,* Kathryn Abrams, *Gender Discrimination and the Transformation of Workplace Norms,* 42 Vand. L. Rev, 1183, 1206 (1989) ("If judges continue to strive for the ostensibly objective perspective in assessing sexual harassment claims, then they will succeed primarily in entrenching the male-centered views of harassment that prevail in many workplaces"); Ehrenreich, *supra* note 2, at 1177 ("My primary purpose is to offer an explanation for how the reasonable person test retains its legitimacy in the face of numerous analytical weaknesses.").

14. *See e.g.,* Ellison v. Brady, 924 F.2d 872, 878 (9th Cir. 1991) (adopting the reasonable woman rather than the reasonable person standard, explaining that "[i]f we only examined whether a reasonable person would engage in allegedly harassing conduct, we would run the risk of reinforcing the prevailing level of discrimination"); Radtke v. Everett, 471 N.W.2d 660, 664 (Mich. App. 1991) ("[W]e believe that in a sexual harassment case involving a woman, the proper perspective to view the offensive conduct from is that of the 'reasonable woman,' not that of the 'reasonable person.'"), *appeal granted,* 487 N.W.2d 762 (Mich. 1992).

15. *See* Alison M. Konrad & Barbara A. Grutek, *Impact of Work Experiences on Attitudes Toward Sexual Harassment,* 31 Admin. Sci. Q. 422 (1986); Gary N. Powell, *Effects of Sex Role Identity and Sex on Definitions of Sexual Harassment,* 14 Sex Roles 9 (1986). *But see* The Roper Org. Inc., *Most Americans Say Sexual Harassment At Work Not A Problem,* Roper Reports No. 92–1 (1992) [hereinafter Roper Poll] (reporting on poll results indicating that, notwithstanding the publicity and public debate attending the Clarence Thomas hearings, sexual harassment in the workplace is not common, and that the vast majority of Americans are satisfied with the way their employers are treating the problem).

16. Lipsett v. University of Puerto Rico, 864 F.2d 881, 898 (1st Cir. 1988).

17. *See* Barbara A. Gutek, Sex and the Workplace (1985).

18. Ehrenreich, *supra* note 2, at 1207 n.10; Lucinda M. Finley, *A Break in the Silence: Including Women's Issues in a Torts Course,* 1 Yale J. L. & Feminism 41, 60 n. 64 (1989).

19. *See* Ehrenreich, *supra* note 2, at 1207–08.

20. *See e.g.,* Hirschfeld v. New Mexico Correction Dep't, 916 F.2d 572, 580 (10th Cir. 1990) ("reasonable person in plaintiff's position would not have felt compelled to resign"); Morgan v. Massachusetts Gen. Hosp., 901 F.2d 186, 193 (1st Cir. 1990) (adopting the "reasonable person" approach); Rabidue v. Osceola Refining Co., 805 F.2d 611, 620 (6th Cir. 1986) (trier of fact, when judging the totality of the circumstances with respect to the asserted abusive and hostile environment must adopt the perspective of a reasonable person's reaction to a similar environment under like circumstances); Bennett

v. New York City Dep't of Corrections, 705 F. Supp. 979, 984 (S.D.N.Y. 1989) (if evidence leads a reasonable person in a similar situation to find the environment offensive, then liability should attach under Title VII); Hollis v. Fleetguard, Inc., 668 F. Supp. 631, 636–37 (M.D. Tenn. 1987) (if reasonable person would not have been affected by the alleged harassing behavior, the claim fails).

21. *See e.g.,* Andrews v. City of Philadelphia, 895 F.2d 1469, 1483 (3rd Cir. 1990) (maintaining that the subjective factor is crucial because it shows that the alleged conduct injured the particular plaintiff and the objective standard protects the employer from the "hypersensitive" employee); Robinson v. Jacksonville Shipyards, Inc., 760 F. Supp. 1486, 1524 (M.D. Fla. 1991) (concluding that the question of whether the harassment affected the victim should be judged from the perspective of both the victim and that of a reasonable woman). Several Seventh Circuit cases have held that the trial court should apply both an objective and subjective analysis to evaluate the likely effect of the defendant's conduct upon a reasonable person's ability to perform his or her work and upon his or her well-being, as well as the actual effect upon the particular plaintiff bringing the claim. *See* King v. Board of Regents, 898 F.2d 533 (7th Circuit 1990); Dockter v. Rudolf Wolff Futures, Inc., 913 F.2d 456 (7th Cir. 1990); Brooms v. Regal Tube Co. 881 F.2d 412 (7th Cir. 1989). For the most part, there is no practical difference between this subjective/objective approach and the "reasonable woman" approach. In both cases, the victim must establish both that she individually was offended and that a reasonable woman would also be offended.

22. *See* Lipsett v. University of Puerto Rico, 864 F.2d 881, 989 (1st Cir. 1988).

23. *See* Ellison v. Brady, 924 F.2d 872, 878 (9th Cir. 1991) (holding that a female plaintiff states a prima facie case of hostile environment when she alleges conduct that a reasonable woman would consider severe and pervasive); Andrews v. City of Philadelphia, 895 F.2d 1469, 1482 (3d Cir. 1990) (standard should be that of the reasonable person of the same sex); Yates v. Avco Corp., 819 F.2d 630, 637 (6th Cir. 1987) (holding that, in a sexual harassment case, "it seems

only reasonable" that the person standing in the shoes of the employee should be the reasonable woman); Rabidue v. Osceola Refining Co., 805 F.2d 611, 626 (6th Cir. 1986) (Keith, J., dissenting in part and concurring in part) (advocating a reasonable victim/woman standard); Robinson v. Jacksonville Shipyards, Inc., 760 F. Supp. 1486, 1523 (M.D. Fla 1991) (noting significance of the fact that certain conduct affects women more than men).

24. 924 F.2d 872 (9th Cir. 1991).

25. News reports commenting on *Ellison* included the following: Michelle Galen, *Ending Sexual Harassment: Business Is Getting the Message,* Bus. Wk., Mar. 18, 1991, at 98–100; Ruth Marcus, *When Is Flirting At Work Sexual Harassment?,* Wash. Post, Feb. 28, 1991, at A32; and Georgia Sargeant, *Sexual Harassment Cases Still Murky,* 27 Trial 14 (1991).

26. *Ellison,* 924 F.2d at 879.

27. *See infra* notes 30–152 and accompanying text.

28. *See infra* notes 153–180 and accompanying text.

29. *See infra* notes 181–292 and accompanying text.

[*Editors' note:* Sections I and II of the original text were not excerpted for our present purposes. The reader is referred to the original text for the complete set of footnotes.]

181. . . . the Civil Rights Act of 1991 authorizes compensatory and punitive damages for cases involving *intentional* sexual discrimination in employment. *See* Civil Rights Act of 1991, Pub. L. No. 102–166, § 102, 105 Stat. 1071, 1072 (1991) (to be codified at 42 U.S.C. § 1981a).

182. *See e.g.,* Riger, *supra* note 5, at 497 (citing U.S. Merit Systems Protection Board, *Sexual harassment in the federal workplace: Is it a problem?* (1981)) (first comprehensive natonal survey of sexual harassment among federal employees determined that roughly 40% of working women report having experienced sexual harassment, and updated study in 1988 found that frequency of harassment had remained constant since the original study).

183. *See* Lipsett v. University of Puerto Rico, 864 F.2d 881, 898 n. 19 (1st Cir. 1988) (citing a number of studies documenting sexual harassment in the workplace, including one that main-

tains that nearly 50% of working women are sexually harassed on the job).

184. *See* Ronni Sandroff, *Sexual Harassment: The Inside Story,* Working Woman, June 1992, at 47, 48 (survey by Working Woman Magazine found that 60% of women who responded reported being sexually harassed).

185. *See* David E. Terpstra & Susan E. Cook, *Complainant Characteristics and Reported Behaviors and Consequences Associated with Formal Sexual Harassment Charges,* 38 Personnel Psychol. 559, 559 (1985).

186. *See* Sandroff, *supra* note 184, at 48.

187. *See id.*; *see also* Riger, *supra* note 5, at 497 (citing several studies that "[w]omen with low power and status, whether due to lower age, being single or divorced, or being in a marginal position in the organization are more likely to be harassed").

188. *See* Riger, *supra* note 5, at 497.

189. *See e.g.,* Sandroff, *supra* note 184, at 47, 50 (according to *Working Woman* survey, among women who have been harassed, "only 40 percent told the harasser to stop, and just 26 percent reported the harassment"); Riger, *supra* note 5, at 497 (noting that "[d]espite the high rates found in surveys of sexual harassment of women, few complaints are pursued through official grievance procedures").

190. *See* Jane Gross, *Suffering in Silence No More: Fighting Sexual Harassment,* N.Y. Times, July 13, 1992, at A1, D10.

191. *See* H.R. Rep. No 40(I), 102d Cong., 1st Sess. 68 (1991), *reprinted* in 1991 U.S.C.C.A.N. 549, 606 n.63.

192. *See* Gross, *supra* note 190, at D10.

193. *See id.*

194. *See id.*

195. Sandroff, *supra* note 184, at 49 (quoting a Washingtron professor).

196. *See e.g.,* Ellison v. Brady, 924 F.2d 872, 878–79 (9th Cir. 1991) ("[C]omplete understanding of the victim's view requires, among other things, an analysis of the different perspectives of men and women. Conduct that many men consider unobjectionable may offend many women."); Andrews v. City of Philadelphia, 895 F.2d 1469, 1486 (3d Cir. 1990) ("Although men may find [obscene language and pornography] harmless

and innocent, it is highly possible that women may feel otherwise."); Lipsett v. University of Puerto Rico, 864 F.2d 881, 898 (1st Cir. 1988):

A male supervisor might believe, for example, that it is legitimate for him to tell a female subordinate that she has a "great figure" or "nice legs." The female subordinate, however, may find such comments offensive. Such a situation presents a dilemma for both the man and the woman; the man may not realize that his comments are offensive, and the woman may be fearful of criticizing her supervisor.

id.; Radtke v. Everett, 471 N.W.2d 660, 664 (Mich. Ct. App. 1991):

[I]t is important to analyze and understand the different perspectives of men and women. [B]ecause of their historical vulnerability in the work force, women are more likely to regard a verbal or physical sexual encounter as a coercive and degrading reminder that the woman involved is viewed more as an object of sexual desire than as a credible coworker deserving of respect.

(citations omitted), *appeal granted,* 487 N. W.2d 762 (Mich. 1992).

197. *See e.g.,* Ehrenreich, *supra* note 2, at 1207–1208 (noting that men tend to view some forms of sexual harassment as "harmless social interactions to which only overly sensitive women would object"); Staton & Sinner, *supra* note 2, at 10 (arguing that Title VII should apply to behavior that many men would not "even realize is inappropriate, or which may have been well-intentioned"); Riger, *supra,* note 5, at 499 ("Men tend to find sexual overtures from women at work to be flattering, whereas women find similar approaches from men to be insulting. . . . Whatever the cause, a reasonable man and a reasonable woman are likely to differ in their judgments of whether a particular behavior constitutes sexual harassment."); Abrams, *supra* note 13, at 1203 (noting that a "characteristically male view, which depicts sexual taunts, inquiries or magazines as a comparatively harmless amusement . . . pervades many recent court opinions").

198. Ehrenreich, *supra* note 2, at 1194–95.

199. *See supra* note 62.

62. Under the Civil Rights Act of 1964, there was no provision for a jury trial. The Civil Rights Act of 1991, however, provides for a jury trial in cases involving intentional discrimination in which the plaintiff requests compensatory and punitive damages. *See* Civil Rights Act of 1991, Pub. L. No. 102–166, § 102, 105 Stat. 1071, 1072 (1991) (to be codified at 42 U.S.C. § 1981a). The introduction of jury trials and the expansion of damages available under Title VII are two of the most significant aspects of the new Act. The addition of these provisions fundamentally changes the legal model underlying federal discrimination laws. The new Act, in providing for expanded money damages, moves these causes of action away from a format in which the goal is conciliation and improvement of employer-employee relations and toward the more adversarial format of a civil trial for tort damages. *See* Committee on Continuing Professional Educ., ALI-ABA, *The Civil Rights Act of 1991,* at 22 (1992) (compilation of materials addressing the 1991 Civil Rights Act amendments).

200. *See infra* notes 242–60 and accompanying text.

201. *See, e.g.,* Carol Gilligan. In a Different Voice: Psychological Theory and Women's Development (1982) (arguing that men and women approach moral decision-making from different perspectives); Deborah Tannen, You Just Don't Understand: Women and Men in Conversation 17 (1990) (recognizing that men and women approach conversations from different perspectives); Abrams, *supra* note 13, at 1187–97 (citing a number of feminist scholars who perceive differences on a number of dimensions between the sexes and stating that "[d]escribing the world as if socially created gender differences did not exist seems to me a strained and misleading undertaking"); Riger, *supra* note 5, at 499 (citing a number of analyses that recognize "clear-cut and persistent" gender differences in the perception of what constitutes sexual harassment).

202. Tannen, *supra* note 201, at 17.

203. *Id.* at 43.

204. Abrams, *supra* note 13, at 1205.

205. *Id.*

206. *See* Roper Poll, *supra* note 15.

207. *Id.* at 1.

208. According to the *Ellison* court:

We adopt the perspective of a reasonable woman primarily because we believe that a sex-blind reasonable person standard tends to be male-biased and tends to systematically ignore the experiences of women. . . . Instead, a gender-conscious examination of sexual harassment enables women to participate in the workplace on an equal footing with men.

Ellison v. Brady, 924 F.2d 872, 879 (9th Cir. 1991).

209. According to Professor Ronald Collins, one of the first references to the phrase is found in Sir William Jones's 1796 work on the law of bailments. *See* Collins, *supra* note 11, at 312–13.

210. Alan Patrick Herbert, Misleading Cases in the Common Law 13 (1928) (quoted in Collins, *supra* note 11, at 315).

211. *See* Collins, *supra* note 11, at 316 (citing Daniels v. Clegg, 28 Mich. 32, 41–42 (1873)).

212. Informal evidence of this trend is found in the fact that a Lexis search for the term "reasonable person" in federal appeals court opinions published after 1990 was not allowed to proceed because it would have retrieved more than 1,000 cases. In contrast, the same search for "reasonable man" found only 86 cases.

213. According to Professor Collins, the "reasonable man" standard was the recognized standard for reviewing culpable conduct in administrative law, bailment law, constitutional law, contract law, criminal law, and the law of trusts. It was also the traditional measure in the study of legal ethics. *See* Collins, *supra* note 11, at 313.

214. *See id.* at 314.

215. The "ideal but not perfect" standard serves as a model for judging the conduct of those accused of committing torts, not for gauging the appropriate response of those against whom torts are committed. Arguably an "ideal but not perfect" reasonable person or reasonable woman would be less vulnerable to sexual harassment than would be a more typical individual.

216. *See, e.g.,* Ellison v. Brady, 924 F.2d 872, 879 (9th Cir. 1991) (employers need not "accommodate the idiosyncratic concerns of the rare hyper-

sensitive employee"); Robinson v. Jacksonville Shipyards, Inc., 118 F.R.D. 525, 530 (M.D. Fla. 1988) ("Title VII liability attaches when the case is proved as to the reasonable person, and it does not extend further based on any hypersensitivity of a particular plaintiff."); Zabkowicz v. West Bend Co., 589 F. Supp. 780, 784 (E.D. Wis. 1984) ("Title VII does not serve as a vehicle for vindicating the petty slights suffered by the hypersensitive."); Radtke v. Everett, 471 N.W.2d 660, 665 (Mich. Ct. App. 1991) (plaintiff cannot prevail if she has an "idiosyncratic or hypersensitive" reaction to co-workers behavior), *appeal granted,* 487 N.W.2d 762 (Mich. 1992).

217. *See, e.g.,* Reed v. Shepard, 939 F.2d 484 (7th Cir. 1991) (no sexual harassment where court found "[b]y any objective standard, the behavior of the male [co-workers] toward Reed revealed at trial was, to say the least, repulsive. But apparently not to Reed. . . . [S]he . . . relished reciprocating in kind."); Christoforou v. Ryder Truck Rental, Inc., 668 F. Supp. 294, 301 (S.D.N.Y. 1987) (plaintiff admitted that instances of alleged harassing behavior did not interfere with her work ability), *cited with approval in Robinson,* 118 F.R.D. at 530; Loftin-Boggs v. City of Meridian, 633 F. Supp. 1323, 1327 (S.D. Miss. 1986) (plaintiff contributed to and apparently enjoyed situation alleged to be harassing behavior), *cited in Robinson,* 118 F.R.D. at 530.

218. Historically, of course, courts did adopt one view—the reasonable man standard—to the exclusion of all other perspectives. *See* Collins, *supra* note 11, at 312–15. We find no support for such an approach today, however.

219. *See supra* notes 195–205 and accompanying text.

220. *See, e.g.,* Roper Poll, *supra* note 15 and accompanying text (surveying perceptions of men and women regarding what constitutes sexual harassment). As noted by Burns W. Roper, chairman of the Roper Organization,

[t]he most significant finding to me is how similarly men and women view the issue of sexual harassment. While sexual harassment may be hard to define in the abstract, both sexes seem to know it when they see it—and neither men nor women think harassment is rampant in their own workplaces.

Id. at 2.

221. *See supra* notes 13–15 and accompanying text.

222. *See supra* notes 195–208 and accompanying text.

223. . . . *But see* Roper Poll, *supra* note 15 and accompanying text.

224. To say that this is the direction in which the courts seem headed is not to say that a majority has yet accepted the reasonable women standard. We also note that the EEOC, always an influential voice in this area, phrases its test differently. The agency evaluates the harasser's conduct from "the objective standpoint of a 'reasonable person,' " but also insists that "[t]he reasonable person standard should consider the victim's perspective." Policy Guidance on Current Issues, *supra* note 6, at 102–03.

225. Ellison v. Brady, 924 F.2d 872, 879, n.12 (9th Cir. 1991) (citation omitted).

226. *See* Radtke v. Everett, 471 N.W.2d 660, 665 n.10 (Mich. Ct. App. 1991), *appeal granted,* 487 N.W.2d 762 (Mich. 1992).

227. *See* Andrews v. City of Philadelphia, 895 F.2d 1469, 1485–86 (3d Cir. 1990).

228. *See id.;* Robinson v. Jacksonville Shipyards, Inc., 118 F.R.D. 525, 530–31 (M.D. Fla. 1988). *But see* Bennett v. Corroon & Black Corp., 845 F.2d 104, 106 (5th Cir. 1988) (expressing disagreement with district court's determination that presence of obscene drawing of plaintiff on walls of men's room constituted harassment), *cert denied,* 489 U.S. 1020.

229. *See* Lipsett v. University of Puerto Rico, 864 F.2d 881, 898 (1st Cir. 1988) (hypothetical example cited by court to illustrate behavior considered innocent by male supervisor, but offensive to a female subordinate); *accord* Ellison v. Brady, 924 F.2d 872, 878 (9th cir. 1991).

230. *See Ellison,* 924 F.2d at 880.

231. Ehrenreich, *supra* note 2, at 1208. Professor Ehrenreich argues that the "persistent behavior of this 'milder' sort is just as disturbing to many women as is overt quid pro quo harassment." *Id.* (citation omitted).

232. Abrams, *supra* note 13, at 1206. Abrams states that "If these . . . forms of employment discrimination against women are to be corrected, and if the norms that permit them to flourish are to be modified, then courts must employ a standard that reflects women's perceptions of sexual harassment." *Id.*

233. Riger, *supra* note 5, at 503.

234. *Id.*

235. *See* Roper Poll, *supra* note 15 and accompanying text.

236. Restatement (Second) of Torts § 402A(2)(a) (1965). This section imposes liability on product sellers "although the seller has exercised all possible care in the preparation and sale of his product." *Id.*

237. EEOC Guidelines, *supra* note 33, § 1604.11 (a) (3) (emphasis added).

  33. Equal Employment Opportunity Comm'n, Guidelines on Discrimination Because of Sex, 28 C.F.R. § 1604.11 (1992) [hereinafter EEOC Guidelines]. The EEOC Guidelines are interpretive regulations. Although they do not have the force of law, they have been relied on by a number of courts in sexual harassment cases. See Downes v. Federal Aviation Admin., 775 F.2d 288 (Fed. Cir. 1985); Henson v. City of Dundee 682 F.2d 897 (11th Cir. 1982); Bundy v. Jackson, 641 F.2d 934 (D.C. Cir. 1981). In the first opportunity that the Supreme Court took to discuss the legal effect of the EEOC Guidelines, the Court stated that the Guidelines "'while not controlling upon the courts by reason of their authority, do constitute a body of experience and informed judgment to which courts and litigants may properly resort for guidance,'" Meritor Sav. Bank v. Vinson, 477 U.S. 57, 65 (1986) (quoting General Elec. Co. v. Gilbert, 429 U.S. 125, 141–42 (1976), quoting in turn, Skidmore v. Swift & Co., 323 U.S. 134, 140 (1944)).

238. Ellison v. Brady, 924 F.2d 872, 880 (9th Cir. 1991) (citation omitted); *see also* Harris v. International Paper Co., 765 F. Supp. 1509, 1515 (D. Me.) ("Victims need establish neither the fault nor the discriminatory intent of their employers and co-workers to succeed under Title VII."), *vacated in part for other reasons,* 765 F. Supp. 1529 (1991); Staton & Sinner, *supra* note 2, at 9 ("Title VII was not designed to be a fault-based scheme.").

239. *See* Keeton et al., *supra* note 11, at 536. According to the authors:

> Tort liability never has been inconsistent with the ignorance which is bliss, or the good intentions with which hell is said to be paved. A trespasser is not excused by the honest, reasonable belief that the land is his own; a bona-fide purchaser of stolen goods is held liable for conversion; the publisher of a libel commits a tort, although he has no means of knowing the defamatory nature of his words. There are many situations in which a careful person is held liable for an entirely reasonable mistake. In all this there is nothing new. Socially, and legally, these defendants are at fault; whether they are individually so, in spite of the fact that they are blameless, appears to be entirely a matter of definition, rather than of substance, and the argument leads only to a pointless dispute over the meaning of a word.

> *Id.* (footnotes omitted).

240. *See generaly id.* at 534–83 (overview of strict liability).

241. *See id.* at 535–36. As the authors argue:

> There is a broader sense in which "fault" means nothing more than a departure from a standard of conduct required of a person by society for the protection of his neighbors; and if the departure is an innocent one, and the defendant cannot help it, it is none the less a departure, and a social wrong. The distinction still remains between the person who has deviated from the standard, and the person who has not.

> *Id.* (footnote omitted).

242. For example, the question of whether a killing was done intentionally, recklessly, or unwittingly can make the difference between a defendant being convicted for murder or walking free.

243. *See* Civil Rights Act of 1991, Pub. L. No. 102–166, § 102, 105 Stat. 1072 (1991) (to be codified at 42 U.S.C. § 1981a); Equal Employment Opportunity Comm'n Policy Guidance on Application of Damages Provisions of the Civil Rights Act of 1991 to Pending Charges and Pre-Act Conduct, N-915.002 (BNA) 441–42 (Dec. 27, 1991).

244. *See* Civil Rights Act of 1991, Pub. L. No. 102–166, § 102, 105 Stat. 1071, 1072 (1991) (to be codified at 42 U.S.C. § 1981a).

245. 42 U.S.C. § 1981 (1988).

246. In particularly egregious cases, plaintiffs could also recover punitive damages. *See* Patterson v. McLean Credit Union, 491 U.S. 164 (1989), *cited in* H.R. Rep. No. 40(I), 102d Cong., 1st

Sess. 65 (1991); Johnson v. Railway Express Agency, Inc., 421 U.S. 454, 460 (1975).

247. *See* Civil Rights Act of 1991, Pub. L. No. 102–166 § 102, 105 Stat. 1071, 1072 (1991) (to be codified as 42 U.S.C. § 1981a).

248. Unlike race discrimination cases, for which there are no limits on recoveries, damages for cases involving intentional discrimination under the 1991 Civil Rights Act are capped, with the cap limits determined by the number of persons employed by the defendant. *See* Civil Rights Act of 1991, Pub. L. No. 102–166, § 102, 105 Stat. 1071, 1073 (1991) (to be codified at 42 U.S.C. § 1981b(3)).

249. Ellison v. Brady, 924 F.2d 872, 880 (9th Cir. 1991).

250. The two leading disparate treatment cases are a Supreme Court case, Watson v. Fort Worth Bank and Trust, 487 U.S. 977 (1988), and the case discussed in the subsequent paragraphs, Texas Dep't of Community Affairs v. Burdine, 450 U.S. 248 (1981).

251. 450 U.S. 248 (1981).

252. *See id.* at 252–53 The Court first articulated these standards for Title VII cases in McDonnell Douglas Corp. v. Green, 411 U.S. 792 (1973). For an example of how a court applies these general guidelines to determine whether a prima facie case exists, see Ramsey v. American Air Filter Co., 772 F.2d 1303, 1307–09 (7th Cir. 1985).

253. *See* Riordan v. Kempiners, 831 F.2d 690, 696 (7th Cir. 1987).

254. *See, e.g.,* Lindahl v. Air France, 930 F.2d 1434, 1437 (9th Cir. 1991) (employee has burden of showing that employer's reason for denial of promotion was "pretext" for discrimination); Billups v. Methodist Hosp. of Chicago, 922 F.2d 1300, 1303 (7th Cir. 1991) ("pretext" may be demonstrated either directly by persuading court that discriminatory reason more likely motivated employer, or indirectly by showing that employer's proffered reason is unworthy of belief); Hayes v. Invesco, Inc., 907 F.2d 853, 858 (8th Cir. 1990) (overruling district court's determination that employer's reason for differential treatment of black clinical nursing instructor was "pretextual").

255. *See* Hill v. Mississippi State Employment Serv., 918 F.2d 1233 (5th Cir. 1990), *cert. denied,* 112

S. Ct. 188 (1991); Mullen v. Princess Anne Volunteer Fire Co., Inc., 853 F.2d 1130 (4th Cir. 1988); Springer v. Seamen, 821 F.2d 871 (1st Cir. 1987).

256. *See* Holder v. City of Raleigh, 867 F.2d 823 (4th Cir. 1989).

257. *See, e.g.,* Morgan v. Massachusetts Gen. Hosp., 901 F.2d 186, 189–90 (1st Cir. 1990) (where employer terminated black employees on possibly mistaken assumption that employee had instigated a fight with co-worker, fact that employer might have been mistaken tended to negate discriminatory intent so long as hospital acted in good faith); Pollard v. Rea Magnet Wire Co., 824 F.2d 557, 559 (7th Cir. 1987) (where employer's reason for alleged discriminatory act was honestly described, but poorly founded, court will not find discriminatory intent), *cert. denied,* 484 U.S. 977 (1988); Wrenn v. Gould, 808 F.2d 493, 502 (6th Cir. 1987) (in evaluating discriminatory intent, court should look to employer's motivation, not applicant's perceptions or even objective assessment of what qualifications are required for particular position); Linder v. Prudential Ins. Co., 743 F. Supp. 1237, 1245 (W.D. Tex. 1990) (employer's action, if based upon sincere belief in business necessity, does not constitute discriminatory intent even where court concludes that employer acted improperly); Howze v. Adams, 689 F. Supp. 20, 25 (D.D.C. 1988) (fact that employer's decision violated federal personnel law did not demonstrate discriminatory intent); Grier v. Casey, 643 F. Supp. 298, 309 (W.D.N.C. 1986) (to find that employer's action was non-discriminatory, trier of fact need only determine that employer had good faith belief that employee's performance was unsatisfactory and that asserted reason for the action was not a mere pretext for discrimination).

258. *See* Keeton et al., *supra* note 11, at 37.

259. For example, where the defendant, over the protests of the plaintiff, tried to set a broken arm and caused severe harm. *See id.*

260. *See id.*

261. According to Ehrenreich:

   [A]ll acts by any one group (or individual) are inevitably harmful to others. One side's freedom can always be seen as the other side's loss of security, one side's equal treatment can seem like the other's unequal treatment, one group's pursuit of its own interest can always be called intolerance of any other group that is affected by that pursuit.

Ehrenreich, *supra* note 2, at 1221 (footnote omitted). Although we hesitate to look at the world as one huge "zero-sum" game, we agree with Ehrenreich that major policy shifts often require painful trade-offs among competing interests.

262. *See supra* notes 225–30 and accompanying text.

263. Our experience as faculty in a business school has sensitized us to the challenges that face corporate officials in addressing new workplace rules. Because most laws present "gray zones" in which it is not clear whether one's practices comply with the rules, companies often try to insulate themselves from liability by drawing "bright line" rules that bar conduct that even hints of a potential violation.

264. Needless to say, kissing under mistletoe at an office Christmas party would be forbidden under this sort of rule.

265. *See infra* note 279.

266. *See* Ehrenreich, *supra* note 2, at 1207.

267. A company might, for example, define "sexual staring" as any glance at an employee that exceeds one second or that is directed below the employee's neck. The question then becomes how to enforce the rule—perhaps by hiring office enforcers or using office informants!

268. Again, a "bright line" rule such as this would work to insulate a company from liability because, the company hopes, it would eliminate any vagueness or ambiguity regarding what constitutes a "dirty" joke or a joke that demeans women.

269. We do not suggest that Title VII is the only area of the law that requires employers to deal with changing and vague standards. Publishers, for example, face evolving "contemporary community standards" that define what constitutes obscenity. *See* Miller v. California, 413 U.S. 15, 24 (1973). We suspect, however, that the lines defining what constitutes obscenity under the many Supreme Court decisions in this area are somewhat clearer for publishing companies than are the boundaries separating acceptable from unacceptable conduct toward employees under recent Title VII decisions.

270. *See* EEOC Guidelines [*supra* note 33,] § 1604.2 for the agency's rules regarding "sex as a bona fide occupational qualification."

271. 112 S. Ct. 2538 (1992).

272. *Id.* at 2548.

273. For example, Title VII has typically been interpreted as covering only certain categories of discrimination, such as race, color, sex, or national origin. Thus, Title VII protects an employee against racial taunts or abusive sexual slurs, but not, say, against co-workers who mock his southern accent of his "Southerness." *See* Williams v. Frank, 757 F. Supp. 112, 120 (D. Mass. 1991).

274. Under this doctrine, regulations that legitimately target conduct incidentally accompanying speech do not violate the First Amendment so long as the regulations are not directed at the content of the speech. *See* United States v. O'Brien, 391 U.S. 367, 376 (1968). According to the *R.A.V.* majority, the key to the constitutionality of such "speech/conduct" regulations is that the government "does not target conduct on the basis of its expressive content." *R.A.V.*, 112 S. Ct. at 2546-47.

275. According to Justice White:

Title VII is similar to the St. Paul ordinance that the majority condemns because "it impose(s) special prohibitions on those speakers who express views on disfavored subjects." . . . Under the broad principle the Court uses to decide the present case, hostile work environment claims based on sexual harassment should fail First Amendment review; because a general ban on harassment in the workplace would cover the problem of sexual harassment, any attempt to proscribe the subcategory of sexually harassing expression would violate the First Amendment.

R.A.V., 112 St. Ct. at 2557 (alteration in original) (citation omitted). Moreover, according to Justice White, the speech regulated in hostile environment cases *is* the conduct that is prohibited in many cases, and penalizing this expression under Title VII "reaches beyond any 'incidental' affect on speech." *Id.*

276. *See* Kingsley R. Browne, *Title VII as Censorship: Hostile-Environment Harassment and the First Amendment,* 52 Ohio St. L.J. 481 (1991);

see also Cathleen M. Mogan, *Current Hostile Environment Sexual Harassment Law: Time to Stop Defendants From Having Their Cake and Eating It Too,* 6 Notre Dame J.L. Ethics & Pub. Pol'y 543, 571–73 (1992) (discussing the "grinding tension" between freedom of expression and the rights of women and minorities).

277. Browne, *supra* note 276, at 515.

278. *Id.* at 549 (quoting Whitney v. California, 274 U.S. 357, 375 (1927) (Brandeis, J., concurring)).

279. *Id.* According to Browne:

It is but a small step from requiring a person to refrain from expressing beliefs in the hope that he will cease to hold them to requiring a person to express beliefs in the hope that he will begin to hold them. If the state may justify a prohibition on a person's saying "blacks are inferior" by pointing to the effect of the prohibition on a person's beliefs, the state should have equivalent power to require that a person affirm a belief in racial equality on the ground that repeated affirmation will cause the person to come to believe it, and, once having come to believe it, to conform his actions to his newly acquired beliefs. . . . In addition to its Orwellian overtones, the assumption that beliefs can be altered by forbidding expression is probably wrong.

Id. at 549–50. One recent law review comment dismisses Browne's concerns by arguing that restricting sexually explicit photographs and other behavior found to be sexually harassing should occur only in work situations that have been traditionally male dominated or in workplaces where the sexes are segregated by job. *See* Amy Horton, Comment, *Of Supervision, Centerfolds, and Censorship: Sexual Harassment, the First Amendment, and the Contours of Title VII,* 46 U. Miami L. Rev. 403, 448 (1991). Although qualifying restrictions on speech and expression in this limited way has a surface appeal, one might question the wisdom of conditioning the right to free expression upon whether it makes those exposed to it uncomfortable. Free speech ought not be restricted simply because others find it offensive. Moreover, we see no evidence that supporters of restrictions on speech and expression in the name of reducing sexual harassment accept the limitations

suggested by Ms. Horton. *See, e.g.,* Dana S. Connell, *Effective Sexual Harassment Policies: Unexpected Lessons from* Jacksonville Shipyards, 17 Employee Relations L.J. 191 (Autumn 1991) (urging employers generally to adopt rules barring the display *or possession of* "sexually suggestive" materials). One approach cited with approval by Connell defines "sexually suggestive materials" as those that depict "a person of either sex who is not fully clothed or in clothes that are not suited to or ordinarily accepted for the accomplishment of routine work in and around the [workplace] and who is posed for the obvious purpose of displaying or drawing attention to private portions of his or her body." *Id.* at 200–01.

280. 765 F. Supp. 1509 (D. Me.), *vacated in part for other reasons,* 765 F. Supp. 1529 (1991).

281. *Id.* at 1516 n.12.

282. 947 F.2d 147 (5th Cir. 1991), *cert. denied,* 112 S. Ct. 3028 (1992).

283. *See id.* at 158 (5th Cir. 1991). According to the majority, the cross did not violate the establishment clause given the length of time it had used the insignia, and given that it had no proselytizing effect and did not endorse religion. *See id.*

284. Judge Goldberg argued that:

Majoritarian adherents, construing a government action devoid of religious purpose, may not perceive the endorsement message that the minority receives with stinging clarity. Only through sensitivity to the nonadherent can we effect the constitutional values inherent in the Religion Clauses. *Cf.* Ellison v. Brady, 924 F.2d 872, 878–80 (9th Cir. 1991) (adopting perspective of "reasonable woman" in order to effect statutory aim of sex discrimination statute). Yet, by insisting that the test be an objective one—a "reasonable nonadherent" test—the endorsement inquiry retains the ability to discount the perceptions of a hypersensitive plaintiff.

Murray, 947 F.2d at 165 (Goldberg, J., dissenting).

285. *See* William B. Johnson, Hudson Institute, *Workforce 2000: Work and Workers For the Twenty-first Century* (1987). This report from the Hudson Institute, which forecasts substantial demographic changes, has sometimes been

misinterpreted to indicate that white males will no longer be in the majority in the year 2000. This is incorrect. What will change is the mix of new entrants in the workforce. By the year 2000, nonwhite, women, and immigrants will make up more than five-sixths of the new entrants in the job market. *See id.* at 85–103. Only 15% of new entrants to the labor force in the years 1987 to 2000 will be native white males, compared to 47% in 1987. *See id,* at xiii.

286 *See, e.g.,* Enrenreich, *supra* note 2, at 1217–19 (recognizing, but failing to suggest solutions to, such conflicts).

287. As stated by the *Ellison* court:

We adopt the perspective of a reasonable woman primarily because we believe that a sex-blind reasonable person standard tends to be male-biased and tends to systematically ignore the experiences of women. . . . [A] gender-conscious examination of sexual harassment enables women to participate in the workplace on an equal footing with men.

Ellison v. Brady, 924 F.2d 872, 879 (9th Cir. 1991).

288. Professor Deborah A. Stone offers what we believe to be a view typical of many current commentaries. According to Professor Stone, in determining which group's standard of behavior should prevail in a harassment case, the test should: "reflect how the action looks to the weaker party, given the real disparity of power. It is a mockery of the liberal ideal of autonomy to interpret a potentially coercive relationship from the point of view of the person who has the power to coerce." Deborah A. Stone, *Race, Gender, and the Supreme Court,* The American Prospect 63, 69 (Winter 1992). Her view is widely shared. *See e.g.,* Riger, *supra* note 5, at 503 (arguing that in deciding which sex's definition of harassment should prevail, policymakers "need to learn to 'think like a woman'" in order to equalize power in the workplace); Ruth Colker, *Anti-Subordination Above All; Sex, Race, and Equal Protection,* 61 N.Y.U. L. Rev. 1003 (1986) (advocating an "anti-subordina-

tion" policy that removes any policy which contributes in intent or affect to the subordination of a historically dominated group).

289. In criticizing this approach, Professor Browne notes:

Ironically, though couched in terms of discriminatory treatment, the real claim in many harassment cases is that the work atmosphere did *not* change in response to the addition of women (or minorities) to the environment. The rationale is that conduct that appears harmless to mean may be offensive to women, although such reasoning seems inconsistent, at least superficially, with the view that Title VII "rejects the notion of 'romantic paternalism' towards women." For example, the court in *Andrews v. City of Philadelphia* rejected the argument that the environment was not a hostile one because "a police station need not be run like a day care center," stating that neither should it have "the ambience of a nineteenth century military barracks," although an all-male police station having such an ambiance would certainly not violate Title VII. The court also noted that although men might find the obscenity and pornography that pervaded the workplace "harmless and innocent," women might well "feel otherwise," and such expression may be "highly offensive to a woman who seeks to deal with her fellow employees and clients with professional dignity and without the barrier of sexual differentiation and abuse." *As a consequence, a locker room atmosphere that was perfectly legal before the entry of women into the job becomes illegal thereafter.*

Browne, *supra* note 276, at 487–88 (emphasis added) (footnotes omitted).

290. Stone, *supra* note 288, at 69.

291. Of course, any of these behaviors, if carried to an extreme, can present a problem that might justify a lawsuit. But feminist writers such as Ehrenreich, Riger, and Abrams also argue that milder versions of these behaviors should be considered sexual harassment. *See supra* notes 231–34 and accompanying text.

292. Tannen, *supra* note 201, at 297–98.

READING 5-5

The Power and Reasons Behind Sexual Harassment: An Employer's Guide to Solutions

Donna M. Stringer
Helen Remick
Jan Salisbury
Angela B. Ginorio

Sexual harassment has become a major concern to employers as they have become aware of its financial, environmental and morale costs in the workplace.

The literature on sexual harassment generally characterizes it as an abuse of either role or sexual power. For example, role power is abused when an employer demands sexual activity as a condition of hiring an applicant. Sexual power is abused if an applicant uses sexual attractiveness to promise sexual favors in exchange for being hired. Two major motivators for harassment, then, are to obtain sexual activity and/or to abuse or increase one's power. These two motivators are not, of course, mutually exclusive.

We believe that sex and power are the primary components of sexual harassment but the issues are more complex than has generally been acknowledged in the sexual harassment literature. Sociologists have developed models of power which, when applied to sexual harassment, lead to a better understanding of the issue. Types of power which can affect sexual harassment include achieved power (that which someone earns), ascribed power (that which is given to someone and cannot be taken away) and situational power (that which depends on the situation in which one is). Each of these types of power also has several sources: achieved power,

Source: Public Personnel Management, 19 (1) (Spring, 1990) 43–52. Reproduced with Permission of Public Personnel Management, published by the International Personnel Management Association, Alexandria, VA.

for example, can come from money, role or position, and information. These types and sources of power are used for a variety of reasons to sexually harass others. Management solutions, if they are to be effective, must result from a careful analysis of each individual case to include both the power issues and the underlying individual reasons behind the sexual harassment.

Sexual harassment in the workplace is not acceptable regardless of the power issues or the motivation. The harasser must be disciplined for the harassment in a way that directly communicates in no uncertain terms that such behavior will not be tolerated. To avoid sexual harassment's costly consequences and minimize its frequency, employers need to identify and understand both the reason for the harassment and the specific form of power being abused.

In this paper we apply the model of achieved, ascribed and situational power to sexual harassment and propose effective employer responses for seven specific reasons for sexual harassment we have observed.

THE QUESTION OF POWER

Achieved Power

Achieved power is a form of power one earns through some effort. Sources of achieved power in the workplace include *information, salary (money) and formal role power (title or position).* Persons who have valued information have more power than those who do not; those who are paid higher salaries are generally perceived as having more power than those who are paid less; higher status roles carry more power than lower status roles.

Perhaps the most obvious source of power for people to understand as it relates to sexual harassment is that of *formal role power* based on a person's rank or position within the organization. Abuse of this type of power is widely seen as inappropriate and thus the easiest for management to take action against when it occurs.

Understanding achieved power can help managers to take effective actions.

The difficulty with achieved power comes when someone uses his/her success in an abusive way to sexually harass someone else. Complicating this issue is the fact that the power role may be so new that the harasser may not see himself/herself as having any power. Further, the harasser's power may only be relative to the victim and not to the entire organization so it may be easy to deny that he/she has power at all. And, of course, the harasser may be unconsciously attempting to reduce current or future competition through sexual harassment. Helping the harasser understand how such behaviors negatively impact the victim may lead to changed behaviors. We have found it effective to discuss this abuse of power with the harasser as a fairness issue: it is simply not fair to use power you worked so hard to achieve to impact negatively another person's chances for career, financial or emotional success. This attempt at helping the harasser understand must not occur, of course, without other disciplinary measures. Discipline is appropriate for the illegal activity of sexual harassment which has occurred; understanding how unfair use of power can affect others can prevent future acts.

Ascribed Power

Ascribed power is an attributed characteristic, or something which the person has no control over and cannot change. Two sources of ascribed power relevant to the workplace include *gender and ethnicity*. When handling sexual harassment which involves ascribed power, one must be particularly careful to help the harasser understand how his/her gender or ethnicity impacts the harassment without seeming to blame the person for his or her gender or ethnicity which, of course, cannot be changed.

Gender power is fundamental to sexual harassment. Virtually all research indicates that this culture attributes more power to men simply because of their gender. In work settings men are viewed as more competent, responsible, committed and valuable than women. When a male harasser uses his "natural" gender power, it is difficult for a female victim to resist or report harassment; his word will virtually always be given more weight than hers.

Gender power makes women with achieved power particularly vulnerable to sexual harassment. Even when a woman has role, information or money power in an organization, she does not have access to the societal value placed on the male gender. It is gender power that allows male subordinates to harass the female supervisor with impunity; and while she has the formal role power within the organization, this rarely outweighs his gender power which makes it hard for her to report any harassment. The usual reacton to these women when they report harassment is to disregard her complaint saying that she had the formal power to stop it if she had really wanted to, or to believe that she was harassed and that she was unable to stop it, in which case the validity of her formal role power will be questioned—that is, she should not have such formal power if cannot even stop a harasser!

While societal values have begun to change, employers must understand that differential values placed on men and women by most Americans continue to impact the workplace. To deny these value differences is to misunderstand much of the foundation of sexual harassment in today's workplace. Until men and women are equally valued by society, women (even "powerful" women) will be at a disadvantage in the workplace as it relates to sexual harassment.

Ethnic Power

Ethnic power can also affect sexual harassment. Because whites are more powerful and valued in this culture than people of color, complaints or concerns of ethnic minority victims are often not taken as seriously, investigated as appropriately, or reprimanded as strongly as those complaints of white victims. Ethnic minority harassers of white women, on the other hand, are often disciplined more severely. Finally, many victims do not report an ethnic minority harasser out of fear that either the victim will be challenged with accusations of racism or out of fear that the harasser will be unduly disciplined.

Ascribed and Achieved Powers Combined

There are two sources of power which impact sexual harassment which are of particular interest because they combine ascribed and achieved powers. These sources of power are *sexuality* and *physical size and strength.* These emphasize the biological differences between men and women and, similar to those sources already discussed, can be mitigated by understanding. With these sources it is important to identify clearly the ascribed characteristics, help the person understand how those characteristics affect power relationships, validate the power they have worked so hard to achieve, and clarify how power can be enjoyed without unfairly using it against other people.

The first source of combined ascribed and achieved powers is *sexuality.* One's sexual organs are biologically determined while one's perception of sexuality and sexual practices are learned through one's family, religion and culture. Exchange of sexual access for power is a common thread in our cultural fabric. It is also obvious that both genders have sexuality with which to barter. When sex and power are exchanged in the workplace, however, it is often sexual harassment and may involve abuse of sexual power in two ways: a person with some form of power may demand sex from a less powerful person or a person with little power may offer sexuality in exchange for access to power. From examination of material from employers, courts and counselors it appears that men usually fall into the former category and women fall into the latter. In other words, men and women usually act on sex and power differently in the workplace which is a critical factor

for employers trying to understand sexual harassment and design appropriate responses.

If a man has achieved forms of power (role status, information, money) in the workplace and abuses this power to successfully sexually harass women, his perceived power increases. That is, people become more likely to give him what he wants because "he must have a lot of power if he can continually get away with sexual harassment." This holds true, of course, whether he actually harasses or merely tells others that he does. In addition to the fear implicit in such compliance, many men will actually admire him for getting away with behaviors they may only fantasize about.

It is rare that women use achieved power in the workplace to sexually harass subordinates—women in power rarely see sexuality as appropriate to the workplace. Research tells us that women who have power in the workplace are often not perceived as sexually attractive and therefore are not likely to be harassed by men around them. Most women who have achieved power are not willing to risk losing it in order to gain sexual access to someone in the workplace. Some women have, however, used their sexuality inappropriately to obtain legitimate power. Women, by virtue of their generally lower cultural status, are more likely than men to be involved in sexual harassment in the form of offering sex for information, money, or status.

The differences, then, in how men and women use sexuality and power in the workplace is that men are most likely to use achieved power to obtain sex, or get away with sexual harassment while women are more likely to use sex to obtain achieved forms of power. Both behaviors are inappropriate.

Physical size and strength are underrated as sources of power but are strong factors in many sexual harassment situations. These forms also combine ascribed (size) and achieved (strength) powers and must be understood in the context of male/female differences. Because most men are larger and stronger than most women, some men may consciously or unconsciously use their size to intimidate or control women whom they are harassing. The size and strength difference also affects how much resistance a woman may feel she can offer without incurring physical injury. This fear of injury by someone larger is exacerbated if a victim has had an earlier history of physical or sexual assault in the form of incest, rape or spouse abuse. Women in nontraditional jobs who have worked hard to achieve the physical strength required to succeed are often fearful of reporting harassment because this may be interpreted as an admission that they cannot do their job: if she is not strong enough to stop harassment, she certainly cannot be strong enough to stay on the job.

Situational Power

And finally, situational power is that which may occur in one situation but not in another. Women may feel free to harass a lone man in a work setting, for example, even if they would not consider such behavior if they were in a social setting, or if several men were in the work setting.

Numbers and territoriality are primary sources of situational power in the workplace. This subtle form of power can be used against a person who is the only one, or one of few, of their "kind" within a work setting: the only woman, the only ethnic minority, the only lesbian or gay man. Abuse of this form of power is usually motivated by wanting to retain the homogeneous work setting—wanting the "outsider" to leave. In sexual harassment this takes the form of focusing on the person's gender or sexual orientation to define him/her as different, not competent, or not to be taken seriously. While the entire work group may not participate in this harassment, the mere existence of a "we/they" atmosphere based on numbers will make it possible for one or more employees to use the power of numbers and territoriality to harass the outsider. This form of power is most frequently found in nontraditional work settings: construction, fire fighting, police work and upper management for women and nursing, teaching, clerical work for men. Unfortunately, this type of harassment frequently is not reported because the victim does not want to do anything to further separate himself/herself from work colleagues. In addition, the victim has often had to become "sexless" to succeed at a traditional job and is therefore literally not able to see herself/himself as "sexually" harassed.

Looking at these power sources individually can lead to very simple conclusions: male bosses are more powerful than female secretaries because they have more information, money, role status and gender-role status. Analyses become more complex. Of course, when (as is often the case in today's workplace) people are outside of roles we traditionally understand, for example, if the boss is female and some of her subordinates are males who have more information than she does by virtue of their longevity with the organization, the question regarding who has the power becomes very complex.

REASONS FOR HARASSMENT OCCURRING

Abuse of power to obtain sexual favors has been discussed above as well as throughout sexual harassment literature. As indicated earlier, in this form of harassment the harasser abuses power, usually formal role power, to intimidate an employee into a sexual relationship. Because this person usually has formal role power assigned by the employer, there is a clear legal liability to the employer.

The only effective employer response is immediate corrective action, from verbal reprimand to termination depending on the frequency and intensity of harassment which has occurred. Repeated incidents must result in the employer removing the harasser's formal role power through demotion or termination. Since the basis for the harassment is the harasser's achieved power, the employer must remove access to that power. Such action not only protects the employer from legal liabilities but it also sends a clear message to the remainder of the workforce that such behavior will not be tolerated by the employer, thus decreasing the chances of other people with such power abusing it.

Sex used to obtain power is most likely to occur when a person offers sex in exchange for money, status or information. This harassment is usually more difficult for the employer to take action against because it is hard for the person with status to substantiate why he/she did not simply use his/her formal power to say "no" to the offer.

The most appropriate employer response here is to refuse the harasser the power he/she is seeking and to provide training for the victim in how to give strong, effective "no's" to future offers. It may also be appropriate to move the harasser elsewhere in the organization where he/she will not have the sought-after job, salary, or information. Employers must also, however, avoid the temptation of widely publicizing this particular type of harassment because it lends to the frequent concern managers have that they will become victims of harassment or victims of false accusations of harassment. To focus on these few cases will be to avoid the fact that the majority of sexual harassment cases involve abuse of power, not a grab for power.

Power used to decrease the power of the victim is another common reason for sexual harassment. In this instance, the harasser rarely expects or demands a sexual relationship. Rather, the intent is to embarrass or intimidate the victim in such a way that her/his credibility, competence, or power is decreased. Examples of this form of sexual harassment include the constant sexual jokes or stories or comments about a person's body. This form of harassment is most common for nontraditional employees such as women in skilled crafts and trades, women in upper level management, women fire fighters or police officers, and male nurses or secretaries.

Employer responses to this form of harassment should begin with proactive planning: <u>preparing the workforce for the arrival of nontraditional employees with specific, nonambiguous policies and statements from management</u> regarding support for those employees. This may not be enough and harassment may occur anyway. This type of harassment can often be extremely dangerous physically and carries high liability for the employer should someone be injured. With this form of harassment, victims frequently hesitate to report it because to do so will even further alienate them from their peers. At the point problems formally reach management they are often out of control; management must, therefore, watch carefully for any signs that it is occurring. If such harassment occurs, management must continue demanding and demonstrating support for the nontraditional employee while effectively reprimanding and/or disciplining harassers.

Employers looking for solutions to such harassment frequently find they cannot simply reassign the harasser or victim to another work site because only one such unit exists. In this case, solutions require more creativity such as retraining one or both persons for new careers or arranging for an employee "trade" with another employer.

Personal crisis in the life of the harasser is another reason for harassment occurring. This is generally someone experiencing a life crisis such as aging, divorce, or monetary problems. These problems may create self doubt about one's value as a "real" man or woman as defined by society. These persons may attempt to regain their self identity by asserting their sexuality—sometimes through sexual harassment. The emphasis in this harassment is two-fold: to obtain sexual access and to regain the harasser's sense of personal power through confirming his/her gender identity. This form of harassment is both harder and easier for employers to deal with than other forms: it is harder because co-workers often feel sorry for the person and protect him/her; it is easier to bring to a successful solution. However, because once harassers are confronted they almost always stop the harassment.

It is the employer's responsibility to make sexual harassment unacceptable as a resolution to personal crisis. This form of harassment is time limited: it begins when the personal crisis begins and ends when the crisis is over. Understanding the source of this harassment allows the victim or the employer to identify a solution. First, one must tell the harasser to discontinue the harassment; secondly, the employer should suggest (and provide if there is a PAGE employee assistance program available) appropriate counseling to help the harasser resolve the personal crisis.

Sexual attraction gone wrong is a fifth reason for harassment occurring. It is important to note, of course, that mutual attraction between two employees or co-workers is NOT sexual harassment. If the attraction is only one way and non-reciprocal, however, it is or can become sexual harassment. Very often this form of harassment begins with a mutual attraction and/or relationship followed loss of interest by one person. The still-interested person then continues to pursue a relationship in such a way that it ultimately becomes harassing and affects the victim's ability to work and/or her or his work environment.

The employer's response here must be to stop the work-related harassment by setting clear guidelines and expectations as it would with other forms of sexual harassment. The employer must keep in mind that this is NOT simply a "personal matter" when the behaviors make the work environment hostile and unproductive. Referring one or both parties to counseling for resolution of the personal relationship may also be appropriate. Some are now arguing that employers are well advised to have a strict non-fraternization policy although there are strong opponents who cite legal and practical objections to the viability of this approach. As long as people work together there are likely to be mutual at-

tractions; as the work force is integrated in ever increasing numbers and in new occupations, employers will need to have the skills and knowledge to help employees differentiate appropriate from inappropriate behaviors in the workplace. Employers will need to take firm positions on which behaviors are acceptable in the workplace and stay out of employees' personal relationships. At the same time, however, employers must know that personal relationships will occur and be prepared to assist employees in dealing with such relationships when they begin to impact the workplace.

Genuine deviance must also be recognized as the cause for some sexual harassment. Alcohol or substance abuse, character disorders, and other socially deviant behavior patterns can lead a person to become a chronic sexual harasser in the workplace. Deviant harassers typically harass more than one person, often successively as victims leave the workplace (either quitting or being fired because of the impacts of the harassment) and are replaced by the next victim. These harassers can be charming, convincing liars, and often present a grandiose picture of their personal and organizational power. A high proportion of harassers who end up in court fit this pattern because they tend to harass employees in more serious ways, including physical contact and retaliation for rejection of their attentions.

It is particularly important with these harassers that the employer act immediately and powerfully. The harasser must be disciplined for the harassment in a way that directly communicates in no uncertain terms that such behavior will not be tolerated. Since the probability of repetition is high in these cases, both the harassment and the disciplinary action should be carefully documented and the next violation met with dismissal. If multiple situations are found during investigation of a complaint, dismissal may be an appropriate first step. The employer may also wish to suggest that professional assistance is appropriate for the harasser.

And finally, a form of sexual harassment is one we term *"a genuine attempt to create new rules for new roles."* This form of harassment can occur when a male is genuinely trying to welcome a female into a work setting but does not know how. Consequently, he may attempt to show acceptance through sexual jokes, touching, comments, or other sexual behavior. Men and women know the rules for traditional roles. Consider some of those role relationships: daughter/father; wife/husband; teacher/student; priest/nun; boss/secretary; doctor/nurse; waitress/customer, etc. Each of these roles has a set of rules which establish both the power relationship and the sexual relationship expected between the two people. The dilemma for us now is that men and women are working in new relationships and we have not established a set of rules which help us understand how to behave. If the man's behavior is inappropriate and the woman points this out and asks for some behavior changes and he complies, there will probably be no further problem. If, on the other hand, she asks for changes and he refuses, legally-defined sexual harassment may exist.

Employers can best respond to this type of harassment through prevention: training classes and policies recognizing women's entry into the workforce and outlining expected behaviors should help. If problems do occur in spite of the proactive work, simple counseling with the man (sometimes with the woman present, depending on the situation) will usually terminate this type of behavior before it becomes defined as sexual harassment.

CONCLUSIONS

While each of the seven reasons for sexual harassment can be viewed as an abuse of some form of power, there are other issues to be considered. Through understanding the complexity of power, sexual relationships and motivation, employers and policy makers will be better equipped to develop appropriate and effective solutions to sexual harassment. This will allow elimination of legal and financial hazards and development of a dynamic, highly motivating work environment.

REFERENCES

Abbey, Antonia & Melby, Christian, "The effects of nonverbal cues on gender differences in perceptions of sexual intent," *Sex Roles,* 15, 1986, 283–298.

Brown, Roger, *Social Psychology,* New York: The Free Press, 1965.

Gutek, Barbara A., *Sex and the Workplace,* San Francisco: Jossey-Bass, Inc., 1985.

Livingston, Joy A., "Responses to sexual harassment on the job: legal, organizational, and individual actions," *Journal of Social Issues,* 38(4), 1982, 5–22.

MacKinnon, Catherine, *Sexual harassment of working women: A case of sex discrimination,* New Haven, Conn.: Yale University Press, 1979.

Renick, James C., "Sexual harassment at work: Why it happens, what to do about it," *Personnel Journal,* August, 1980, 658–662.

"Whose Job Is It Anyway?" Employee Security and Employer Rights

INTRODUCTION

"Employment-at-will" (EAW) is a shorthand for an ethical and legal theory that purports to describe the appropriate relationship between employers and employees. According to EAW, employment is a contractual relationship, resting on the free consent of both parties. As such and as long as the terms of the contract are not violated, it may be terminated at the will of either party for any reason or for no reason at all. A wrongful termination occurs only when either party ends the relationship in violation of one of the contract's explicit terms.

A utilitarian assessment that, in comparison to other economic systems, capitalism produces more net good, in terms both of wealth and of general human flourishing, is central to EAW's ethical justification. Guided only by the principles of voluntary exchange, buyers, sellers, producers, and consumers work together, almost unwittingly, to produce socially beneficial goods. The freedom of employees to work where and for whom they will and of employers to hire and discharge employees as they see fit means businesses will function efficiently and

productively, generating social utility. Any interference with this finely tuned mechanism, by the government or anyone else, will only disrupt it.

"At-will" underscores the importance placed on the rights of each party, particularly the right to free association and the right to enter into contracts freely, rights anchored in Kant's insistence on the respect due the autonomy of human beings. Employees have the right to select the persons and organizations for whom they will work and, unless they have explicit contractual obligations to the contrary, to leave those employers whenever they wish. Similarly, employers have the right to select their employees according to whatever criteria they wish to use and, unless they have explicit contractual obligations to the contrary, to retain and discharge those employees as they deem appropriate.

Respect for property rights is integral to EAW's ethical justification. A business's capital is the property of its owners, and they are free to use it as they wish. Likewise, employees own their skills and labor and are free to use them as they wish. Once employers choose to sell or rent their skills and labor to an employer, in effect they become the employer's to use.

While EAW has its supporters, there are naturally detractors as well. Some of the arguments they advance are as follows.

1. EAW can be construed as intrinsically unfair because it appears to allow employers to violate the common morality's prohibition against inflicting harm without an ethically valid justification. Firing a long-term, loyal, productive employee for no reason, or for no good reason, seems to EAW's opponents so unfair that any ethical arguments in support of EAW cannot bear the burden of proof.

2. Critics note that it is extraordinarily difficult, from a utilitarian perspective, to analyze and compute the benefits and harms resulting from EAW, particularly if the social and financial costs of worker insecurity and unemployment to society at large are taken into account. In addition, some critics question whether an organizational culture that permits workers to be discharged arbitrarily provides an environment in which efficiency and productivity can flourish.

3. EAW's appeals to freedom of association and contract make sense only on the assumption that employers and employees enjoy equal independence and bargaining power in negotiating contracts. In reality, the playing field is not level; employers, by virtue of their wealth and power, often have a significantly superior bargaining position and thus enjoy more options and more freedom than employees. After all, an employee frequently needs a job much more than any given employer needs that employee. That being the case, EAW is not an agreement between free equals.

4. EAW's opponents object to its assessment of property rights on two grounds. First, although they are part of the production process, **human** resources enjoy an ethical status different from that of nonhuman capital. Discharging an employee is not the same as discarding a tool. EAW overlooks that difference. Second, critics argue that EAW fails to acknowledge the fact that an employee may well have a **property right** to his or her job. The United States Supreme Court has affirmed this right in the case of public employees and has found that the Fourteenth Amendment's protection of property extends to their employment. Why shouldn't private employees enjoy the same rights and protections?

Whatever the merits of these arguments and the weight of the tradition that rests upon them, the past sixty years in the United States have witnessed a considerable erosion of both the theory and practice of employment-at-will. The growth of organized labor, along with legislation and court decisions in the areas of labor and antidiscrimination law, have significantly limited traditional employer prerogatives. Currently, the legal situation is fluid. Different states recognize different exceptions to EAW, based on grounds of public policy, the existence of an implied contract, and the good faith and fair dealing that ought to characterize any contractual relation. In addition, new legislation is under consideration, such as the proposed Model Employment Termination Act, which attempts to balance the interests and rights of employers and employees. Although its terms are controversial, and, to date, it has not generated legal, political, or ethical consensus, the very fact that it has been seriously considered and debated indicates how dramatically the status of EAW has changed.

Concerns about lawsuits, as well as considerations of ethics and employee morale, have prompted many employers to think hard about issues of fairness in personnel decisions, particularly when terminating an employee. Although guaranteed access to due process is neither required nor prohibited by EAW, many people consider it crucial to fairness in the workplace, and many employers have incorporated it into their personnel procedures. Some of the readings in this chapter propose, on grounds both of ethics and employee morale, that employers hold themselves to higher standards of behavior than those required by EAW.

★ ★ ★

In this chapter's readings, **Clinton O. Longenecker** and **Frederick R. Post** describe the legal and financial risks that wrongful discharge lawsuits present to employers and discuss four "termination traps" into which the managers whom they surveyed think businesses can easily fall. **Michael J. Phillips** analyzes and appraises the conflicting economic and ethical claims made about EAW and concludes that the fairest policy would recognize that employees have a right to be protected from arbitrary discharge, and that, under certain circumstances, they also have a right to waive that protection. **Robert J. Paul** and **James B. Townsend** review the evolution of restrictions on EAW and propose several proactive measures that companies can take to protect themselves from lawsuits without endangering employee loyalty and morale or damaging their own reputations.

CASE: The Daycare Dilemma

Susan sat at her desk wondering what to do about her latest dilemma. As the director of the University Children's Center (UCC), it seemed there was always some crisis or emergency facing the center. What with caring for seventy children in three different centers, dealing with their parents and families, a staff of fourteen teachers and administrators, and thirty-plus student workers, the possibilities sometimes seemed endless. Today, it appeared, would be no exception.

Daryl, the head teacher at the center, had come to work with some disturbing news. "Have you seen the paper yet?" he inquired. "No," Susan answered. "Why? Is there something I need to see?" "Maybe you had better take a look at this," he answered, showing her the first page of the second section of the local paper. There, in a prominent place on the page, was an article describing the arrest of several university students for the possession and sale of drugs. The article did not go into great detail, but the names and addresses of all the students were printed. Susan read the article, but it took a few minutes before she made the connection. It appeared as if one of the students arrested, Bob Bradley, was an employee of the center. "Is this our Bob?" she asked. "I'm pretty sure it is," answered Daryl, "but you can check his address in the personnel file if you want to be sure." Reluctantly Susan retrieved Bob's personnel file. There was no doubt the address was the same.

Source: This case was written by Linda Lerner, Tennessee Technological University, and is used here with her permission.

"How terrible," Susan murmured. "How do you think he got into this? I have always liked Bob, and he has been such a good worker. I wonder if we will see him? It says they were released on bail. I wonder what he's going to do?" A whole host of questions crossed Susan's mind, but it appeared that Daryl had something more to add. "I didn't see the article." he said. "Margaret gave it to me when I picked her up. Leave it to her to pick up on something like this so quickly."

Margaret was the center's "grandma." She was an elderly widow who had worked at the center for about five years. A calm and loving presence, she was a most valued employee. Working about six hours a day, three days a week, she spent most of her time with the 3- to 5-year olds, who delighted in her presence. Typically, Margaret did not participate in staff meetings or engage in extraneous conversation with the adults for that matter. As she would say, "I just come to be with the children."

"She is very upset," Daryl said. "Margaret is adamant that Bob not be allowed near the children again. She said she was not judging him, but that the children had to be protected, and that meant that he should not be around them." At the moment, Susan was not sure that would be a problem. Bob might not show up at all, or, if he did, he might realize himself that continuing to work with the children would not be such a good idea. On the other hand, she wondered how Bob was handling all of this. He had worked at the center for almost two years and was well liked by everyone. If he did not appear, surely some of the older children would ask for him. Moreover, the staff was very close and had always maintained a caring and protective environment for everyone, children and staff alike. It would not be easy simply to cut Bob off. Susan wondered if she should try to contact him or just wait and see if he contacted them.

BACKGROUND

Susan Langley had been director of UCC for four years. University Children's Center provides day-care services for infants, toddlers, and preschoolers up to the age of six years. UCC is located on the campus of a medium-sized state university in a small midwestern town. Administered and staffed by the university, it provides day-care services to university students and staff as well as to residents of the surrounding communities. The university is located in a town of approximately 15,000 and has a student population of 12,000. The surrounding area has a population in excess of 60,000.

UCC is the only day-care center in this university community, although several large centers operate in the surrounding areas. The need for day-care in the area far exceeds the supply, so there is little competition for clients. In fact, the centers frequently work together to help parents locate acceptable child care, and the directors of the various centers are well known to each other. In many respects this is a close-knit community, particularly among the directors of the not-for-profit centers. Most of these centers receive public money to provide day-care to low-income families, and approximately forty of the centers statewide are members of a state day-care directors' association that represents the interests of day-care to state government. The center directors place a premium on providing high-quality child care and have worked together on many issues affecting day-care. Three of the local centers are members of the association.

In addition to day-care centers, child care is also offered through family day-care homes, where a smaller number of children can be cared for by individuals. UCC has developed a network of day-care homes through which it provides resources, supplies, support, and referrals to family day-care providers. The state provides a limited amount of money to support the family day-care homes, and UCC has been awarded a grant to provide this service. Through the network UCC has become well known to this part of the day-care community.

UCC provides day-care to approximately seventy children through three day-care programs that it operates directly. The main center is located in a university-owned building on the college campus. Other space is donated by a local church. Approximately 40 percent of the clients receive some financial assistance through state funding for day-care. All the centers are licensed by the state and must adhere to state day-care standards as well as fire and safety regulations. UCC has always prided itself on its good reputation and its standing in the community. Many parents come to the university specifically because they want their children to attend UCC. Both students and staff have recognized UCC for the quality of its staff and services.

From the university standpoint, UCC provides two important services. The center provides needed day-care for students and staff. Over the years both groups have pushed for additional funds for day-care, and the university has responded with increased support. From an educational standpoint UCC is also a place where students can be trained and employed. The center has served as a training site for early childhood teachers and interns. In addition, the center has always employed a large number of students. The center is considered a prime place to work on campus, and it has always received many more applications for work than there were jobs. The students are considered a valuable resource, and many work for several years at the center before they graduate.

All students go through a brief orientation and training program and then receive mostly on-the-job supervision. Students who do not receive good evaluations are not rehired the following year. Bob had worked at UCC for almost two years. Susan did not know if he had exhibited any signs or symptoms of taking drugs. But then, as the centers had grown, she was not as able to keep up with all the student workers. She would have to talk to Joan, his primary supervisor. She did know that he was well liked by both the staff and the children. Many of the parents felt that having male child care workers on staff was a plus since many of the children lived in single-parent households, usually without a father present. Finding enough men who were interested in working at a day-care center was not always easy.

THE STAFF MEETING

The issue of dealing with Bob unfortunately came up sooner than Susan had anticipated. That afternoon Bob appeared at his regular work time and went directly into the playroom and became involved with the children. He did not appear particularly distressed or preoccupied; in fact he appeared to be his usual self. Deciding the issue could not wait, Susan asked Bob if she could speak with him in her office. As they walked upstairs Bob became noticeably silent. When they got upstairs, Susan asked him directly about the article in the paper. At that point Bob became very distressed and said, yes, that he had been arrested. He said he felt like he had ruined his whole life. He did not deny his involvement in the drug activity and implicitly accepted responsibility. He did not know how he would face his father, he said, who would be utterly disappointed in him. He felt he had destroyed his opportunity to continue in school and with that any opportunity to do anything

with his life. Bob became more distraught as he talked. He felt he had no reason to live any more and pleaded with Susan to allow him to come to the center. His connection to the center, he said, was the only thing in his life that made any sense. It was his lifeline.

Susan was torn between her obligation to the children and her desire to provide some support for Bob. She said she would have to speak with the rest of the staff, and they would make a decision regarding his employment at the center. She would support him in any way possible, but she could make no promises. She would meet with the staff the next day, and then they would talk again.

The staff meeting was set for the following day. Susan described her meeting with Bob. Daryl responded first. "While I wish to support Bob," he said, "I feel our first responsibility is to the children. I do not feel he is a threat to the children, but I am concerned about Margaret's feelings. She is unyielding in her opinion that Bob has betrayed our trust and that we cannot continue to have him around the children. I respect Margaret and feel we must consider her feelings. She has been a member of our staff for a long time and has never wavered in her concern for the children. I could not betray her trust in us, and I would find it impossible to have Bob here even when Margaret is off if we decide that is the course we will take." For Allison the issue was similar. "I am not opposed to having Bob here, but I would be if it hurt Margaret. Still, I would like to help Bob in some way. He is reaching out to us and may feel that he has no one else right now." Joan was Bob's supervising teacher. She noted that he had seemed distracted at times, and she had wondered if anything was wrong. While she had observed some changes in behavior, she had never judged him incapable of carrying out his responsibilities. She was comfortable working with him and was willing to continuing supervising him. She would not permit him to continue working if it appeared in any way that he could not do his job.

While most of the discussion centered on Bob and his ability to work with the children and, in particular, on Margaret's feelings, Susan also had some other concerns. None of the parents seemed aware of the situation, and no one had said anything to her. Would she be betraying their trust to allow Bob to continue at the center? Were there other threats that she had ignored? Was there some solution that she had not considered? Was she underestimating the reaction of others if they found out about Bob? Finally, did she and the staff have any obligation to Bob? It would be at least five or six months until his trial, and it did not appear that Bob was simply going to disappear.

The Management Termination Trap

Clinton O. Longenecker
Frederick R. Post

"When you fire managers these days you better have your ducks in a row if they come after you with a lawsuit. . . . The problem is the way we deal with managers before we let them go can create a legal trap for the organization and all too often. . . . When you look at the number of lawsuits plaintiffs are winning, the out-of-court settlements, and the size of the awards, it is a testimony that organizations need to take a serious look at the process used to terminate managerial personnel."

—A vice president of human resources

In these challenging economic times there is nothing rare or even unusual about a manager being fired or terminated for poor performance. Under increasing competitive pressure from home and abroad, organizations require better performance on the part of all their members. As such, greater pressure is exerted on managers at all levels to be more effective and efficient in leading their operations. Modern managers must show a strong bottom line, enhance product quality, increase employee involvement, foster innovation, and satisfy their customers' ever-increasing demands.

As the nature of managerial work becomes more complex and demanding, many would argue that the probability of a manager failing increases significantly. When a manager fails to obtain results or perform duties in a manner commensurate with the firm's current needs, employers frequently exercise their right to terminate the manager for cause. *The Wall Street Journal* and other business publications regularly carry accounts of *Fortune 500* companies

Source: Business Horizons, May-June, 1994, 71–79. Used with permission.

terminating upper-level managers. But today there is an emerging pattern: managers are suing their former employers for unlawful termination.

While terminating management personnel is still viewed as an inherent employer right based upon the employment-at-will doctrine, there has been a significant erosion in the common-law rule that says a company can fire a person for whatever reason it deems appropriate—good, bad, or no reason at all. A variety of theories of recovery have emerged—some quite traditional and some new and innovative—that enable discharged employees to obtain such monetary remedies as back pay, front pay, and punitive damages. These theories include breach of an implied contract, promissory estoppel, negligence in appraisal, defamation, fraud, intentional infliction of emotional distress, and invasion of privacy. Many theories stem from court-created exceptions to the at-will doctrine. Most wrongful discharge lawsuits contain multiple theories of recovery and represent an expensive, time-consuming, and complicated distraction from the activities of trying to run a competitive organization.

Albrecht (1991), characterizing employment law as one of the key forces transforming American civil law in the last two decades, accurately summarized the situation:

By the early to mid-1980s, employers and courts of law were staggering under a plethora of wrongful discharge cases, and each day brought new limitations to the perceived rights of employers to run the workplace as they thought best. Riding the at-will horse for so long had calloused some employers against the painful personal consequences of employee termination. Egregious factual circumstances gave courts of law the moral incentive to protect employees where they might otherwise have declined. The law of wrongful discharge and its attendant claims for relief became the labor law issue of the 1980s.

In our present dynamic economic environment, disgruntled managers who have been terminated by their organizations and are suffering a loss of position, income, and career advancement are suing their former employers and winning both in and out of the courtroom with increasing frequency. A new class of managerial litigants is now aggressively utilizing the legal machinery available within administrative agencies and federal and state court systems to challenge the decisions that have left them unemployed, with damaging organizational consequences.

In this article we discuss why terminated managers resort to wrongful discharge lawsuits. We review the findings of in-depth interviews with 200 middle- and upper-level managers that clearly identify four problematic organizational behavioral patterns that exist in managing supervisory personnel. Finally, we offer some practical advice to help organizations and managers avoid the costly mistake of being caught up in wrongful discharge litigation.

THE SCOPE OF THE PROBLEM

To grasp the full significance of this transformation of American civil law and the resulting devastating financial and operational impact upon corporate America, we should review some statistics that depict the phenomenon. Geyelin (1990) conservatively estimated that 150,000 employees are unjustly discharged every year. A 1988 Rand Corporation study, which examined California jury verdicts in 120 wrongly discharge cases between 1980 and 1986, made the following relevant observations:

- 89.3 percent of plaintiffs were white;
- 68.6 percent of plaintiffs were male;
- 53.4 percent were either "executives" or "middle management";
- plaintiffs prevailed in 67.5 percent of the cases;
- the average monetary award for a plaintiff was $646,855; and
- plaintiffs were successful in obtaining punitive damage awards in 40 percent of the cases (Geyelin 1990).

A 1991 study by the Bureau of National Affairs determined that more than 25,000 wrongful discharge cases are pending in federal and state court systems, and that the number of these types of cases doubled between 1982 and 1987. The large multi-state labor law firm of Jackson, Lewis, Schnitzler, and Krupman discovered that 50 percent of 1,014 surveyed industrial managers who had terminated employees were faced with legal action in response to those terminations.

While these numbers may be telling, the full scope of the problem is difficult to calculate for several reasons. First, legal experts in this field strongly believe that a substantial proportion of unlawful discharge lawsuits involving managerial personnel are settled out of court to avoid costly legal fees, unpredictable jury awards, and unwanted adverse publicity. Second, the organizational consequences are difficult to calculate in terms of lost productivity, focus, and morale. A director of human resource management of a *Fortune 500* organization recently commented, "When the former director of marketing was suing us because he was fired, it was like there was a black cloud hanging over that entire department and everyone felt it."

The response by corporate management to these striking trends has been varied. Some believe that lawyers should be involved in all hiring and firing decisions. Others believe that instead of terminating managerial employees, expensive settlement packages of severance benefits should be negotiated in trade for the employee's written waiver of any future legal action. We assert that neither approach is necessary if the issue of termination is taken seriously, is handled in a professional manner, and takes into account some of the problematic practices of managing and leading managers.

Why Do Managers Sue?

The obvious question to ask is, "Why are managers increasingly willing to sue their former employers?" Although there is no single answer, we believe that there are a variety of useful explanations based upon societal and economic trends that organizations must attempt to understand. First, managers are more aware of their workplace rights than ever before; using litigation to protect one's rights is commonly accepted. Second, there is an abundance of lawyers, and with the resulting increase in competition within the practice of law, more lawyers are willing to consider such a potentially lucrative area. As an indication of this trend, an interest group called the National Employment Lawyers Association (NELA) has been established for the purpose of sharing information, strategies, and data on employment law litigation—including wrongful discharge suits. Third, when a manager believes that being fired will make it more difficult to find another job of equivalent value, the manager may be more willing to consider litigation. This consideration is particularly germane when the job market is flat or stagnant or the professional reputation of the discharged manager has been damaged. Fourth, when a manager has not been forewarned that termination is possible or forthcoming without performance improvement and is shocked or surprised by the action, the likelihood of litigation increases based on a desire for vindication. This is especially true when a manager believes that basic due process has been ignored by the former employer.

An important organizational concern must therefore be addressed as management terminations increase and managers are more willing to sue their former employers. In our opening quote, a vice president of human resources stated, "When you fire a manager these days you'd better have your ducks in a row." There is increasing evidence that organizations simply do not have their "ducks in a row" when they terminate management personnel. This exposes the organization to what we call the "management termination trap."

THE TERMINATION TRAP

The management termination trap has its roots in the way companies manage their managerial personnel before firing them. This includes the actions taken leading up to the termination. In many firms, guidelines and procedures for effective human resource management are adhered to in terminating lower-level salaried and hourly employees. But the same guidelines often are not followed with the same vigilance in dealing with management personnel, thus opening the door for the "trap" that leads to wrongful discharge litigation.

A substantial body of academic and practitioner literature details the steps organizations need to follow in an employee termination to allow an individual due process. There is also an abundance of information and advice available to organizations, which if followed can protect them by discouraging terminated employees from filing a wrongful discharge lawsuit and help them defend themselves in the event of litigation.

Although this is a fluid and dynamic area of the law that varies by state, there is a nucleus of accepted guidelines to protect against a wrongful discharge:

- Ensure that employment applications and employee handbooks are precise and do not represent an implied contract.
- Provide clearly defined work rules, standards, and expectations of performance.
- Maintain accurate documentation of employees' performance.
- Provide progressive discipline and feedback that allow employees the opportunity to improve their performance.
- Apply performance standards consistently to all organization members, thereby avoiding favoritism.
- Investigate the causes of performance problems or work rule violations.
- Provide clear examples and explanations of why termination is taking place.
- Document both sides of the situation.

These guidelines are not exhaustive, but they do represent practices that protect employers from the likelihood of wrongful discharge litigation. We argue that a termination trap exists for many firms because of a lack of proficiency in applying several of these critical principles when terminating unsatisfactory managers.

Our Study

To understand this issue better, we recently conducted in-depth interviews with 200 managers from 18 large service and manufacturing firms in the United States. These managers were from companies in the transportation, steel, automotive, electronics, medical, communications, and building products industries. Participating managers represented 14 different functional areas; 54 percent were senior managers and 46 percent were middle managers. Participants averaged 17 years of managerial experience and were 46 years old. The purpose of these interviews was to explore how managers felt they were managed by their superiors and assess their perceptions on a host of human resource management issues. During these semi-structured interviews, managers were asked to discuss their observations and experiences freely during their managerial careers and provide specific examples when possible.

A content analysis of the interviews was conducted and each of the findings presented below was discussed by at least 65 percent of the managers in this study. Direct quotes from interviews are used where appropriate. Managers identified four patterns of managerial behavior that create a potential legal termination trap for the organization when discharging managers for poor performance. Specific examples from recent legal cases will be discussed in relationship to each finding to illustrate the linkage between these findings and current legal precedent.

Trap One: Managers' Performance Standards Are Often Poorly Defined.

"Assumptions are frequently made that managers know exactly what their duties should be, what their responsibilities are, what goals they ought to be pursuing. . . . [O]rganizations are guilty of not clarifying, in no uncertain terms, what they expect

of managers—which makes it tough to objectively assess their performance."

Managerial work, which is complex and dynamic, is frequently performed by individuals with a strong desire for autonomy and a high tolerance for ambiguity. Yet the respondents in our study made it clear that, for any number of reasons, upper-level managers often do not adequately clarify what they expect from their subordinate managers in terms of overall performance. When clear standards and expectations of managerial performance are not established, there is no unambiguous basis on which to hold a manager accountable. In the short run, lack of clarity on this issue can have a debilitating impact on a manager's performance. In the long run, this practice can create vulnerability for the organization if a termination occurs.

In the recent case of *Burrill v. GTE Government Systems Corp.,* plaintiff Burrill was hired as the manager for GTE's Colorado facility. Burrill was hired to solve a series of problems that his employer, a government contractor, was experiencing with its prime customer, the United States. But he was given no explicit job description with his position. He was subsequently terminated—allegedly "laid off"—based on what he claimed was actually a discharge for alleged poor performance. Burrill filed a wrongful discharge suit against the company. At the conclusion of all pretrial preparation, which had consisted of depositions, interrogatories, and the exchange of documentation from Burrill's personnel files, the defendant employer filed a summary judgment motion to have the case dismissed. GTE Government Systems Corp. argued that, as a matter of law, the plaintiff employee could not prove his case.

The employer's position was based upon Burrill's at-will status, the absence of any implied employment contract, the absence of any representations made to Burrill to initially induce him to take the position, the company's supposed compliance with the provisions of its supervisor's personnel handbook, and the absence of any express covenant of good faith and fair dealing in the company's policies, which it had allegedly violated. The court, however, overruled the company's motion for dismissal of the case and ordered it to trial. Noting that there were so many discrepancies and uncertainties about what was expected of Burrill in his management position—whether he was laid off or discharged, whether the company had complied with its own termination procedures, whether statements made to Burrill had created an implied contract, and whether Burrill had relied upon the company's positive assertions in the handbook—the court concluded that such factual discrepancies demonstrated a likelihood that Burrill could prove his case, that it could not be dismissed as a matter of law, and that these issues must be resolved by a jury.

This case effectively illustrates that when clear standards and performance expectations have never been established for a manager, a subsequent discharge often becomes indefensible, placing the defendant organization in the unenviable position of having to raise an abundance of technical legal arguments. Because there was no basis—as a matter of law—for being able to justify and explain Burrill's discharge in performance terminology, the case was ordered to trial.

Trap Two: Accurate Documentation of a Manager's Actual Performance Frequently Does Not Exist.

"Documentation is the key to lawful termination. . . . A lot of times organizations are real sloppy about appraisals and reviews with managers. . . . Second, when appraisal documentation does exist, it is not an accurate reflection of the manager's performance, especially because of politics or if they have problems. . . . [W]hen it is time to provide evidence of performance failure, it does not exist, and this creates big problems in the termination process."

One of the most critical aspects of terminating any employee is documenting evidence of poor performance. Managers in this study made it clear that all too often actual documentation of poor management performance does not exist in a form that helps the organization justify its decision. Managers identified two specific problems:

(a) performance appraisals are frequently not conducted with managerial personnel in a systematic and objective fashion to create written documentation; and

(b) when they are conducted they frequently sidestep or avoid identifying specific performance problems in writing.

Managers also suggested that written appraisals are frequently done in a fashion that is more optimistic or positive than the actual face-to-face appraisal review with the subordinate manager. As one manager commented, "Written performance reviews rarely capture exactly what was said in our meeting . . . so the accuracy can be a question mark we all create for ourselves." It appears that managers are exceedingly reluctant to put anything in writing that has the potential of damaging someone's career. Yet inflating the written review by failing to address specific performance problems opens the door to litigation when specific documentation of performance failure is needed. In addition, inflated performance reviews can be used against the organization to prove that it has wrongly terminated a manager whose performance is at least satisfactory.

To illustrate the danger of this practice, in *McNeil v. Economics Laboratory,* the plaintiff executive prevailed against his former employer because of prior positive performance evaluations and an absence of any written documentation in the personnel records that demonstrated any adverse managerial performance. The defendant employer contended that the basis for the termination was a series of poor working relationships between McNeil, his coworkers, and customers. After the trial court dismissed these contentions as merely pretextual, the appellate court affirmed that decision, noting that "the conduct to which [the] defendant refers should be accorded little weight because it . . . was not thought to be serious enough to be recorded in his monthly or yearly appraisals."

A similar pattern of consistently high ratings over a 23-year career existed in *Chamberlain v. Bissell, Inc.,* where the plaintiff manager also prevailed in wrongful discharge litigation. Not until his final performance review did Chamberlain receive any hints that there were performance problems. Even then there were no documented assertions that termination was being considered. The court concluded that these omissions in the appraisal process by the company constituted "negligence in the evaluation and discharge of Chamberlain without giving him prior notice of the intent to discharge him." The court further noted that the failure by the company to document the plaintiff's actual management performance coupled with "22 years of adequate service tended to create a heightened sense of job security on his part." By failing to place accurate written documentation about Chamberlain in his personnel file and also to notify him about his unsatisfactory performance, the employer was found liable for wrongful discharge.

Trap Three: Withholding Performance Feedback Limits a Manager's Opportunity to Correct Deficient Performance.

"For anyone's performance to improve or change they need feedback and specific feedback at that, especially managers. . . . [W]ithholding that information discourages good performers and allows poor performers to falsely believe they are doing fine—which creates long-term problems, potentially leading up to dismissal."

Managers in this study claimed that performance feedback was often ignored in the managerial ranks. They clearly stated that the absence of feedback was a specific point of frustration that caused them to operate "in the dark" too often in terms of knowing where they stood with their superiors. Managerial performance feedback is a critical issue in the termination process because the organization should be able to demonstrate that it gave the manager time to improve performance as well as specific information on how to do so. Without letting managers know where they stand—specifically and regularly—organizations are opening themselves up to performance problems and making it difficult to prove the basis for their actions if termination becomes necessary.

In both the *McNeil* and *Chamberlain* cases, the employers were found liable partly because they failed to discuss alleged performance deficiencies with the manager, thereby giving him no opportunity to correct the problems. In *McNeil,* the court observed that in addition to the lack of written documentation in his performance appraisal about deficiencies, there were no warnings by McNeil's supervisor "that his conduct would not be tolerated." In *Chamberlain,* the court concluded that even though good cause existed for the manager's discharge, the firm's failure to tell him about his problems, advise him of its intent to terminate his employment, and inform him what he might do to save his job was itself actionable negligence, which enabled the plaintiff to prevail in the discharge litigation. As to the employer's withholding of information, the court wrote that the appraiser "was in a position to eliminate all doubt concerning Chamberlain's status, and, further, to provide Chamberlain with the greatest possible incentive to reform his conduct and improve his performance. There was no reason for [the appraiser] not to take the necessary step of informing Chamberlain, and his failure to do so may properly be labeled as negligent in the circumstances of this case."

Trap Four: Managerial Politics Can Undermine the Link Between Actual Performance and Human Resource Decisions.

"We make decisions around here that frequently let politics rule the day. For example, promote a guy just to get rid of him, transfer someone to make room for someone else we like, give a person a better rating than they deserve to get their loyalty. . . . [P]olitics is a bigger part of a lot of HR decisions than most people will admit, and that is where real trouble starts—especially in a termination."

Organizations are by nature political. Managers use their power and influence to protect their personal and organizational self-interest. The respondents in our study regularly cited examples of promotions, demotions, transfers, rewards, and terminations based on issues other than the individual's actual contributions to the organization. It was widely accepted among participants in this study that politics or the potential misuse of power to protect self-interest was simply "part . . . of life in the managerial ranks."

Yet it is in this area that managerial terminations possess the greatest legal threat to an organization, because both the issues of performance and right to due process have been cast aside for some darker agenda. The link between actual performance and the resulting personnel decision has been severed. This places the firm in an indefensible position should the termination lead to litigation. Although the frequency of this action was not articulated in these interviews, managers cited numerous examples of colleagues who had been whacked, pink-slipped, dismissed, or summarily discharged for reasons they believed fell into the political category.

When an individual is dismissed for less than objective, unbiased, and well-documented reasons, the organization is in legal jeopardy. Conversely, when politics is deemphasized and the termination is the result of specific performance-based criterion that the terminated manager has failed to meet, after timely advance notice about the deficiencies in performance, the organization will be able to defend its termination decision. The case of *Selsor v. Callaghan & Co.* illustrates how objective procedures will lead to a defense victory in litigation. Interestingly, the defendant corporation was a legal book and research materials publisher—which might explain why its management practices conformed well with existing legal requirements for a successful defense to wrongful discharge allegations.

Plaintiff Selsor was hired as the advertising manager for the corporation in 1971 when he was 46 years old. As a result of the company being acquired in 1979, efforts were made to expand its share of the legal publications market. This included the hiring of Cochran, the new vice president of marketing. Cochran conducted Selsor's annual performance appraisals. In the June 1981 appraisal, Selsor received an overall satisfactory appraisal that contained compliments based on his years of experience and his positive attitude as well as specific suggestions for improvement. The suggestions stated that Selsor needed to solicit competitive bids for advertising and become more cost-effective. Selsor was told that his performance in these two areas would be monitored by Cochran because cutting costs was an important part of Selsor's job. In September 1981, Cochran met with Selsor again and noted that in response to these deficiencies, Selsor had set unrealistic time-tables, was time-oriented rather than task-oriented, had not solicited advertising bids successfully, and had not been assertive enough with outsiders.

Three months later, in December 1981, Cochran concluded that the deficiencies had still not been remedied. So he decided to hire a new assistant advertising manager who would assume the managerial aspects of Selsor's job, allowing Selsor to devote his energies to the more creative side of advertising. The new person, Gold, assumed most of the management tasks that Selsor had been unable to accomplish. Although Gold and Selsor initially worked well together, a personality conflict soon developed because Gold was an effective manager, accomplishing the cost cutting and streamlining tasks that Selsor had previously been unable or unwilling to do. Even though Selsor, in his new position of "production coordinator," retained his prior salary and all benefits, he became unhappy and unproductive.

In April 1983, after five three-month time periods had passed during which there had been increasing problems with Selsor's performance, he was placed on 30 days' probation and his several mistakes and deficiencies listed. Selsor asked to be transferred to another job in the company and then took a two-week vacation. Upon his return, he was told there were no other jobs. In response, he resigned his position. Shortly thereafter, he filed a wrongful discharge lawsuit against Callaghan & Co., alleging age discrimination because he was 59 years old.

Before the trial, after depositions, interrogatories, and other procedural devices had enabled both parties to understand the factual basis for the legal theories claimed to support the basis for their respective positions, the defendant corporation filed a motion for summary judgment seeking dismissal of the lawsuit as a matter of law. The essence of Callaghan's position was that Selsor could not prove he was performing well enough to satisfy its legitimate expectations. Considering the unrebuttable documentation in Selsor's personnel records over a two-year period, the court concluded that the uncontradicted evidence supported the conclusion that Selsor was not meeting his employer's legitimate expectations, rather than the termination decision being based upon biased, politically motivated action.

The court further noted, "While Selsor received satisfactory overall reviews in the past, the criticisms of his work were consistent even in these satisfactory reviews. . . . It is clear that Callaghan has met its burden of articulating lawful reasons for firing Selsor." The court observed that "a great mass of undisputed evidence supports this explanation." The court dismissed the lawsuit as a matter of law, not even allowing the case to go to trial. This is in complete contrast to *Burrill v. GTE Government Systems Corp.,* in which the employer offered no legitimate performance-based explanations for its termination decision and was ordered to trial.

In this case, Callaghan & Co. successfully demonstrated to the court that plaintiff Selsor could not prove he was performing his job adequately, using the two years of documentation that had been developed regarding his deficiencies and the repeated efforts by his superior, Cochran, to counsel him on how to remedy his deficiencies. Even in the potentially "political" environment of personality conflicts, restructured job duties based on uncorrected past problems, and certainly understandable ongoing emotional tensions between Cochran, Gold, and Selsor, the court ruled as a matter of law that the two years of documentation in Selsor's personnel file supported the management termination decision.

AVOIDING THE TERMINATION TRAP

> "It sounds very popular to say this, but it is the truth. . . . [It]t always goes back to basics. Managers that ignore the basics in the human resource arena usually hurt the company, and they can kill you when it comes to termination. . . . [T]o avoid problems in terminating managers, stick to the basics and avoid the ambiguity and politics that surround so many managerial jobs in this country."

The management termination trap generally does not exist because of poorly run human resource departments or companies not having access to the information that tells them how to avoid a wrongful discharge lawsuit. Firms create legal traps for themselves because of the very way they lead and manage their managers. The issues and frustrations raised by the 200 managers in our research reflect the dominant belief that managers are self-starting, self-directing, and autonomous individuals—or they would not be managers. Good managers are generally self-starting, often to an extraordinary degree, but they are also employees of the firm who both want and need input, clear performance standards, and regular feedback about their performance. When the organizational practices set out as follows are present, the management termination trap has been set.

The termination trap is created when those who manage other managerial personnel do not provide them with critical guidance, feedback, and fairness in treatment—the hallmarks of any good working relationship. When these important behavioral practices are neglected or ignored, the manager in charge has hurt the ability of subordinates to succeed and has potentially made the organization more vulnerable in the likelihood of a termination. In the words of one vice president in this study, "It's not that we don't know what to do, it is just that we don't do it. . . . We don't apply a lot of good management and human resource practices to our managerial personnel."

If you are a human resource specialist or a practicing manager, this is one of those specific instances when good preventive legal practice and good management practice come together nicely. To enhance the performance of managerial personnel and to avoid the management termination trap, a manager would be well served to follow the guidelines spelled out below.

1. Make sure managers have clearly defined goals and duties. When managers do not have a clear sense of focus and direction their performance can suffer, especially when asked to do more with less. Failing to clarify a manager's duties and goals can have disastrous motivational and organization consequences. Managers need a flexibly framed picture of what their superiors expect them to accomplish. A personal strategic plan for the use of each managerial resource should be developed that includes a nucleus of critical job duties and specific, measurable, attainable, results-oriented, time-oriented (SMART) goals. Targeted job responsibilities and SMART goals remove some of the ambiguity of managerial work and provide a defined basis for measuring a manager's contribution.

2. Provide honest, specific, and ongoing performance feedback to managers. To avoid management performance problems, provide feedback regularly to reinforce good performance and give the manager an opportunity to be aware of performance problems and take appropriate corrective action before a crisis. Providing regular feedback demonstrates the firm's commitment to helping its managers succeed. Moreover, it demonstrates a pattern of interaction that reduces the likelihood of a manager being shocked or blindsided when told that the employment relationship is over.

3. Conduct regular, candid, and systematic performance reviews. The comments made by the participants in our study strongly suggest that there is need for a great deal of improvement in the way organizations frequently evaluate managerial personnel. For reviews to be effective, they must be timely, structured, and honest. The documentation they create must be an accurate reflection of the manager's actual performance. To do otherwise is to create problems for all parties concerned. If formal performance reviews are not professionally conducted, the organization loses a potentially strong tool for defending itself in a wrongful discharge lawsuit. If the reviews are artificially inflated, lack specifics, or use ambiguous language, they can be used against the employer's position in a lawsuit.

4. When "management style" problems exist, focus on identifying specific problematic behaviors and actions. If a manager is going to be terminated because of an ineffective management style, two warnings are in order. First, make sure that specific problematic behaviors and actions have been previously pointed out to the manager in question. Second, give the manager an opportunity to turn his or her performance around by providing a sufficient period of time for change and plenty of feedback counseling during that time. To terminate a manager for a "caustic management style," or for "failing to be assertive enough," or for not "looking beyond the numbers," without providing specific examples of inappropriate behavior and a time period within which to improve that behavior is grounds for a lawsuit, especially if the manager has a documented history during prior performance appraisals of at least satisfactory performance.

5. Keep politics out of the management termination equation. Politics often cause people to look at factors other than those that are most obvious. For an organization to be on safe ground when terminating a manager, it must have a clear basis on which to judge performance, be able to document poor performance, be able to demonstrate that the manager knew of problems and had an opportunity to respond, and be able to make the causal link between the particular human resource decision and the manager's performance. By definition, politics frequently involves bringing in additional information that has little to do with correct legal action. To terminate a manager to simply eliminate a dissident, or to replace someone with another person who is more loyal, or to summarily punish a manager, opens the door to litigation. Human resource managers can play a valuable role in helping line managers test their motives to ensure that contemplated termination decisions are actually warranted. Politics and management terminations are a volatile mix.

The termination process is typically a painful one for all parties concerned, especially when the person being released is a manager. The process can become more painful when it is not properly executed. The loss of income, position, and career can have devastating effects on peo-

ple who have been used to a certain measure of organizational prestige. Managers are more willing than ever to use litigation to protect or retain these commodities.

Firms are too often lax in the way they guide and manage their own management personnel. This laziness creates a legal trap that can spring shut on the company with a wrongful discharge lawsuit. The only real protection against such action is to be prepared. And the only real way for a firm to be properly prepared is to apply effective management practices to its own managerial personnel. This simply makes good business and legal sense. To underscore this point, we close with a kernel of wisdom from one of our participant executives: "In my opinion, it is rare to find examples where the legal stuff and good management fit together . . . but when it comes to terminating a manager or avoiding a performance problem, good management and the law both make it clear that focus, feedback, honesty, solid documentation, and fair play work."

REFERENCES

Warren H. Albrecht, Jr., "The Changing Face of Employment Law and the Practical Lawyer," *North Dakota Law Review,* 67 (1991): 469–470.

Burrill v. GTE Government Services Corp., D.C. COLO, 91-A-2172. September 10, 1992. 7 IER 1435 (1992).

Chamberlain v. Bissell Inc., 547 F. Supp. 1067 (1982). Milo Geyelin. "Fired Managers Winning More Lawsuits," *Wall Street Journal,* September 7, 1989, p. B1.

McNeil v. Economics Laboratory, Inc., 800 F.2d. 111 (7th Cir. 1986).

Selsor v. Callaghan & Co., 609 F. Supp. 1003 (1985).

READING 6-2

Toward a Middle Way in the Polarized Debate over Employment at Will

Michael J. Phillips

INTRODUCTION

In August of 1991, the National Conference of Commissioners on Uniform State Laws issued a Draft Uniform Employment-Termination Act.[1] This model act, which displaces most common law claims for wrongful discharge where it applies,[2] generally makes it illegal for employers with five or more employees[3] to terminate protected workers without good cause.[4] Alleged violations of this good cause requirement are subject to arbitration.[5] However, an employer and its employee can waive the good cause standard by express written agreement.[6]

The model act's provisions are controversial,[7] and at this writing its prospects of adoption seem poor.[8] Thus, the near-term future promises further chapters in the cacophonous ethical and policy debate over employment at will.[9] This debate began in earnest when common law recoveries for wrongful discharge began to become more frequent some twenty years ago. By now, its protagonists are familiar actors on the American legal and policy scene. At one end of the stage stand libertarians, law-and-economics writers, and other observers who generally see employment at will as a good thing.[10] At the other are employee rights advocates who tend to regard the doctrine as an anachronism that can work serious harm on workers.[11] Generally speaking, neither set of writers fully considers the other's arguments. The result is a polarized "dialogue" over discharge policy.

Source: American Business Law Journal (1992). Reprinted with permission.

This article is an ethical analysis of employment at will that tries to stake out a position between the extremes which dominate academic discussion of the subject. That position, briefly, is that while a just cause standard should replace employment at will as the common law baseline, the law also should strive to maximize competition over discharge terms by increasing employee's awareness of those terms. The article begins by briefly summarizing employment at will's history and the emergence of common law wrongful discharge actions in the 1970s and 1980s. Then it considers the blizzard of conflicting economic/utilitarian claims made about the doctrine. Finding these inconclusive, I then examine it at length from a "rights" perspective. This portion of the article argues that while employees have a moral right to be discharged only for good cause, they also can contract that right away. Because the typical indefinite-term employment agreement is not such a contract, however, employment at will cannot stand. After this, I consider the virtues and possible vices of agreements by which employees expressly contract away their discharge rights, arguing that such agreements should be enforceable if they meet stringent conspicuousness/disclosure tests. The aim of this recommendation is to increase employer competition over discharge terms.

As will become apparent throughout the article, my conclusions have presuppositions that are unpopular within one or both camps in the war over employment at will. Contrary to many in each group, for example, the article maintains that people are different and can rationally desire different discharge policies. It also parts company with many foes of employment at will by arguing that, so far as discharge terms are concerned, disparities in bargaining power do not pervade employment markets. Nonetheless, the article asserts that government intervention is needed if employees are to possess sufficient information for those markets to function tolerably well. The model act could be an example of such intervention.

BACKGROUND MATTERS

The Emergence of Employment at Will

Subject to certain exceptions, medieval English courts usually construed an indefinite-term employment contract as a hiring for one year.[12] Some nineteenth century American courts continued this construction.[13] Others rejected it while still finding indefinite-term employment contracts obligatory for some period or under some circumstances.[14] Not until the last quarter of the nineteenth century did courts begin to read such contracts as terminable at will. The first statement of this new rule apparently came in Horace G. Wood's 1877 employment law treatise.

> With us the rule is inflexible, that a general or indefinite hiring is *prima facie* a hiring at will, and if the servant seeks to make it out a yearly hiring, the burden is on him to establish it by proof. A hiring at so much a day, a week, month or year, no time being specified, is an indefinite hiring, and no presumption attaches that it was for a day even, but only at the rate fixed for whatever time the party may serve. It is competent for either party to show what the mutual understanding of the parties was in reference to the matter; but unless their understanding was mutual that the service was to extend for a certain fixed and definite period, it is an indefinite hiring and is determinable at the will of either party . . .[15]

Although Wood cited several cases for his at-will rule, commentators have argued that they do not support it.[16] But the point hardly matters, for by early in this century employment at will was the general rule throughout the United States.[17]

Employment at will, then, gives either party to an employment contract for an indefinite duration the freedom to terminate that contract at any time and for any reason without incurring liability. According to one much-quoted statement of the rule, it allows an employer to discharge indefinite-duration employees "for good cause, for no cause, or even for cause morally wrong, without being thereby guilty of legal wrong."[18]

Among the contracts considered sufficiently indefinite to be at-will are agreements for "steady," "regular," and even "permanent" employment.[19] Of course, as the quotation from Wood seems to recognize, discharged at-will employees can recover the reasonable value of the services they actually perform.[20] And as that quotation makes clear, employment at will does not prevent the parties from contracting for a fixed term. Such contracts can be implied as well as express.[21]

The Rule's Retreat

Throughout the twentieth century, the range of firings covered by employment at will has steadily been reduced by statutes[22] and common law rules[23] proscribing termination in certain circumstances. Perhaps more important, however, the three judge-made claims that have come to comprise a common law of unjust dismissal or wrongful discharge. These three claims, at least one of which has been adopted by most states,[24] are: (1) the public policy exception, (2) the implied covenant of good faith and fair dealing, and (3) a trio of theories under which employers are bound to their express or implied-in-fact statements about discharge policy.

Public Policy Claims Although estimates of its adoption vary, the public policy exception to employment at will probably has been recognized in at least forty states.[25] Under that exception, which usually is regarded as a tort claim,[26] discharged employees can recover if that dismissal "jeopardize[s] a specific public policy interest of the state."[27] Most often, the relevant public policy must be one articulated by a constitution or statute,[28] but sometimes other forms of positive law are permissible sources as well.[29]

Successful claims under the public policy exception generally break down into three categories. The first involves dismissals motivated by employees' refusal to commit unlawful acts such as perjury and antitrust violations.[30] The second, involving firings for the performance of important public obligations, is exemplified by discharges for employees' performing jury duty, being subpoenaed to testify before a grand jury, or engaging in whistleblowing.[31] The third category involves employees who are discharged for exercising a statutory right or privilege; examples including filing a workers' compensation claim, joining a labor union, and refusing to take an illegal lie-detector test.[32]

The Implied Covenant of Good Faith and Fair Dealing *Restatement (Second) of Contracts* section 205 says: "Every contract imposes upon each party a duty of good faith and fair dealing in its performance and its enforcement."[33] This implied covenant of good faith and fair dealing now is a general rule of contract law.[34] Among its several applications[35] is its utilization as a theory of recovery for wrongful discharge.[36] All things considered, however, the implied covenant of good faith and fair dealing clearly is the least important of the three major common law exceptions to employment at will.

The first reason for the implied covenant's relative insignificance is that probably no more than a dozen states clearly recognize it in the wrongful dismissal context.[37] The second is that in some of these states it affords discharged employees little protection. On one reading of the covenant, it guarantees only that the parties' agreed common purpose and justified expectations be satisfied.[38] In an at-will relationship, this purpose and those expectations apparently are that both parties can terminate the relationship at any time and for any reason. If so, how can an arbitrary dismissal violate the covenant?[39] To be sure, the covenant also can be read as imposing community-based good-faith norms that are external to the parties' actual agreement.[40] And a few courts have given employees significant protection by reading it exactly this way.[41]

Employer Liability for Express and Implied-in-Fact Statements The third major exception to employment at will involves three distinct rationales with a common bottom line: that employers are liable for breaking their express or implied-in-fact promises about discharge policy. Courts in at least thirty-four states have embraced this exception in some form.[42] Most often, the promises in question are expressly stated in employee handbooks or policy manuals; but they also are expressed in benefit plans, are made as oral or written assurances about job security, and even are implied from business custom and usage.[43]

The first rationale courts use to impose such liability is called the implied-in-fact contract exception to employment at will. Earlier, we saw that the at-will rule is inapplicable if the parties impliedly contract to the contrary.[44] Unlike implied-in-law promises such as the implied covenant of good faith and fair dealing, such implied-in-fact agreements or terms are derived from an employer's express statements about discharge policy, its personnel practices, industry practices, business customs, the nature of the job, the employee's longevity of service, and the employer's record in keeping its past promises.[45] Our second rationale, unilateral contract theory, applies mainly to express promises in handbooks and manuals.[46] Under this rationale, such promises are construed as offers for a unilateral contract—offers employees can accept by beginning or continuing to perform the employer's requested services.[47] Finally, courts sometimes foreswear contract doctrine and bind employers to their promises by frankly invoking public policy.[48]

Critical Reaction and Recent Developments

Since the late 1960s, at least, scholarly reactions to the developments just described generally have been positive, and evaluations of employment at will correspondingly negative. As one prominent dissenter from this consensus has conceded: "The judicial erosion of the older position has been spurred on by academic commentators, who have been almost unanimous in their condemnation of the at-will relationship, often treating it as an archaic relic that should be jettisoned along with other vestiges of nineteenth-century laissez-faire."[49] Nonetheless, employment at will has not been without its modern defenders.[50]

Some recent developments on the wrongful discharge front suggest that the defenders may be gaining ground. For one thing, a few states still refuse to adopt any of the three common law exceptions to employment at will.[51] In others where the exceptions appeared solidly entrenched, courts have scaled them back.[52] Also, many courts have enabled employers to reduce their liability for their own express statements by enforcing at-will clauses or disclaimers of wrongful discharge liability in employment applications, employment contracts, and employee handbooks.[53]

Other recent developments are a mixed bag for both the friends and the foes of employment at will. Due partly to escalating damage recoveries and the costs they generate,[54] Montana now regulates wrongful discharge recoveries by statute, limiting damages in the process.[55] Partly for the same reason,[56] the new uniform act— with its good-cause standard, its arbitration scheme, and its disclaimer provisions—has emerged.[57]

UTILITARIAN INCONCLUSIONS

Introduction

With the legal pendulum arguably beginning to swing back toward employers and with the model act's emergence, perhaps it is time for yet another ethical/policy analysis of employment at will. When trying to evaluate that doctrine, one must decide where to begin among the array of claims the debate over discharge policy has gen-

erated. For reasons that hopefully will become apparent, I begin with the moral theory that, despite its ups and downs, arguably has dominated Anglo-American moral philosophy over the past 150 years. I refer of course to utilitarianism.

Even though it has been subjected to innumerable criticisms,[58] and even though some philosophers assert that it is trumped by rights claims,[59] utilitarianism—or *utility,* at least—has proven hard to kill.[60] Contemporary philosophers continue to advocate it.[61] It probably best justifies the common belief that wealth-maximization is an important ethical criterion.[62] For example, America's continuing preoccupation with aggregate dollar measures of economic health finds its most natural justification in utilitarianism, because most people seem to derive utility from the material things greater wealth enables them to obtain.

Of course, utility need not be the *sole* criterion for evaluating actions. Instead, utility-based claims might be weighed against other moral claims when making decisions.[63] However, such balancing exercises, while perhaps inevitable, obviously present difficulties. Thus, if there are solid utilitarian arguments for or against employment at will, and if other ethical criteria point in a different direction, severe problems confront anyone who attempts an ethical analysis of the doctrine. But here, at least, such problems do not exist. The reason is my judgment that the literature on employment at will does not permit us to reach any firm conclusions about its implications for utility.

Claims and Counterclaims

How do employment at will and its competitors compare from a utilitarian standpoint? To begin, I assume that employment at will promotes economic efficiency, wealth, and utility when employers use the doctrine to terminate employees on genuinely competitive, profit-maximizing grounds. For present purposes, however, this conclusion is unimportant because the at-will doctrine's major competitors normally allow such terminations as well. This almost certainly is true of the three common-law exceptions just described. Also, most versions of the just-cause standard appear to countenance good-faith discharges based on reasonable economic considerations.[64] Employment at will's defenders, however, make other economic attacks on alternatives such as a good-cause standard. For example, such standards impose all the costs associated with increased litigation.[65] More importantly, the threat of such litigation or of arbitration tends to lessen employers' ability and willingness to fire incompetent employees, and also may reduce workplace discipline.[66] For these reasons, it also forces employers to expend more resources in evaluating the employees they hire and in other preventative measures.[67] The resulting costs mean losses in wealth for *someone*,[68] and arguably mean less overall utility than would otherwise be the case.

To all of this, employment at will's foes reply that many countries with greater job protections than the United States also outstrip the U.S. in productivity and economic growth.[69] Of course, the doctrine's defenders can counter that many factors influence a nation's economic performance, and that America's output would be even lower were it to completely abandon employment at will. But employment at will's detractors can reply that this is just an unprovable surmise. They can also adduce reasons why greater job protection might increase productivity. Under such a regime, they sometimes assert, workers perform better because they are more secure, more content, and more loyal to their employers.[70] For such reasons, and because employees with job security would perceive fellow workers as colleagues rather than rivals, business enterprises would be more efficient.[71] Also, legal protections against wrongful discharge reduce the number of utterly arbitrary terminations—firings that tend to diminish efficiency, wealth, and utility.[72]

The foes of employment at will also can adduce some noneconomic reasons for believing that a just-cause standard would generate more utility than the at-will rule. As the previous paragraph suggests, they probably believe that employees' daily lives would be *happier* under that standard. If so, those employees would have more utility, other things being equal. Similarly, more enlightened dismissal standards would reduce the number of arbitrary firings and thus reduce the severe economic and emotional costs of such firings for both their victims and those individuals' families.[73] In this connection, foes of the at-will rule also raise an argument which is less utilitarian than equitable: that despite the rule's facial neutrality between employer and employee, in its practical operation it generates far more pain for the latter.[74]

To this last argument, however, employment at will's defenders have a rejoinder. As we will see later,[75] employees may receive greater compensation in return for the risks an at-will relationship creates, and thereby may achieve a net positive balance in their collective utility account.[76] In fact, the defenders go on to challenge the whole notion that employees would be better off were employment at will to disappear. Occasionally, they argue, the doctrine benefits certain people in the long run by enabling employers to discharge them from positions for which they were unsuited but from which they are unwilling to leave.[77] By the same token, it enables employers to hire marginal people—and thus gives those people a chance to show what they can do—because they can easily be discharged if they do not work out.[78] More generally, employment at will maximizes employers' ability to match employee and job. Because a just-cause standard can make firing marginal employees too risky or too expensive, for example, it both reduces efficiency *and* frustrates the advancement of superior workers who would otherwise have replaced them.[79] Finally, and most importantly, the costs created by protecting employees against unjust dismissals may mean greater unemployment.[80]

An Evaluation

If I were forced to guess, the preceding section's claims and counterclaims would lead me to conclude that employment at will is superior to the alternatives from a utilitarian perspective, perhaps considerably so. But I do not *know* this, and I surely cannot *prove* it. Indeed, the main reason behind the guess is my suspicion that increased job rights will tend to reduce wages and/or employment over the long haul. Also, I am skeptical about the have-your-cake-and-eat-it attitude expressed by those who argue that good-cause discharge policies are both humane *and* wealth-maximizing. However, these are not compelling arguments, and they will not convince someone who wants to believe the contrary. Indeed, the difficulties presented by any serious utilitarian analysis of employment at will make it unlikely that such an analysis would force anyone to abandon his or her prejudices.

In sketching these difficulties, perhaps the place to begin is with economists' familiar aversion to interpersonal comparisons of utility.[81] If this objection is valid, it might preclude a utilitarian analysis of employment at will even if every person affected by the doctrine provides a personal "utility score" rating its consequences for him or her alone.[82] However, maybe we sometimes can make fairly reliable seat-of-the-pants judgments of utility. On act-utilitarian grounds,[83] at least, I probably would be justified in torturing a terrorist to get him to reveal where he has hidden the vial of deadly bacteria whose release will soon bring a lethal plague to New York City. This would seem true even if the terrorist sincerely tells me that the torture is causing him infinite pain—more than any aggregate of people could possibly suffer. But such rough judgments appear difficult in the present context. One reason is the apples-and-oranges utility comparisons the previous arguments force upon us: for example, rating the satisfactions resulting from alleged economic gains against the satisfactions presumably generated by greater job security.

Conceivably, however, all these different satisfactions and dissatisfactions could be quantified and made the subject of a massive attempted cost-benefit analysis.[84] But even if they could be quantified it would be difficult to determine how much of each is likely to occur. Assuming that job protection generates all the disutilities claimed by employment at will's defenders, just what is their magnitude? Similarly, what is the magnitude of the suffering produced by arbitrary firings and the prospect of such firings? Turning to overall systemic effects, finally, it is not even clear whether the consequences of either legal regime would be positive or negative. The conflict over employment at will's implications for economic growth is part of a broader question on which equally credentialed experts disagree. At the most general level, that question might be posed as follows: which system—pure laissez-faire or some Japanese-style corporate state—will be more productive over the long haul?

A RIGHTS ANALYSIS OF EMPLOYMENT AT WILL

Despite my skepticism about the project's viability, far be it from me to say that no one can determine utilitarianism's implications for employment at will. Here, my only certainty is that *I* cannot make the determination. For this reason, utilitarian arguments do not figure prominently throughout the remainder of this article. In their absence, utilitarianism's main modern competitor—rights theory—takes center stage.

The Right Not to Suffer Arbitrary Dismissal

The no-cause or bad-cause dismissals permitted by employment at will can be attacked from various ethical perspectives. For example, an utterly arbitrary firing strikes most people as intrinsically unjust. Generalizing this and similar moral perceptions, the British intuitionist W. D.

Ross included among his presumptively binding "prima facie duties" obligations of *justice*—obligations aimed in part at preventing "a distribution of pleasure or happiness (or of the means thereto) which is not in accordance with the merit of the persons concerned."[85] Such terminations also have been attacked on what apparently are communitarian grounds. To one legal writer, for instance, an employer's duty to terminate only for good cause somehow arises out of the employment relationship itself.[86] Finally, employment at will can be attacked under the formulation of Kant's categorical imperative[87] which asserts that one should "[a]ct in such a way that you always treat humanity, whether in your own person or in the person of any other, never simply as a means, but always at the same time as an end."[88] Although its specific implications are not completely clear, this formulation of the imperative has been taken to mean that we should avoid harming others, should actively promote their welfare, should respect their rights, and should appeal to their rational nature when we try to use them for our ends.[89] The arbitrary dismissals permitted by employment at will arguably conflict with these duties. As Patricia Werhane has argued, "[t]reating employees 'at will' is analogous to considering an employee as a piece of property at the disposal of the employer, because arbitrary firing treats rational persons as things."[90]

Thus, three distinct ethical perspectives (intuitionism, communitarianism, Kantianism) might support the notion that employers or their managers[91] have a moral duty to avoid arbitrary firings or to discharge only for good cause. Although this roll call of ethical theories does not definitively establish the duty, it at least is evidence in that direction. And if we eschew probabilistic arguments for ethical propositions—or for anything else—by demanding conclusive demonstrations of their truth, we most likely will attain no knowledge whatever. Assuming, then, that employers or their managers have such a duty, how should the "ought" it contains be stated? In the business ethics literature on employment at will, that "ought" usually is described in terms of *rights*. Specifically, it is affirmed that no-cause discharges are wrong because they violate employee rights to receive substantive and/or procedural justice before being terminated.[92] Because A's duty to B usually can be redescribed as B's right against A,[93] this usage seems unexceptionable. Perhaps its prevalence can be explained by today's individualistic climate, in which all moral obligations seem to reduce to "rights talk."

Can Employees Contract the Right Away?

Introduction   If employees have a moral right not to suffer arbitrary discharge, it would seem that no at-will relationship could be justified, because such a relationship would permit arbitrary firings. But this discharge right may sometimes conflict with *other* rights—for example, rights of liberty or autonomy.[94] If these rights mean anything, they mean that people should be free to contract on the terms they desire. Thus, if employees can contract away their right not to be arbitrarily discharged, and if an indefinite-term employment contract is such an agreement, employment at will might find a rights-based justification after all. In this lengthy subsection, I consider the first of these positions; the next subsection treats the second. Basically, I maintain that: (1) employees ought to be allowed to contract away their right against arbitrary discharge, but (2) the typical at-will employment agreement is not such a contract.

Our present concern, then, is whether employees can rightly contract away their right to be fired only for good cause. Some foes of employment at will answer this question in the negative. Joseph R. Des Jardins and John J. McCall, for example, advance a conception of employee rights which "places prior constraints on the content of employment contracts in such a way as to limit the contracting powers of prospective employees. Thus, . . . an employee right to due process before dismissal is an entitlement which the employer is not free to bargain away in exchange for other goods."[95] How can this position be justified? Conceivably, one could assert that the right not to be arbitrarily dismissed is by its nature inalienable, but the assertion is extremely implausible.[96] Writers on that subject, however, frequently identify two other situations in which otherwise-alienable rights should not be yielded: (1) where their relinquishment is involuntary, and (2) where it is irrational.[97] Foes of employment at will often make analogous arguments. First, they claim that freedom of contract is meaningless in the employer-employee context because employers have vastly superior bargaining power and thus can force employees to accept their terms.[98] Thus, the right to contract away one's dismissal rights really is a "right" to have that choice dictated in advance by one's employer. Second, employment at will's foes say that even if employer and employee bargain on equal terms, there is no rational reason for the employee to accept an at-will arrangement. I now consider each argument in turn.

When Do Employers Have Superior Bargaining Power Regarding Discharge Terms?

Nowhere is the mutual incomprehension between employment at will's foes and its friends more evident than on the question whether employers and employees have relatively equal bargaining power. The former group tends to deny the existence of such power, while to the latter group it is ubiquitous. For example, Lawrence Blades's much-cited 1967 attack on employment at will opened with this paragraph:

It is a widely accepted proposition that large corporations now pose a threat to individual freedom comparable to that which would be posed if governmental power were unchecked. The proposition need not, however, be limited to the mammoth business corporation, for the freedom of the individual is threatened whenever he becomes dependent upon a private entity possessing greater

power than himself. Foremost among the relationships of which this generality is true is that of employer and employee.[99]

By way of comparison, Richard Epstein's 1984 defense of employment at will asserts:

The account thus far given of the contract at will in no way depends upon any notion of an inherent inequality of bargaining power that pervades all employment contracts. Indeed, if such an inequality did govern the employment relationship, we should expect to see conditions that exist in no labor market. Wages should be driven to zero, for no matter what their previous level, the employer could use his (inexhaustible) bargaining power to reduce them further, until the zero level was reached.[100]

Of much the same mind is Ian Maitland, who observes that "many of the accounts of rights in the workplace seem to assume pervasive market failure which leaves employers free to do pretty much what they want."[101] But in reality "employers' discretion to unilaterally determine terms and conditions of employment is drastically limited by the market."[102]

Aside from Epstein's apparent belief that bargaining power is an all-or-nothing proposition, I tend to agree with him and with Maitland so far as the discharge terms of employment contracts are concerned. But the qualifier is important, for inquiries about unequal bargaining power should be context-specific. The main reason for my conclusion that employers generally lack the power to dictate discharge terms to their employees is the unpersuasiveness of the reasons such power is said to exist. More bluntly, it is difficult to identify a reliable answer to the question: "Where does this pervasive employer power come from?" Before considering the various alleged bases of that power, however, it is useful to examine two assumptions on which the image of the all-powerful employer often seems to be based. The first is the view that the absence of genuine bargaining over a contract term implies that the party offering the term imposed it through superior power. The second is the notion that superior size *of itself* creates superior bargaining power. Having half-consciously embraced each assumption at one time or another, maybe I am credible when I assert that neither makes much sense.

Two Dubious Assumptions One difference between those who maintain that employers have superior power and those who assert the contrary is that members of the former group tend to focus on the bargaining process between employer and employee, while their opponents stress the systematic (mainly market) factors that make employers offer the terms they do. People of the first kind sometimes appear to believe the following proposition: if an employee cannot meaningfully bargain with her employer, the employer has superior power. For example, consider Peter Linzer's response to Epstein's claim that turn-of-the-century employees should have been able to extract extra compensation from employers who required them to sign a yellow-dog contract.[103] "One visualizes the pre-New Deal job applicant saying, 'What will you give me for the yellow dog clause?' One suspects that the answer would have been 'I'll give you a job.'"[104] Maybe Linzer is correct in assuming that pre-New Deal employers had sufficient power to impose a yellow-dog contract without paying for it, but he provides no justification for that assumption. In particular, he ignores the possibility that the wages offered by such employers *already* were increased to reflect that clause. He also ignores other factors that may have influenced those wages—for example, competitors who offer better pay. However, he does consider what is probably the most important such factor: employees' ability to walk away if they find an employer's terms unacceptable. "Epstein," Linzer says, "argues that employees were thus well-served because they could always quit en masse and

join a union. He does not explain where they would find work."[105] Maybe they would find it—at suitable terms—with their former employer, who by hypothesis would be left without a labor force. In any event, their options—and their employer's options—would largely be determined by labor market conditions at the time and place in question.

The extreme implausibility of the idea that the absence of meaningful bargaining means unequal bargaining power should become apparent when we consider how common such situations are. If inflexibility on terms is a sign of superior power, we all are being exploited by grocery stores, restaurants, movie theatres, and innumerable other such establishments. As will become evident later, moreover, large firms often have more or less innocent reasons for refusing to budge from their standardized terms.[106] However, foes of employment at will might point out that, unlike grocery stores and restaurants, employers often are *big* by any measure, and invariably are bigger than their employees. By doing so, however, they make the second erroneous assumption that colors so much thinking about bargaining power: its equation with size per se. By size per se, I mean size *in itself*—size abstracted from every tangible advantage it might produce.[107] For example, although IBM undoubtedly is big and assuredly has political and social influence, how can it dictate an at-will clause to me? Can it draft me to work for it? Can it force me to remain in its employ if I dislike its terms? For the company to get such power, something else besides size obviously is required.

Standard Forms and Express At-Will Clauses One "something else" afforded by size involves the statement and packaging of contract terms. As is well-known, large (and not-so-large) firms often possess (or can purchase) the skills to structure their relations with third parties under standard-form contracts of adhesion that are offered on a take-it-or-leave-it basis.[108] Unless the firm gets leverage from another source, however, it may be inaccurate to describe this imposition of standard-form terms as an exercise of superior bargaining *power.* Here the "power" in question generally results from the other's party's lack of opportunity to read the form, the complicated language in which its terms are stated, and the way that language is presented or packaged on the form—and not from something akin to coercion.[109] Nonetheless, such situations do afford the "stronger" party a practical ability to dictate its preferred term.

Because indefinite-term employment contracts traditionally were deemed at-will, employers once did not have to use standard forms to impose that relationship. Since the emergence of the three common-law theories of wrongful discharge, however, firms often have used disclaimers of wrongful discharge liability or at-will clauses that resemble standard-form terms in some respects.[110] These clauses sometimes appear in employment applications,[111] but most often are placed in employee handbooks or policy manuals.[112] Although their presentation varies considerably, only infrequently are they genuinely conspicuous.[113] In addition, a disclaimer often appears along with promises of job security that conflict with it and that tend to reduce its comprehensibility even if it is conspicuous and is read.[114] But many courts enforce at-will clauses nonetheless.[115] As a rule, though, they do so only in suits involving a claim that an employer has violated one of its express or implied-in-fact promises—and not in public policy cases or cases involving the implied covenant of good faith and fair dealing.[116] In cases where disclaimers are enforced, employers effectively are allowed to take away with one hand what they apparently promised with the other.[117]

Do employers which use disclaimers have such an advantage over employees that nothing could every justify enforcing the clause? A suffi-

ciently pervasive independent source of power-as-coercion would create such an advantage, but presently it is absent by hypothesis. Also absent here is another practical edge often possessed by a party who uses a standard form: complex terms. With at-will clauses, we deal with a matter almost anyone can understand. Surely Epstein was close to the mark when he said that "[a]n employee who knows he can quit at will understands what it means to be fired at will, even though he may not like it after the fact."[118] However, the packaging of many disclaimers—their inconspicuousness and their conjunction with promises of job security—raises serious questions about employees' ability to recognize them and understand their full impact. But as argued later in this article, the solution to this problem is not to ban disclaimers outright, but to create conditions under which they are likely to be read and understood.[119]

Monopsony Another bargaining edge correlated with superior size is that larger employers are more likely to have the market power necessary to become a monopsonist—a monopoly or oligopoly purchaser of labor.[120] A monopsony position gives an employer a bargaining edge over its workers.[121] Because some employees have more bargaining power than their employers,[122] monopsony obviously is not universal. When might it exist? Economists who study labor markets typically list several possibilities. The first and most obvious, well illustrated by the traditional company town, is the situation where one firm is the sole employer within a particular locality.[123] A second is collusive agreement among employers.[124] A third, discussed below, occurs when an "employer who uses highly specialized workers is . . . the only employer in a labor market who employs workers in certain occupations."[125] Monopsony may also exist in certain specific situations involving one or more of the previous factors.[126]

Are such monopsony possibilities common today? Labor market economists seem skeptical that they appear very frequently.[127] One reason is workers' increased geographical mobility, which effectively expands the relevant territorial market and dilutes the effects of employer concentration within a smaller market.[128] Another is the relative infrequency of anticompetitive agreements[129] and (more importantly) the difficulty of enforcing them when they do exist.[130] In most cases, moreover, monopsony usually requires a high degree of employer concentration within a particular area—a situation in which one firm or a few firms hire a large fraction of the labor force within that area. Apparently, such concentration is uncommon.[131]

The remaining monopsonistic possibility, specialization, sometimes is mentioned as a source of employer power by foes of employment at will.[132] The assumption underlying this argument is that specialized jobs require unique skills that are relatively difficult to obtain. Thus employees who possess such skills can only market them with one employer or a small group of employers, cannot easily acquire new skills, and have little leverage because they have few options. But clearly this argument cuts both ways. The very factor that weakens the employee's position—the difficulty of acquiring new skills—also makes specialized employees valuable to employers. As Posner observes, "precisely because this [specialized] employee is more productive than a new replacement would be, he can threaten the employer with quitting. . . . It is a game of chicken, likely to end in a stand-off. . . ."[133]

Should Employees Have to Be Mobile?   Monopsony, then, seems relative uncommon in the United States today. Nonetheless, some instances of the phenomenon undoubtedly exist. The most common examples probably are situations in which a few employers dominate a local labor market. For reasons discussed in the next subsection, such cases do not seriously dis-turbed my overall argument in this article. But they do pose a problem that may deserve a short, if somewhat inconclusive, digression. Friends of employment at will could maintain that even where a local labor market is dominated by a few employers, most workers nonetheless have a genuine option: to leave the area and to seek better employment elsewhere. And if they fail to utilize that option, no one should claim that they were *forced* to accept at-will employment because their employers possessed superior bargaining power. The rejoinder to all this, of course, is that in many cases it is unreasonable to expect people to uproot themselves. This being so, the rejoinder would continue, their local employers *do* have power over them.

In some cases of this kind, it seems reasonably clear that genuine monopsonistic power exists. In local labor markets with few employers, for example, those employers most likely have superior power over employees who face high relocation costs or are ignorant of alternative job opportunities.[134] But these hardly are the most common reasons why people remain tied to a particular locality. For example, communal identifications (e.g., roots in a particular community or family ties) and regional attachments (e.g., one's love for the ocean) may prevent them from seeking better employment prospects elsewhere.[135] Because such attachments surely have value, it might be maintained that people should not be required to forego them in situations where they are especially strong. In other words, the affectional constraints such attachments impose should be treated like the constraints imposed by excessively high relocation costs or ignorance of alternative job opportunities. If so, these affectional constraints might fairly be regarded as a source of superior employer power. This would be true even though the people in question are not directly compelled to accept their employers' terms, and are least negatively free from a proffered at-will arrangement because there is no external impediment to their moving elsewhere.[136]

One somewhat rhetorical reply to this line of argument is to reclassify affectional ties as mere *preferences.* On this view, whatever "power" employers thus acquire is simply the price such "situated" employees must pay to realize their preferences. If, for example, Sam Sailor is forced to accept at-will employment due to his desire to remain in the monopsonistic town of Seaside City, that is Sam's choice and he should have to bear the consequences. This rejoinder, however, seems less compelling where the "preferences" in question are familial bonds or longstanding, deep-rooted attachments to a locality. Here, though, another rejoinder—one involving the third-party effects of rights against wrongful discharge—comes into play. If we regard affectional ties as a source of superior employer power, then any "situated self's" agreement to contract away her moral right against wrongful discharge is tainted by that power. Thus, the agreement should be invalid and the employee should retain her right. But as we have seen, employers who are forced to recognize the right incur extra costs.[137] Those costs may be borne by the employee (in the form of a less attractive compensation or benefits package), by the employer and/or its shareholders, or by consumers of the employer's products to whom the costs are passed on.[138] In the first case, employees effectively pay for their desire to remain in a certain area. But in the last two situations, third parties absorb the expense of giving employees their rights and preserving their affectional ties. On what basis should these third parties be required to do so? On what basis, that is, should they be forced to subsidize someone else's affections and attachments? Perhaps it could be argued that people have a "right to roots" that trumps the third parties' right to their money, and also overcomes any countervailing utilitarian claims. Perhaps the same result could be reached via a communitarian argument: for example, that the *quid pro quo* for my subsidizing your roots is your subsidizing mine. To my knowledge, however, neither argument

has been made by the foes of employment at will. And it is doubtful whether either argument's aims could be realized without economic costs.

Why Would Employees Choose to Be Employed at Will?   The preceding subsection did not maintain that employers never exercise superior bargaining power over their employees. Rather, the argument was that such inequalities are not sufficiently pervasive to justify a flat ban on employees' alienation of their job rights. Freedom of contract, almost everyone assumes, is a very important right, one not to be restricted for trivial reasons.[139] Thus, those who argue that employees never can contract away their dismissal rights face a stiff burden of proof. They could prevail were they able to show that employees always bargain at a disadvantage, but this is implausible in the extreme. They also might prevail if they could show that employees are so often at a disadvantage that an across-the-board ban on the alienation of discharge rights is cheaper and/or more accurate than case-by-case adjudication of claims that employers wielded superior power. But if the preceding section's arguments are sound, relative *equality* is more the rule than the exception. And the judicial system is not without tools for handling the situations where this generalization fails to hold.[140]

But foes of employment at will have at least one more arrow in their quiver. Occasionally, they argue that employees cannot be allowed to alienate their right to a nonarbitrary discharge because no rational person would ever voluntarily accept an at-will relationship. After cataloguing employment at will's disadvantages for employees, Werhane concludes that "it is hard to imagine that rational people would agree in advance to being fired arbitrarily in an employment contract."[141] Her argument might be attacked as paternalistic, but this begs the question whether paternalism sometimes is justified. If it is accurate, moreover, the argument undermines my contention that employer and employee tend to deal on relatively equal terms. If employment at will is genuinely irrational, few employees would voluntarily accept it. Thus, its prevalence must be explained on other grounds, and the obvious explanation is that employers use their superior power to impose it.

Unfortunately, for employment at will's enemies, there are at least three reasons why rational employees might freely agree to an employment relation that either party can terminate at any time and for any reason. Serving as a backdrop to them all, perhaps, is the likelihood that because most employers are more or less rational most of the time, they are unlikely to arbitrarily fire productive workers.[142] The first reason employees might rationally choose to be employed at will is that because it enables them to quit whenever they desire, they can escape employers who abuse the relationship by making excessive demands on them.[143] For the same reason, employers may be deterred from making such demands. Secondly, employment at will gives employees the flexibility to end the employment without liability whenever better opportunities present themselves. As Epstein says:

> The contract at will is also a sensible private adaptation to the problem of imperfect information over time. In sharp contrast to the purchase of standard goods, an inspection of the job before acceptance is far less likely to guarantee its quality thereafter. The future is not clearly known. More important, employees, like employers, *know what they do not know.* They are not faced with a bolt from the blue, with an "unknown unknown." Rather they face a known unknown for which they can plan. The at-will contract is an essential part of that planning because it allows both sides to take a wait-and-see attitude to their relationship so that new and more accurate choices can be made on the strength of improved information.[144]

As Epstein's statement suggests, employers have interests that are roughly analogous to these two employee interests. That is, employers would rationally prefer employment at will because it enables them to remove troublesome, unproductive, or unneeded workers; and to deter malingering by the threat of easy discharge. Thus, we can see why a rational employer and a rational employee who bargain from positions of perfect equality might agree on an at-will relationship.

Common to both preceding arguments was the assumption that by agreeing to be fired at will, employees also get the power to quit with impunity themselves. But why would they so agree if they already have this power? Why should they give up their discharge rights to get something they already have? Earlier, I argued that employers are morally obligated not to terminate their employees, but I said nothing to indicate that employees have a similar duty toward their employers. This subject apparently has received little discussion in the literature on employment at will.[145] But if workers can terminate at will and their employers cannot, neither of the two previous points would make it rational for them to agree to an at-will relationship.

Even under this assumption, however, there is a third reason why employees might agree to let employers fire them at will: *money.* Earlier, we saw that good-cause termination imposes costs on employers, and that some or all of those costs would fall on them.[146] If so, employers may want to offer employees some or all of those extra costs in increased wages, if employees will eliminate the source of the costs by agreeing that they can be fired at will. On the other hand, if the costs fall wholly or largely on employees in the form of lower wages, they might want to increase their pay by relinquishing their discharge rights. Of course, whether an employee would make either hypothetical deal depends on the relative value she attaches to money and risk. Almost certainly, however, some would sign on. As Maitland states:

Presumably, if the price is right, some workers will be willing to accept the greater insecurity of [employment at will]. This may be particularly true, for example, of younger, footloose and fancy-free workers with marketable skills. It is also likely to be truer in a metropolitan area (with ample alternative employment opportunities) than a small town and when the economic outlook is good.[147]

In reply, foes of employment at will might urge that, because rights claims always trump claims based on utility, employees simply cannot be allowed to alienate their rights for mere money.[148] But even if this argument's shaky premise is granted, another right—the worker's autonomy-based freedom-of-contract right—is relevant here. Employees would exercise this right when making the hypothetical deal just sketched. Who are business ethicists to deny them this option?

Does an Indefinite-Term Employment Agreement Contract the Right Away?

From the preceding discussion, two general propositions emerge. First, as argued at the very beginning of this section, employees have a moral right not to be terminated on an arbitrary basis. Second, because employees might rationally agree to be employed at will and because employers generally lack the ability to impose that relationship, employees can justifiably contract their right away, thus rendering themselves terminable at will. Under the employment-at-will rule, employees have this status when their employment contract lacks a definite time term. But is an indefinite-term agreement sufficient to contract away employee discharge rights, and thus to provide an ethical basis for employment at will?

Interpretive Criteria As Epstein observes, the previous question involves "a rule of construction in response to the perennial question of gaps in contract language: what term should be

implied in the absence of explicit agreement on the question of duration or grounds for termination?"[149] Under general contract law, at least two considerations are relevant in resolving this question. The first is the fairness of each rival construction, as measured by community standards.[150] Although I have not polled the American people on employment at will, I find it difficult to believe that most would seriously disagree with the broad conclusions I have advanced. Roughly speaking, these are: (1) that it is wrong to fire someone for bad reasons or no reason and that employees therefore have a moral right not to be arbitrarily discharged, and (2) that they can contract away this right under appropriate circumstances. In any event, my conclusions are not without support from moral theory, from the nature of the employer-employee relation, and from economic considerations surrounding that relation. Thus, I maintain, the "ethical" construction of an employment contract is one that respects an employee's right not to be arbitrarily terminated, unless the parties agree otherwise. As a result, the worth of a particular judicial construction depends on what the parties actually wanted, with the right to a nonarbitrary dismissal serving as the fallback position. The second interpretive consideration supplied by general contract law counsels that we employ the construction which would be most frequently adopted by the parties over a broad range of cases, were the issue brought to their attention.[151] This criterion obviously resembles the first part of our previous criterion.

Our general question, then, is something like the following: would many or most employers and employees choose employment at will if the question were brought to their attention at the time the employment contract is formed? If the question cannot clearly be answered, the typical at-will employment cannot be regarded as a contract whereby employees contract away their right against wrongful discharge. In that case, this moral right, which serves as a kind of default position, sets the standard the law should follow. Although the matter may not be completely certain, I assume that employers generally would desire an at-will relationship if given a choice. In determining how to construe an indefinite-term employment contract, therefore, our main concern is the desires of employees.

Do Most Employees Want At-Will Employment? As noted earlier, critics of employment at will sometimes appear sure that they know what discharge policy employees would pick if provided a genuine choice. As it turns out, much the same is true of their (allegedly) laissez-faire adversaries. The main difference, of course, is that the two sides disagree about the nature of that choice. In arguing that most employees want, or rationally would want, an at-will relationship, employment at will's defenders appear to make three more or less distinguishable arguments. Each is unpersuasive.

The Argument from the Alleged Prevalence of At-Will Relations As we have seen, at least some employees are likely to desire an at-will relationship. But how many? Even though Epstein explicitly recognizes that employment at will is not for everyone,[152] he obviously thinks that the bulk of informed employees would and should choose that relationship. In arguing that point, Epstein and other defenders of employment at will argue from its alleged prevalence to its basis in employees' genuine interests. "It is hardly plausible," he asserts, "that contracts at will could be so pervasive in all businesses and at all levels if they did not serve the interests of employees as well as employers."[153] To Maitland, "there is good reason for concluding that the prevalence of [employment at will] does accurately reflect workers' preferences for wages over contractually guaranteed protections against unfair dismissal."[154]

The main problem with the Epstein-Maitland argument is the uncertainty surrounding its premise. Given the longstanding prevalence of just-cause discharge in union contracts and in public employment, plus the emergence of common law wrongful discharge claims and miscellaneous statutory restrictions on certain firings, is employment at will really so pervasive? Apparently, Epstein and Maitland are arguing that if at-will employment really is onerous, worker discontent surely would have compelled courts or legislatures to make changes. To some degree, however, those changes *have* been made, and different public attitudes are a plausible explanation for the changes.

The Argument from Rationality But Epstein and those like him have other reasons for believing that most employees would or should choose employment at will. The most important of these reverses an earlier argument advanced by the doctrine's enemies. Rather than wondering how any sane employee would ever choose to be employed at will, its defenders tend to believe that at-will employment is virtually the only rational choice. As Epstein observes, he must rebut the common view that "the contract at will is so unfair and one-sided that it cannot be the outcome of a rational set of bargaining processes. . . ."[155] To do so, he must "explain why rational people would enter into such a contract, if not all the time, then at least most of it."[156] The three arguments sketched earlier are Epstein's and Maitland's attempts at such an explanation.[157]

The problem with this position, however, is that these arguments tend to presuppose people of a certain character, with certain interests and values. In other words, while the arguments show why a rational employee *might* choose to be employed at will, they do not demonstrate why *most* rational employees would do so. Consider for example Maitland's suggestion that employment at will is apt to be favored by younger, footloose, fancy-free urban workers with marketable skills.[158] Its obvious corollary is that less well-endowed workers who are older, more rooted, and more risk-averse should tend to favor job protection over money. Are such interests, drives, and values irrational? The dominant modern (i.e., post-1600) conception of reason sees it as a faculty that tells us how to realize our ends, but does not say what those ends should be.[159] If this instrumental conception of reason is the correct one, it is difficult to see how preferring job security to money can be called irrational. Nor is it obviously irrational in a looser sense of the term—in the sense, for example, that irrational actions are those we cannot imagine sane people performing. Since when is it insane to sacrifice some of one's pay to help keep one's job?

The Argument from the Alleged Nature of Most People Nonetheless, employment at will's defenders might have a last line of defense. Even if there is nothing irrational about rejecting an at-will relation, perhaps most people *really are* tough, mobile, wealth-maximizers who prefer money and other benefits over job security. We have already seen reasons to suspect that this assumption is false.[160] If such people preponderate, why is just-cause discharge so common in union contracts and in public employment? Why do we have a common law of wrongful discharge that most likely increases employers' costs and may negatively affect wages in some cases?[161] If employees generally are unconcerned about job security, finally, why do employers so often make express promises on the subject?[162]

Conclusions Unlike many commentators on employment at will, I am not sure whether most people would prefer an at-will relation and the better compensation package it can provide, or would prefer more job security and less money instead. Indeed, I suspect that some employees are uncertain about their preferences, or watch those preferences change with time and circum-

stances. In part, this individual uncertainty exists because the relevant choices—e.g., *how much* extra money? *how much* extra job security?—tend to be context-specific. If I had to guess, however, my guess would be that if confronted with an explicit choice over a range of circumstances, a majority of Americans would value job security over increased pay. If accurate, this guess might support reading some limitations on employers' power to arbitrarily discharge their employees into indefinite-term employment agreements. But even if my guess is wrong, it still is difficult to argue that most employees favor employment at will. In the resulting uncertainty, we cannot read an employment contract for an indefinite term as an agreement that either party can terminate the relationship at any time and for any reason. Instead, we come full circle by adopting the default position with which this section began: that employers are morally obligated not to arbitrarily terminate their employees and that the law should reflect that obligation.

MAXIMIZING INFORMED CHOICES ABOUT DISCHARGE POLICY

In the previous section, I argued that: (1) employees have a right not to be arbitrarily discharged, a right the law should respect; (2) because inequalities in bargaining power do not pervade employment markets and because employees might rationally choose to be employed at will, they can contract away that right; and (3) the typical at-will agreement is not such a contract. If that analysis is correct, employment at will is not morally justified, and the common law ought to adopt some kind of good-cause test instead. But as the previous section makes clear, such a test obviously is deficient too. The reason is the inability of a uniform good-cause standard to accommodate employers and employees who would prefer an at-will arrangement.[163] But the analysis also suggested a way around this difficulty. Absent disparities in bargaining power, employers and employees who desire different discharge standards should be allowed to contract to that effect.[164]

The Virtues of Individualized Contracts

Underlying the previous paragraph's conclusions is a simple assumption: that no uniformly valid discharge policy exists. Where feasible, therefore, the law should try to promote informed employer-employee contracting on that subject. This policy recognizes that people are different and that they seek to realize different values, goals, and interests through their employment relationships. Therefore, it respects their autonomy. For much the same reason, the policy also should maximize utility between the parties, although not necessarily societally.[165]

Problems with Individualized Contracts

Despite its attractiveness, a strategy of promoting individualized discharge contracts terms faces difficulties. At first blush, there is reason to doubt how often such contracts can happen. And even if they do occur, they will not attain their ends if employees lack adequate notice and information about the employer's terms, or simply lack the ability to care for themselves even if such information is provided. I now consider these difficulties.

Transaction Costs It is almost certain that many employers would offer employees at-will terms were a good-cause standard the common-law baseline. Indeed, they often do so now,[166] and a good-cause standard should spur them to greater efforts. But transaction costs may well prevent employers from contracting on an individualized basis with each of their employees.[167] For example, administrative and record-keeping expenses may prevent large employers with many employees from dealing with those employees one-by-one.[168] Individualized deals regarding discharge terms also could defeat some of the aims firms try to achieve by using standard forms. These include: (1) facilitating better communication and coordination among departments, (2) enabling the optimal policies to be imposed uniformly throughout the firm, and (3) preventing subordinates from thwarting those policies by cutting their own deals with third parties.[169]

Thus, employers who expressly contract on discharge terms are likely to offer their employees one uniform term. If so, how can individualized contracts occur? The answer is that the problems just identified do not preclude *different employers* from offering different discharge terms and from competing with each other on that basis (as well as on common terms such as salary). As Maitland has argued:

> If employers were generally to heed business ethicists and to institute workplace due process in cases of dismissals—and to take the increased costs or reduced efficiency out of workers paychecks—then they would expose themselves to the pirating of their workers by other (less scrupulous?) employers who would give workers what they wanted instead of respecting their rights.
>
> If, on the other hand, many of the workers not currently protected against unfair dismissal would in fact prefer guarantees of workplace due process—*and* would be willing to pay for it—then such guarantees would be at an effective recruiting tool for an entrepreneurial employer. That is, employers are driven by their own self-interest to offer a package of benefits and rights that will attract and retain employees.[170]

As noted earlier, the result of such competition could be the maximum satisfaction of individual preferences and, for that reason, maximum utility as between the parties.[171]

Would employers actually behave as Maitland suggests? Because employees differ in how they weigh job security against the other elements in employers' rights/benefits packages, there should be a demand for different packages. But since employers seem inclined to disclaim whenever possible, perhaps they would not respond to the segment of the work force that values job security. However, employers—often those same employers—also make express promises about job security. Under the tough conspicuousness/disclosure requirements advocated later in this article,[172] such firms could not promise job protection and then successfully disclaim it. As a result, they effectively would have to choose between workers who strongly value job security and workers who rate money or other benefits more highly. Absent successful collusion, some of these employers almost certainly would aim their rights/benefits packages at particular segments of the labor force. And in most circumstances, collusive agreements among employers should be very difficult to create and maintain.[173] The reasons include the number of relevant employers, the difficulties this poses for forming and enforcing any agreement on the terms they offer workers, and their incentive to cheat on such agreements.

The Need for Full and Conspicuous Disclosure of Discharge Terms   Earlier, I argued that disparities in bargaining power do not pervade employment markets. Where they exist, of course, they are a basis for invalidating contracts whereby employees deal away their discharge rights.[174] In addition to power-as-coercion, however, employers also can gain a practical edge if employees do not understand the terms they offer. As related earlier, this probably happens when employers make inconspicuous disclaimers of wrongful discharge liability, and/or weaken understanding of those disclaimers by including promises of job security as well.[175] As also noted at that point, courts tend to enforce such clauses. Because the aim of individualized contracts is to maximize employees' ability to obtain the employment terms that suit them, these tendencies are most unfortunate. They obviously tend to defeat employees' ability to ascertain the terms offered them, and thus to get the employment relationship they prefer.

For these reasons, courts must crack down on employers by imposing much tougher tests for enforcing at-will clauses. In another piece,[176] I suggest several such tests. The most important is that employers only be allowed to disclaim in a separate, signed writing that conspicuously describes the employment relation as at-will and does so in a fairly colloquial way. This requirement means that disclaimers in employee handbooks or policy manuals simply would not be enforced. Also, even if an employer's disclaimer meets the previous tests, it should not be enforced where the employer makes a promise about discharge policy in a writing (such as a manual) that states a centrally-dictated company policy, the promise is inconsistent with the disclaimer, and the promise would create liability in isolation from the disclaimer. The main aim of this rule is to stop employers from inducing employees to think they have, or might have, job security when in fact they do not. By refusing to enforce at-will clauses when they fail to meet these tests, courts force employers to state their discharge terms in a fashion calculated to maximize the chance that employees will read and comprehend them.

Can Employees Care for Themselves? Will They?   From the preceding discussion, it appears that my recommended approach—a disclaimable just-cause standard with tough conspicuousness and disclosure standards—may increase competition over discharge terms and give employees more genuine options. Even so, one can question whether workers could or would make good use of the opportunity. One possible argument that they could not analogizes at-will clauses to standard-form terms such as insurance and credit-card contracts, or to implied warranty disclaimers. In such cases, it is arguable that the complexity of the contract's subject-matter and/or the relevant law justify the imposition of standardized terms because only the most alert, informed, and industrious consumers could possibly understand, digest, and assimilate the relevant information.[177] But as Epstein observed earlier, almost anyone can understand what it means to be employed at will.[178]

Another variant on the argument from employee incapacity stresses that workers tend not to act in their true interests when they consider terms of employment.[179] As one observer maintains:

Employees may for a variety of reasons misperceive their best interests at the outset of the employment relationship. For example, employees may tend to discount substantially the risk of wrongful discharge, and as a result systematically undervalue job security. This reflects a common psychological response; since most people prefer not to think about the possibility of disaster, employees understandably tend to disregard the possibility of job loss. In addition, most employees have only limited access to information about personnel relations in a firm and are unable to "shop around" by comparing the firm's relative turnover rate and firing histories. Companies further contribute to the employee's predicament by promoting an image of job security that is not completely accurate. Either a false sense of security or a failure to realize the risks involved may therefore lead employees to seek wage increases rather than forgo some immediate benefits in return for an appropriate level of job protection.[180]

Thus the law must approximate "the accommodation that the parties would have reached had they actually bargained over the unsettled term."[181] Unsurprisingly, that accommodation turns out to be an implied duty that employers only terminate their employees in good faith.[182]

Although one could argue with the author's reasons why people tend to discount the risk of being wrongfully fired and to undervalue job security when considering discharge terms, none of them are ridiculous. When considering them, however, we also should recall that rational, self-interested employers normally have little reason to fire productive employees.[183] Thus, the probability of being unjustly terminated may be so low that it would be difficult for an em-

ployee to underestimate it.[184] In any event, the main problem with the author's argument is that its conclusion (a dictated employer duty to terminate only in good faith) does not follow from its premise. In other words, even if employees misperceive their interests when entertaining discharge terms, it does not follow that they should be forced to accept job protection. The reason, once again, is that there is no one optimum discharge policy that all fully rational minds would invariably be drawn to accept. When deciding upon her preferred discharge policy, a rational employee presumably multiplies the magnitude of a firing's disutility by its probability. Because the disutility of being arbitrarily fired varies from individual to individual, it is difficult to see how academic writers can authoritatively pronounce on the subject. Similarly, people often react differently to an agreed-upon probability of harm. Thus, even an utterly rational employee with perfect information might agree to contract away her discharge rights. More importantly, even if employees systematically underrate the risks of being wrongfully dismissed, many of them still might opt for an at-will relationship were we able to correct for this bias.

A final argument for employee incapacity might assert that even if workers can approach at-will clauses knowingly and rationally, they simply may not bother. For example, how many people really read their employee handbooks with care? In fashioning standards for enforcing at-will clauses, however, I went some way toward heading off such problems by requiring a very conspicuous and blunt disclaimer on a separated signed writing. Still, some employees no doubt will pay little attention to an at-will clause even in this instance. Such employees, however, may be relatively unconcerned—perhaps justifiably unconcerned—about the possibility of a wrongful discharge. And why should their unconcern or inattention justify dictating terms to those who *do* know and care? Finally, if we differentiate the former group from the latter by letting employees escape a conspicuous at-will clause on the basis that they did not read it, we give them an incentive to lie on an issue where their testimony is critical.

CONCLUSION

As readers may have observed, the Draft Uniform Employment-Termination Act's provisions roughly parallel the discharge rules recommended here. Those provisions do so by: (1) establishing a good cause standard for permissible discharges, and (2) allowing that standard to be waived by express written agreement.[185] Thus, the preceding ethical analysis helps justify some features of the model act. However, my suggested standards for the placement, statement, conspicuousness, and authentication of enforceable at-will clauses[186] are absent from its disclaimer provision.[187]

The act's drafters say that its "underlying theme or basic philosophy" is "one of compromise—an equitable tradeoff of competing interests."[188] In that philosophy, and in the eclecticism just noted, the model act obviously departs from most of the ethical/policy commentary on employment at will and the absolutist positions to which it tends. But if this article's ethical analysis is on the mark, the act's drafters did rather well without much heeding either the employee rights enthusiasts or their law-and-economics adversaries. In particular, they seem to have avoided each side's main vices: excessive confidence about the nature of human beings and the discharge policy rational employees would choose, and a resulting overeagerness to read those assumptions into the law of wrongful discharge.

In thus criticizing the main tendencies in the "dialogue" over employment at will, I do not proceed from some set of rigid antipaternalist principles. This article is not a libertarian manifesto, and it does not reject all forms of legal paternalism in the employment relation or anywhere else. But individual issues must be considered on their own merits. In the case of employee dismissal policy, the arguments for a dictated legal solution are not very compelling. This is true regardless of whether the preferred solution is to infer an at-will relationship from an indefinite-term employment contract, or to impose an across-the-board good-cause standard. Indeed, reflection on the inadequacies of each extreme soon leads one to a stance that seems radical within the polarized ethical debate over employee discharge policy.[189] It induces one to conclude that because there is no "right" discharge policy for everyone, the law should try to encourage a modicum of genuine individual choice on the subject.

NOTES

1. Draft Uniform Employment-Termination Act, August 2–9, 1991, *in* Lab. Rel. Rep. (BNA), Ind. Empl. Rights Manual, at 540:21–540:41 [hereinafter cited as Model Act]. The Individual Employment Rights Manual is hereinafter cited as IERM. Throughout, I cite to the August 2–9 drafting committee version of the act. On August 8, 1991, the commissioners approved a model law that is substantially similar to the August 2–9 draft. But a motion to approve the draft as a uniform law was defeated. *Id.* at 540:21. The historical and background statements that precede the act suggest several reasons for its promulgation. These include the uncertainties created by existing wrongful discharge law; the inherent desirability of state-by-state uniformity; the very high recoveries some discharged employees have received; the tendency for successful plaintiffs to be from middle- or upper-level management rather than from the rank-and-file; and the cost, delays, and unpredictability of wrongful discharge suits. *Id.* at 540:21, 540:23. The act's basic philosophy is said to be "one of compromise—an equitable

tradeoff of competing interests." *Id.* at 540:23. For background commentary regarding uniform wrongful discharge legislation, see, e.g., Henry H. Perritt, Jr., *Wrongful Dismissal Legislation,* 35 UCLA L. REV 65 (1987). For post-promulgation commentary on the act, *see, e.g., "Tell It to the Arbitrator",* BUS. WK. (Nov. 4, 1991), at 109; Randall Samborn, *At-Will Doctrine Under Fire: Model Act Divides Employment Bar,* NAT'L L.J., October 14, 1991, at 1.

2. Model Act., *supra* note 1, § 2(b). However, the act does not displace termination rights or claims arising under: (1) state or federal statutes or administrative regulations, (2) a collective bargaining agreement, and (3) an express written or oral agreement relating to employment. *Id.* § 2(d). Employees not subject to the act's provisions generally retain their common-law wrongful discharge rights (unless superseded by some other law). *Id.* § 2(c).

3. *Id.* § 1(2). Section 1(2) defines an employer as a "person" that "employs five or more employees . . . for each working day in each of 20 or more calendar weeks in the current or next preceding calendar year, excluding any employee who is the parent, spouse, child, or other member of the employer's immediate family." The term "person" means an individual, corporation, business trust, estate, trust, partnership, association, joint venture, or any other legal or commercial entity. *Id.* § 1(7). The coverage of government employees is left to local option. *Id.,* Comment, paragraph (7).

4. *Id.* § 3(a). This provision, however, applies only to employees who have been employed by the same employer for a total period of at least one year, and who have worked for the employer for at least 520 hours during the 26 weeks preceding the termination. *Id.* § 3(b).

    The act defines good cause as: (1) a reasonable basis for termination in view of relevant factors and circumstances, or (2) the exercise of good-faith business judgment by the employer. *Id.* § 1(4). Specific examples of good cause firings under the first option include those based on an employee's theft, assault, on-the-job fighting, destruction of property, on-the-job use or possession of drugs or alcohol, insubordination, excessive absenteeism or tardiness, incompetence, lack of productivity, inadequate job performance, and neglect of duty. *Id.,* Comment, paragraph 4. Regarding the second option, the comment adds that "an employer's decision as to the economic goals and methodologies of the enterprise and the size and composition of the work force . . . shall be governed by honest business judgment."

5. *See id.* §§ 5–7. The remedies an arbitrator can award basically are limited to: (1) reinstatement, (2) backpay, (3) a severance payment, and/or (4) attorney's fees and costs. *Id.* § 7(b).

6. *Id.* § 4(b). However, an employer must agree that if an employee is discharged for reasons other than willful misconduct, it will give him severance pay equalling at least one month's wages for each full year of employment, up to a maximum total payment of thirty months' pay. *Id.* A valid agreement under this subsection constitutes a waiver by both employer and employee of the right to a civil trial regarding disputes about the nature of the termination. *Id.* In addition, a valid and appropriately drafted waiver probably would disclaim the employee's common-law wrongful discharge rights. *See id.* § 2(b) (common-law wrongful-discharge claims are extinguished when an employee is subject to a severance pay agreement under § 4(b)).

7. *See, e.g.,* Samborn, *supra* note 1, at 1.

8. *E.g.,* Elletta S. Callahan, *The Public Policy Exception to the Employment at Will Rule Comes of Age: A Proposed Framework for Analysis,* 29 AM. BUS. L.J. 481, 517 (1991) (quoting a source describing the act as "basically dead" even before the Commission approved it). Of course, nonuniform state statutory responses also are possible and already have been enacted. *See* MONT. CODE. ANN. §§ 39–2–901 to 39–2–914 (1992) imposing various standards for covered discharges, including a good-cause standard, while also limiting damage recoveries and permitting arbitration for wrongful discharge claims). *See also* P.R. LAWS ANN. tit. 29, § 185a (1985) (establishing a good-cause standard, and basing indemnity for its violation on the employee's length of service).

9. The traditional formulation of the familiar doc-

trine of employment at will says that either party to an employment contract of indefinite duration can terminate the contract without liability for good cause, for bad cause, or for no cause whatever. *See infra* text accompanying notes 15, 18.

10. Articles that tend to fit this description include Richard A. Epstein, *In Defense of the Contract at Will,* 51 U. CHI. L. REV. 946 (1984); Mayer G. Freed & Daniel D. Polsby, *Just Cause for Termination Rules and Economic Efficiency,* 38 EMORY, L.J. 1097 (1989); Lary S. Larson, *Why We Should Not Abandon the Presumption That Employment is Terminable at Will,* 23 IDAHO L. REV. 219 (1986–87); Ian Maitland, *Rights in the Workplace: A Nozickian Argument,* 8 J. BUS. ETHICS 951 (1989); Richard A. Posner, *Hegel and Employment at Will: A Comment,* 10 CARDOZO L. REV. 1625 (1989); Richard W. Power, *A Defense of the Employment at Will Rule,* 27 ST. LOUIS U. L.J. 881 (1983).

11. Legal articles that more or less fit this description include Lawrence E. Blades, *Employment at Will Vs. Individual Freedom: On Limiting the Abusive Exercise of Employer Power,* 67 COLUM. L. REV. 1404 (1967); Peter Linzer, *The Decline of Assent: At-Will Employment as a Case Study of the Breakdown of Private Law Theory,* 20 GA. L. REV. 323, 375–424 (1986); Ellen Rust Peirce, Richard A. Mann, & Barry S. Roberts, *Employee Termination At Will: A Principled Approach,* 28 VILL. L. REV. 1, 36–50 (1982–83); Clyde W. Summers, *Individual Protection Against Unjust Dismissal: Time for a Statute,* 62 VA. L. REV. 481 (1976); Note, *Protecting At-Will Employees Against Wrongful Discharge: The Duty to Terminate Only in Good Faith,* 93 HARV. L. REV. 1816, 1828–44 (1980). Several business ethics works sound the same general line. *See, e.g.,* PATRICIA H. WERHANE, PERSONS, RIGHTS, AND CORPORATIONS ch. 4 (paperback ed. 1985); Joseph Des Jardins, *Fairness and Employment-At-Will,* 16 J. SOC. PHIL. 31 (1985); Joseph R. Des Jardins & John J. McCall, *A Defense of Employee Rights,* 4 J. BUS. ETHICS 367, 369 (1985).

12. *E.g.,* Jay M. Feinman, *The Development of the Employment at Will Rule,* 20 AM. J. LEGAL HIST. 118, 119–21 (1976). Even within the one-year period, however, the contract also could be terminated, if reasonable notice was given. *Id.* at 121. The contract also could be terminated for just cause. Daniel A. Matthews, Note, *A Common Law Action for the Abusively Discharged Employee,* 26 HASTINGS L.J. 1435, 1439 (1975).

13. *E.g.,* Matthews, *supra* note 12, at 1439.

14. *See generally* Feinman, *supra* note 12, at 122–24 (sketching the confusion). For example, some courts presumed that the hiring could continue for a time equal to the employee's pay period, while others made the matter a fact question for the jury. Kelly McWilliams, Note, *The Employment Handbook as a Contractual Limitation on the Employment at Will Doctrine,* 31 VILL. L. REV. 335, 338 n. 10 (1986).

15. HORACE G. WOOD, A TREATISE ON THE LAW OF MASTER AND SERVANT § 134, at 272 (1877) (footnotes omitted).

16. J. Peter Shapiro & James F. Tune, *Implied Contract Rights to Job Security,* 26 STAN. L. REV. 335, 341–42 n.54 (1974).

17. *E.g.,* Feinman, supra note 12, at 126.

18. Payne v. Western & Atlantic R.R., 81 Tenn. 507, 519–20 (1884).

19. John W. Blackburn, *Restricted Employer Discharge Rights: A Changing Concept of Employment at Will,* 17 AM. BUS. L.J. 467, 467–68 (1980).

20. Wood said that an indefinite hiring is "only at the rate fixed for whatever time the party may serve." *See Supra* text accompanying note 15. Even if that rate somehow were deemed unreasonable, quasi-contract can justify an employee's ability to recover the reasonable value of her services.

21. *See, e.g.,* Larson, *supra* note 10, at 221–24.

22. Perhaps the most significant example is federal labor law, which has generated a collective bargaining system through which most union contracts have come to include just-cause termination provisions that are enforced through arbitration. *See, e.g.,* Summers, *supra* note 11, at 482–83, 491–92, 499–508. By now, moreover, federal, state, and even local employees may enjoy some protection against arbitrary discharge. *E.g., id.* at 497–98; Note, *Protecting*

Employees at Will Against Wrongful Discharge: The Public Policy Exception, 96 HARV. L. REV. 1931, 1934 (1983). Federal employment discrimination law also constitutes a major exception to the at-will rule. *E.g.,* 29 U.S.C. § 623(a) (1988) (age discrimination); 42 U.S.C. § 2000e2(a) (1988) (race, color, religion, sex, and national origin discrimination); 42 U.S.C.A. § 12112(a) (1992 pamphlet) (discrimination based on disbility). For some miscellaneous statutes that encroach upon the rule, *see, e.g.,* Summers, *supra,* at 492–97; Matthews, *supra* note 12, at 1446–47; McWilliams, *supra* note 14, at 343. *See also* 29 U.S.C.A. § 2002 (Supp. 1992) (prohibited firings under the Employee Polygraph Protection Act).

23. For example, promissory estoppel has been used to circumvent the at-will rule. *See, e.g.,* Cheryl V. Brady, Note, *Ravello v. County of Hawaii: Promissory Estoppel and the Employment-at-Will Doctrine,* 8 U. HAWAII L. REV. 163 (1986). Also, some firings may create international tort liability. *See, e.g.,* McWilliams, *supra* note 14, at 344–45 (intentional interference with contractual relations, defamation, invasion of privacy, misrepresentation, and intentional infliction of emotional distress).

24. *See* IERM, *supra* note 1, at 505:51–505:52, containing a 1991 chart which suggests that no more than five states still refuse to adopt any of the three major common-law wrongful discharge theories.

25. *Compare id.* (listing eleven states that have not definitely recognize the theory) *with* Henry J. Perritt, *Implied Covenant: Anachronism or Augur?,* 20 SETON HALL L. REV. 683, 687 (1990) (courts in all but six states have adopted the public policy exception).

26. *E.g.,* Kenneth T. Lopatka, *The Emerging Law of Wrongful Discharge—A Quadrennial Assessment of the Labor Law Issue of the 80s,* 40 BUS. LAW. 1, 16 (1984). For this reason, plaintiffs who succeed under the public policy theory may recover compensatory and punitive damages. *Id.*

27. Perritt, *supra* note 25, at 687.

28. *E.g.,* Lopatka, *supra* note 26, at 14–16.

29. *E.g.,* Henry H. Perritt, Jr., *The Future of Wrongful Dismissal Claims: Where Does Employer Self-Interest Lie?,* 58 U. CIN. L. REV. 397, 398

(1989) (state or federal constitution, statute, administrative regulation or common law).

30. *See, e.g.,* Lopatka, *supra* note 26, at 7 and cases cited therein.

31. *See, e.g., id.* at 8–11 & n.40; Note, *supra* note 22, at 1937 and cases cited in each.

32. *See, e.g.,* Lopatka, *supra* note 26, at 11; Note, *supra* note 22, at 1937 and cases cited in each.

33. RESTATEMENT (SECOND) OF CONTRACTS § 205 (1981).

34. *E.g.,* E. ALLAN FARNSWORTH, CONTRACTS § 7.17 (1982).

35. For example, its application to insurance contracts. Lopatka, *supra* note 26, at 23.

36. In this particular application, the implied covenant sometimes is treated as a tort theory of recovery. *See, e.g., id.* at 25.

37. *See* IERM, *supra* note 1, at 505:51–505:52. *Cf.* Perritt, *supra* note 25, at 690, 699, 702–06 (discussing cases from about a dozen states that recognize the covenant in some form).

38. RESTATEMENT (SECOND) OF CONTRACTS § 205, comment a (1981); Lopatka, *supra* note 26, at 23 (implied covenant imposes duty that neither party do anything that injures the other's right to receive the benefits of the agreement).

39. *See, e.g.,* Wagenseller v. Scottsdale Memorial Hosp., 710 P.2d 1025, 1040 (Ariz. 1985) (where the court made much this argument). What protection, then, does this reading of the implied covenant afford? The court suggested that it protects employees from discharges based on an employer's desire to avoid paying benefits the employee already has earned, and that it also would obligate employers to provide suitable working conditions and to pay employees for work they actually have done. *Id.* For some other limitations on the implied covenant of good faith and fair dealing, see Perritt, *supra* note 25, at 702–06.

40. Immediately after stating the proposition in *supra* text accompanying note 38, RESTATEMENT (SECOND) OF CONTRACTS § 205, comment a (1981) says that the covenant "excludes a variety of types of conduct characterized as involving 'bad faith' because they violate community standards of decency, fairness, or reasonableness."

41. *E.g.,* Monge v. Beebe Rubber Co., 316 A.2d 549, 551 (N.H. 1974).

42. *See* IERM, *supra* note 1, at 505:51–505:52. *But see* Perritt, *supra* note 29, at 411 (claiming that courts in virtually every state have adopted the implied-in-fact promise theory described below).

43. *See* Lopatka, *supra* note 26, at 19.

44. *See supra,* note 21 and accompanying text.

45. *See, e.g.,* Folcy v. Interactive Data Corp., 765 P.2d 373, 387 (Cal. 1988); Larson, *supra* note 10, at 230–31. Besides *Foley,* cases applying the implied-in-fact contract theory include Leikvold v. Valley View Hosp., 688 P.2d 170, 174 (Ariz. 1984); Morriss v. Coleman Co., 738 P.2d 841, 848–49 (Kan. 1987).

46. On this rationale, see generally Michael A. Chagares, Comment, *Limiting the Employment-at-Will Rule: Enforcing Policy Manual Promises Through Unilateral Contract Analysis,* 16 SETON HALL L. REV. 465, 477–89 (1986).

47. *See, e.g.,* Duldulao v. St. Mary of Nazareth Hosp., 505 N.E.2d 314, 318–19 (Ill. 1987); Lewis v. Equitable Life Assurance Soc'y, 389 N.W.2d 876, 882–83 (Minn. 1986).

48. *See, e.g.,* Toussaint v. Blue Cross & Blue Shield, 292 N.W.2d 880, 892 (Mich. 1980). *See also* Thompson v. St. Regis Paper Co., 685 P.2d 1081, 1087–88 (Wash. 1984). *Toussaint,* however, may have been tacitly overruled by a recent Michigan case. *See* Rowe v. Montgomery Ward & Co., 473 N.W.2d 268, 289 (1991) (Cavenaugh, J., dissenting) (suggesting as much about the majority opinion in the case).

49. Epstein, *supra* note 10, at 948.

50. *See* the sources cited *supra* in note 10.

51. *See supra* note 24 (suggesting that as many as five states still refuse to adopt any of the three major exceptions).

52. *See, e.g.,* Foley v. Interactive Data Corp., 765 P.2d 373, 379–80, 389–401 (1988) (rejecting a public policy claim because the policy the employer allegedly violated was insufficiently "public," and also holding that the implied covenant of good faith and fair dealing is not a tort claim); Rowe v. Montgomery Ward & Co., 473 N.W.2d 268, 289 (Mich. 1991) (Cavenaugh, C.J., dissenting) (asserting that the majority in the case had virtually overruled the *Toussaint* decision cited in *supra* note 48).

53. *See* Michael J. Phillips, *Disclaimers of Wrongful Discharge Liability: Time for a Crackdown* [in press with the WASHINGTON UNIVERSITY LAW QUARTERLY]. The literature on this subject tends to consist of pieces advising employers how to avoid having to follow their own promises about discharge policy. *See, e.g.,* Michael A. Chagares, *Utilization of the Disclaimer as an Effective Means to Define the Employment Relationship,* 17 HOFSTRA L. REV. 365, 380–99 (1989); John D. Coombe, *Employee Handbooks: Asset or Liability?,* 12 EMPLOYER REL. L.J. 4, 15–16 (1986); James G. Frierson, *How To Fire Without Getting Burned,* 67 PERSONNEL 44 (Sept., 1990); Kenneth R. Gilberg, *Employee Terminations: Risky Business,* 32 PERSONNEL ADMINISTRATOR 40 (March, 1987); William H. Holley, Jr. & Roger S. Wolters, *An Employment-at-Will Vulnerability Audit,* 66 PERSONNEL J. 130, 136 (April, 1987); Maureen Reidy Witt & Sandra R. Goldman, *Avoiding Liability in Employee Handbooks,* 14 EMPLOYEE REL. L.J. 5, 12–17 (1988); Cynthia Weber Scherb, Note, *The Use of Disclaimers to Avoid Employer Liability Under Employee Handbook Provisions,* 12 J. CORP. L. 105 (1986).

54. *See* Jonathan Tompkins, *Legislating the Employment Relationship: Montana's Wrongful-Discharge Law,* 14 EMPLOYEE REL. L.J. 387, 392 (1988).

55. *See supra* note 8.

56. *See, e.g., Tell It to the Arbitrator, supra* note 1, at 109.

57. *See supra* notes 1–8 and accompanying text.

58. Because I later conclude that we cannot now determine employment at will's implications for utility, I fortunately need not list and consider those criticisms. For a sampling, see, e.g., G.E. MOORE, PRINCIPIA ETHICA ch. 3 (1903); RICHARD A. POSNER, THE ECONOMICS OF JUSTICE 51–60 (paperback ed. 1983); JAMES RACHELS, THE ELEMENTS OF MORAL PHILOSOPHY chs. 7–8 (1986); Bernard Williams, *A Critique of Utilitarianism,* in J.J.C. SMART & BERNARD WILLIAMS (EDS.), UTILITARIANISM: FOR AND AGAINST 75–150 (paperback ed. 1973).

59. *See, e.g.,* ALAN H. GOLDMAN, THE MORAL FOUNDATIONS OF PROFESSIONAL ETHICS 24–27 (paperback ed. 1980).

60. *E.g.,* RACHELS, *supra* note 58, at 101 (there is a sense in which no moral philosopher can completely reject utilitarianism, because all must admit that the consequences of actions are extremely important).

61. *See, e.g.,* Russell Hardin, *The Utilitarian Logic of Liberalism,* 97 ETHICS 47 (1984); J.J.C. Smart, *An Outline of a System of Utilitarian Ethics,* in SMART & WILLIAMS, *supra* note 58, at 3–74.

62. *See, e.g.,* RONALD DWORKIN, A MATTER OF PRINCIPLE 245–46 (1985) (commenting on the work of Richard Posner). *But see* POSNER, *supra* note 58, at 51–87 (trying to give wealth-maximization an ethical basis distinct from utilitarianism, but in my judgment failing adequately to do so).

63. *See, e.g.,* WILLIAM K. FRANKENA, ETHICS 35 (paperback ed. 1963) (advocating a "mixed deontological theory" in which the claims of utility somehow are balanced against the claims of justice); W.D. ROSS, THE RIGHT AND THE GOOD 18–22 (1930) (sketching several classes of prima facie duties, each of them binding unless outweighed by another prima facie duty against which it is intuitionistically weighed; and including among them duties of beneficence, which include duties to make other beings better in terms of pleasure).

64. *E.g.,* Model Act, *supra* note 1, § 1(4)(ii); Note, *Employer Opportunism and the Need for a Just Cause Standard,* 103 HARV. L. REV. 510, 511 (1989). *See supra* note 4.

65. *E.g.,* Posner, *supra* note 10, at 1633. However, a recent study by the RAND Institute for Civil Justice suggests that such "direct legal costs" are not excessive. *See* JAMES N. DERTOUZOS & LYNN A. KAROLY, LABOR-MARKET RESPONSES TO EMPLOYER LIABILITY 35–36 (1992) [hereinafter cited as Rand Study]. The authors estimate that in California in 1987, the average litigation-related cost per at-will employee (included awards or settlements, plus legal expenses) was ten dollars; the "expected legal cost" of terminating one at-will employee was about $100.

66. *E.g.,* Posner, *supra* note 10, at 1633.

67. *E.g., id.* at 1634 (employers would search longer before hiring a worker). The Rand Study, *supra* note 65, reached the conclusion that legally-enforced job protection generates greater costs of doing business by an interesting, if indirect, route. First, the study found that after states adopt the most pro-employee tort-based versions of the implied covenant of good faith and fair dealing or a broad version of the public policy exception, aggregate employment within the state drops significantly (on the order of two to five percent). *Id.* at 62; *see id.* at 46–61. From this, the study surmised that employers must have incurred significant "indirect" costs brought about by new human-resource practices made in response to changes in the law. *Id.* at 63. However, the authors admitted that as yet there are no case studies directly documenting those changed practices and those costs. *Id.* at 65. In fact, given the relatively low direct legal expenses attributable to the common law exceptions, *see supra* note 65, the authors wondered why the exceptions would produce so profound a response. As they put it: "Personnel managers may be reacting to perceived rather than actual legal risks." *Id.* at 64.

68. This loss might be borne by employees themselves. *See, e.g.,* Freed & Polsby, *supra* note 10, at 1102 (monopoly employers who are legally compelled to provide job tenure would institute an offsetting wage reduction, thus leaving their labor costs unchanged). As will be discussed later, however, it is unlikely that many employers have a monopoly—technically, a monopsony or oligopsony—position. *See infra* notes 120–33 and accompanying text. In cases where an employer lacks the power to impose an offsetting wage reduction, the costs will fall somewhere else. *See, e.g.,* Jeffrey Harrison, *The "New" Terminable-at-Will Employment Contract: An Interest and Cost Incidence Analysis,* 69 IOWA L. REV. 327, 342–44 (1984) (costs of increased job security not borne by employees are absorbed by employer, or by consumers of employer's products or services).

69. *E.g.,* Peirce, Mann, & Roberts, *supra* note 11, at 43.

70. *E.g.,* Note, *supra* note 11, at 1834–35.

71. *See* Freed & Polsby, *supra* note 10, at 1104 (merely stating the argument).

72. *E.g.,* Note, *supra* note 11, at 1834.

73. *E.g., id.* at 1833–34; Peirce, Mann, & Roberts, *supra* note 11, at 44–45.

74. *E.g.,* Des Jardins, *supra* note 11, at 35–37.

75. *See infra* notes 146–47 and accompanying text.

76. *Cf.* Posner, *supra* note 11, at 1631, who asserts that under employment at will it is not clear whether a firing "on average [will] hurt the employee more than a quit will hurt the employer," because "the employee may be compensated ex ante for this risk (for example, by being paid a higher wage)."

77. Power, *supra* note 10, at 892.

78. *Id.* at 892–93. *See also* Epstein, *supra* note 10, at 972.

79. *See* Power, *supra* note 10, at 891.

80. *E.g.,* Posner, *supra* note 10, at 1634 (because just-cause discharge increases employers' labor costs, they hire less, automate more, and relocate their plants to foreign countries). On those costs, see *supra* notes 65–68 and accompanying text. In fact, a recent study claims that signficant drops in aggregate employment followed states' adoption of pro-employee versions of the exceptions to employment at will. *See supra* note 67.

81. *E.g.,* WALTER NICHOLSON, MICROECONOMIC THEORY: BASIC PRINCIPLES AND EXTENSIONS 77–78 (4th ed. 1989).

82. "If one person reports that a steak dinner provides a utility of '5' and another reports that the same dinner offers a utility of '100,' we cannot say which individual values the dinner more since they could be using very different scales." *Id.*

83. Act-utilitarianism asserts that the criterion for the rightness or wrongness of an act is *that act's* consequences for aggregate utility. The main alternative, rule-utilitarianism, asserts that the criterion for the rightness or wrongness of an act is its congruence with the *rule* that would maximize aggregate utility if consistently followed in like circumstances. *See* Smart, *supra* note 58, at 9.

84. RAND Study, *supra* note 65, at 64–65 tries to discuss the costs and benefits of employment at will's common-law exceptions, but the discussion is brief and inconclusive.

85. Ross, *supra* note 63, at 21.

86. *See* Linzer, *supra* note 11, at 326–27, 334, 367–69, 390, 419–20 (speaking both legally and normatively). One problem with such arguments, however, is the familiar logical gulf between "is" and "ought": how do moral obligations derive from a relationship that at first glance seems a mere *fact*? Even if this hurdle is surmounted, how does the relationship between employer and employee give rise to *this particular* obligation (a duty to fire only for good cause) rather than some other duty?

87. Due to the familiar charge that it is indeterminate in its application, I will not consider Kant's various "universalization" formulations of the imperative. For such criticisms, see, e.g., ALASDAIR MACINTYRE, A SHORT HISTORY OF ETHICS 197–98 (paperback ed. 1966); RACHELS, *supra* note 58, at 108–09 (paperback ed. 1986).

88. IMMANUEL KANT, GROUNDWORK OF THE METAPHYSIC OF MORALS 96 (H.J. Paton tr., Harper Torchbook ed. 1964) (italics omitted).

89. *See* RACHELS, *supra* note 58, at 116–17.

90. WERHANE, *supra* note 11, at 89.

91. I say "employers or their managers" in order to avoid discussing whether corporations and other business entities are "moral persons": the kinds of entities that themselves can have moral duties, duties which may differ from those of their human components.

92. WERHANE, *supra* note 11, at 143 (procedural guarantee of explanation from employer plus substantive right to good reasons for firing); Des Jardins, *supra* note 11, at 32–33 (due process right to be terminated only on a nonarbitrary basis); David R. Hiley, *Employee Rights and the Doctrine of At Will Employment,* 4 BUS. & PROF. ETHICS J. 1, 3 (1985) (property right to same effect).

93. *See e.g.,* MICHAEL J. PERRY, MORALITY, POLITICS, AND LAW 187 (paperback ed. 1988).

94. *See* WERHANE, *supra* note 11, at 17–18 (recognizing these rights).

95. Des Jardins & McCall, *supra* note 11, at 369.

96. The term "inalienable right," of course, has been variously defined. Here, I treat inalienable rights as rights which their possessors cannot justifiably yield, even if the relinquishment is knowing and voluntary. *E.g.,* Joel Feinberg, *Vol-*

untary Euthanasia and the Inalienable Right to Life, 7 PHIL. & PUB. AFFAIRS 93, 112, 113 (1978) (defining the term this way). Some contemporary philosophers apparently maintain that *no* rights are inalienable. *See* John O. Nelson, *Are There Inalienable Rights?,* 64 PHILOSOPHY 519 (1989); Marvin Schiller, *Are There Any Inalienable Rights?,* 79 ETHICS 309 (1969); Donald Van De Veer, *Are Human Rights Alienable?,* 37 PHIL. STUD. 165 (1980). While perhaps avoiding this categorical position, others have concluded that some very important rights can be alienated—for example, the right to life, *see* Lance K. Stell, *Dueling and the Right to Life,* 90 ETHICS 7 (1979), and the right not to be someone's slave, ROBERT NOZICK, ANARCHY, STATE, AND UTOPIA 331 (paperback ed. 1974).

In addition, the right not to be arbitrarily fired seems remote from the rights some other philosophers *have* regarded as inalienable: for example, the rights to life, to be free from torture, and to liberty or a set of basic liberties. *See, e.g.,* J.S. MILL, UTILITARIANISM, ON LIBERTY, AND CONSIDERATIONS ON REPRESENTATIVE GOVERNMENT 171–72 (Everyman's Library paperback ed. 1972) (right to liberty); A. John Simmons, *Inalienable Rights and Locke's Treatises,* 12 PHIL. & PUB. AFFAIRS 175, 182–83 (1983) (mentioning all the named rights as favorite candidates for inalienability over time, without endorsing their inalienability).

Finally, the claim that employee dismissal rights are inalienable seems implausible when we consider the criteria sometimes adduced for identifying such inalienable rights, if any, as exist. One of these is the notion that inalienable rights are those people possess simply by virtue of their humanity. *E.g.,* Simmons, *supra,* at 187–88 (not necessarily endorsing their view). Although this criterion's meaning and application are unclear, one can identify numerous rights that seem more essential to a person's "humanity" than the right not to be fired without good cause, and that also may be alienable. Another possible criterion is the irrationality of yielding a particular right. *E.g., id.* at 201–04. This test is discussed extensively below. *See infra* notes 140–48 and accompanying text,

where it is concluded that in certain cases it is eminently rational to deal away one's right not to be arbitrarily fired.

97. *E.g.,* David Archard, *Freedom Not To Be Free: The Case of the Slavery Contract in J.S. Mill's On Liberty,* 40 PHIL. Q. 453, 455 (1990) (involuntariness, ignorance, coercion, and mental incompetence, *inter alia,* valid reasons not to enforce agreement); Joel Feinberg, *Legal Paternalism,* 1 CANADIAN J. PHIL. 105, 110 (1971) (equating voluntariness with full information and the absence of compulsion).

98. *E.g.,* Peter Stone Partee, *Reversing the Presumption of Employment at Will,* 44 VAND. L. REV. 689, 702 (1991) (commentators most often identify unequal bargaining power as the market failure responsible for causing the prevalence of at-will employment).

99. Blades, *supra* note 11, at 1404.

100. Epstein, *supra* note 10, at 973. Epstein did devote about four pages to the bargaining power question, but he did not discuss any of the reasons usually advanced to explain why employers have superior power over their employees. *See id,* at 973–77.

101. Maitland, *supra* note 10, at 954.

102. *Id.*

103. Epstein's argument appeared in Richard A. Epstein, *A Common Law for Labor Relations: A Critique of the New Deal Labor Legislation,* 92 YALE L.J. 1357, 1382 (1983).

104. Linzer, *supra* note 11, at 414.

105. *Id.*

106. *See infra* notes 167–69 and accompanying text.

107. Courts sometimes seem to use superior size as a proxy for superior bargaining power. *See, e.g.,* A & M Produce Co. v. FMC Corp., 186 Cal, Rptr. 114, 125 (1982) (in the unconscionability context). *See also* Michael J. Phillips, *Unconscionability and Article 2 Implied Warranty Disclaimers,* 62 CHI.-KENT L. REV. 199, 235–36 (1985) (explaining a number of unconscionability cases involving disclaimers of implied warranty liability between commercial parties on this basis).

108. The classic account is Friedrich Kessler, *Contracts of Adhesion—Some Thoughts About Freedom of Contract,* 43 COLUM. L. REV. 629 (1943).

109. *See* FARNSWORTH, *supra* note 34, at 294–95 (distinguishing these two forms of "power").

110. *See* the sources cited in *supra* note 53. These sources provide considerable additional support for the generalizations in the remainder of this paragraph.

111. *E.g.,* Therrien v. United Airlines, Inc., 670 F. Supp. 1517, 1519 (D. Colo. 1987).

112. *E.g.,* Bailey v. Perkins Restaurants, Inc., 398 N.W.2d 120, 121 (N.D. 1986).

113. *See* Phillips, *supra* note 53 (dealing specifically with this factor).

114. Indeed, disclaimers normally are used in an effort to negate an employer's specific promises. *See infra* text accompanying note 116.

115. For numerous examples, see Phillips, *supra* note 53.

116. Nonetheless, a few courts have allowed disclaimers to block recovery under the implied covenant of good faith and fair dealing. *See id.* But these invariably involve the weak version of the covenant, *see supra* notes 38–39 and accompanying text, described earlier.

117. *E.g.,* Small v. Springs Indus., Inc., 357 S.E.2d 452, 454 (S.C. 1988) (employers should not be allowed to issue potentially misleading personnel manuals while reserving the right to disregard them at their option).

118. Epstein, *supra* note 10, at 955.

119. See *infra* text following note 175.

120. *E.g.,* Harrison, *supra* note 68, at 351–52 & n.129. Sometimes the situation where only one purchaser of labor exists is called a monopsony, and the situation where several buyers exist is called an oligopsony. *E.g.,* SAUL D. HOFFMAN, LABOR MARKET ECONOMICS 47 (1986).

121. *E.g.,* HOFFMAN, *supra* note 120, at 48–49 (in monopsony, balance of power shifts toward employer, and outcomes are clearly less favorable to workers). The countervailing power of a union, however, can check an employer's monopsony power. *See, e.g., id.* at 49. Here, however, we are not concerned with unionized employment, because labor contracts typically provide for just-cause discharge.

122. "Employees sometimes exercise market power. For example, many employers will compete to offer jobs to persons such as Clint Eastwood or Lee Iacocca. . . . Anyone who has a skill that is "in shortage—repairing BMWs, grinding contact lenses for sea lions, writing MS-DOS software—has the upper hand in bargaining." Freed & Polsby, *supra* note 10, at 1101.

123. *E.g.,* BELTON M. FLEISHER & THOMAS J. KNIESNER, LABOR ECONOMICS: THEORY, EVIDENCE, AND POLICY 204 (3d ed. 1970); DANIEL S. HAMERMESH & ALBERT REES, THE ECONOMICS OF WORK AND PAY 121–22 (3d ed. 1984); HOFFMAN, *supra* note 120, at 49.

124. *E.g.,* FLEISHER & KNIESNER, *supra* note 123, at 204; HAMERMESH & REES, *supra* note 123, at 122. The traditional pattern in professional sports is a possible example. *See, e.g.,* FLEISHER & KNIESNER, *supra* note 123, at 213–18; HAMERMESH & REES, *supra* note 123, at 120–21.

125. HAMERMESH & REES, *supra* note 123, at 122.

126. One possible example is nursing. First, nursing is a specialized skill. Second, most nurses work for hospitals, and in many areas there are only a few hospital-employers within the relevant territorial market. Third, married nurses with a working spouse often have little mobility. *See* HOFFMAN, *supra* note 120, at 53–54.

127. *E.g.,* FLEISHER & KNIESNER, *supra* note 123, at 213 ("we feel confident that monopsony is not widespread today"); HAMERMESH & REES, *supra* note 123, at 121 ("[t]here is some reason to think that the monopsony case has been given more attention in textbooks and the economics literature than its actual importance would warrant"); HOFFMAN, *supra* note 120, at 49 (unclear "whether monopsony today is common enough to constitute a serious problem"); *id.* at 52 ("[p]ure monopsony is almost certainly less common today that [sic] it was 75 to 100 years ago").

128. "Modern roads and relatively cheap used automobiles make workers quite mobile, so that the company town is largely a thing of the past." FLEISHER & KNIESNER, *supra,* note 123, at 213. "It is now practical and common for American workers to commute up to 25 miles to work, and very few employers provide the bulk of employment within a 25-mile radius of their establishments." HAMERMESH & REES, *supra* note 123, at 122.

129. *E.g.*, FLEISHER & KNIESNER, *supra* note 123, at 213 (employer collusion does not seem widespread).

130. "[T]hese agreements must be very difficult to enforce. . . . When labor markets become tight, the temptation for the parties to collusive agreements to violate or evade them probably becomes irresistible." HAMERMESH & REES, *supra* note 123, at 122. The authors also note that such agreements are unnecessary in loose labor markets, because in that case there is an abundance of labor and no upward pressure on wages or other employment terms. *Id.*

131. *See* FLEISHER & KNIESNER, *supra* note 123, at 212–13.

132. *E.g.*, Blades, *supra* note 11, at 1405. In addition, sometimes it is maintained that the unemployment which is a more or less permanent feature of the U.S. economy gives employers a bargaining edge. In such an environment, the foes of employment at will say, "it is meaningless to maintain that an employee who has no alternative employment available has the freedom to leave his job." Peirce, Mann, & Roberts, *supra* note 11, at 38–39. For this reason, the employee has to accept his employer's terms. But while the argument seems true as far as it goes, how far does it go? For one thing, how often does the postulated condition—no alternative employment—really exist? Sometimes, after all, employees (especially valuable employees) have desirable options. Even if all that is available is a less desirable job, that option still puts some limits on an employer's ability to extract onerous terms.

Admittedly, however, *some* segment of the work force presumably will be without options if unemployment is at any finite percentage. But aside from the possibility that some of the affected people do not desire work, this is not necessarily a permanent status. Overall, though, it may be true that employers have a general edge if, say, 100 workers are chasing 95 jobs. But *how much* of an edge? And in which segments of the labor market?

133. Posner, *supra* note 11, at 1632. *See also* HAMERMESH & REES, *supra* note 123, at 122:

In this case [specialization], . . . the monopsony power is bilateral. The workers have nowhere else to go without leaving the area, but the employer has no local labor supply beyond present employees. Attempting to exploit this position beyond obtaining a fair return on investment in specialized training will increase the movement of workers to other areas and could produce losses on past investment in them.

134. RICHARD A. POSNER, ECONOMIC ANALYSIS OF LAW 300 (3d ed. 1986).

135. The arguments made immediately below also may apply to the situations, if any, where an employer's monopsony power is wholly or partially based on employees' possession of specialized skills and the difficulty they face in acquiring new skills. Here, the foes of employment at will essentially would be arguing that, beyond a certain point, employees should not be required to acquire new skills that they are hypothetically capable of acquiring.

136. On negative freedom, *see e.g.*, ISAIAH BERLIN, FOUR ESSAYS ON LIBERTY 122 (paperback ed. 1969) (one is negatively free when no one interferes with his activity).

137. *See supra* notes 65–68 and accompanying text.

138. *See, e.g.*, Harrison, supra note 68, at 342–44; Note, *supra* note 11, at 1829 n.77.

139. *See supra* note 94 and accompanying text (linking freedom of contract to autonomy).

140. *See infra* note 174.

141. WERHANE, *supra* note 11, at 91.

142. *Cf.* Maitland, *supra* note 10, at 953 (employees' preference for employment at will may derive in part from their perception that most employers do not abuse the doctrine).

143. *See* Epstein, *supra* note 10, at 966–67.

144. *Id.* at 969.

145. *Compare* WERHANE, supra note 11, at 151 (asymmetry of rights between employer and employee justified because employer exercises power over employee) and Des Jardins, *supra* note 11, at 35–37 (due process for employees, but not for employers, is justified because arbitrary termination of relationship causes greater harm to employees than to employers on average) *with* Posner, *supra* note 10, at 1631 (allow-

ing employee to demand a reason for being fired logically entails employer's right to demand the same when employee quits; result is that employee may be chained to a bad job). In response to the point made by Des Jardins, Posner replies that "the employee may be compensated ex ante for this risk (for example, by being paid a higher wage)." Posner, *supra* note 10, at 1631.

146. *See supra* notes 65–68 and accompanying text.
147. Maitland, *supra* note 10, at 952.
148. *Cf.* Des Jardins, *supra* note 71, at 35 ("since we are concerned here with people and not objects, supply and demand is an improper means for establishing value").
149. Epstein, *supra* note 10, at 951.
150. *E.g.,* RESTATEMENT (SECOND) OF CONTRACTS § 204, comment d (1981) (in supplying an omitted essential term, courts should supply "a term which comports with community standards of fairness and policy" when the parties clearly have not agreed). *Cf.* Epstein, *supra* note 10, at 951, 952 (suggesting, *inter alia,* a construction's good sense and inherent desirability as criteria).
151. *E.g.,* RESTATEMENT (SECOND) OF CONTRACTS § 204, comment d (1981) ("probability that a particular term would have been used if the question had been raised" a factor in determining which omitted essential term to suply); Epstein, *supra* note 10, at 951 (rule of construction should reflect "the dominant practice in a given class of cases").
152. "The contract at will is not ideal for every employment relation. No court of legislature should ever command its use." Epstein, *supra* note 10, at 951. *See also id.* at 951–52 (recognizing that parties always can contract out of the preferred construction of indefinite-term employment agreements).
153. *Id.* at 955.
154. Maitland, *supra* note 10, at 953.
155. Epstein, *supra* note 11, at 956.
156. *Id.*
157. *See supra* notes 142–48 and accompanying text.
158. *See supra* text accompanying note 147.
159. *See, e.g.,* ROBERTO MANGABEIRA UNGER, KNOWLEDGE, AND POLITICS 38–46 (1975).

160. In addition to the points made below, some isolated anecdotal evidence suggests the same. *See* Raymond L. Hilgert, *How At-Will Statements Hurt Employers,* 67 PERSONNEL J. 75 (February, 1988). Here, Professor Hilgert reports on an unscientific informal survey of sixty business students. When asked whether they would sign a job application containing an at-will statement, eighty percent of the students said that they would do so if this was necessary to obtain a job. In addition, all sixty said that, all other things being equal, they would prefer employment with a firm that did not require them to sign such a statement. Finally, various students regarded an employer's imposition of such terms as insensitive, demeaning, and domineering. However, Professor Hilgert apparently did not ask his students whether they would sign an at-will statement to get higher pay.
161. *See supra* notes 65–68 and accompanying text.
162. *See supra* notes 53, 110–17 and accompanying text.
163. *See* Partee, *supra* note 98, at 708–09 (making a similar argument).
164. For somewhat similar reasons, Peter Stone Partee makes a recommendation that parallels mine in certain respects. The recommendation is that courts scrap employment at will and establish a rebuttable presumption that employees can be fired only for just cause. *Id.* at 709. An employer could rebut the presumption by proving: (1) that it lacks monopoly [i.e., monopsony] power over the employee in question, and (2) some kind of at-will agreement. *Id.* The apparent reason for Partee's first requirement is that he does not consider the extent to which disparities in bargaining power actually characterize employment markets, instead remaining agnostic on the subject and on several occasions treating such disparities as a genuine possibility. *See generally id.* at 702–11. My general position, on the other hand, is that superior employer power is more the exception than the rule. *See generally supra* notes 103–33 and accompanying text. Of course, I do contemplate judicial intervention in cases where such power exists. *See infra* note 174 and accompanying text.

165. According to economists, a voluntary transaction between fully informed parties produces an allocation of resources that makes at least one party better off in dollar terms and no one worse off, assuming that the transaction has no effect on third parties. POSNER, *supra* note 134, at 12. Here, of course, I am assuming that greater wealth usually means greater utility, all other things being equal.

166. *See supra* notes 53, 110–17 and accompanying text.

167. *See, e.g.,* Harrison, *supra* note 68, at 356; Note, *supra* note 11, at 1830–31.

168. Harrison, *supra* note 68, at 356.

169. *See* Todd Rakoff, *Contracts of Adhesion: An Essay in Reconstruction,* 96 HARV. L. REV. 1174, 1222–23 (1983). *See also* RESTATEMENT (SECOND) OF CONTRACTS § 211, comments a, b (1981).

170. Maitland, *supra* note 10, at 952–53.

171. *See supra* note 165 and surrounding text.

172. *See infra* note 176 and following text.

173. *See supra* note 130 and accompanying text.

174. This probably can best be accomplished through the doctrine of common-law unconscionability. *E.g.,* FARNSWORTH, *supra* note 34, at 315. And where the dismissal was unjust, courts should have little difficulty finding substantive unconscionability.

175. *See supra* notes 110–17 and accompanying text.

176. *See* Phillips, *supra* note 53.

177. *See, e.g.,* Phillips, *supra* note 107, at 243 (arguing that freedom of contract cannot justify the enforcement of implied warranty disclaimers because consumers cannot understand their meaning and legal significance).

178. *See supra* text accompanying note 118.

179. Another reason why individualized contracting allegedly would fail to advance employee's interests is that such contracting undercuts their ability to bargain collectively and to get better terms for everyone from such bargaining. *See* Des Jardins & McCall, *supra* note 11, at 373. For example, it is argued that workers' shared interest in working nine (rather than ten or more) hours a day can only be achieved by suppressing individualized bargaining. *See* Hardin, *supra* note 61, at 58–62 (1986) (discussing Mill's argument to that effect). But even if the argument is correct in that situation, it has no application here. As I have been arguing all along, there simply is no discharge policy that is right for all employees. As a result, there is no collective interest of the kind postulated, save perhaps the interest in free, fully informed competition.

180. Note, *supra* note 11, at 1831–32.

181. *Id.* at 1833.

182. *See id.* at 1833–43.

183. *See supra* text accompanying note 142.

184. *See* Freed & Polsby, *supra* note 10, at 1105–07. Using data provided by foes of employment at will, the authors calculate yearly probabilities of .000154, .005768, and .002083 for various types of wrongful discharges. *Id.* at 1106–07. They also introduce a psychological study purporting to show that people overestimate the present disvalue of low-probability losses. *Id.* at 1107.

185. *See supra* notes 1–6 and accompanying text.

186. *See supra* text following note 176.

187. *See* Model Act, *supra* note 1, § 4(b) and Comment to § 4. However, the comment does say that section 4's intent is "not to allow so-called 'contracts of adhesion' to be used to waive or otherwise circumvent employee's rights under the Act." Also, section 4(b) gives employers some disincentive to disclaim by requiring them to agree to a graduated series of severance payments in the same writing containing the disclaimer. *See supra* note 6. The comment suggests that, as a practical matter, this provision will largely limit disclaimers' use to "management personnel, key professionals, and other persons not subject to periodic layoff." The reason is that workers laid off for more than two months can treat the layoff as a "termination" under the act, and thus trigger the severance pay provision. *See* Uniform Act, *supra* note 1, §§ 1(8)(ii), 4(b) and the comment to section 4.

188. IERM, *supra* note 1, at 540:23 ("Background and Summary" portion of Commissioners' opening statement to the model act).

189. *But see* Partee, *supra* note 98, at 708–11 and *supra* note 164 (outlining recommendations not dissimilar from those made here).

READING 6-3

Wrongful Termination: Balancing Employer and Employee Rights—A Summary with Recommendations

Robert J. Paul
James B. Townsend

INTRODUCTION

Since the emergence in 1978 of uniform guidelines on employee selection, nondiscriminatory employment decision making has been addressed extensively in the literature. Recent attention has shifted to the final stage of the employment process, termination. Whereas prior to 1980 an employer's right to terminate for any cause was virtually unchallenged, the judicial environment has changed, and wrongful termination has become one of the hottest issues in the workplace. Terminated employees often sue, and frequently they win. A Rand study estimates that employees in wrongful termination suits win 68% of the cases, and jury awards average more than $600,000 (Culbert & McDonough, 1990).

The purpose of this article is to review the background and legal framework of wrongful termination and to offer some guidelines to help employers avoid this emerging employment problem.

BACKGROUND

Traditionally, American courts have ruled that when workers are hired for indefinite intervals, either employer or employee can terminate the relationship at any time for any reason (Wood, 1886). This employment relationship, known as

Source: Employee Responsibilities and Rights Journal, 6(1) (1993), 69–82. Reprinted with permission of Plenum Publishing Corporation.

the "employment at will" or "termination-at-will" doctrine, is based on the principle that duration of employment is a matter of contract between free agents. Either party may sever the relationship at will, when there is no stated duration. Proponents of the doctrine hold that it promotes freedom in the labor market and increased labor productivity because either party can break the employment relationship for any reason and enter into a new, more satisfactory one. The "at will" doctrine is still pervasive and covers about 65% of American workers (Youngblood & Bierman, 1985). Thus, most of the work force has neither statutory nor expressed contractual protection against arbitrary discharge (Brake, 1982). However, three factors are eroding the "at-will" doctrine: (1) employee rights legislation; (2) the grievance and arbitration processes in union-management contracts, which cover about 17% of the American labor force; and (3) various court decisions (Koys, Briggs & Grenig, 1987).

The number of employees discharged annually is estimated at about 1% of the labor force. However, given greater employee awareness of workplace rights and their increasing willingness to seek legal solutions, this small percentage of the labor force accounts for large legal expenditures by employers. The situation is exacerbated by the erroneous belief that employees are without safeguards against arbitrary discharge and therefore must seek protection through wrongful termination suits. In this context, then, this article examines the legal framework that governs "termination at will."

THE LEGAL FRAMEWORK OF "TERMINATION AT WILL"

The doctrine of "termination at will" in America arose out of the master and servant laws of Great Britain. American doctrine, however, deviated from British law, which was based on both the terms of employment intended and the mutual obligation of reasonable notice. The

American concept of "termination at will," in contrast, turned toward the developing contract law and encompassed social, political, and economic forces. This change of focus fostered an individualistic laissez-faire approach to employment relations.

An employer's freedom to "terminate-at-will" is no longer *carte blanche* but is restricted by five general types of rules: statutory, arbitral, contractual, constitutional, and judicial (Youngblood & Bierman, 1985). A summary of each type follows.

Statutory Protection

Table I summarizes major federal laws concerning termination. Legal scholars have often attacked the "termination-at-will" doctrine because of the incongruity of the doctrine when ranged against other rules that protect specific groups of workers from unjust discharge (Peck, 1979). Federal courts seem to follow a situational approach, balancing the value of management prerogatives against the value of employee job security. Courts have tended to favor employee rights, unless it can be shown that termination was essential to the financial well-being of the firm (Buckley & Weitzel, 1988). "Termination-at-will" cases are heard in state courts, unless the firm is engaged in interstate commerce or the issues in dispute involve federal law.

In addition to federal statutes which restrict employee discharge, state statutes also limit an employer's right to discharge at will. Although many states still adhere to the "termination-at-will" doctrine, they differ widely in their interpretations of permitted exceptions. These exceptions are discussed under judicial protection, but first a look at arbitral protection.

Arbitral Protection

Protection is normally established where the collective bargaining agreement prohibits discharge without "just cause." Where the agreement contains no such statements, arbitrators may still infer such protection from other clauses such as seniority or grievance procedures (Hill & Sinicropi, 1981).

Arbitration of discharge claims has produced a considerable body of common law. That body has produced some principles concerning "just cause" discharge which can serve as guidelines. These are in summary as follows:

1. *Employee right to know what is prohibited.* Did the employer give the employee forewarning or knowledge of the disciplinary consequences of his or her conduct?
2. *Management's right to manage.* Were company rules reasonably related to orderly, efficient, and safe operation of the enterprise and the performance expected of the employee?
3. *Procedural fairness.* Did the company make an effort to fairly and objectively investigate the rule violation or disobedience of a management order?
4. *Right to equal treatment.* Have company rules, orders, and penalties been applied consistently to all employees?
5. *Corrective discipline.* Did management's punishment fit the crime, given the seriousness of the offense and the seniority of the employee (Youngblood & Bierman, 1985)?

Violations will probably result in an arbitrator's ruling that "just cause" did not exist. The consistency of arbitrators' rulings had led some scholars to advocate arbitration as a means of avoiding the potential consequences of wrongful termination. Although only about 17% of the labor force is unionized, arbitral protection is much more widespread. Nonunionized firms may also submit labor-management disputes to arbitration, and nonunion employees can avail themselves of union procedures in unionized plants.

Contractual Protection

Traditionally, employers have resisted employment contracts because they are thought to re-

TABLE 1

MAJOR FEDERAL STATUTES PROVIDING PROTECTION FROM EMPLOYMENT TERMINATION

Statute	Protection legislated
Railway Labor Act (1926)	Protection from discharge for union-related activities
National Labor Relations Act (1935)	Negotiated agreements providing for arbitration on unjust discharge disputes
Title VII of the Civil Rights Act (1964, 1972, 1978)	Protection from unjust discharge based on race, color, religion, sex, or national origin
Civil Service Reform Act (1978)	Just cause protection from discharge, grievance procedures, and appeal processes
Fair Labor Standards Act (1938)	Prohibits discharge for filing a complaint under the statute
Age Discrimination in Employment Act (1967, 1987)	Prohibits age-based discharge of persons over 40 years old
Rehabilitation Act (1973)	Prohibits federal contractors of federally supported programs from discriminating against handicapped persons
Vietnam Eva Veterans Readjustment Assistance Act (1979, 1982)	Provides veterans with protection from discharge from civilian service
Occupational Safety and Health Act (1970)	Prohibits discharge of employees in Railway reprisal for exercising their rights under these acts
Safety Act (1982)	
Energy Reorganization Act (1974)	Protect employees from discharge for instituting or testifying at proceedings against an employer in relation to these Acts
Clean Air Act (1981)	
Federal Water Pollution Control Act (1978)	
Employee Retirement Income Security Act (1974)	Prohibits discharge of employees to avoid the attainment of vested pension rights
Consumer Credit Protection Act (1982)	Prohibits discharge of employees for garnishment of wages for an indebtedness
Judiciary and Judicial Procedure Act (1982)	Prohibits discharge of employees who serve on juries in federal court

strict employers' right of control, to overformalize the employment relationship, and to tie the employer to an unproductive employee for the duration of the contract (Gumbel & Hoover, 1990). While these concerns may be valid, recent legal precedents with regard to wrongful termination make an employment contract valuable in employee recruitment and retention. A contract may also prevent costly legal problems, should the employment relationship become onerous to either party. A written contract, clarifying as it does the employment relationship by specifying the parties' obligations, can prevent a court's drafting terms and conditions of employment.

Employer resistance to employment contracts also has been based on the premise that in the absence of a written agreement, the employment relationship was subject to termination by either party for any reason. The impact of federal and state law has eroded this premise. Even more significant, however, is the trend by state courts to diminish the "at-will" doctrine still further by inferring contractual obligation from the employment relationship itself (Gumbel & Hoover, 1990). A December 1988 Bureau of National Affairs survey showed that courts in at least 39 states and the Virgin Islands have ruled that an employee simply cannot be terminated "at will."

Constitutional Protection

The 5th and 14th Amendments entitle public employees to constitutional protection. Constitutional protection implies that since employees have a property right in a job, they cannot be deprived of it without due process (French, 1990). Thus, an employee in the public sector is entitled to a hearing and a statement of the reasons for discharge. Constitutional protection therefore limits the power of government over its employees. Public sector employees enjoy the full range of constitutional rights on the job and are less subject to arbitrary or discriminatory employment practices than their private sector counterparts. This inherent protection has been enhanced by specific legislation (see Table I) which provides "just cause" protection, grievance procedures and appeal processes.

Judicial Protection

Although a state by state analysis reveals increasing activism, "termination at will" still governs employment. While many states adhere to the doctrine, others have made exceptions for one or more of the following reasons: (1) termination violated some aspect of public policy, (2) an implied contract prohibiting termination without good reason existed, (3) the employer committed a wrongful act under tort law, or (4) other exceptions. Exceptions follow.

Public Policy These exceptions hold that an employee's discharge is contrary to established public policy. What constitutes public policy has been subject to varying judicial interpretation.

Generally, it must be shown that the employer was guilty of bad faith, malice, or retaliation. Three employee defenses are normally available when public policy related discharges are contested. First, employees must show that they have been asked to commit an unlawful act (e.g., commit perjury). A second defense is that the employee was performing an important obligation or whistle blowing (e.g., jury duty or supplying information to the police about a law violation by the employer). A third defense is that an employee was exercising a statutory right or privilege (e.g., filing a worker's compensation claim).

The problem of varying judicial interpretation of public policy exceptions to "termination-at-will" involves an analysis of state laws, the state constitution, and other court rulings. Another problem with public policy exceptions is that they may be unknown to lower-level, less skilled employees who perceive and define fair treatment differently. Table II summarizes public policy issues that protect employees from arbitrary dismissal.

Implied Contracts The implied contract exception to the "termination-at-will" doctrine holds that statements in employee handbooks, job application forms, employment interviews, and/or personnel policies create a contract (Koys *et al.,* 1987). Such statements modify the "termination-at-will" relationship by implying that termination will be for "just cause" rather than merely any cause. This exception also holds that all contracts contain an implied agreement of good faith and fair dealing, requiring the parties to abide by the contract.

Handbooks, job application forms, realistic job previews, and personnel policies are excellent methods for employers to promote a sense of community with their employees and at the same time to establish the rules of the employment relationship. By following these rules employers can minimize legal risks with regard to "termination at will."

TABLE II

PUBLIC POLICY ISSUES PROTECTING EMPLOYEES FROM ARBITRARY DISCHARGE[a]

- Whistleblowing (e.g., opposing and publicizing policies or practices that violate laws such as the antitrust, consumer protection, or environmental protection laws)

- Garnishment for any one indebtedness

- Complaining or testifying about equal pay or wage/hour law violations

- Complaining or testifying about safety hazards and/or refusing an assignment because of the belief that the assignment is dangerous

- Engaging in union activities, provided there is no violence or unlawful behavior

- Engaging in concerted activity to protest wages, working conditions, or safety hazards

- Filing a worker's compensation claim

- Filing unfair labor practice charges with the NLRB or a state agency

- Cooperation in the investigation of a charge

- Reporting Occupational Safety and Health Administration (OSHA) violations

[a] *Source:* Schuler and Huber (1990), p. 470.

Before reviewing handbooks, employers need to consider two basic tenets: (1) Employees do not sue because of the handbook per se. Rather, they become involved in a disagreement and perceive mistreatment. The handbook simply becomes the mechanism for addressing this perceived mistreatment. (2) In constructing the handbook, employers should not overreact to the fear of litigation. The handbook should strike a balance between language that reduces the risk of liability and language that conveys a positive tone. With that in mind, the following guidelines are offered (Johnson & Gardner, 1989):

1. *Review annually with counsel.* Review and update the employee handbook at least annually. Not only should policies be revised to comply with current law and corporate goals, but outdated and inappropriate provisions must be discarded.

2. *Evaluate language judiciously.* Each word must be examined before it is included.

3. *Include restrictive clauses.* Include acknowledgment, amendment, and disclaimer clauses in employee documents.

4. *Say what you mean.* Include only those provisions that managers are willing to follow routinely and apply consistently.

Tort Law The third category of exceptions to the "termination-at-will" doctrine involves tortious behavior by an employer. Tortious conduct occurs when someone harms another without justification. The person suffering tortious harm from unlawful acts of another may bring suit and recover damages from the perpetrator of the act. Under tort law former employees have argued that their discharges unjustifiably produced wanton violent emotional distress or defamed their character. All states consider these acts grounds for legal action in some situations, but not all states consider employment termination as one of these situations.

Tort law exceptions include (in some states) the following:

1. *Emotional distress.* A former employee may sue for intentional infliction of emotional distress. Thus, a discharged employee may seek damages for outrageous acts related to discharge (e.g., firing an employee for dating an employee of a competing firm).

2. *Defamation.* Employees may bring suit against their former employer, claiming that they were defamed by the distribution of untrue information that harmed their reputation (e.g., an employer falsely states that an employee was discharged for theft).

3. *Interference with a contractual relationship.* A discharged employee may sue when a third party intentionally and unjustifiably interferes with a contractual employment relationship between other parties (e.g., a

bus terminal company tells a bus line that unless it fires a driver, it will be denied use of the bus terminal).

Other Judicial Exceptions   Other common law exceptions to the "termination-at-will" doctrine, however infrequently used, demonstrate how judicial rulings have eroded the doctrine. An example is illustrative. The legal doctrine of "promissory estoppel" has been applied to unjust termination in instances where the employee claims that he/she was induced to work for the employer (e.g., through enticing recruiting tactics) and relied on this inducement, only to be subsequently discharged and suffer deleterious consequences.

Implications for Practitioners

Although courts vary in interpretation of the legal aspects of "termination at will," some trends can be identified. First, most states recognize public policy exceptions to "termination at will," and the number is growing. Second, state courts have increasingly held that statements in employee handbooks, application forms, and personnel policies constitute implied contracts of employment. Oral promises and implied contracts of good faith and fair dealing as exceptions to the "termination-at-will" doctrine are untested. Defamation and third party interference charges show no identifiable trend.

Employer Responses

Employers may adopt either reactive or proactive responses to the threat of wrongful termination charges.

Reactive Responses   These focus on court rulings, laws, and congressional hearings as a basis for building a system to limit exposure to legal action. They advocate avoiding potential liability by promising nothing, issuing disclaimers and statements that employment is "at will," and they even get employees to sign a waiver of rights as a condition of employment. Included is a careful analysis of application forms, employee handbooks, and personnel policy statements to be sure that these contain no language that might imply an employment relationship other than "at will" (Johnson & Gardner, 1989).

Even so, this presents problems because of controversy over the impact of "termination at will" on employee loyalty (Wilhelm, 1990; Roth, 1990). Its opponents argue that the use of disclaimers and employee waivers reduces loyalty and respect for the company. It is also held that these diminish a company's good public image and leave a poor impression on job applicants as well as on employees. Employers can achieve the same results by less onerous means such as writing personnel manuals that do not imply contracts, including "at-will" statements, and retaining the right to change policy at any time. Finally, it is held that a society that values and protects the rights of citizens through fair treatment and due process should rightfully extend those same rights to the work place.

Proactive Responses   These focus on court rulings, laws, and congressional hearings to build a system that recognizes and maximizes the intent and purpose of the law. Although there are actions that management might take to prevent unjust dismissal lawsuits (employment contracts, an open door policy, participative management, profit sharing, idea incentive programs, egalitarian parking and dining facilities, severance pay, and special perks and benefits), four areas of possible action seem especially critical: performance appraisals, employee communications, disciplinary procedures, and dispute handling (Scarpello & Ledvinka, 1988).

Performance Appraisals. Since appraisals are the basis for employment decisions, including the decision to terminate, they are subject to scrutiny by the Equal Employment Opportunity Commission and the courts. Such scrutiny focuses on how evaluation procedures are applied within the organization. Appraisal procedures must be used in a fair and unbiased manner and provide a logical and consistent basis for termination (e.g., consistently good performance reviews would not support a decision to terminate for inadequate performance). Consistency between evidence and action taken is important, since courts are gradually moving the right of "termination at will" in the direction of termination for good cause.

Based on a review of court decisions, Bernardin and Beatty (1984) have provided a checklist for evaluating the soundness of a performance evaluation system:

- Standards for evaluation should be based on job analysis.
- Performance standards should be communicated to employees.
- Employees should be evaluated on specific categories of job performance.
- Performance categories (criteria) and standards should be defined in behavioral terms and supported by objective, observable evidence.
- Individual raters should be assessed for validity in their ratings.
- When possible, more than one rater should be used, particularly when ratings are to be closely tied to important personnel decisions.
- Documentation of extreme ratings should be required.
- A formal appeal process should be established.

An employer can minimize the possibility of a wrongful termination suit, or at least put the firm in a better position to defend itself successfully and at reduced cost by using a few common sense rules (Kaplan, 1989). First, specify the rules, taking care not to promise or imply more than one is willing to deliver. Second, be candid with employees, giving them regular, accurate evaluations of performance. Third, put

employees on notice, honestly and directly. The notice should explain the reasons and set a specific time period to make corrections and/or improvements. Fourth, consider options other than termination for employees who are not performing satisfactorily. Finally, discharge if no other option is possible. Reasons for termination should be carefully documented. Demonstrated fairness is the key.

Employee Communications. Contract theory is inconsistent with dismissal when employers have given assurances of job security. The obvious solution is to avoid giving any such assurances, but this solution has its costs. It may reduce the sense of job security among employees, and this in turn may reduce commitment, create morale problems and precipitate unionization. Employers should review all public statements and publications with counsel and train interviewers to avoid statements which imply employment security.

Disciplinary Procedures. Employee discipline has essentially the same objectives as performance appraisal: to encourage individual behavior that contributes to organizational goal achievement. Performance appraisal achieves this objective by providing employees feedback about their performance, whereas traditional discipline does so by punishing poor performance. Newer methods of discipline tend to borrow from both approaches and emphasize counseling and communication. These methods are based on two criteria for due process of law: (1) the exercise of power should be based on objective rules rather than the personal preferences of those in power, and (2) the rules should respect the commonly accepted rights of the person over whom power is exercised (Scarpello & Ledvinka, 1988). (Of course there is disagreement over commonly accepted rights in "termination-at-will" situations.) Based on these criteria Scarpello and Ledvinka (1988) believe that the following are characteristics of a good progressive disciplinary system:

- *Specific rules,* which leave no doubt about when they have been violated.
- *Job-related rules,* which are reasonably related to the employee's work or to some other legitimate organizational objective.
- *Clearly stated punishments,* which leave no doubt about the consequences of violating those rules.
- *Punishments that fit the crime,* which mean that the infraction should be severe enough to warrant the disciplinary action taken.
- *Careful investigation,* which ensures that the rules really were violated.
- *Prompt and consistent* enforcement of rules.
- *Documentation* of all observed rule violations and disciplinary actions taken.
- *Specific statement of the offence* in communicating with the employee.
- *Discussion confined to the problem at hand* which does not question the employee's overall worth.
- *Effective communication* of rules and punishments.
- *Advance warning* of any change in rules.
- *An appeals process.*

Dispute Handling. Only unionized firms traditionally had formal procedures for handling employee-employer disputes. In nonunionized firms the process tended to be informal, involving "see your supervisor" or "open door" policies. Since these policies represent chain of command approaches, employees often view them as ineffective. Legal trends have emboldened employees and convinced employers that more formal procedures are necessary.

One such procedure is to establish a dispute-handling system independent of and outside the chain of command. Such a system would normally involve either a representative grievance committee that is advisory to line management or provide for the appeal of grievances to an outside arbitrator. Key elements of a successful internal dispute resolution system are as follows (Westin, 1983):

- Visible top management commitment to fair treatment and fair process.
- Merit-oriented personnel policies.
- A complaint and appeal system that fits the company culture, work force, organization, and dynamics.
- Management acceptance of dispute resolution as a positive and valuable process.
- Full and frequent advertising of the system to all employees.
- Protection of employees using system against open or covert reprisal.
- Professional management of the system—no place for amateurs.
- Training of supervisors, line managers, and middle managers to live with and profit from the system.
- Acceptance of the duty to correct manager misconduct and policy weaknesses.
- Periodic employee surveys to measure employee satisfactions and concerns with the system.
- Recognition of a turbulent business and social environment that will inevitably create disputes for the system to resolve (e.g., office and factory automation).
- A formal system without legalism.

Independent dispute-handling processes can benefit both employers and employees. They can enhance employer reputation for fair dealing, improve company loyalty and provide for low cost conflict resolution. Such procedures can also improve employee job security and job satisfaction and provide protection against arbitrary management action. Gaining these benefits requires that the firm overcome management resistance to change and to the loss of power.

Just Cause Dismissal

Despite the large number of laws, acts, and court dicta protecting employees from "termination at will," employers still retain the right to terminate without cause. This right is being eroded in the direction of termination for good cause. Although termination for good cause has not been an explicitly accepted doctrine in nonunion organizations, judicial decisions suggest the following grounds for discharge (Culbert & McDonough, 1990).

Malfeasance   Malfeasance involves issues of wrongdoing or dishonesty, which violate specified corporate practices, rules of professional conduct, or civil, regulatory, or criminal law. Examples include theft of money or materials, falsification of records, slander, bribery, lying, and favoritism for personal gain. Also covered are immoral, indecent, or improper behavior including blatant sexism, misuse of alcohol or drugs, endangering personnel, or exposing the firm to civil or criminal action by financially injuring someone or knowingly violating rules and statutes that govern the firm's operations.

Malfeasance dismissal is normally not difficult to justify. However, employers must be diligent in documenting facts and reasons and demonstrate responsible behavior toward the accused. Employers should follow three steps when accusations are made: (1) attempt to uncover the other side of the story, (2) gather substantiating evidence, and (3) confront the accused. Difficulties may arise in malfeasance situations because it is not possible to provide a complete list of terminable offenses. Employers may also find it difficult to apply standards consistently to all employees.

Inadequate Performance   Failure to terminate for incompetence that fails to respond to training or accommodation can harm productivity and demoralize employees. Employers must send clear, accurate messages regarding performance appraisal. An earlier discussion of implicit contract noted that many disputes arise because managers create expectations that an employee can be terminated only for good cause. Inconsistency between feedback and action as well as a failure to document performance inadequacies can also be sources of trouble. Finally, employers have an obligation to provide training and support in an attempt to improve inadequate performance.

Job Elimination   The basic logic of job elimination is an employer's argument that labor and capital must be mixed efficiently to maintain profitable operation. However, employers who use job elimination as a method of avoiding documentation in a desire to eliminate an undesirable employee may exact a heavy toll in employee trust and loyalty.

Job elimination seems legitimate when corporations downsize or engage in corporate restructuring. Downsizing is defended by the economic logic of changing market conditions, international competition, and changing technology. Courts traditionally have accepted this logic, and firms have acted to sustain it by offering generous severance allowances and reemployment assistance. However, bargaining agreements and trade legislation are moving toward greater employee job security.

Team Fit   Team fit is an ill-defined concept in which an employer attempts to employ people who conform to his/her own leadership style or formula for success. Used as a justification for dismissal, team fit often involves flagrant abuse of managerial choice. This abuse stems from two basic factors: (1) A manager makes no attempt to distinguish between those changes required for team effectiveness and those based on personal whim; or (2) a manager is unable to distinguish between poor team fit and an inability to manage an otherwise competent employee.

Although team fit is a nebulous concept requiring management latitude, some guidelines are appropriate: (1) Civil rights laws must be respected; (2) the change must be based primarily on business reasons; (3) reasonable attempts must be made to accommodate employees who do not fit in (offering other company positions, etc.); and (4) those who are terminated must suffer no quantifiable damage or financial loss (Culbert & McDonough, 1990). Thus, employers need a framework to guide discussion of the subjectivity that invariably exists in team fit decisions. The key features of such a framework are openness and demonstrated fairness to those affected by changes.

The maze of legislation and common law and the large element of judgment in interpretation complicate compliance with the "termination-at-will" doctrine. To aid the manager in making sense of the apparent chaos, some guidelines are offered.

Some Guidelines—A Summary

Laws, judicial precedents, and employment trends permit drafting guidelines for employers who wish to educe the incidence of wrongful termination litigation (Slahor, 1989):

- Employers need to tighten their personnel policies to be sure that employees are evaluated at least annually. If an employee is showing evidence of incompetence on the job, the employee must receive a warning or notice of that incompetency, and the employer must provide the employee a chance to improve the performance. All evaluation should be reduced to writing and reviewed. Evaluations should be signed by the employee.
- Employers should keep careful records of all actions such as employee evaluations, copies of warnings or notices, copies of memos outlining how improvement should be accomplished, and so on. Efforts at counseling or discipline must be kept confidential so that the employee cannot claim to have been defamed in front of other employees or third parties.
- Employers should analyze employee handbooks. The handbook must neither state nor imply that employment continues just because an employee is "part of the family" of the

company, is loyal, or has long-term service. An employee should learn, through the handbook, exactly what is expected in the employer-employee relationship. Handbooks should contain a statement that they are not contracts. Alterations to handbooks should be flagged to present employees by having them sign a statement indicating they are aware of the changes.

- Employers must be sure that the company's policy about probationary periods of employment is clear, so that an employee cannot infer that once past the probationary period hurdle the job is "safe." Employers must state that promotions, raises, commendations, and other advancements will be based on merit only.
- Employers should screen job applicants thoroughly to be sure that only the best-qualified and most competent person is selected for the job opening. The job application itself should contain no express or implied guarantees that the employer does not want to offer.
- Employers must set an employment policy, establishing either a good cause termination policy or a pure at-will relationship. All those who deal with employees within the organization must be instructed to state or write only the practices or comments that match the firm's employment policy.
- Employees terminated should be treated with fairness and tact. The case should be reviewed before the employee is fired. The company's attorney should be consulted. A supervisor should meet privately with the employee to discuss the reasons for termination and allow the employee to comment.

These guidelines demonstrate that employer protection from wrongful termination litigation requires good personnel management practices. Fair play, careful hiring, specific instructions, accurate and honest performance appraisals, open commmunication, due process, and attention to laws have been part of progressive human resource management for many years.

REFERENCES

Bernardin, H., & Beatty, R. (1984). *Performance Appraisal: Assessing Human Behavior at Work,* 672–673, Boston, MA: Kent Publishing Co.

Brake, C. (1982). Limiting the right to terminate-at-will: Have the courts forgotten the employer? *Vanderbilt Law Review,* 201–243.

Buckley, M., & Weitzel, W. (1988). In Ferris, G., Rowland, K., & Buckley, M. (Eds.), *Employing at Will, Human Resources Management,* (2nd Ed.), 454–459, Needham, MA: Allyn & Bacon.

Culbert, S. & McDonough, J. (1990). Wrongful termination and the reasonable manager: Balancing fair play and effectiveness. *Sloan Management Review,* Summer 39–46.

French, W. (1990). *Human Resources Management,* 2nd Ed., 593, Boston, MA: Houghton Mifflin Co.

Gumbel, J., & Hoover, J. (1990). Employment contracts: An option to consider. *Labor Law Journal,* March, 175–177.

Hill, M., & Sinicropi, A. (1981). *Remedies in Arbitration.* Washington, D.C.: BNA Books.

Johnson, P., & Gardner, S. (1989). Legal pitfalls in employee handbooks. *SAM Advanced Journal,* Spring, 42–46.

Kaplan, A. (1989). How to fire without fear: Wrongful discharge litigation in the post-employment-at-will era. *Personnel Administrator,* September, 74–76.

Koys, D., Briggs, S., & Grenig, J. (1987). State court disparity on employment-at-will. *Personnel Psychology, 40,* 565–577.

Peck, C. (1979). Unjust discharges from employment: A necessary change in the law. *Ohio State Law Journal,* 40, 1–49.

Roth, T. (1990). Productivity does not suffer. *Human Resources Magazine,* September, 89.

Scarpello, V., & Ledvinka, J. (1988). *Personnel/human resource management: Environments and functions,* 671–703, Boston, MA: PWS-Kent Publishing Co.

Schuler, R., & Huber, V. (1990). *Personnel and Human Resource Management,* 470, 4th Ed., St. Paul, MN: West Publishing Co.

Slahor, S. (1989). Wrongful termination—The California story. *Supervision,* May, 3–6.

Westin, A. (1983). New techniques for resolving employee disputes in non-union firms: An empirical report on changing corporate practices and options. In Bardash, J., & Kauf, J. B. (Eds.) *Unjust Dismissal 1983: Litigating, Settling and Avoiding Claims,* 262, New York: Practicing Law Institute.

Wilhelm, P. (1990). Employment-at-will harms productivity. *Human Resources Magazine,* September, 88.

Wood, H. (1886). *A Treatise on the Law of Master and Servant.* (2nd Ed.), San Francisco: Bancroft-Whitney.

Youngblood, S., & Bierman, L. (1985). An introduction to employement-at-will, human resources management, (2nd Ed. 1990), Ferris, G., Rowland, K. & Buckley, M. (Eds.), Needham Heights, MA: Allyn & Bacon Publisher.

"Good Job—You're Fired." Downsizing and Its Impact

INTRODUCTION

Driven by the pressures of general economic uncertainty and instability, of highly charged domestic and global competitive environments, and of the need to reduce redundant staffing in merged or acquired firms, America's largest employers have laid off millions of employees in recent years. It is conservatively estimated that more than 1,130,000 workers were laid off in 1993 and 1994, averaging almost 1,500 *per day*. Not surprisingly, a recent *USA Today* survey (March, 1995) reports that job insecurity is the major source of employee stress. Many of these layoffs occurred as a result of economic downturns. However, many others have occurred in times of recovery and general prosperity, thus signaling a basic restructuring of how a significant number of Americans earn their livings and organize their careers.

Although layoffs have become common, managers should not become insensitive to the human costs involved. Even when they help to cut costs and increase productivity, layoffs are still traumatic for employees, their families, and their communities. Layoffs raise important ethical questions and dilemmas, particularly with respect to why and how they take place. The "why" involves evaluating the reasons a layoff is considered advisable or necessary; the "how" concerns the steps managers take to implement a layoff decision. Most managers are involved in the latter type of decision. Questions of utility, respect for persons, justice, and fairness should all be considered.

Since layoffs obviously inflict significant harms on employees and communities, why they are undertaken is ethically important. From a utilitarian perspective, such harms are legitimate only if they are *necessary* either to produce a greater good or to prevent a greater harm. For example, it is intuitively clear that a layoff is ethically justified if it is the only alternative to a company's going out of business. If there are other alternatives, then utilitarians insist that each be examined and its beneficial and harmful consequences weighed. Questions of fairness also need to be addressed. If some stakeholders (e.g., stockholders and senior management) benefit, while others (e.g., employees and communities) suffer, the issue of whether and how such a disparity can be ethically justified needs consideration.

How a layoff is managed is equally important. The loss of a job, especially as the result of circumstances beyond an employee's control, is a blow to a person's financial and psychological security and to his or her self-esteem. Kantian concerns for the dignity and autonomy of layoff victims is reflected in the Worker Adjustment and Retraining Notification Act of 1988, which requires that, under ordinary circumstances, employees receive enough warning of an impending layoff that they can begin to make alternative plans. While this is a legal minimum of respect, sound ethics may well demand more.

At this point, Kantian and utilitarian considerations converge. If a layoff is necessary and the resulting harms are ethically justified, utilitarians will insist that reasonable steps be taken to minimize its burdens. Outplacement programs, psychological counseling, job fairs, and severance packages are all tactics that companies can use to mitigate the harms of a layoff.

Considerations of justice are crucial to the ethical assessment not only of the "why" of the layoff, but also of the "how." Stockholders, managers, departing employees, "survivors," affected communities—in short, anyone who is affected by the layoff—has an ethical right to have his or her needs taken into consideration in balancing the layoff's harms and benefits. How will the benefits and, particularly, the harms be distributed? What standards of justice are most appropriate in this context? Both ethical and legal considerations prohibit the discriminatory distribution of benefits and harms (e.g., on the basis of age).

The difficulty lies in determining how to proceed fairly. As we pointed out in Chapter 1, organizational theorists have identified eighteen standards of justice to which people appeal in making or evaluating decisions. It should come as no surprise then that reasonable and ethical people disagree on how principles of justice should be applied with respect to layoffs (e.g., concerning the relative importance of seniority, performance evaluations, or membership in a protected class). Managers concerned with the ethical dimensions of their actions need to examine closely and to discuss thoroughly what standards of fairness are appropriate in evaluating the outcomes of their decisions (e.g., should the burdens of the layoff be shared equally or according to some other criterion?), the procedures they follow (e.g., should employees have a voice in making layoff decisions?), and the system itself (e.g., what role should a company's affirmative action policy have in determining who is terminated?).

Clearly, managerial and ethical reflections are intertwined. In today's economic climate, difficult decisions must be made only after careful reflection. The effects of a downsizing on the "survivors" are crucial to whether or not the organization's goals are achieved and whether or not the business recovers its health. If the remaining employees believe that the layoffs were unnecessary or were carried out in a harsh, disrespectful, insensitive, or unfair way, they will be demoralized and distrustful, and effectiveness may well suffer. On the other hand, if layoffs were seen as necessary and as carried out in a manner consistent with ethical principles of fairness and respect, "survivors" may well be motivated to commit themselves further to the organization and its goals.

★ ★ ★

In the readings selected for this chapter, **Robert J. Samuelson** surveys the current business climate and argues that the time of the "good corporation," one that blends the roles of fierce economic competitor and welfare state for its workers, has passed. His obituary notes further that the full social impact of its passing has not yet been felt. The contributors to the symposium, "Is the Good Corporation Dead?" in *Business and Society Review,* ranging from libertarian (**Doug Bandow**) to liberal (**Robert B. Reich**) to communitarian (**Tom Chappell**), debate Samuelson's view and discuss whether downsizing has indeed buried corporate social responsibility. **Brian N. Bulger** and **Carolyn Curtis Gessner** examine the different strategies (voluntary and involuntary) that companies can use to achieve a reduction in their work forces, and they explore in detail the legal liabilities of each and the steps for reducing them, particularly in the area of age discrimination. **Joel Brockner** points out the crucial role that fairness plays in mitigating the harmful effects of layoffs. His article gives managers a number of practical suggestions for conducting layoffs fairly, treating "victims" with compassion and respect, and encouraging "survivors" to cope with, and even to profit from, the changes in their work environment. **Daniel C. Feldman** and **Carrie C. Leana** advance several proposals designed to help employers and managers avoid the legal, public-relations, and organizational dangers of poorly managed layoffs. In their view, both ethics and principles of sound management dictate that companies should, as far as possible, mitigate the harmful effects of a layoff (by providing adequate advance notice, fair severance pay and extended benefits, opportunities for retraining, and outplacement services), implement the layoff fairly, and pay attention to the stress and discomfort of the "survivors."

CASE: Layoffs at Alexo Plastics

Bill Armbruster shook his head and read the memo again. He'd been with Alexo Plastics for fifteen years and had served as head of the Technical Support Group (TSG) in the firm's marketing department for the past four years. Several times in the past year there had been rumors of large-scale layoffs, but none had been carried out to date. But Mike Ross's memo left no room for doubt that layoffs were imminent. Current business conditions and competitive pressures within the industry meant that Alexo needed to reduce its staff positions by as much as 33 percent. Consequently, Bill was told via memo to reduce his six-person group by two.

BILL ARMBRUSTER AND THE LAYOFFS

In Bill's eight years in the marketing department, he had been promoted twice, most recently to his present job as TSG department head. He had started as a marketing analyst and had been promoted to product development manager prior to his present assignment. TSG's mandate was to provide a wide range of consulting services to Alexo customers who were attempting to develop new products from materials supplied by Alexo. Thus, TSG played a key role in developing or solidifying several strategic alliances involving Alexo and its major customers.

The company had grown steadily over the past five years, and some talented people had

Source: This case was prepared by Dr. Gerald McCarthy with help from Joy Durand, research assistant, as a basis for class discussion rather than to illustrate either effective or ineffective handling of an administrative situation. This case is largely fictional but represents a composite of actual events.

been added to Marketing and TSG to handle the increased workload. Thinking about these people and their many contributions to Alexo saddened Bill. Adding to his concern was the way in which he had learned of the layoffs—a "surprise" memo from someone with whom he interacted daily. Bill would have expected Mike to come to him and discuss the layoffs in person before sending an official memo.

Early in the day after he received the memo, Bill arranged a meeting with Mike. Bill expressed surprise that the news about the layoffs came to him in a formal letter. Because he and Mike had been friends for many years, Bill didn't hesitate to tell him that he was more than a little annoyed that he hadn't learned about the layoffs sooner, and in a less formal manner. Bill explained that he did not think his department could perform its important mission with only four people. Bill asked if there was any way that TSG could be exempted from the cuts. Mike told him in an uncharacteristically abrupt way that Bill had no choice but to lay off two people. Bill left Mike's office more annoyed and frustrated than when he went in. Mike had been no help at all in easing the stress Bill felt. It wasn't like Mike to be so secretive or so abrupt with his department heads.

THE TECHNICAL SUPPORT GROUP

Bill was upset with the prospect of laying off two people from his department. His six-person department was effective and reasonably close-knit. There were many projects with larger customers in which the entire Technical Support

Group needed to work together. They often consulted with one another. They interacted well and were able to generate creative ideas to solve difficult problems brought to them by customers. Bill considered the impact of the layoffs on his group's functioning and thought about each member of his department. He didn't want those laid off to feel resentful towards him, and he hated the idea of being the "bad guy." Bill also wanted to do his best to preserve the positive work environment that had developed since he became department head. He knew that this would be difficult to manage.

NANCY O'COIN

His train of thought was interrupted when his de facto second-in-command, Nancy O'Coin, stopped in to remind him that he had a meeting with the head of new product development in fifteen minutes. Bill admired Nancy's efficiency and had often remarked how much more smoothly the department functioned in the three years since Nancy had joined TSG. He had recommended her for two extraordinary salary increases, both of which had been approved, one just two months ago. Alexo had few women in managerial positions, and Nancy was clearly on a "fast track" to join that small group.

Nancy was a hard worker with an outgoing personality. She worked well with Bill. She was not afraid to voice her opinions to him if she had a different viewpoint, though she was very tactful. Bill had come to rely on Nancy's memory and organization, as well. She was also very highly regarded by Alexo customers. Would he even consider laying off Nancy? He'd often wondered how the department had gotten along without her. But it *had,* though less effectively.

Returning to his office after the meeting, he didn't stop to talk with people as he usually did. He went directly to his desk and began reviewing the other people in his department. Whom would he lay off?

PHIL ESPOSITO

Phil Esposito, fifty-eight years old, had been with the company for twenty-eight years. Phil had the longest tenure and the highest salary of the six-member staff. He had lost some of his enthusiasm, and his job performance had slipped slightly in the past year. Phil always received excellent reviews from customers, not just for his work ethic but because he was a veteran in the industry. No one would ever think of questioning Phil's loyalty, integrity, or professionalism. In addition, he was highly respected by his coworkers. Bill remembered how Phil had taught him the ropes when he was new to the firm and how supportive he had been when Bill was promoted to department head. On the other hand, Phil's age and length of service qualified him for Alexo's early retirement plan, which would not be available to anyone else in the department. However, Bill didn't know if Phil was interested in early retirement.

Bill was concerned that Phil might not adapt well to "life after layoffs" in TSG. Another employee in the department had mentioned that Phil had been talking a lot recently about how much Alexo had changed from the good old days when he had first joined the firm. It just wasn't the same company it used to be, Phil had stated. Phil had even submitted a somewhat bitter memo to Mike Ross expressing his opinion that the company was going downhill.

AL JENSEN

Bill's thoughts then turned to Al Jensen. At forty-eight, he was ten years younger than Esposito but had been with the company nearly as long, starting during his college years. A conscientious worker, he lacked Phil's savvy but brought more energy to the job. About the only thing Bill could fault him for was a "prickly attitude," which made him, on occasion, difficult to work with. Al was moody and often kept to himself. But no one could dispute his competence. Al's real passion was in the technical challenge of the job itself. He was not a people person and not the most socially adept individual Bill had ever met. Bill was certain that, if Al was one of the four "survivors" in TSG, he would continue to do his job with the enthusiasm he had always shown.

ALICE FORD

Bill didn't "connect well" with Alice Ford. Alice was thirty and had been at Alexo for five years. She was intelligent and knew Alexo's products, as well as the manufacturing technologies and processes of Alexo's customers, better than anyone in the department. She was perceived as abrasive by coworkers and as arrogant by customers. Bill had discussed these perceptions with Alice, and recently she was getting higher marks from both groups. She had mentioned to Bill on several occasions that she was under a great deal of stress, as a single mother with two young children. She often needed to leave early to pick up one of her children from preschool or music lessons. Recently, she had met with Bill to discuss the possibility of rearranging her work schedule so that she could spend more time with her children. Should she be one of the ones to go? Her technical skills were superb, and, with the proper coaching, she could develop into a great asset to the company.

RICH TIEDLINGER

Bill had hired Rich Tiedlinger, twenty-four years old, just over a year ago. Rich's technical abilities were strong though not as strong as Alice's. He was clearly the most energetic and likeable member of the department. He was working toward his MBA in a well regarded university's evening program. His still made mistakes, but his attitude almost made up for them. His gung-ho approach did not wear well with the older members of the group, especially Al, though even he thought that Rich contributed to

esprit de corps of the department. His enthusiasm seemed to be an intangible asset to the group. To some, Rich seemed a born leader of the "rah rah" variety. Would he fine-tune his leadership skills at Alexo or elsewhere?

He was clearly ambitious and Bill wondered how long he was likely to stay at Alexo. Bill was willing to bet that Rich would go on to bigger and better things in the years to come, maybe even Bill's position if given the right opportunity.

PHIL GONZALES

The sixth member of his group was Phil Gonzales, thirty-three years old. Bill genuinely admired Phil. He had worked his way up through the blue-collar ranks at Alexo, had taken night courses at a local community college, and had been in his present job for two years.

Bill knew that Phil had moved up in the company, at least in part, due to a conscious Alexo strategy to improve relations with the city's growing Hispanic community, who made up an increasing percentage of Alexo's work force. More new Hispanic managers had been appointed last year than ever before. And Bill knew that the company's policy on providing opportunities for minorities was as important as its policy on opportunities for women. Phil was a role model for other Hispanic workers in the firm. He knew everyone from the shop floor to the executive offices and was respected for the high quality of his work in TSG.

DECISION TIME

There is no way around it, Bill thought. This is going to be awful, but I have to do it. Since he could not avoid laying off two workers, he wanted to make sure that what he did was done professionally, with a fairness and sensitivity that these people deserved. Bill knew also that it would make his job a lot easier if one or two of them would leave voluntarily, either taking early retirement or pursuing other opportunities—inside or outside the firm. Of course, there were possible negatives in this approach; maybe the wrong people would leave. Would that be right from the perspective of the firm and the effectiveness of TSG? He picked up a blank pad of paper and began to write down his thoughts.

R.I.P.: The Good Corporation

Robert J. Samuelson

IBM's fall from grace is more than a big business story. It also represents last rites for the "good corporation." This was our ideal of what all American companies might become. They would marry profitmaking and social responsibility, economic efficiency and enlightened labor relations. IBM was the model. It seemed to do everything right, and its present troubles (including its first layoffs) have shattered the vision with unmistakable finality.

The resulting psychic void explains much of today's sense of economic insecurity. The spread of the "good corporation" was supposed to provide stable jobs and generous fringe benefits—health insurance and pensions—for more and more Americans. Instead, the process is sliding into reverse. As companies strive to stay competitive, they are shedding workers, encouraging early retirement and cutting fringe benefits. Consider:

- In 1979, 55 percent of full-time male workers had employer-paid pensions. By 1988, that had dropped to 49 percent, according to the Labor Department.
- Health-insurance coverage is eroding, and workers must pay more of the premiums. A study by Foster Higgins, a consulting firm, finds that nearly four fifths of companies now require employees to pay an average of $107 a month for family coverage, up from $69 in 1989.
- Companies are also trimming—or eliminating—health insurance for retirees. In 1992, about half of workers in companies with more than 200 employees were promised retiree

Source: Newsweek, July 5, 1993, 41 and © 1993, Newsweek, Inc. All rights reserved. Reprinted with permission.

benefits, down from two thirds in 1983, reports the consulting firm KPMG Peat Marwick.

The once-imagined vision of universal benefits and secure jobs is fading. It is not that executive suites have suddenly been hijacked by meanspirited monsters who have replaced the previous compassionate saints. Both images are obviously overdrawn. Countless companies still make ample profits while treating their workers well, as a recent book ("The 100 Best Companies to Work for in America") shows.

There's 3M, which allows many employees to devote 15 percent of their time to projects of their own choosing. One recent payoff: Post-It note pads. There's Merck, which has pioneered major drugs and has such a good reputation that it receives 150,000 job applications a year. There's Motorola, which has invested massively in worker training.

Nor is it true that stable jobs have vanished. Among men, the typical worker between the ages of 45 and 54 has been with his present employer 12 years. About a third have been there 20 years or more. As more women pursue careers, their job tenure is actually increasing. Still, something has changed. What's gone is a sense of confidence, a faith that jobs—or careers—are permanent. The anxiety may exaggerate the reality, but it is keenly felt.

The idea of the "good corporation" assumed that superior American management could easily blend two roles: the company as a fierce economic competitor, and the company as a welfare state for its workers. There seemed to be no conflict. Stable jobs and ample fringe benefits would make workers loyal, and loyal workers would make companies prosper. IBM is hardly the first company to disappoint the ideal. The unraveling really started in the 1970s with troubles at firms like Penn Central and Chrysler.

But IBM's downfall has special meaning, because it seemed the best of the best. No company, regardless of how prosperous, now seems permanently safe from upheaval. We overestimated the process of U.S. management and underestimated the disruptive power of market changes, from new technologies to foreign competitors. We also found that corporate generosity does not automatically create corporate competence. Companies where life became too cushy often lapsed into overconfident mediocrity.

Welfare state: In some ways, these changes have been healthy. The new insecurity—more realistic than the old complacency—often motivates managers and workers to keep their companies viable. But in another sense, the changes have left us adrift. We now lack a clear concept of what "good management" means. It used to be benevolent shrewdness. Does it now include necessary cruelty: axing one third of the company to save the other two thirds?

What also has been wounded is our idea of the welfare state. Since World War II this has always been an unofficial blend of private and government benefits. As more firms became "good companies," we thought, more workers would receive welfare benefits (health insurance, pensions). Government would protect only the poor, disabled and aged. Companies had become spontaneous instruments of social policy: for a citizenry suspicious of government, this seemed just fine.

There were always some groups that didn't fit easily into this welfare system, as Mary E. O'Connell of Northeastern University writes in The American Prospect magazine. These included workers in low-paying industries with high labor turnover and women who moved between the home and paid work. But these excluded groups are now increasingly joined by full-time career workers, whose companies either aren't offering comprehensive benefits or are cutting back. Gaps in the social safety net widen.

What to do? The impending health-care debate is partially a product of this breakdown.

People increasingly fear losing health insurance, so government may mandate—or provide directly—the coverage. Parental-leave legislation (requiring time off for new parents) reflected the same impulse. If companies don't do the right thing, then government will make them. But, of course, it isn't that simple.

Governments that saddle companies with more labor costs ultimately discourage companies from hiring. And mandated benefits, whether paid by government with payroll taxes or simply imposed on business by regulation, are higher labor costs. The effect is the same as an increase in the minimum wage: if the wage rises too high, companies won't hire workers who seem worth less. Europe has drifted disastrously down this path. In 1970, its unemployment was 2.6 percent; now it is about 11 percent.

So the death of the "good corporation" poses hard issues. There are many good companies, but many don't reach our ideal and some that now do won't in the future. We are discovering the world as it is, not as we wished it to be.

READING 7-2

Is the Good Corporation Dead?: A *BSR* Symposium

In a recent column in *Newsweek,* Robert J. Samuelson wrote an obituary for corporate social responsibility. "IBM's fall from grace . . . represents the last rites for the 'good corporation,'" wrote Samuelson. "This was our ideal of what all American companies might become. They would marry profit making and social responsibility, economic efficiency, and enlight-

Source: Business and Society Review, 87 (Fall 1993), 9-17. Reprinted with permission of *Business and Society Review.*

ened labor relations. IBM was the model. It seemed to do everything right and its present troubles (including its first layoffs) have shattered the vision with unmistakable finality. . . .

"The spread of the good corporation was supposed to provide stable jobs and generous fringe benefits—health insurance and pensions—for more and more Americans. Instead, the process is sliding into reverse. As companies strive to stay competitive, they are shedding workers, encouraging early retirement, and cutting fringe benefits."

Business and Society Review asked a number of scholars, businesspeople, and commentators for their reaction to Samuelson's conclusion. We posed three questions: Is Samuelson right? Do recent layoffs at IBM, Procter & Gamble, and other major companies signal the end of secure jobs with good benefits? Can companies continue to be good employers and good corporate citizens when there is so much competition?

Here are the responses:

STEWARDSHIP OF THE FUTURE

Robert B. Reich *is the U.S. secretary of labor. He responded:*

American companies used to honor an implicit contract between top managers and workers: If a worker made a good effort to do her job, she could count on keeping it as long as the firm stayed in business. To many workers' dismay, however, this contract is being rapidly abandoned. U.S. manufacturers dropped 275,000 workers from their payrolls last year, even though profits were rising.

Why is this so? Why are most businesses seemingly moving away from the good corporate citizen role, instead seeking better performance by reducing middle management, subcontracting functions done more cheaply outside, and automating routine operations? Clearly increased competition is the driving force, but a recent survey in *The Wall Street Journal* showed that corporate downsizing frequently does not achieve the higher levels of increased productivity, profits, and customer service companies had initially hoped.

In fact, companies that downsize invite problems that show up later in the bottom line. Cutbacks may cause these companies to forfeit both the morale and loyalty of the remaining employees, and the knowledge and experience of those whose jobs were eliminated.

Ultimately, these losses can amount to fewer innovations in the future, as less job security and accumulated knowledge provide little incentive for workers to go the extra mile.

Cumulative Results

If downsizing can affect individual companies so dramatically, the cumulative results from these activities at the national level are even more startling. Both the unemployed and those threatened with job loss consume less, produce less, pay fewer taxes, and cost more in unemployment insurance benefits.

Even when employee cuts meet the test of profitability, companies may be overlooking strategies to improve productivity without layoffs. These strategies, which produce a distinctly different and decidedly more valuable organization, include: providing both on-the-job and formal training, giving front-line workers substantial authority over production and sales; offering employment security by tying wages to profits or productivity; and making needed cuts through normal attrition, while offering assistance to help workers find new jobs.

Many studies demonstrate the effectiveness of these strategies, especially when used in combination rather than singly. A survey of 700 firms from all major industries also found that companies utilizing one or more of these strategies had higher annual shareholder returns and higher gross return on capital between 1986 and 1991 than companies that did not.

The Clinton Administration is working on a comprehensive plan to help the unemployed and address these issues. But we must all make a bigger choice in the future. If we choose downsizing alone, we may indeed increase profitability for the moment, but we will essentially do little more for the work force than reallocate it. If we choose to invest in the workers we employ, we can enhance the value of their skills, insights, and inherent capacities to produce wealth.

Ultimately, we must remember that none of us is a bystander in this grand economic tournament. We must all take a hard look at how the game is being played to decide whether downsizing is good for the company or the country in the long term. Stewardship of the future, after all, is the responsibility of us all.

IN SEARCH OF THE GOOD CORPORATION

Milton Moskowitz *is a* Business and Society Review *senior editor. He responded:*

Having spent twenty-five years in search of the "good corporation," I had the wind knocked out of me by Robert Samuelson's comments, which were, as always, insightful. I came across them on the morning of June 30 when they appeared in *The Washington Post.* Robert Levering and I were in Washington on that day to brief Secretary of Commerce Ronald Brown on the findings of our book, *The 100 Best Companies to Work For in America.* I thought: "Have I wasted the last twenty-five years of my life?"

We did reassure the secretary that we thought it is possible to run a company that makes money and treats employees well. Indeed, we told him that in our view a company would, over the long haul, perform better if it had a workplace where trust, fairness, and friendliness were core values. And we were able to cite studies that indicated the publicly held companies on our roster outperformed the stock market averages. So, I am not ready yet to write off the good corporation, although I recognize the logic of Samuelson's argument.

But isn't it true that there is nothing new about this debate? It has been going on since the dawn of the Industrial Revolution. And doesn't it have a lot to do with the nature of the economic system which we call capitalism? Those who were appalled by the excesses of this system used to rally behind the socialist banner, as I once did. But now socialism has been discredited across the world. Today, even China and Russia embrace the market system. As a result, the good corporation has to carry the freight for those hoping to improve conditions for working people.

The problem, as Samuelson acutely illustrated with IBM as an example, is that capitalism places a high premium on winning. This is a game where winning is everything. If you lose, you're outta here, no matter how good a guy you are. That is the system we have in place—and it was useful for Samuelson to have reminded us of that.

EMPLOYABILITY SECURITY

Rosabeth Moss Kanter *holds the Class of 1960 Chair as Professor at the Harvard Business School, where she has taught since 1986. Her eleven influential books include* When Giants Learn to Dance: Mastering the Challenges of Strategy, Management and Careers in the 1990s; The Change Masters; *and most recently,* The Challenge of Organizational Change.[1] *She responded:*

For many people in the twentieth century, careers were constituted by institutions. Large employers were expected to provide—and guarantee—jobs, benefits, and upward mobility. Long-term employment has long been considered a central component of high-commitment, high-productivity work systems. And corporate

Source: "Employability Security" from *Men and Women of the Corporation* by Rosabeth Moss Kanter. Copyright © 1977 by Rosabeth Moss Kanter. Reprinted by permission of Basic-Books, a division of HarperCollins Publishers, Inc.

entitlements, from health benefits to pensions, were based on an assumption of longevity, especially as U.S. employers were expected to offer benefits guaranteed by governments in other countries.

Now recessionary pressures and sweeping industrial transformations are forcing large companies to downsize—a euphemism that masks the human turmoil involved. Even in Japan, the bastion of lifetime employment in big businesses where nearly three quarters of the country's 60 million workers stayed with one employer throughout their working life, cutbacks and layoffs beginning in 1992 have been shaking the social contract.

The job-tenure ideal of the past is colliding with the job-insecurity reality of the present. Institutionally dependent careers are declining; self-reliant careers as professionals and entrepreneurs are proliferating, increasing the burdens on people. And women are joining men as peers in nearly every corner of the labor market, bringing new issues—inclusion, empowerment, accommodations to family needs—at a time when companies are struggling to stay afloat.

Churn and Displacement

The United States has been fortunate in not depending solely on large enterprises. America has a vibrant entrepreneurial economy, a small business sector that creates a higher proportion of jobs than are similarly created in European nations. But employment in smaller organizations is inherently less secure, especially given the high failure rate of new small businesses, and such jobs often come without the benefits and safeguards mandated for companies with more than fifty employees. Some Americans count on entrepreneurs to pull the country out of the economic doldrums as large companies sputter and downsize. But an entrepreneurial economy is full of churn and displacement—and the fate of small companies is often linked to the fate of big ones which they supply and service.

New policies must reflect new forms of security while embracing the emerging realities of flexibility, mobility, and change.

Upgrading Skills

If security no longer comes from being employed, it must come from being employable. Employability security—the knowledge that today's work will enhance the person's value in terms of future opportunities—is a promise that can be made and kept. Employability security comes from the chance to accumulate human capital—skills and reputation—that can be invested in new opportunities as they arise. No matter what changes take place, persons whose pool of intellectual capital or expertise is high are in a better position to find gainful employment—with the current company or with another company or on their own.

For example, a senior executive developing new ventures for a materials company offered no guarantees of continued employment to the people he recruited, promising instead, "If they give the new business a whirl, they will be a better and more saleable person for it." The proof of his proposition: He left three years later to join a rapidly growing venture capital firm.

In many high-tech firms, people already acknowledge the new reality. They bet their future on continuing hard work and growth in skills that match changes in the industry, finding security in their own ability to generate income, perhaps as entrepreneurs themselves someday. Companies come and go, but technical know-how can still find a home. What makes the current company attractive are learning opportunities—chances to grow in skills, to prove and improve one's capacity—that enhance the person's ability to keep employable. Challenging jobs on significant projects are more important, in this calculus, than promises about the future or benefits programs contingent on long service.

Even in cases in which employment security is promised, the employment guarantee is only possible because of programs aimed at ensuring employability. Companies can offer to invest in retraining and career counseling to upgrade people's skills continually so they will always be employable, though specific jobs might disappear and they might have to prove their ability to contribute to the company over and over again throughout their careers.

Continuing upgrading of skills and pursuit of new opportunities is a lifelong proposition even inside a single corporation, an essential part of the corporate fitness regime for global competition. And in the wake of restructuring and downsizing, when large employers shed jobs in bundles of ten thousand, the same proposition needs to be extended outside the corporation, as President Clinton's campaign platform acknowledged. Social safety nets need to be extended to help people upgrade skills and deal with the costs of transition as they seek new jobs or plan new businesses. Helping men and women succeed as mobile professionals is a matter of public self-interest.

A society that encourages investment in human capital via continuing education, training, and support for new venture creation can help people feel secure even when they move across companies or invent their own jobs.

Writing the Employability Security Contract

It is time for a new social contract based on the new realities. It should show people what the company is willing to do to help them build their own futures. It should be an explicit statement of how much people are valued. And it should be a commitment to specific actions made possible by public policies.

Imagine an agreement that every manager would sign and give to every person in the company that would read something like this:

"Our company faces competitive world markets and rapidly changing technology. We need the flexibility to add or delete products, open or close facilities, and redeploy the work force. Although we cannot guarantee tenure in any particular job or even future employment, we will

work to ensure that all our people are fully employable—sought out for new jobs here and elsewhere.

"We promise to increase opportunity and power for our entire, diverse work force. We will:

- Recruit for the potential to increase in competence, not simply to narrow skills to fill today's slots.
- Offer ample learning opportunities, from formal training to lunchtime seminars—the equivalent of three weeks a year.
- Provide challenging jobs and rotating assignments that allow growth in skills even without promotion to higher jobs.
- Measure performance beyond accounting numbers and share the data to allow learning by doing and continuous improvement—turning everyone into self-guided professionals.
- Retrain employees as soon as jobs become obsolete.
- Emphasize team building, to help our diverse work force appreciate and utilize fully each other's skills.
- Recognize and reward individual and team achievements, thereby building external reputations and offering tangible indicators of value.
- Provide three-month educational sabbaticals, external internships, or personal time-out every five years.
- Find growth opportunities in our network of suppliers, customers, and venture partners.
- Ensure that pensions and benefits are portable, so that people have safety nets for the future even if they seek employment elsewhere.
- Help people be productive while carrying family responsibilities, through flex-time, provision for sick children, and renewal breaks between major assignments.
- Measure the building of human capital and the capabilities of our people as thoroughly and frequently as we measure the building and use of financial capital.

- Encourage entrepreneurship—new ventures within our company or outside that help our people start businesses and create alternative sources of employment.
- Tap our people's ideas to develop innovations that lower costs, serve customers, and create new markets—the best foundation for business growth and continuing employment, and the source of funds to reinvest in continuous learning."

Policies like these could renew loyalty, commitment, and productivity for all men and women, of corporations both large and small, as they struggle to create jobs, wealth, and well-being in the global economy.

A SAD BUT NEEDED CHANGE

J. H. Foegen *is professor of business at Winona (Minnesota) State University and has published more than 360 articles including occasional contributions to* Business and Society Review. *He responded:*

Certainly there is some truth to Samuelson's arguments but his conclusion seems overdrawn and unduly pessimistic. Even mighty IBM, important as it is, represents far less than the whole economy; it never did call the tune for such a complexity. Many firms probably did not even consider IBM a viable role model.

Samuelson's key words, I think, are "ideal" and "might," as in "our ideal of what all American companies might become." Arguably, it was never possible for all to be—or even to become—like IBM. Many firms have always been smaller, less profitable, and less able to afford what many still see as the luxury of social responsibility. In the competitive jungle, survival alone is a major accomplishment.

In any case, the spice of business life, as well as life in general, is variety. Despite the fact that most new businesses fail, the action remains largely theirs: opportunities to fill unmet needs, to profit from leading-edge innovations, and, maybe for a few, eventually to become like an

IBM. Small firms also continue to be significant job producers that offset job losses from technological progress, greater efficiency, downsizing, and shifts in industry fortunes.

Admirable as was Big Blue in its glory days, the company and its managers were not and could not be perfect. Cynics might add that, when you are number one, there is no way to go but down. Even vaunted IBM could not expect to be king of the hill indefinitely. (Do not forget, however, that despite current problems the firm is hardly a has-been. *Business Week's* October 4, 1993 cover story, "Rethinking IBM," is only one of many articles so attesting.)

In short, "good" corporations are still possible. In fact, today's "leaning-down" efforts constitute a sad but much-needed scrambling to regain lost competitiveness, to do what, with hindsight, was probably preventable. Such efforts, if successfully completed, can produce a new round of good, IBM-like jobs, with economic security, generous benefits, and even social responsibility in all its guises.

The most tragic thing about the situation is not the troubles in Armonk per se. Rather, as is so often the case, the economic adjustments are still borne by workers more than by managers and owners. Top executives in some companies received large increases in salaries and stock options while workers were being let go.

A main difference between yesterday and today is that currently, middle-age and white-collar types are hurting too, along with young workers and blue-collar employees. The pain is no less—at IBM or anywhere else it is faced.

DON'T CONFUSE BAD BUSINESS DECISIONS WITH SOCIAL RESPONSIBILITY

Joan Bavaria *is president of Franklin Research & Development and cochair of CERES. She responded:*

Frequently throughout recorded history, there have been proclamations, assertions, and declarations by those who claim to have some unique insight into truth, whether that insight is gleaned by divine intervention, careful scrutiny of evidence, or simply the strength of a hysterical voice. Chicken Little, you recall, was certain that the sky was falling when an apple descended from a tree in the wrong place at the wrong time. Faced with a similar phenomenon, Isaac Newton came to an entirely different conclusion. In his *Newsweek* column, Robert J. Samuelson, in calling socially responsible management dead, seems to be coming from an intellectual process similar to Chicken Little's.

Before the decade of the 1980s brought back a robber baron mentality reminiscent of the last century, companies were never asked to become "welfare systems." Pensions and health benefits are compensation for work done. They are not welfare. Workers and their employers bargain for packages of benefits rather than for simple wages because we decided as a society to provide insurance against indigence in old age and needless suffering from lack of health care.

Missing the Mark

IBM and other companies that are now cutting work forces and benefits do so for various complex reasons. Due to artificially low costs of transportation and exponentially more efficient communications systems, the economy has become, almost overnight, global. Transnational companies are no longer forced to stay within defined geographical areas in the search for workers. The result is we are exporting nonsupervisory jobs out of this country at an incredible rate through different employment abroad or indirect outsourcing of manufacturing to foreign firms. Lester Thurow estimates that after correcting for inflation, the wages of nonsupervisory U.S. workers have fallen 19 percent in the past nineteen years despite a 25 percent increase in the real per capita gross domestic product (GDP).

At the same time nonsupervisory workers were losing economic ground, total executive compensation including limousines, fancy dinners, and lucrative stock options that do not appear as expense items on income statements rose exponentially. In 1990, the average ratio of a chief executive's salary to that of a blue-collar worker at major Japanese automobile companies was twenty to one. In the United States, it was 192 to one. IBM managers participated handsomely in this windfall. This is not, in my view, socially responsible.

More important, IBM missed the mark technologically. It did not move with innovators to develop software, and fell victim to what has become the commodity-like market for computers. The company's culture of tradition, authority, and white-shirted conformity probably contributed to this disaster.

Plenty of companies continue to treat their workers extremely well and do not fall victim to competitive pressures. It is wrong to assume a correlation between socially responsible employment practices and bad business decisions.

Rather than herald the demise of social responsibility in corporate management, Samuelson should question excesses in management compensation and the ability of corporate or political cultures to respond to constantly shifting external environments. The world as it is can become the world as we wish it to be with a little hard work.

SHOULD WE EVEN BOTHER TO MOURN?

Doug Bandow *is a senior fellow at the Cato Institute and a contributing editor to the* Freeman *magazine. He responded:*

Is the good corporation dead? And if so, should we be happy or sad? At first blush, the answer to the first question appears to be yes. As for the second, some people probably do not understand how one could even ask it. Yet the answers are more difficult than they might at first appear.

The real issue is the nature of employment. Is a job an entitlement? If so, then we rightly mourn the possible passage of the private welfare state, the company that offers stable, life-long employment plus the full range of generous benefits. If not, however, then we should applaud a move back towards individual rather than corporate responsibility.

Despite the recent emphasis on business "social responsibility," we should not forget that companies are merely one of many different social institutions. Business' prime obligation is to supply goods and services to willing buyers. In doing so, firms should respect the rights of others, but a potential employee has no moral claim to be hired—or, if hired, to be guaranteed forty years of employment, receive a certain level of health insurance, or expect anything else.

Rather, these issues should be decided by negotiation between employers and employees. Bargaining is particularly important since a firm's decision to act "responsibly" always involves trade-offs. Money for health care benefits and pensions does not come out of thin air, but reduces that available to provide salaries. Job stability, too, has an economic cost. Different employees will prefer different benefit packages.

Still, to some the competitive pressures that are forcing even major companies to retrench appear to be unfairly reducing workers' options. Yet high salaries alone do not guarantee a high standard of living. Precisely these same pressures are pushing down prices and creating more product and service alternatives, allowing people to live better even with less money. In short, people are more likely to prosper in open markets that encourage adaptation and innovation.

This does not mean that change is painless. But no one has a right to avoid change, or to make other people pay the cost of change. Thus, the end of firms as a generous private adjunct to the public welfare state does not mean the end of the good corporation, since the fairness of a company's dealings with its employees should not be defined by its level of benefits. Nor does this change mean the end of the good society as long as two points are emphasized. First, people need to recognize that the ultimate responsibility

for their and their family's future lies with them, not their employer or their government. That is, people need to save and invest, purchase disability and health insurance, create their own retirement funds, and otherwise prepare for an uncertain future.

Second, people need to work together to establish a social safety net to care for those who prove most vulnerable to a world of change. That means private charity for those in need as well as the sort of fraternal associations that existed before the Great Depression to help prevent people from becoming impoverished. In these ways, people's desire for greater stability could be manifested by demonstrating greater responsibility as individuals, families, and communities.

Should we mourn the passing of the good corporation? Japan is asking this question too, as firms begin laying off workers and linking pay to performance. The answer is no. For many people, the end of the welfare corporation will be painful. But responsibility for one's own security and that of one's family does not properly lie with either business or government. If people take up this challenge, the ongoing economic changes, painful as they are, will end up moving us closer to the good society.

THE PURSUIT OF GOODNESS

Tom Chappell *is president of Tom's of Maine and author of the just-published book,* The Soul of a Business: Managing for Profit and the Common Good *(Bantam. New York). He responded:*

Tom's of Maine, the country's leading producer of natural personal care products, is a relatively small company with eighty employees and retail sales approaching $20 million. How can we compete with Procter & Gamble and others that can afford to spend $80 million on advertising alone? In simple numbers, we can't. Instead, we look to our beliefs and to our mission to create our own distinct identity. We practice what I call "common good capitalism." It's working for us, and our sales are growing at a five-year compounded average of 20 percent.

Common good capitalism is the practice of managing your business with multiple aims: the pursuit of profit and the intentional pursuit of goodness. It calls on business to break down the traditional barriers between corporate values and the most fundamental values of society—respect for people, nature, and community—so they may guide and inform our business decisions. The result? Greater competitive advantage for your company. It succeeds because its products, services, and business practices reflect the basic values that are important to consumers today.

The fundamental idea behind common good capitalism is that for business to prosper today, goodness must be pursued with the same intention with which we pursue profit. But just what is goodness? And how can business put it into practice?

At its core, goodness is the demonstration of care and concern for people, nature, and community. It is not something we can take for granted but must be actively sought and created. Most important, goodness must be created in connection with others, for it is in relation to other people that we find goodness. This definition may sound far too philosophical for the realities of business, but relationships—with your customers, your employees, and your suppliers—are the very foundation of business.

When you respect your customers, you get better feedback on products and issues. If employees feel that everyone is being open and honest and working toward the same goals, then you get more creative problem solving and better answers. When your vendors trust and respect you, you get better service. When you consider your community and the environment in decision making, you gain marketplace respect and support in return. In short, you gain the competitive edge and your business succeeds. Customers do not want to choose between price, quality, and companies they believe in and respect.

Putting common good capitalism into practice means finding a practical path between seemingly incompatible values—profits versus respect and competition versus goodness. Common good capitalism is not about balance or compromise. Rather, it is the process of finding a middle ground that keeps competing aims in view but finds a new, creative way to integrate them into a single act or decision. You don't have to sell your soul to make your numbers.

That is not to say that common good capitalism is easy. There is no right way or sure-fire business plan. Common good capitalism is a journey in which every business must find its own answers. When there is conflict, there must be creativity. Although finding a new way is often more difficult, the result is always worth the effort—for people, our environment, and profits.

NOTES

1. This article is based on the 1993 Afterword to *Men and Women of the Corporation* (Basic Books, New York.) Copyright © 1993 by Rosabeth Moss Kanter.

READING 7-3

Sign of the Times: Implementing Reductions in Force

Brian W. Bulger
Carolyn Curtis Gessner

In the past few years, the increasing uncertainty and instability of doing business in the United States have forced many companies to reduce their work forces dramatically. The need to cut employees can arise from a variety of factors,

Source: Sign of the Times: Implementing Reductions in Force, Brian Bulger and Carolyn Curtiss Gessner, copyright © 1991–1992. *Employee Relations Law Journal, 17* (3) (Winter, 1991-92), 431-447. Printed by permission of John Wiley & Sons, Inc.

including economic and competitive pressures on in-house costs, mergers or acquisitions that result in duplicative staffing, or perceptions that the company should become "lean and mean" to be an aggressive presence in the marketplace. Whatever the reasons, reductions in force may bring about the desired results. However, such drastic actions carry problematic consequences that employers must recognize and evaluate before making reductions.

In particular, reductions in force (RIFs) frequently lead to litigation against the company by its terminated employees. Such suits are not limited to employees who were "formally" discharged; constructive discharge claims have been brought by individuals who left their jobs under the auspices of ostensibly "voluntary" early retirement or incentive plans. Management personnel over the age of forty often bring suits under federal and/or state age discrimination laws. These lawsuits can be difficult for employers to win and extremely expensive to lose, as age discrimination claimants are generally entitled to jury trials and may receive back pay, front pay, and liquidated damages.

For these reasons, as well as the more fundamental priorities of fairness and employee morale, an employer considering an RIF should move cautiously. Its decisions must be based on demonstrable, objective factors. This article examines the steps employers should follow in implementing RIFs and points to the potential problems that must be avoided to avert age discrimination liability.

EVALUATING THE EMPLOYER'S OPTIONS

As a preliminary step, employers should strongly consider whether actions other than RIFs will have the desired effects on business strength. Such a self-examination works both prospectively and retrospectively: it gives the employer a clearer understanding of its needs before drastic actions are taken, and it may serve as evidence of the employer's good faith should RIF decisions ever be challenged[1] in

order to maintain employee morale and forestall future liability, the employer should endeavor to show that it did not want to terminate employees, but that it, in fact, had no other reasonable options.

Such a self-examination begins with pinpointing the business needs that drive the inclination to make cuts.[2] By targeting problem areas, alternatives may be more effectively developed and evaluated, and narrowly tailored decisions may be more easily defended.

Alternatives to drastic reductions can be contemplated in a series of stages. The first stage includes steps that may generate some improvement in the employer's financial picture, such as:

- *Implementing nonemployment cost reductions*—Trimming waste in the company's overhead is a logical first step in controlling costs, although a well-managed company will likely find the actual savings generated by such cuts to be limited.
- *Exploring methods to increase productivity and/or profitability*—Although most companies seek to improve these factors continually, the pressure of potential staff reductions may act as an added incentive to change traditional performance patterns.
- *Examining whether usual attrition rates will yield sufficient vacancies to meet reduction needs*—In a workplace with significant turnover and relatively interchangeable job responsibilities, leaving jobs open after employees depart may remove some economic pressure. Realistically, though, fewer employees are likely to leave voluntarily during periods of declining opportunity in the job market, so historic attrition rates may not provide an accurate picture of the future.

Unfortunately, these tactics will not usually lead to sufficient improvement in an employer's economic position. If this is the case, the employer may opt to move on to the second stage of alternatives. These options have a first-hand economic impact on employees, but are less financially devastating than involuntary RIFs. In addition, this class of options includes creative opportunities for job restructuring or early retirement, options that may appeal to some employees while saving the employer money at the same time. Such options include:

- Pay freezes or reductions
- Shorter work hours or weeks
- Short-term temporary shutdowns or layoffs
- Job sharing
- Voluntary leaves of absence
- Incentive or early retirement programs

Again, these types of actions may not lead to the dramatic cost savings the employer requires. However, the consideration and implementation of such programs demonstrate the employer's good faith and may decrease the number of involuntary terminations to be made later. In most cases, therefore, employers will want to attempt some form of voluntary reduction before deciding whether to move on to the third stage, involuntary terminations.

VOLUNTARY SEPARATIONS

Voluntary separations, either through a job "buy-out" program or an early retirement incentive "window," have significant advantages over involuntary terminations. Foremost among these advantages is the mutual satisfaction engendered by truly voluntary programs, especially when the program eliminates the need for involuntary RIFs: the employee chooses the path he or she wishes to follow, and the employer is not forced to make—and defend—often painful decisions about cutting individual employees. The resulting sense of certainty and increased morale can significantly help the company weather economically difficult periods.

Obviously, however, these programs have their downsides. On the most basic level, incentives are expensive in the short term[4] and potentially impractical for employers strapped for cash. Even more troubling in the long run, the employer lacks firm control over who will leave

the company if the program is truly voluntary. Although the employer may limit its incentive offer to specified classes of employees, such distinctions need to be based on objective, verifiable business needs.[5] Employers must also recognize that some employees may accept the incentive offer, but then sue for constructive discharge (that is, allege that they were coerced into resigning or retiring). The employer can best protect against such litigation in two ways: first, by designing an incentive program that strongly communicates its voluntary nature, and second, by incorporating severance agreements, waivers, and/or releases in the incentive program.[6] Both of these important factors are discussed in more detail in the following sections.

Designing a Voluntary Separation Program

A company's decision to implement incentive programs requires the consideration of a variety of factors. Intended results, program costs, and the potential impact on business operations all should be evaluated assuming various levels of participation. Educated guesses generally can be made as to which groups will find the offer too good to pass up, allowing the employer to identify potential problems that might result from the loss of key personnel. Such projections also allow for an analysis of the company on a before and after (hypothetical) basis, which may reveal the potential impact of a proposed plan on the company's race, age, and gender demographics. Such studies are usually discoverable in litigation, but will not be considered evidence of unlawful discrimination if properly linked to objective business needs.[7]

Given that these documents are discoverable, all records of studies should reflect the unbiased goals of the program. Documents that imply that the company wants only older people to retire could be used to support allegations that improper age bias motivates the company's plan. As far as possible, calculations should be made using only average statistics to avoid the impression that a particular age group has been targeted for cuts. Keep in mind that a company may be sued for implementing a plan that has an unnecessarily detrimental impact on a protected group.[8]

On balance, although some analysis is obviously necessary and beneficial, this is an area in which the employer should not attempt to study exhaustively every possible, if unlikely, outcome. Rather, relatively brief studies of costs, alternatives, and potential impact should be undertaken, and the employer should be prepared to demonstrate that, based on those studies, it designed a plan that contained the most justifiable combination of factors, with little detrimental impact upon a selected group. Of course, so long as the plan is truly voluntary, and is not accompanied with "wink and a nod" communications about which employees should stay or leave, arguments about adverse impact should have little weight with a court.[9]

Legal Barriers to Voluntary Separation Plans

Before implementing any kind of incentive plan, an employer may have to overcome a variety of statutory and common law obstacles. For example, state and federal antidiscrimination statutes will prohibit the implementation of plans that are motivated by unlawful bias. The Employee Retirement Income Security Act (ERISA) may also impose requirements for reporting, disclosure, and claims procedures.[10] In addition, the employer should consider whether employees affected by the offer are covered by express employment agreements or implied agreements, such as those created by employee handbooks or oral representations. Similarly, existing welfare plans, retirement plans, collective bargaining agreements, and personnel policies may need to be modified before an incentive program can be implemented. In particular, employers will need to consider the age discrimination issues raised by voluntary retirement plans.

Treatment of Voluntary Plans under the OWBPA

Employers that have used early retirement incentive plans over the past few years have had to cope with dramatically fluctuating legal standards. Prior to 1989, programs that set age limits for eligibility presented a prima facie case of age discrimination, which the employer then was forced to rebut by showing that the program was a "bona fide employee benefit plan . . . [and] not a subterfuge to evade the purposes of [the ADEA].[11] The Supreme Court upset this standard with its 1989 decision in *Public Employees Retirement System of Ohio v. Betts,* 492 U.S. 158, in which the Court found that the ADEA did not generally prohibit age discrimination in employee benefits plans.

In October 1990, Congress enacted the Older Workers Benefit Protection Act (OWBPA) to erase *Betts's* impact on employee rights. The OWBPA specifically amends the ADEA to include all employee benefits and bona fide employee benefit plans in the class of "compensation, terms, conditions or privileges of employment," which employers are prohibited from allocating discriminatorily. The so-called anti-*Betts* provisions became immediately effective for new benefit plans on the day of enactment (October 16, 1990) and became applicable to plans that preexisted the OWBPA on April 14, 1991.

The OWBPA contains several provisions of special interest to employers designing incentive programs. First, the Act expressly allows employers to set minimum ages for eligibility in early (or, for that matter, normal) retirement benefit plans. Additionally, the Act invokes a historic EEOC rule known as the "Equal Benefit or Equal Cost" standard. Under this rule, an employer is required to provide older workers with benefits at least equal to those provided to younger employees, *unless* it can be determined that providing an equal benefit to the older worker is more costly than to the younger person. Finally, as mentioned previously, the Act heavily regulates the terms under which an employee's voluntary waiver may be enforced.

Pros and Cons of Requiring Waivers of ADEA Claims

Some elements of strategy to be considered in deciding whether or not to seek an Agreement and Release of Claims as part of a voluntary (or involuntary) RIF include the following:

1. Requesting the release is likely to expose those employees who are considering, or are likely to consider, a lawsuit in response to their termination. A refusal to sign may identify not only troubled employees but problem areas in the workplace. Early disclosure of these potential plaintiffs and their areas of concern may enable the employer to prepare an early defense. On the other hand, seeking the release may arouse employee concerns and suspicions where there previously had been none and may alert employees to claims that they may never have realized they had.
2. The release itself may have certain psychological value in deterring later litigation. Some employees may feel compelled to live with the choice they made in signing the release.
3. Although even an employee who signs a release may choose to disavow it and sue, the existence of a release enables the employer to insist that the primary issue of any litigation must be the validity of the release.

OWBPA'S waiver provision seeks to guarantee that employees signing separation agreements have every opportunity to consider their potential litigation options. Specifically, waivers will not be valid unless they are "knowing and voluntary," a standard that requires the employer, among other things, to allow for a waiting period before and after the document's execution, advise the employee of the names of other employees covered by the incentive plan,

and urge the employee to consult with an attorney before signing the waiver.

The requirement that other covered employees be identified is particularly problematic, as it basically allows the employee to have cost-free discovery of company information prior to the inception of a lawsuit. Consequently, the employer must take care in designing its plan to avoid even the appearance of discriminatory impact or other impropriety. On the other hand, the employer's obligation to advise the employee to consult with legal counsel actually is less of a detriment to the employer's position than it might appear in the abstract. The involvement of counsel has always served to enhance the enforceability of waivers, and plaintiffs' attorneys may help the employee to view his or her situation objectively and realistically, rather than emotionally.

Guaranteeing Voluntariness

As mentioned earlier, employees who accept incentive separation offers will sometimes turn around and sue their former employers, claiming that they were forced to resign involuntarily. If the employer had the foresight to obtain a waiver of claims from the employee, the voluntariness of the waiver will also be challenged. To preserve the position it hopes to achieve through its voluntary separation program, the company should take all available steps to ensure that the plan is truly voluntary and document those efforts fully.[12]

At the outset, the employer should publicize the plan, emphasizing its voluntary nature. If possible to do so truthfully, the employer also should attempt to squelch rumors that those who do not leave voluntarily will be fired later. This avoids a "gun to the head" argument if constructive discharge is alleged afterwards. However, if further reductions are anticipated, the employer should be frank in presenting the company's prospects and future.[13]

As word of the plan is being spread, great care should be taken to instruct managers not to steer the decisions of employees. The company must avoid giving employees the impression that they must leave now or be fired later or, just as importantly, giving the impression that some employees are untouchable. Either situation will create significant problems in subsequent litigation. As one court colorfully noted, "to accept the reasoning . . . that a person's acceptance of an early retirement package is voluntary when faced with a 'choice' between the Scylla of forced retirement or the Charybdis of discharge . . . is to turn a blind eye to the take it or leave it nature of such an offer."[14]

Once the plan has been publicized, the employer should encourage interested individuals to bring questions to designated personnel who have been thoroughly instructed on the applicable laws. Some companies send follow-up information only to interested employees and do not further solicit employees who do not respond.

Another technique is to hire an outside financial consultant or accountant to advise employees about the plan. The consultant should be instructed to use his or her own judgment in advising employees, with the understanding that the company has no interest in obtaining anything other than a truly voluntary decision to leave or stay. The consultant should, however, keep a record of the advice given to an employee. This approach can be good for employee morale and foster confidence in the incentive program and the company. Moreover, an employee who is advised by an outside consultant that a program is "too good to refuse" will have a hard time proving coercion or that separation was really a constructive discharge.

In publicizing the plan, expiration dates must be clearly stated. Although the OWBPA does impose applicable time requirements, in particular the forty-five-day consideration period for incentive and early retirement agreements, the plan cannot be allowed to hang indefinitely. A reasonable deadline or "window" should be set, balancing the needs of the employees to deliberate over this major decision with the pressing financial or other structural needs experienced by the company. Without such a firm deadline, employees may sit out the pending offer in hopes that a better deal will come along.

Oversubscription

Sometimes voluntary separation incentive plans are too successful for the employer's good. Cost considerations or the loss of too many key employees may make a voluntary plan prohibitively expensive if many more employees choose to leave than were anticipated. The employer may consider leaving itself an "out" by offering the plan with the condition that if too many employees express interest, of if an entire area seems likely to lose all its key personnel, the plan may be modified or rescinded. This approach carries very serious risks, however. If an employer wishes to use an oversubscription clause, it should be prepared to defend the refusal to allow any group or individual to participate with legitimate business reasons.

On balance, this approach is not recommended. If problems are serious enough to justify reducing the work force, they probably are serious enough for the company to be able to lose even a relatively large number of "key" employees. Quite often, employers are amazed at how drastically the work force can be reduced without a significant decline in productivity. In short, a company may be better advised to let the cuts run too deep rather than too shallow, which at least avoids the need for more cuts later.

Structuring Severance Pay Plans

Certain special problems come into play when designing severance pay plans. Some employers wish to pay severance only to employees who cannot take advantage of retirement benefits and have accordingly limited participation to those younger than retirement age.

This is another area in which the OWBPA is leaving its mark. Under the new Act, employers are prohibited from allocating offers of severance pay strictly on the basis of age. However, severance payments may be reduced by the value of any retiree health benefits received by an employee who is eligible for an immediate pension. Such an offset may also include any additional pension benefits provided to employees entitled to an immediate and unreduced pension. The clarification of rights and duties presented in the OWBPA is intended to eliminate the case law confusion that arose under the former distinction between "simple fringe benefits" and "complex benefit schemes."[15]

INVOLUNTARY REDUCTIONS

Unfortunately, even after all other voluntary means have been exhausted, it may still be necessary to conduct an involuntary reduction in force to meet the business needs of the company. The potential for legal action by employees who are involuntarily terminated is, of course, much higher.[16] Therefore, the employer must be prepared to defend each individual non-retention decision as well as the overall impact of its reduction upon various protected groups.[17]

Designing the RIF Plan

Whether or not a proposed RIF follows a voluntary program, the company should conduct an analysis of the need for and size of the RIF. This study should be performed by senior management, particularly if the RIF is large. The involvement of senior management serves both internal and external purposes: lower-level officials may have personal interests in the RIF, and juries expect involvement of senior management in decisions of this importance.

At the outset, the pre-RIF work force should be analyzed in terms of protected groups (that is, race, sex, and age). Age studies should not simply categorize employees as over/under forty, but should cover various age brackets. This study can and should be undertaken pursuant to a directive from senior management that the

company's policy is to conduct the RIF in the fairest, most objective manner it can and avoid any significant adverse impact upon protected groups. From this overall picture, smaller segments can be studied to determine the employment picture by division, department, job classification, and so on. Ultimately, these materials will be used for an impact study of the effects of the RIF.

At the next step, management will lay out a plan for determining who is to be retained or let go. This plan should be written with assistance of counsel and with the determination that following the plan strictly is the best way to defend against litigation.[18]

Formulating the plan consists primarily of determining the best means for deciding retention issues. To the extent possible, the first focus of any plan is on what jobs or job functions generally need to be eliminated or retained. This may be easy, as, for example, when an entire product line has suffered a serious drop in sales, necessitating large cutbacks for that line. In most cases, however, the employer is looking for across-the-board cuts of the work force, often coupled with a redesigned organization. The plan should designate management committees to study and then apply the plan's imperatives.

Conducting Job Studies

Following development of the RIF general plan, management should undertake an intensive study of job functions, without regard to the identities of incumbents.[19] Normally, the plan will designate a committee to handle this task. Written instructions should be provided to the committee, detailing the factors to be considered in whether to consolidate or eliminate jobs or job functions. The committee should not consider the individual strengths and weaknesses of the employer's incumbent personnel in reaching these decisions. Rather, factors that should be studied include types of duties performed and time spent on performance, overlaps among jobs or departments, availability of qualified personnel for such positions, and so on.[20] A caveat is necessary here because an analysis of cost considerations may be used to suggest age discrimination, as more highly paid employees generally are older and more senior.

The committee should be instructed to determine which jobs or tasks can be eliminated, consolidated, or reduced, and which should be retained. An analysis can be made of the likelihood of meeting the business goals through the proposed changes, which can be used by senior management to decide whether further study and cuts are necessary before proceeding to the next step. The committee also should be instructed to prepare detailed job descriptions that include necessary and preferred qualifications. These descriptions can then be used to evaluate the fitness of particular employees for the remaining jobs.

Evaluating Individual Employees

Once a new structure has been decided upon after a study of job functions, management can move to the next step—determining which individuals are to be retained to fill the remaining jobs. Most often, the initial evaluation is done by the manager of a particular area. However, many companies have used committees to evaluate personnel or to pass on initial recommendations, whereas others have experimented with peer review systems.

Whether an evaluation is conducted by an individual or a committee, the standards of evaluation must be clear and documented in writing. Similarly, evaluations should be written or otherwise documented. Of course, written evaluations will be important issues in subsequent litigation, so evaluators must be thoroughly trained in evaluation procedures. "Smoking gun" memoranda are common at this stage—for example, "This is really a young man's game, and Joe's not cut out for it anymore." Even otherwise neutral words like "dynamic" or "aggressive" can be deemed code words for youthfulness in the context of an age discrimination lawsuit.[21]

An important question to be faced is whether evaluators will consult previous performance evaluations or if a whole new system is to be used for the RIF. It is a simple fact that because most managers are not completely candid in the yearly appraisals, "grade inflation" inevitably creeps into the system. Moreover, the previous evaluation system may be so vague or subjective that it has little value in defending against discrimination claims. There are advantages to using existing appraisals, however, because not only do they lend some historical perspective to the differences among employees,[22] but perhaps even more importantly, employees generally will have failed to contest past adverse comments.[23] Additionally, failure to consult existing evaluations may be held against the company.[24]

Whether or not previous evaluations are consulted, employers should consider also adopting a special RIF evaluation system. The goal of this system is to rank employees relative to one another, and numerical rating systems are used frequently. Inconsistencies with previous ratings, however, may be difficult to explain.[25]

Instructions as to factors for consideration, and their relative weights, should be given to evaluators.[26] These factors should include performance ratings, particular skills, and other objective criteria. Additionally, consideration of seniority will serve to negate any implication of discrimination, such as years of service.[27] Employers are cautioned, however, not to base decisions on the relative salaries paid to incumbent employees, because courts have construed such considerations as a proxy for age discrimination.[28] A particularly instructive case is *Stendebach v. CPC International,* 691 F.2d 735 (5th Cir. 1982), certiorari denied, 461 U.S. 944 (1983), in which a committee prepared a list of qualifications for each position, designed a rating system using those qualifications, and numerically rated each candidate. In case of a tie, older employees were retained. Final decisions were then reviewed by corporate headquarters for adverse impact. On that basis, the Court found that the former employee had failed to raise a substantial issue of fact and affirmed summary judgment for the employer.

Reviewing the Proposed RIF'S Impact on Protected Groups

Once the initial evaluator has finished ranking employees and made retention/nonretention recommendations, a review must be conducted to determine whether adverse impact or some other form of discrimination is operating. This review should be conducted by senior personnel familiar with the legal definitions and implications of discrimination. The review may be conducted by a committee, balanced to ensure representation of protected groups.

The reviewing committee should be instructed, first, to evaluate the rankings by cross-checking evaluations against the instructions, job descriptions, and relevant performance documents.[29] Next, retention decisions should be evaluated against the pre-RIF work force makeup to determine if protected groups are adversely affected. If adverse impact is found, it may be necessary to check each individual decision and evaluator carefully for indications of bias, and to review job descriptions and evaluation criteria to ensure that they are nondiscriminatory.[30]

Reconsideration of the process or of particular retention decisions may be necessary at this point. Be aware, though, that employers are under no affirmative duty to create another job for, or bump another employee in deference to, an employee from a protected age group.[31] Moreover, even a drop in the overall age of the remaining employees may not support an inference that a particular employee was discharged because of age.[32]

Separations

Once the review process is completed, the employer may proceed with implementation of separations. Practices will vary among employers, but every effort should be made to respect the dignity of individuals and to reduce feelings of anger toward the company.

If individual managers are to announce separations, they should be trained to do so. Separation should be accompanied by explanation of company benefits available, and outplacement assistance is a virtual requirement in these situations. Exit interviews should be required, and the employer may want to establish a formal appeal process for separation decisions. All interview sessions should be documented so that a record of statements made to the employee is available in the event of litigation.

Communications

At *all* steps in the RIF process the employer should be communicating with employees. At the outset the reasons for cuts, together with the need for a certain number of cuts, should be communicated. Once a plan is adopted, it should be publicized. The employer may even want to solicit suggestions about the plan from employees. Criteria to be used in decisions should be published, and an appeal process may be instituted and employees so advised.

Although an active communications program contains the risk of communicating improper statements, a well-developed program can reduce employee anxiety and anger by demonstrating the necessity and fairness of the RIF. When coupled with significant severance benefits, effective communication may reduce the chance of RIF litigation by many employees.

Post-RIF

Don't, Don't, Don't replace employees terminated in the course of an RIF within (at least) a year. The employees *will* find out about such replacements, which then act as a catalyst to lawsuits and enhance an employee's claim that the RIF was a pretext for unlawful discrimination.[33]

Ideally, a tight hiring freeze should be imposed after an RIF. If new hires are needed, consideration should be given first to employees terminated in the RIF. The employer may wish to establish a priority placement list consisting of terminated employees who will be rehired if positions open up.[34] In particular, employers should not deny a job opening to an over-forty employee on the sole basis that he or she may be "overqualified" for the position, as courts may view that as simply another "code word" for age bias. For example, in *Taggart v. Time, Inc.,* 924 F.2d 43 (2d Cir. 1991), the court said that "denying employment to an older job applicant because he or she has too much experience, training or education is simply to employ a euphemism to mask the real reason for refusal, namely, in the eyes of the employer the applicant is too old." The *Taggart* decision notes that the usual rationale for not hiring overqualified individuals, that is, a concern that such employees will leave at the first preferable opportunity, does not hold true for older employees, whose mobility is greatly diminished. In a similar decision issued shortly after *Taggart,* the Second Circuit ruled that an employer's refusal to "underemploy" employees in lower-echelon positions did not rebut the employee's prima facie case of age discrimination.[35]

Employees should be asked to state particular positions, geographic areas, and salary ranges for which they wish to be considered, rather than allowing completely open consideration. If this process is used, however, it is important not to raise employees' hopes unduly. As before, be sure managers are cautioned against making loaded statements to employees or ex-employees after the RIF is implemented.

Throughout the process of considering its options, the employer must take care to document thoroughly the investigations, studies, and evaluations it undertakes. Any judge or jury will expect a medium-sized or large company to be able to present a paper trail proving that a genuine business need requires drastic measures, like an RIF.

The goal of such a paper trail is to reflect the company's actual needs, its concern for its employees, and the objectivity of its plans. It should not, however, whitewash the facts. Rather, documents should contain frank analyses of the size of reductions necessary to achieve the desired ends and, if applicable, the inability of methods short of an RIF to attain them.[36] Keep in mind that documents prepared for these purposes will usually be discoverable in court. Objective, unbiased documentation will go a long way toward showing the employer's good faith.[37]

Juries tend to be much less likely than judges to accept management's judgment that an RIF was necessary. If jurors are not completely satisfied that an employer pursued all available options, they may seek to punish the employer regardless of whether the employee manages to prove unlawful discrimination.[38] To combat this predisposition against employers, management should strive to maintain concrete, objective evidence of the basis for its decisions and why other options would be ineffective.

CONCLUSION

There is no one "right" way to conduct a reduction in force. However, employers should study carefully various alternatives within the framework of the law in their jurisdiction and their own particular circumstances. A well-defined plan keyed to business reasons for cutbacks, coupled with fair, objective evaluation of employees for retention, is the best way to avoid or defeat legal challenges by former employees.

NOTES

1. See *Cannistra v. FAA,* 24 FEP Cases 162 (D. D.C. 1979).
2. See *Cooper v. Cook Paint & Varnish Co.,* 563 F. Supp. 1146 (W.D. Mo. 1983); *Parcinski v. Outlet Co.,* 673 F.2d 34 (2d Cir. 1982), cert. denied, 459 U.S. 1103 (1982).

3. As will be discussed in the following section, incentive and early retirement programs carry a range of potential complications. Such plans therefore should be implemented very carefully and with sufficient study.

4. An employer cannot make an involuntary termination appear voluntary by paying the employee retirement or other benefits to which he or she would be entitled anyway. See *McMahon v. Libbey-Owens-Ford Co.,* 870 F.2d 1073, 1077 (6th Cir. 1979). Additionally, waivers or releases executed by employees in the course of such programs will not be enforceable without extra consideration. Employers should therefore expect to offer significant benefits over and above previous entitlements in connection with their separation incentive programs.

5. See *Bodnar v. Synpol, Inc.,* 843 F.2d 190, 193 (5th Cir. 1987), cert. denied, 488 U.S. 908 (1988).

6. Note that the OWBPA has significantly altered the consequences of seeking waivers and releases from employees.

7. See, e.g., *Kesselring v. United Technologies Corp.,* No. C2-89-622, 1991 WL 847 (S.D. Ohio, Jan. 7, 1991); *Stanojev v. Ebasco,* 643 F.2d 914 (2d Cir. 1981); *Marson v. Jones & Laughlin Steel Co.,* 523 F. Supp. 503 (E.D. Wis. 1981); *Stendebach* (cited on p. 325); *Earley v. Champion Int'l Corp.,* 907 F.2d 1077 (11th Cir. 1990); *Wilson v. Firestone Tire & Rubber Co.,* 932 F.2d 510, 514 (6th Cir. 1991).

8. See *EEOC v. Chrysler Corp.,* 733 F.2d 1183 (6th Cir. 1983); *Polstorff v. Fletcher,* 452 F. Supp. 17 (N.D. Ala. 1978).

9. See e.g., *Russell v. Teledyne Ohio Steel,* 892 F.2d 1044 (table; text in Westlaw) (6th Cir. 1990) (statistics as to employees who voluntarily retired could not be used to prove adverse impact or treatment on basis of age).

10. In some instances, it may be possible to avoid the detailed participation, vesting, funding, reporting, and disclosure requirements of ERISA on the premise that the severance pay plan is a payroll practice rather than an employee benefit plan subject to such requirements. In other instances, however, the employer may desire (and it may be required by ERISA) to regard the severance pay arrangement as an employee welfare benefit plan under ERISA, which subjects the arrangement to certain reporting and disclosure requirements and a more formal claim review procedure.

11. 29 U.S.C. § 623(a)(1) and (f)(2).

12. In an interpretive statement by the managers of the Senate bill that became the OWBPA, the importance of voluntariness was made abundantly clear: "Because, by definition, early retirement incentive plans are made available exclusively to older workers, relevant circumstances must be carefully examined to ensure that older workers make a voluntary decision." The statement emphasizes the length of time given for employees to choose, the disclosure of accurate and complete information regarding the plan's benefits to employees, and the presence of any threats or coercive statements as factors determining voluntariness. (Reprinted in 17 Pens. Rep. (BNA) 43, Special Supp., 10/22/90.)

13. Such honesty will not imply age bias unless the actual risks to the employee's job are caused by age bias. See *Harris v. Mallinckrodt,* 886 F.2d 170 (8th Cir. 1989); but contrast *Stamley v. Southern Bell Telephone & Telegraph Co.,* 859 F.2d 855 (11th Cir. 1988) (employer's coercive actions demonstrated that employee's election of retirement was not voluntary) and *Colgan v. Fisher Scientific Co.,* 935 F.2d 1407 (3d Cir. 1991) (poor performance evaluation given to formerly highly rated employee soon after he declined offer of early retirement raised an inference of age discrimination).

14. *Hebert v. Mohawk Rubber Co.,* 872 F.2d 1104 (1st Cir. 1989); see also *Tribble v. Westinghouse Electric Co.,* 669 F.2d 1193 (8th Cir. 1982), cert. denied, 460 U.S. 1080 (1982); *Henn v. Nat'l Geographic Soc'y* 819 F.2d 824 (7th Cir. 1987), cert. denied, 484 U.S. 964 (1987).

15. See e.g., *EEOC v. Borden's, Inc.,* 724 F.2d 1390 (9th Cir. 1984); contrast *Britt v. E.I. Dupont de Nemours & Co., Inc.,* 768 F.2d 593 (4th Cir. 1985).

16. Although this article does not focus on the intricacies of discrimination litigation, the expense and exposure of such litigation cannot be overlooked. The overlapping administrative and judicial review procedures can take years to resolve. *See Astoria Federal Savings and Loan Association v. Solimino,* 111 S. Ct. 2166 (1991) (employer who won dismissal of discrimination

charge at state agency level could still be subject to a federal court lawsuit; agency's findings are not preclusive). A recent Supreme Court decision opened the door to arbitration of age discrimination cases pursuant to written agreement. *Gilmer v. Interstate/Johnson Lane Corp.,* 111 S. Ct. 1647 (1991). However, *Gilmer* relied significantly on arbitration procedures used in the securities industry and failed to decide whether the Federal Arbitration Act's exception was applicable due to the nature of the agreement at issue, which the Court characterized as being with a third party rather than an employer.

17. Although not the primary focus of this article, employers must be cognizant of legal barriers besides the ADEA that restrict employers' rights to conduct RIFs. For example, the Worker Adjustment and Retraining Notification Act requires advance notice of large layoffs to be given to employees and their collective bargaining representatives. Also, foreign-owned companies particularly should be aware of the risk of national origin discrimination charges if RIF decisions take a heavier toll on American employees than on foreign personnel working in the United States.

18. See *Gill v. Union Carbide Corp.,* 368 F. Supp. 364 (E.D. Tenn. 1973).

19. See *Holley v. Sanyo Mfg, Inc.,* 771 F.2d 1161 (8th Cir. 1985); *Wilbur v. Southern Galvanizing Co.,* 34 FEP Cases 1468 (D. Md. 1983).

20. See e.g., *Guinn v. Elec. Data Systems, Inc.,* 752 F. Supp. 713 (S.D. W. Va. 1990); *Rose v. Wells Fargo & Co.,* 902 F.2d 1417 (9th Cir. 1990).

21. See, e.g., *Nobler v. Beth Israel Medical Center,* 702 F. Supp. 1023 (S.D.N.Y. 1990) (comments about need for "new blood," a "fresh face," a "new outlook," and "the best leadership into the new century"); *Taggart* (cited on p. 326) (description of job applicant as "overqualified"); but see *Rose v. Wells Fargo* (cited in note 20), 902 F.2d 1417 (9th Cir. 1990) and *Lindsey v. Baxter Healthcare Corp.,* No. 88 C 10395, 1991 WL 9018 (N.D. Ill. 1991) (phrase "good old boys" not evidence of discrimination).

22. See, e.g., *Conkwright v. Westinghouse Elec. Co.,* 739 F. Supp. 1006 (D. Md. 1990). But note that primary weight should be given to evaluations of the employee in his or her current position, if at all possible. *Connelly v. Bank of Boston.* No. 90-1160, 1991 WL 6464 (1st Cir. January 28, 1991).

23. It may be noted that, for litigation purposes, "an employee's denial of specific events which form the basis of the employer's evaluation may be sufficient to create a genuine issue of fact. . . . However, the fact that the employee takes issue in general terms with the employer's overall evaluation is not sufficient to create a triable issue on pretext." *Komel v. Jewel Cos.,* 874 F.2d 472, 474-475 (7th Cir. 1989) (citations omitted).

24. See *Duffy v. Wheeling Pittsburgh Steel Corp.,* 738 F.2d 1393 (3d Cir. 1984), cert. denied, 469 U.S. 1087 (1984).

25. See *EEOC v. Consol Edison,* 25 FEP Cases 537 (S.D.N.Y. 1981).

26. See *Brito v. Zia Co.,* 478 F.2d 1200 (10th Cir. 1973).

27. This is not to say that decisions based on seniority are in reality based on age. See *Ludovicy v. Dunkirk Radiator Corp.,* 922 F.2d 109, 111 (2d Cir. 1990).

28. See, e.g., *Metz v. Transit Mix, Inc.,* 828 F.2d 1202 (7th Cir. 1987).

29. See *Grabb v. Bendix Corp.,* 666 F. Supp. 1223 (N.D. Ind. 1986); *Holley v. Sanyo,* 771 F.2d 1161 (8th Cir. 1985). As discussed previously, information regarding such a review generally is discoverable, although it will not have a negative impact on the employer's case if conducted properly. As the Seventh Circuit Court of Appeals recently noted in a different context, "a trier of fact may not infer action from knowledge alone." *Visser v. Packer Eng'g Corp.,* 924 F.2d 655, 658 (7th Cir. 1991).

30. See *Cazzola v. Codman & Shurtleruff, Inc.,* 751 F.2d 53 (1st Cir. 1984); *Graham v. F.B. Leopold Co.,* 779 F.2d 170 (3d Cir. 1985).

31. *Tice v. Lampert Yards, Inc.,* 761 F.2d 1210 (7th Cir. 1985); *Ridenour v. Lawson Co.,* 791 F.2d 52 (6th Cir. 1986).

32. *Kier v. Commercial Union Ins. Co.,* 808 F.2d 1254 (7th Cir. 1987).

33. The continuing performance of some of the terminated employee's duties does not necessarily show that the person was actually replaced. See *Kesserling* (cited in note 7) ("[A] person is not replaced when another employee is assigned to

perform the plaintiff's duties in addition to other duties, or when the work is redistributed among other existing employees already performing related work."); see also *Barnes v. Gencorp, Inc.,* 896 F.2d 1457 (6th Cir. 1990); *Schuler v. Polaroid Corp.,* 848 F.2d 276 (1st Cir. 1988). Contrast *Moody v. Pepsi-Cola Metro. Bottling Co., Inc.,* 915 F.2d 201 (6th Cir. 1990) (evidence of replacement, coupled with employer's conflicting evidence regarding its reasons for RIF, supported jury's verdict in plaintiff's favor); *Johnston v. American Vision Center,* No. CV-86-2504, 55 EPD (CCH) ¶ 40,471 (E.D. N.Y. 1990) (employer's objective evidence of economic motivation for RIF's effect on plaintiff does not justify summary judgment, where plaintiff was replaced a few months after RIF).

34. Keep in mind that decisions about who to rehire carry the risk of creating liability just like any hiring decision. See *Sischo-Nownejad v. Merced Community College,* 934 F.2d 1104 (9th Cir. 1991) (same standards of proof apply to discriminatory hiring and discriminatory discharge actions under Title VII and ADEA).

35. *Binder v. Long Island Lighting Co.,* 933 F.2d 187 (2d Cir. 1991). The dramatic pronouncements made in *Taggart* and *Binder* have been tempered to some extent by the subsequent decision in *Bay v. Times Mirror Magazines, Inc.,* 936 F.2d 112 (2d Cir. 1991). For a thorough analysis of the impact of these decisions, see Kandel, 'Overqualified' or 'Appropriately Qualified': New ADEA Risks," 17 *Empl. Rel. L.J.* 287 (Autumn 1991).

36. See *EEOC v. Ingersoll Johnson Steel Co.,* 583 F. Supp. 983 (S.D. Ind. 1984).

37. See, e.g., *Parcinski v. Outlet Co.,* 673 F.2d 34 (2d Cir. 1984); *Sahadi v. Reynolds Chem.,* 636 F.2d 1116 (6th Cir. 1980); *Lucas v. Dover Corp.,* 857 F.2d 1397 (10th Cir. 1988). Contrast *Cannistra* (cited in note 1) (even though employer showed need for improved efficiency, failure to prove that employer considered all options failed to rebut discriminatory impact analysis).

38. The ADEA provides a claimant with the right to seek pay, reinstatement (or in some circuits, front pay), and liquidated damages equal to double the back pay amount in cases of willful discrimination. Obviously, suits brought by well-paid man-

agers can easily involve claims for damages in the hundreds of thousands of dollars.

READING 7-4

Managing the Effects of Layoffs on Survivors

Joel Brockner

Consider the following reactions of two middle-level managers who had recently survived layoffs in their respective organizations:

> You give years of your life to this place, and what do you get for it? I used to think that my job was secure as long as I put in a good day's work. Well, you can forget about that. Plus, the way that they handled the layoff was really unfair. I used to be real gung-ho about working here, but if that's the way they're going to treat people, then they shouldn't expect to get much out of me.

> This is something that the company should have done a long time ago. I feel bad that some people had to be let go, but frankly, they, like the organization, will probably be better off for it over the longer haul. This place is much more ready to tackle the challenge of the 90s; we may have more work to do as a result of the cutbacks, but it's much more interesting than before.

Layoffs were a pervasive workforce reduction strategy in corporate America in the 1980s, and there is every indication that this trend will continue for the foreseeable future. According to a survey of managers attending the American Management Association's (AMA) annual convention in 1989, more than half of the companies

Source: Reprinted from the *California Management Review,* Vol 34, No. 2. By permission of the Regents.

represented had experienced downsizing within the past four years; an even greater percentage anticipated that their companies would downsize within the next few years.[1] According to *The New York Times,* many major American companies in numerous industries announced significant job cuts for 1991, including Sears, General Dynamics, General Motors, Citicorp, Pan Am, Digital Equipment, Hills Department Stores, and Aetna Life & Casualty. The specter of layoffs is omnipresent in the public sector as well.[2] As this article was being prepared, many state and local governments were facing massive layoffs.

Most of the research on layoffs has studied their underlying causes, or their effects on the individuals who lost their jobs. Overlooked was the highly practical matter of how both the productivity and morale of the individuals who did not lose their jobs were affected by the layoffs.[3] After all, it is the reactions of the employees who remain—hereafter referred to as the survivors—that will dictate the organization's effectiveness.

The opening quotations suggest that there is no simple or single answer to the question "What effects do layoffs have on survivors?" As exemplified by the first quotation, some managers report that the layoffs have a decidedly negative effect on their subordinates' productivity, morale, and overall commitment to the organization. Reactions similar to those described in the second quotation, while less frequent, also have been reported. Adding to this apparent confusion, some managers report that their subordinates respond very differently even within the same organization or work group.

If the factors that influence survivors' reactions can be identified, then managers will be able to make more informed decisions about how to handle layoffs. Many of the determinants of survivors' reactions are factors that managers can influence. If the layoffs are mismanaged, thereby hampering survivors' productivity and morale, then the organization stands to lose a sizeable portion of the savings it hoped to achieve by introducing layoffs. Consequently, it is incumbent upon executives of a downsizing organization to plan and implement layoffs with special attention devoted to their impact on those who remain.

FACTORS AFFECTING SURVIVORS' REACTIONS

The Role of Perceived Fairness Survivors' perceptions of the fairness of the layoff are determined by their beliefs about *why* the layoff occurred as well as *how* the layoff was implemented. The general finding emerging from numerous studies is that survivors react more favorably to the extent that they believe that the layoff is fair. While the previous statement should come as no surprise, far less obvious is the fact that survivors' fairness judgments are influenced by a wide range of issues. Some of the fairness-related questions survivors ask include:

• *Is the layoff justified?* Survivors need to believe that the layoff is truly necessary rather than, for example, caused by managerial greed or incompetence. If other firms within the organization's reference groups also are downsizing, then survivors are more likely to believe that the layoff is justified. In addition, if top management clearly considered alternative cost-cutting measures (e.g., attrition, hiring and wage freezes) before deciding upon layoffs, then the layoffs are likely to be received as more justified. One former CEO of a major supermarket chain tried whenever possible to reduce non-personnel costs before resorting to layoffs. One virtue of this cost-cutting strategy is that when layoffs were introduced in this organization, survivors were more likely to view them as justified.

• *Is the layoff congruent with corporate culture?* IBM has adopted a policy of full employment, in which every attempt is made to retrain and redeploy employees whose jobs are eliminated. Moreover, when the workforce at IBM needs to be reduced—IBM announced that it planned to cut 14,000 jobs in 1991 to bring its workforce to 359,000, down nearly 12% from its employment peak of 406,000 in 1986—IBM chooses attrition, early retirement, and other voluntary resignation incentives. At other companies, employment security is an integral part of their informal organization or corporate culture. When these companies choose to implement layoffs—as many so-called paternalistic organizations did in the 1980s (e.g., Kodak, AT&T) and now in the 1990s (e.g., Digital Equipment)—they violate employees' beliefs about the nature of the corporate culture. Layoffs perceived to be inconsistent with corporate culture break the "psychological contract" between employer and employee, and therefore they are more likely to be seen as unfair.[4]

• *Did the organization provide ample advanced notice?* If people are going to lose their jobs due to layoffs, it would seem only fair that they receive adequate advanced notice. In fact, proponents of the federally enacted plant closing law—which requires employers to give at least 60 days advanced notice in the case of plant closings or large-scale layoffs—argued their case in the name of justice. As Senator Howard Metzenbaum (D-Ohio), the bill's chief sponsor, put it: "[60 days notice] should be the law of the land. It's the fair and humane thing to do." In announcing in 1991 that it would close one of its assembly plants in 1993, General Motors said that the long lead time was to allow the laid-off workers to have "the fullest opportunity for planning for their future."

Of course, what constitutes "ample" advanced notice is likely to vary considerably from one situation to the next. Furthermore, top management will have to weigh the need to provide enough advanced notice against the sometimes justified concern that they may pay the price for providing *too much* advanced notice (in the form of employee slowdown or sabotage). Consider this, however: prior to the passage of the plant closing law, the *average* amount of advanced notification provided to employees that they were about to lose their jobs was one week! It seems likely that in many of these instances laid-off workers could have been given greater advanced notice (i.e., they could have been treated more fairly) with little or no additional cost to the organization.

• *In implementing the layoff, how well did the organization attend to the details?* It would seem that survivors would be highly concerned with the fact that a layoff occurred, and not so interested in the nitty-gritty details of how the news was delivered. However, research has shown that survivors' reactions do depend to a significant extent on the apparently trivial details of implementation.[5] One example of how *not* to communicate the layoff was provided by a petroleum company in which employees were brought together for a meeting. Each employee was given an envelope with the letter A or B on it. The A's were told to stay put, while the B's were ushered into an adjacent room. Then, en masse, the B's were told that they were being laid off. Another example of how *not* to do it was the experience of employees at a communications company, in which the word of layoffs was leaked to the press *before* the people to be laid off were told. As a result, some people learned that they were about to lose their jobs over the radio while driving home from work.

These implementaton details affect survivors largely because of their symbolic meaning. People need to be treated with dignity and respect, especially during a painful procedure such as downsizing. The way in which the organization implements the layoff may seem trivial, but the message conveyed in their actions is anything but trivial. Thus, the organization that "sweats the details" of implementation is communicating (to both layoff victims and survivors) that it respects the personhood of its employees; as a result, the layoff will be perceived as more fair.[6]

• *Did management provide a clear and adequate explanation of the reasons for the layoffs?*

When the organization takes the time to provide adequate reasons for the layoffs, survivors will judge the process as more fair. The content of the explanation may include valid arguments for the necessity of the layoffs which previously uninformed survivors may not have thought about before. Also, the mere fact that the organization took the time and effort to explain—independent of the content of the explanation—itself symbolizes to survivors that they are being treated in a dignified and respectful way.[7]

• *Were cutbacks shared at higher managerial levels?* A theme emerging thus far is that survivors' fairness judgments depend upon both the substance and style of how the layoff is handled. It is important to do the right thing (substance), and to do things right (style). If the organization is downsizing, then it is especially important for higher levels of management to become cost-conscious, too. For example, when International Harvester was undergoing severe downsizing in 1981, the company forgave loans of its president and chief executive officer (worth more than $2 million). Even though these arrangements were part of the executives' compensation package when they were hired years earlier, somehow it just seemed unfair for top managers to benefit greatly at the same time that the corporation was undergoing severe downsizing. Said one survivor: "Morale is zero. We see Lee Iacocca working for a dollar a year and the general feeling is that our top guys are lapping up the gravy." Another commented that "the company could not be in such trouble if it paid top executives millions of dollars a year."[8] To avoid such reactions, turnaround specialist John Whitney advocates that senior management take pay cuts before (or while) the rank and file are being laid off.

• *What decision rule was used to determine which employees would be laid off versus chosen to remain?* Some of the typical decision rules include merit, seniority, or function. No one decision rule is inherently more fair than the other. Depending upon the corporation's strat-egy, history, and culture, each may be viewed as most legitimate, at least some of the time. For example, if the post-layoff strategy is to specialize in areas emphasizing certain functional units rather than others, then the decision about who goes or stays is likely to be determined by function. If seniority has historically been the basis for making resource allocations in the organization, and the organization does not wish to buck that tradition, then the decision about who goes or stays may be determined appropriately by seniority.

Perhaps just as important as the content of the decision rule is the way that it is implemented. Consistency and accuracy are two hallmarks of a fairly implemented decision rule.[9] Thus, if merit is the basis for one, then it should be the basis for all. Exceptions may be allowed, but if so it is incumbent to explain why. Moreover, if merit is the chosen basis, then it is crucial that the procedure used be a valid representation of merit. For example, one organization intended to downsize on the basis of merit; performance appraisal ratings were used to distinguish the good from the not-so-good performers. However, the accuracy of the performance appraisal system in this particular organization was viewed as dubious by many, both layoff victims and survivors alike. As a result, the well-intentioned decision to downsize on the basis of merit was viewed as unfair.

• *Did the organization provide tangible caretaking services to help soften the blow for those laid off?* Tangible signs of caretaking include severance pay, outplacement counseling and other forms of helping those laid off find comparable employment elsewhere, and continuation of health insurance and other benefits beyond the date of severance. It is no secret that certain individuals receive more caretaking than others; layoff victims with high status in the organization usually are provided more than their lower-status counterparts. Furthermore, certain organizations do more for their layoff victims than others. For example, when the Defense Department canceled the Navy's A-12 program in January 1991, many subcontractors laid off workers. Subcontractor A did relatively little to take care of the layoff victims, although the company held "two job fairs and contacted possible employers."[10] In sharp contrast, Subcontractor B "ran a hot line, took out full-page newspaper ads inviting prospective employers to call, and set up a resource center with word processors, fax machines, and other facilities for job hunting."[11] In addition, Subcontractor B reportedly provided greater severance pay than Subcontractor A. Although it is possible for a downsizing organization to be too generous in its caretaking of layoff victims—as in the case of a financial services institution who provided so much to the layoff victims that some survivors felt envious!—in general, survivors are more likely to view the layoff as fair if they see concrete evidence of the organization providing for those laid off.

• *Did the organization involve its employees in the layoff decision process?* For some of the many decisions associated with layoffs, employees should participate in the process. For example, prior to downsizing, certain organizations actually seek input from their workforces on how to cut costs. This practice has two benefits. First, employees may have creative solutions on how to do more with less without necessarily having to resort to layoffs. Second, if the employees do opt for layoffs, they are more likely to view them as fair (than if the very same layoffs were autocratically imposed upon them).

In sum, these questions describe some of the fairness-related issues of concern to survivors. In general, survivors' productivity and morale will be greater to the extent that they view the layoffs as fair. Furthermore, perceived fairness is especially likely to affect survivors' reactions under certain specific conditions, such as:

• *When survivors are close to the layoff victims.* Prior to the layoffs, survivors may have developed close professional or personal relation-

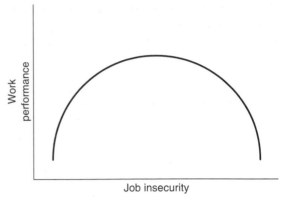

FIGURE 1
The Effect of Job Insecurity on Work Performance.

ships with the layoff victims. For instance, survivors may have worked interdependently with them for a long period of time. They may live in the same community, and therefore spend time socializing either on or off the job. Survivors may have been laid off in the past themselves, further promoting feelings of identification with the layoff victims. In several studies we found that survivors who were close to those laid off felt that the layoff was more unfair, worked less hard, and became less committed to the organization, relative to survivors who had more distant relationships with the layoff victims.[12] Therefore, when survivors feel attached to the layoff victims (e.g., as in a tightly knit, cohesive group), it is especially important that the layoffs be handled fairly.

• *When survivors are committed to the organization.* In a recent address to the Wall Street Human Resources Conference, James Jones, the CEO of the American Stock Exchange, pointed out that people need to feel that they are part of and contributing to a larger collective. One outgrowth of peoples' need for group membership is that they expect and want to be treated fairly by the collectives to which they belong. Consider the situation of survivors who felt very loyal to the organization prior to the layoff. If they believed that the layoff was handled fairly, their commitment to the organization should be confirmed. However, our research suggests that if these same persons believed that the layoff was unfair, then their loyalty dropped sharply, even more so than survivors who were less committed at the outset and viewed the layoff as unfair.[13] Put differently, the higher they are (in their prior loyalty to the organization), the harder they fall (if they believe the layoff was unfair). Thus, layoff managers who handle the process unfairly may run the risk of alienating the survivors they least wish to alienate: those who were very loyal to the organization at the outset.

The Role of Changed Working Conditions

Survivors are influenced not only by the perceived fairness of the layoff, but also by changes in their work setting which often accompany layoffs. Some of these changes represent perceived sources of threat, others perceived sources of opportunity. The general finding emerging from research, not surprisingly, is that survivors' productivity and morale decline more if the changes are believed to represent threats rather than opportunities. Some of the more specific concerns survivors have about changes in the workplace include:

• *How much should I worry about the possibility of further layoffs?* Survivors' job insecurity generally increases after layoffs. This is understandable, since many organizations downsize in waves rather than on a one-shot basis. The threat of additional layoffs by itself, however, does not lead to job insecurity. Insecurity is experienced when survivors also believe that if additional layoffs were to occur, there would be little they could do to counteract the negative effects of job loss.[14] For example, individuals who expect to lose their jobs during the anticipated next round of layoffs will not necessarily feel insecure if they know that they will be able to find a comparable job elsewhere.

High levels of job insecurity lead to negative effects on survivors' productivity and morale. However, there is some evidence that a moderate amount of job insecurity actually leads to greater productivity (but not morale), relative to that caused by low levels of job insecurity. In fact, in one downsizing organization the relationship between job insecurity and work performance took the form of an inverted-U, as shown in Figure 1.[15] The results in Figure 1 raise some interesting and important questions for layoff managers. Is it better for survivors to feel moderate rather than low levels of job insecurity? Figure 1 suggests that moderate job insecurity leads to greater work performance than does low job insecurity. However, it is possible that the organization would pay the price (of moderate job insecurity) in some other way. For example, in that very same sample it was found—but not reported in Figure 1—that survivors' loyalty to the organization was lower when their job insecurity was at a moderate rather than low level.

• *How does my job compare to the one that I had before the layoffs?* Many survivors are likely to find that their job has changed. First, the sheer volume of their workload often increases. With fewer people to do the work, the remaining employees may find that they have more to do. This tendency was observed in a sample of middle managers from a wide variety of downsizing organizations. When asked to describe how their jobs had changed over the years, surviving middle managers reported a sharp increase in the size of their workload; they reported working longer hours and taking fewer vacation days. These results were hinted at in a more recent and larger-scale survey conducted by the Wyatt Company, which polled 1,005 corporations employing more than four million people. Nearly all of them (86%) had downsized within the past five years, but less than half (42%) had eliminated the amount of work that their employees had to do.

Second, the nature of the work that survivors perform invariably changes. The same group of middle managers who reported an increase in the quantity of their work also reported that the job had become *more* intrinsically enjoyable. They experienced greater *autonomy* than before, and they also felt that there was more *variety* in their jobs, two attributes that have been shown to increase the intrinsic enjoyability of work. Thus, this group of middle managers experienced both negative and positive changes in their work: the quantity of the work increased (representing a source of threat), but so did its intrinsic quality (representing a source of opportunity).

• *What is my future here?* Layoffs often have the effect of making unclear survivors' future prospects within the organization. For example, consider the plight of first-level supervisors in a downsizing organization who had hoped to be promoted to the ranks of middle management within the next few years. The organization had eliminated many middle management positions during its most recent layoffs, leaving survivors uncertain about their future opportunities within the organization. In other situations, survivors may believe that new career options exist as a result of their organization's recent downsizing. In short, survivors' reactions will depend upon their beliefs about how their career prospects—either within the organization or outside of it—have changed, relative to what they were before the layoff.

• *What are the reactions of my fellow survivors?* In times of stress or uncertainty, people often take cues from their co-workers to help them determine what they should be thinking and doing. Not only are survivors keenly attentive to *objective* changes in their work environment (i.e., whether their workload has increased, or whether their career opportunities have diminished), but they are acutely aware of their fellow survivors' *reactions to* the new work environment. For example, they monitor whether their fellow survivors seem more or less withdrawn from the organization. Their own reactions along these dimensions are determined to a significant extent by those of fellow survivors, particularly those in their immediate work group.[16]

PRACTICAL IMPLICATIONS: THE EFFECTIVE MANAGEMENT OF LAYOFFS

To elicit the most positive reactions among survivors, managers need to: conduct the layoff fairly; help survivors cope with the negative changes (i.e., threats) in the workplace; and encourage survivors to focus on the positive changes (i.e., opportunities) in the work setting. Appropriate managerial action steps can be meaningfully divided into three categories: those taken before, during, and after the layoff.

Before the Layoff

• *Evaluate the relationship between the layoff and corporate strategy and culture.* As dramatic as their effects may be, layoffs are only one of the many factors that will affect the short- and long-term health of the organization. Top managers need to determine the relationship between layoffs and these other factors, most notably corporate strategy and culture. Layoffs generally reflect the organization's strategy of improved productivity through (labor) cost containment. Whereas cost containment may be an appropriate strategy at least some of the time, it may not be optimal all of the time. For example, J.H. Heinz enacted a cost-cutting strategy (e.g., layoffs, plant closings) throughout the 1980s with considerable financial success. However, its surviving workforce was becoming increasingly alienated, product quality was slipping, and waste was high. Three years ago, Heinz changed the emphasis in its strategy from cost containment to total quality management (TQM). This strategic shift led Heinz to *increase* its workforce in certain instances. Under the cost containment strategy:

> Heinz had cut the workforce at its StarKist tuna canning factories. . . . But the fish cleaners were so overworked that they were leaving literally tons

of meat on the bone every day. . . . StarKist managers slowed down the production lines, hired 400 hourly workers and 15 supervisors, and retrained the entire workforce. . . . All told, StarKist increased labor costs by $5 million but cut out $15 million in wastage. Net saving: $10 million annually.[17]

In short, layoffs should be a logical consequence of corporate strategy. If that strategy is poorly defined prior to the adoption of layoffs, then the latter are less likely to be the answer to the firm's short- or long-term problems. Layoffs are a means to an end; corporate strategy helps to define that end. Furthermore, if the strategy suggests that downsizing is warranted, the organization would do well to consider other cost-saving options (e.g., attrition, hiring or wage freezes, or early retirement) instead of, or in addition to, layoffs. These alternatives to layoffs generally are less drastic and therefore may be less likely to send shock waves throughout the organization.[18]

The intricate relationship between layoffs and corporate culture also needs to be thought through prior to the adoption of layoffs. Given the existing culture of the firm, top managers need to evaluate whether layoffs should be implemented, and if so, how they should be implemented. Some managers may decide that the culture of the organization is so strong that it precludes the possibility of involuntary layoffs (e.g., IBM). This is not to say that the decisions regarding whether to lay off or how to implement layoffs *always* need to be consistent with the corporate culture. Indeed, sometimes layoffs are undertaken in order to change the existing culture. For example, some organizations with previously paternalistic cultures have taken the unusual step of laying off workers *precisely because* they wanted to change the culture to be more hard-driving and aggressive. However, if the decision to lay off (or the ways in which the layoffs are implemented) are seen as incongruent with the existing corporate culture, they are more likely to be experienced by survivors as

unfair. Of course, management may be able to counteract such perceptions by handling smoothly the other fairness-related issues (e.g., advanced notice, clear explanation of the reasons for the layoff, adequate caretaking of the layoff victims).

• ***Provide ample advanced notice.*** By providing ample advanced notice, the organization stands to benefit because: the victims of the layoff should exit more gracefully, making them less likely to file wrongful discharge lawsuits (favorable victim reactions should also enhance the organization's reputation and future recruiting efforts); and the survivors of the layoff will be more appreciative, leading to better productivity or morale.

• ***Identify key people and solicit their commitment to the new organization.*** Key people come in several varieties. First, there are the "star" performers whom the organization will wish to retain for obvious reasons. Second, there are the "opinion leaders" whose viewpoints have reverberating effects on those around them. Given that survivors take their cues from one another about how they should respond, it is especially important for the opinion leaders to have relatively upbeat reactions to the layoff.

Several action steps may help solicit the commitment of key people to the new organization. For example, they need to be told exactly what their role will be and how important that role is to the success of the downsizing effort. In addition, they can participate in the organizational restructuring decisions or serve on task forces.

• ***Prepare supervisors and managers for the layoffs.*** Those who implement the often difficult layoff process need to be prepared, both for what to expect and how to behave. They should expect their surviving subordinates to feel a wide range of emotions, including anxiety, anger, relief, guilt, and envy. Many people will feel two or more of these emotions simultaneously. Furthermore, some of these emotions may not seem to make sense. Consider the case of "survivor guilt." People usually feel guilty when they believe that they have done something wrong. Survivors may say to themselves, "Well, I haven't done anything wrong. Why, then, do I feel guilty?" The mere fact that survivors fared better than those laid off can produce guilt feelings, particularly when survivors believe that they, rather than the layoff victims, just as easily could have been the ones who were laid off. It is important for managers and supervisors not to be surprised when and if survivors express emotional pain, even feelings that seem irrational. Survivors' painful emotional states are more likely to become destructive (to themselves and the organization) when they are invalidated, i.e., denied or derogated as not making sense. Therefore, layoff managers who anticipate their subordinates' emotional pain are more likely to give them the room they need to have their feelings, and thereby keep such emotions from having harmful effects.

Further complicating matters is that those responsible for implementing the layoffs often do a notoriously poor job. First, most implementers do not *want* to face the painful task of telling people that they are about to lose their jobs. People generally do not like to be the bearers of bad news, and layoff managers are no exception. Indeed, managers often say that the most difficult part of their job is telling people that they are being terminated, especially when those being let go have performed reasonably well in the past. As a result of their discomfort, implementers could mishandle the process. For example, they may be evasive, and thereby accused of being unfair for not "being straight" with their subordinates. Other implementers react to their discomfort by coming on too strong, thereby running the risk of being seen as unfair for not treating people with dignity and respect.

Second, most implementers lack the *ability* to handle layoffs smoothly. Whereas some are naturally talented at handling the process, others will only become proficient through experience. However, layoffs are relatively rare events

within organizations, occurring perhaps yearly or less often. Consequently, implementers often do not reap the benefit of the learning that goes along with doing something repeatedly.

Preparing supervisors and managers for what they need to do is no small matter. Given their unwillingness or inability to implement the layoffs well, they need to be trained in how to behave. Perhaps committees could be established whose mandate it is to develop an appropriate plan of action. As in the case of most behaviors, practice makes perfect; therefore managers and supervisors may benefit from rehearsing or role-playing what they plan to do as they implement the layoffs.

During the Layoff

• *Give full information.* Once the workforce has learned that layoffs will occur, they will be hungry for information. Some of their questions pertain to events in the immediate future, including: Who will be laid off? When will the layoffs occur? Why are they happening? Will they happen again? How will the organization decide who goes and who stays? What does the organization plan to do to soften the blow for those laid off? Other questions refer to events that are likely to unfold over time, such as: What will life be like here after the layoffs? Can management be trusted? One school of managerial thought is that employees should be told as little as possible, i.e., that if management provided information then they would only be putting counterproductive ideas in the minds of the workforce. However, during stressful times such as layoffs, the workforce *already* is likely to have counterproductive fantasies about what is taking place. By not providing information, management allows these fantasies to feed on themselves. First, within survivors' minds they are likely to fill in the blanks with beliefs damaging to the organization. Trust in the organization often is reduced during layoffs, causing survivors to believe that management is guilty until proven innocent. Second, survivors take cues from each other; thus, the grapevine provides another mechanism through which survivors' beliefs can spin out of control, unless they are counteracted by accurate information.

Clearly, there are certain things that managers may be unwilling or unable to discuss with the surviving workforce. Even here, however, survivors are likely to feel that they were treated more fairly if management acknowledged those issues about which it could not provide information; this would be especially true if managers provided a clear and adequate explanation of why they were unwilling or unable to disclose the information. In short, all of the uncertainties brought on by the layoffs will cause survivors to try to make sense of what is happening, both in the short and long term. People need to know both concrete details about the immediate future, as well as information that symbolizes what they can expect from the organization over time. For these reasons, management needs to be especially attentive to both the substance and style of its communications.

• *Overcommunicate.* Layoff managers need to make the information sought by survivors as vivid as possible. Managers could feel frustrated because they know that they communicated information to survivors, only to discover that their message was not heard. The distracting nature of the post-layoff work environment makes it necessary for management to overcommunicate pertinent information. For example, wherever possible important information should be communicated in a face-to-face manner. Furthermore, information deemed to be important should be communicated more than once, and in different ways. To reinforce its communications, some organizations make use of an in-house TV network (as Ford Motor Company does), or utilize an electronic newsletter (as Bethlehem Steel does) so that people working at computer terminals can receive information in a timely manner. The key assumption that managers need to make

in order to overcommunicate is the following: just because information was *sent* to the surviving workforce does not ensure that said information was *heard* by the workforce. Moreover, if the intended message is not heard, the grapevine is likely to become the primary source of information—information that is erroneous or damaging to the organization more often than not.

• *Provide assistance.* Layoffs directly threaten the economic well-being of those laid off, and indirectly threaten that of the survivors (who may be wondering whether they are the next to go). Therefore, it is important for the organization to provide concrete assistance to help ease the pain. Severance pay and outplacement counseling are obvious examples of tangible help. Some downsizing organizations temporarily beef up their Employee Assistance Programs, in order to handle the increased demand on that function that layoffs often produce. The direct cost of these and other tangible caretaking provisions can be considerable to the downsizing organization. However, these costs may be offset to some extent by the positive effects they have on the survivors (as well as the victims) of job loss.

It is also crucial for management to communicate (again, overcommunicate) to survivors what is being done concretely to help the layoff victims. A major consumer products company that I know of actually provided considerable tangible resources to the layoff victims, only to discover that the surviving workforce still reacted rather negatively. When questioned about what they communicated to the survivors about the assistance provided to the layoff victims, management responded that they had said nothing at all. In not communicating with the survivors about this issue, management missed an opportunity to show its commitment to its employees, even as it was in the process of separating some of them from the organization. This is not to say that survivors need to know every detail about such things as the layoff victims' severance package or outplacement counseling. Moreover, if the organization were overly generous to the layoff victims, then survivors could feel resentful that they were not laid off themselves. Still, survivors need to be reassured that the victims are being provided for, and management needs to be sure to communicate that.

• *Treat victims and survivors with dignity and respect.* One way to treat victims respectfully is by providing tangible forms of assistance, such as severance pay and outplacement counseling. However, the seemingly inconsequential details of *what* was told to victims and survivors, *how* things were said to them, *when* they were told, and *where* they were when they received the news also determine whether the workforce feels that it has been treated with dignity. Furthermore, the direct costs to the organization of handling these apparently trivial details are far less than those associated with the more concrete forms of caretaking such as severance pay and outplacement counseling.

One question that downsizing organizations often face is how to combine the tangible forms of caretaking (such as severance pay) with the intangible forms of caretaking (such as treating the victims and survivors in a humane, dignified way). Obviously, the more that the organization can provide on both of these dimensions, the more favorably survivors will respond to the layoff. Perhaps the most interesting and managerially useful finding to emerge from several studies is that: if survivors felt that the *procedures* used to implement the layoff were fair—that is, ample advanced notice was given, clear explanations of the reasons for the layoff were provided, and the news was delivered in a respectful way—then the impact of the more costly forms of caretaking (such as severance pay) on survivors' reactions was greatly reduced. In other words, survivors generally reacted much more favorably if they felt that the organization was generous rather than stingy in the concrete provisions (e.g., severance pay) it

offered to the layoff victims. Such a finding should come as no surprise. However, if the layoff was implemented in a procedurally fair manner, then survivors' reactions did not depend *nearly as much* on the amount of concrete, tangible assistance that the organization provided to the layoff victims. Only when survivors believed that the procedures used to implement the layoff were unfair did their reactions depend greatly upon the amount of concrete assistance offered to those laid off.[19]

This is not to say that downsizing organizations need not concern themselves with providing concrete assistance to the layoff victims. Indeed, if the organization concentrated its efforts solely on the fairness of its downsizing procedures and offered little or nothing in the way of concrete assistance to those laid off, then survivors are likely to react quite negatively. However, once a certain threshold level of concrete assistance has been provided, then the layoff may be handled in a more *cost effective* way not by providing additional concrete assistance to the layoff victims, but rather by ensuring that the procedures used to implement the layoffs were perceived by survivors to be fair.

• *Increase managerial accessibility.* In stressful times such as layoffs, survivors feel confused and upset. A frequent managerial response to the turmoil caused by layoffs is to become more withdrawn from the surviving workforce. In some ways, the withdrawal of managers is understandable. After all, they may feel more self-preoccupied because of their own worries and fears. Furthermore, most of us would just as soon not be involved in communicating bad news to the people with whom we work. However, management at all levels needs to increase rather than decrease its accessibility to the surviving workforce. Information goes a long way towards helping many people cope with stressful circumstances. At one downsizing organization, top level managers increased their frequency of MBWA—management by walking around. Another one instituted a special hotline number that survivors could call to have their questions immediately addressed. A third organization went to extra efforts to publicize its already-existing open-door policy.

• *Use ceremony to facilitate the transition.* Sociologists have noted that important changes in peoples' lives are accompanied by a formal ceremony recognizing the transition. It is somehow easier to accept transitions when people take the time to recognize that their world has changed and to acknowledge their feelings associated with that change, such as grief, anxiety, and guilt. Ceremonies provide people with an opportunity to acknowledge change and their reactions to it. Ceremonies in the survivor setting can take any of a number of forms. For example, small groups of survivors can go out to lunch with the understanding that the purpose of the meeting is to discuss the impending change in the workplace. Or, the organization may hold special meetings *on company time* during which the changes associated with the layoff are acknowledged, and survivors are encouraged to share their reactions to the changes. Of course, these meetings must be organized and led by people with a good deal of interpersonal sensitivity and skill.

One potential drawback to the latter idea is that if the ceremony is done on company time on a large scale basis—as it probably should—it may at first appear to cost the organization a considerable amount of person-hours. However, survivors already are highly distracted from their daily tasks at this point in the layoff process. Hence, the opportunity cost of having them participate in the ceremony is greatly reduced, and should be more than recouped in the form of more favorable survivor reactions.

After the Layoff

After the layoffs the surviving workforce will need to regroup. A number of action steps may facilitate this process. Although these steps represent generally sound management practice, the layoff setting represents a specific situation in which it is important to follow these recommendations. Although these steps should be *implemented* after the layoffs, their *planning* needs to occur prior to the implementation of the layoffs.

• *Soliciting employee input.* As soon as management believes that the acute trauma of the layoff has subsided somewhat, survivors should be given every opportunity to play an active role in shaping the post-layoff work environment. Some organizations (e.g., General Electric's "Workout" program) have cultivated participatory processes in which survivors are encouraged to make suggestions on how the organization can do more (work) with less (workers). One organization went so far as to set aside money saved from the downsizing to reward survivors who made useful suggestions on how to work more efficiently. Employee input becomes especially crucial after stressful events such as layoffs. After all, the survivors have just witnessed an event that threatens their sense of control. Perceived control may be restored at least somewhat if survivors are actively involved in decisions that will affect them in the aftermath of the layoff.

• *Rightsizing.* A common complaint among survivors is that they not only have to do their own jobs, but significant portions of the work previously performed by those laid off. Just as the organization needs to think through its strategy to decide whether layoffs are appropriate, so too must it evaluate whether the tasks undertaken by survivors are appropriate to the strategy. Some downsizing organizations (in the minority, to be sure) recently have taken a hard look at eliminating low value work. They compared the work that they *should* concentrate on (based upon their strategy) with the tasks that survivors *actually* were doing. Not surprisingly, the latter often were very different from the former. The next step was to do away with those aspects of the workload that were no longer seen as necessary. For example, Oryx, an oil and gas producer based in Dallas, "junked 25% of all internal reports, reduced from 20 to four the number of signatures required on requests for capital expenditures, and compressed from seven months to six weeks the time it took to produce the annual budget.[20] After undergoing layoffs, the group at Colgate-Palmolive discovered that "instead of concentrating on how to make teeth whiter or clothes brighter, scientists were expending too much energy on supervising and reporting. Researchers at different locations were duplicating one another's efforts. They also were preoccupied with designing new factories, a task that had little to do with the tech group's responsibility for inventing and improving products."[21] Colgate-Palmolive took the necessary steps to ensure that surviving scientists were concentrating their efforts on the work that needed to be done. This was achieved in part by eliminating some of the work that they were doing prior to the layoff that was no longer viewed as useful.

Habitual behavior is hard to change. Nevertheless, more and more downsizing organizations are learning that "because that's the way we have always done things around here" is not ample justification for having certain tasks included in survivors' job descriptions. By eliminating low value work, the organization benefits in numerous ways, not the least of which is that survivors are less likely to feel overwhelmed by a workload that includes all of their previous responsibilities plus that of some of their recently departed co-workers.

• *Job enrichment.* Survivors' reactions depend not only on the change in the volume of quantity of their workload relative to before the layoffs, but also on the change in the quality or enjoyability of their jobs. If their work has become more intrinsically interesting, then their productivity and morale should increase.[22] Kodak, for example, involves employees in decision making, has them work in teams (which

leads to greater variety and reduced isolation), and teaches them how to check their own work (so that they receive feedback on a more regular basis). The post-layoff environment provides especially fertile ground for redesigning the work survivors do so as to make it more psychologically interesting—a process known as job enrichment. Just as the organization needs to examine *what* work its employees are doing as it attempts to rightsize, so too should it look at *how* the work is being done, which may lead to creative ways to make the work more interesting. When survivors' jobs have been altered (to make them more interesting), the organization may have to incur the additional expense of training survivors to handle their new responsibilities. For example, five years ago an employee at Kodak, Daniel Cardinale, "did nothing but operate a punch press eight hours a day. Now he coaches fellow team members in statistical process control, meets with suppliers, interviews prospective recruits, and helps manage just-in-time inventory."[23] The cost of training Cardinale and his colleagues has paid for itself handsomely; it now takes one shift to accomplish the same work that used to be done in three shifts.

• *Make certain that survivors recognize new opportunities.* If done correctly, layoffs represent only part of a larger scale organizational change. Therefore, the opportunities for success that accompanied the old ways of doing things may no longer be present. Unfortunately, many survivors falsely conclude that "there just aren't *any* opportunities around here anymore," a perception that spurs their productivity and morale. In reality, the organization may provide many opportunities (or positive sources of change) in the aftermath of the layoff, but these opportunities may be quite *different* from those that existed previously. Therefore, the organization's responsibility is to make explicit to survivors: the opportunities present in the post-layoff environment, which may range from new ways to work more successfully and happily on a day-in, day-out basis, to methods to enhance one's career prospects (either within the organization or beyond) over the longer haul; and what survivors need to do to capitalize on these potential opportunities. To highlight the opportunities present (and ways to achieve them), managers may do any of the following:

- Have survivors work at "achievable" goals and tasks. The upset caused by layoffs makes most survivors hungry for a success experience. One way to increase survivors' chances for success is by assigning goals and tasks that they are likely to achieve. On the assumption that numerous tasks could be undertaken in the post-layoff environment, it is important that at least some of them provide survivors with the opportunity for a win, however small. With their self-confidence somewhat renewed, they should be better equipped to tackle some of the more difficult challenges that the post-layoff environment inevitably will pose.
- Publicize the rewards provided to survivors for the new behavior you wish to encourage. People learn a lot simply by watching the outcome of others' behaviors. If survivors know that others have been rewarded for taking the steps necessary to help the organization adapt to the layoffs, they should be more likely to do so themselves. Publicly announced rewards are especially needed to encourage survivors to undertake new behaviors. Recall the earlier example of the downsizing organization that financially rewarded survivors who made useful suggestions on how to improve productivity. Not only were people rewarded for their creative ideas, but also the accolades they received were made visible throughout the organization. This publicity campaign had the effect of showing survivors what was in it for them to work towards furthering the organization's goals.
- Make new career paths explicit. Most of us are motivated by the psychology of hope: the

expectation and wish that our future work situation will be better than (or at least as good as) the present one. However, the massive restructurings that often accompany layoffs could leave survivors uncertain about their longer term prospects within the organization. Therefore, it is important to make clear to survivors—especially the star performers—the new sources of rewards in the organization, as well as the ways to achieve those rewards. Some downsizing organizations even provide career counseling to survivors, which focuses less on highlighting the opportunities within the organization and more on encouraging individuals to clarify their personal values and hone their self-marketing skills. At first blush, this practice seems unwise in that it may encourage talented survivors to find a better position in a different organization. However, as William Bridges, a noted change management consultant, commented, even if this service "does give a few people what they need to leave, that is a small cost to pay for the empowerment and revitalization of the great mass of the survivors who will remain. These are the people the organization is depending on, and nothing less than their all-out effort on the organization's behalf will suffice."

CONCLUDING COMMENTS

The managerial prescriptions presented here are general; they will apply to the majority of downsizing organizations most of the time. Each situation has its idiosyncrasies, so the architects of the layoffs will need to evaluate carefully the appropriateness of the various recommendations to their particular circumstances. Managers should be forewarned of the long recovery period that survivors invariably need to adapt to layoffs. *There is no quick fix.* Even if the recommendations offered are implemented properly, layoff managers should prepare themselves for an adjustment period measured more appropriately in terms of years than in months or weeks. For all of their potential turmoil, however, downsizing and layoffs represent *opportunities* for the organization to dramatically improve its health over the long haul. Contributing to this optimistic outlook is the fact that many determinants of survivors' reactions are factors that managers can control. Therefore, as they undertake this arduous but critical change management process, executives need to remember that what they do will have a significant effect on survivors' productivity and morale, and ultimately on the effectiveness and vitality of the organization.

REFERENCES

1. Right Associates, "Managing Change in the 90s," *The Right Research* (1990).
2. *The New York Times,* April 15, 1991.
3. Joel Brockner, "The Effects of Work Layoffs on Survivors: Research, Theory, and Practice," in Barry M. Staw and Larry L. Cummings, eds., *Research in Organizational Behavior,* Vol. 10 (Greenwich, CT: JAI Press, 1988), pp. 213-255; Joel Brockner and Jerald Greenberg, "The Impact of Layoffs on Survivors: An Organizational Justice Perspective," in John S. Carroll, ed., *Applied Social Psychology and Organizational Settings* (Hillsdale, NJ: Erlbaum, 1990), pp. 45-75; Joel Brockner and Batia M. Wiesenfeld, "Living on the Edge (of Social and Organizational Psychology): The Effects of Job Layoffs on Those Who Remain," in J. Keith Murnigham, ed., *Social Psychology in Organizations: Advances in Theory and Research* (Englewood, NJ: Prentice-Hall, 1992).
4. Denise M. Rousseau, "Psychological and Implied Contracts in Organizations," *Employee Rights and Responsibilities,* 2 (1989): 121-139.
5. Joel Brockner, Mary Konovsky, Rochelle Cooper-Schneider, and Robert Folger, "The Interactive Effects of Procedural Justice and Outcome Negativity on the Victims and Survivors of Job Loss," manuscript under review, 1992.
6. Tom R. Tyler and Robert J. Bies, "Beyond Formal Procedures: The Interpersonal Context of Procedural Justice," in John S. Carroll, ed., op. cit.
7. Robert J. Bies, "The Predicament of Injustice: The Management of Moral Outrage," in Larry L.

Cummings and Barry M. Staw, *Research in Organizational Behavior,* Vol. 9 (Greenwich, CT: JAI Press, 1988), pp. 289-319.
8. Todd Jick, "Navistar: Managing Change," Harvard Business School Case N9-490-003, 1989.
9. Gerald S. Leventhal, "The Distribution of Rewards and Resources in Groups and Organizations," in Leonard Berkowitz and Elaine Walster, eds., *Advances in Experimental Social Psychology,* Vol. 9 (New York, NY: Academic Press, 1976), pp. 91-131.
10. *The Washington Post,* February 17, 1991.
11. Ibid.
12. Joel Brockner, Steven Grover, Thomas Reed, Rocki Lee DeWitt, and Michael O'Malley, "Survivors' Reactions to Job Layoffs: We Get By With a Little Help from Our Friends," *Administrative Science Quarterly,* 32 (1987): 526-541.
13. Joel Brockner, Tom R. Tyler, and Rochelle Cooper-Schneider, "The Effects of Prior Commitment to an Institution on Reactions to Perceived Unfairness: The Higher They Are, The Harder They Fall," manuscript under review, 1992.
14. Leonard Greenhalgh and Zev Rosenblatt, "Job Insecurity: Toward Conceptual Clarity," *Academy of Management Review,* 9 (1984): 438-448.
15. Joel Brockner, Steven Grover, Thomas Reed, and Rocki Lee DeWitt, "Layoffs, Job Insecurity and Survivors' Work Effort: Evidence of an Inverted-U Relationship," *Academy of Management Journal,* in press.
16. Gerald R. Salancik and Jeffrey Pfeffer, "A Social Information Processing Approach to Job Attitudes and Task Design," *Administrative Science Quarterly* 23 (1978): 224-253.
17. *Business Week,* April 9, 1990.
18. Leonard Greenhalgh, Anne T. Lawrence, and Robert I. Sutton, "Determinants of Workforce Reduction Strategies in Declining Organizations," *Academy of Management Review,* 13 (1988): 241-254.
19. Brockner, Konovsky, Cooper-Schneider, and Folger, op. cit.
20. *Fortune,* April 9, 1990, p. 43.
21. Ibid.
22. J. Richard Hackman and Greg R. Oldham, *Work Redesign* (Reading, MA: Addison-Wesley, 1980).
23. *Fortune,* April 9, 1990, p. 48.

READING 7-5

Managing Layoffs in the '90s

Daniel C. Feldman
Carrie R. Leana

Most managers are reluctant to lay off workers, and do so only as a last resort. Yet work force reductions are all too common. Blue-collar workers have long been subject to layoffs, and substantial declines in employment in Rustbelt industries continue. During the 1980s, employment by the "big three" auto manufacturers dropped nearly 25 percent, and U.S. Steel alone laid off more than 35,000 workers during that same decade.

In addition, since 1980, more than half of the 1,000 largest corporations in the United States have undergone some form of reorganization that has caused widespread layoffs of *white-collar* workers. General Electric, for instance, closed 73 plants and offices, eliminating tens of thousands of jobs, and ITT cut its labor force by 100,000, including 66 percent of its headquarters staff. More than half a million blue-collar and white-collar jobs were eliminated in the United States in 1991 alone.

The sheer volume and diversity of work force reductions are making it more important than ever for managers to learn to handle layoffs effectively.

The issue of layoffs has also become more complicated. Several court cases have sharply curtailed the employment-at-will doctrine, i.e., employers are no longer completely free to fire and terminate as they deem best for their corporations.

In addition, layoffs are now much likelier to be challenged legally. The courts have been sympathetic to suits of laid-off employees alleging age and sex discrimination and those filed on the basis of defamation of character.

Moreover, work force reductions have begun to hurt some companies' reputations in the community. In 1987, Chrysler's Christmas closing of its Kenosha, Wisconsin, plant received extensive adverse publicity on prime-time network news. Prior layoffs at Atari and the network news stations themselves also generated substantial negative publicity. Goodwill has been lost particularly when the public believed laid-off employees had been treated harshly.

In addition, work force reductions that are handled poorly can lead to decreased productivity and poor morale among "survivors," those employees who remain on their jobs after others have been laid off. When layoffs are handled poorly, survivors may become highly dissatisfied, and may search for new jobs themselves, lose their motivation to go the extra mile at work, or become anxious that future layoffs will claim them, too.

Managers should also be concerned with the impact of layoffs on employees and their families for humanitarian reasons. Layoffs can have substantial negative effects on both the psychological well-being and the physical health of laid-off workers. In some cases, layoffs have contributed to marital difficulties and problems with children.

For all these reasons, learning how to manage layoffs effectively is critical for both human resources managers and general managers.

Advance notification, severance pay and extended benefits, retraining programs, and outplacement programs are four corporate interventions that have been used most frequently to soften the effects of layoffs.

ADVANCE NOTIFICATION

Of all the corporate programs, none has received as much recent attention as advance notification. Estimates from the early 1980s suggest that 80 percent of the corporations that laid off workers

5¢/'/3

provided less than four weeks' notice of impending terminations, and many gave less than a few hours' notice, even to professional employees.[1]

The Worker Adjustment and Retraining Notification (WARN) Act of 1988 is federal legislation that generally requires employers to give at least 60-days notice when a plant closing or downsizing will result in the laying off of at least 50 employees or one-third of the work force. This legislation provides for an exception, however, if "unforeseeable business circumstances" prevent the employer from meeting the requirement. Moreover, although the law asks employers to consult in good faith with employees for a "mutually satisfactory alternative" to layoffs, the employer is not required to *implement* that alternative.

But even this loophole did not prevent an outcry from many corporate officers and business associations against the 1988 WARN Act, ample testimony to the degree of opposition management has historically taken to advance notice.[2] Management has justified its stand in several ways. Many managers oppose advance notice because they fear laid-off workers will lower productivity, engage in work slowdowns, or commit industrial sabotage. Other managers fear laid-off workers will seek employment elsewhere before the organization is ready to terminate them, leaving the closing facility shorthanded at a time it will be most difficult to replace labor. A third reason management is opposed to advance notice is that it fears competitors will be able to take advantage of such information to make further inroads in their business. Finally, managers do not like restrictions that might reduce their discretion in business decision making, i.e., they do not want to be locked into a course of action any sooner than they have to be.[3]

Despite these fears, however, the evidence is that advance notice has very few adverse consequences for corporations. The announcement of an impending plant shutdown does create an initial shock, but employee reactions do not generally result in any perceptible decreases in productivity.[4] Indeed, in some cases productivity has actually *increased* after the announcement, as employees worked even harder in an attempt to persuade management to reverse its decision and keep the plant open.[5] Research also suggests that quit rates after announcements of impending layoffs are actually quite low,[6] especially when the layoffs threaten plants located in small or depressed labor markets where alternative job opportunities generally are limited. Under these circumstances, workers see quitting early as probably increasing the length of their layoffs. Moreover, there is little evidence advance notification causes large losses in market share; rather, it is the loss of market share that created the necessity of the layoff in the first place.

Furthermore, there is substantial evidence advance notification does have *positive* consequences for workers faced with layoffs. These individuals have more time to search for jobs before they become unemployed, decreasing the length of time they will be without work. They have some advance warning to cut back current spending and defer major purchases, decreasing the likelihood of financial disaster.[7] They have time to get over the initial shock of job loss before going out on the job market, increasing their chances of successfully obtaining reemployment.

In some cases, failure to provide advance notification can cause extreme and unnecessary hardships for laid-off workers, as workers that we interviewed noted.

- I feel top management did not keep us informed enough about current conditions that might end up with a layoff. In my case, I had just turned down a job two weeks before my layoff. I had no indication [the termination] was coming.
- I'm very bitter about the manner in which the mills were closed. No warning, no one cared. There should be a better way than the way

they went about it. It was a very traumatic experience.

- The company should have done more to prepare the workers prior to the shutdown of the mills. Enough was not done in these areas.
- Since purchasing a new home . . . before the plant was shut down without warning, I was forced to go bankrupt. Now it is hard to start all over again.
- I was not informed about maybe moving to another plant. I knew nothing of the [training] program and I lost the chance to go to school again.

Advance notification may benefit the company as well. It allows more time for manpower planning under reduced employment, and more time for phasing out operations in cases of plant shutdowns. Also, employees may respond less negatively to layoffs if they feel the company is attempting to buffer them from the adverse consequences of job loss.[8]

There may also be some positive goodwill advantages to giving advance layoff notification. For example, at Atari, laid-off employees complained about abrupt terminations, claiming such treatment made it more difficult for them to secure other jobs. These workers felt longer advance notice would have made it possible for them to secure new jobs without the stigma of unemployment.[9]

In response, Atari's vice-president commented: "Frankly, I can't see anything out of the ordinary about asking a person to leave in two days in the world of big business. Most people can pack up an office in five minutes. I don't have much sympathy for anyone complaining about the time to get out." Such posturing gained substantial ill-will in the business community.[10] Stock brokerage firms received similarly bad press when they laid off thousands of employees after the stock crash of October 1987; many of these employees were asked to leave by 5 p.m. of the day they were notified.

In contrast, Union Carbide, Ford, and Electrolux all gave 6 months' to a year's advance notice, as well as other types of assistance (e.g., training, outplacement, and counseling).[11] In some locations, IBM and American Hospital Supply were able (1) to use carefully scheduled layoffs that kept jobs open for "skeleton crews" at other facilities, (2) to hire laid-off workers on a contract basis, and (3) to significantly compensate the last group of employees to leave with overtime pay for their efforts. In so doing, these corporations were respected for protecting and taking care of former employees.[12]

SEVERANCE PAY AND EXTENDED BENEFITS

Like advance notification, severance pay and extended benefits allow workers whose jobs have been eliminated to weather the financial difficulties of unemployment. Those who received such benefits frequently commented that the financial assistance reduced the need for their spouses to work full time, reduced the pressure to grab any job that came along simply to obtain cash, and provided some resources for the household while the worker went back for training for a new career.

Most important, though, many workers feel the company owes them some restitution for their years of service. Our respondents had many bitter comments about being thrown out with very little to show for their efforts.

- I resent the fact that I was not paid my severance pay from USX, especially when the company was not going to call me back.
- My pension payments were drastically reduced because [the company] defaulted on its premium payments.
- I worked for [the company] for 14 years and I have never received 1 cent [of pension]. That was not fair, and I still feel cheated.
- I had only two and a half years to go for re-

tirement, and had to settle for a big cut in pension. Because of my age I could not find full-time work; I had to settle for part-time. Because of shifting me from one department to another, I was not able to get training benefits.

- The last few years of my service with U.S. Steel, even though I had over 25 years with the company, I was frequently laid-off, so it was almost impossible to put away money into savings. Also, it affected my pension payment. Now whatever I had in savings is exhausted and my pension barely covers my utilities and taxes.

- I could not get any severance pay because they said I didn't work long enough. . . . I thought, when you work in a place that closes up, you get severance pay regardless of the time you put in. I didn't receive anything.

Another benefit of severance pay and extended benefits is that it reduces the need for the unemployed to seek additional governmental financial assistance—an activity that is distinctly unpleasant to most people, as our respondents noted.

- The people in these government offices make you feel like you are the scum of the earth for trying to get help. They really knock your self-esteem down. The people in these agencies need to realize they, too, could be on the other side of the counter. All I want is to be treated with some respect. It is not my fault I was laid off, and I'm tired of making excuses for it.

- The main thing I learned is that for every good program like the Job Training Partnership Act, there is an office like the unemployment office working against you.

- I had a great deal of trouble dealing with the state getting my training benefits . . . my checks are always three weeks late or have been stopped. It is very hard to get someone to listen or help when you try to help yourself the honest way.

When blue-collar workers do not have a union contract, they generally fare least well in the area of severance pay and benefits. It is mainly at this level that employers have held the line. Unfortunately, these blue-collar workers are the ones most in need of such benefits.

Because many blue-collar workers cannot afford major pay cuts without falling below the poverty level, adequate severance pay and continuation of health and life insurance programs are essential. A major problem arises, however, when the layoffs are due to financial difficulties in the corporation: those employees who need such economic support do not receive it because the organization itself is bankrupt. To guard against this problem, it has been suggested that companies in particularly volatile sectors of the economy such as high-tech manufacturing and steel commit money during profitable quarters to fund severance pay and extended benefits during economic downturns.[13]

Traditionally, companies have been much more concerned with giving severance pay and extended benefits to managerial and professional employees than to blue-collar workers. After corporate restructuring, for instance, Exxon gave many executives up to 6 months' salary as severance pay. In other corporations, laid-off executives are also likely to be handsomely compensated—often very handsomely indeed.[14] Partly from guilt and partly in fear of an increasingly litigious executive work force, corporations shower many top-level managers with generous severance packages. The so-called employment-at-will doctrine (that companies can hire and fire at will) often does not seem to apply. Each year, displaced executives are collecting in excess of $30 million in damage awards and settlements and that does not include damages awarded for age discrimination. Thus, companies are very reluctant to lay off high-level managers, especially those over age 50, without considerable benefits.[15]

Middle- and lower-level managers have not been treated nearly as generously. The best deal most middle managers can count on is a week's severance pay for every year worked. Thus, if a middle manager is earning $50,000 a year and has worked 20 years, his or her severance pay would be $20,000—just enough to make it through the 6 months the typical middle-manager is unemployed.[16] Other companies are less generous. For example, International Harvester expected its laid-off managers to apply for unemployment benefits, and deducted the severance pay checks by the amount of those benefits (roughly $100 per week).[17]

RETRAINING PROGRAMS

Another kind of assistance firms can provide to laid-off employees is training. Particularly for firms in declining industries and occupations, simply encouraging workers to go out and find new jobs misses the mark. These individuals need considerable retraining in order to obtain satisfactory new employment. In our studies, fewer than a quarter of the respondents had received any training from their companies after they were laid off. Many, however, undertook training or went back to school with government assistance or on their own—often with very positive results. Getting retrained can help unemployed workers reduce the amount of time between jobs.[18] Enrollment in training programs can also have psychological benefits. Training programs give unemployed workers some structure to the day, provide them with regular work-related activity, and allow them opportunities for increased social contact.

• In some ways, the layoff has been a blessing in disguise. I am now in a field which has always seemed interesting, though I had never imagined ever working in it. But having been forced into it, so to speak, things are looking up. It is not unreasonable to expect to double my former income or earn even more within two years.

• I feel that working is very important, not only to support myself, but also to keep busy. I am planning on taking some night classes soon.

Despite these positive accounts, many who could have benefited from retraining did not get it. There were two dominant reasons why. First, many were intimidated by the prospect of going back to school. Some had not been good students earlier in life and others were afraid that in the wake of a job loss, they could not withstand another failure. Still others, particularly older workers, felt that getting more education at their stage in life would be futile, especially since they perceived there were so few "good" jobs of any sort for people their age. Second, many employees couldn't afford to go back to school because of insufficient benefits or because they had to work two jobs and had no time left in the day for school as well. The comments of some of our study participants express many of these concerns.

• Although I was eligible for education benefits, I could not utilize them because I was employed full time. Even though I greatly desire more education, I could not afford not to work full time without losing my home.

• I started retraining, but before starting my classes I went to work part time and needed to be available all hours. I felt it was more important to my family to pick up any work available.

• I wasn't sure what field to pursue anyway and I am not very academic. I learn much easier by experience, not a blackboard.

• I feel I need further education to get anywhere in a job situation, but I'm very afraid of failing. That would be like the final crushing blow. I think I would just give up then. So I have not enrolled in any courses.

What these comments suggest is that for retraining programs to be effective, many must also be structured to take into account employees' anxieties about failure and intimidation in the classroom. Moreover, our research suggests that retraining programs are more effective when combined with severance pay and other financial assistance programs so employees will not be forced to forgo or interrupt their education out of financial necessity. Finally, training should ideally be something that is ongoing throughout a person's career. Recent initiatives like the new Career Development Program jointly sponsored by the Steelworkers union and major companies in the steel industry provide ongoing educational development opportunities for individuals while they are still employed.

OUTPLACEMENT PROGRAMS

Within the business community, the company intervention that has received substantial attention has been outplacement, "a series of services to terminated employees to minimize any period of unemployment following termination."[19] As this definition suggests, outplacement is not a specific program or service but instead encompasses a variety of services such as résumé-writing workshops, career-counseling sessions, and direct-placement assistance. Because the content and length of these programs vary so greatly from corporation to corporation, hard empirical evidence on their effectiveness has lagged behind their favorable publicity.[20]

There have been several noteworthy outplacement programs. At AT&T, the company did not implement layoffs after its reorganization until it had first asked for volunteers to leave the company with increased financial incentives. Then it attempted to relocate within the company those employees who didn't want to leave but whose positions were slated as surplus. Finally, for those employees who were forced out, AT&T paid for a full-service outplacement package that included programs from individual career counseling to the printing of business cards.[21] Wang likewise provided its laid-off employees with office space, telephones, personal comput-

ers, job search workshops, and other auxiliary services for up to six months after termination.

Brown and Williamson, a company in the United Kingdom, helped relocate employees, provided vocational training and very generous separation pay, and continued life and medical insurance. Electrolux involved state and local agencies in finding workers new jobs, provided retirement planning, offered some of the laid-off workers transfers or moving assistance and gave paid time-off for job interviewing.[22] When The Stroh Brewery Company closed its 70-year-old facility in Detroit, it set up different transition centers for hourly and salaried employees. These centers provided skill testing and assessment, individualized counseling and job-search assistance, and computerized job banks. One year after the plant closing, all of the salaried employees and 98 percent of the hourly employees had found jobs.[23]

Cooperation between the private and public sectors has resulted in some impressive outplacement services, too. For instance, Bethlehem Steel Corporation joined the State of Pennsylvania and the U.S. Department of Labor to establish the Career Continuation Center with offices in Johnstown and Bethlehem. These centers contained bulletin boards with job listings, 25 desks with telephones, and secretarial services. Laid-off workers could also participate in two-day seminars on job-seeking techniques, as well as one-on-one counseling. At the Bethlehem Center, nearly two-thirds of the employees obtained jobs within 90 days.[24]

After the *Challenger* disaster, Brevard Community College set up a similar center with federal funds to assist laid-off aerospace workers.

When Ford laid off more than 2,000 employees in Ontario, it set up 2 Manpower Adjustment Committees for salaried and hourly employees. Members of these committees came from Ford's corporate staff, the United Auto Workers union, and Canada Manpower Consultative Services. After obtaining specific information from laid-off workers about job skills, experience, and job preferences, these Manpower Adjustment Committees contacted 130 firms by letter and 2,000 smaller companies by telephone. This innovative program found new employment for nearly 85 percent of the displaced workers.[25]

Not quite so impressive are those outplacement programs that are well-intentioned but too narrow in scope or poorly executed.[26] For instance, laid-off employees of NBC complained that that network's résumé-writing workshops were "conducted by a youngster in the personnel department who didn't realize that seasoned professionals don't get jobs by sending out résumés." Similarly, an institutional sales trader at Lehman Bros. (who was let go when Lehman Bros. was bought by Shearson/American Express) agreed that while Lehman had set up a "base of operations" for him, the office had only one phone for three people, so employees couldn't seriously make or take calls.[27]

Some of the weakest outplacement activities are those that have the veneer of helpfulness but which are perceived as manipulative or punitive by workers. General Motors' "Mainstream" activities have received much attention in this regard. The Mainstream program was designed to help persuade managers to leave and to ease the process, but several employees initiated litigation. A planner claims that he and seven other managers who didn't "volunteer" to leave were put in a specially-created area that was bare except for desks and telephones, where they stayed for four months with no work assignments. A draftsman who didn't volunteer to leave says that for his defiance, he has been put at a desk in front of his boss' office where he files product-description manuals in binders. And an engineer who didn't volunteer to leave has been assigned to wiping down oil drums.[28]

Not having an outplacement program, or having a poorly designed one, can increase the likelihood that employees will sue over job loss. At Atari, 400 former workers filed a $13.6 million class-action suit for damages related to their layoffs. At Singer Company, 700 former employees filed a class-action suit seeking $28 million, contending that Singer reneged on a previous agreement to invest $2 million in upgrading their New Jersey plant. Singer eventually settled out of court. Before Western Electric was permitted to close its plant in Kearny, New Jersey, a federal judge required the company to create a $7 million fund for the 2,000 women who were to be displaced.[29]

Our own research suggests that outplacement activities can be quite beneficial. Several of our respondents noted that outplacement activities gave them the added stimulus to seek further education, to get into a more suitable occupation, or to relocate to an area with a healthier economy. Outplacement activities can also provide some of the same positive secondary consequences as training, i.e., they can give workers structure to their day, companionship and social support, and a signal from the company that it supports employee efforts to obtain reemployment. All of these may help reduce the anxiety levels of laid-off workers enough to allow them to cope with job loss effectively.[30]

Research on outplacement suggests two other points. First, one very valuable facet of an outplacement program is the temporary base of operations from which laid-off workers can job hunt, and receive clerical and technical support for writing résumés. Secondly, mainly anecdotal evidence suggests that counseling and career planning activities are better implemented after the layoffs are finalized, and on a one-to-one basis.

COMPANY INTERVENTIONS

Our research points out several important issues about the role of corporate interventions in the lives of workers who have been laid off.

First, corporate interventions play a relatively small role in directly influencing whether former employees get satisfactorily reemployed elsewhere. Demographic factors (age, education) and labor market factors (level of unemployment, skill level of occupation) play a much greater role in whether workers get satisfactorily reemployed or have good prospects for doing so.

Second, corporate interventions play a larger role in influencing laid-off workers' coping strategies. Corporate interventions seem to energize workers to engage in more active coping, which in turn leads to a better reemployment picture.

Third, to the extent corporate interventions do play a role in influencing adjustment to life without work, they do so by facilitating coping behavior that leads to reemployment. Corporate interventions do not, in and of themselves, lead to less psychological distress or more life satisfaction, because coping itself is stressful and often anxiety-arousing. Thus, although corporate interventions do provide workers with some structured activities and social interaction, they also energize workers to engage in activities they find inherently unpleasant.

Fourth, different corporate interventions seem to be differentially effective among job categories. Because unemployed white-collar workers are likelier to be searching only for new jobs, outplacement assistance tends to be more critical to them. Because unemployed blue-collar workers are likelier to be changing occupations, retraining tends to be more critical to them. Since unemployment is likely to be shorter-term for white-collar than blue-collar workers, extended benefits are more critical for blue-collar workers. Losing a job without notice is stressful for anyone, but it entails the greater financial hardship for the lower-paid, blue-collar worker.

LAYOFFS IMPLEMENTATION

How layoffs are implemented also plays a major role in how individual workers respond to becoming unemployed.[31] Repeatedly, our respondents commented on how angry they were about how they had been let go.

- I feel betrayed. We were told about several contracts and work being transferred from subdivisions of this company only last year. Now there is nothing. I was lied to.
- In my opinion, it was all company politics.
- The process of reducing the work force at my company could have been handled more tactfully and with greater concern for the individual.

Management needs to address five issues when they implement a layoff: (1) criteria for layoffs, (2) role of performance evaluations in layoff decisions, (3) fair treatment of laid-off workers, (4) fair recommendations to potential employers, and (5) attention to the stress and discomfort of the "survivors."

Criteria for Layoffs

Our studies produced substantial evidence that laid-off employees believed their terminations were arbitrary or biased. Many employees attributed their layoffs to age bias. Many workers also believe that top management spares barely competent management personnel while greatly slashing the number of lower-level employees.

- The company did not exercise good judgment in laying off lower-paid employees while keeping an overabundance of much higher-paid management and supervisory personnel.
- It distressed me greatly to see people's lives being literally ruined careerwise by management personnel who had little or no contact with these individuals [but who] had complete control over their futures.

The same phenomenon can be seen even when layoffs are caused by mergers and acquisitions or by corporate restructuring. At NBC, for instance, a female associate producer was laid off from her job—and then discovered that all but one of the people laid off in her unit were women. NBC countered that men and women were laid off in equal numbers in the network's total corporate layoff.[32] Independent of the legal issues of gender discrimination involved, however, the perception of bias remained.

To avoid these perceptions, *it is important for management to make clear, both in words and behavior, the criteria for terminations, regardless of whether they are seniority, merit, or job category.* Otherwise, management leaves itself open to legal action from those who are laid off, ill-will from the public, and justified distrust from those who remain.

Role of Performance Evaluations

Contributing greatly to the feeling of arbitrariness or bias in the layoff procedures are perceptions that employee performance evaluations are not used at all, or are purposely downgraded to justify terminations. In our study, 75 percent of the survey respondents had received "outstanding" or "excellent" on their last performance appraisal—and yet they had been let go. As one manager noted, "Inaccurate and untrue performance appraisals were used in support of company layoff goals—a very cavalier attitude toward dedicated, long-term employees. The human aspects were gruesome . . ."

Recently, Professors C. O. Longenecker, D. A. Gioia, and H. P. Sims detailed just how political the performance appraisal process can be. They found that managers are greatly influenced by political considerations when completing performance appraisals, i.e., they inflate them to maximize merit increases, and deflate them to speed up a termination process. The executives in the Longenecker study were quite open about the political pressures they felt.

- There is really no getting around the fact that whenever I evaluate one of my people, I stop and think about the impact—the ramifications of my decisions on my relationship with the guy and his future here.
- When I rate my people, it doesn't take place in a vacuum, so you have to ask yourself what the purpose of the process is. . . . I use this thing to my advantage; I know my people and

what it takes to keep them going—and that is what this is all about.[33]

When layoffs occur, all the political games used to justify performance results come open for inspection. The negative spin-off effects for top management prove embarrassing; the adverse consequences for laid-off employees who were unaware of the political rating (or who chose to pretend they did not exist) are disastrous. Corporations need to make sure performance evaluations accurately reflect employee abilities. Otherwise, they risk not only litigation but also the loss of their best talent and the retention of marginally competent members of a "good-old-boy" network.[34]

Fair Treatment of Laid-Off Workers

Several researchers found that one of the most important executive actions for managing human resources during layoffs is treating laid-off employees with dignity and social support. The effective managers in their study gave terminated employees accurate and honest information so they could make better decisions about the future. Effective managers also spent time talking with laid-off employees, allowing them to vent some of their anger and frustration. Such actions on the part of executives helped terminated workers cope more realistically and face a job hunt with more self-confidence and self-esteem.

- He [the boss] was firm, honest, and open. He didn't tolerate saboteurs and rabble-rousers who really heat up rather than help the situation. I respected his fair but direct style of acting professional.
- He was easy to talk to, made me feel comfortable. He just paid attention to my concerns and uncertainty.
- She set up a workshop on her own for résumé preparation and interviewing skills.
- She paid a friend of hers—a personnel director from another firm—to spend three hours

on three different nights to help get our act together.[35]

In contrast, there have been some very unpleasant episodes involving laid-off employees' being mistreated. Professors R.I. Sutton, K.M. Eisenhardt, and J.V. Jucker, for instance, document problems with Atari in 1982 and 1983, just before it was sold by Warner Communications.[36]

- The manager gave the production employees directions to Sunnyvale High School and told them to be there on Friday, February 25. [When they arrived], he collected their badges, and the production workers were escorted off the premises.
- Top management went around and spoke to everybody. What they said was, "Now we've gotten rid of all the rummies and the company's strong and all the good people are left." And they never should have said that. They should have said, "Because of business problems, we have had to let people go." But they said, "We've gotten rid of all the scum," and that wasn't the case at all. And everybody knew it, and everybody resented it. So it just got worse and worse.

Sutton, Eisenhardt, and Jucker also suggest several strategies for treating employees with dignity during layoffs.

1. Employees should be able to say goodbye to co-workers, and to express their anger and sorrow.
2. They should not be denigrated to their peers after their departure.
3. Laid-off employees should be given the bad news in person and by people they know, not through the mail or from managers they've never heard of.[37]

Treating departing employees with dignity and compassion is better for the laid-off workers themselves, better for the employees who remain, and better for the company's public image.

Fair Recommendations to Potential Employers

More and more lawsuits are being filed by terminated employees who feel they are not being fairly recommended for employment in other corporations. In 1986, the suits filed by discharged employees against former bosses accounted for about a third of all defamation actions.[38] In the aftermath of layoffs, it is particularly important for executives to be sensitive to the legal implications of negative recommendations for terminated employees.

A well-publicized instance of termination resulting in litigation is the case of Buck v. Frank B. Hall & Co.[39] A Hall executive told a detective posing as a representative of a prospective employer that Buck was "a Jekyll-and-Hyde person, a classic sociopath." Buck sued his former employer for malicious slander and libel, and collected $605,000 in lost wages and a $1.3 million penalty.

Indeed, counseling companies on both small- and large-scale layoffs in order to avoid discrimination suits has recently become an important phase of employment law.[40] Because of the many legal ramifications of layoffs—not only in terms of recommendations, but also in terms of renegotiating contracts and pension plans—many corporations are using the services of "undertaker" firms. These companies advise clients on the legal technicalities of laying off employees, financial incentives for management personnel, and other human resource problems that occur during a reorganization.[41]

Handling "Survivors" of Layoffs

From the viewpoint of the laid-off workers, losing the social support of friends and colleagues at work is one of the most distressing aspects of job loss. But for the companies dealing with layoffs, there is also the other side of the issue: those employees who survive often are upset and angry, too.[42] They miss their departed colleagues and are frequently angry with management for having caused the layoff, for having mishandled the layoff process, or for speaking disparagingly about the departed workers. The productivity of survivors may also decrease. Workers lost time discussing their emotions, speculating on whether more layoffs will be forthcoming, and, often, looking for new jobs of their own.[43] Survivors are especially negatively affected when they identify closely with the layoff victims and feel the laid-off workers were inadequately compensated.[44]

Because of these problems, firms have taken some positive, concrete actions to lift morale and instill trust in survivors. Consulting firms like Eclecon and Good-measure advise corporations, first, to give employees relatively easy work for a week or so after the layoffs, and then to give them new, challenging assignments to distract them. Companies like AT&T have followed these strategies with success.[45]

The survivor problem should also sensitize management to two other issues. First, layoffs should not be intermittent, sporadic, or extended over long periods of time. Second, the number of job changes for survivors after the layoffs should be kept to a minimum.

These policies will help to stabilize employee concerns and reduce needless anxiety and apprehension. At Amax, Inc., unfortunately, a series of layoffs occurred over a four-year period, each accompanied by management's claim that the company was now "lean and mean." Such actions only served to further demoralize workers.[46]

CONCLUSION

As distasteful as the announcement and implementation of layoffs may be, it is critical that management confront these issues. Managers need to understand how layoffs affect employees and how to manage work force reductions more effectively. Our research suggests several points for managers to keep in mind.

First, management should seriously consider alternatives to layoffs, and, if layoffs are unavoidable, the number of people to be laid off should be reduced as much as possible.

Second, corporations should offer employees a variety of assistance programs to help them find new employment in the long run and to cope with unemployment in the short run.

Third, corporations should follow specific procedures to treat laid-off employees humanely, and to decrease losses in morale and productivity among survivors.

Fourth, corporations should work cooperatively with unions, governmental agencies, and the local community to minimize the negative aftereffects of layoffs.

Layoffs of blue-collar workers as a result of deindustrialization of manufacturing, and layoffs of white-collar employees as a result of acquisitions, are likely to continue. Managers need to think carefully about the consequences of such layoffs, and to take actions to reduce the emotional suffering and financial hardships layoffs can create.

NOTES

1. H. G. Kaufman, *Professionals in Search of Work: Coping with the Stress of Job Loss and Unemployment* (New York: John Wiley & Sons, 1982).
2. J. T. Addison, "The Controversy over Advance Notice Legislation in the United States," *British Journal of Industrial Relations* 27 (1989): 235-63.
3. J. J. Chrisman, A. B. Carroll, and E. J. Gatewood, "What's Wrong with Plant Closing Legislation and Industrial Policy," *Business Horizons* 28 (1985): 28-37.
4. R. G. Ehrenberg and G. H. Jakubson, "Advance Notification of Plant Closings: Does It Matter?" *Industrial Relations* 26 (1989): 60-71; J. T. Addison and P. Portugal, "The Effect of Advance Notification of Plant Closings on Unemployment," *Industrial and Labor Relations Review* 41 (1987): 3-16, 43-45, 49.

5. A. R. Weber and D. P. Taylor, "Procedures for Employee Displacement: Advance Notice of a Plant Shutdown," *Journal of Business* 36 (1963): 312-15.

6. J. Fedrau, "Easing the Worker's Transition from Job Loss to Employment," *Monthly Labor Review* 107 (1984): 38-40; B. Harrison, "Plant Closures: Efforts to Cushion the Blow," *Monthly Labor Review* 107 (1984): 41-43; M. L. Sweet, *Industrial Location Policy for Economic Revitalization: National and International Perspectives* (New York: Praeger, 1981); R. Hershey, "Effects of Anticipated Job Loss on Employee Behavior," *Journal of Applied Psychology* 56 (1972): 273-75.

7. Ehrenberg and Jakubson, "Advance Notification"; Addison and Portugal, "The Effect of Advance Notification."

8. C. R. Leana and J. M. Ivancevich, "Involuntary Job Loss: Institutional Interventions and a Research Agenda," *Academy of Management Review* 12 (1987): 301-12.

9. M. Langley, "Many Middle Managers Fight Back as More Firms Trim Work Forces," *Wall Street Journal,* 29 November 1984, p. 55.

10. R. I. Sutton, K. M. Eisenhardt, and J. V. Jucker, "Managing Organizational Decline: Lessons from Atari," *Organizational Dynamics,* 14 (1986): 17-29.

11. A. Kinicki, J. Bracker, R. Kreitner, C. Lockwood, and D. Lemak, "Socially Responsible Plant Closings," *Personnel Administrator,* No. 6 (June 1987): 116-28.

12. Langley, "Many Middle Managers Fight Back."

13. J. C. Latack and J. B. Dozier, "After the Ax Falls: Job Loss as a Career Transition," *Academy of Management Review* 11 (1986): 375-92.

14. A. Bennett, "After the Merger, More CEO's Left in Uneasy Spot: Looking for Work," *Wall Street Journal,* 3 February 1987, p. 35.

15. C. H. Deutsch, "Why Being Fired Is Losing Its Taint," *New York Times,* 24 January 1988, pp. 3-11.

16. F. Kessler, "Managers Without a Company," *Fortune,* 28 October 1985, pp. 51-56.

17. Ibid.

18. Kaufman, *Professionals in Search of Work.*

19. J. Scherba, "Outplacement as a Personnel Responsibility," *Personnel* 50 (1973): 40-44.

20. C. R. Leana and D. C. Feldman, "Individual Responses to Job Loss: Perceptions, Reactions, and Coping Behaviors," *Journal of Management* 14 (1988): 5-19.

21. Langley, "Many Middle Managers Fight Back."

22. Kinicki et al., "Socially Responisble Plant Closings."

23. J. Jannotta, "Stroh's Outplacement Success," *Management Review* 76 (1987): 52-53.

24. J. S. DeMott, "After the Mills Shut Down," *Time,* 15 August 1983, p. 46.

25. Kinicki et al., "Socially Responsible Plant Closings."

26. C. R. Leana and D. C. Feldman, "When Mergers Force Layoffs: Some Lessons about Managing the Human Resource Problems," *Human Resource Planning* 12 (1989): 123-40.

27. Langley, "Many Middle Managers Fight Back."

28. A. K. Naj, "GM Now Is Plagued with Drop in Morale as Payrolls Are Cut," *Wall Street Journal,* 26 May 1987, pp. 1, 18.

29. Kinicki et al., "Socially Responsible Plant Closings."

30. Leana and Ivancevich, "Involuntary Job Loss"; Leana and Feldman, "Individual Responses to Job Loss."

31. Leana and Feldman, "Individual Responses to Job Loss"; Leana and Feldman, "When Mergers Force Layoffs."

32. Langley, "Many Middle Managers Fight Back."

33. C. O. Longenecker, D. A. Gioia, and H. P. Sims, "Behind the Mask: The Politics of Employee Appraisal," *Academy of Management Executive* 1 (1987): 183-94.

34. Leana and Feldman, "Individual Responses to Job Loss"; Leana and Feldman, "When Mergers Force Layoffs."

35. D. M. Schweiger, J. M. Ivancevich, and F. R. Power, "Executive Actions for Managing Human Resources Before and After Acquisition," *Academy of Management Executive* 1 (1987): 127-38.

36. R. I. Sutton, K. M. Eisenhardt, and J. V. Jucker, "Managing Organizational Decline: Lessons from Atari," *Organizational Dynamics* 14 (1986): 17-29.

37. Ibid.

38. G. Stricharchuk, "Fired Employees Turn the Reason for Dismissal into a Legal Weapon," *Wall Street Journal,* 2 October 1986, p. 33.

39. J. B. Copeland, "The Revenge of the Fired," *Newsweek,* 16 February 1987, pp. 46-47.

40. Langley, "Many Middle Managers Fight Back."

41. W. C. Putnam, "Undertaker Helps Businesses Close Down," *Gainesville Sun,* 27 April 1987, p. 8C.

42. J. Brockner, S. Grover, T. Reed, R. DeWitt and M. O'Malley, "Survivors' Reactions to Layoffs: We Get By with a Little Help from Our Friends," *Administrative Science Quarterly* 32 (1987): 526-41: L. Greenhalgh and Z. Rosenblatt, "Job Insecurity: Toward Conceptual Clarity," *Academy of Management Review* 9 (1984): 438-48.

43. Naj, "GM Now Is Plagued."

44. L. Reibstein, "Survivors of Layoffs Receive Help to Lift Morale and Reinstill Trust," *Wall Street Journal,* 5 December 1985, p. 33.

45. Ibid.

46. S. G. Harris and R. I. Sutton, "Functions of Parting Ceremonies in Dying Organizations," *Academy of Management Journal* 29 (1986): 5-30.

CHAPTER 8

"Whose Side Is Big Brother On?" Electronic Monitoring and Employee Privacy

INTRODUCTION

According to Supreme Court Justice Louis Brandeis, privacy is "the right most valued by civilized men." Kant's claim that every human being is entitled to a respect worthy of his or her dignity carries over to our insistence that we have a right to privacy and that other people have a duty to "respect" it. In our personal lives, we are deeply offended if someone, without our permission, inspects our belongings, reads our mail, or listens in on our conversations.

Modern technologies pose unprecedented risks to privacy; it is now possible to obtain, store, evaluate, and disseminate large amounts of personal data. Our financial status, our physical health, our psychological well-being, even our moral beliefs are, in the right circumstances, available for inspection. Because drug testing, health screening, polygraph testing, video monitoring, e-mail scanning, and computer monitoring all give employers access to their employees' backgrounds, personal habits, and work performance, many employees believe that their right to privacy is at risk.

Yet, as with most rights, the right to privacy is not absolute. Employees give up some, but not all, of their expectations of privacy when they come to work. Employers have a legitimate interest in knowing about their employees. Owners or managers of business enterprises have a right and a legitimate responsibility to take steps to prevent theft, protect proprietary information, and insure efficiency in the production and delivery of their goods and services. Informed hiring decisions and adequate supervision and appraisal of work performance are essential to the exercise of managerial rights and responsibilities.

The readings in this chapter discuss the ethical and managerial issues involved in the electronic monitoring of employees. Three sorts of electronic monitoring are customary in the workplace: video surveillance, telephone monitoring, and computer monitoring, each with its different uses (and potential abuses). For example, video surveillance is often adopted in the shipping industry and in retail stores in order to prevent theft; the use of telephone monitoring to observe how customers are served is widespread in the service industries; and computer monitoring of the performance of individual employees is common in companies that process large amounts of information. This chapter's ethical analyses and recommendations are often illustrated by reference to computer monitoring, although they are more generally applicable.

Critics of electronic monitoring appeal to a variety of ethical and managerial considerations to support their position. In particular they argue that:

1. Video surveillance and telephone monitoring, unless carefully restricted, easily intrude on areas of legitimate employee privacy (e.g., employee lounges, restrooms, and private telephone conversations).
2. The assumption of pervasive electronic monitoring is that employees are untrustworthy and need to be constantly watched, which not only erodes employees' self-esteem but also undermines their loyalty.
3. Computer monitoring can be used to establish production standards and a work tempo that are so stressful that employees' physical health and psychological well-being are threatened.
4. Since the use of computer monitoring in the evaluation of employee performance focuses only on quantitative measurements (e.g., the number of keystrokes per minute or information requests handled per hour) and ignores considerations of quality, it may represent a one-sided and unfair performance measure.

On the other hand, supporters of monitoring believe that its benefits (e.g., increased productivity, better accounting controls, more informed personnel decisions, etc.) to both employers and employees outweigh its costs. More specifically, they maintain that:

1. Employers have a basic right to control the output and quality of work in their workplaces. If they believe that electronic monitoring aids them in preventing theft and in improving productivity and the quality of their services, they have the right to use it.
2. Electronic monitoring can be a valuable training tool that provides employees with feedback needed to enhance their performance.
3. Because it is thoroughly objective, electronic monitoring provides a fair and accurate measurement of an employee's performance and eliminates many of the subjective and biased factors that contribute to unfair evaluations.

Fairness is a central element in this discussion. As we have seen in Chapter 1, fairness considers, among other things, the distribution of benefits and burdens. If employees believe that most of the likely benefits of electronic monitoring will accrue to owners and managers and that most of the likely burdens will fall on them, they will perceive the process as unfair. However, if the benefits are fairly distributed, the employees are involved in a meaningful way in designing the system, and the privacy rights of employees are respected, electronic monitoring can be implemented in an ethically and managerially sound fashion. Ethically, the following questions need to be addressed (Boatright, 1993, p. 193) (and, in fact, guide the discussions in our selected readings).

1. What kind of information will be collected?
2. How will the information be collected?
3. How will the accuracy and completeness of the information be guaranteed?
4. Who will have access to the information? What access will employees have?
5. To what use will the information be put?
6. What safeguards will employees have against misuse of the information?

★ ★ ★

In this chapter's readings, **Kristin Bell DeTienne** emphasizes the benefits of electronic monitoring, when it is humanely employed. To

Ernest Kallman, the central issue is the amount of control that electronic monitoring gives management and the risk to employee privacy. He reviews arguments both for (e.g., increased productivity, more efficient accounting) and against electronic monitoring (e.g., privacy, employee stress, fairness) and proposes a series of ethical and managerial guidelines to govern its use. **Kenneth A. Jenero** and **Lynn D. Mapes-Riordan** examine relevant case law and suggest how employers can fairly balance interests and reduce their legal risks. **Andrew Clement,** after reviewing the sweeping future possibilities of "fishbowl" surveillance, compares the protection of employee interests prevalent in the European community with that in North America and makes several proposals to balance employer and employee interests and rights.

REFERENCES

Boatright, John. (1993) *Ethics and the Conduct of Business,* Englewood Cliffs: Prentice-Hall.

CASE: Jim Boyd at Redlow Corporation

Jim Boyd, the vice president for management information systems (MIS) at Redlow Corporation, felt pleased but slightly uneasy about his meeting earlier that day with Jeff Neal, the head technical services representative from ExecSystems, Inc. (ESI). The two firms had enjoyed a long and productive relationship, with Redlow buying all of its computer hardware and most of its software from ESI over the last ten years. Neal had worked on the Redlow account for nearly five years and had become a valuable source of technical expertise to Jim and the Redlow management team. But now, as he thought back to their meeting, Jim didn't know quite what to make of the new software that Jeff had brought to his attention.

REDLOW CORPORATION

Redlow, a mid-sized company based in Chicago, was established in 1969 by two graduates of a midwestern engineering school. The company staked its claim in the health-care industry by developing innovative products designed to speed up claims processing for its customers. In addition, it provided a claims processing service for smaller clients.

Redlow had developed a positive reputation within the health-care industry over the past several years. The atmosphere within the company reflected its good reputation outside. There was a cohesiveness within departments that allowed Redlow to run smoothly, even during high-enrollment months and fiscal year end. Managers prided themselves on the company's achievements and employee empowerment. Employees had opportunities within the company for advancement to management, supported by a commitment from the firm to develop employee skills across several departments and specialty areas. Redlow preferred to hire from within for management positions. Jim Boyd himself had started his career at Redlow in accounting but moved to MIS just five years ago. It was a different industry now than it had been ten or twelve years ago, Jim thought. Employees needed to work at a faster pace than ever before. It was important for Redlow to stay on top of its industry segment with a combination of accuracy, accountability, and speed. To Jim Boyd, this was an important challenge.

THE NEW SOFTWARE OPPORTUNITY

Jeff told Jim, in their meeting, about an innovative piece of software that he (Jeff) claimed could significantly improve the productivity of the 125-person data entry staff at Redlow. As Jeff described the software, Jim was impressed by its capacity to continuously monitor each worker's performance (down to the number of keystrokes per minute), to compare worker's outputs, to generate "exception reports" by the hour, and to generate "feedback messages" to each worker, informing them, for example, that they had slowed their earlier pace and urging them to work faster.

Source: This case was prepared by Joy Durand, research assistant, under the supervision of Professor Edward Ottensmeyer as the basis for class discussion rather than to illustrate either effective or ineffective handling of an administrative situation. The case is fictional but represents a composite of actual events.

CEO INPUT

Jim was extremely interested in improving productivity in the staff service departments at Redlow and had held a lengthy discussion with the CEO, John Turner, about it at his recent budget presentation. It was clear that John was looking to Jim to take a leadership role in productivity improvement in this area of the firm.

John had a few concerns about monitoring that he mentioned during the meeting. He emphasized the need to improve productivity and security while not generating resentment. Monitoring could be a very emotionally charged issue and had to be presented in the right way to workers, he told Jim. He was concerned about morale and the stress levels that might be associated with closer monitoring. He predicted a higher level of competition among data entry workers if monitoring was linked to rewards and discussed that possibility with Jim. The CEO gave Jim a set of articles about electronic monitoring. He asked Jim to read them and consider the implications. Jim was excited to get the project into motion. He hoped his reading about electronic monitoring would help him sort through the issues involved.

DEPARTMENTAL OPERATIONS

In reflecting upon his department, Jim noted that the turnover rate for the data entry positions was averaging nearly 10 percent per month. This undermined consistency within the department and increased costs. Training for the positions was time-consuming, as was the recruitment process. To recruit and train a new employee cost the company $2500 per employee. With this cost and the 10 percent per month turnover rate, the company was losing nearly $400,000 a year. Jim was enthusiastic about the prospect of improving productivity. If the monitoring software was effective, this was a great opportunity to take the initiative and increase output in data entry, as well as to impress the CEO.

Data entry work was very routine and could easily be described as boring. There was no technologically sophisticated monitoring system in place at present, and performance on the job was measured simply by the number of standardized entries per day. Deviations from "normal" performance were measured, and, if they persisted for more than a week, a supervisor would meet with the worker to point out the substandard performance.

The turnover rate was the highest in the company; the average compensation was the lowest. The department consisted primarily of women, ranging in age from late teens to early fifties. The twelve men in the department had the same duties and responsibilities, as well as the same compensation, as the women. Should an employee stay with data entry for six months and earn good reviews, she or he had an opportunity to advance to assistant floor manager.

Employee reviews of their work conducted periodically by the human resources department, indicated that the data entry department, as a whole, thought of their jobs as dull and ranked them low in motivation. Most saw data entry as a "dead-end" job, although some satisfaction came from personal relationships with coworkers and supervisors. They ranked trust with the company and top management highly. Jim was concerned about altering the few positive opinions about their jobs and about Redlow by adding "invisible managers" (i.e., electronic monitoring) to the mix.

JEFF NEAL'S SALES PITCH

In a follow-up phone conversation with Jeff, Jim began to see the software in a more favorable light. Jeff presented the many positive features and advantages of the new software. This approach was innovative, he said, and "at the forefront of industry practice." He offered testimonials from other firms that had recently purchased and installed the software, including rave reviews from a few CEOs, which pointed out cost-cutting efficiencies, increased work output, and enhanced supervision as the system's greatest advantages.

To Jim, an especially attractive aspect of the software was its database capabilities—an ability to chart each employee and compare his or her performance with others doing the same job. The system just needed to be "told" which employees to monitor on an hourly, daily, or continuous basis, and comprehensive data and reports could be printed out and available for analysis on demand. The software would chart high and low productivity times by averaging the employee's keystrokes. It recognized differences in keystrokes, thus, for example, constant repetition, such as hitting one letter over and over for several minutes at a time, would be noted in the charting sequences. It had the capability to chart individual employees, as well as the department's performance as a group.

Regarding "on-screen messaging," the software could be set to send out messages, such as "faster pace needed" during low productivity times—early in the morning, after lunch, or late afternoon. The on-screen messages could either be uniform or personalized for each employee. The software had the capability to change messages during the day as well as to rotate messages on a random basis.

Crucial to its usefulness was the ability of the software to expand as the company grew. Jeff had learned from managers in other companies that many of them had expanded the software into other parts of their companies within several months of installment. Jim immediately thought that the perfect places to implement the software after a trial six months in data entry would be in the quality assurance and claims adjustment departments. These departments were input-oriented, and performance efficiency was essential.

JIM'S UNEASINESS

Jim learned from Jeff that the system had been implemented recently by Mallord, Inc., a competitor regarded as the industry technology trendsetter. Still, Jim had some nagging concerns about the software. Was it right to monitor workers this way? What about the "on-screen messages" capability? Was it too intrusive? Would this new technology lead to greater productivity and be fair to the workers?

Jim reviewed the articles that John had given him. They were informative and helpful. Several companies utilizing electronic monitoring were described, and their feedback was available. Some firms, such as a competitor health-care company, used the monitoring to aid in measuring time off and attendance. Monitoring systems greatly improved the airline industry's ability to take reservations quickly and accurately.

There were also some negatives noted. Among other things, employees often felt that they were being spied on or that the company did not trust them. The stress level of employees under these monitoring systems had been shown to increase. And there were worries that it might also discourage social relationships on the job. These did not seem unrealistic expectations to Jim.

JIM'S DECISION

Jim felt that he had done his homework on this issue, and that he was getting closer to a decision. As he casually glanced at his crowded inbox, he noticed an item from John Turner. It was a copy of a *Wall Street Journal* article titled "Productivity: Key to US Global Competitiveness." The CEO had scrawled in the margin, "Anything new in your shop?" He also thought about a short conversation he had with his wife a few days earlier. After hearing what he had told her about the monitoring software, she had asked a question that stuck in his mind—Would you want your boss to do that to you?

Source: This case was prepared by Joy Durand, research assistant, under the supervision of Professor Edward Ottensmeyer as the basis for class discussion rather than to illustrate either effective or ineffective handling of an administrative situation. The case is fictional but represents a composite of actual events.

Big Brother or Friendly Coach? Computer Monitoring in the 21st Century

Kristen Bell DeTienne

Picture this as the workplace of the future: A computer tells you if you are making too many typos and suggests that you take a break from typing. Or it tells your boss if you are talking to a customer. Or taking too long a break. Or what you are saying on the phone. Through a computer, your boss can see what you are doing every minute and every second while you are at work.

Does this description sound like a portrayal of the far-off future? It isn't. It's today. Currently, as many as 26 million workers in the United States are monitored in their jobs, and this number will increase as computers are used more and more within companies and as the cost of these monitoring systems goes down. By the end of the decade, as many as 30 million people may be constantly monitored in their jobs. But exactly how will these monitoring systems change in the next 20 years, and how will they affect workers?

Alan Westin, a professor at Columbia University, believes that monitoring can be done in a humane fashion if employees are guaranteed several rights, including access to all information gathered through monitoring. Furthermore, it can be motivational to give employees personal access to this information. As Michael J. Smith, a professor at the University of Wisconsin–Madison, asserts, "Information given to the supervisor often turns out to be a club, but when

it goes directly to the worker, it can become a positive motivator."

EVASION-PROOF MONITORING

Computer monitoring in the future will have fewer of the loopholes that today's employees discover and use to circumvent company rules and regulations governing their actions. Systems will become increasingly more complex and be able to prevent much of the evasion and game playing that goes on now.

A look at the reservation offices at the major airlines helps to illustrate the meaning of computer loopholes. All of the major airlines have computerized reservation systems, and they use computers to monitor the reservation agents' work. The agents are assigned specific time periods for breaks, and except for these assigned times, the agents are not to leave their seats.

To enforce these rules, computers keep track of the agents' actions. However, the computer only keeps a record of the agents' average time between calls and their average time during calls. The agents are allowed a short time between calls to enter information from the call into the computer system. The airlines examine the agents' records to make sure the elapsed time between calls is not too large (usually not over a minute).

However, some agents have discovered that, if they keep customers on the line while they enter information (thus keeping their time between calls to only one second), they can take an additional five-minute break every two hours. Agents can take this additional break because the computer only keeps track of the average time between calls. More sophisticated future monitoring systems will keep records of actual times, not just the average time between calls.

There will be two main implications of this trend. First, the computers will be able to prevent certain employees from evading the system. As a result, employees who do not take advan-

Source: The Futurist, September-October, 1993, 33-37. Reprinted with permission from *The Futurist,* published by the World Future Society, 7910 Wordmont Avenue, Suite 450, Bethesda, Maryland 20814.

tage of the system will no longer resent the unfair work habits of their co-workers. Second, employees who are accustomed to evading the monitoring system may no longer be able to tolerate it. Unable to use loopholes as a coping mechanism, some employees may suffer from higher levels of stress and fatigue.

SUGGESTIONS FOR IMPROVING PERFORMANCE

Advanced computer systems will be able to make suggestions based on information that the employee enters. Not only will these computers keep closer tabs on employees, but based on this added information, the computer will be able to help employees do their jobs more effectively.

Hotel reservation agents, for instance, are required to remember a great deal of information about current joint ventures and promotions. They are trained to know what types of service or package deals should be offered to which customers. Often, agents are reminded at the start of each shift about the promotions currently being offered. However, sometimes the agents forget to tell the customers about these programs.

In the future, prompts will appear on the computer screen to remind agents of promotions. Let's say that Hotel A is involved in a joint venture with Car Rental Agency B to offer a discount on car rental for customers who stay in Hotel A in either Miami or Houston. If an agent uses the computer to answer a customer's inquiry about reserving a hotel room in Miami or Houston, the computer will remind the employee about the promotion and then provide the details.

Overall, the use of prompts will be positive, for employees will not have to worry as much about remembering countless details. Other implications will depend on a particular organization's use of this technology. For example, if the organization uses the prompts to inform employees every time they take too long on a trans-action or fall below the group average, there may be more negative outcomes.

INFORMATION FOR SELF-EVALUATION

New technology will also give employees access to information about their own performance. Few monitoring systems that are currently operating can do this. In the future, employees will be able to check their own performance and to compare it with that of their co-workers.

This knowledge could increase employee performance and efficiency. For example, a study conducted by Christopher Earley in 1988 indicated that computer-based feedback has a greater impact on an employee's performance if he or she receives it directly from the computer system than if it is provided by a supervisor. The largest implication of this trend is positive. Employees will be given access to all information gathered in monitoring.

NEW FOCUS ON RESULTS

Monitoring will be seen as part of a more results-oriented focus in companies of the future. Currently, most employees who are monitored are given specific instructions they must follow while doing their jobs. This often leads to a focus on the means rather than the ends. In the future, companies will allow employees more personal freedom in *how* they accomplish their objectives.

An examination of the telemarketing industry provides an illustration of the results-oriented focus. Many telemarketers are given a script that they must follow when selling their product. These scripts have been developed based on the techniques that tend to be the most effective for most telemarketers on most customers. Instead of being required to use scripts and step-by-step instructions, future employees will be given tips on methods that tend to be most effective, trained to use these methods, and then allowed to choose the method that works best for them.

As long as the means are ethical and portray a positive image for the company, performance will be measured by examining the ends. In the future, more organizations will concentrate on the desired results, rather than forcing every employee to use the exact same technique.

The major implication of the growing emphasis on results will be positive. The increased freedom regarding how they do their job will tend to motivate workers. However, a difficulty lies in the supervisor's qualitative evaluation of an employee's work. Most organizations that use computers to count the number of keystrokes or transactions also use "electronic spies" to randomly listen in on calls to make sure that both the quantity and the quality of the work are high. These electronic spies may have personal preferences about techniques that should or should not be used and may be subjective in their qualitative evaluations of employee performance.

COMPUTERS AS COACHES

Information gathered via computer monitoring will increasingly be used to coach employees. Currently, many organizations use the information gathered as a basis for criticism. Companies will begin to realize that it is more motivating for employees to be coached rather than reproached.

Current monitoring systems fail as coaches. For instance, in one case involving a major U.S. airline, reservation agents were monitored electronically to make sure they stayed within the allotted time for restroom breaks. They were permitted a total of 12 minutes for restroom breaks during a seven-and-a-half-hour period. If an agent spent over 12 minutes a day for breaks, it was grounds for a disciplinary warning.

One employee was threatened with firing because she spent 13 minutes over her allotted time. This employee said that her supervisor "told me that while I was in the bathroom my co-workers were taking extra calls to make up for my 'abusive' work habits."

After this incident, the reservation agent suffered a nervous breakdown, which she blamed on "bathroom break harassment." A manager at the airline argued that the supervisors were "not spying on workers but trying to enhance their competitive position."

In the future, companies that use monitoring will recognize the need to be more sensitive to the messages that they send to their employees. If companies are too harsh, they will lose in the long run due to increased turnover, absenteeism, medical costs, and worker's compensation claims. Supervisors will have to work as coaches rather than critics whenever possible, and employees should receive helpful feedback on their performance.

The implication of this trend is positive in that it overcomes two of the biggest complaints about the current use of monitoring: (1) that the results are used only for work speedups, and (2) that too much emphasis is placed on the quantity of work rather than the quality. If supervisors primarily use coaching information to motivate employees, both the company and the workers will benefit.

COMPUTERS AS TEAM FACILITATORS

Monitoring systems can also facilitate group work and team-oriented approaches. Instead of using computer monitoring to pit employee against employee, companies will begin to use more team-centered competitions. Many times it is more productive for an employee to work as part of a team than individually. Although there will be an increase in individual accountability, companies will also realize that occasionally putting employees into groups can be a refreshing and motivating change of pace.

Computers will help managers decide which employees should be teamed together. To take another example from the airlines, one employee may be especially skilled at selling seats, while another is good at calming irate customers. If employees with different strengths are placed on the same team, they will be able to learn from each other. In addition, the computer will help managers to decide when more agents are needed on the phone and when business is slow enough to allow some agents to go home early.

Many of the implications of this trend are positive. Employees may feel increased camaraderie, enjoy learning from each other, have higher job satisfaction, discover how to perform their jobs more effectively, and experience less stress if they are evaluated as a team rather than individually. In fact, many companies in Europe are already monitoring groups rather than individuals.

Some implications of this trend are negative, however. Employees may feel less satisfied if they are placed in teams on the basis of statistical probabilities rather than on their personal preferences. They may rely too much on other members of their team to perform at high levels. And they may form coalitions with the other members of their team only and feel less commitment to the organization as a whole. Also, organizations may have difficulty rewarding individual effort. This could especially be a problem in the United States, where most people place more emphasis on individual achievement rather than group accomplishments.

PAY AND PERFORMANCE

Computer monitoring will permit companies to tie compensation more closely to employee performance. Along with increased individual accountability will come an increase in individual rewards.

Examples of tying pay to performance include innovative new benefits programs being implemented at IBM, Merck & Co., and Nu Skin International. These companies and many others are realizing that monetary rewards can motivate employees by instilling within them the idea that company-desired behaviors (in this case, high performance) lead to employee-desired outcomes (higher pay).

There are both positive and negative implications to this trend. The positive is that employees will feel as though they are being rewarded on the basis of objective criteria rather than subjective evaluation by their supervisors. On the other hand, companies will face the challenge of creating a balanced measure of the quantity and the quality of service provided by employees. If pay is tied exclusively to the quantity of service provided, the organization will eventually suffer due to a low quality of customer service. Thus, organizations will need to develop detailed performance-appraisal systems that examine all factors of performance, including both how much and how well the employee works.

MONITORING WORKERS AT HOME

Some employees who are monitored will work at home. Although not all jobs can be done at home, some companies will allow and even encourage employees to work at home rather than

---

Nine Forecasts for Computer Monitoring

1. Monitoring systems will become "evasion-proof."
2. Monitoring systems will provide suggestions to employees for performance improvement.
3. Monitoring systems will give employees access to information about their own performance.
4. Monitoring will be used as part of a results-oriented focus.
5. Monitoring will primarily be used as a coaching device.
6. Monitoring systems will facilitate group work and team-oriented approaches to work.
7. Pay will be more closely connected with employee performance.
8. The number of electronically monitored employees who work at home will increase.
9. There will be increased attempts to pass legislation that regulates monitoring.

in the office. These companies can save money if they do not have to provide rooms in which employees perform their jobs.

Some employees who perform data-entry tasks can be paid per transaction or per keystroke as monitored by the computer. These employees can work in their own homes, at their own pace, and their work can be evaluated at a later time by supervisors in the company's office. Because of the financial advantages of allowing employees to work at home, this practice will become more common in the next 10 years.

There will be many positive implications of working at home. For individuals, there will be an increase in autonomy, a reduced amount of time spent commuting, and, in some cases, more flexibility regarding child-care options. For companies, there will be lower costs associated with providing a place for employees to work, less hassle associated with interpersonal conflicts in the office, and an increased potential to attract segments of the work force that may otherwise remain unemployed.

Conversely, there may be negative implications for both employees and companies. For individuals there may be less feedback received, a greater feeling of social isolation, impaired personal and professional development, and reduced opportunities for promotion. Organizations may experience increased difficulty in establishing objective criteria for evaluating employee performance and deciding which ones to promote. Companies may also find it harder to identify employees who do not perform their jobs the way that the organization prefers.

REGULATING COMPUTER MONITORING

There will be increased attempts to pass legislation that regulates employee monitoring via computers. As long as companies use technology to monitor human work, some humans will react negatively to the procedure and demand protection through legislation. The issues will focus on management's desire to know "who is doing what" in the office and an employee's right to privacy and human dignity.

Recently, several attempts have been made to pass legislation that limits the use of monitoring. If it is legal for companies to use insensitive or unfair monitoring practices, companies that do will be less profitable because of an increase in turnover, absenteeism, stress-related illnesses, and so on. On the other hand, if companies are legally restricted in their use of technological methods for evaluating performance, many will achieve the same ends through the use of regular human supervision.

Both positive and negative implications can arise from increased legislation. On the positive side, such regulation may ensure the humane treatment of all employees, regardless of the organization for which they work. Legislation may protect many employees' right to privacy, which may otherwise be neglected. On the negative side, some legislation could make it difficult for companies to compensate employees in a fair and equitable manner. Also, legislation could unfairly restrain some organizations that need information gathered by monitoring to remain competitive in the global market.

In the future, the most successful companies will be those that treat their employees equitably and respectfully. As John Sculley, the chairman of Apple Computer, has noted, "Instead of emulating the autocratic, invincible models of the past, successful managers must lead by inspiring individuals." Although risks of abuse are real, computer monitoring can indeed inspire some employees to achieve excellence.

READING 8-2

Electronic Monitoring of Employees: Issues & Guidelines

Ernest Kallman

INTRODUCTION

Considerable controversy surrounds the use of computers by management for electronic monitoring of employee productivity. The central issue is whether or not the amount of control that this technology places in management's possession is so intrusive that it constitutes an invasion of employee privacy. A more practical issue from management's perspective is the negative effect on productivity when employees believe that their privacy is being violated. This paper evaluates these issues and proposes a balance between control and privacy that can enable management to successfully utilize electronic monitoring to achieve increased productivity without invading privacy.

Electronic monitoring means the use of specialized computer software for the capture and analysis of data to measure the quantity of work being done by employees using computer terminals. Examples include the counting of keystrokes by data entry clerks or the number of calls taken by a telephone operator or an airline reservationist. EM results in the ability of management to use computers to monitor, supervise and evaluate employee performances electronically. It is a major step toward the automation of employee control.

The scope of EM systems is large and increasing rapidly. In 1987, the Office of Technology Assessment (OTA) estimated that 20 to 35 percent of terminal users are being monitored

Source: Reprinted with permission from the Association for Systems Management, *Journal of Systems Management,* June 1993, Volume #44 Issue #6. Author Ernest Kallman.

(27, p. 40), and that this represents several million employees being monitored in 60,000 companies. Michael Smith at the University of Wisconsin estimates that "by the year 2000, there will be 30 to 40 million terminal users and as many as 50 to 75 percent of them will be monitored" (4). This trend will definitely change the way supervision is performed. It is, therefore, critically important that today's management understand how to deal with the issue of EM technology and privacy.

ARGUMENTS IN FAVOR OF EM

Authorities (courts, legislatures, etc.) have historically allowed employers broad rights of observation and record keeping when monitoring workers in the factory or office (27, p. 13). These rights are based on the employer ownership of the premises at which the work is done and on the basic right of management to control the work process. Proponents contend that EM is simply an extension of their right to control the business.

Management's primary argument for installing EM is to increase productivity (23, 26, p. 128, 27, p. 34). The large capital investments for computer systems are frequently justified on promised productivity increases. EM is often viewed as a control to help ensure that these increases are achieved.

Henriques (11) cites more accurate cost accounting as a second management argument for EM. More exact measurement and control of employee output enables companies to do a better job in pricing of goods and services. In some cases, Sherizen (23) found that this can also be an internal company practice as when companies are using chargeback systems to monitor costs within their own company.

The third major argument for EM is that it allows management to do a better job of personnel management (9, 12). First, they reason no bias is involved because this approach is an impartial method of collecting performance data. The computer records results with absolute accuracy regardless of race, age, gender or any other characteristic of the employee (11). Secondly, it helps establish fair performance expectations because the computer fairly and accurately records individual productivity figures. An advantage of accurate work quantity measurements is that it enhances the ability of management to reward high-achieving employees through incentive pay for exceeding work quotas (12). Finally, Grant and Higgins (9) contend that this approach improves the performance appraisal process. The consistency and objectivity of EM performance measurement provides an improvement over traditional evaluations based on subjective and intermittent data collected by human supervisors. EM performance data is also available more quickly and frequently, thus increasing the employee's awareness of individual productivity. In addition, the ability to provide negative feedback in a non-threatening manner may be better with these systems because the data is not subjective.

CRITICISMS OF EM

The primary criticism of monitoring is that it is an invasion of worker privacy. Other criticisms are derived from the privacy issue and include concerns such as the creation of employee stress, and the "fairness" in the application of the approach.

Unions and some authors have compared the use of EM with George Orwell's Big Brother in the workplace (5, 9). The fear is that overzealous employers will get carried away with information gathering to the point of exceeding the boundary between work performance and privacy. As an AT&T telephone operator explains "I can't even go to the bathroom without being watched. I have to put up a flag at my terminal, wait until the restroom is empty, sign out, sign back in and remove my flag" (19).

Two aspects of this monitoring make it different from traditional work supervision and rein-

force the big brother perception. First, it is continuous, whereas the traditional approach is intermittent (26, p. 130). This means that everything that the employee does, from taking regular rest breaks to restroom breaks, is timed to the second. In addition, the worker has no control over (or, in some cases, even knowledge of) when monitoring occurs and how the information is to be used. This contrasts with traditional monitoring which is easy for a worker to detect since it usually entails the physical presence of the supervisor. According to Brown (5), EM is, therefore, perceived by employees as being covert and conveys a lack of trust by management. This perception erodes mutual trust and loyalty, and thus demotivates employees rather than encouraging them toward more conscientious effort.

Opponents of EM have made very limited progress with the privacy issue in persuading government authorities to support their opposition to EM systems. The OTA (26, p. 181) says that the privacy argument isn't appropriate because the work is done on the employer's premises in a group setting. In addition, supervision has traditionally been an aspect of the employer-employee relationship and the collection of quantitative data has been used for a long time in evaluating and compensating performance.

As a result of their inability to make progress with the privacy argument, opponents of EM have shifted their focus to the effects on employees of continuous monitoring and the resultant lack of personal privacy. One of the primary effects cited is mental stress. Sheridan (22) believes that job stress could emerge as the most important public health problem related to office automation. Continual monitoring puts pressure on the employee to work at a machine-established pace. This leads to anxiety, fatigue and apprehension from knowing that he or she will be expected to work at a machine paced level for the whole day.

The effects of stress on health include musculoskeletal aches and pains, visual difficulties and psychological complaints (22). At AT&T, where monitoring is widely used, stress-related emotional disorders have resulted in job counseling for approximately 25 percent of the monitored workforce (19). This leads to increased absenteeism and turnover, decreases in performance and even acts of sabotage (26, p. 128); all of which subverts management's goal of higher productivity.

According to Nussbaum and duRivage (19), stress is also caused by excessive production quotas and work speedups. The ability of management to count key strokes down to the split second enables managers to increase production and piece rate standards. This causes work speedups that result in lower pay for more work, or even dismissal for those employees who are unable to keep up with the new standards. This stress is further compounded by the posting of individual scores in an effort to promote competition.

In the traditional office, the OTA (26, p. 135) found that the social environment of the office helped act as a buffer to help reduce stress. However, when EM is introduced, a higher level of stress is produced and because there is a tendency for workers to spend more time at a computer terminal, there is less opportunity for social interaction and stress reduction. Thus, stress is not only increased, but also intensified.

Karon (14) and Nussbaum and duRivage (19) believe that EM leads to poor management. They say that employers who install EM also tend to adopt scientific management principles which support the concept of breaking a task into greatly simplified units. They contend that this approach is not appropriate for designing office work. Instead of learning from the now discredited experiences in the factory, office managers are embracing the worst abuses of the assembly line and imposing them on office workers. This leads to an overdependence on "the numbers" as the sole measure of an employee's performance. Human assessments of an employee's performance, based on a supervisor's opinion of non-quantifiable aspects of a job, are practically eliminated. This results in a very narrow and incomplete appraisal of an employee's total contribution to the company.

Susser (25) says that EM systems can cause lower morale, increased turnover and absenteeism as well as lower product quality and poor customer service. According to Nussbaum and duRivage (19), some workers, when forced to meet unrealistic production goals, cut off customers, enter incomplete data and even drop paper clips into equipment to slow it down. In view of its potential disadvantages and their consequences, it is apparent that management must carefully evaluate EM prior to proceeding with its implementation.

LEGAL CONSIDERATIONS

As noted above, critics of EM have increasingly linked it with workplace stress. In the last ten years, worker's compensation claims for mental and emotional stress have grown dramatically as have the number of lawsuits seeking damages under various tort theories (24, p. 579). As a result, the cost of providing financial compensation to employees for stress related disabilities and injuries has increased dramatically.

While the issue of privacy invasion is frequently addressed in these cases, Susser says that the real issue relates to the fairness with which the EM systems are applied in the work place (24). Since workers are usually not included in the design and implementation of EM systems, they don't perceive any fairness and are thus generally hostile toward them.

The OTA (27, p. 111) proposes that fairness involves three considerations: 1) the work standards, 2) the measurement process, and 3) the methods of applying measurements to the evaluation of employees. Work standards should reflect the average capacities of the specific work force and indicate whether the standards will create unhealthy stress for the employees. The measurement process relates to whether or not workers are told and, if so, whether they understand how the measurements are being done. The third area of employee evaluation concerns the inclusion of quality as well as quantity criteria and whether there is a way to adjust expectations when unusual conditions arise such as system downtime or other problems. The OTA research suggests that agreement between employers and employees on these issues helps workers accept EM and reduce stress.

Although there are presently few laws specifically constraining the monitoring practices of private sector employers, Dworkin (8) has found that several state legislatures do have bills under consideration. The essence of most of these bills is worker notification of the monitoring. Massachusetts has one of the most comprehensive bills under consideration. This legislation (H4457) has been filed by the Massachusetts Coalition on New Office Technology—a coalition of over 40 unions and organizations—and is intended to serve as a model for the rest of the country. It does not prohibit EM, but rather is intended to prevent abuses by establishing public policy guidelines to ensure protection of employer's civil liberties. (17)

There are four "rights" that the bill seeks to establish:

1. Right to Know

Employees have a right to know if and how monitoring is being used. The bill requires written notification of: what kinds of monitoring are being used, how frequently it will occur, and how the information is used.

2. Right to Privacy

Monitoring can only be used to collect information which is relevant to work performance. Access to that information should be restricted.

3. Right to Due Process

The bill requires that an employee has access to all information collected through monitoring. If any action (performance evaluation, disciplinary action, etc.) is to be taken on the basis of this information, the employee must be shown the information soon enough to be able to remember what took place at the time. Employees would have the option of entering a written comment into the record.

4. Right to Human Dignity

Monitoring cannot be the exclusive basis for performance evaluation or disciplinary action. The premise is that there is a human side to every job that a computer cannot evaluate.

Dworkin (8) says that legislation regulating computer monitoring appears likely to pass. This is because much of the proposed legislation focuses on notifying employees of the monitoring, and not the stress issue. In essence, the legislation is not significantly different from proposals from business groups. Thus, business is not aggressively fighting the legislation because it is perceived as being reasonably moderate.

MANAGEMENT GUIDELINES

Research suggests that there are some very specific guidelines that management can follow that will greatly enhance the probability of success.

Seek worker involvement: According to Nath and Gilmore (18), employees' resistance will be greatly reduced if they are provided with an opportunity for personal input in two critical areas. First, active employee input should be encouraged during the systems planning and design. Baetz (2) recommends that an effective way to achieve this is with some or all employees being involved with participative design and evaluation teams. By using this approach, companies have found that employee understanding and cooperation are very greatly increased. Secondly, after the system has been implemented, a "quality circle" consisting of employees should be formed. The purpose of the group is to provide management with feedback on the operational equity within the system. This helps to reduce the perception that the system is "too invasive" and enhances the belief that it is an equitable representation of individual performance.

Decide what information is really needed: EM provides management with an unparalleled capability relative to the scope and quantity of information it is able to collect on workers. Because of a "more is better" mentality, Nath and Gilmore (18) believe many managers are tempted to gather more information than they really need. However, it is not necessarily the quantity, but the quality and relevancy of information that is really important.

Nath and Gilmore (18) also say that humans need a certain amount of privacy. Having a computer record on how often they go to the restroom, take medicine, or attend to personal needs is demeaning and insulting. Workers who feel their privacy is invaded will leave if they can. This increases turnover. Ironically, in high turnover situations, it's often the best and most productive employees who will leave because they are better able to find alternative employment. Thus, the quality of the work force could decline over time. By collecting only needed data, the chances of offending workers and spurring unwanted turnover are reduced.

Employee notification: Make sure that all employees understand when and how their work is being monitored and why measurement is necessary (6, 8, 27).

Strive for fairness: The OTA (27, p. 111) found that the major difference between employee protests over invasion of privacy and acceptance of EM depended on the level of agreement between employees and employers on the issue of fairness. Three key aspects of this issue are involved. The fairness of standards, the measurement process employed, and the way in which measurements are used in employee evaluations.

Employee data access: Provide employees with access to their records and regular, support-

ive feedback. Access can either be on-line or through weekly or monthly reports. There should be a procedure for error discovery and correction.

Implement a reward-for-performance policy: Reward individuals appropriately through either incentive pay, public recognition or promotions. Make sure that the performance measurements include quality or subjective factors if applicable to the position (18, 24).

Use statistics to inspire group competition: Be very careful about using statistics to motivate individual competition. Posting all individual scores can backfire by making those employees who score below average angry and stressed. If handled sensitively, group competition will not only increase productivity, but also morale and camaraderie (24, 27).

Don't "inch up" production standards: Employees resent managers who "inch up" production standards so the employees have to work harder and harder to achieve the same rate of pay. This is a very poor management technique that leads employees to feel that they are working under "sweat shop" conditions (19, 24).

Provide facilities for social interaction: According to the OTA (26, p. 135), the office is a social environment and can be an important factor in worker job satisfaction. Because they are electronically monitored, workers may spend so much time at a terminal that social isolation results from a lack of opportunity to interact with others. Social isolation has been shown to be associated with depression, anxiety, job dissatisfaction, and muscular fatigue and psychosomatic symptoms. As a result, management needs to provide lounges and discussion rooms to break the routine of social isolation.

Provide supervisory training on performance feedback: Chalykoff and Kochan (6) found that managers can have substantial control over employees' responses to Electronic Monitoring. Those managers who use principles of good performance appraisal and feedback can minimize the negative effects of EM. As a result, there can be a significant return in terms of employee satisfaction and reduced turnover for supervisory training pertaining to characteristics of good performance feedback.

SUMMARY

As computer use continues to increase so will the appeal of electronic monitoring. The trend will be driven by management's desire to achieve increased productivity based on the perception that Electronic Monitoring will provide an element of control which will contribute to higher employee outputs. EM will be further spurred by new applications of technology which lend themselves to monitoring and measurement. These include the increased use of retail point of sale systems and the trend toward working at home via remote computer terminals.

However, imposing an EM system without proper planning can cause a number of undesirable results. Among these are employee resistance to what they see as an invasion of their privacy by the EM system. Their reaction to this may be merely low morale and griping or may take more active forms like sabotage. EM can cause stress levels to rise significantly sometimes causing illnesses for which the company could be held financially liable. And finally, there is the threat from restrictive legislation which will at least require employers to notify those affected about the EM system and its use.

The burden is clearly on management to balance these conflicting perceptions and objectives. The key is in how management does its job. The same EM technology has been a success and a failure depending on the organization in which it was applied. In many instances success seems to be related to situations where management shared the responsibility for the planning and implementation of the EM system with those who were affected by it. The requirements in the proposed Massachusetts legislation provide a minimum starting point. The guidelines offered in this paper provide management with a fuller framework within which to plan and build their EM systems. These, together with good management practice, should go a long way to resolving the issues surrounding electronic monitoring.

SELECTED REFERENCES

1. Angel, N. Faye. "Evaluating Employees By Computer." Personnel Administrator, November, 1989, pp. 67-72.
2. Baetz, Mary L. Planning For People In The Electronic Office. Homewood, IL: Dow Jones-Irvin, 1985.
3. Betts, Mitch. "VDT Monitoring Under Stress." Computerworld, January 21, 1991, pp. 1, 14.
4. Brophy, Beth. "New Technology, High Anxiety." U.S. News & World Report, September 29, 1986, pp. 54-55.
5. Brown, Tom, "We need managers, not Big Brothers." Industry Week, September 29, 1986, p. 13.
6. Chalykoff, John and Kochan, T. A. "Computer-aided Monitoring: Its Influence on Employee Job Satisfaction and Turnover." Personnel Psychology, Winter, 1989, pp. 807-829.
7. Collins, Joseph E. "OTA Report on Electronic Monitoring." Data Management, December, 1987, p. 7.
8. Dworkin, T.M. "Protecting Private Employees from Enhanced Monitoring: Legislative Approaches," American Business Law Journal, Spring, 1990, pp. 59-85.
9. Grant, R. and Higgins, C. "Monitoring Service Workers via Computer: The Effect on Employees, Productivity and Service." National Productivity Review, Spring, 1989, pp. 101-112.
10. Grant, R. "Computerized Performance Monitors: Are they Costing You Customers?" Sloan Management Review, Spring, 1988, pp. 39-45.
11. Henriques, Vico E. "In Defense of Computer Monitoring." Industry Week, July 7, 1986, p. 14.
12. Henriques, Vico E. "Hallmark of a Computer's Measurement Is Fairness." The Office, May, 1987, pp. 40-44.
13. Hoer, John. "Privacy." Business Week, March 28, 1988, pp. 61-68.

14. Karon Paul. "In Pursuit of Productivity: Computer Monitoring of PC Workers." PC Week, June 2, 1987, p. 77.

15. Kraut, Robert E. and Dumais, Susan. "Computerization and the quality of working life: the role of control." Proceedings of the ACM Conference on Office Information Systems, Cambridge, MA, April 25-27, 1990, p. 56-68.

16. Long, Richard J. New Office Information Technology: Human and Managerial Implications. London: Croom Helm, 1987.

17. Massachusetts Coalition on New Office Technology. "H4457-Bill Summary, Electronic Monitoring: Supervision or Surveillance", March, 1991.

18. Nath, R. and Gilmore, B. "Managing Computerized Supervisory Systems." Management Solutions, July, 1987, pp. 4-11.

19. Nussbaum, Karen and duRivage, V. "Computer Monitoring: Mis-management by Remote Control." Business and Society Review. November, 1985, p. 16-20.

20. Piturro, Marlene. "Employee Performance Monitoring or Meddling." Management Review, May, 1989, pp. 31-33.

21. Piturro, Marlene. "Electronic Monitoring." Information Center, July, 1990, pp. 26-31.

22. Sheridan, Peter. "Electronic Monitoring: Stress Producer for VDT Operators." Occupational Hazards, April, 1986, pp. 39-53.

23. Sherizen, Sanford. "Work Monitoring: Productivity at what cost to privacy?" Computerworld, July 7, 1986, p. 55.

24. Susser, Peter. "Electronic Monitoring in the Private Sector." Employee Relations, Spring, 1988, pp. 575-595.

25. Susser, Peter. "Modern Office Technology and Employee Relations." Employment Relations Today, Spring, 1988, pp. 9-17.

26. U.S. Congress, Office of Technology Assessment. Automation of America's Offices. OTA-CIT-287. Washington, DC: U.S. Government Printing Office, December, 1985.

27. U.S. Congress, Office of Technology Assessment. The Electronic Supervisor: New Technology, New Tensions, OTA-CIT-333, 2 volumes, Washington, DC: U.S. Government Printing Office, September, 1987.

READING 8-3

Electronic Monitoring of Employees and the Elusive "Right to Privacy"

Kenneth A. Jenero
Lynne D. Mapes-Riordan

Privacy has been coined the "workplace issue of the 1990s."[1] Modern technology has led to the development of many sophisticated methods for employers to monitor employees, inside and outside the workplace, without their knowledge. Employees regularly are monitored through their telephones, through their computers, and through advanced video surveillance equipment. The purposes for such monitoring range from the evaluation of individual employee productivity, to the analysis of overall organizational performance, to the investigation of theft and other conduct adverse to the employer's interest.

Although estimates vary, as many as twenty-six million workers may be affected by one or more forms of electronic monitoring.[2] By all indications, that number will rise steadily as the types of positions subject to monitoring increase and as the expense of doing so decreases. The Gartner Group, a Stamford, Connecticut computer data analysis firm, is banking on such growth and expects sales of its computer surveillance programs to expand at a rate of about 50 percent a year until at least 1996.[3]

The three basic forms of electronic monitoring used by employers are (1) service observation, (2) computerized work measurement, and (3) video and other electronic surveillance. *Service observation* refers to the practice of electronically monitoring employee job performance—most commonly through the use of

Source: "Electronic Monitoring and the Elusive Right to Privacy," Kenneth Jenero and Lynne Mapes-Riordan, Employee Relations Law Journal, copyright © 1992. Reprinted by permission of John Wiley & Sons, Inc.

telephones or other listening devices. For example, employers often monitor telephone conversations between employees and customers by either simultaneously listening-in or by recording the conversations for later review. Telephone monitoring is used extensively with customer service and sales employees, such as airline reservationists and catalog telemarketers. However, professionals—including brokers on Wall Street—increasingly are finding themselves subject to telephone monitoring.[4]

In general, service observation is used for one of three distinct reasons. First, it enables employers to enhance the quality of their services by ensuring that employees are providing customers with accurate information, on a timely basis, and in a courteous manner. Second, it enables employers to train employees and to evaluate the accuracy, speed, and quality of individual employee performance. Third, it enables employers to collect valuable information that can be used to assess broader organizational or operational performance.

Telephone monitoring—the most prevalent form of service observation—itself has many variations, depending on the particular employer's business objectives. The monitoring can be conducted secretly or with notice to the employees. It can be conducted systematically, as part of a plan of routine monitoring, or only sporadically, in response to a specialized need. Similarly, it can extend to all of the employer's telephone lines or only to lines dedicated exclusively to business use, and then, to all or only some of the calls made on those lines.

Computerized work measurement refers to the practice of monitoring an employee's computer screen as he or she works and collecting data about the employee's work performance for later review. Technology is providing employers with innovative ways of monitoring employees through their computers. New software products such as "Peek and Spy," produced by Networking Dynamics Corp., of Glendale, California, allow employers the choice of "peeking" in on an employee's computer screen with the employee's knowledge or "spying" on the employee's screen without his or her knowledge.

Employees in positions involving work that is repetitive and easily quantifiable, such as in the customer service and data processing industries, are most frequently subject to computerized work measurement. However, more and more executive level employees are being subjected to such monitoring as software programs are developed to analyze executive "tasks." Once linked to a central network, the personal computer purchased by the executive to impress his or her superiors with his or her turn-around time on a given project becomes a vehicle for constant monitoring by those superiors.

Employers use computerized work measurement to achieve several objectives. As with service observation, computerized work measurement enables employers to evaluate the performance of individual employees. For example, employers can determine how many telephone calls the employee handled in an hour, the average length of each call, and the result of the call (for example, whether the call resulted in a reservation or sale). Similarly, employers can determine the number of keystrokes made by a data processing employee in a given period of time. In fact, it has been reported that one airline employer based its reservationists' raises on several numerical factors derived from computer monitoring, including the time between calls and the percentage of time spent working at the computer.[5] The data collected through computerized work measurement also can be used by employers to establish productivity and other output standards on both an individual-employee and organization-wide basis.

Video and other electronic surveillance is used for various purposes in virtually all industries. For example, retailers use video surveillance to guard against theft by employees, as well as consumers. Employers whose operations involve assembly lines use video surveillance to record the production process and the movement of workers within the plant. This information, in turn, can be used to develop time or production standards, or safer or more efficient manufacturing methods. In addition, employers, across industry lines, regularly employ video surveillance measures in connection with the investigation of suspected theft, fradulent employment practices, breaches of loyalty, and other violations of work rules and regulations. To this extent, the employer's surveillance measures sometimes extend beyond the four walls of the workplace.

A BACKLASH FROM EMPLOYEES

As the use of new and more effective forms of electronic monitoring increases, so inevitably will the number and frequency of related legal challenges. Employees, unions, and employee advocacy groups already have complained that these technologically advanced monitoring systems unnecessarily trammel the privacy and autonomy of employees and adversely affect their physical well-being. According to the critics, the impersonal and unceasing nature of the monitoring serves both to increase employee stress and to minimize the importance of individual work patterns.

These complaints recently have started to translate into lawsuits seeking to vindicate the employees' "right to privacy." For example, two cases currently pending in the California courts raise issues about an employer's ability lawfully to intercept its employees' electronic mail messages.[6] More recently, Northern Telecom, Inc., of Nashville, Tennessee, agreed to settle a class action suit filed by the Communications Workers of America on behalf of employees who allegedly were subjected to secret electronic monitoring over a thirteen-year period. Under the terms of the settlement, the company reportedly agreed to pay $50,000 to individual plaintiffs, $125,000 for attorney's fees, and $200,000 toward class claims by employees and members of the public whose conversations may have been recorded secretly over telephone lines or on the premises of the company's Nashville plant.[7]

This article addresses the legal parameters of electronic monitoring of employees in the public and private sectors. Specifically, it discusses the potential sources of protection of employee "privacy rights," including federal and state constitutions, state common law, and federal and state wiretapping statutes. It then reviews proposed federal legislation designed to protect employees against surreptitious workplace monitoring and concludes with recommendations for employers to minimize their exposure to liability arising out of the use of electronic monitoring systems.

CONSTITUTIONAL PRIVACY RIGHTS

The Fourth Amendment to the U.S. Constitution provides that "[t]he right of the people to be secure in their persons, houses, papers, and effects, against *unreasonable searches and seizures,* shall not be violated . . ." (emphasis added). The Amendment guarantees an individual's privacy, dignity, and security against certain arbitrary and intrusive acts by government entities.[8] This guarantee extends to the actions of government entities at the state and local, as well as the federal, levels.[9] Moreover, it applies not only when government entities are acting in a law enforcement capacity, but also when they are acting *as employers.*[10] Thus, the Fourth Amendment provides a source of protection for the privacy rights of *public sector* employees.[11]

It is well established that electronic surveillance, including the monitoring or recording of telephonic communications, may constitute a "search" or "seizure" within the meaning of the Fourth Amendment.[12] Whether the Fourth Amendment is implicated depends initially on whether the asserted search or seizure—for example, the electronic surveillance—infringes on a *"reasonable expectation of privacy."* This determination must be made in light of all the surrounding circumstances, including the context in which the search is conducted, the uses to which the searched area or item have been put, and society's understanding regarding the extent to which such area or item deserves protection from governmental intrusion.[13]

Assuming the existence of a reasonable expectation of privacy, the focus then shifts to the reasonableness of the particular search or seizure at issue. By its terms, the Fourth Amendment does not proscribe all searches or seizures, but only those that are "unreasonable." The determination of what is reasonable likewise "depends on all the circumstances surrounding the search or seizure and the nature of the search or seizure itself."[14] Ultimately, this determination requires a "balancing [of] the nature and quality of the intrusion on the individual's Fourth Amendment interests against the importance of the governmental interests alleged to justify the intrusion."[15]

The U.S. Supreme Court has yet to consider the Fourth Amendment's particular application to the electronic surveillance of public employees by a government employer. However, in *O'Connor v. Ortega*, 480 U.S. 709 (1987), the Court addressed the Amendment's applicability in the related context of a government employer's search of a public employee's office, desk, and file cabinets. In so doing, the Court established the parameters of the Fourth Amendment's protection of a public employee's right to privacy *in the workplace.*

Dr. Ortega had been employed by a California state hospital as Chief of Professional Education for seventeen years. In that position, he was responsible for training young physicians in psychiatric residency programs. When allegations arose regarding various improprieties in Ortega's management of the residency program, the hospital's "investigative team"' conducted a search of Ortega's office. During the search, several personal items—including a Valentine's Day card, photograph, book of poetry, and billing documents relating to one of his private patients—were seized from Ortega's desk and file cabinets. Ortega, who subsequently was terminated, sued the hospital, alleging that this search and seizure violated his right to privacy guaranteed by the Fourth Amendment.

In reviewing Ortega's claim, the Supreme Court began by specifically rejecting the hospital's contention "that public employees can never have a reasonable expectation of privacy in their place of work." The Court noted that individuals do not lose their Fourth Amendment rights merely because they work for a government entity and that their personal effects are not removed from the scope of the Amendment's protection merely because they are brought into the workplace. However, the Court also noted that an employee's expectation of privacy necessarily must be assessed in "the context of the employment relation," including the "operational realities" of the particular workplace at issue.

In some cases, for example, an employee's expectation of privacy may be reduced by virtue of actual office practices or by legitimate regulation. In others, an office might be so open to fellow employees or the public that no expectation of privacy would be reasonable. Indeed, because of the great variety of work environments in the public sector, the Court held that "the question whether an employee has a reasonable expectation of privacy must be addressed on a case-by-case basis."

Turning to Ortega's particular case, a majority of the Court concluded that he had a reasonable expectation of privacy in his office, as well as his desk and file cabinets. In support of this conclusion, the Court noted that Ortega did not share his office, desk or file cabinets with any other employees; that none of the files relating to the hospital's residency training program were kept in his office; and that Ortega had kept a variety of personal materials in his office throughout the seventeen-year period during which he occupied it. Furthermore, there was no evidence that the hospital had established a regulation or policy discouraging employees from storing personal effects in their offices.

After determining that Ortega had a reasonable expectation of privacy, the Court directed its attention to the question of whether the hospital's conduct was "unreasonable" and, thus, violative of the Fourth Amendment. According to the Court, the answer to this question required a balancing of the invasion of the public employee's expectation of privacy in the workplace against the government employer's need for supervision, control, and efficient operation of the workplace. This need, the Court noted, was particularly compelling when the employer was conducting a search for noninvestigatory *work-related* reasons or for evidence of suspected *work-related* misconduct. Therefore, the constitutional propriety of searches in such cases was to be judged by the deferential standard of "reasonableness under all the circumstances."

The Court explained that this standard required that any search be reasonable, both at its inception and in its scope. A search of an employee's office by a supervisor ordinarily would be *justified at its inception* if: (1) there were reasonable grounds for suspecting that the search would turn up evidence of the employee's work-related misconduct, or (2) the search was necessary for a noninvestigatory work-related purpose, such as to retrieve a needed file. A search ordinarily would be *permissible in scope* when the breadth and intrusiveness of the search were reasonably related to the accomplishment of its underlying objectives. Because there were insufficient facts in the record to determine whether the search of Dr. Ortega's office satisfied the applicable standard of reasonableness, the Court remanded the case for further evidentiary proceedings.

In *Ortega,* the Court found it unnecessary to decide whether "*individualized suspicion*" of misconduct was an essential element of the constitutional "reasonableness" standard because the hospital, in fact, had such suspicion with respect to Dr. Ortega. However, the Court subse-

quently addressed the issue in *Skinner v. Railway Labor Executives Association,* 489 U.S. 602 (1989), which involved mandatory drug and alcohol testing of employees in *safety-sensitive* positions. After concluding that the subject blood and urine tests constituted "searches" under the Fourth Amendment, the Court nevertheless held that they properly could be conducted without a prerequisite showing of individualized suspicion. The Court stated that it would consider a search to be reasonable despite the absence of individualized suspicion "in limited circumstances"—such as those presented in *Skinner*—"where the privacy interests implicated by the search are minimal, and where an important governmental interest furthered by the intrusion would be placed in jeopardy by a requirement of individualized suspicion[.]"[16]

Subsequently, in *Burka v. New York City Transit Authority,* 739 F. Supp. 814 (S.D. N.Y. 1990), a federal district court held that the Fourth Amendment required individualized suspicion for mandatory drug testing of public employees in *non-safety-sensitive* positions. According to the court, the absence of safety sensitivity served both to increase the employees' expectations of privacy and to reduce the government's interests by eliminating the presence of a "special need" for the testing.[17] It seems clear, therefore, that individualized suspicion justifying the particular intrusion at issue will be required in the great majority of cases in which an employee's Fourth Amendment rights are implicated.

However, several lower court decisions also demonstrate the principle expressed in *Ortega* that an employee's expectation of privacy may be reduced or eliminated by virtue of legitimate regulation, office practices, or the operational realities of the workplace. For example, in *American Postal Workers Union v. United States Postal Service,* 871 F. 2d 556 (6th Cir. 1989), the employees had signed waivers advising them that their lockers were subject to random inspection by authorized postal officials. In addition, the collective bargaining contracts covering the employees provided for random inspection of lockers under specified circumstances (for example, when there was reasonable cause to suspect criminal activity). Relying specifically on the referenced waiver and contract provision, the court concluded that the employees "had no reasonable expectation of privacy in their respective lockers that was protected by the Fourth Amendment."

More directly on point is the case of *Simmons v. Southwestern Bell Telephone Company,* 452 F. Supp. 392 (W.D. Ok. 1978). The plaintiff, Simmons, worked as a deskman at Bell's test center. As such, he was one of several employees assigned to a testboard—a large, complex panel where all trouble reports from customers were received, cleared, dispatched, and closed. Bell's supervisors monitored the use of the testboard telephones for service quality checks, checking work in progress, assisting the deskmen, and other business purposes. The deskmen, including Simmons, knew that the testboard telephones were monitored. Furthermore, the plaintiff was aware of Bell's written policy that personal calls were not allowed to be made to or from the testboard and that other telephones, not subject to service monitoring, were available for such calls. In fact, Simmons had been warned repeatedly about his use of the testboard telephones for personal calls.

The plaintiff ultimately brought an action against Bell alleging, among other things, that its monitoring of his personal calls on the testboard telephones violated his constitutional right to privacy. The court dismissed this part of the plaintiff's action because Bell, as a private employer, was not subject to the proscriptions of the Fourth Amendment. However, the court went on to state that, in any event, the Fourth Amendment protected "only a *reasonable expectation* of privacy." It then observed that under the circumstances—including, specifically, the plaintiff's knowledge that his conversations on the testboard telephones could be, and in fact

were, monitored—the plaintiff could have no reasonable expectation of privacy in those conversations. At the same time, the court noted that it would have had little difficulty finding a violation if Bell had monitored the plaintiff's conversations on the telephones designated for *personal calls.*

The case law thus establishes that the Fourth Amendment provides at least a limited source of protection for public sector employees against electronic surveillance by government employers. Its application in any given case will depend on an analysis of all of the surrounding circumstances relative to: (1) the existence of a reasonable expectation of privacy on the part of the employee, and (2) the reasonableness of the employer's surveillance. Nevertheless, certain general principles can be stated.

Pure service observation, computerized work measurement, and other electronic surveillance limited to the employee's job performance or other job-related activities in the workplace almost certainly will not implicate the Fourth Amendment's protections. Employees in such cases will be unable to make the minimum threshold showing of a reasonable expectation of privacy, particularly when they have been given notice of the nature and extent of the employer's surveillance. However, even without such notice the Fourth Amendment likely will afford no protection because pure service observation, computerized work measurement, and similar forms of electronic surveillance, by their very nature, are relatively unintrusive. Moreover, such surveillance generally can be justified on the basis of the employer's legitimate interests in training, evaluating, or supervising its employees, or otherwise enhancing the safety or efficiency of its operations.

The likelihood that the Fourth Amendment's protections will come into play increases in direct proportion to the extent to which the employer's surveillance infringes on an employee's *personal* conversations or activities inside or outside the workplace. As the surveillance moves away from strictly work-related matters of legitimate interest to the employer, it necessarily moves into areas in which the employee has a heightened expectation of privacy. It is much more likely, therefore, that the employer will be put to the test of demonstrating the "reasonableness" of its surveillance, in terms of both its inception and scope. In all but the rarest of cases, individualized suspicion of misconduct or other circumstances justifying the surveillance will be required to meet this test. Without it, indiscriminate surveillance of personal conversations or activities—whether inside or outside the workplace—almost certainly will be "unreasonable" and violative of the right of privacy guaranteed by the Fourth Amendment.

STATE CONSTITUTIONS

Most states have constitutional provisions that embody the Fourth Amendment's proscription against unreasonable searches and seizures. In addition, ten states have adopted specific privacy guarantees in their respective constitutions.[18] Like the Fourth Amendment, these state constitutional provisions generally restrict the actions of government entities only. Thus, they provide another source of protection for public sector employees, subject to essentially the same "reasonable expectation of privacy" and "balancing of interest" tests applicable under the Fourth Amendment. However, they generally provide no protection for employees in the private sector.[19]

The state of California appears to be the only exception. The California courts have held that the right to privacy in the California constitution applies with equal force to *private and public* sector employers.[20] They also have held that the state constitution prohibits all incursions into individual privacy unless justified by a *"compelling interest."* This test places a heavier burden on California employers than the Fourth Amendment privacy analysis, which generally

requires only a showing of "reasonableness" under the circumstances.[21] As a result, California employees in both the public and private sectors are the beneficiaries of enhanced privacy rights.

The California constitution has not been applied specifically in the context of electronic monitoring or surveillance of employees. However, its application in other workplace contexts—including random drug tests and preemployment psychological screens—aptly demonstrates the heavy burden that the "compelling interest" test imposes on California employers. Although this burden is not likely to change the legal result in cases involving pure service observation and computerized work measurement, it may well render unconstitutional other types of electronic surveillance that could withstand scrutiny under the Fourth Amendment's less burdensome "reasonableness" standard.

For example, in *Luck v. Southern Pacific Transportation Company,* 218 Cal. App. 3d 1, 267 Cal. Rptr. 618 (1990), a California court of appeals held that a private employer engaged in the operation of a railroad had no compelling interest in randomly testing a computer programmer for drug use. The employer had advanced a number of safety and non-safety-related interests in support of its drug testing policy, including deterrence, efficiency, competence, creating a drug-free environment, enforcing rules against drug use, and ensuring public confidence in the integrity of the railroad industry. The court, however, held that the employer had failed to prove a *"clear, direct nexus"* between the programmer's job duties and any of the interests asserted in support of the drug testing policy. Accordingly, they could not be considered "compelling interests" sufficient to justify an intrusion on the programmer's privacy rights.

A similar conclusion was reached in *Soroka v. Dayton-Hudson Corporation,* 235 Cal. App. 3d 654, 1 Cal. Rptr. 2d 77 (1991). The appellate court there held that the employer had failed to establish a compelling interest to justify its practice of requiring security officers to pass a pre-employment psychological screen that included intrusive questions about an applicant's religious beliefs and sexual orientation. Significantly, the trial court—which erroneously had applied the lesser "reasonableness" standard—had endorsed the employer's use of the screen as a legitimate means of securing psychologically fit applicants for important security positions. Thus, in this case, the difference in the applicable legal standard in fact contributed to a different result that afforded greater protection for the employee's privacy rights.

COMMON LAW PRIVACY RIGHTS

The common law right of privacy actually is comprised of four separate causes of action, three of which are relevant in the employment context: (1) intrusion upon seclusion, (2) publicity given to one's private life, and (3) publicity placing a person in a false light. The privacy claim most likely to be asserted in response to electronic surveillance of employees is intrusion upon seclusion. However, the publicity-based privacy claims may be invoked in connection with an employer's disclosure of information obtained through the surveillance. In addition, employees sometimes have attempted to state an independent invasion of privacy claim based generally on the nebulous concept of "public policy."

Section 652B of the Restatement (Second) of Torts (1977) defines the tort of intrusion upon seclusion as follows:

> One who intentionally intrudes, physically or otherwise, upon the solitude or seclusion of another or his private affairs or concerns, is subject to liability to the other for invasion of his privacy, if the intrusion would be highly offensive to a reasonable person.

Under this definition, proof of three essential elements is required to state a valid claim of intrusion upon seclusion: (1) an intrusion, (2) into a private matter, (3) that is highly offensive to a reasonable person. Electronic surveillance, including the monitoring or recording of telephonic communications, generally is viewed as an "intrusion" sufficient to establish the first element of the prima facie case.[22] However, given the operational realities of the workplace and the variety of legitimate business interests abounding to employers in the employment context, employees often will be unable to establish the second and/or third elements of the prima facie case.

Indeed, the tort of intrusion would appear to be particularly unavailing in cases of pure service observation, computerized work measurement, or other electronic surveillance limited to the employee's job performance or job-related activities in the workplace. An employee would be hard-pressed to assert either: (1) that he or she has a protectable privacy interest in the tasks that he or she performs for his or her employer, with the employer's equipment, on the employer's premises, during compensated working hours; or (2) that the employer's conduct in monitoring the performance of those tasks, for legitimate business purposes, through relatively unintrusive forms of electronic surveillance, is "highly offensive." The courts' decisions in *Thomas v. General Electric Company,* 207 F. Supp. 792 (W.D. Ky. 1962), and *Barksdale v. International Business Machines Corporation,* 620 F. Supp. 1380 (W.D. N.C. 1985), support this conclusion.

The plaintiff in *Thomas* alleged that his employer had violated his common law right to privacy by taking motion pictures of him, without his consent, while at work and in the discharge of his customary duties. The evidence established that this was done pursuant to the employer's long-standing practice of taking pictures of the layout of equipment and machinery, and the movement of employees while engaged in their jobs, as aids in the development of time standards and safer, more efficient manufacturing methods and processes. The court summarily dismissed the plaintiff's invasion of privacy claim, citing the absence of proof that the pictures were taken for other than the legitimate purpose articulated by the employer and the absence of case law forbidding an employer from using such means to improve the efficiency and safety of its operations.

The plaintiffs in *Barksdale* were several individuals who had been hired as temporary employees to participate in a study conducted by IBM ostensibly to determine the best overall arrangement of computer terminals, viewing angles, and viewing distances. Their lawsuit alleged that IBM had misrepresented the true nature of the study; that they really were the subjects of "an experiment in testing the levels of human tolerance"; and that IBM had invaded their privacy "by eliciting responses from them through its study that it otherwise would not have been able to obtain." In dismissing the invasion of privacy claim, the court succinctly stated:

> The Defendant's observation and recording of the number of errors the Plaintiffs made in the tasks they were instructed to perform can hardly be considered an intrusion upon the Plaintiffs' "solitude or seclusion . . . or [their] private affairs or concerns."

High-tech service observation and computerized work measurement are essentially advanced versions of the basic observation, surveillance, and information-gathering conducted by the employers in *Thomas* and *Barksdale*. Technologically advanced workplace monitoring techniques do not become any more actionable under the tort of intrusion upon seclusion by virtue of their enhanced level of sophistication and effectiveness. As long as the monitoring is limited to job performance and related activities in the workplace, it is highly unlikely that it will be deemed either intrusive on an employee's "private affairs" or "highly offensive" for purposes of common law invasion of privacy claim.

Furthermore, the courts specifically have recognized that an employee's common law right of privacy is limited by an employer's countervailing rights arising out of the employment relationship. Included among these is the right to engage in investigation of employees suspected of illegality, fraud, or other misconduct committed in the course of employment.[23] In exercising this right, employers even have been allowed to conduct reasonable surveillance of employees outside the workplace.

In *McClain v. Boise Cascade Corporation,* 271 Ore. 549, 533, P. 2d 343 (1975), for example, the court dismissed an invasion of privacy claim brought against an employer that had taken eighteen rolls of movie film of an employee suspected of filing a fraudulent workers' compensation claim. The movies, which were taken without the employee's knowledge, showed him engaged in various activities around his home. In dismissing the employee's claim, the court relied on the "well established" principle that "one who seeks to recover damages for alleged injuries must expect that his claim will be investigated and waives his right of privacy to the extent of a reasonable investigation."[24]

Some courts—specifically in the state of Michigan—have gone further and allowed employers to "use intrusive and even objectionable means to obtain employment-related information about . . . employee[s]."[25] An illustrative case is *Saldana v. Kelsey-Hayes Company,* 178 Mich. App. 230, 443 N.W. 2d 382 (Mich. App. 1989). There, the employer engaged a private firm to investigate an injured employee suspected of "malingering." During the course of several days of surveillance, the investigators "tailed" the employee and observed him in his home through an open window with the assistance of a high-power camera lens.

On these facts, the court assumed that the employee had established two of the three essential elements of a claim for intrusion upon seclusion (that is, actual intrusions by means highly objectionable to a reasonable person).

Nevertheless, the court dismissed the claim because the employee had failed to establish the intrusions "were into matters which [he] had a right to keep private." The court stated that the employee's privacy was subject to the legitimate interest of his employer in investigating suspicions that his work-related disability was a pretext, and concluded that "the surveillance of [the employee] at his home involved matters which [the employer] had a legitimate right to investigate."

Barring a major shift in the development of the tort of intrusion upon seclusion, it stands to be of relatively little value to employees subjected to electronic surveillance inside and even outside the workplace. That is not to say, however, that it is totally useless to employees. It will provide a source of protection for employees in those extreme cases in which the employer's surveillance unduly infringes on personal conversations or activities without sufficient business justification. For example, employees subjected to surveillance in such highly private areas as restrooms and lounges almost certainly would be able to state a valid cause of action for intrusion upon seclusion.[26] Employees subjected to unreasonable and obtrusive surveillance in their homes similarly would have a valid tort claim.[27] The indiscriminate surveillance of employees' personal conversations or activities—whether inside or outside the workplace—similarly would subject the employer to liability in tort for invasion of privacy.[28]

As noted above, two publicity-based invasion of privacy claims also are potentially applicable in the employment context. The first of these claims—publicity given to one's private life—is stated when an individual gives publicity to a matter concerning the private life of another that would be highly offensive to a reasonable person and is of no legitimate concern to the public. The second claim—publicity placing a person in a false light—generally is stated when publicity is given to a matter that places another in a false light which would be highly offensive to a rea-

sonable person. In the electronic surveillance context, these claims might be invoked in response to the employer's disclosure of information obtained through the surveillance, rather than by virtue of the act of surveillance itself.

However, these publicity-based invasion of privacy claims typically have met with very limited success in the employment setting. As is true in connection with the related claim of intrusion upon seclusion, employees often find it difficult to establish the existence of "private matters" warranting common law protection or of employer conduct that is sufficiently outrageous to meet the "highly offensive" standard. Moreover, the publicity-based claims, by definition, require the additional showing of *public disclosure* of a private or false matter. Specifically, this requires proof that "the matter is made public, by communicating it to the public at large, or to so many persons that the matter must be regarded as substantially certain to become one of public knowledge.[29]

The inability to establish the requisite public disclosure often has proven fatal to employees' publicity-based invasion of privacy claims. For example, in *Beard v. Akzona, Incorporated,* 517 F. Supp. 128 (E.D. Tn. 1981), the plaintiff alleged that her employer had violated her right to privacy by disclosing the contents of wiretapped telephone communications that had been secured by her husband during his investigation into her suspected "affair" with a coworker. For purposes of its decision, the court assumed both that the private facts surrounding the plaintiff's relations with a coworker were not a legitimate concern to the public and that their disclosure would be highly offensive. However, the evidence showed that these private facts had been disclosed to only five individuals, all of whom were members of the employer's management staff and who had some job-related connection to the employees involved. Accordingly, the court dismissed the plaintiff's claim because she had failed to show "the extent of publicity necessary to give rise to liability for invasion of her privacy."[30]

In addition to these traditional common law invasion of privacy claims, employees occasionally have attempted to bring actions premised on generalized notions of "public policy." For the most part, the courts have been unwilling to open the door to these vague public policy-based privacy claims. In *Borse v. Piece Goods Shop,* 758 F. Supp. 263 (E.D. Pa. 1991), for example, the court held that the privacy protections embodied in the First and Fourth Amendments to the U.S. Constitution did not create a clearly mandated public policy that would provide the basis for a wrongful discharge action under Pennsylvania law. The plaintiff in *Borse* had asserted that her discharge for refusing to sign a consent form agreeing to drug and alcohol testing and personal property searches as a condition of continued employment violated her public policy-based right to privacy. A similar claim was rejected under Connecticut law in *Johnson v. Carpenter Technology Corp.,* 723 F. Supp. 180 (D. Conn. 1989).

However, in *Cordle v. General Hugh Mercer Corp.,* 325 S.E. 2d 111 (S. Ct. W. Va. 1984), the Supreme Court of West Virginia recognized the existence of a public policy against unreasonable invasions of privacy, which was violated by an employee's discharge for refusing to submit to a random polygraph examination as a condition of continued employment. At the same time, the court specifically noted that the privacy right of employees under this public policy is not absolute. Rather, in each case the employee's right must be balanced against the legitimate, countervailing business interests of the employer.[31] The court thus adopted a standard for evaluating private employee public policy-based invasion of privacy claims that is essentially the same as the "balancing of interests" analysis applied in public employee cases brought under the Fourth Amendment.

FEDERAL WIRETAPPING STATUTE

In 1968, Congress enacted Title III of the Omnibus Crime Control and Safe Streets Act "to protect effectively the privacy of wire and oral communications, to protect the integrity of court and administrative proceedings, and to prevent the obstruction of interstate commerce. . . ."[32] Although the focus of the Act was on the use of wiretapping and electronic surveillance by law enforcement officials, its prohibitions encompass the interception, disclosure, and intentional use of oral, wire, and electronic communications by both *private and public* parties without prior judicial authorization.

Title III, as amended by the Electronic Communications Privacy Act of 1986, is enforced through criminal prosecutions and civil actions. The Act specifically provides that individuals whose communications are intercepted, disclosed, or used in violation of the statute may recover damages equal to the greater of: (1) the sum of the individual's actual damages and any profits the violator made as a result of the violation, or (2) statutory damages in the amount of $100 a day or $10,000, whichever is greater. Punitive damages, reasonable attorney's fees, and other litigation costs also are recoverable, making violations of the Act potentially very costly.

Under the Act, the interception of telephone conversations or other oral, wire, or electronic communications is unlawful only if accomplished through the use of an "electronic, mechanical, or other device." It is not unlawful simply to listen to or overhear an oral communication with the naked ear. Furthermore, the interception of *oral* communications is prohibited only to the extent that the speaker exhibits "an expectation that the communication is not subject to interception under circumstances justifying such an expectation." This limitation does not apply with respect to *wire or electronic* communications, which generally are protected against interception unless a specific exception is shown. Two such exceptions are particularly relevant in the employment context. The first—the "prior consent" exception—applies to the interception of oral, wire, and electronic communications. The second—the "business use" exception—applies only to wire and electronic communications.

The Prior Consent Exception

The "prior consent" exception appears in Section 2511(2)(d) of the Act, which states:

> It shall not be unlawful under this chapter for a person not acting under color of law to intercept a wire, oral, or electronic communication where such person is a party to the communication or where one of the parties to the communication has given prior consent to such interception unless such communication is intercepted for the purpose of committing any criminal or tortious act in violation of the Constitution or laws of the United States or of any State.

The language and legislative history of Section 2511(2)(d) make clear that it applies only if one of the *individuals directly participating* in the communication consents to its interception. An employer, therefore, cannot rely on its own consent to invoke the "prior consent" exception with respect to telephone conversations between its employees and third parties.[33] Furthermore, as demonstrated by the decisions in *Watkins v. L.M. Berry & Company,* 704 F.2d 577 (11th Cir. 1983), and *Jandak v. Village of Brookfield,* 520 F. Supp. 815 (N.D. Ill. 1981), the "prior consent" exception has been construed very narrowly in the employment context.

Watkins involved an employee who was hired to work as a sales representative soliciting Yellow Pages advertising over the telephone. The employer had an established policy—of which all employees were informed—of monitoring solicitation calls as part of its regular training program. The monitoring was accomplished through a standard extension telephone located in the supervisor's office. Employees were permitted to make personal calls on the employer's telephones, but specifically were told that such calls would not be monitored except to the extent necessary to determine whether they were of a personal or business nature.

During her lunch hour, Watkins received a telephone call at work from a friend. Shortly into the conversation, Watkins was asked about a job interview she had the previous evening with another company. In response, she stated that the interview had gone well and that she was very interested in the job. Unbeknownst to Watkins, her supervisor had monitored the call from the extension telephone in her office. The supervisor then reported the contents of the call to her manager, who, in turn, contacted Watkins and asked that she not leave her job. Upon inquiring, Watkins learned that the manager knew about her recent job interview because her supervisor had monitored the conversation between Watkins and her friend.

Watkins later sued her employer, alleging that it unlawfully intercepted her personal telephone call. In defense, the employer argued that Watkins had consented to the interception by accepting the sales position with full knowledge of the telephone monitoring policy. The court, however, rejected this defense, finding that Watkins had neither expressly nor impliedly consented to interception of the *particular* call at issue.

The court first noted that Watkins had not consented to a policy of general monitoring of all telephone calls. Rather, her consent was limited to a policy of monitoring *sales* calls. Her consent also encompassed the *inadvertent* interception of *personal* calls, but only for as long as necessary to determine the nature of the call. Therefore, if the supervisor's monitoring went beyond that point, it exceeded the scope of any actual consent given by Watkins.

Turning to the issue of implied consent, the court noted that Title III's "strong purpose to protect individual privacy" would be thwarted "if consent could routinely be implied from circumstances." Therefore, "knowledge of the *capability* of monitoring alone cannot be considered implied consent." Furthermore, the evidence in Watkin's case failed to establish that she impliedly consented to a scheme of telephone monitoring broader than that to which she actually consented. The court then concluded as follows:

> We . . . hold that consent within the meaning of Section 2511(2)(d) is not necessarily an all or nothing proposition: it can be limited. It is the task of the trier of fact to determine the scope of the consent and to decide whether and to which extent the interception exceeded that consent.

The concept of implied consent was explored further in *Jandak.* The plaintiff in that case was a private citizen who charged the Village of Brookfield with unlawfully intercepting her personal telephone conversation with an officer of the Brookfield Police Department. The subject conversation occurred on a police department telephone line used for investigative purposes. Pursuant to the department's established practice, all conversations on this telephone line routinely were recorded.

In response to the plaintiff's charge, the Village attempted to invoke the "prior consent" exception. Specifically, it asserted that its police officer, who was one of the parties to the telephone conversation, had actually or impliedly consented to its interception. The court refused to find actual consent, noting that the police officer denied both that he had consented to interception of the particular conversation at issue and that he had knowledge of the department's routine recording of conversations on the telephone line used to call the plaintiff.

On the issue of implied consent, the court found that the circumstances—including the department's routine, non-surreptitious monitoring of all calls on the investigative line, and the police officer's specific training and job history—established that the officer "should have known that calls on the line he used were monitored." Nevertheless, the court rejected the Village's "prior consent" defense. According to the court, consent could be "implied in fact, from surrounding circumstances indicating that the party knowingly agreed to the [monitoring]." However, it would go far beyond the Act's language

and legislative history to allow consent to be "implied in law," based solely on a finding that the party "reasonably should have known" of the monitoring. The court, therefore, specifically declined to read the "prior consent" exception so expansively.

The Business Use Exception

The "business use" exception appears in Section 2510(5)(a)(i) of the Act, which states:

> "[E]lectronic, mechanical, or other device" means any device or apparatus which can be used to intercept a wire, oral, or electronic communication *other than*—
>   (a) any telephone or telegraph instrument, equipment or facility, or any component thereof, (i) furnished to the subscriber or user by a provider of wire or electronic communication service in the ordinary course of its business and being used by the subscriber or user in the ordinary course of its business[.]

This "business use" exception effectively "legalizes" much of the workplace telephone monitoring conducted by employers. It does so by exempting from the Act's coverage interceptions of wire or electronic communications accomplished through equipment used by a telephone subscriber in the ordinary course of its business. Such equipment includes standard extension telephones, as well as more sophisticated communication and dispatching systems, furnished by providers of wire or electronic communication services.[34]

Application of the "business use" exception to standard workplace telephone monitoring practices is demonstrated by *James v. Newspaper Agency Corp.,* 591 F.2d 579 (10th Cir. 1979). James worked in the newspaper's accounting/credit department as a collector of so-called transient advertising accounts. All of the telephones in James's department were monitored through the use of equipment installed by the Bell system. When the monitoring system was installed, all affected employees, including

James, were notified in writing. The newspaper's supervisory personnel used the system to monitor business calls for the purpose of providing training and instruction to employees and protecting them against abusive calls. In summarily dismissing James's lawsuit challenging the legality of the newspaper's monitoring system, the court stated that it "[came] squarely within the exception provided in 18 U.S.C. §§2510(5)(a)."

The "business use" exception, however, is not without limits. In order to invoke the exception, an employer must demonstrate that its monitoring, in fact, was conducted "in the ordinary course of business." As the court noted in *Watkins,* it is not enough for an employer "to show that its general policy is justifiable as part of the ordinary course of business." An employer also must show that the *particular* interception at issue was in the ordinary course of business. This, in turn, requires proof that the subject matter of the intercepted communication is one in which the employer has a "legal interest."

In *Watkins,* for example, the court rejected the employer's attempt to invoke the "business use" exception in connection with its interception of a telephone conversation in which an employee discussed her interest in an alternative job with another company. The court observed that if an intercepted call is a *business call,* then monitoring it is "in the ordinary course of business." However, if it is a *personal* call, then the monitoring is "probably, but not certainly, *not* in the ordinary course of business." According to the court, the evidence strongly suggested that Watkins's call was a personal call inasmuch as she had not made the call in the performance of her job duties; she, in fact, had received the call; the caller was a friend; and the topics discussed were mainly social.

The court also specifically rejected the argument that Watkins's call necessarily was "in the ordinary course of business" because it concerned a matter—that is, her interview with an-

other company—that was "of interest and concern" to her employer. As the court stated:

> The phrase "in the ordinary course of business" cannot be expanded to mean anything that interests a company. . . . [The employer] might have been curious about Watkins' plans, but it had no *legal interest* in them. Watkins was at liberty to resign at will and so at liberty to interview with other companies. Her interview was thus a personal matter, neither in pursuit nor to the legal detriment of [the employer's] business. To expand the business extension exemption as broadly as [the employer] suggest[s] would permit monitoring of obviously personal and very private calls[.] [emphasis added]

The court then concluded its decision by affirmatively addressing the extent to which a personal call could be monitored without losing the protection of the "business use" exception. According to the court, a personal call could be monitored only to the extent necessary to guard against unauthorized use of the telephone or to determine whether a call is personal or not. In other words, "a personal call may be [monitored] in the ordinary course of business to determine its nature but never its contents."

The courts have been fairly liberal in their construction of "legal interests" sufficient to justify an employer's monitoring of employee communications "in the ordinary course of business." In *Briggs v. American Air Filter Co., Inc.,* 630 F.2d 414 (5th Cir. 1980), the court upheld the monitoring and recording of part of a telephone conversation in which a salesman discussed the employer's business with a former employee who was engaged in the operation of a competing business. In so doing, the court noted that the call admittedly was of a business nature and that the employer's monitoring was "limited in purpose and time." The evidence established that the employer had "particular suspicions" about confidential information being disclosed to a business competitor; had warned the salesman not to disclose such information; had reason to believe that he continued to disclose the information; knew that the telephone call at issue was with an agent of a competitor; and listened-in on the extension phone only as long as the call involved the type of information that it feared was being disclosed.

In *Epps v. St. Mary's Hospital of Athens, Inc.,* 802 F.2d 412 (11th Cir. 1986), the court concluded that the "business use" exception applied to the interception and recording of a telephone conversation that occurred during office hours, between co-employees, over a specialized extension which connected the employer's principal office to a substation, and concerned "scurrilous remarks about supervisory employees in their capacities as supervisors." The court stated that "the potential contamination of a working environment is a matter in which the employer has a legal interest."

Similarly, in *Burnett v. The State of Texas,* 789 S.W. 2d 376 (Tex. App. 1990), the court held that the "business use" exemption protected the use of an extension telephone to intercept the call of an employee who was under investigation for suspected theft of the employer's merchandise. In support of its holding, the court noted that it was against the employer's policy for an employee to use the telephones for personal calls. Furthermore, as in *Briggs,* the employer had "specific suspicions" about the employee and listened-in on her call only long enough to confirm that she was arranging a pick-up for stolen merchandise.

Employers have not fared as well, however, when their monitoring lacked appropriate substantive or temporal limitations and, thus, unreasonably intruded on the employees' personal communications. For example, the courts in *Awbrey v. Great Atlantic & Pacific Tea Company,* 505 F. Supp. 604 (N.D. Ga. 1980), and *Abel v. Bonfanti,* 625 F. Supp. 263 (S.D. N.Y. 1985), refused to dismiss claims of illegal wiretapping predicated on the employer's alleged surreptitious and indiscriminate monitoring of business telephones from which employees regularly made personal calls. More recently, in

Deal v. Spears, 780 F. Supp. 191 (W.D. Ark. 1991), the court held that the "business use" exception did not apply, even though the employer began recording calls out of a legitimate concern about thefts at its store, because the vast majority of calls recorded were of a personal nature.

In *Deal,* the owners of a liquor store suspected an employee—Sibbie Deal—of being involved in the theft of $16,000. After conferring with a police officer, the owners decided to install a device to monitor the store's telephone. It was their hope that an employee would make an admission about the theft. The owners used a recording machine connected to an extension telephone in their residence, which shared a single line with the liquor store. The machine automatically recorded all incoming and outgoing calls without any notice to the callers.

Through the use of the recording device, the owners learned that Deal improperly had sold a keg to her boyfriend at a discounted price and had attempted to involve a third party in a cover-up of the transaction. The owners subsequently fired Deal, after playing the relevant portion of the recording in the presence of Deal and two other employees. Deal, joined by her boyfriend, then sued the owners, alleging that they had unlawfully intercepted and disclosed their personal telephone calls.

As noted above, the court rejected the owners' attempt to invoke the "business use" exception. The facts showed that the vast majority of calls recorded by the owners were not business-related. Many of the calls, in fact, included sexually explicit conversations between Deal and her boyfriend, both of whom were married to other individuals at the time. The owners, moreover, took no steps to limit their intrusion on the callers' privacy. Indeed, besides listening to all of the calls, one of the owners informed the callers' respective spouses of the provocative content of the calls. The court itself described the case as one of "sex, lies and audio tapes." It then awarded Deal and her boyfriend $20,000 each in statutory damages—$10,000 for the unlawful interception of their calls and an additional $10,000 for the unlawful disclosure of the calls to their spouses.

The Reasonable Expectation of Noninterception

Title III of the Act prohibits the interception of oral communications, as well as wire and electronic communications. However, individuals alleging the unlawful interception of *oral* communications have an additional evidentiary burden not present in other cases. Section 2510(2) of the Act specifically requires such individuals to show that: (1) they had an expectation that their oral communications were not subject to interception, and (2) their expectation was justified under the circumstances. This "expectation of noninterception" requirement was addressed in *Walker v. Darby*, 911 F.2d 1573 (11th Cir. 1990).

In *Walker*, a black postal employee sued three of his white supervisors, claiming that they unlawfully had placed a "bug" at his work station to intercept his conversations. The employee alleged that the "bugging" was part of a racially-motivated campaign to have his employment terminated. In upholding the employee's claim against a motion to dismiss, the court noted that the issue under Section 2510(2) of the Act was not whether the employee had a "reasonable expectation of privacy" in his work area. Rather, the issue was whether he had a "reasonable expectation of noninterception" of his communications. As the court explained:

> [The] courts distinguish between an expectation of privacy and the expectation of noninterception that is discussed in §2510(2). We agree that there is a difference between a public employee having a reasonable expectation of privacy in personal conversations taking place in the workplace and having a reasonable expectation that those conversations will not be intercepted by a device which allows them to be overheard inside an office in another area of the building.

Turning to the case at hand, the court concluded that the employee had presented suffi-

cient evidence of this "expectation of noninterception" to warrant the trial of his claim. The court first noted that the employee had established a subjective expectation of noninterception through his affidavit stating, inter alia, that he never gave permission to anyone to intercept or monitor conversations taking place at his work station. It then noted that his subjective expectation of noninterception appeared to be objectively reasonable under the circumstances. According to the court, although the employee might have expected conversations uttered in a normal tone of voice to be overheard by those standing nearby, "it is highly unlikely that he would have expected his conversations to be electronically intercepted and monitored in another part of the building."

Interestingly, the court in *Walker* allowed the employee's claim to proceed to trial even though he had failed to present evidence of the specific contents of the conversations allegedly intercepted. The court observed that because eavesdropping is surreptitious by nature, its victims often will lack direct evidence of the particular conversations intercepted. Therefore, requiring individuals to produce such evidence in order to state a valid claim under the Act would serve only to reward the eavesdropper for the stealthiness of his or her invasions. Although an individual must prove that his or her conversations, in fact, were intercepted, the court concluded that this could be accomplished through *circumstantial* evidence. Direct proof of the contents of the intercepted communications was not required.

STATE WIRETAPPING STATUTES

South Carolina appears to be the only state that has not enacted statutory limitations on electronic surveillance and monitoring by private individuals and entities. Most of the state statutes are fashioned after the Title III of the federal Act and, thus, include both the "prior consent" and "business use" exceptions. However, a limited number of state statutes do not contain a consent exception.[35]

The statutes that permit eavesdropping or wiretapping with the consent of a party to the conversation vary a great deal with respect to the proper scope of the consent exception. Several state statutes specifically require the consent of *all* parties to the conversation in order to invoke the exception.[36] But, a number of these statutes, which on their face require the consent of all parties, have been interpreted by the courts to require only the consent of one of the parties to the conversation. The Delaware and Illinois statutes are examples.[37]

Because the state statutory approaches vary and several state statutes have been judicially interpreted in ways that defy their express terms, it is important for employers to review the applicable state law before monitoring or recording employees' oral, wire, or electronic communications. Like the federal statute, the state statutes generally provide for both criminal penalties and civil damages. Therefore, ignoring the state statutes could prove costly.

PROPOSED FEDERAL LEGISLATION

As discussed above, there currently are few legal restrictions on an employer's ability to engage in pure service observation, computerized work measurement, or other forms of electronic surveillance limited to an employee's job performance. Furthermore, other than the statutory prohibitions against discrimination, there generally are no restrictions on the uses to which an employer may put the information it gathers, including discipline or discharge of employees determined to be performing below acceptable standards. Since 1987, there have been several unsuccessful efforts to pass federal legislation designed to strike a balance between the employer's right to monitor employees in the workplace and the employee's expectation of privacy.[38]

In 1991, these legislative efforts were renewed through the proposed Privacy for Consumers and Workers Act, HR 1218. The Act was introduced in the House of Representatives by Representative Pat Williams (D-Montana). A companion bill was introduced in the Senate by Senator Paul Simon (D-Illinois). The Act specifically is designed to address the privacy, stress, and individual autonomy concerns expressed by employees subjected to electronic monitoring. In February 1992, the Act, which reportedly has 135 cosponsors, was passed out of the House Education and Labor Subcommittee on Labor Management Relations.

Under the Act, employers are required to give affected applicants and employees written notice of any existing electronic monitoring practices. This notice must include the following information: (1) the forms of electronic monitoring used by the employer; (2) the personal data collected through the monitoring ("personal data" are data that can be readily associated with an individual because of a name, identifying mark, or description); (3) the frequency of each form of monitoring; (4) the uses of the personal data collected; (5) the interpretation of statistical printouts or other compilations of the information collected; (6) the employer's existing production standards and work performance expectations; and (7) the methods used to establish production standards and work performance expectations on the basis of the information collected through the monitoring.

Another major provision of the Act requires employers to notify employees that they are being electronically monitored *at the time* the monitoring is taking place. This notice, which must be given at periodic intervals, must be in the form of a signal light, beeping tone, verbal notification, or other form of visual or aural notice. This specific notice is not required, however, if the employer continuously monitors the employee during the employee's shift.

Two other substantive provisions of the Act attempt to give employees some control over the use of the data collected. One provision requires employers to permit employees access to all personal data obtained through the monitoring. The other provision prohibits employers from evaluating any employee solely on the basis of personal data obtained through the monitoring, unless the employee has the opportunity to review the data within a reasonable time after it is obtained. Employees thus are given the opportunity to challenge the data, to question the employer's interpretation of the data, and to rectify any related misunderstandings.

Employers that have voiced concern over the Act's requirements have done so on essentially two bases. First, they argue that giving employees specific notice when they are being monitored will result in the employees "shaping up" temporarily and will not produce an accurate portrait of their overall performance. Second, the employers argue that requiring notice will destroy their ability to identify employees involved in both on-site and off-site fraud, such as fraudulent workers' compensation claims. However, a recent revision to the Act may alleviate the latter concern by permitting secret monitoring of an individual employee if the employer has "reasonable cause" to suspect wrongdoing.

Proponents and opponents of the Act both have expressed some interest in a compromise that would involve providing employees with only general notice of the employer's monitoring practices, without specific notice at the time the monitoring is conducted. This general notice would serve to let the employees know that they are subject to monitoring during certain hours or during certain tasks, but would not alert them to the specific occasions when their work, in fact, is being monitored. This approach may well provide the balance of employer and employee interests necessary for passage of the Act this year.

SUGGESTIONS FOR EMPLOYERS

Although an employer's right to engage in service observation, computerized work measurement, and other electronic surveillance of employees is largely unrestricted, it is not entirely without limits. Employees have a protected zone of privacy—albeit relatively narrow—even inside the workplace. Monitoring employees' personal calls, eavesdropping on their private communications, videotaping employees in highly private areas, or otherwise exceeding reasonable substantive and temporal limitations on the scope of the monitoring may well subject employers to liability under existing constitutional, common law, or statutory prohibitions. Furthermore, the protection afforded to employees' "privacy rights" necessarily increases as the employer's monitoring extends beyond purely work-related matters or moves outside the workplace.

Employers also should note that the law in this area is in a developmental stage. In addition to the ongoing federal legislative effort to curb surreptitious workplace monitoring, there likely will be a flurry of similar activity at the state and local levels. Moreover, if privacy truly is the "workplace issue of the 1990s," we can expect a substantial increase in the number of lawsuits seeking to stretch the limits of existing legal theories to provide greater protection for the rights of employees. In the past, the courts have exhibited great ingenuity in expanding the common law to address changing social needs. As evidence, we need only look at the various "public policy" and "good faith" exceptions carved out by the courts in response to the perceived harshness of the previously accepted doctrine of "at-will" employment, which left employers free to discharge employees summarily without warning, notice, or cause.

There is yet another reason for employers to proceed cautiously in the area of electronic monitoring of employees. Although this article has focused only on the *legality* of employee monitoring, the question of "fairness" should not be overlooked. It is the perception of unfairness that often motivates employees to seek union representation and compels courts to create new law. Thus, if for no reason other than their economic self-interest, employers would be well-advised to consider the "fairness" issue when developing and implementing electronic monitoring programs.

The suggestions that follow arc designed principally to assist employers in minimizing their exposure to liability arising out of the electronic monitoring of employees. In part, they are based on lessons learned from "right to privacy" cases decided under federal and state constitutions. Because the legal analysis applied in those cases involves a balancing of employer and employee interests, several of the corresponding suggestions necessarily will promote the "fairness" of the employer's monitoring practices.

• *Determine the applicable federal and state laws.*

As noted in this article, the specific legal restrictions applicable in any given case will depend not only on whether the employer operates in the public or private sector, but also on the particular states in which the employer conducts its business. Constitutional and statutory provisions, as well as common law developments, may vary substantially from state to state.

• *Provide employees with prior written notice of the nature and extent of the applicable monitoring practices.*

Giving employees such notice, when consistent with the employer's business objectives, will serve to reduce or eliminate any "reasonable expectation of privacy." The notice need not bc givcn specifically at the time the monitoring is conducted, but should at least advise the employees that they are subject to specified monitoring practices. To further protect their interests, employers could secure signed waivers from employees acknowledging the employers' right to engage in electronic monitoring.

• *Be prepared to justify the monitoring from its inception.*

Employers should be able to demonstrate that the monitoring was initiated to serve legitimate business interests. In cases of service observation and computerized work measurement, this simply may be the need to effectively train, evaluate, and supervise employees in the performance of their jobs. However, when monitoring is conducted for specific investigatory purposes, the employer should be prepared to establish

that it had "individualized suspicion" of the employee's involvement in conduct adverse to its "legal interests."

• *Observe reasonable temporal and geographical limitations on the scope of the monitoring.*

Fmployers should be able to demonstrate that any monitoring was only as broad as necessary to fulfill the legitimate business interests which justified its inception.

• *Be sensitive to employee "privacy rights."*

Monitoring should not extend into highly private areas in the workplace, such as restrooms and lounges. In addition, monitoring generally should be limited to the workplace, unless there is a compelling, work-related reason for moving it outside the workplace (for example, the investigation of fraudulent or unlawful conduct arising out of the employment relationship). Even then, the monitoring should be reasonable in scope and relatively unobtrusive.

• *Limit telephone monitoring and similar forms of electronic surveillance as necessary to preserve the "business use" exception.*

Employers should ensure that any such monitoring is "in the ordinary course of [their] business." This requires a showing that: (1) the monitoring policy generally is justifiable on the basis of the employer's legitimate business needs, and (2) the subject matter of each monitored communication is one in which the employer has a "legal interest." Where possible, it is best to monitor only those telephone lines that, with the employee's knowledge, are dedicated exclusively to business use. Employers should strictly enforce their policies against the use of such business lines for personal calls, through disciplinary action if necessary. In any event, the employer's monitoring should cease as soon as any particular call has been identified as personal in nature. In all but the rarest of cases (for example, when actual or implied consent is present), employers should not engage in the indiscriminate monitoring of all incoming or outgoing calls on lines used by employees.

• *Do not "bug" employees' offices or otherwise surreptitiously intercept their oral communications.*

Employers cannot invoke the "business use" exception in connection with the interception of oral communications. Furthermore, in the absence of actual consent, it will be extremely difficult for employers to show that the employee lacked a reasonable expectation of "noninterception" of his or her oral communications inside or outside the workplace.

• *Adopt reasonable procedural safeguards concerning the use and disclosure of information gathered through monitoring.*

When appropriate, employees should be allowed access to the information gathered, as well as an opportunity to rebut the information or its interpretation by the employer. This is particularly true in cases in which the information is being used as the basis for disciplinary action. Obviously, employers should use any such information gathered through monitoring only for lawful purposes. In addition, disclosure of the information should be limited to those management representatives or law enforcement officials who have a legitimate "need to know" about it in the performance of their duties.

• *Train supervisors, managers, and security personnel regarding the applicable legal restrictions.*

As is always the case, merely having lawful policies is not enough. Ultimately, an employer's liability will turn on whether its electronic monitoring policies were applied lawfully and evenhandedly by those responsible for doing so.

NOTES

1. Linowes and Spencer, "Privacy: The Workplace Issue of the '90s," 23 *John Marshall L. Rev.* 591-620 (Summer 1990) and Reuben, "Privacy: The Issue of the 90s: California's Right to Privacy Is Coming out of the Bedroom to the Workplace and Beyond," 10 *Cal. Law.* 38(c) (March 1990).
2. Nussbaum, "Workers under Surveillance," 26 *Computer World* 21 (January 6, 1992).

3. Bylinsky, "How Companies Spy on Employees," 124 *Fortune* 140 (November 4, 1991).
4. Id.
5. Id.
6. Rhonda Hall and Bonita Burke filed suit against their employer, Nissan Motor Corporation U.S.A., in late 1991 claiming that they were improperly dismissed for their usage of the company's electronic mail network. Alana Shoars has sued Epson America Inc. for dismissing her after she complained about a supervisor's reading and printing out of electronic mail messages between two employees. Rifkin, "Do Employees Have a Right to Electronic Privacy?," *N.Y. Times,* December 8, 1991, at A8.
7. BNA, "Northern Telecom Settles with CWA on Monitoring," 7 *Individual Employment Rights* 1 (March 10, 1992).
8. *Camara v. Municipal Court,* 387 U.S. 523, 528 (1967). See also *Delaware v. Prouse,* 440 U.S. 648, 653-54 (1979); *United States v. Martinez-Fuerte,* 428 U.S. 543, 554 (1976).
9. The strictures of the Fourth Amendment are applied to units of state and local government through the Fourteenth Amendment.
10. See *Ortega* (cited on p. 378), *National Treasury Employees Union v. Von Raab,* 489 U.S. 656 (1989); *American Postal Workers* (cited on p. 379).
11. Private sector employees generally enjoy no privacy rights derived from the Fourth Amendment. There is a limited exception, however, in cases in which the private employer acts under color of state or federal law as a result of the involvement of law enforcement officials or the application of federal regulations. See, e.g., *Skinner* (cited on p. 379) (Fourth Amendment applied to private railroads requiring breath and urine tests in reliance on drug/alcohol testing regulations promulgated by the Federal Railroad Administration).
12. See *Katz v. United States,* 389 U.S. 347, 353 (1967); *Berger v. New York,* 388 U.S. 41, 51 (1967); *United States v. Domme,* 753 F.2d 950, 952 (11th Cir. 1985); *United States v. Agrusa,* 541 F.2d 690, 698 (8th Cir. 1976); *United States v. King,* 536 F. Supp. 253, 266 (C.D. Cal. 1982).
13. See *Ortega* (cited on p. 378) at 715; *American Postal Workers* (cited on p. 379) at 559-60; *United States v. McIntyre,* 582 F.2d 1221, 1223-

24 (9th Cir. 1978); *Simmons* (cited on p. 378) at 392, 394.

14. *Skinner* (cited on p. 379) at 619, citing *United States v. Montoya de Hernandez,* 473 U.S. 531, 537 (1985).

15. *Ortega* (cited on p. 378) at 719, citing *United States v. Place,* 462 U.S. 696, 703 (1983) and *Camara* (cited in note 8) at 536-37.

16. See also *Von Raab* (cited in note 10) at 668.

17. See also *National Treasury Employees Union v. Lyng,* 706 F. Supp. 934, 949-50 (D.D.C. 1988); *Bangert v. Hodel,* 705 F. Supp. 643, 645, 650-51 (D.D.C. 1989).

18. The relevant states are Alaska, Arizona, California, Florida, Hawaii, Illinois, Lousiana, Montana, South Carolina, and Washington.

19. See, e.g, *Bianco v. American Broadcasting Co., Inc.,* 470 F. Supp. 182, 187 (N.D. Ill. 1979) (Right to be secure against "unreasonable . . . invasions of privacy or interceptions of communications by eavesdropping devices or other means," as set forth in Article I, Section 6 of the Illinois Constitution, is a limitation only on governmental activity).

20. See *Wilkinson v. Times Mirror Corp.,* 215 Cal. App. 3d 1034, 264 Cal. Rptr. 194 (1989); *Semore v. Pool,* 217 Cal. App. 3d 1087, 266 Cal. Rptr. 280 (1990); *Luck* (cited on p. 381); *Soroka* cited on p. 381).

21. See *Luck* (cited on p. 381) at 20; *Soroka* (cited on p. 381) at 1 Cal. Rptr. 2d at 86.

22. See, e.g., *Awbrey* (cited on p 390) (wiretapping); *LaCrone v. Ohio Bell Tel.,* 182 N.E. 2d 15 (Ohio App. 1961) (wiretapping); *Fowler v. Southern Bell Tel. & Tel. Co.,* 343 F.2d 150 (5th Cir. 1965) (wiretapping); *Nader v. General Motors Corp.,* 25 N.Y.S. 2d 560, 255 N.E. 2d 763, 307 N.Y.S. 2d 647 (N.Y. App. 1970) (wiretapping); *Beard* (cited on p. 85) (wiretapping); *Pemberton v. Bethlehem Steel Corp.,* 66, Md. App. 133, 502 A. 2d 1101 (1986) (electronic listening device); *Saldana* (cited on p. 383) (high-power camera lens); *Doe by Doe v. B.P.S. Guard Servs., Inc.,* 945 F.2d 1422 (8th Cir. 1991) (videotape surveillance cameras).

23. See *McClain* (cited on p. 383); *Saldana* (cited on p. 383); *Catania v. Eastern Airlines, Inc.,* 381 So. 2d 265 (Fla. App. 1980).

24. See also *Tucker v. American Employers' Ins. Co.,* 171 So. 2d 437 (Fla. App. 1965); *Souder v. Pendleton Detectives, Inc.,* 88 So. 2d 716 (La. App. 1956); *Saldana* (cited on p. 383).

25. *Baggs v. Eagle-Picher Indus., Inc.,* 1992 U.S. App. LEXIS 2769 (6th Cir. 1992).

26. See, e.g., *Doe by Doe* (cited in note 22) (Common law invasion of privacy claim stated by fashion show models subjected to video camera surveillance while changing clothes in makeshift dressing area). See also *K-Mart Corp. v. Trotti,* 677 S.W. 2d 632 (Tex. App. 1984) (Common law invasion of privacy claim stated by employee whose locker and purse were searched by employer).

27. See, e.g., *Beard* (cited on p. 384) (Court assumed that wiretapping of employee's home telephone would provide basis for common law invasion of privacy claim, but found no evidence that the employer had engaged in such conduct); *Ford Motor Co. v. Williams,* 108 Ga. App. 21, 132 S.E. 2d 206 (1963) (Common law invasion of privacy claim stated by individual whose home was entered by defendant); *Pemberton* (cited in note 22) (Common law invasion of privacy claim stated by union bargaining agent subjected to electronic surveillance while in his motel room).

28. See, e.g, *Awbrey* (cited on p. 390) at 606, 609-10 (Employer's indiscriminate wiretapping of store business telephones from which employees regularly made personal calls provided the basis for civil action for invasion of privacy under Georgia law).

29. Restatement (Second) of Torts, §652D, Comment a. (1977).

30. See also *Gentry v. E.I. Dupont de Nemours and Co., Inc.,* 733 S.W. 2d 71 (Tenn. App. 1987); *Barr v. Arco Chem. Corp.,* 529 F. Supp. 1277, 1280 (S.D. Tx. 1982); *Vogel v. W.T. Grant Co.,* 458 Pa. 12, 327 A. 2d 133, 137-38 (1974); *Tureen v. Equifax, Inc.,* 571 F.2d 411, 419 (8th Cir 1978).

31. See also *Golden v. Board of Educ. of the County of Harrison,* 285 S.E. 2d 665 (S. Ct. W. Va. 1981).

32. Section 801 Pub. L. 90-351.

33. 1968 U.S. Code Cong. & Admin. News 2112, 2182, citing *United States v. Pasha,* 332 F.2d 193 (7th Cir.), cert. denied, 379 U.S. 839 (1964).

34. See, e.g, *Watkins* (cited on p. 386) (standard extension telephone); *Jandak* (cited on p. 386) (ten-line communications system with recording capability); *Epps* (cited on p. 389) (communications console connecting dispatch office to various substations).

35. The relevant states are Arkansas, Kansas, New Hampshire, and Rhode Island.
36. The relevant states are California, Delaware, Florida, Illinois, Lousiana, Maryland, Massachusetts, Michigan, Montana, Oregon, Pennsylvania, and Washington.
37. See *United States v. Vespe,* 389 F. Supp. 1359, 1372 (D. Del.), aff'd, 520 F. 2d 1369 (3d Cir. 1975), cert. denied, 423 U.S. 105 (1976); *People v. Beardsley,* 115 Ill. 2d 47, 104 Ill. Dec. 789, 503 N.E. 2d 346, 350 (1986).
38. See discussion of prior legislative efforts in Susser, "Electronic Monitoring in the Private Sector: How Closely Should Employers Supervise Their Workers?" 13 *Empl. Rel. L.J.* 589 (Spring 1988).

READING 8-4

Electronic Workplace Surveillance: Sweatshops and Fishbowls

Andrew Clement

1. INTRODUCTION

A key feature of the "Information Society" is the increasingly central role that detailed information created during the production and distribution of goods and services plays in management. Nowhere is this process applied more thoroughly than in the internal workings of highly computerized organizations. As Zuboff (1988) has noted, the radical innovation that information technology offers managers lies not in its ability to automate production, but rather to generate vast quantities of production information that can be used in turn for controlling the work

Source: Reprinted with permission from the *Canadian Journal of Information Science,* Vol. 17, No. 4, December, 1994, pp. 18-45.

processes. Information on rates, times, delays, calls answered, keys pressed, messages sent, transactions entered, and so on have for the first time become instantly and cheaply available. When analyzed appropriately, this information about the performance of machines and workers can be very valuable for improving management. On the other hand, it provides the basis for surveillance of individuals unprecedented in its scope and detail. This potential invasion of personal privacy raises an Orwellian spectre attended by public controversy; see, for example, recent articles in *Time* (Lacayo 1991), *Business Week* (Hafner et al. 1988; Rothfeder et al. 1990), *Globe and Mail* (List 1986), *Harvard Business Review* (Marx et al. 1990), *New York Times* (Kilborn 1990; Rifkin 1991), *Toronto Star* (Papp 1991). With the spread of computerization, the proper use of this burgeoning information resource is of concern to those who design, manage, or work with information systems.

This paper examines the phenomenon of electronic surveillance. After defining the term, we will survey the range of settings, particularly in Canada, where it is practised. These vary from the sweatshop-like conditions that telephone operators experience to the more indirect monitoring practices that can create a "fishbowl" environment for workers in any highly computerized workplace. A discussion of the managerial rationales for electronic monitoring is then counterposed with a survey of the negative human and organizational implications. Finally we examine the various avenues for remedying the potentially deleterious aspects of electronic surveillance.

2. ELECTRONIC SURVEILLANCE AT WORK

While close supervision is a longstanding workplace practice, automated forms of keeping track of employee activities are relatively new, and generally accepted definitions for the phenomena are only just being developed. As recently as 1979 a Discussion Paper on Electronic Surveillance prepared by the Ontario Ministry of Labour defined electronic surveillance without any mention of data processing techniques (Ontario Ministry of Labour 1979). The discussion at that time was almost entirely on the use of video cameras, whereas now the major concern is the use of computers to record and analyze employee performance. To incorporate this data processing aspect, we define electronic work monitoring as "the computerized collection, storage, analysis and reporting of information about employees' workplace activities" (Clement 1984, 260; U.S. Congress 1987). This becomes "surveillance," to use Rule and Brantley's terminology, when managers systematically monitor individual staff members' job performance with an eye to ensuring compliance with management expectations (Rule and Brantley 1992). Within this broad definition, we will focus mainly on data about employees obtained directly through their interaction with computerized equipment.

As the technique of supervision becomes more computerized, its form is changing. In the past it was often necessary for supervisors to observe the work in person or have employees fill out forms to record the amount of work done during specific time periods. Now it is feasible to generate such statistics directly from the use of the automated equipment. This has the advantages of not interfering with productive workflow; of being more detailed, reliable, and accurate; of reducing possible employee resentment over filling out personal work records; and of being cheaper and faster to process since the data are already in machine-readable form. Results can be available immediately and at a distance. As computer-based surveillance becomes easier to conduct as an unobtrusive byproduct of the work process, its use is likely to spread. It is precise, fine-grained, relentless, and increasingly pervasive.

Although automated forms of surveillance cover a wide range of settings and modes of application, they were first developed in work situations characterized by high volumes of generally routine transactions performed by operators using online systems. Let us look at surveillance aspects of three automated systems and how they have been used in managing employees. These are among the most frequently mentioned cases of electronic surveillance, and, as we shall see, attempts to ameliorate these practices illustrate the more general obstacles to reform.

Telephone Operators

Probably the foremost example of automated workplace surveillance is to be found in telephone companies. Telephone operators at large central offices have for a long time been closely monitored in their work. However, when the old "cord boards" at Bell Canada offices were replaced by the Traffic Operator Position System (TOPS), not only was the routing of calls speeded up, but operators found that monitoring had been intensified. Instead of connecting calls by manually inserting plugs into sockets and then filling in billing tickets, all operators work at the keyboard of a VDT. Each keystroke is timed and recorded, and various statistical measures are continuously calculated. The president of a local of the Communication Workers of Canada reports:

> With the touch of a few keys, management is delivered 76 pieces of data on an operator's performance. The manager is aware of the operator's overall performance in terms of average work time per call and what percentage of the time the operator was away from the machine.
>
> If in the opinion of management, the operator is not meeting objectives, [he or she] can be questioned with respect to the average number of seconds required to depress the first key after a customer comes on the line, the average number of letters per entry, the average number of corrections per call, the average number of seconds to key the data, and much more. (Larter 1984)

The main statistic used to evaluate operator performance is Average Working Time (AWT).

For TOPS, the target level fluctuates around 25 seconds per call, depending on the time of day. For directory assistance calls, Bell managers expect operators to maintain AWTs that are much lower still.

Airline Reservation Agents

The airline industry was one of the first to make extensive use of online systems. Air Canada's Reservec II, introduced in 1970, was a leading system that dramatically sped up the reservation process. However, management could not exploit its new surveillance possibilities until several years later when modifications to record the sales and call timing behaviour of passenger agents were added. The submission to the Labour Canada Task Force on Micro-electronics and Employment by the association that represented 4500 airline employees (CALEA) describes the additional capabilities:

> Contained in Reservec II is an automatic process designed to collect performance data on each individual passenger agent. The monthly Passenger Agent Sales Effectiveness Reports (P.A.S.E.R.) indicate PNRs (passenger name record) booked, PNRs modified, number of passengers per PNR, tickets-by-mail arranged, hotels and cars booked, and passenger revenue generated. The monthly reports compare the individual passenger agent's productivity to that of his or her entire team (15-18 agents) . . .
>
> STAR (System for Telephone Administration Response) is a computerized information system that interfaces with the automatic distributor. From the time an agent is plugged into STAR, his or her telephone time is measured. STAR identifies call volumes, and call lengths. It measures the amount of time the telephone release button is pushed which is considered time used by the agent to clean up a file or "fatigue" time. STAR also monitors an agent's lunch and coffee breaks by calculating the amount of time his or her phone jack is removed. (Canadian Airline Employees Association 1982)

At Air Canada's Toronto office, agents are expected to be "inline" with or waiting for customers for at least 80% of the seven-hour work shift (Robertson and Wareham 1990). Failure to meet these standards can be grounds for supervisors to initiate "coaching and counselling" sessions and ultimately disciplinary action. At Pacific Western Airlines (before its merger with CP Air to form Canadian Airlines International), the Reservation Handbook stated that agents will receive individual counselling if they do not reach the expected standard. If performance is below 80% of the norm for longer than sixty days, then "disciplinary action including possible discharge will take place." American Airline's well-known SABRE system is used even more intensively to regulate agent performance and behaviour (Garson 1988; Kilborn 1990).

Airlines are not alone in using Automatic Call Distributors (ACD). By 1981, Rockwell International claimed that ACDs were in use in "almost the entire airline industry, offices, hotels, credit card companies, car rental agencies, newspapers, banks, insurance companies and public utilities" (*Globe and Mail* 1981). In each setting is the potential to use it for monitoring individual worker performance.

Data-Entry Clerks

The job of "data entry" is probably the most routinized and finely monitored job involving computers. Keystroke counting has been practised for decades (Hoos 1961), but with the use of online key-edit systems the collection and processing of performance statistics is easier and more intensive.

The Ontario Health Insurance Plan processes massive volumes of premiums and billing transactions. Until recently these have been handled by regional data centres throughout the province. In 1985, management in the Mississauga office informed all data-entry clerks that those who persistently failed to meet the "minimum acceptable level" of 11,400 keystrokes per hour would be demoted and eventually fired (McDermott 1987, 34). Though the memo was subsequently withdrawn in the face of more than twenty-five grievances, the production standard remained informally in effect. Performance statistics in comparison to the 11,400 figure continued to be posted each Monday morning. In one office, each person's score was posted daily.

Similar performance standards and production regimes can also be found in large private-sector firms. At the Toronto headquarters of a major Canadian life insurance firm, management pays data-entry clerks according to individual production performance and raised the hourly quota from 11,500 keystrokes to 13,000 when it began to record non-keying breaks. The data-entry supervisor compared her section to a "sweatshop" run on a piecework basis (Clement 1986, 5-10).

These are but three of the most prominent examples of the use by managers of fine-grained computer generated data to ensure the compliance of their employees. It is difficult to assess how widespread this phenomenon is, but the best estimates come from the extensive study conducted by the U.S. Congress Office of Technology Assessment (OTA). Its report, *The Electronic Supervisor,* lists seven office jobs that are "often subject to work measurement from production data gathered through electronic monitoring"—routine clerical jobs dealing with word processing, data entry, telephone operation, customer service, insurance claims, telemarketing, mail, and bank proofs (U.S. Congress 1987, 29). OTA estimates that in the U.S., 20-35% of all clerical employees are electronically monitored for pay, promotion, or discipline purposes, as are up to another 5% of managerial, professional, and technical workers. Altogether this amounts to five to eight million employees. Rule and Brantley (1992), in their survey of 186 firms in the New York City area selected in a random sample stratified by size, industrial sector, and district, found that clerical workers were not disproportionately represented among those subject to monitoring.

Comparably detailed studies of Canadian workplaces have not been conducted, but the data available are consistent with those above. Grant and Higgins (1991) surveyed fifty-one ser-

vice-sector firms and received responses from 1,489 clerks providing direct service to customers. Of these, 35% reported being subject to some form of computerized performance monitoring. The Ontario Federation of Labour reports that a survey of conference attendees showed 20% of its members experiencing electronic surveillance. Among government and crown corporation employees, the figure rises to 38% (Archer 1985). Monitoring is not restricted to office jobs. Increasingly truck, train, and bus drivers, meter readers, retail sales clerks, and machine operators of many kinds are also finding that they are supervised in part on the basis of data they generate as a byproduct of their work.

Most of the jobs referred to above as being most susceptible to electronic monitoring have in common several characteristics that favour a "people driving" approach to the application of computer technology, to use Bjorn-Andersen's apt term (1983). They all involve the processing of large volumes of routine transactions by employees (largely women) performing low-status jobs for which formal skills or credentials are not required. In these important respects they represent the modern electronic-office versions of the classic sweatshops and assembly lines.

However, as the U.S. data cited above indicate, it is not just the relatively routine jobs that are the subject of close electronic scrutiny. As online systems are being used more widely, application of other techniques of electronic monitoring, characterized by rapid and remote access to detailed, up-to-date employee information, are becoming feasible in a growing number of areas of work that do not necessarily share the characteristics of those just described. It is now becoming commonplace for employees, regardless of position and function, to interact with a range of computerized systems that play generic, infrastructural roles. Among the most widespread of these are systems for data access and security, physical access and security, time and attendance recording, telephone call accounting, and electronic mail. Each of these is rapidly becoming taken for granted in modern workplaces and they each produce an enduring and detailed record of employee behaviour. For example, when anyone signs into or out of on-line systems or particular databases, a log entry is often made so that errors or security violations can be later traced. Similar records are created when anyone enters buildings or rooms requiring special identity cards or passwords. In some cases these are connected to time and attendance systems used in calculating payroll and monitoring employee absence. One company that sells such a system, Hecon Canada, advertised its product with the slogan *"It's 11:00 a.m. Do you know where your employees are?"* (*Canadian Office* 1983, 55).

Just as conventional time clocks are converted through computerization into data generating instruments capable of monitoring employees, so too are company telephone systems. Most modern PBX (private branch exchange) systems incorporate Station Message Detail Recording (SMDR) features capable of reporting who calls whom, when, and for how long. Mitel Corporation advertised that its early SUPERSWITCH product was a "very thorough informer" and could be used to identify personal use and "long talkers" (Mitel 1980). Such language may be less acceptable a decade later, but the practices it implies are unlikely to have disappeared (U.S. Congress 1987).

Electronic mail (email) services take the monitoring potential a step further by making it possible to capture the content of interaction with the computer systems as well as the purely transactional data discussed so far (times, volumes, etc.). Since email requires the (temporary) storage of messages, someone with appropriate authorization or the ability to impersonate an email user, can readily and unobtrusively view an individual's correspondence. This is not a widespread phenomenon, but several incidents have been reported, with two U.S. cases heading for trial as violations of privacy and employment laws (Glen 1991; *Harvard Law Review* 1991; Rifkin 1991). Zuboff has described how in a

multinational drug company, a flourishing discussion about "women's professional improvement" conducted via a closed computer conference quickly died out once it became known that more senior managers had started collecting transcripts and asking questions (1988, 382-83). In a related vein, key evidence in the Iran-Contra hearings was provided by archived copies of White House email that were overlooked in the destruction of records prior to the investigation. A Canadian university provides another interesting illustration of the surveillance potential of email. In an attempt to discourage cheating on programming assignments, a professor developed a program, appropriately called SNOOP, which would regularly copy all messages of students in a course to the appropriate instructors. When these interception capabilities were announced, a lively, but inconclusive, debate via email ensued.

It is not just in office settings that the minute activities of employees create an electronic text of their workday that can be read by managers. This practice is now routine in some highly computerized industrial installations. Zuboff (1988) describes in considerable detail how the activities of workers in settings as diverse as a pulp mill and a telephone switching centre are electronically recorded. Managers used these data in a range of activities that included promotions, assigning workloads, fine tuning production schedules, accelerating individual learning, and assigning responsibility for breakdowns.

A further step in creating work environments in which employees produce a detailed electronic trace of their activities arises from proposals for implementing "media spaces." Still experimental, these involve linking work areas via computer-controlled audio and video communications paths (Borning and Travers 1991; Mantei et al. 1991). In conjunction with the wearing of "active badges," which permit the continuous tracking of the individual's movements, these highly computerized work environments are designed to enable employees to get in touch with each other via a variety of channels wherever they happen to be. Although the initiative for developing these environments has generally come from researchers for their own experimental use rather than for managerial oversight, the abundant potential in this latter area is obvious.

As computers become increasingly "ubiquitous," even though they may disappear from direct view (*New York Times* 1991; Weiser 1991), we should thus expect that ever more information about employees will be routinely collected and available for scrutiny. When data from this widening range of sources are integrated and analyzed by means of sophisticated database query languages, they can yield fine-grained profiles of individual employee behaviour that can be used in situations far from what was originally intended. In an informational sense, the workplace becomes transparent, with virtually everything one does potentially on view by others. Metaphorically, it could become like working in a "fishbowl."

This "fishbowl" approach differs from "sweatshop" surveillance in a number of important respects (see Table 1). In informationally transparent workplaces, all employees, and not just specific lower-level job classes, can be monitored. Behaviour covering a wide range of tasks, not just production performance on routine operations, can be scrutinized. Expected standards do not have to be defined ahead of time and applied uniformly across categories of employees, but remain as the tacit-intentions behind ad hoc queries about specific individuals and incidents.

These differences define the two forms of surveillance not as mutually exclusive alternatives but rather as opposite ends of the electronic surveillance spectrum. At this point, sweatshop surveillance is more evident than fishbowl surveillance.

However, the spread of techniques enabling the latter, which can affect a wider range of employees, should raise concerns about potential deleterious effects. The degree to which it does in practice depends on many factors other than the technical ones on which we have focused so far. Among the most important of these are the managerial intentions and the wider organizational milieu that drive the growth of monitoring capabilities as well as their transformation into surveillance practices. It is to these that we now turn.

3. MANAGERIAL RATIONALES—THE PARADIGM OF CONTROL

The key to understanding the growth and implications of electronic surveillance lies not in the technologies of monitoring nor in the personalities of the managers who may put them into action. Though both of these are important, of greater significance is the history and ethos of modern management. The close monitoring of

TABLE 1

"SWEATSHOP" VERSUS "FISHBOWL" SURVEILLANCE

	Sweatshop	Fishbowl
Tasks	High volume, routine (e.g., data entry)	General
Occupations	Lower level (clerical, sales)	General (clerical, managerial, professional)
Application	Special purpose	General purpose
Queries	Structured, predefined (e.g., AWT)	Ad hoc
Measures	Production performance (calls connected, value of flights booked)	Behavioural (who contacted, time worked)

employee behaviour represents a logical extension of the central management paradigm—pursuit of control over all relevant aspects of the business enterprise. Indeed, some believe that "to manage is to control." Cybernetician Stafford Beer terms management "the profession of control" (1959). From their different perspectives, Braverman (1974) and Chandler (1977) have both traced the development of the principles of managerial control and their central role in modern industrial enterprise. Beniger (1986) identifies management's success in resolving multiple crises of control in the material goods systems as the revolutionary innovation that ushered in the present industrial era. Mowshowitz (1983) similarly observes that the pursuit of control is a "technocultural paradigm" deeply embedded in Western civilization.

While pursuing control is central to the management of modern enterprises, it is not simply an end in itself. Control is a prerequisite for the efficient and effective performance that competitive organizations rely on for their survival. Whatever strategy is followed, whether it is mass production of low-cost goods or the customized creation of high-value-added services, effective control over the core functions is essential for long-term viability. The less certain the environment, the more critical this internal control becomes.

There are many ways to pursue control, but they all rely fundamentally upon principles of effective control first articulated in the work of Weiner (1947) and Ashby (1956). Their formal model of control involves sensors, regulators, and effectors linked via information feedback loops. Organizational performance and environment are sensed and compared with goals, decisions on appropriate action are made, and instructions issued. The more information that can be collected and the more quickly a response formulated, the more effectively control can be achieved in the face of uncertainty.

The prodigious ability of computers to handle massive volumes of information for programmed decision making largely accounts for their widespread application in controlling critical aspects of the enterprise involving money, materials, and people (e.g., in systems for accounting, inventory control, payroll) (Rule and Attewell 1989). If tasks are well understood, goals clearly identified, and employees regarded principally as human resources who take their place alongside the other factors of production, then it appears obvious, even natural, that employees should be closely monitored by the same computerized techniques. Indeed, given that people are typically the least reliable components of a production system, there is added incentive to ensure they are performing to expectations. Computerized "sweatshop" surveillance, as described above, is thus a straightforward, if extreme, application of this theory of control. It is also a direct descendant of the principles of scientific management that constitute the traditional mainstream of management practice. However, this technique is relatively simplistic, and from a managerial perspective is limited in its effectiveness. As Attewell (1987) points out, sweatshop surveillance is very unlikely to become general in computerized workplaces. One important reason is that many jobs cannot be so narrowly routinized and fragmented, with goals neatly quantified and the contributions of collaborating individuals clearly distinguished. More subtle and contextually sensitive techniques for exercising control are needed in such settings. Because of the way transparency can encourage compliance with a wider range of expectations with little need for overt intervention, it is here that the fishbowl approach has much to offer.

This broader view of control draws upon the notion of the "panopticon," a remarkable social engineering innovation that Jeremy Bentham proposed as a means for social betterment in the last century (see Foucault 1979; Robins and Webster 1988; Zuboff 1988). The panopticon is essentially an architecture for social control in which a central unseen authority maintains a potentially continuous watch over a large number of individuals who are encouraged to assume that their every act is available for inspection and remedial intervention. To avoid confrontation, the individual becomes self-monitoring in compliance with expectations. Transparency thus contributes to the internalization of control.

Integrated communications and information technologies free the application of this panoptic principle from the constraints of physical architecture and permit its extension to intensively computerized settings (Robins and Webster 1988). Beyond the obvious advantages of automating the supervision function, there are several factors related to the changing nature of work that are fuelling this process. As production work shifts away from the creation of physical objects and becomes more abstract, data-based methods are in some cases the only way to measure individual performance. This same imperative applies when workers are linked via computer rather than meeting in person. Remote, abstract work calls for remote, abstract supervision.

Scientific management is of course not the only approach to control favoured by managers. Since before the emergence of the Human Relations school in the 1930s, managers have been concerned about employee motivation and socialization. An important concern about close surveillance from this perspective is that it can harm employee morale and even provoke active resistance. Automating surveillance offers advantages in this regard by avoiding some of the objections employees have with conventional forms of supervision. There is no need for them to perform extra work involved in recording production outcomes, and the objective, quantitative nature of the data can serve to protect employees from the arbitrariness to which human supervision is prone. Computer-generated statistics offer an objective performance record less susceptible to the favouritism or discrimination that employees have often complained about. If the results are presented to employees in a way that enables them to learn more about the production process and improve their performance, electronic monitoring may be positively wel-

comed and contribute to improved morale. Such a reaction depends on the degree to which employees perceive this performance feedback as legitimate and not mainly as a device to reinforce their subordination. It also raises the question of the role of power as a motive for surveillance.

While the major rationale for computerizing surveillance is to improve organizational effectiveness and efficiency, its contribution to maintaining hierarchical social relations cannot be ignored. The characteristically asymmetric flow of information about employees to their supervisors confers an obvious advantage on the latter in their mutual dealings. Quite apart from any improvements in organizational performance, some managers will see the ability to preserve authority as an important attraction of this technique. If computerized surveillance is seen in this light, it would not be the first time that technologies have been developed for their labour-disciplining features and not simply for technical efficiency (Marglin 1974; Noble 1984).

It should be noted that although enhanced control over employees may often be an important managerial objective in computerization, it is not always the most significant motive (Kling and Iacono 1985). But nor does it have to be for computerized surveillance to spread. Both Zuboff's in-depth study of a few highly computerized enterprises and Rule and Brantley's more representative sample survey in the New York area indicate that the development of computerized surveillance emerges indirectly as a by-product of managements' broader attempts to rationalize and control production. As Zuboff notes:

> The techniques of panoptic power were typically developed after the fact, by coincidence and by accident, as managers discovered ways to colonize an already functioning portion of the technological infrastructure and use it to satisfy their felt needs for additional certainty and control. (1988, 324)

The case of Air Canada described above offers a further illustration. It suggests that the spread of computerized surveillance is likely to be incremental rather than abrupt, and uneven rather than uniform. But this opportunistic evolution also suggests that there are few intrinsic limits to its ultimate scope, since the need for control remains insatiable and the opportunities for monitoring are continuing to expand. As long as organizations face an increasingly competitive, turbulent environment while work grows ever more complex, abstract, spatially distributed, and computerized, the pressure on managers to take advantage of these new panoptic capabilities for control can only intensify.

4. ADVERSE HUMAN, ORGANIZATIONAL, AND SOCIAL IMPLICATIONS

In our society, with its claims to liberal democratic norms, close observation of an individual is widely regarded as an infringement of basic human rights. Detailed surveillance of adults by whatever means is considered degrading and an affront to human dignity. It is only children, invalids, criminals, and slaves who historically have been watched every moment. Using a machine to do the watching adds an explicit depersonalizing element that conjures up one of the most potent dystopian images of this century— George Orwell's "Big Brother." It is therefore little wonder that the subject of computer surveillance is so controversial. The essence of this debate is aptly captured in the words of the arbitrator in the widely reported Puretex case:

> In the use of electronic surveillance, it is apparent that we confront conflicting social values of considerable significance. There is on the one hand the principle of the right to privacy and beyond that the more general idea, of which the right to privacy is only one facet, of the crucial importance of preserving and nurturing the historically fragile concept of human dignity . . . On the other side of the issue are simply considerations of efficiency in dealing with social problems. (Ellis 1979)

While these remarks were made in the context of video surveillance, they apply equally well to the automated case.

Within this broadly cultural objection to automated surveillance, employees and others have raised a wide range of more specific, but interrelated, complaints. We begin our exploration by considering the implications for individual employees and then move through workplace relationships to the world beyond.

Self-Concept

Closely tied to the threat to the concept of human dignity is the negative effect of surveillance on the self-concept of an individual employee. Implicit in the use of any device that monitors the activity of an adult is the presumption that he or she is not entitled to be left alone. This is captured in a statement by an airline reservation agent:

> I . . . feel that the Company doesn't trust me, that's why they have this machine that watches me. It sure doesn't do much for my self-esteem. (personal interview 1984)

In Quebec, a telephone operator expressed frustration at being "spied upon" (Mosco and Zureik 1987, 77) by means of the detailed measurements within the TOPS system. An OHIP data-entry operator expressed similar sentiments when she wrote to management that its memo reminding workers of the 11,400 keystroke standard was "demoralizing, humiliating and degrading" (McDermott 1987, 35).

Health and Safety/Stress

It is clear that automated surveillance does not pose a direct threat to employee health or safety in the same way that working with toxic chemicals or heavy objects obviously does. However, the indirect effects may nevertheless be quite significant. Particularly in the case of routine work, close monitoring of employee performance is used to maintain high uniform rates of production. When the work involves the repetition of a relatively fixed pattern of physical motions (such as keying), prolonged work at a rapid pace can lead to repetitive strain injuries such as carpal tunnel syndrome and tendinitis.

In a study of the OHIP data-entry operators, forty-three out of forty-seven interviewees felt that had health problems related to their work. Musculo-skeletal complaints were the most common, focusing on the back, wrists, hands, and fingers (McDermott 1987).

A more general health problem that has been linked with automated surveillance is stress. Stress is a normal physiological response, but when it becomes chronic it can lead to mental and physical exhaustion, anxiety, and depression. In extreme cases it leads to serious illnesses such as coronary heart disease, high blood pressure, and ulcers. A study conducted by Bell Canada of its operators found that "AWT-items were most strongly linked to job stress by operators" and concluded that "it is likely that current AWT and monitoring practices have a negative effect on health" (Bell Canada 1987, 36). Another study of operators conducted in four provinces showed similar high stress levels and a specific link between monitoring and stress (Mosco and Zureik 1987). An investigation by Manitoba Telephone System, into the widely reported complaints by operators of "shock-like" incidents, found that the equipment was not at fault, as had originally been suspected. Instead, a high-level engineering and medical review concluded that the primary cause of the symptoms was "occupational stress." Both management and the union were convinced that this was for the most part due to the "highly repetitive, closely measured, high productivity" nature of operators' tasks (Manitoba Telephone System 1990, 2). Numerous studies in the U.S. (cited in U.S. Congress 1987) have also repeatedly pointed to a connection between computerized surveillance and job stress.

Stress not only arises from performing work under pressure, but is also linked to the amount of discretion employees exercise in their activities. A study by the National Institute of Occupational Safety and Health (NIOSH) found that clerical VDT operators showed higher stress levels than any other group of workers NIOSH had ever measured, including those popularly regarded as under high stress, such as air traffic controllers (NIOSH 1981). Part of the explanation for this finding is that although other occupations may be under more pressure given the serious consequences of mistakes, clerical workers experience greater stress since they have very little autonomy or control over their work. Surveillance systems, regardless of the routineness of the work, are typically used by management to remove effective control from employees and in this way contribute to unwelcome job stress (U.S. Congress 1987).

Workplace Relations

Automated surveillance can be detrimental not only to employees individually but also to the relationships among employees and between employees and their supervisors. Particularly when used to increase production, surveillance systems discourage social intercourse while encouraging employees to compete against each other in their race to avoid coming near the bottom of performance ratings. In one OHIP office, an operator described the daily posting of individual performance results as "pitting us against each other and embarrassing people." Another unpopular, and short-lived, management tactic was to reward high performers with roses. One recipient said she "felt like a fool carrying them out. My friend said to me, 'So what are we—chopped liver?'" (McDermott 1987, 36). Practices of this sort inhibit maintenance of the good interpersonal relationships that are often one of the more rewarding aspects of working life.

Social relationships between employees and their supervisors can also suffer. Automated surveillance makes increasingly possible what Zuboff terms "remote supervision." She reports that in one automated switching office, "most foremen acknowledged that they sometimes found themselves 'supervising' workers whom they had never seen" (1988, 332). Electronic monitoring takes over some of the work of supervisors, permitting them to take on increased spans of control, further distancing themselves from individual employees. Greater emphasis on quantitative, rather than on more "human" qualitative aspects of performance, is also encouraged by the use of electronically gathered statistics. All of these factors contribute to feelings of impersonality and formality. This process erodes the mutual understanding of personal problems and needs, hence undermining the reciprocity essential to effective working relations.

The spread of automated forms of surveillance can also have a detrimental effect on workplace relations at the labour/management level. New surveillance techniques often represent an attempt by managers to further remove effective control of the productive process from the employees who do the work and vest it in higher ranks of the organization. Although this result will be favoured by those who support the principle of managerial rights, organized labour and those who seek a greater democratization of work do not welcome the shift in control towards management. They will regard it as a setback in establishing the rights of workers to have a say in how enterprises are run.

Customer Service

Going beyond the workplace to consider the relationship between organizations and the people they are expected to serve, we can see further deleterious implications of automated surveillance. As work is speeded up and employees are made more conscious of the imperative to produce immediately quantifiable results, the more qualitative aspects are likely to suffer (Grant et al. 1988; Irving et al. 1986). Telephone operators, reservation agents, and other service workers report that because of the need to maintain monitored performance at high levels, they are less able to devote their attention to providing a good quality of service to their customers. In the Bell Canada study cited above, it was "difficulty in serving customers well and still keeping AWT down" that was found to be the most significant contributor to stress, with 70% of operators reporting this a factor to a "large or very large extent" (Bell Canada 1987, p. 17). Handling com-

plicated cases and emergencies often takes longer than dealing with a normal call and is more emotionally demanding, but the extra effort is not credited in automated accounting schemes. The degradation in service is also evident in the more routine transactions. As operators sound increasingly harassed and anxious to move on quickly, customers can begin to feel pressure on themselves to make calls brief and "efficient" and end up obtaining inadequate service.

Democratic Institutions

A further area of concern about the spread of automated workplace surveillance is the impact on democratic institutions in society. People's activities as citizens are influenced over time by their experiences at work. Participating fully in a democratic society requires practice in exercising initiative and thinking for oneself. Close surveillance stifles independent effort by promoting excessive conformance to norms established by higher-level authorities. Malinconico, summarizing Zuboff's findings on the supervision aspects of computer-mediated work, notes:

> People using on-line systems tended to limit their risk-taking behaviour, particularly with respect to deviation from standard practice. Conformity with the most complete prescriptions of a standard is a relatively unassailable practice. Less than complete adherence exposes one to the risk of defending the judgments upon which rests the decision to deviate from the standard. (1983)

Since many people find it hard to argue against the authoritative model embodied by the automated system, they tend to favour alternatives that are least likely to need justification. Zuboff further notes that automated forms of supervision may hide the real human authority behind the system since employees "can tend to see technology less as an instrument of authority than a source of it" (1982).

Automated surveillance is certainly not alone as a means for promoting conformity, obscuring power relations, and habituating submission to technical systems of control, but no one concerned for the viability of democratic institutions can welcome the spread of such a coercive technique in the workplace. This spread is particularly troublesome in the context of what some observers see as a general trend to a "surveillance society" based on information technology (Flaherty 1989; Gandy 1989). Gary Marx (1986) is concerned in particular that as democratic societies rely less on physical means of social control, they are using surveillance techniques to replace them with less violent forms that are also dangerous but more difficult to guard against.

It should be clear in this discussion that it is not mainly the use of computer systems *per se* that is responsible for these adverse implications. While computerization influences the character of the surveillance process, permits its wider application, and provides a potent symbolic focus for reaction, what is problematic is how management sometimes chooses to utilize the technique. Few question the legitimacy of managers' obtaining current and detailed information on production and organizational performance. The objections arise when this practice is applied to people in a way that is intrusive or otherwise violates common notions of personal privacy. As noted earlier, the conflict is between individual and collective human rights in the workplace, and management rights.

5. REMEDIAL POSSIBILITIES

As surveillance practices are intensified and spread, there are signs that opposition to them is increasing and remedial actions are being more vigorously sought. Alan Westin, a leading American authority on privacy protection, notes that privacy protection in the public realm:

> . . . has been the result not of *noblesse oblige* by organizational managers but of determined political campaigns by various privacy advocates and a strong concern over privacy by the publics of democratic nations. (1983)

Analogously we must expect that much of the initiative for workplace reforms will come from employees and their organizations.

Worker Resistance

Though automated surveillance is unpopular among many workers, the very nature of the settings in which it is most practised discourages individuals from articulating their objections and actively promoting alternatives. Instead, workplace reactions tend to be less overt, consisting mainly of passive resistance and sometimes sabotage. The most general reaction to unwelcome surveillance is a lowering of morale, with consequent loss of performance as people perform to the minimum that they can get away with. Workers will also attempt to "work around" those aspects of the measuring system that they find objectionable. In one insurance company, claims processing clerks reported that they routinely bypass standard procedures to "fool" the monitoring system into giving them credit for performing work that is not otherwise counted (Grant et al. 1988, 43). OHIP data-entry operators similarly took evasive action when managers attempted to tighten up the way in which keystrokes rates were calculated. Instead of dividing total keystrokes by the standard number of hours in the work week, management introduced a "time available" measure according to how long operators machines were actually turned on. The response by many operators was simply to switch their machines off every time they were not keying—even for ten or fifteen seconds. Management in the larger centres countered by introducing equipment that could not be turned off individually, but only centrally. In other settings they established that a minimum of 1,700 minutes per week be spent keying. Some operators, immediately began keeping their fingers on the space bar during breaks to keep their numbers looking good (Clement and McDermott 1991).

In some cases management has reacted to resistance by abandoning or lessening their surveillance practices (Irving et al. 1986); however, we see from this example that it can also lead to an unproductive cycle of measure and counter-measure. In either case, these forms of resistance are limited in their potential to lead to substantive, widespread reform. In addition to individualized, covert reaction, workers also turn to collective forms of action where individuals are better protected, greater force can be exerted, and the issue can be addressed more comprehensively.

Collective Bargaining

Several Canadian unions representing workers particularly subject to computerized surveillance have made it an important issue for collective bargaining. So far, the Canadian Union of Postal Workers (CUPW) is the only major Canadian union to have negotiated contract language that protects its members from individualized work monitoring. After two weeks of national strike action in 1975 in which work measurement was a major issue, the following provision was agreed upon:

> 39.10 Group Measurement
> It is recognized that volume measurement is necessary to obtain an objective evaluation of the level of production of employees in an office or section. In the application of this article, there shall be no group measurement of employees for a homogeneous group of ten (10) employees or less.

This clause has been highly contentious—it was removed at a time strikes were prohibited by law and has subsequently been reinstated. The Communications and Electrical Workers of Canada (CWC) has throughout the 1980s attempted to negotiate with Bell Canada similar limitations on individualized performance measures and monitoring. In 1986/87, a joint labour/management health and safety committee oversaw the Operator Stress Study (Bell Canada 1987), which highlighted the negative effects of

AWT-related practices and monitoring. These were still major issues in the 1988 strike, which lasted ten days (Edwards 1988), and although no formal resolution was achieved, Bell did agree on a trial to end the use of individual AWT measurement and instead assess production on the basis of group performance (Coutts 1989). After one year of the experiment, a Bell study showed that operators felt less stressed, service quality had increased, and morale had improved significantly without adverse effect on productivity (Coutts 1990). However, in spite of these results and the sustained pressure from the union, Bell still did not agree to formalize this arrangement in contract language in the 1991 bargaining.

A similar story has taken place in negotiations between Air Canada and the Canadian Auto Workers (CAW), which now represents the reservation agents. Bargaining resulted in a Letter of Understanding that sought to reduce stress by limiting the use of individual performance statistics. In particular, discipline was excluded as a "primary" purpose for this data collection. However, a 1990 study conducted by the union indicated that about 40% of agents felt that the electronic measurement and call monitoring were still used for this purpose (Robertson and Wareham 1990).

Perhaps the most successful of such initiatives to reform highly routinized, closely monitored jobs is the "Trial Office" project at Manitoba Telephone System, which was instituted after it was found that shocks were caused not by equipment failure but by the excessively stressful working conditions. A joint management/labour team established a new operator services office for experimenting with a wide range of job design innovations. Among these were the transfer of major supervisor functions to the operators and the elimination of individual AWT reports. The Trial Office has been the source of several significant job changes implemented in 1990 throughout Operator Services following the ratification of a joint Memorandum of Agreement (Manitoba Telephone System and Communications and Electrical Workers of Canada internal document 1990). It is still operating after three years.

Because of the legislation governing most government workers in Ontario (the Crown Employees Collective Bargaining Act—CECBA), the Ontario Public Service Employees Union (OPSEU), which represents the OHIP data-entry operators discussed earlier, is prohibited from bargaining over technological changes. In seeking a way around these legal restrictions, OPSEU has tried unsuccessfully to have the issue of surveillance resolved by the Ontario Ombudsman. On its fourth appeal to the Ontario Public Service Labour Relations Tribunal, it was successful in obtaining the right to bargain over the elimination of electronic monitoring. The government opposed this move on the grounds that the proposal "infringes the Employers' exclusive jurisdiction to determine work methods and procedures and appraisals" (OPSLRT 1989, 13); nevertheless, the Tribunal agreed with the union's position that its main objective was to protect the health and safety of its members, and hence within the bargaining scope of CECBA. However, since this 1989 ruling it has made no progress on actual bargaining, partly because most of the data-entry jobs have themselves been eliminated.

Overall, Canadian unions have made remarkably slow progress in bargaining protection from automated workplace surveillance. Even when research indicates that performance need not suffer, relatively powerful, persistent unions have been unable to negotiate effective contract language on this matter. Their failure likely reflects a great reluctance on the part of management to concede on issues that reduce the "management rights" provisions common to all collective agreements. It suggests that collective bargaining as a forum is limited in its promise for substantial reform. The alternative is to seek protection through legislation. For the approximately 60% of Canadian workers who are not unionized, including the great majority of private-sector office workers, legislation offers the only formal protective mechanism.

Legislation

The most obvious place to seek legal protection from surveillance is in privacy legislation; yet it has proven to be of little help. In the U.S., what privacy rights citizens have in the public arena do not extend to the workplace. This position was expressed in an extreme form by an American arbitrator in the case of FMC Corp. vs. UAW:

> The right of privacy concerns an individual's right not to have his statements, actions, etc., made public without his consent. But this serves only to protect him against the publication of his PRIVATE statements of PRIVATE actions. It should be evident that an employee's actions during working hours are NOT PRIVATE actions. (Mittenthal 1966)

In Canada, with its weaker constitutional notions of privacy, the situation is no better. A private legal opinion (1983) on the subject of electronic employee surveillance, which considered the common-law right to privacy, criminal law limitations to electronic surveillance (e.g., wiretapping), constitutional law limitations (e.g., Charter of Rights and Freedoms), and human rights legislation (e.g., Canadian Human Rights Code), advised a union representing telephone operators that:

> . . . electronic performance monitoring and the subsequent use of the information obtained is within the bounds of management rights. *Legal* redress is most unlikely. (emphasis in original)

More recently, David Flaherty has noted that although "the federal Charter of Rights and Freedoms is not explicit about privacy, certain sections have been used by the Supreme Court of Canada to recognize a right to privacy" (1991, 844). He observes, however, that so far such judgments apply primarily to "government" action and not the workplace (1992, personal communication). Since existing laws provide virtually no protection, several proposals have been made for legislation that specifically restricts electronic surveillance of individual workers. The 1982 Labour Canada Task Force on Microelectronics and Employment heard submissions on this matter and concluded:

> . . . close monitoring of work is an employment practice based on mistrust and lack of respect for basic human dignity. It is an infringement on the rights of the individual, an undesirable precedent that might be extended to other environments unless restrictions are put in place now. We strongly recommend that this practice be prohibited by law.

However, these recommendations were not accepted by the federal government, and legislation introduced in British Columbia, Ontario, and Saskatchewan to ban individual monitoring has failed to pass.

In the U.S., legislation with the more modest goals of requiring employers to inform workers of impending monitoring and provide them with access to their records has fared little better. A West Virginia law was passed in 1983, but then repealed in 1986 when AT&T threatened to build a new management centre in another state (U.S. Congress 1987). Similar legislation, entitled The Privacy of Consumers and Workers Act, is currently before the U.S. Congress (*Harvard Law Review* 1991; Lacayo 1991).

European legislation provides an interesting contrast to these faltering North American initiatives. In countries with co-determination laws, Acts promoting a healthy work environment express the aim of avoiding individualized monitoring but leave it up to labour and management to work out the details. For instance, Section 22 of regulations implementing Norway's Act Respecting Worker's Protection and Work Environment (1977) states:

> Registration of data for quantity and quality of work for the individual employee shall preferably be avoided.

While monitoring is generally restricted to the group level, in some cases unions have agreed to individual monitoring to prevent theft. In Germany, Works Councils consisting of worker representatives elected at every enterprise with more than nineteen employees, are empowered by law to co-determine:

> . . . the introduction and use of technical installations that are intended to monitor conduct or performance of employees. (U.S. Congress 1987, 123)

In 1986, the Supreme Labour Court ruled that even the mere *capability* of monitoring was sufficient to require Works Council approval for the introduction of technology. This is in keeping with the Constitutional Court's recognition in 1983 of the "fundamental right of informational self-determination" (Flaherty 1989, 46). According to a leading German Data Commissioner, the Constitution thus gives individuals, in the workplace as elsewhere, "the right to decide when and under what circumstances [their] personal data may be processed" (Flaherty 1989, 377).

All European Community (EC) countries must also conform to the privacy protection conventions adopted by the Council of Europe and its successor, the Council of the European Communities. Unlike North American laws, this legislation is comprehensive in scope—applying both to the private and public sectors and all data subjects, whether as citizens, consumers, or employees. According to the official recommendations made to member states, "personal data covers any information relating to an identified individual." Systems for the handling of such personal data must conform to the generally accepted principles of fair information practice. Furthermore, "employers should, in advance, fully inform and consult their employees or the representatives of the latter about the introduction or adaptation of automated systems for the collection and use of personal data of employees." Where this consultation "reveals a possibility of infringement of employees' right to respect for privacy and human dignity," employee agreement must also be sought (Council of Europe 1989, 27). A more recent and more broadly focused Directive of the Council of the EC, which attempts to harmonize data protection legislation among member states, further strengthens the universality of privacy principles—notably the necessity for the informed consent of the data subject (Council of the EC 1990).

North Americans might be the indirect beneficiaries of this European legislation. Since all companies operating in the EC have to abide by these directives, and since the transmission of personal data, including electronic funds transfer, to countries that do not have "adequate" privacy protection is prohibited, there will be growing pressure to bring Canadian legislation up to this standard (Rideout 1992). Even if this requirement leads to nothing more than a simple recognition that employees have privacy rights that are not automatically superseded by management rights, that would be welcome progress.

Privacy Principles in Information Systems, Work, and Organization Design

Regardless of whatever collective agreements or legislation may become established, what matters ultimately is the nature of the jobs that employees actually perform. Their nature depends upon the design of information systems, the related work practices, and their organizational context. This conception obviously takes us well beyond considerations relating only to computerized surveillance, but the above discussion does suggest some specific design principles concerning the creation and use of information about employees to guide this wider design effort. The aim is to take fuller advantage of the new managerial possibilities offered by computerized performance monitoring while minimizing its harmful effects. Principles should be applicable across a range of work settings and surveillance practices—from sweatshops to fishbowls.

Although the complete avoidance of individual monitoring is in important respects a worth-

while goal, it is likely an infeasible and too drastic approach in many settings. It is an attempt to avoid potentially objectionable surveillance practices by eliminating the source of data upon which surveillance depends. In this regard, it is similar to gun control legislation, which is based on regulating access to devices as a means of regulating socially unacceptable behaviour. However, unlike with guns, the technology of electronic monitoring is often an intrinsic part of everyday production and plays an essential operational role. Even in the sweatshop settings of most intense surveillance, to isolate the adverse effects of monitoring from other aspects of the job design, such as work pace and monotony, is difficult. Furthermore, as we have seen pragmatically, management will not, except in the most extreme cases, give up what it sees as its fundamental right to measure the performance of individual employees. Indeed, few would argue that managers cannot take reasonable steps to determine how well employees are performing in the jobs they were hired to do. What we seek instead are more subtle approaches for achieving a balance between employee and managerial information interests in various situations. Such approaches should result in information handling practices that respect employees' needs for privacy, dignity, and autonomy while providing managers with the information they need to guide the overall enterprise. These practices may act as a check on excessive managerial authority, but without challenging its legitimate role.

An appropriate starting point for the design of computerized workplaces is the recognition that employees have a right to privacy based on the fundamental notions of informational self-determination and informed consent. At a minimum, this means that the widely recognized principles of "fair information practice" (Flaherty 1989) apply to information on individuals when at work as much as in their dealings as citizens with governments. Each employee should be informed of all individualized data collection and the purposes to which it would be put. Collection, processing, and retention of personal data should be kept to the minimum necessary for meeting legitimate, well-defined management aims. In particular, information that was merely suggestive of work performance should be avoided (Rule, personal communication). Purposes other than the stated ones would not be permitted without employee approval. Records would be open to the employee, who could also challenge them and have them corrected if deemed necessary.

Such fair information principles should be welcomed by many managers. They should not be seen simply as an additional burden, but as entirely consistent with sound, efficient information management. While they may prevent some ad hoc "snooping" in fishbowl environments, they do little to inhibit employee surveillance. Indeed, by helping avoid blatant abuse, they can make monitoring more legitimate and hence facilitate its wider acceptance.

However, because these principles do not in themselves actually affect the jobs concerned, they are limited in their value for reforming surveillance practices. They were developed initially to regulate relatively static information stored in permanent databases. In work settings time scales can be much shorter—especially in multi-media fishbowl settings, where sensitive data may be broadcast instantly to large numbers of people without ever being stored. Hence principles for dealing with the timing of access need also to be considered. The relative sequencing of information access by managers and employees is likely to be very important.

Task feedback offers a prime example of how electronically obtained information may serve to lessen the need for managerial surveillance. It is a well-established principle of good job design that employees need timely feedback to be able to regulate their own performance effectively. If this feedback arrives mainly via supervisors when performance is poor, it is inevitably burdened by the potential for reproach and coercion. Employees should have immediate, neutral feedback on how well they are doing, and in the case of quantitative measures such feedback is best provided directly from the computerized systems. As employees in several studies cited earlier (Clement and McDermott 1991; Irving et al. 1986; Robertson and Wareham 1990) have requested, they should be able to view any of the data they have generated, and see how they compare with co-workers and with established norms. This procedure would help restore some of the self-monitoring capabilities that are an intrinsic part of manual work but have to be deliberately built into computerized systems (Matthews 1989, 119). With appropriate measures, employees should be able to regulate their own activities to meet managerial expectations while reducing the need for supervisory intervention. Indeed, as employees are better able to manage their own performance, the cost of providing thorough feedback could be offset by lower supervision costs.

A further step away form surveillance involves designing the reporting system so that as long as employees are able to maintain results that are within previously established limits, supervisors would not have access to fine-grained statistics about them. Monthly or annual performance reviews would of course still be possible, but they would use data aggregated over the relevant time period. With this preferential access to information, employees could negotiate their own "privacy zones" within which they could exercise a significant degree of autonomy in carrying out work tasks. The same principle could be applied to work groups, enabling greater local self-management. Fishbowl environments could be especially suitable for group self-management, whereby a wide range of performance and behavioural information would be readily available to all members as a way to maintain the mutual awareness useful for coordinated activity. Adopting a principle of reciprocal access rights would help maintain equity within the group and limit the dangers from wider dissemination. Information would only be made available to those who in turn provided like access (Borning and Travers 1991).

These informational principles of workplace privacy—fair information practices, preferential feedback, and reciprocity—are intended to provide a useful framework for designing the monitoring aspects of computerized jobs. However, they do not address the equally vital question of the design process itself. As the European co-determination legislation explicitly recognizes, whenever systems are introduced that are capable of monitoring individual employees, the employees must have an effective voice in their development. For other reasons too, there is growing attention to the value of having users participate directly in systems development. This interest is being accompanied by an expanding body of knowledge about how it can be done (Bjerknes, Ehn and Kyng 1987; Greenbaum and Kyng 1991).

6. CONCLUSIONS

A central challenge in dealing with workplace computerization is how to take best advantage of the "informating" potential of computer-based production techniques (Zuboff 1988). Computerized employee surveillance is perhaps the area in which this issue is posed most sharply. On the one hand it represents a potent means for violating the privacy of employees and subordinating them to managerial authority—whether in a drive to enhance production or promote conformity to official norms. On the other hand, it provides the technical means for new forms of management in which employees can exercise greater influence over production. Computerized monitoring could provide a valuable ingredient for the democratic operation of modern, thoroughly computerized enterprises.

The experience with electronic surveillance in Canada over the past decade does not offer grounds for optimism that the latter vision will soon prove to be the norm. The protracted struggles and slow progress in reforming the most visible examples of computerized surveillance indicate that well-established patterns of managerial authority will not be relinquished easily. In the absence of a fundamental change in approach, the continued spread of information technologies suggests that computerized surveillance will likely grow and with it the ongoing controversy. We should expect the calls for legislation and approaches to systems development that recognize the rights of people to privacy and control in the workplace to intensify. They are a welcome sign and should be encouraged.

While the debate shows little sign of resolution, one thing does seem clear. Information technologies now offer great flexibility in terms of who has access to what employee information and when. The computerized jobs and organizations we are creating are less and less constrained by particular technological forms. Increasingly they reflect social choices about workplace relations in an advanced information society.

REFERENCES

Archer, Lawrence. 1985. I saw what you did and I know who you are. *Canadian Business,* November: 76-82.

Ashby, W. Ross. 1956. *Introduction to cybernetics.* University Paperbacks.

Attewell, Paul. 1987. Big Brother and the sweatshop: Computer surveillance in the automated office. *Sociological Theory,* Spring: 87-99.

Beer, Stafford. 1959. *Cybernetics and management.* New York: John Wiley and Sons.

Bell Canada Ltd. 1987. *Operator stress survey—a corporate health and safety committee report.* Communications and Electrical Workers of Canada, Bell Canada Ltd.

Beniger, James. 1991. *The control revolution: Technical and economic origins of the information society.* Boston: Harvard University Press.

Bjerknes, Gro, Pelle Ehn, and Morten Kyng. 1987. *Computers and democracy: A Scandinavian challenge.* Aldershot: Avebury.

Bjorn-Andersen, Niels. 1983. Office work. In *New Office technology: Human and organizational aspects,* ed. H.J. Otway and M. Peltu.

Borning, Alan, and Michael Travers. 1991. Two approaches to casual interaction over computer and video networks. In *Proceedings of CHI'91, New Orleans, April 28-May 2,* 13-19. New York: ACM.

Braverman, Harry. 1974. *Labour and monopoly capital.* New York: Monthly Review Press.

Canadian Airline Employees Association. 1982. *Submission to the Task Force on Micro-Electronics and Employment.* Halifax: Canadian Airline Employees Association.

Canadian Office. 1983. Advertisement for Hecon Canada, 55.

Chandler, Alfred D. 1977. *The visible hand: The managerial revolution in American business.* Boston: Harvard University Press.

Clement, Andrew. 1984. Electronic management: The new technology of workplace surveillance. *Proceedings of the Canadian Information Processing Society National Conference, Calgary, May 9-11,* 259-68.

Clement, Andrew. 1986. Managerial control and on-line processing at a large insurance firm. Ph.D. dissertation, Dept. of Computer Science, University of Toronto.

Clement, Andrew, and Patricia McDermott. 1991. Electronic monitoring: Worker reaction and design alternatives. In *Information system, work and organization design,* ed. P. van den Besselaar, A. Clement, and P. Jarvinen, 187-99. Amsterdam: North-Holland.

Council of Europe, Committee of Ministers. 1989. Protection of personal data used for employment purposes. *Transnational Data and Communications Report* 12(3): 26-28.

Council of the European Communities. 1990. Proposal for a Council Directive concerning the protection of individuals in relation to the processing of personal data. *Official Journal of the European Communities* 90/C 277/03, 5 November: 3-12.

Coutts, Jane. 1989. Bell stops snooping on its operators. *Globe and Mail,* 14 September.

Coutts, Jane. 1990. Bell finds morale improved since monitoring stopped. *Globe and Mail,* 22 February, A14.

Edwards, Peter. 1988. Big Brother control over jobs bugs Bell workers. *Toronto Star,* 6 July, A20.

Ellis, S.R. 1979. Re Puretex Knitting Co. Ltd. 23 Ontario LAC (2d), 14.

Flaherty, David H. 1989. *Protecting privacy in surveillance societies.* Chapel Hill: University of North Carolina Press.

Flaherty, David H. 1991. On the utility of constitutional rights to privacy and data protection. *Case Western Reserve Law Review* 41: 831-55.

Foucault, Michel. 1977. *Discipline and punish.* Pantheon.

Gandy, Oscar. 1989. The surveillance society: Information technology and bureaucratic control. *Journal of Communication* 39(3): 61-77.

Garson, Barbara. 1988. *The electronic sweatshop: How computers are turning the office of the future into the factory of the past.* New York: Simon and Shuster.

Glen, Ron. 1991. E-mail voyeurism. *Canadian Datasystems,* October: 57-58.

Globe and Mail. 1981. Rockwell International advertisement, 2 September.

Grant, Rebecca A., and Chris A. Higgins. 1991. The impact of computerized performance monitoring on service work: Testing a causal model. *Information Systems Research* 2(2): 116-42.

Grant, Rebecca A., Christopher A. Higgins, and Richard H. Irving. 1988. Computerized performance monitors: Are they costing you customers? *Sloan Management Review* 29(3): 31-45.

Greenbaum, Joan, and Morten Kyng. 1991. *Design at work: Cooperative design of computer systems.* Lawrence Erlbaum.

Hafner, Katie, Susan Garland, and John Hoerr. 1988. Privacy: Companies are delving further into employees' personal lives—and workers are fighting harder for the right to be left alone. *Business Week,* 28 March, 61-68.

Harvard Law Review (Editorial). 1991. Addressing the new hazards of the high technology workplace. *Harvard Law Review* 104: 1896-1916.

Hoos, Ida. 1961. *Automation in the office.* Washington.

Irving, R.H., C.A. Higgins, and F.R. Safayeni. 1986. Computerized performance monitoring systems: Use and abuse. *Communications of the ACM* 29(8): 794-801.

Kilborn, Peter T. 1990. Workers using computers find a supervisor inside. *New York Times,* 23 December, 1-13.

Kling, Rob, and Suzi Iacono. 1984. Computerization as an occasion for social control. *Journal of Social Issues* 40(3): 77-96.

Labour Canada. Task Force on Micro-Electronics and Employment. 1982. *In the chips: Opportunities, people, partnerships: Report of the Labour Canada Task Force on Micro-Electronics and Employment.* Ottawa: Labour Canada.

Lacayo, Richard. 1991. Nowhere to hide: Using computers, high-tech gadgets and mountains of data, a growing army of snoops is waging an assault on America's privacy. *Time,* 11 November, 40-46.

Larter, George. 1984. Electronic monitoring causes VDT stress. *VDT Newsletter* 2(3): 2.

List, Wilfred. 1986. Electronic monitoring sparks new debate in the workplace. *Globe and Mail,* 26 September, B2.

Malinconico, S. Michael. 1983. Hearing the resistance. *Library Journal,* 15 January: 111-113.

Mantei, M., R. Baecker, A. Sellen, W. Buxton, T. Milligan, and B. Wellman. 1991. Experiences in the use of a media space. In *Proceedings of CHI'91, New Orleans, April 28-May 2,* 203-208. New York: ACM.

Marglin, Stephen. 1974. What do bosses do? The origins and functions of hierarchy in capitalist production. *Review of Radical Political Economics* 6(Summer): 60-112.

Marx, Gary T. 1986. The iron fist and the velvet glove: Totalitarian potentials within democratic structures. In *The social fabric: Dimensions and issues,* ed. James E. Short, 1235-62. Beverly Hills, CA: Sage Publications.

Marx, Gary T., J. Moderow, SW. Zuboff, B. Howard, and K. Nussbaum. 1990. The case of the omniscient organization: Dominion-Swann management acquires technology to support employees— or control them? *Harvard Business Review,* March/April: 12-30.

Mathews, John. 1989. *Tools of change: New technology and the democratisation of work.* Sydney, NSW: Pluto Press.

McDermott, Patricia. 1987. *The differential impact of computerization on office workers: A qualitative investigation of 'screen assisted' VDT users.* Toronto: Ontario Public Service Employees Union.

Mitel Corporation. 1980. *SUPERSWITCH product bulletin.* Mitel Corporation.

Mittenthal, Richard. 1966. FMC Corp. vs. U.A.W. 66-1 CCH Lab Arb Awards, para. 8287.

Mosco, Vincent, and Elia Zureik. 1987. Computers and the workplace: Technological change in the telephone industry. Part III: Summary and analysis of depth interviews, 75-126. Unpublished manuscript.

Mowshowitz, Abbe. 1983. *Social change in the computer revolution.* Troy, NY: Rensselaer Polytechnic Institute, Science and Technology Studies Division.

NIOSH. 1981. Health consequences of video viewing. San Francisco study. *National Institute for Occupational Safety and Health,* February.

Noble, David F. 1984. *Forces of production: A social history of industrial automation.* New York: Knopf.

Ontario Ministry of Labour, Research Branch. 1979. *Electronic surveillance: A discussion paper.* Toronto: Ontario Ministry of Labour, Research Branch.

Papp, Leslie. 1991. Working under the electronic eye: Is it Big Brother or a necessary management tool? *Toronto Star,* 27, D1-D5.

Rideout, Vanda. 1992. *The Implications of Information Technology on Personal Privacy, Report to Strategic Planning Division,* Ottawa: Department of Communications.

Rifkin, Glenn. 1991. Do employees have a right to electronic privacy? *New York Times,* 8 December, F8.

Robertson, David, and Jeff Waveham. 1990. *Technological change: Air Canada customer sales and service.* CAW Technology Report. Don Mills, ON: CAW.

Robins, Kevin, and Frank Webster. 1991. Cybernetic capitalism. In *The Political Economy of Information,* ed. Vincent Mosco and Janet Wasko. Madison: University of Wisconsin Press.

Rothfeder, Jeffrey, Michele Galen, and Lisa Driscoll. 1990. Is your boss spying on you? High-tech snooping in 'the electronic sweatshop'. *Business Week,* 15 January: 74-75.

Rule, James, and Paul Attewell. 1989. What do computers do? *Social Problems* 36(3): 225-41.

Rule, James, and Peter Brantley. 1992. Computerized surveillance in the workplace: Forms and distributions. *Sociological Forum* 7(3).

U.S. Congress, OTA. 1987. *The electronic supervisor: New technology, new tensions.* Washington: OTA-CIT-333, U.S. Government Printing Office.

Weiner, Norbert. 1948. *Cybernetics or control and communication in the animal and machine.* Cambridge: MIT Press.

Weiser, Mark. 1991. The computer for the 21st century. *Scientific American,* September: 94-104.

Westin, Alan. 1983. New issues in privacy in the eighties. In *Information Processing '83,* ed. Mason, 733-39. Amsterdam: North Holland.

Zuboff, Shoshana. 1982. New worlds of computer mediated work. *Harvard Business Review,* September/October: 142-52.

Zuboff, Shoshana. 1988. *In the age of the smart machine: The future of work and power.* Basic Books.

CHAPTER 9

"Somebody's Going to Get Hurt." Whistleblowing: Employee Loyalty and Dissent

INTRODUCTION

In many instances, whistleblowers have brought the ethical lapses of corporations and government agencies before the public eye. Through their efforts we have learned about unsafe products, government waste, corporate fraud, kickbacks, lax safety inspections, and so on. In some ways, it all seems very clear—the heroic individual versus the System, moral David versus corporate Goliath. We imagine that whistleblowers would be treated as public heroes. Surprisingly, they are villainized, not lionized, which should alert us to the possibility that there is more involved in whistleblowing than meets the eye.

The origin of the term "whistleblowing" is the action of a sports official blowing a whistle to call time out and to assess a penalty when a rules infraction occurs. Though the metaphor is straightforward, the concept and definition of whistleblowing are variously interpreted. Two types of whistleblowing are either explicitly drawn or implied in all of the readings in this chapter. **Internal** whistleblowing occurs when a member of an organization reports suspected wrongdoing *within* the organization, either

through the customary chain of command (e.g., reporting it to his or her supervisor) or outside the chain of command (e.g., reporting it to a higher-up, such as a company ethics officer or an ombudsperson). The **external** whistleblower reports his or her observations and assessments to someone *outside* the company (e.g., a government official, reporter, or lawyer) who the whistleblower believes can either help correct the wrongs being done or prevent future harms.

Both types of whistleblower are accused of being the "class snitch," though the charge is more often leveled against the external whistleblower. The whistleblower's detractors allege that he or she has a duty to be a member of a team, to be loyal—a formal duty to the organization and an informal duty to colleagues—and that he or she fails to live up to that duty. Consider one such description from the former chairman of the board of General Motors.

Some critics are now busy eroding another support of free enterprise—the loyalty of a management team, with its unifying values of cooperative work. Some of the enemies of business now encourage an employee to be disloyal to the enterprise. They want to create suspicion and disharmony, and pry into the proprietary interests of the business. However this is labelled—industrial espionage, whistleblowing, or professional responsibility—it is another tactic for spreading disunity and creating conflict (James Roche, qtd. in Boatright, 1993, p. 134).

As intemperate as such language sounds, the critics do have a point. In their roles as employees or managers people do have a legal and ethical duty of loyalty to the organizations for which and in which they work; they have an obligation to promote the best interests of those firms and businesses that pay their salaries.

What the critics fail to see, however, is that these ethical duties, though real, are *prima facie,* that is, as we saw in Chapter 1, they can be overridden by other, more ethically pressing, obligations and duties. Critics of whistleblowers often base their argument on a mistaken version of utilitarianism; that is, in their calculation of benefits and harms they restrict the people whose interests are taken into account to members of the organization. The whistleblower reminds them and us that this is too narrow. Members of the larger community have a right to have their interests taken into account as well. Corporate benefit does not justify public harm.

Whistleblowing must be viewed from the perspectives of the organization, the whistleblower him- or herself, and the general public. Each has its interests, its rights, and its responsibilities. The organization has a right to the loyalty and commitment of its employees. At the same time, it has an obligation to protect the interests of the public whom it serves and to create a culture in which its employees can protect those public interests without being considered disloyal or suffering reprisals.

Whistleblowers have rights and obligations to themselves, their families, their employers, and the public. Weighing these different obligations and rights is often an extraordinarily difficult task, but it is one that the conscientious whistleblower must undertake. Similarly, organizational managers have a responsibility to their

employees to provide safe and fair avenues for them to communicate suspected wrongdoing. This responsibility is consistent not only with the manager's fiduciary obligation to key stakeholders (e.g., stockholders), but also with the long-term success of the enterprise. Those who study whistleblowing point out that, while whistleblowers may cause short-term discomfort to top managers forced to deal with difficult realities, they often speak for the higher ideals of the organization and the longer-term perspective.

★ ★ ★

In the readings that we have selected, **Barbara Ettore** relates several anecdotes showing the risks involved to the career of the whistleblower, which to her is evidence of a deficiency of ethics in business life and in American culture in general. **Marcia Miceli** and **Janet Near** agree with Ettore's assessment and point out that organizations need to take a proactive position with respect to issues that create the need for whistleblowing, focusing on ways to create a climate that encourages employees to recognize and to respond to wrongdoing. In short, they must find ways to insure that *internal* whistleblowing is effective. **Kevin Smith** and **John Oseth** examine society's response to the perception that "unscrupulous business practices may jeopardize important public interests." After exploring the different federal and state statutes, common-law protections, and sentencing guidelines designed to protect whistleblowers from reprisals and to encourage businesses and other organizations to promote internal whistleblowing, they suggest several concrete steps that businesses and managers can take to stay within the law. **Mike Martin** recalls the career and social risks to which the whistleblower is exposed and argues that he or she has both a right and a duty to take the personal burdens of whistleblowing into account in her or his ethical analysis and decision-making. In weighing Martin's opinions you may wish to consider the views of John Simon and his coauthors (presented in Chapter 1) concerning the conditions under which we have a positive ethical duty to help an individual or group.

REFERENCES

Boatright, John. (1993) *Ethics and the Conduct of Business.* Englewood Cliffs: Prentice-Hall.

CASE: Jill LeBlanc and the Research Grant

Jill LeBlanc was stunned. She had just been fired, and she didn't know what to do. Her supervisor and mentor, Dr. Bill Elliott, had just informed her that, because of an incident that took place while she was working on the renovation of the computer lab, she "no longer enjoyed his full confidence." He told her that he appreciated her abilities and the work she had done, but that her services would no longer be required. He added that he hoped that there would be no hard feelings and that he would be glad to serve as a reference in any future job search. As she left his office, she wondered about the events of the past two years and what she should do next.

BACKGROUND

Three years earlier, Jill had gone to work for the Department of Naval Architecture at Northern Virginia State University after she had received her undergraduate degree from the same department and university. She had worked as a research assistant on various departmental research projects for those three years and had hopes of continuing such work throughout her doctoral program, which she had begun in the previous academic year. The project she was now working on was funded by a three-year grant from a large federal agency and involved the development of specialized software for use

Source: Pradeep Viswarkumar and Joy Durand prepared this case under the supervision of Professor Edward Ottensmeyer as a basis for class discussion rather than to illustrate either effective or ineffective handling of an administrative situation. The case is based on actual events, but the names of individuals and organizations have been disguised.

in naval architecture. She was very pleased to be involved with such a sophisticated endeavor and excited to be working under the supervision of Dr. Bill Elliott, who, at thirty-seven, had already developed a considerable reputation in the field. She was particularly grateful that Dr. Elliott had taken an interest in her career and had organized her work assignments with an eye to enhancing her professional growth.

Research projects of this type were crucial both to the department and to the university, and there was intense competition among universities to obtain them. This was the first such grant awarded to the Department of Naval Architecture. It represented a significant source of support; in particular, the capital equipment acquired for the project would be retained by the department when the project was completed. The success of the current project was crucial in clearing the way for the approval of the next one, which was being prepared for submission. Jill hoped that the next project would be approved by the time their current work was completed, since her job depended upon the availability of grant funds like these.

Dr. Bill Elliott was himself a graduate of Northern Virginia and had returned there to join the faculty after receiving his doctorate from a prestigious university. An energetic and gifted man, he had been named Chair of the department five years ago and had since built the department's resources and reputation. He had been the key person involved in obtaining the software contract. In addition, he served as a consultant to a number of shipyards and frequently asked Jill to assist him on these outside projects. She was grateful for both the experience and the extra money.

Dr. Elliott, as principal investigator on the grant, had full control of the use of the project funds. He had decided that the department's computer equipment needed to be upgraded, not only to complete the current project but to give the department the resources to compete successfully for future projects.

The usual procedure for beginning work of this sort was to request sealed bids from prospective suppliers. These bids were then evaluated, and the supplier that had the lowest bid and met all of the technical criteria was awarded the contract. During the bidding process, representatives from the competing suppliers visited and talked to the people who would make the funding decisions. This was to insure the bidder fully understood what the department was looking for. The suppliers used these visits to strike up personal relationships with departmental representatives, in the hope that it would give them an "edge" when decisions were being made. The department, for its part, could make use of the visits to make sure that it fully understood the bidders' proposals.

THE PROJECT

The initial phase of the project was to proceed in two stages. The first involved the purchase and installation of five state-of-the-art computer workstations to provide support during the time the lab would be closed for renovations. The second stage called for the purchase and installation of a specialized mini-computer, linked to twenty-five terminals. The company that Dr. Elliott chose to supply the personal computers in the first stage was a new firm. Jill remembered that the firm had been very anxious to get the contract since it wanted to establish contacts at the university so that it could compete more efficiently with older, more established suppliers for future projects.

Jill had no concerns with the process until the machines were delivered. On checking the computers she found that they did not have the memory requirements specified in the contract. She informed Dr. Elliott of what she had discovered, but he seemed unconcerned and simply told her that he would take care of the situation. A month passed. When Jill mentioned it again to Dr. Elliott, he said that he had talked to the local sales representative and that the matter would be rectified soon. Another month went by and nothing happened.

Meanwhile, on her own initiative, Jill called the local representative twice and, upon mentioning the memory problem, got what she saw as evasive replies. She was genuinely concerned, in part because Dr. Elliott seemed preoccupied with other matters. Finally, after consulting with a colleague in the university purchasing department, Jill wrote a letter to the company's regional headquarters and informed them of the situation and her intention to bring it to the attention of university authorities. Less than a week after she sent the letter, Jill was called into Dr. Elliott's office. He reminded her that he, not she, was the project coordinator, and that he had already resolved the matter with the local sales representative. All her letter had done, he said, was to create confusion.

Puzzled and feeling chastised, Jill left the office. The renovation of the computer facilities proceeded according to plan, and everyone congratulated Dr. Elliott on the splendid job he had done. With the renovation behind them, Jill concentrated on completing the remaining stages of the project. She noticed a certain "coolness" in Dr. Elliott's behavior toward her, but chalked it up to her having overstepped her responsibilities with the computer supplier.

As the second year of the project was coming to an end, Jill was preparing the data for the progress report required by the funding agency. In the course of this work, she reviewed the files of the renovation project. She noticed that the original bids of the winning computer supplier, of which there were photocopies, differed from the bids that were finally submitted. She suspected that after the bids were opened someone had allowed the firm to resubmit its bids so that it would be marginally lower than the other bids. As she remembered it, no one had access to these files during this period other than Dr. Elliott. But Jill reminded herself that she couldn't be absolutely sure of this.

JILL'S DILEMMA

Jill was unsure of what to think or what to do. After a week of fretting about her discovery, she decided to approach a faculty member in the same department whom she felt she could trust. After listening to her story, he told her that she had no real evidence of any wrongdoing, and that apparent bookkeeping "glitches" were fairly common with grant funds. He asked her to take a realistic look at what she might achieve by pursuing the matter. He advised her further that if she hoped to continue working in the department on future projects, it might be better for her to do the job for which she was hired and not worry about what he termed "peripheral matters" like purchasing computer equipment. Even if something were "slightly amiss," he said that she would not get much support from anyone in the department since everyone was delighted with Bill Elliott's leadership.

Jill came away from this meeting uncertain what, if anything, she might do. As she was considering her options the following morning, she received a note from Dr. Elliott asking her to come to his office for a short meeting. Four hours later, the fateful meeting took place, and she lost her job.

JILL AND THE ETHICS OFFICE

After her meeting with Dr. Elliott, Jill was very upset and not at all sure she had done anything

to deserve this fate. The next day, still troubled and disappointed, she arranged a meeting with the university ethics officer. Mary O'Brien met with Jill immediately. Jill was not sure whether she could trust Mary, since she felt she had already been burned once by a faculty member whom she had trusted. Jill decided to tell Mary the full story. She began by saying that she worked for a faculty member in the university (Jill did not say who it was) who she thought was guilty of wrongdoing. She also explained that he was a well-respected, tenured faculty member. Jill added that the suspected wrongdoing had to do with the use of grant funds by this faculty member.

Jill asked Mary if she should even bother to report a well-respected member of the university community for wrongdoing. What were the implications of reporting it? Jill said that she was not really sure who was to blame. Maybe the faculty member she had spoken to, before she was fired, was right in saying that Jill had no proof of any wrongdoing. Mary listened to Jill's summary of the events, did not ask Jill to "name names," explained to her the university's procedures, and gave her three forms that Jill would need to submit if she wanted to proceed to the next stage—fact-finding followed by a confidential hearing involving herself, the faculty member, and a three-member review committee made up of administrators and faculty members.

Jill left Mary's office feeling slightly better for having explained her situation to someone. Jill was still not certain whether or not she had done anything wrong or whether Dr. Elliott had legitimate reasons for firing her. Jill spent the evening alone in her apartment trying to sort out the pros and cons of her next steps. The faculty member she had spoken with specifically told her that no formal complaints would do any good because of Elliott's reputation and position. This faculty member would argue that she should simply ignore the situation. On the other hand, because she had been fired, she was angry about being treated unfairly. What did she have to lose by reporting her suspicions to university authorities or even to the funding agency? She might even get her job back. But, Jill reminded herself, Dr. Elliott would surely be consulted by potential employers in her own upcoming job search. She would certainly benefit from a positive letter from him. That possibility would surely fly out the window if she requested a formal investigation and hearing.

Whistleblowers: Who's the Real Bad Guy?

Barbara Ettorre

The popular notion persists that whistleblowers are crazy and vengeful malcontents.

This goes against overwhelming statistics that show they are well-educated, well-liked and committed employees, generally in middle-to-senior-level posts. Yet, with all too few exceptions, whistleblowers continue to be ostracized and humiliated by the companies they hope to improve. Worse, in more than half of whistleblowing instances, the charges are ignored.

When an employee steps forward and legitimately accuses an organization of wrongdoing, it can bring out the worst in everyone. The hierarchy—right up the line to the CEO and the board, if the allegations are serious enough—may enact one of several scenarios: The company may instigate a cover-up. It could make the whistleblower (instead of the allegations) the issue by trying to discredit the individual. It could retaliate against the whistleblower. Or, in perhaps the most insidious of the lot, the company could pretend to listen, appoint the whistleblower to solve the problem, deny access to needed information—and make the whistleblower the scapegoat when the wrongdoing persists.

Fear of bad publicity, expensive litigation and loss of business can make a company hostile and defensive, usually at the expense of the whistleblower's personal or professional reputation. The individual's coworkers get suspicious and angry because their expertise or ethics may be

suspect. The whistleblower's family becomes anxious and insecure: "If we lose that paycheck, what happens to us?"

Then, of course, there is the whistleblower, who has stepped forward to tell the truth, despite a jumble of contradictory emotions and fears. Feelings of disloyalty are at war with those of obligation and, possibly, outrage at something very wrong in the company and frustration that no one seems to want to listen.

If that employee has blown the whistle not only on his or her boss but also on the company by taking the case outside to other authorities or to the media, the harsh truth is that this represents a failure on everybody's part. It means the business had not allowed the normal use of communications from the bottom up and that reporting procedures had not worked—or that the whistleblower had not found them to be receptive.

The sad fact is that in today's supposedly enlightened business world, corporate America continues to treat its whistleblowers poorly. The notion persists that it is disloyal and irresponsible to criticize one's employer, notwithstanding the fact that the company has done wrong. Making matters worse is the thicket of often contradictory state and federal laws and procedures. These can help or hinder the whistleblower in the recovery of damages, in reinstating his or her job—even in addressing the company's wrongdoing itself.

Consider a few whistleblowing cases, some ending more happily than others:

- Chester Walsh, a former employee at GE Aircraft Engine, a division of General Electric Company, gathered information for four years to expose a defense contract fraud at the company. Senior company executives and an Israeli general were accused of a scheme to divert U.S. funds in connection with a contract involving Israel's purchase of GE jet engines. Last year, a federal judge awarded Walsh $11.5 million under provisions of the False

Source: Reprinted, by permission of publisher, from *Management Review,* May 1994 © 1995. American Management Association. All rights reserved.

Claims Act, a federal statute permitting employees to sue their employers on behalf of the government and to collect as much as a quarter of the assessments and fines. During the tortuous legal process, Walsh was vilified as an employee just out for the money.

- Allan McDonald and Roger Boisjoly, engineers at Morton Thiokol Inc., testified before the Rogers Commission investigating the 1986 Challenger shuttle disaster that there had been ongoing problems with the rocket's O-rings and that they had urged their supervisors and NASA officials to postpone the fatal launch. Following their testimony, the engineers were demoted to menial jobs. Only the intervention of the Commission members got them reinstated.

- Billie Garde, a Census Bureau employee in Oklahoma in 1980 and a single mother of two, was ordered by her supervisor to misrepresent civil-service test scores so he could hire incompetents. Garde, a former schoolteacher, also was directed to recruit female ex-students as sex partners for visiting political officials. When she refused and blew the whistle, her manager fired her and helped her ex-husband win custody of the children. Garde eventually regained custody with the help of whistleblower advocates. She attended law school and now, as a Houston attorney, represents whistleblowers.

- Last year, an administrative law judge for the U.S. Labor Department found that managers at the Oak Ridge National Laboratory had retaliated against a technician who had expressed concerned about radiation exposure

there. The worker, Charles D. Varnadore, had undergone colon cancer surgery in 1989 and had subsequently appeared on television to voice distress about the prevalence of cancer among his colleagues and the lax protection against radiation. His supervisors transferred Varnadore to a room full of toxic and radioactive substances and gave him useless work. Martin Marietta Energy Systems, which runs the lab for the U.S. Department of Energy, was ordered to pay Varnadore damages, the amount to be set by Labor Secretary Robert B. Reich.

- A. Ernest Fitzgerald, an Air Force financial analyst, battled the military because of its wasteful practices during several administrations. President Nixon fired Fitzgerald in 1969 after he exposed a $2 billion overrun in an Air Force contract. (Fitzgerald was reinstated by court order, but it took him until 1982 to be restored to his old job.) He was the kind of civil servant the Pentagon loved to hate: He testified before Congress about $7 claw hammers costing $436 and 25-cent washers purchased for $693 each. Resentful coworkers christened Fitzgerald and his staff "attic fanatics" because of their cramped upper-floor Pentagon offices.

A PROBLEM, YOU SAY? YOU'RE FIRED.

Discussions with experts, advocates, human resource professionals and public interest groups about how organizations treat employee whistleblowers illuminate a dismal picture. Other than outright dismissal, retaliation can and does in-

---

Briefcase

The good news is, there are methods in place at a growing number of corporations for employees to report wrongdoing. The bad news is, businesses usually es-

tablish these procedures after someone has blown the whistle—and they continue to mismanage whistleblowing.

clude demotion, false complaints about job performance, reassignment and relocation, assignment of unsympathetic coworkers or supervisors and otherwise making the job difficult, withholding of pension, orders to undergo psychological examination, investigation of finances and personal life, and harassment of family and friends.

"The menu of reprisals is limited only to the imagination," says Thomas Devine, legal director of the Government Accountability Project (GAP), a Washington-based public-interest watchdog group that assists and represents both government and corporate whistleblowers.

Donald R. Soeken, who has been counseling whistleblowers since 1978, puts it directly: "If you blow the whistle on somebody below you, you'll get a pat on the back. Above you? You'll be fired."

Soeken was a therapist at a public service health clinic when he realized that federal agencies were using fitness-for-duty psychiatric examinations to weed out whistleblowers. The strategy, he found, was to find the individuals eligible for disability discharges, ending their whistleblowing claims. The object was to discredit their testimony and to make them appear crazy. Soeken's subsequent testimony before Congress helped abolish these examinations from some of the federal system, although the practice persists.

While retaliation is still business-as-usual, a surprisingly large number of whistleblowing charges die from benign neglect. "As a proportion, retaliation isn't done in even half the instances," says Marcia P. Miceli, associate dean for academic programs and professor of human resources at Ohio State University. She and a colleague, Indiana University Professor Janet P. Near, have written extensively on whistleblowing, including *Blowing the Whistle* (Lexington Books, 1992).

"The typical response is to ignore the charges," Miceli continues. "Corporations will say there is no merit in them, but corporations need to communicate and explain their actions—even when they do find no merit."

In the midst of such unremitting negatives, surely there must be some ray of hope, some enlightened companies that not only foster communication among employees who are compelled to report problems, but also encourage them to come forward. After all, the past few years have seen a meteoric rise in ethics programs and all the trappings of compliance systems that go into them, including confidential hotlines and employee surveys, ombudspersons and neutral-party inspector generals. Then, why is whistle-blowing still treated as it was in the Dark Ages?

To answer this, we need to ponder some of the larger ideas that motivate ethical behavior in America.

The United States has been weaned on the notion that there are no moral absolutes, that whatever works is true or right, say the philosophers. We have been conditioned to think that what may be right for one person may not necessarily be right for another. Human beings, say the behaviorists, are products of genetics and environment, with little or no self-determination. The only thing meaningful is what you can measure.

"Put this all together and you have a picture that leaves out the immeasurables of ethics, religion and aesthetics," says W. Michael Hoffman, director of the Center for Business Ethics at Bentley College and a professor of philosophy. "Ethics are a matter of personal, rather than community, choice. A lot of society works on the myth that 'telling on someone is bad.'"

Professor Hoffman goes on to say that shared accountability and responsibility as part of an organization are not valued today. The American corporation has operated on the basis of goals set from the top, with little input from below. Employees have been encouraged to put their shoulders to the wheel and not to complain. There are signs that this mentality is slowly changing: increased corporate interest in participatory management, flattened hierarchies, work teams and shared goals. But it will be decades before these elements shape and define the typical organization.

Meanwhile, a whistleblower persists as someone who tattles and who presumes to judge the whole organization, causing resentment of supervisors and coworkers alike. In fact, a whistleblower's colleagues often can be the biggest problem—stonewalling any investigation of the charges, for example, or shunning the whistleblower and spreading rumors about the individual's professional or personal life. It is not without irony that in some companies, employees have taken to calling the ethics hotline "1-800-RAT-FINK."

HERO OR TATTLETALE?

"We need to begin to turn tattletales into moral heroes," Professor Hoffman declares.

The epithets of "rat fink," "tattletale" and "snitch" notwithstanding, it would certainly seem that the concept of shared responsibility moves enough people to come forward and blow the whistle when they see something wrong in their workplace. Statistics aren't reliable, but there are arguably at least several hundred thousand whistleblowing incidents annually, in all walks of organizational life—ranging from the "I think my coworker is stealing office supplies" calls to the ethics hotline, to full-blown charges of widespread fraud with documentation quietly accumulated over several years.

Understandably, most lesser whistleblowing charges do not reach the media because they are not grievous and, in the best cases, are handled by companies' ethical compliance programs. But serious whistleblowing can go unreported because, under pressure, whistleblowers recant their allegations, for instance, or because they become too discouraged or intimidated.

Clearly, whistleblowing presents knotty problems for the manager. If, however, an organization really wants to encourage its employees to come forward with critical disclosures, there are ways to make the process easier, say the experts.

Companies must begin to set up a climate conducive to responsible whistleblowing. One big step, suggested by Miceli, is to select an arbiter who is highly trusted by all and who is visible.

Additionally, what steps to take when reporting wrongdoing and what evidence is needed should be laid out for every employee to know—preferably in writing, with input from all levels. If issues arise, they should be resolved in a timely way. Companies should communicate to all workers the actions they took and why. When appropriate, whistleblowers should be praised and rewarded for their actions. In turn, employees need to be apprised of their rights and ethical responsibilities as members of an organization.

"I'm an optimistic person," says Professor Miceli. "If an organization really wants to encourage whistleblowing, there are ways. But I'm pessimistic, too. I wish I could really see companies doing so."

LEGAL AID

Mistreated employees have legal avenues for redress, although many of these laws are enforced by the same systems in which the charges originated. Nevertheless, there are signs that whistleblowers will be afforded some protection from employer reprisals. One of the biggest stumbling blocks has been that whistleblower protection laws have evolved inconsistently. There is no coherent body of law that protects all whistleblowers—state, municipal, federal and corporate (both public and private companies), says GAP's Devine. And, some laws protect better than others. As Devine says, "With or without legal changes, it is a fact of life that when you bite the hand that feeds you, it tends to slap you, at the least."

This may be alleviated by a bill expected to be introduced by Representative Patsy T. Mink (D-Hawaii) this spring. The proposal attempts to be a comprehensive whistleblowing code for corporate, municipal, federal and state employ-

"Would I Do It Again? You Bet"

When Robert A. Bugai realized that he would have to blow the whistle in the early '80s, he made a "premeditated and deliberate" decision to learn about what he was getting into. "I took the time to find out," says Bugai, 37. "I researched whistleblowing at the library. I sat down and considered the cost—mentally, financially, physically, emotionally and spiritually."

When Bugai decided to go ahead, he blew the whistle on college marketers, which he figures is currently a $140 million market. These are firms hired by advertising agencies to get their clients' products and services (credit cards, car rentals, periodicals, grooming aids, dorm room supplies, apparel) to college students.

Beginning as a student in 1974, Bugai worked on a commission basis for various college marketing firms, supplying placards, posters,

product samples, magazines, stand-up card displays and other ad tools to be placed on college campuses. Trouble was, Bugai had found the products and ad messages weren't reaching the intended audience.

Bugai found that campus representatives were filling out job completion forms—while posters and other sales materials and samples languished undistributed in campus storage closets and basements and empty vandalized merchandise racks went unrepaired and unfilled. Posters were ripped off bulletin boards and were not replaced. College newspaper organizations, which had payment contracts with marketers for inserting their clients' ads in newspapers, were not being paid.

Bugai went back to the library, taught himself investigative techniques and went to the clients, documenting his charges with pho-

tographs and legitimately retrieved samples, many of them bearing original wrappings and shipping documents. Twice he was taken to court by the marketers, but both cases were settled before trial. When threatened with a court action, Bugai would write a polite thank-you letter saying how honored he was to have such a formidable opponent. "I wasn't going to be nasty," he says. "I wanted to give positive reinforcement to other whistleblowers."

In 1985, Bugai made his expertise formal by founding College Marketing Intelligence, based in North Arlington, N.J., offering advice, competitive intelligence and marketing programs on his own. "I would encourage people who are thinking of being whistleblowers to think about the real cost involved," he says. "Would I do it again? You bet."

If You Are Blowing the Whistle

There is a wealth of advice available from ex-whistleblowers, counsellors and advocates. The following strategies are from the Government Accountability Project:

- Talk everything over first with your family or loved ones.
- In a non-accusatory manner, first try to work within the system, involving several layers of management, before going outside the organization. Be aware that sounding the alarm may trigger a cover-up.
- Develop a specific record—keep a factual log, documenting both wrongdoing and any harassment you receive.
- Make a detailed memorandum for the record, when

you need a permanent record of an important event or conversation. Sign it, date it, and, if possible, have someone witness it. If you believe your word will be challenged, you can apply the "poor person's copyright": mail a copy to yourself, and keep it, unopened, until it is needed.
- Pinpoint and copy key records before drawing attention to your allegations. You may be denied access later.
- Create a larger support circle, a constituency of those outside the organization who would benefit from the exposure of your allegations.
- Seek the help of specialists, organizations that assist whistleblowers.

ees who are alleging violations of federal law. Some 200 companies and public policy groups have petitioned Congress to extend whistleblowing protection.

Mink's proposal stipulates a due process hearing by a U.S. Department of Labor administrator. Also, the case must be adjudicated by legal standards of the Whistleblower Protection Act of 1989. In part, it says that if an employee alleges he or she was discriminated against because of whistleblowing as a contributing factor, the employer has to prove legitimate independent grounds for its actions. Additionally, when a whistleblower files a reprisal complaint, the allegations of wrongdoing will simultaneously be forwarded to law enforcement and federal agencies for investigation.

Congress is slowly showing some muscle. Last year it refused to re-authorize the U.S. Office of Special Counsel. It was created in 1978, ostensibly to assist federal employee whistleblowers, but the OSC had been widely criticized for hampering and intimidating them over the years.

Yet, the False Claims Act has been criticized as counterproductive because it provides monetary incentives to employees to bypass internal reporting systems, while the Federal Sentencing Guidelines . . . require corporations to set up these systems. In addition, recent amendments to the act have stipulated that if wrongdoing isn't reported immediately, the whistleblower has less of a right to share in eventual damages.

HERE'S WHAT YOU GET

What happens to whistleblowers after the fact? It is like getting a divorce, says Mary Louise Cohen, a partner at Washington-based Phillips, Cohen & Goldstein, and an advocate for whistleblowers in false claims cases. "They may have had 25 years at the company. They give up their identities and fulfilling relationships."

Counsellor Soeken and other experts advise whistleblowers to leave their careers and to start fresh in other lines of work—because their actions have efficiently blacklisted them. Most whistleblowers, while avowing they would sound the alarm again under the same circumstances, would rather never have gone through the turmoil, even if they were vindicated and if they received millions of dollars in settlement. They wish the occasion to blow the whistle—the wrongdoing—had never occurred.

But at least one whistleblower says he wouldn't do it again. In 1975, William C. Bush, then a 50-year-old aerospace engineer in the National Aeronautics and Space Administration (NASA), challenged agency policies that kept workers inactive.

Workbook

Few managers are ever comfortable hearing from their subordinates that a problem exists in the company. As a manager, how can you develop an atmosphere in which it would be likely your people will come to you if they know of wrongdoing? Here are a few timeless suggestions:

- Don't play favorites, above or below you.
- Keep an open-door policy so that your staff knows you are available and accessible. Ivory towers have fallen; you should already be listening to your people every day.

- Maintain confidentiality on unimportant matters; when important matters come along, your employees will know they can trust you.
- Appreciate that, for most employees, it takes courage to come to a supervisor with a problem.
- Investigate all allegations, and if appropriate, act on them. Document what you do and communicate your actions to the employee.
- Show by example that you believe ethics are paramount.

Threatened with dismissal, Bush saw his grade level reduced and his salary cut by $10,000. He was eventually given a clerical job. It took more than three years for him to be reinstated.

Bush also blew the whistle on a private NASA directive (later rescinded) disallowing executive leadership training programs for employees after age 40. Eventually, the Supreme Court ruled 9-0 against Bush, saying that federal employees did not have the constitutional right to blow the whistle.

Bush retired from NASA in 1986 and now suffers from several stress-related illnesses he says were brought on by continual harassment. One of the country's best-known former whistleblowers, he has maintained a support network for others and has pleaded their causes to members of Congress, the press and concerned organizations. Although less active now, Bush says he still receives a couple calls a week from whistleblowers.

"Hell, no, I wouldn't do it again," Bush asserts. "I ruined my life, my wife's life. And, I wouldn't do it anonymously, either. There is no protection whatsoever."

READING 9-2

Whistleblowing: Reaping the Benefits

Marcia P. Miceli
Janet P. Near

. . . Recently, an employee at a large hospital provided physical evidence to his superiors that bacteria that cause pneumonia and other serious diseases were growing in anesthesia equipment.

Source: Academy of Management Executive, 8 (3) (1994), 65–72. Used with permission.

The equipment was not cleaned following each use, thus risking the already precarious health of patients using the same equipment. Despite the considerable dangers posed by the practice of failing to clean the equipment, the employee was not thanked for being vigilant about safety. Instead, he was asked whether he personally could provide the funds necessary to do the cleaning, since "times were tough" at the hospital. No changes were made, the employee was reprimanded, and his access to sections of the hospital were restricted.

Aside from the obvious ethical and legal concerns, this incident raises concerns that the hospital's leaders displayed a very short-sighted approach to management: they ignored the wrongdoing. If even one patient were seriously harmed by the negligence, the amount the hospital would pay in losing a lawsuit would far outweigh any amount that routine cleaning and maintenance would cost. Employees who came into contact with the contaminated instruments were also at risk; lost sick days cost the hospital. Further, hospital managers should have wondered, if unsafe conditions were discovered in the anesthesia equipment, might there be similar or more hazardous conditions elsewhere in the hospital?

The hospital also ran several additional risks in reprimanding the employee rather than making immediate corrections and thanking him for his attentiveness and concern. First, some state laws proscribe retaliation against whistleblowers. The monetary damages awarded to the whistleblower who proves retaliation can be sizeable.[1] Further, if the employee, frustrated by the lack of response, called a local reporter who publicized the wrongdoing, the adverse publicity would damage the hospital for many years to come. An external report might bring more scrutiny by inspectors and other authorities of all hospital operations, leading to fines, or perhaps additional legislative action to curb hospital managers' discretion. In addition, if the hospital's culture becomes one that tolerates or encourages wrongdoing and discourages the appropriate exercise of rights and execution of responsibilities, it is less likely to be attractive to or retain the loyalty of productive and satisfied employees.

Unfortunately, many companies are perceived as taking a "do nothing" perspective in dealing with reports of wrongdoing. Surveys of employees reveal that most of them expect that if they were to report an observed wrongdoing, nothing would happen.[2] Paradoxically, even if management believes that the whistleblower is incorrect in his or her allegations, or that the person is a chronic complainer,[3] a do nothing approach presents many of the same risks as a retaliatory one. Similarly, adopting policies designed to protect whistleblowers from retaliation is desirable but difficult to enforce. Preventing or reducing wrongdoing in the first place may be a more effective strategy than "doing nothing" or than concentrating solely on protection for whistleblowers. Therefore, we believe managers should give some thought to alternative approaches.

AVOIDING THE NEED FOR EXTERNAL WHISTLEBLOWING

Management can be proactive in creating a positive climate for correcting wrongdoing. However, eliminating wrongdoing will not necessarily eliminate external whistleblowing, since individuals' perceptions of and beliefs about what constitutes wrongdoing vary. Nonetheless, firms that are proactive will be at a competitive advantage.

Defining Wrongdoing and Its Consequences

It is essential for top management to recognize the importance of bringing together all parties who play a role in establishing a climate that encourages organizational members to recognize and respond effectively to wrongdoing. Providing an opportunity for a variety of perspectives to be shared is quite valuable. Internal auditors, for example, have insights into the points at which the control process breaks down and the temptation for wrongdoing can be too great. External auditors can view the organization perhaps more objectively and with comparative data from other organizations. They can also suggest strategies that have worked in similar organizations, as can human resource professionals who keep abreast of the literature in their field and network effectively. Legal counsel can address the implications of the ideas generated through this process and suggest other effective strategies. Together, they provide a richer and more comprehensive resource for top management.

Managers need to focus on several key questions, including:

- What kind of an organization are we?
- What are our values and standards?
- What are our ethical obligations?
- What are the costs and benefits of enacting our values and meeting our standards?
- What are we willing to do to ensure that our values and standards are upheld in practice?

By exploring and answering such questions candidly, managers will be able to clarify their beliefs about what constitutes wrongdoing and help identify potential problem areas.

It is essential that activities that primarily harm parties other than the company or its stockholders, such as discrimination, safety violations, or pollution, be addressed. All too often, codes of ethics emphasize wrongdoing against the company but say little about wrongdoing that hurts other stakeholders.[4] On the other hand, seeking to define wrongdoing too specifically may actually be counterproductive. Giving employees checklists for wrongdoing can result in a mindless application of the rules, while ignoring important new signals.[5] Generally, we have found that it is best to view the process of defining wrongdoing as ongoing and changing.

Communicating Policies and Codes of Ethics

Ideally, codes of ethics and other policies that relate to wrongdoing should spell out more specifically—but without inappropriate rigidity—what activities are considered wrong. A policy that provides specific examples of questionable activities is more easily understood by employees and will result in fewer unfounded complaints than one that does not.

Codes and formal policies should also specify what actions are desired. For example, to whom should employees report a potential wrongdoing—their boss, the personnel department, a corporate attorney, or an internal auditor? Research suggests that establishing policies that define appropriate responses to perceived wrongdoing can encourage internal whistleblowing.[6] Obviously, complaint recipients must be brought into the structuring process at an early stage and ongoing training and support must be provided as they advise employees.

However, simply publishing policies or codes is not enough. Policies must be clearly communicated and become part of the organizational culture and reward system, with training provided to help organization members take the initiative in reporting wrongdoing. One caution: our research found that employees who observed wrongdoing within the last year were far less satisfied with their jobs than those who had not made such observations. Hence, care should be taken to ensure that employees understand that the purpose of such training is to improve the work climate in the *future* rather than to point the finger at past incidents.[7] Employee notices, such as posters, can also be used to keep awareness levels high. For example, Pacific Gas & Electric San Luis Obispo posts notices imploring workers to tell supervisors or the Nuclear Regulatory Commission immediately—without fear of retribution—if they see something amiss.[8] Further, executives and supervisors must model values they want employees to emulate, rather than simply communicating policies and procedures to which they do not appear committed. When employees believe such policies are only receiving "lip service" from management, they quickly become cynical.

ENCOURAGING INTERNAL WHISTLEBLOWING

Encouraging internal whistleblowing must go beyond defining only certain jobs as "watchdog" roles. Everyone must understand what types of activities are considered wrong and what he or she should do when it is observed. However, peer reporting may also increase levels of mistrust among colleagues.[9] Broad areas of responsibility and important concerns must be explained, perhaps in a written question-and-answer format indicating what to do when an employee believes that a violation has taken place.

While there are costs to encouraging individuals to monitor and report wrongdoing, such costs are generally lower than those incurred when wrongdoing is not detected early. In one case, an internal auditor at a large hospital reported to us that he saved the firm $300,000 a year when he found the Director of Pharmacy engaged in stealing drugs from the hospital and reselling them.

Complaint Recipients

Practically all wrongdoing that is eventually reported externally is first reported internally, suggesting that responsiveness to an initial complaint is a key factor in avoiding external reporting. Victims are not always required by law to use internal complaint channels before turning to an external party. Employees may sue or complain to an equal employment enforcement agency without first providing the employer with an opportunity for self-correction. Our own research indicates that wrongdoing involving harm to the public or employees and wrongdoing involving employee theft are more likely to result in external whistleblowing than are other types of wrongdoing.[10] Therefore, managers who can reduce these types of wrongdoing may succeed in encouraging whistleblowers to use internal channels only.

Not surprisingly, research indicates that employees with greater knowledge of effective internal channels of complaint are more likely to engage in internal whistleblowing.[11] This suggests that the complaint process should be as clear as possible to all employees.[12] The issues of trust and access are also important. If the corporate attorney is unknown to the employee or is far away geographically, it is unlikely that the employee will feel comfortable raising sensitive issues with him or her, and may feel intimidated due to status differences.

If a supervisor is directly involved in the wrongdoing, or feels compelled to take management's side, then the employee would be forced to think twice before proceeding higher in the hierarchy. In such cases, communication systems that circumvent the chain of command, such as use of an ombudsman, can help. Battelle Memorial Institute developed such a system for the National Aeronautic and Space Administration (NASA), in 1987, at Kennedy Space Center, following the explosion of the space shuttle *Challenger*.[13] According to Michael Hanley, the project manager, "the system enables anyone working on the shuttle project to alert NASA to any potential safety problem while maintaining their anonymity." The program is designed to reduce the fear that whistleblowing will lead to reprisals, a theme that had been sounded in the aftermath of the *Challenger* disaster.

While employee assistance programs (EAPs) are ostensibly designed to help employees with performance problems stemming from psychological problems, alcoholism, drug abuse, family stresses and the like, they may also treat employees whose problems stem from workplace wrongdoing. It is imperative that the EAP not be used by management to victimize an already vulnerable party.[14] EAP counselors should be trained in procedures to be used when they suspect that a referral has been made to harass a potential whistleblower, and when employees refer themselves in response to the stress that pursuing a complaint may have provoked.

One often overlooked complaint recipient is the trainer or internal organizational development consultant. These individuals may have opportunities to hear expressions of employee concerns. During training or focus group sessions, for example, suspicions of wrongdoing might be expressed, even when these issues are not the planned topic for the sessions. Trainers could be surprised at such expressions and may not know how to handle them, particularly where confidentiality has been promised to participants. Therefore, companies should develop policies for responding to these incidents, and they should train the trainers accordingly. Similarly, external consultants or audit teams may have difficulty resolving ethical dilemmas about whether to report information given to them in confidence by employees. Development of policies for such instances should be undertaken.[15]

Utilizing Alternative Reporting Mechanisms

Employees may feel more comfortable reporting unethical or illegal behavior through the suggestion system rather than to other recipients, particularly when anonymous suggestions are accepted. To accommodate individual differences in communication preferences, suggestion systems can allow for either oral or written media. IBM has an "open door" policy under which employees are urged to carry complaints all the way up the corporate ladder. IBM receives up to 18,000 letters a year from workers making confidential complaints under a "Speak Up" program. Bank of America in San Francisco encourages its employees to subject complaints or reports through its "Open Line" program. The program's coordinator contacts the whistleblower at home to gather information in complete confidence and then confronts the accused person for a response.[16]

Another potential method for handling whistleblowing complaints is arbitration. Traditionally, arbitration serves as the last step of a grievance procedure in unionized settings in both private and public sector organizations. Both parties agree to allow the arbitrator to decide the grievance. The American Arbitration Association estimates the cost to be $200 to $1500 per case with two to three months for resolution.[17] This can be contrasted with the case of Bertrand Berube, a federal whistleblower. Resolving concerns he raised cost an estimated $200,000 to $700,000 and exhausted six years in the court system. Reducing the time in resolution lessens opportunities for retaliation against the whistleblower and the stress of uncertainty imposed on all parties. Obviously, companies must look closely at how the arbitration process can be adapted to accommodate questions of unethical behavior in addition to disputes concerning more traditional issues such as excessive absences and pay disputes.

Frequently, a complaint can be settled out of court by an in-house review panel, thereby saving costs. In 1983, General Electric's Columbia, Maryland, plant initiated a panel process for its hourly employees.[18] Of course, not all complaints concern wrongdoing, but some do. Employees with complaints are encouraged by GE to first try to resolve it on a one-to-one basis with the supervisor. If that is unsuccessful (about one third of the time), the next step is to bring the complaint to the peer review panel, comprised of five individuals. Three are hourly employees, drawn at random from about sixty hourly employees. The other two are management representatives who are permanently assigned to the panel. These panelists are specially trained in dispute resolution techniques. GE reports that the number of grievances has far outpaced the number of complaints filed in the previous five years during the so-called "open door" policy when employees were free to complain to management. A survey shows that eighty-two percent of the plant's staff was satisfied with the peer review process. GE attributes the success of the program to the placing of power in the hands of the hourly employees, which removes the management insulation of the supervisor from the consequences of unfair practices.

Managerial Actions

Traditionally, managers are advised not to retaliate against whistleblowers. Though certainly retaliation can be devastating and must be avoided, research shows consistently that concern about potential retaliation is not a primary influence in the decision to blow the whistle. A much more important factor is the individual's belief that something will be done to correct the problem. Therefore, the most important thing managers can do is to show that the company will do something in response to the complaint. If the complaint is valid, correcting the problem and showing employees that the problem has been corrected sends a powerful message. Likewise, if no action is warranted, it is equally important to explain to employees why management has chosen not to act. We also advise managers to resist the understandable temptation to dismiss complaints by denigrating the whistleblower and instead to focus on the validity of the complaint itself. There is evidence that many whistleblowers are high performers who are relatively well paid and who feel compelled to report wrongdoing by their own sense of morality, and they generally believe that they are required by their jobs to do so.[19,20] Consequently, managers in companies that have taken care to devise fair and effective responses to whistleblowers should be carefully trained in the company's procedures for handling such issues and the need to be considerate of employee rights.[21]

On the other hand, the possibility of abuse by employees who claim to be whistleblowers but are merely disgruntled poor performers is real. Nonetheless, steps can be taken to protect managers from such abuses. First, it is recommended that managers leave a paper trail in performance appraisal. Second, companies should institute a progressive disciplinary system built into the performance appraisal process. For example, poor performance may initially be followed by counseling. Later incidents may engender warnings or written reprimands. If the poor performance persists, it would be followed by suspensions or other actions. Third, where firing is contemplated, managers should refer questions to a third party, who will objectively review any termination process to make sure the documentation is complete and that the termination was driven by appropriate reasons.

Incentives

The research is rather consistent in showing that the most powerful incentive a company can offer potential whistleblowers is its willingness to correct wrongdoing. However, some firms have also offered more direct incentives. First Interstate Bank of California in Los Angeles maintains a code of ethics, and bank officials encourage employees to report suspected violations and recognize them with letters of commendation. Hughes Tool Co. of Houston has offered rewards of up to $10,000 leading to the arrest and conviction of oilfield thieves, often members of the company.[22] General Motors has offered cash rewards to get information about leaks of sensitive future product information. Several retail chains, including Bloomingdale's, Inc., are using rewards to get information on employee theft. While it may seem straightforward that adding rewards would increase the likelihood of whistleblowing, unanticipated negative consequences should be considered. For example, if the whistleblower is viewed by others as having blown the whistle primarily to get a bonus, they may view the person as a "fink," ostracizing him or her from the group.

Under the False Claims Amendments Act of 1986, whistleblowers are permitted to receive monetary rewards. In one reported case, a physician left a clinic and sued it and a former colleague for allegedly defrauding Medicare by billing for procedures that were more expensive than those actually performed. Even though the

financial incentives for the physician were fifteen to twenty-five percent of a multimillion-dollar judgment, he reportedly said his only concern was the ethics involved.[23]

Curiously, whistleblowers are frequently quoted as claiming that the financial incentives played no role in their decision to blow the whistle. In our analyses of data from federal employees, very few organization members reported that cash awards would encourage them to blow the whistle. On the other hand, there is some evidence that the possibility of large awards has spurred whistleblowing. Before the False Claims Act was revised in 1986 to facilitate large rewards, cases under this Act averaged ten per year. By late 1989 the number of suits filed since the revisions became effective was 198.

Reaping the Benefits

Whistleblowing presents a dilemma for many managers, and may often be viewed as a threat. But, in an era of increasing recognition of the benefits of employee involvement, we believe that it is time for managers to see that many whistleblowers can be a valuable resource. If they are viewed as committed employees who can provide useful information and solutions to problems, managers can take action in many ways that benefit their companies.

NOTES

Portions of this article are based on our book, *Blowing the Whistle* (Lexington, MA: Lexington Books, 1992). Permission has been granted by Lexington. We thank the associate editor and two anonymous reviewers for their helpful comments.

1. T. M. Dworkin and J. P. Near, "Whistleblowing Statutes: Are They Working?" *American Business Law Journal*, 25(2), 1987, 241–264.
2. United States Merit Systems Protection Board (USMSPB), *Whistleblowing and the Federal Employee* (1981), and *Blowing the Whistle in the Federal Government: A Comparative Analysis of 1980 and 1983 Survey Findings* (1984), (Washington, DC: U.S. Government Printing Office); J. P. Keenan, *First-level Managers and Whistle-*

blowing: An Exploratory Study of Individual and Organizational Influences. Working paper, School of Business-Management Institute, University of Wisconsin, Madison, 1990.

3. Research to date has supported some of the myths about whistleblowers but discounted others. For example, whistleblowers as a group are not disgruntled "wackos" trying to gain notoriety, but instead, conscientious high performers who are alarmed when they perceive wrongdoing by members of their firm. Likewise, most whistleblowers are not greatly deterred by the threat of retaliation. Rather, they act because they believe that the wrongdoing is so egregious as to be intolerable—and they assume that someone at high levels would like to know about it. See M. P. Miceli and J. P. Near, *Blowing the Whistle* (Lexington, MA: Lexington Books, 1992).

4. M. C. Mathews, "Codes of Ethics: Organizational Behavior and Misbehavior," in W. C. Frederick (Ed.), *Research in Corporate Social Performance and Policy,* Vol. 9 (Greenwich, CT: JAI Press, 1987), 107–130.

5. K. V. Pincus, "The Efficacy of a Red Flags Questionnaire for Assessing the Possibility of Fraud," *Accounting, Organizations, and Society,* 14, 1989, 153–163.

6. T. R. Barnett, D. S. Cochran, and G. S. Taylor, "The Relationship Between Internal Dissent Policies and Employee Whistleblowing: An Exploratory Study," paper presented at the 50th annual meeting of the Academy of Management, San Francisco, 1990.

7. Miceli and Near, *op. cit.*

8. J. L. Sheler, "When Employees [sic] Squeal on Fellow Workers," *U.S. News & World Report,* November 16, 1981, 81–82.

9. L. K. Trevino and B. Victor, "Peer Reporting of Unethical Behavior: A Social Context Perspective," *Academy of Management Journal,* 35, 1992, 38–64.

10. Miceli and Near, *op cit.*

11. M. P. Miceli and J. P. Near, "The Relationships Among Beliefs, Organizational Position, and Whistleblowing Status: A Discriminant Analysis," *Academy of Management Journal,* 27, 1984, 687–705.

12. On the other hand, research suggests that different potential recipients or types of communication attempts may be needed to evoke reporting from different persons. See M. P. Miceli and J. P. Near, "Characteristics of Organizational Climate and Perceived Wrongdoing Associated with Whistleblowing Decisions," *Personnel Psychology,* 38, 1985, 525–544.

13. D. Shingler, "Battelle Program Attracts NASA Whistleblowers," *Business First of Greater Columbus,* 4(3), October 5, 1987, 9.

14. There have been alleged abuses of the psychiatric examination policy in the military. See W. V. Kennedy, "Military Uses Exam to Curb Whistleblowers," *Christian Science Monitor,* November 29, 1987, B1.

15. We are grateful to Judith Tansky for these suggestions.

16. Sheler, *op. cit.*

17. "Control your Liability to Keep Out of Court," *Personnel Administrator,* 33(3), March 1988, 44.

18. M. I. Finney, "A Good Idea—Five Years Later," *Personnel Administrator,* 33(3), 1988, 38–44.

19. M. P. Miceli and J. P. Near, "Individual and Situational Correlates of Whistleblowing," *Personnel Psychology,* 41, 1988, 267–282.

20. M. P. Miceli, J. P. Near, and C. Schwenk, "Who Blows the Whistle and Why?" *Industrial and Labor Relations Review,* 45, 1991, 113–130.

21. See Note 17.

22. Sheler, *op. cit.*

23. "Doctor May Profit in Medicare Fraud Suit Against Ex-Colleague," *The New York Times,* September 10, 1987, 3.

The Whistleblowing Era: A Management Perspective

Kevin M. Smith
John M. Oseth

In the last decade, one of the most prominent features to emerge on the legal landscape has been the whistleblowing phenomenon—the increasing propensity of company employees to report suspected illegal activity, or conduct simply perceived to be improper, to internal or external authorities and the tendency of legislatures and courts to encourage and protect employees who blow whistles on their employers or coworkers.

Indeed, through the 1980s whistleblower provisions became a central component of a wide range of federal and state legislation aimed at shielding employees from employer reprisals. There was similar ferment in the judiciary, especially as a result of wrongful discharge suits by employees seeking to take advantage of "public policy" exceptions to the traditional doctrine of at-will employment.[1] In part, the energy for these developments derived from an increased perception that unscrupulous business activity may jeopardize important public interests. Concerns about federal procurement integrity, consumer safety, and environmental protections, for instance, have appreciably widened the sphere of government regulation of business and have markedly expanded the norms and expectations against which corporate conduct is measured.[2] Also significant has been the appearance of the U.S. Sentencing Commission's sentencing guidelines for organizations, which treat an employer's handling of whistleblowing as a barometer of a corporation's commitment to compliance with applicable law and regulations.[3]

All this has occurred despite a marked lack of consensus concerning the whistleblowing activities that should be protected and how best to encourage the desired conduct. What is clear, however, is that employers face a variety of challenges as a result of the last decade's developments: how, in general, to maximize compliance with law and the applicable regulatory framework (and thereby reduce vulnerability to whistleblowing), how to deal with employees who report improprieties or illegalities, and how to minimize the risks of wrongful discharge suits or other litigation in which employees seek by a variety of means to hold their employers accountable for alleged wrongdoing. This article surveys the legislative and judicial landscape and offers guidelines for employers on how to deal with the whistleblower phenomenon and the various protections that have grown up around it.

DEFINITIONS AND PERCEPTIONS: THRESHOLD ISSUES

There is no uniformly applied concept of whistleblowing in any sphere—in legislatures, courts, or academia. Some observers define it narrowly as the reporting of suspected illegal activity, while others prefer an all-encompassing definition that includes a broad range of employee complaints or activity, including reports concerning possible illegality, refusal to participate in illegal conduct, reports concerning violations of professional codes of conduct, reports concerning product defects or other circumstances dangerous to the public health and safety, reports that are volunteered and reports that respond to queries, reports to managers within the company and reports to outsiders (including nongovernment entities), and even incipient whistleblowing situations where *no* report of wrongdoing has been made but an employee had the opportunity to observe potentially objectionable conduct.[4]

Whatever the governing concept of whistleblowing in any particular jurisdiction, every employer must confront certain concrete and un-avoidable realities about this phenomenon.

First, it is all too easy for managers, human resource personnel, and coworkers to regard whistleblowers as disloyal troublemakers. The perspective that seeks to protect whistleblowers, however, regards them as important instruments of the public interest who take significant risks in order to perform a civic duty or service. That attitude can be analogized to the early days of Title VII and other far-reaching social legislation. Even the most problematic employees can take refuge in that aura of public service. Thus an employer's disciplinary instincts in any situations involving reports of irregularities must be appropriately constrained by an appreciation of this "public-service" rationale underlying whistleblower protections.

Second, employers must realize that whistleblowers are ubiquitous. They see what any and all employees can see—and in many cases they can observe much more than corporate leaders can. All company activity and all employee conduct are at least potentially subject to their surveillance. Additionally, at least in theory, they are the most knowledgeable critics a company could encounter, having acquired firsthand familiarity with the policies, procedures, and activities they challenge. In fact, a whistleblower may be a company's expert in the area spotlighted by his or her allegations of wrongdoing.

On the other hand, for a variety of reasons, employee whistleblowers may not actually be so knowledgeable about the activities they observe and report about. Indeed, the reality for many employers is that complicated organizational structures divide employees' knowledge and expertise into functional compartments and vertical layers of supervision—which tends to isolate employees from work performed by others and from central policy-making dynamics.

Operational units, moreover, may be geographically dispersed, and removed in any event from the employer's headquarters, where the most important decisions are made. In those situations it is difficult for workers to understand fully how their activities fit into a larger pattern of policy and strategy within their own enterprise, let alone in the industry at large. It is even more difficult for employees at operational levels to develop broad comprehension of applicable public policies, laws, and governmental regulations. If employees' perceptives are flawed because they misunderstand the activities they observe or the rules that apply to those activities, they can easily misperceive employer motives and conduct, and consequently they may object to essentially unobjectionable conduct.

Finally, employee whistleblowers are subject to all human failings, and some may in fact blow their whistles in bad faith, or at least with mixed motives. They may have grievances (articulated or not) against the employer other than concern about company wrongdoing, and those other complaints may be the source of their reportorial energy.

This means, of course that even the most conscientious employer, with the most thoughtfully developed program of compliance with law and public policy, cannot be sure of eliminating all whistleblower complaints. Ultimately all prudent employers return to the original proposition: no matter where an employer operates nor what the content of any applicable laws may be, the whistleblowing phenomenon presents distinctive challenges that are unlikely to recede in the foreseeable future.

STATUTORY PROTECTIONS AND INCENTIVES

At both the federal and the state level, legislatures have enacted a variety of whistleblower protections over the last decade.

Federal Statutes

Over two dozen federal statutes now protect and/or encourage whistleblowers in the private and public sectors.[5] Most address agendas other than protection of whistleblowers but include protection against employer reprisals for employees who report violations of the statutes.

The approach taken in the Water Pollution Control Act is typical: it contains a provision that protects an employee from employer retaliation because of the employee's participation in a proceeding under the statute or in other activity carrying out the purposes of the Act. Similar provisions appear in the Migrant and Seasonal Agricultural Workers Act, the Occupational Safety and Health Act, the Age Discrimination in Employment Act, the Federal Surface Mining Act, the Clean Air Act, and the Comprehensive Environmental Response, Compensation and Liability Act.

Federal employees who report wrongdoing are protected under the combined provisions of the Civil Service Reform Act of 1978, which prohibits termination based on whistleblower conduct, and the Whistleblower Protection Act of 1989, which added protection for employees who report violations of law, rule, or regulation, gross waste and mismanagement, or danger to public health or safety. These statutes protect whistleblowing to any person, but they provide a specific channel for reporting—an Office of the Special Counsel, which is charged to ensure whistleblowers do not experience reprisals as well as to investigate reports of wrongdoing.

In the private sector, the federal statutes having whistleblower protection clauses cover a wide range of employee situations, and they reach many employers in a variety of industries. Even so, there is considerable sentiment among scholars and legislators that the protection available to persons who report violations of federal law or regulations is insufficient.[6] Thus, despite the diversity of existing legislation, or more accurately because of the *patchwork* of law that has resulted from past legislative efforts, proposals to expand and generalize such protections have repeatedly been offered in the Congress.

In 1992, for instance, one such proposal, H.R. 1664, would have extended protection to every private sector employee and every state and local government employee from employment retaliation motivated to any degree by whistleblowing activity, which was defined essentially as (1) assisting an employer in complying with federal law, (2) refusing to violate federal law, or (3) disclosing evidence that an employer is violating federal law or mismanaging its business with respect to a federal program. Such proposals have generated considerable debate concerning the efficacy of existing protections and the advisability of adding more, but to this point they have not succeeded.[7]

The federal whistleblower protections noted above generally prohibit retaliation against employees who report activities violating the statutes or who assist in enforcement proceedings or exercise rights granted thereunder. Another approach at the federal level, however, has been to provide not only protections but also *incentives* for employees to come forward with disclosures about wrongdoing. Under the Federal Civil False Claims Act, notably, whistleblowers can bring suit on behalf of the United States against their employer for presenting false or fraudulent claims for payment to the federal government. The statute allows these employees to retain a substantial—and potentially enormous—bounty from the proceeds of the suit for their effort to defend professedly public interests.[8]

Although the idea of providing financial rewards to stimulate suits against employers is not universally applauded,[9] this statute remains a fixture in the federal government's overall enforcement arsenal—and in terms of popularity with private claimants it may now rival RICO litigation. The statute even contains its own whistleblowing provision, Section 3730(h), which protects investigating, initiating, and testifying in a civil false claims action, and under which a wrongfully discharged employee may recover double back pay and win reinstatement.

State Statutes

The majority of states have now enacted whistleblower statutes protecting state or local governmental employees; at least seventeen have enacted statutes that protect private sector employees.[10]

Although there are significant variations from state to state, such statutes typically protect disclosures regarding violations or suspected violations of law (federal, state, or local), and they may also focus on areas of special concern like public health and safety. Frequently they require complaints to be made in good faith (that is, they confer no protection for self-interested or malicious charges or for allegations that the employee has made no reasonable effort to substantiate). Some statutes specify how the disclosure must be made (written or oral), and some designate the government agencies to which reports may be made. Some also require whistleblowers to report their complaints internally to the employer and to give the employer a reasonable opportunity to correct the violation.

A few states even protect "embryonic whistleblowers"—persons who have not disclosed irregularities but who might have been close to doing so at the time of an adverse employment action (for example, demotion, transfer, or discharge). Overall, prevention of retaliation is the main tool the states have employed to protect whistleblowers' activities; remedies typically include reinstatement of a lost position and imposition of penalties on the employer.[11]

State statutes protect what many may regard as "mainstream" whistleblowing—reports about violations of laws, rules, or regulations. Generally, the states have not protected private sector employees who complain about waste or mismanagement within the employer's organization, nor have they enacted protections for employees who complain that their employers have violated ethical norms.[12] In addition, state statutes typically protect whistleblowing to a government agency or the employer but not disclosures that are made to third parties, such as the media or interest groups.

As in the Congress, state legislatures increasingly are interested in whistleblower issues—and continue to expand protections to encompass additional categories of employees and kinds of reporting conduct. For instance, 1992 saw major whistleblower initiatives in Connecti-

cut, Florida, North Carolina, Oklahoma, Utah, and Washington.[13]

COMMON LAW PROTECTIONS

In many states, additional protection for whistleblowing is found in court decisions that place whistleblowers within a "public policy" exception to the traditional doctrine that either the employee or the employer may terminate the employment relationship at any time, "at will."

Public policy-based restrictions on an employer's right to terminate an at-will employee were first recognized in a 1959 California case, *Petermann v. Teamsters,* 174 Cal. App. 2d 184, 344 P.2d 25 (Cal. Dist. Ct. App.). Petermann had alleged that he was fired because he had testified—truthfully—before a state legislative committee that had subpoenaed him, after his employer had instructed him to lie. The case thus presented a whistleblowing scenario, and the court came down firmly on the side of the whistleblower, even though his employment was terminable at will. The court held essentially that the state's public policy clearly was to encourage, not discourage, truthful testimony and that the law therefore must remove whatever impediments to that objective it encounters. In the decades following the *Petermann* decision, most states have recognized some sort of public policy exception to the employment-at-will doctrine.[14]

Generally, when a public policy exception has been recognized, an employee may sue in tort against an employer for wrongful discharge if the employee is terminated for engaging in some activity that the state seeks to promote as a matter of public policy. The contours of the exception vary considerably from jurisdiction to jurisdiction, notably as to the sources of the public policy (for example, legislated versus court-made) that may justify an exception to the traditional doctrine and the nature of the conduct that is protected. Seen in the large, however, the decisions that recognize the exception have protected employees who refuse to participate in illegal conduct, perform an important public duty, exercise a legal right or interest, expose an employer's wrongdoing, perform an act that public policy encourages, or refuse to do something that public policy discourages.[15]

Many courts have explicitly extended the public policy exception to whistleblowing situations, following California's lead; a few, however, have expressly declined to do so or have limited it to public sector employees. Where courts have extended the public policy exception to whistleblowers, the reasoning uniformly is premised on the idea of an overarching public interest. A Kansas case, *Palmer v. Brown,* 752 P.2d 685 (1988), for instance, involved an employee's claim that she had been terminated for reporting fraudulent Medicaid billing practices. Observing that Medicaid fraud is a crime under both federal and Kansas law and that Kansas public policy encouraged citizens to report crimes, the court held: "We have no hesitation in holding termination of an employee in retaliation for the good faith reporting of a serious infraction of such rules, regulations, or the law by a co-worker or an employer to either company management or law enforcement officials (whistleblowing) is an actionable tort."[16]

Efforts to extend the public policy exception to whistleblowers are often resisted by employers' defense counsel on several grounds: no specific statute or constitutional provision required the activity the employee engaged in; no specifically illegal conduct was involved; or the reports conveyed only suspicions or pointed to conduct that was trivial.[17] Where states have refused to recognize the exception, they have prominently cited two reasons: (1) strict adherence to the at-will doctrine and (2) reluctance to pronounce on matters that the state legislature has not addressed.[18]

SENTENCING GUIDELINES

Statutory and common law protections for whistleblowing employees have provided substantial incentives for employers to develop sys-

tematic ways of handling employee reports of wrongdoing—and indeed to foster an organizational culture in which wrongdoing itself is discouraged. In the last few years, moreover, the Organizational Sentencing Guidelines (OSG) developed by the U.S. Sentencing Commission have added new incentives by focusing attention on (and rewarding) the extent to which an employer has developed a self-governance system that addresses (and indeed works to eliminate) whistleblowers' concerns.

The guidelines establish a method to be used by judges in imposing fines on employers (and corporate officials) for violations of federal law. Their importance is not limited to the sentencing phase of criminal proceedings, however. They embody the analytical approach commonly used by federal prosecutors in determining whether to bring criminal charges against a target company and in choosing the severity of the charges brought. Thus, compliance programs that meet the requirements of the guidelines for criminal sentencing purposes may also help protect employers from civil and administrative sanctions under regulatory statutes.

Under the guidelines, an effective compliance program includes these features:

- Written standards of conduct that are reasonably capable of reducing the prospect of criminal behavior
- Overall compliance responsibility assigned to a high-level official
- Personnel policies that prevent persons having a propensity to engage in proscribed activity from having duties with substantial discretionary authority
- Communications and training programs for employees concerning conduct standards
- Internal monitoring and auditing systems designed to detect problematic conduct, *including a reporting mechanism that employees can use without fear of retribution*
- Disciplinary measures consistently applied
- Self-corrective measures where needed, to prevent non-complying conduct and to adjust

the reporting and compliance program as may be required

The Sentencing Commission thus constructed a compliance paradigm that has at its center a positive receptivity to whistleblowing, which is precisely the opposite of the resistance of the instinct for reprisal that has been the concern of statutory whistleblower protections and the common law "public policy" exceptions to the at-will employment doctrine.

Although the guidelines contemplate establishment of a multifaceted corporate compliance system, they make it clear that a credible program must provide internal channels for employees to complain about possible improprieties, without fear of retribution and with confidence that the matter will be treated seriously. Accordingly, to take advantage of the guidelines an employer must adopt mechanisms to promote, not discourage, internal reporting of perceived irregularities and to facilitate corrective action in the event that reports prove well-founded.

AN EFFECTIVE MANAGEMENT STRATEGY

As the foregoing discussion has indicated, the law as it has developed over the last decade seeks to promote a workplace environment that is hospitable to whistleblowing activities. To that end, it employs incentives in the form of both sticks and carrots to induce employers to create such an environment. The sticks include wrongful discharge litigation risks and burdens—amplified by the weight of law enforcement scrutiny in some circumstances. The carrots include potentially favorable assessment of the employer's intentions, in the event that those intentions *are* scrutinized by law enforcement officials and judges, so long as the employer has instituted a credible compliance regime.

In light of those incentives, what steps should prudent employers take to minimize risks and exposures in the whistleblowing era? The most fundamental advisory is the obvious one: an employer's key managers and human resources personnel must understand the applicable legal landscape. They must be familiar not only with the regulatory framework governing company operations, but also with whistleblower protections that apply where the company operates. Thus, training is of paramount importance. But beyond an appreciation of the legal terrain, two approaches recommend themselves to employers: they should aim first to create an overall compliance culture within the company by systematically fostering requisite attitudes and institutions, and in such a program they should incorporate steps that encourage potential whistleblowers to become more (not less) informed about business operations and thereby to channel their energies in productive directions.

Molding Organizational Culture

The analysis of the sentencing guidelines described above indicates that employers must develop a climate that both discourages illegal (or other objectionable) conduct and promotes internal reporting and resolution of wrongdoing allegations. Such a "corporate compliance" effort has both attitudinal and institutional dimensions and in general requires three fundamental commitments.

The first is more or less a matter of internal policy and posture: the employer must accord its compliance-related goals (and accommodation to whistleblowing protections) equal stature with—and at times explicit priority over—traditional private sector management objectives. Managers and human resources personnel must recognize, essentially, that elevating perceived public interests, and government policies that serve those interests, is not in conflict with a business calculus ordinarily focused intensely on the bottom line. In doing so, employers should find that appropriate policies and training can provide confidence that decisions and activities can be defended under standards government officials recognize and respect.

The second commitment the typical employer would have to make is organizational or structural: it should declare its attitude about compliance with law and regulation in a central compliance manager's charter and consolidate relevant functions under that individual. Such a charter would be developed explicitly to prevent and detect wrongdoing, ensure regulatory compliance, and eliminate other improprieties. The individual entrusted with that charter must similarly be given the resources commensurate with his or her authority and responsibility. Particularly in large and complex organizations, and among executives accustomed to operating in accordance with balance-sheet calculations and imperatives, these steps may not be easy to take.

A third basic commitment typical employers must make is programmatic: a compliance manager must devise and execute (1) a system of standards, (2) a monitoring strategy that covers appropriate pressure points systematically, and (3) communication channels that facilitate early reporting and correction of what employees perceive as irregularities. The success of this effort depends critically on the nature of the compliance manager's charter and on the support (and participation) of other leaders within the employer's organization. In that respect, all three of these fundamental corporate commitments are interrelated, and weakness in one will undermine them all.

Educating Potential Whistleblowers

As discussed above, under legal standards now prominent an employer's compliance program must provide meaningful and accessible internal channels for employees to lodge complaints about suspected improprieties. Whatever else an employer may choose to incorporate into its operational strategies, it must be receptive to whistleblowers' perspectives and react decisively to address the issues they raise.

True receptivity, of course, requires an openness to mistaken or fanciful reports as well as ones that are on target. Compliance officers, human resources personnel, in-house counsel, and all who are involved in the formal compliance apparatus must vigorously pursue each indication of potential impropriety without prejudging its merits. For most employers, the new realities of the whistleblower era mean that internal investigative systems must become more active, intrusive, and costly than in the past. The potential rewards are also greater than in the past—reduction in legal defense costs (and huge verdicts) associated with whistleblower claims, as well as better reception by regulators when a legitimate problem is uncovered.

Employers can, and should, take steps to improve the *quality* of whistleblowers' reporting, to both internal and external authorities, by reducing the ways in which employees might misperceive or misunderstand the corporate activity they see. The objective here is essentially to ensure that employees' judgments about employer conduct have the right referents: an accurate view of the relevant facts (workplace events) and a clear understanding of the applicable regulatory standards. So informed, employees—without becoming less vigilant for indicators of wrongdoing—should be far less likely to clutter internal complaint channels with dubious reports or suspicions. This again highlights the importance of well-conceived employer-sponsored education and training programs, augmented by less formal dialogue across jurisdictional boundaries in the workplace that, if possible, expose employees to the full spectrum of their employers' operations.

In effect, then, the emerging whistleblower phenomenon requires employers to recognize and implement a corollary of a key principle announced in the sentencing guidelines: that employers should train their employees in ethical matters. Companies should surely do that, but to be most effective such training must occur in the context of some familiarity with the full spectrum of company functions and policies, industry practices and relationships, and the overarching regulatory regime. This broad-gauged view of employees' overall "education" needs can markedly improve an employer's chances of avoiding litigation and other proceedings in which it must defend against serious allegations that stem, at bottom, from the whistleblowers' incomplete knowledge of (1) the employer's activities, systems, policies, and strategies; (2) industry structure and standards; and (3) the government's regulatory framework.

Thus, prudent employers should attempt systematically to broaden (not, as might be the reflexive and defensive response, to narrow) employees' awareness of work-related matters beyond what they do every day. Programs so designed will not only serve useful employee development goals, but will also go far to reduce a company's exposure to unfounded complaints. There is no question, of course, that such initiatives must compete for attention and resources with others more directly productive of profits or cost savings. Accordingly, institutional and attitudinal commitments such as those discussed above will likely be preconditions to their establishment and survival in any employer's organization.

CONCLUSION

What is most critical in the whistleblowing era is for employers to commit the corporate enterprise fully to complying with norms and expectations that are grounded in the public interest and that impose clear costs without offering equally tangible offsetting benefits. In some situations, this commitment may require what amounts to a counter-cultural reordering of an employer's priorities and a reshaping of attitudes, structures, and programs, all in the name of some concept of the public interest. It is doubtlessly true that for such an effort to remain viable over the long haul, it has to be led from the top and sustained by energies that press constantly downward and outward to all people employed in the organization. It is incumbent on human resources personnel and in-house counsel also to play an active leadership role in this process. If the trend toward increasing regulation and scrutiny by both employees and regulators continues, employers not so led are at markedly greater risk in today's legal environment than many may believe.

NOTES

1. The phenomenon has impressed some observers as an increasingly crowded "whistleblower protection bandwagon." See Dworkin and Callahan, "Internal Whistleblowing: Protecting the Interests of the Employee, the Organization, and Society," 29 *Am. Bus. L.J.* 267 (1991).

2. For example, companies now must comply with a broad range of requirements relating to socioeconomic objectives and environmental concerns. See, e.g., Hartman, "How Environmental Compliance Programs May Miss Their Mark," *Nat'l L.J.,* December 14, 1992, at S10.

3. The Organizational Sentencing Guidelines assist judges in sentencing organizations found guilty of federal crimes. U.S. Sentencing Commission, Federal Sentencing Guidelines Manual, §8A1.2 commentary at 362 (1993 ed.).

4. Compare the narrow definition in Tobias, *Litigating Wrongful Discharge Claims,* Vol. 1, §5:14 (Clark Boardman Callaghan, 1991), to the broad definition in Westman, *Whistleblowing: The Law of Retaliatory Discharge,* at 19 (BNA Books, 1991).

5. See Westman, Id. at 188–97, summarizing relevant provisions of twenty-seven statutes.

6. See, e.g., Boyle, "A Review of Whistleblower Protections and Suggestions for Change," 41 *Labor L.J.* 12 (1990).

7. For an overview of perspective pro and con, see the debate on H.R. 1664 in *Hearing on H.R. 1664, Corporate Whistleblower Protection: Hearing Before the Subcomm. on Labor-Management Relations of the House Comm. on Education and Labor,* 102d Cong., 2d Sess. (1992).

8. See e.g., Wartzman, "Northrop Agrees To Pay about $9 Million To Settle Suit by Two Whistle-blowers," *Wall St. J.,* June 24, 1991, at A4. The former employees' bounty in that case could have been up to 25 percent of the government's proceeds.

9. See, e.g., Callahan and Dworkin, "Do Good and Get Rich: Financial Incentives for Whistleblowing and the False Claims Act," 37 *Vill L. Rev.* 273 (1992).

10. Statement of Daniel Westman, in *Hearing on H.R. 1664* (cited in note 7) at 89. States protecting public employee whistleblowers include Alaska, Arizona, California, Colorado, Delaware, Florida, Illinois, Indiana, Iowa, Kansas, Kentucky, Maryland, Missouri, Nevada, New Hampshire, North Carolina, Oklahoma, Oregon, Pennsylvania, South Carolina, Tennessee, Texas, Utah, Washington, West Virginia and Wisconsin. States whose protections cover private sector whistleblowers include California, Connecticut, Florida, Hawaii, Louisiana, Maine, Michigan, Minnesota, New Hampshire, New Jersey, New York, Ohio, Rhode Island, Tennessee and Wisconsin. See also Barnett, "Overview of State Whistleblower Protection Statutes," 43 *Labor L.J.* 440 (1992); Westman (cited in note 4) at 177–87; Dworkin and Callahan (cited in note 1) at 275–80.

11. See Adler and Daniels, "Managing the Whistle-blowing Employee," 8 *The Lab. Law.* 19 (1992), observing that state whistleblower protections vary in the types of activity protected, the types of information that may be disclosed, the entities to which disclosures may be made, the form the disclosures may take, the knowledge and intent of the whistleblower, and other factors of circumstances that may critically affect the availability of protections.

12. Hughes et al., "Counseling the Whistleblower (Part I)," 38 *The Prac. Law,* 37 (June 1992).

13. See the state-by-state survey in *Special Report: State Labor Laws Enacted in 1992,* Daily Labor Report (BNA) No. 72 (April 16, 1993).

14. See, e.g., the survey in R. Greene, et al., 1993 *State by State Guide to Human Resources Law* (1993), at 8–31 to 8–41. In 1992, the Colorado Supreme Court found thirty-seven jurisdictions that recognize a public policy tort exception to the at-will rule and nine jurisdictions that have declined to do so. *Martin Marietta Corp. v. Lorentz,* 823 P.2d 100 (Colo. 1992).

15. The decisions were so summarized in *Hinson v. Cameron,* 742 P.2d 549 (Okla. 1987).

16. See also *Palmateer v. Int'l Harvester Co.,* 421 N.E. 2d 876 (Ill. 1981).

17. Scc, c.g., the arguments offered (unsuccessfully) in *Belline v. K-Mart Corp.,* 940 F.2d 184 (7th Cir. 1991) (public policy favoring exposure of crime protected employee who reported suspicions of criminal conduct to the employer but not to government authorities).

18. See Tobias (cited in note 4) at §5:20.

Whistleblowing: Professionalism, Personal Life, and Shared Responsibility for Safety in Engineering

Mike W. Martin

More than most issues, life and death issues in the professions rivet our attention. Medicine presents us with questions about whether to remove life-support systems and whether to assist the suicide of patients who could live, but with a dubious quality of life. Law disturbs us with the need for defense attorneys to defend clients who they know are morally guilty of murder or rape and who may engage in those crimes again if released. And engineering confronts us with agonizing decisions about whether to whistleblow in order to warn the public of deadly hazards known only to those inside technological corporations.

Source: Business & Professional Ethics Journal, Vol 11 (2) (Spring, 1992): 21–40.

Right off, this interest in whistleblowing tells us something important about engineering. Whistleblowing occurs in all professions, and most of what I say will have general relevance to professional ethics. Only in engineering ethics, however, has whistleblowing been something of a preoccupation. The reason is clear. Engineers work on projects that affect the safety of large numbers of people. As professionals, they live by codes of ethics which ascribe to them a paramount obligation to protect the safety, health, and welfare of the public, an obligation that sometimes implies whistleblowing. As employees of corporations, however, their obligation is to respect the authority of managers who sometimes give insufficient attention to safety matters, and who also severely punish whistleblowers. As a result, there are inevitable conflicts between professional obligations to employers and the public, as well as conflicts between professional and personal life.

I want to take a fresh look at whistleblowing in order to draw attention to some neglected issues concerning the moral relevance of personal life to understanding professional responsibilities. Specifically, the issues concern: personal rights and responsibilities in deciding how to meet professional obligations; increased personal burdens when others involved in collective endeavors fail to meet their responsibilities; the role of the virtues, especially personal integrity, as they bear on "living with oneself"; and personal commitments to moral ideals beyond minimum requirements.

1. DEFINITION AND CASES

By "whistleblowing" I have in mind the actions of employees (or former employees) who identify what they believe to be a significant moral problem concerning their corporation (or corporations they deal with), who convey information about the problem outside approved organizational channels or against pressure from supervisors or colleagues not to do so, with the intention of drawing attention to the problem (whatever further motives they may have).[1] Examples of serious moral problems include felonies, immoral treatment of clients or employees (such as sexual harassment), misuse of public funds, and—my focus here—technological products that are unacceptably dangerous to the public.

I will focus on cases where whistleblowers identify themselves. While anonymous whistleblowing is a legitimate option in some situations, acknowledging one's identity and credentials is usually necessary in order to be taken seriously; in any case, corporations typically have resources to hunt down "leaks" in order to identify whistleblowers.[2] I will discuss both external whistleblowing, where information is passed outside the corporations (for example, to government officials, the press, professional societies), and internal whistleblowing, where information is passed to higher management against corporate policy or one's supervisor's directives.

Let me bring to mind three well-known cases.

1. In 1972 Dan Appelgate wrote a memo to his supervisor, the vice-president of Convair Corporation, telling him in no uncertain terms that the cargo door for the DC-10 airplane was unsafe, making it "inevitable that, in the twenty years ahead of us, DC-10 cargo doors will come open and I would expect this to usually result in the loss of the airplane."[3] As a subcontractor for McDonnell Douglas, Convair had designed the cargo door and the DC-10 fuselage. Applegate was Director of Product Engineering at Convair and the senior engineer in charge of the design. His supervisor did not challenge his technical judgment in the matter, but told him that nothing could be done because of the likely costs to Convair in admitting responsibility for a design error that would need to be fixed by grounding DC-10's. Two years later, the cargo door on a Turkish

DC-10 flying near Paris opened in flight, decompressurizing the cargo area so as to collapse the passenger floor—along which run the controls for the aircraft. All 346 people on board died, a record casualty figure at that time for a single-plane crash. Tens of millions of dollars were paid out in civil suits, but no one was charged with criminal or even unprofessional conduct.

2. Frank Camps was a principal design engineer for the Pinto.[4] Under pressure from management he participated in coaxing the Pinto windshield through government tests by reporting only the rare successful test and by using a Band-Aid fix design that resulted in increased hazard to the gas tank. In 1973, undergoing a crisis of conscience in response to reports of exploding gas tanks, he engaged in internal whistleblowing, writing the first of many memos to top management stating his view that Ford was violating federal safety standards. It took six years before his concerns were finally incorporated into the 1979 model Pinto, after nearly a million Pintos with unsafe windshields and gas tanks were put on the road. Shortly after writing his memos he was given lower performance evaluations, then demoted several times. He resigned in 1978 when it became clear his prospects for advancement at Ford were ended. He filed a law suit based in part on age discrimination, in part on trying to prevent Ford from making him a scapegoat for problems with the Pinto, and in part on trying to draw further attention to the dangers in the Pinto.

3. On January 27, 1986, Roger Boisjoly and other senior engineers at Morton Thiokol firmly recommended that space shuttle *Challenger* not be launched.[5] The temperature at the launch site was substantially below the known safety range for the O-ring seals in the joints of the solid rocket boosters. Top management overrode the recommendation. Early in the launch, the *Chal-*

lenger boosters exploded, killing the seven crew members, to the terrified eyes of millions who watched because schoolteacher Christa McAuliffe was aboard. A month later Boisjoly was called to testify before the Rogers Commission. Against the wishes of management, he offered documents to support his interpretation of the events leading to the disaster—and to rebut the interpretation given by his boss. Over the next months Boisjoly was made to feel increasingly alienated from his coworkers until finally he had to take an extended sick leave. Later, when he desired to find a new job he found himself confronted with companies unwilling to take a chance on a known whistleblower.

As the last two cases suggest, there can be double horrors surrounding whistleblowing: the public horror of lost lives, and the personal horror of responsible whistleblowers who lose their careers. Most whistleblowers undergo serious penalties for "committing the truth." One recent study suggests that two out of three of them suffer harassment, lowered performance evaluations, demotions, punitive transfers, loss of jobs, or blacklisting that can effectively end a career.[6] Horror stories about whistleblowers are not the exception; they are the rule.

2. THREE APPROACHES TO WHISTLEBLOWING ETHICS

The literature on whistleblowing is large and growing. Here I mention three general approaches. The first is to condemn whistleblowers as disloyal troublemakers who "rat" on their companies and undermine teamwork based on the hierarchy of authority within the corporation. Admittedly, whistleblowers' views about safety concerns are sometimes correct, but final decisions about safety belong to management, not engineers. When management errs, the corporation will eventually pick up the costs in law suits and adverse publicity. Members of the public are part of the technological enterprise which both benefits them and exposes them to risks; when things go wrong they (or their surviving family) can always sue.

I once dismissed this attitude as callous, as sheer corporate egoism that misconstrues loyalty to a corporation as an absolute (unexceptionless) moral principle. *If,* however—and it is a big "if"—the public accepts this attitude, as revealed in how it expresses its will through legitimate political processes, then so be it. As will become clear later, I take public responsibilities seriously. If the public refuses to protect whistleblowers, it tacitly accepts the added risks from not having available important safety information. I hope the public will protect the jobs of whistleblowers; more on this later.

A second approach, insightfully defended by Michael Davis,[7] is to regard whistleblowing as a tragedy to be avoided. On occasion whistleblowing may be a necessary evil or even admirable, but it is always bad news all around. It is proof of organizational trouble and management failure; it threatens the careers of managers on whom the whistle is blown; it disrupts collegiality by making colleagues feel resentment toward the whistleblower, and it damages the important informal network of friends at the workplace; it shows the whistleblower lost faith in the organization and its authority, and hence is more likely to be a troublemaker in the future; and it almost always brings severe penalties to whistleblowers who are viewed by employers and colleagues as unfit employees.

I wholeheartedly support efforts to avoid the need for whistleblowing. There are many things that can be done to improve organizations to make whistleblowing unnecessary. Top management can—and must—set a moral tone, and then implement policies that encourage safety concerns (and other bad news) to be communicated freely. Specifically, managers can keep doors open, allowing engineers to convey their

concerns without retribution. Corporations can have in-house ombudspersons and appeal boards, and even a vice-president for corporate ethics. For their part, engineers can learn to be more assertive and effective in making their safety concerns known, learning how to build support from their colleagues. (Could Dan Applegate have pushed harder than he did, or did he just write a memo and drop the matter?) Professional societies should explore the possibility of creating confidential appeal groups where engineers can have their claims heard.

Nevertheless, this second approach is not enough. There will always be corporations and managers willing to cut corners on safety in the pursuit of short-term profit, and there will always be a need for justified whistleblowing. Labelling whistleblowing as a tragedy to be avoided whenever possible should not deflect attention from issues concerning justified whistleblowing.

We need to remind ourselves that responsible whistleblowing is *not* bad news all around. It is very good news for the public which is protected by it. The good news is both episodic and systematic. Episodically, lives are saved directly when professionals speak out, and lives are lost when professionals like Dan Applegate feel they must remain silent in order to keep their jobs. Systematically, lives are saved indirectly by sending a strong message to industry that legally-protected whistleblowing is always available as a last resort when managers too casually override safety concerns for short-term profits. Helpful pressure is put on management to take a more farsighted view of safety, thereby providing a further impetus for unifying corporate self-interest with the production of safe products. (In the DC-10, Pinto, and *Challenger* cases, management made shortsighted decisions that resulted in enormous costs in law suits and damaged company reputations.)

In this day of (sometimes justified) outcry over excessive government regulation, we should not forget the symbolic importance of clear, effective, and enforced laws as a way for society to express its collective vision of a good society.[8] Laws protecting responsible whistle-blowing express the community's resolve to support professionals who act responsibly for public safety. Those laws are also required if the public is to meet its responsibilities in the creation of safe technological products, as I will suggest in a moment.

A third approach is to affirm unequivocally the obligation of engineers (and other professionals) to whistleblow in certain circumstances, and to treat this obligation as paramount—as overriding all other considerations, whatever the sacrifice involved in meeting it. Richard De George gave the classical statement of this view.[9] External whistleblowing, he argued, is obligatory when five conditions are met (by an engineer or other corporate employee):

1. "Serious and considerable harm to the public" is involved;
2. one reports the harm and expresses moral concern to one's immediate superior;
3. one exhausts other channels within the corporation;
4. one has available "documented evidence that would convince a reasonable, impartial observer that one's view of the situation is correct"; and
5. one has "good reasons to believe that by going public the necessary changes will be brought about" to prevent the harm.

De George says that whistleblowing is morally *permissible* when conditions 1-3 are met, and is morally *obligatory* when 1-5 are met.

As critics have pointed out, conditions (4) and (5) seem far too strong. Where serious safety is at stake, there is some obligation to whistleblow even when there are only grounds for hope (not necessarily belief) that whistle-blowing will significantly improve matters, and even when one's documentation is substantial

but less than convincing to every rational person.[10] Indeed, often whistleblowing is intended to prompt authorities to garner otherwise-unavailable evidence through investigations.

Moreover, having a reasonable degree of documentation is a requirement even for permissible whistleblowing—lest one make insupportable allegations that unjustifiably harm the reputations of individuals and corporations. So too is having a reasonable hope for success—lest one waste everyone's time and energy.[11] Hence, De George's sharp separation of requirements for permissibility and obligation begins to collapse. There may be an obligation to whistle-blow when 1-3 are met and the person has some reasonable degree of documentation and reasonable hope for success in bringing about necessary changes.

My main criticism of this third approach, however, is more fundamental. I want to call into question the whole attempt to offer a general rule that tells us when whistleblowing is mandatory, *tout court*. Final judgments about obligations to whistleblow must be made contextually, not as a matter of general rule. And they must take into account the burdens imposed on whistleblowers.[12]

3. THE MORAL RELEVANCE OF PERSONAL LIFE TO PROFESSIONAL DUTY

In my view, there is a strong *prima facie* obligation to whistleblow when one has good reason to believe there is a serious moral problem, has exhausted normal organizational channels (except in emergencies when time precludes that), has available a reasonable amount of documentation, and has reasonable hope of solving the problem by blowing the whistle. Nevertheless, however strong, the obligation is only *prima facie*: It can sometimes have exceptions when it conflicts with other important considerations. Moreover, the considerations which need to be weighed include not only *prima facie* obligations to one's employer, but also considerations about one's personal life. Before they make all-things-considered judgments about whether to whistleblow, engineers may and should consider their responsibilities to their family, other personal obligations which depend on having an income, and their rights to pursue their careers.

Engineers are people, as well as professionals. They have personal obligations to their families, as well as sundry other obligations in personal life which can be met only if they have an income. They also have personal rights to pursue careers. These personal obligations and rights are moral ones, and they legitimately interact with professional obligations in ways that sometimes make it permissible for engineers not to whistleblow, even when they have a *prima facie* obligation to do so. Precisely how these considerations are weighed depends on the particular situation. And here as elsewhere, we must allow room for morally reasonable people to weigh moral factors differently.

In adopting this contextual approach to balancing personal and professional obligations, I am being heretical. Few discussions of whistleblowing take personal considerations seriously, as being morally significant, rather than a matter of nonmoral, prudential concern for self-interest. But responsibilities to family and to others outside the workplace, as well as the right to pursue one's career, are moral considerations, not just prudential ones. Hence further argument is needed to dismiss them as irrelevant or always secondary in this context. I will consider three such arguments.

(i) The *Prevent-Harm Argument* says that morality requires us to prevent harm and in doing so to treat others' interests equally and impartially with our own. This assumption is often associated with utilitarianism, the view that we should always produce the most good for the most people. Strictly, at issue here is "negative utilitarianism," which says we should always act to minimize total harm, treating everyone's interests as equally important with our own. The idea is that even though engineers and their families must suffer, their suffering is outweighed by the lives saved through whistleblowing. Without committing himself to utilitarianism, De George uses a variation of the impartiality requirement to defend his criteria for obligatory whistleblowing: "It is not implausible to claim both that we are morally obliged to prevent harm to others at relatively little expense to ourselves, and that we are morally obliged to prevent great harm to a great many others, even at considerable expense to ourselves."[13]

The demand for strict impartiality in ethics has been under sustained attack during the past two decades, and from many directions.[14] Without attempting to review all those arguments, I can indicate how they block any straightforward move from impartiality to absolute (exceptionless) whistleblowing obligations, thereby undermining the Prevent-Harm Argument. One argument is that a universal requirement of strict impartiality (as opposed to a limited requirement restricted to certain contexts) is self-demeaning. It undermines our ability to give our lives meaning through special projects, careers, and relationships that require the resources which strict impartiality would demand we give away to others. The general moral right to autonomy—the right to pursue our lives in a search for meaning and happiness—implies a right to give considerable emphasis to our personal needs and those of our family.

As an analogy, consider the life-and-death issues surrounding world hunger and scarce medical resources.[15] It can be argued that all of us share a general responsibility (of mutual aid) for dealing with the tragedy of tens of thousands of people who die each day from malnutrition and lack of medical care. As citizens paying taxes that can be used toward this end, and also as philanthropists who voluntarily recognize a responsibility to give to relief organizations, each of us has a *prima facie* obligation to help. But there are limits. Right now, you and I could dramatically lower our lifestyles in order to help save lives by making greater sacrifices. We could even donate one of our kidneys to save a life. Yet we have a right not to do that, a right to give ourselves and our families considerable priority in how we use our resources. Similarly, engineers' rights to pursue their meaning-giving careers, and the projects and relationships made possible by those careers, have relevance in understanding the degree of sacrifice required by a *prima facie,* whistleblowing obligation.

(ii) The *Avoid-Harm Argument* proceeds from the obligation not to cause harm to others. It then points out that engineers are in a position to cause or avoid harm on an unusual scale. As a result, according to Kenneth Alpern, the ordinary moral obligation of due care in avoiding harm to others implies that engineers must "be ready to make greater personal sacrifices than can normally be demanded of other individuals."[16] In particular, according to Gene James, whistleblowing is required when it falls under the general obligation to "prevent unnecessary harm to others" and "to not cause avoidable harm to others," where "harm" means violating their rights.[17]

Of course there is a general obligation not to cause harm. That obligation, however, is so abstract that it tells us little about exactly how much effort and sacrifice is required of us, especially where many people share responsibility for avoiding harm. I have an obligation not to harm others by polluting the environment, but it does not follow that I must stop driving my car at the cost of my job and the opportunities it makes possible for my family. That would be an unfair burden. These abstract difficulties multiply as we turn to the context of engineering practice which involves collective responsibility for technological products.

Engineers work as members of authority-structured teams which sometimes involve hundreds of other professionals who share responsibility for inherently-risky technological projects.[18] Engineers are not the only team-members who have responsibilities to create safe products. Their managers have exactly the same general responsibilities. In fact, they have greater accountability insofar as they are charged with the authority to make final decisions about projects. True, engineers have greater expertise in safety matters and hence have greater responsibilities to identify dangers and convey that information to management. But whatever justifications can be given for engineers to zealously protect public safety also apply to managers. In making the decision to launch the *Challenger,* Jerald Mason, Senior Vice President for Morton Thiokol, is said to have told Robert Lund, "Take off your engineering hat and put on your management hat." Surely this change in headgear did not alter his moral responsibilities for safety.

Dan Applegate and Roger Boisjoly acted responsibly in making unequivocal safety recommendations; their managers failed to act responsibly. Hence their moral dilemmas about whether to whistleblow arose because of unjustified decisions by their superiors. It is fair to ask engineers to pick up the moral slack for managers' irresponsible decisions—as long as we afford them legal protection to prevent their being harassed, fired, and blacklisted. Otherwise, we impose an unfair burden. Government and the general public share responsibility for safety in engineering. They set the rules that business plays by. It is hypocrisy for us to insist that engineers have an obligation to whistleblow to protect us, and then to fail to protect them when they act on the obligation.

(iii) The *Professional-Status Argument* asserts that engineers have special responsibilities as professionals, specified in codes of ethics, which go beyond the general responsibilities incumbent on everyone to prevent and avoid harm, and which override all personal considerations.

Most engineering codes hint at a whistleblowing obligation with wording similar to that of the code of the National Society of Professional Engineers (NSPE):

> Engineers shall at all times recognize that their primary obligation is to protect the safety, health, property and welfare of the public. If their professional judgment is over-ruled under circumstances where the safety, health, property or welfare of the public are endangered, they shall notify their employer or client and such other authority as may be appropriate.[19]

The phrase "as may be appropriate" is ambiguous. Does it mean "when morally justified," or does it mean "as necessary in order to protect the public safety, health, and welfare." The latter interpretation is the most common one, and it clearly implies whistleblowing in some situations, no matter what the personal cost.

I agree that the obligation to protect public safety is an essential professional obligation that deserves emphasis in engineers' work. It is not clear, however, that it is paramount in the technical philosophical sense of overriding all other professional obligations in all situations. In any case, I reject the general assumption that codified professional duties are all that are morally relevant in making whistleblowing decisions. It is quite true that professional considerations require setting aside personal interests in many situations. But it is also true that personal considerations have enormous and legitimate importance in professional life, such as in choosing careers and areas of specialization, choosing and changing jobs, and deciding how far to go in sacrificing family life in pursuing a job and a career.

Spouses have a right to participate in professional decisions such as those involving whistleblowing.[20] At the very least, I would be worried about professionals who do not see the moral importance of consulting their spouses before deciding to engage in acts of whistleblowing

that will seriously affect them and their children. I would be equally worried about critics who condemn engineers for failing to whistleblow without knowing anything about their personal situation.[21]

Where does all this leave us on the issue of engineers' obligations? It is clear there is a minimum standard which engineers must meet. They have strong obligations not to break the law and not to approve projects which are immoral according to standard practice. They also have a *prima facie* obligation to whistleblow in certain situations. Just how strong the whistleblowing responsibility is, all things considered, remains unclear—as long as there are inadequate legal protections.

What is clear is that whistleblowing responsibilities must be understood contextually, weighed against personal rights and responsibilities, and assessed in light of the public's responsibilities to protect whistleblowers. We must look at each situation. Sometimes the penalties for whistleblowing may not be as great as is usually the case, perhaps because some protective laws have been passed, and sometimes family responsibilities and rights to pursue a career may not be seriously affected. But our all-things-considered judgments about whistleblowing are not a matter of general absolute principle that always overrides every other consideration.

Yes, the public has a right to be warned by whistleblowers of dangers—assuming the public is willing to bear its responsibility for passing laws protecting whistleblowers. In order to play their role in respecting that right, engineers should have a legally-backed *right of conscience* to take responsible action in safety matters beyond the corporate walls.[22] As legal protections are increased, as has begun to happen during the past decade,[23] then the relative weight of personal life to professional duty changes. Engineers will be able to whistleblow more often without the kind of suffering to which they have been exposed, and thus the *prima facie* obligation to whistleblow will be less frequently overridden by personal responsibilities.

4. CHARACTER, INTEGRITY, AND PERSONAL IDEALS

Isn't there a danger that denying the existence of absolute, all-things-considered, principles for whistleblowers will further discourage whistleblowing in the public interest? After all, even if we grant my claims about the moral relevance of personal rights and responsibilities, there remains the general tendency for self-interest to unduly bias moral decisions. Until adequate legal protection is secured, won't this contextual approach result in fewer whistleblowers who act from a sense of responsibility? I think not.

If all-things-considered judgments about whistleblowing are not a matter of general rule, they are still a matter of good moral judgment. Good judgment takes into account rules whenever they provide helpful guidance, but essentially it is a product of good character—a character defined by virtues. Character is a further area in which personal aspects of morality bear on engineering ethics, and in the space remaining I want to comment on it.

Virtues are those desirable traits that reveal themselves in all aspects of personality—in attitudes, emotions, desires, and conduct. They are not private merit badges. (To view them as such is the egoistic distortion of self-righteousness.[24]) Instead, virtues are desirable ways of relating to other people, to communities, and to social practices such as engineering. Which virtues are most important for engineers to cultivate?

Here are some of the most significant virtues, sorted into three general categories.[25]

1. *Virtues of self-direction* are those which enable us to guide our lives. They include the *intellectual virtues* which characterize technical expertise: mastery of one's discipline, ability to communicate, skills in reasoning, imagination, ability to discern dangers, a disposition to minimize risk, and humility (understood as a reasonable perspective on one's abilities). They also include *integrity virtues* which promote coherence among one's attitudes, commitments, and conduct based on a core of moral concern. They include honesty, courage, conscientiousness, self-respect, and fidelity to promises and commitments—those in both personal and professional life. And *wisdom* is practical good judgment in making responsible decisions. This good moral judgment, grounded in the experience of concerned and accountable engineers, is essential in balancing the aspirations embedded in the next two sets of virtues.

2. *Team-work virtues* include (a) loyalty: concern for the good of the organization for which one works; (b) collegiality: respect for one's colleagues and a commitment to work with them in shared projects; and (c) cooperativeness: the willingness to make reasonable compromises. Reasonable compromises can be integrity-preserving in that they enable us to meet our responsibilities to maintain relationships in circumstances where there is moral complexity and disagreement, factual uncertainty, and the need to maintain ongoing cooperative activities—exactly the circumstances of engineering practice.[26] Unreasonable compromises are compromising in the pejorative sense: they betray our moral principles and violate our integrity. Only good judgment, not general rules, enable engineers to draw a reasonable line between these two types of compromise.

3. *Public-spirited virtues* are those aimed at the good of others, both clients and the general public affected by one's work. *Justice virtues* concern fair play. One is respect for persons: the disposition to respect people's rights and autonomy, in particular, the rights

not to be injured in ways one does not consent to.

Public-spiritedness can be shown in different degrees, as can all the virtues. This helps us understand the sense of responsibility to protect the public that often motivates whistleblowers. Just as professional ethics has tended to ignore the moral relevance of personal life to professional responsibilities, it has tended to think of professional responsibilities solely in terms of *role responsibilities*—those minimal obligations which all practitioners take on when they enter a given profession. While role responsibilities are sufficiently important to deserve this emphasis, they are not the whole of professional ethics. There are also *ideals* which evoke higher aspirations than the minimum responsibilities.[27] These ideals are important to understanding the committed conduct of whistleblowers.

Depth of commitment to the public good is a familiar theme in whistleblowers' accounts of their ordeals. The depth is manifested in how they connect their self-respect and personal integrity to their commitments to the good of others. Roger Boisjoly, for example, has said that if he had it all to do over again he would make the same decisions because otherwise he "couldn't live with any self respect."[28] Similarly, Frank Camps says he acted from a sense of personal integrity.[29]

Boisjoly, Camps, and whistleblowers like them also report that they acted from a sense of responsibiity. In my view, they probably acted beyond the minimum standard that all engineers are required to meet, given the absence of protective laws and the severity of the personal suffering they had to undergo. Does it follow that they are simply confused about how much was required of them? J.O. Urmson once suggested that moral heroes who claim to be meeting their duties are either muddled in their thinking or excessively modest about their moral zealousness, which has carried them beyond the call of duty.[30]

Urmson, like most post-Kantian philosophers, assumed that obligations are universal, and hence that there could not be personal obligations that only certain individuals have. I hold a different view.[31] There is such a thing as voluntarily assuming a responsibility and doing so because of commitments to (valid) ideals, to a degree beyond what is required of everyone. Sometimes the commitment is shown in career choice and guided by religious ideals: think of Albert Schweitzer or Mother Teresa of Calcutta. Sometimes it is shown in professional life in an unusual degree of *pro bono publico* work. And sometimes it is shown in whistleblowing decisions.

According to this line of thought, whistleblowing done at enormous personal cost, motivated by moral concern for the public good, and exercising good moral judgment is both (a) supererogatory—beyond the general call of duty incumbent on everyone, and (b) appropriately motivated by a sense of responsibility. Such whistleblowers act from a sense that they *must* do what they are doing.[32] Failure to act would constitute a betrayal of the ideal to which they are committed, and also a betrayal of their integrity as a person committed to that ideal.

Here, then, is a further way in which personal life is relevant to professional life. Earlier I drew attention to the importance of personal rights and responsibilities, and to the unfair personal burdens when others involved in collective enterprises fail to meet their responsibilities. Equally important, we need to appreciate the role of personal integrity grounded in supererogatory commitments to ideals. The topic of being able to live with oneself should not be dismissed as a vagary of individual psychology. It concerns the ideals to which we commit ourselves, beyond the minimum standard incumbent on everyone. This appreciation of personal integrity and commitments to ideals is compatible with a primary emphasis on laws that make it possible for professionals to serve the public good without having to make heroic self-sacrifices.[33]

NOTES

1. Cf. Mike W. Martin and Roland Schinzinger, *Ethics in Engineering,* 2d ed. (New York: McGraw-Hill, 1989), p. 213 ff.

2. See Frederick Elliston, "Anonymous Whistleblowing," *Business & Professional Ethics Journal* Vol. 1, No. 2 (Winter 1982): 39–58.

3. Paul Eddy, Elaine Potter, Bruce Page, *Destination Disaster* (New York: Quadrangle, 1976), p. 185.

4. Frank Camps, "Warning an Auto Company About an Unsafe Design," in Alan F. Westin (ed.), *Whistle-Blowing!* (New York: McGraw-Hill, 1981), pp. 119–129.

5. Roger M. Boisjoly, "The Challenger Disaster: Moral Responsibility and the Working Engineer," in Deborah G. Johnson (ed.), *Ethical Issues in Engineering* (Englewood Cliffs, NJ: Prentice Hall, 1991), pp. 6–14.

6. See, e.g., Myron P. Glazer and Penina Migdal Glazer, *The Whistleblowers* (New York: Basic Books, 1989).

7. Michael Davis, "Avoiding the Tragedy of Whistleblowing," *Business & Professional Ethics Journal* Vol. 8, No. 4, (Winter, 1989): 3–19. Davis also draws attention to the potentially negative aspects of laws, as does Sissela Bok in "Whistleblowing and Professional Responsibilities," in D. Callahan and S. Bok (eds.), *Ethics Teaching in Higher Education* (New York: Plenum), pp. 277–295. Those aspects, which include violating corporate privacy, undermining trust and collegiality, and lowering economic efficiency, are serious. But I am convinced that well-framed laws to protect whistleblowers can take them into account. The laws should protect only whistleblowing that meets the conditions for the *prima facie* obligation I state at the beginning of section 3.

8. Robert Nozick drew attention to the symbolic importance of government action in general when he recently abjured the libertarian position he once defended vigorously. *The Examined Life* (New York: Simon and Schuster, 1989), pp. 286–288.

9. The quotes are from Richard T. De George's most recent statement of his view in *Business Ethics,* 3d ed. (New York: Macmillan Publishing, 1990), pp. 208–212. They parallel his view as first stated in "Ethical Responsibilities of Engineers in Large Organizations," *Business & Professional Ethics Journal* Vol. 1, No. 1 (Fall 1981): 1–14. As an example of a far higher demand on engineers see Kenneth D. Alpern, "Moral Responsibility for Engineers," *Business & Professional Ethics Journal* Vol. 2, No. 2 (Winter 1983): 39–47.

10. Gene G. James, "Whistle Blowing: Its Moral Justification," in W. Michael Hoffman and Jennifer Mills Moore (eds.), *Business Ethics,* 2d ed. (New York: McGraw-Hill, 1990), pp. 332–344.

11. David Theo Goldberg, "Tuning in to Whistle Blowing," *Business & Professional Ethics Journal* Vol. 7, No. 2 (Summer, 1988): 85–94.

12. As his reason for conditions (4) and (5), De George cites the fate of whistleblowers who put themselves at great risk: "If there is little likelihood of his success, there is no moral obligation for the engineer to go public. For the harm he or she personally incurs is not offset by the good such action achieves." ("Ethical Responsibilities of Engineers in Large Organizations," p. 7.) Like myself, then, he sees the personal suffering of whistleblowers as morally relevant to understanding professional responsibilities even though, as I go on to argue, he invokes that relevance in the wrong way.

13. De George, *Business Ethics,* p. 214.

14. See especially Bernard Williams, "A Critique of Utilitarianism," in *Utilitarianism for and Against* (Cambridge: Cambridge University Press, 1973) and "Persons, Character, and Morality," in *Moral Luck* (New York: Cambridge University Press, 1981). For samples of more recent discussions see the special edition of *Ethics* 101 (July 1991), devoted to "Impartiality and Ethical Theory."

15. Cf. John Arthur, "Rights and Duty to Bring Aid," in William Aiken and Hugh La Follette (eds.) *World Hunger and Moral Obligation* (Englewood Cliffs, NJ: Prentice-Hall, 1977).

16. Alpern, "Moral Responsibilities for Engineers," p. 39.

17. James, "Whistle Blowing: Its Moral Justification," pp. 334–335.

18. See Martin and Schinzinger, *Ethics in Engineering,* chapter 3. The emphasis on engineers adopt-

ing a wide view of their activities does not imply that they are culpable for all the moral failures of colleagues and managers.

19. National Society of Professional Engineers, Code of Ethics.

20. Cf. Thomas M. Devine and Donald G. Aplin, "Whistleblower Protection—The Gap Between the Law and Reality," *Howard Law Journal* 31 (1988), p. 236.

21. I am glad that the NSPE and other professional codes say what they do in support of responsible whistleblowing, as long as it is understood that professional codes only state professional, not personal and all-things-considered obligations. Codes provide a backing for morally concerned engineers, and they make available to engineers the moral support of an entire profession. At the same time, professional societies need to do far more than most of them have done to support the efforts of conscientious whistleblowers. Beyond moral and political support, and beyond recognition awards, they need to provide economic support in the form of legal funds and job-placement.

22. I defend this right in "Rights of Conscience Inside the Technological Corporation," *Conceptus-Studien, 4: Wissen and Gewissen* (Vienna VWGO, 1986): 179–191.

23. Alan F. Westin offers helpful suggestions about laws protecting whistleblowers in *Whistleblowing*. For a recent overview of the still fragmentary and partial laws protecting whistleblowers, see Rosemary Chalk, "Making the World Safe for Whistle-Blowers," see *Technology Review* 91 (January, 1988): 48–57; and James C. Petersen and Dan Farrell, *Whistleblowing: Ethical and Legal Issues in Expressing Dissent* (Dubuque, Iowa: Kendall/Hunt, 1986).

24. Cf. Edmund L. Pincoffs, *Quandaries and Virtues* (Lawrence, KS: University Press of Kansas, 1986), pp. 112–114.

25. Important discussions of the role of virtues in professional ethics include: John Kultgen, *Ethics and Professionalism* (Philadelphia: University of Pennsylvania Press, 1988); Albert Flores (ed.), *Professional Ideals* (Belmont, CA: Wadsworth, 1988); and Michael D. Bayles, *Professional Ethics,* 2d edition (Belmont, CA: Wadsworth, 1989). John Kekes insightfully discusses the virtues of self-direction in *The Examined Life* (Lewisburg: Bucknell University Press, 1988).

26. Martin Benjamin, *Splitting the Difference* (Lawrence, KS: University Press of Kansas), 1990.

27. On the distinction between moral rules and ideals see Bernard Gert, *Morality* (New York: Oxford University Press, 1988), pp. 160–178.

28. Roger Boisjoly, ibid., p. 14.

29. Frank Camps, ibid., p. 128.

30. J. O. Urmson, "Saints and Heroes," in A. I. Melden (ed.), *Essays in Moral Philosophy* (Seattle: University of Washington Press, 1958), pp. 198–216.

31. Cf. A. I. Melden, "Saints and Supererogation," in *Philosophy and Life: Essays on John Wisdom* (The Hague: Martinus Nijhoff, 1984), pp. 61–81.

32. Harry Frankfurt insightfully discusses this felt "must" as a sign of deep care and commitment in *The Importance of What We Care About* (New York: Cambridge University Press, 1988), pp. 86–88.

33. An earlier version of this paper was read in a lecture series sponsored by the Committee on Ethics in Research at the University of California, Santa Barbara (January 1992). I am grateful for the helpful comments of Jacqueline Hynes and Larry Badash, and also for conversations with Roland Schinzinger on this topic. I am especially grateful for the comments I received from the editor of this journal.

CHAPTER 10

"What's Mine? What's Yours?" Intellectual Property Rights

INTRODUCTION

When we think of property we usually imagine something tangible—the land people own, the cars they drive, or the equipment that belongs to a business—and we have relatively straightforward ideas concerning its use and protection. However, scientific formulae, software designs, marketing plans, and customer lists are examples of another, more complex, type of property: intellectual property. This chapter discusses the ethical and legal issues surrounding its use and protection.

Several factors account for the increasing importance of intellectual property in the current business climate. First, a company's competitive success frequently depends on its ability to be technologically innovative, often making information and knowledge its most valuable assets. Second, the nature of the employer–employee relationship in the United States appears to be changing. In a highly competitive and rapidly changing economy, the long-term employment relationship may be a thing of the past, particularly in the "high-tech" industries. Departing employees regularly take their knowledge and information with them, sometimes to a competitor.

While tangible property has physical location, can usually be easily identified, and is exclusive (i.e., the use of it by one person typically precludes someone else from using it at the same time), intellectual property can be used by different persons at different places at the same time. It is commonly harder to identify than tangible property since it is often intimately related to other ideas and background knowledge and is difficult to disentangle from them.

The ethical and legal issues concerning intellectual property involve weighing the legitimate interests of employers, employees, and society at large. Employers have an interest in their firms' competitive success in the marketplace, in protecting their investments of time and money, and in recruiting and retaining talented employees. Employees have an interest in furthering their careers and in using their knowledge and talents to their best advantage. Society has an interest in the free exchange of information and in securing the benefits of knowledge. Judgments of utility, fairness, and rights all play a role in balancing these interests.

Not everything that a company wishes to claim as its own enjoys the protection of ethics

457

or the law. A company's ability to identify its intellectual property and to establish its proprietorship is essential. Copyrights, patents, and trade secrets are three principal forms of intellectual property; each has its own requirements and each offers its own protection. Because they are the least expensive to obtain and provide the broadest protection, trade secrets are possibly the most effective way to provide protection. However, there is frequently controversy about whether certain information meets the criteria for classification as a trade secret.

The Uniform Trade Secrets Act specifies that, to qualify as a trade secret, information must

1. derive independent economic value, actual or potential, from not being generally known, and not being readily ascertainable by proper means by, other persons who can obtain economic value from its disclosure and use;
2. be the subject of efforts that are reasonable under the circumstances to maintain its secrecy. (Uniform Trade Secrets Act, 14 U. L. A. 433 (1990) 1 (4))

Also considered, according to the *Restatement of Torts* (Section 757), are the extent to which the information is generally known or could be generally known, the economic value that its owner derives from its not being generally known, the amount of time and money that was expended in developing it, and the measures taken to protect its secrecy.

Property rights and the duties of confidentiality are often cited as two important ethical and legal arguments for the protectability of trade secrets. These arguments presuppose that it is possible to identify clearly the property in question and to determine with some precision who has the rights of ownership. Doing so in practice is often difficult.

When trade secrets are already in the employer's possession, the employer's property rights and the employee's duty of confidentiality are fairly clear, at least for the time that the employer takes reasonable steps to protect the information and it does not become commonly known. However, when an employee has been involved in developing the information, it is often difficult to determine precisely the relative contributions, and hence the property rights, of employer and employee. Sometimes these matters are settled contractually, but often, even when there is a contract in place, both legal questions and ethical concerns of fairness arise.

Similarly, it is frequently difficult to distinguish in a particular case between trade secrets and the background knowledge and experience that a potential employee brings to the job. An employee has the right to use such "intellectual capital" to further his or her career interests. In such cases, marking off where an employer's legitimate interests in his or her intellectual property ends and an employee's background skills begin can be very complicated.

In general, society benefits from an increase in its stock of knowledge and has an interest in its continued development. Since it is highly unlikely that companies would invest large amounts of time and money in developing new ideas unless they had some assurance that the results of their work would be protected, utilitarian considerations support the protection surrounding intellectual property. At the same time, employee mobility and the free exchange of ideas not only contribute to the development of this stock of socially valuable knowledge but also to the life satisfaction of many of society's members. Thus, courts attempt to balance carefully the interests of employers, employees, and the public; they also cautiously examine agreements that restrict the post-employment activities of employees. However, managers and employers who recognize the important role that their employees play in the development of their intellectual capital may well be the most effective protection that intellectual property can have.

★ ★ ★

According to **Kathleen Murray,** protecting knowledge has become a problem that departments of human resources are well equipped to manage. HR personnel are the logical ones to establish and enforce security arrangements, to supervise the implementation of legal agreements, to supply training about the use and protection of intellectual property, and to create programs which reward employees' technological achievements. **Miles J. Feldman** examines the terms of the Uniform Trade Secrets Act and concludes that they fail to balance adequately employer and employee interests. He proposes several strategies for improving the law in this area. **Edwin C. Hettinger** and **Lynn Sharpe Paine** both discuss the significant ethical questions concerning intellectual property. Hettinger lists several important differences between intellectual and tangible property and points out some of the difficulties of ethically justifying the exclusive use of intellectual property, particularly trade secrets. Paine disagrees with Hettinger's analysis, arguing that trade secrets must be discussed in a different context from patents and copyrights, and that they can be ethically justified.

CASE: Colin Rhodes At Jansen Chemical, Inc.

Sitting at his new desk, at his new job at Jansen Chemical, Inc., Colin Rhodes contemplated the events that led up to his writing of the draft report he held in his hand.

He reflected upon the information he was about to give to Laura Kraviston. He had promised her a memo detailing a set of manufacturing innovations developed by him and his group at Rontech Industries, his former employer. Colin was well aware of the impact this information could have at Jansen, as well as of the personal recognition that he might receive. He wondered, though, how much information he should share with Laura, and, more fundamentally, whether it was right to share any at all.

JANSEN CHEMICAL: NEW OPPORTUNITIES

In his four months at Jansen Chemical, Colin felt he had made quite a positive impression on the senior executives. He had recently been working closely with Laura Kraviston, vice president of research and development, and had made contact with nearly all of the V.P.s of Jansen's seven other departments. Jansen, founded in 1974, specialized in the sale and development of polymers, as well as furthering research on chemical formulas and compositions. A $400 million corporation employing 650 workers, engineers, and managers, Jansen was at

Source: Joy Durand, research assistant, prepared this case under the supervision of Professor Edward Ottensmeyer as a basis for class discussion rather than to illustrate either effective or ineffective handling of an administrative situation. The case is fictional but is based on a composite of actual events.

the forefront of its industry niche. It was regarded as a hard-charging company that enjoyed the loyalty of its work force, and that paid above-average salaries. When he had first considered a job change, Colin Rhodes had been impressed with Jansen's reputation and the opportunities for professional growth it might provide; the 30 percent salary increase he was later offered solidified this attraction. Jansen was known within its industry as a firm that consistently attracted an aggressive group of engineers, who were the "cream of the crop." Jansen thought of its hiring policies as bringing in "idea makers." Colin felt fortunate and proud to be part of the Jansen team, and hoped to prosper there.

RONTECH INDUSTRIES, INC.: PAST EXPERIENCE

Colin Rhodes had spent his first fifteen years in the field of chemical engineering at Rontech Industries. Rontech, a polymer manufacturer with annual revenues of $150 million, was smaller and more traditionally run than Jansen. Colin developed the view that the real power positions in the company were reserved for members of the Williams family, which had founded Rontech in 1963.

Colin respected Jonathan Williams, the CEO at Rontech, and felt that Rontech was generally a good place to work. But he was frustrated that he was not moving up, in both responsibilities and salary, at a faster pace. During his time at Rontech, Colin had earned a reputation as a hard-driving, efficiency-minded chemical engineer. In his last assignment at Rontech, he managed a team of eleven engineers, responsible for both new product and new process research and development. He enjoyed good rapport with his subordinates and was respected for his creativity and managerial abilities. He gave his most innovative engineers considerable freedom to develop new products and new manufacturing processes.

Colin thought that his performance at Rontech would lead to an appointment as vice president of engineering. When he learned that he had been passed over for the second time for the vice presidency, Colin was ready with his letter of resignation.

THE JOB CHANGE

He focused his job search efforts on Jansen Chemical, a larger California-based polymer maker. Over the course of two months, he was interviewed twice and was subsequently hired by Laura Kraviston, the vice president of R&D, for the position of Senior Engineer. Laura told Colin she was impressed with his experience and his ideas about polymer development and manufacturing. She also informed him of Jansen's policy on intellectual property and trade secrets. She asked him to sign an agreement that he would not release confidential information to competitors, and that he would not compete on a professional basis with Jansen for a period of one year, if he left his position at Jansen. Colin readily agreed to this arrangement, since his new position held so many opportunities, and since he had been offered a severance agreement that would pay him a salary for one year should he be terminated by the firm.

AN OPPORTUNITY AND A DILEMMA

Four weeks into his new job at Jansen, Laura convened a special staff meeting that included Colin and the five other senior engineers who reported to her. The purpose of the meeting was to discuss the R&D contribution to the current year's performance goals—improved market share and profit margins. Laura pointed out that R&D, at a minimum, needed to move faster on three new products under development and push them into the market. Jansen's best customers needed these products, and Jansen wanted to keep them happy. Laura urged everyone to pool their efforts and get moving on these products.

The second major push—R&D's contribution to profit performance—involved achieving greater efficiency and speed in the polymer manufacturing process. This was an area, she admitted, that had not been a top priority in the past few years, because of the need to focus on new products and market share growth. Now, given Jansen's profit targets as well as the shrinking margins of several of its older products, production efficiency had to get more attention. The group's subsequent discussion of ideas on reducing manufacturing costs soon turned to the shape and location of the baffles contained in the reactors. Colin perked up at hearing this. At Rontech he had directed the efforts of a manufacturing engineering team working on exactly the same problem.

Colin approached Laura after the meeting and explained to her that, based on his prior experience at Rontech, he had the expertise to lead a team to work on baffle placement. Laura seemed very interested and asked Colin to draft a short report specifying some of the details, as well as the financial costs and benefits. Colin saw this project as a way to become an "impact player" at Jansen in his first six months at the firm.

When he started assembling his report to Laura, Colin began to think about how he should present some of the information. He recognized a need to proceed with some caution. He had come upon many of the key ideas he would pass on to Laura while managing a team of production engineers at Rontech. He felt that the information was his to use, since he had, after all, headed up the group. He certainly knew how to implement the ideas that had been developed by the team effort. The key features of the innovative process they had crafted, to the best of Colin's knowledge, had not been patented. Colin also reflected on his own interests and rights. He certainly had a right to earn a living; it would also feel good to gain respect among his peers and superiors at Jansen, something he felt had been lacking at Rontech. He was also well aware of the significant profit improvement that this new manufacturing process had given Rontech. Production costs had been reduced by nearly 4 percent, adding over $3 million directly to pre-tax profits.

Colin thought about his years at Rontech. He didn't recall signing any sort of agreement regarding the use of proprietary information. Rontech was a very informal place, without many well developed policies of any kind. He thought more generally about competition among chemical firms. Weren't trade secrets and proprietary information really a thing of the past? With the new generation of information technology, practically anything was at the fingertips of an aggressive engineer if he or she was willing to do the research. The techniques that his group had developed at Rontech surely could be viewed as professional knowledge that was quickly going to become general knowledge within the industry. After all, most of the component parts of the manufacturing innovations at Rontech were already on the market. Couldn't he have acquired the same information at any company, as the head of a similar team?

As Colin looked over his draft report to Laura for a second time, he wondered if he had considered all the benefits and risks of what he was doing. Were there questions he had not asked himself? Were there other people he should bring into his decision making?

HR Takes Steps to Protect Trade Secrets

Kathleen Murray

When employee Eric Francis quit his job in 1990, MAI Systems paid little attention. Francis was one of several customer-service representatives of the Irvine, California-based computer company, and turnover in the department wasn't unusual. Following an uneventful exit interview with human resources officials, Francis left to start a job with MAI rival, Peak Computer, also in Irvine.

It might have ended there. But when Francis' new employer began taking away MAI's business, management took notice. After some checking, MAI learned that Francis was using inside knowledge of MAI's customer lists to make sales. Company officials also suspected he might be relying on MAI's customer specification and repair manuals. Could he do that? Not according to the company's legal department.

In March 1992, MAI sued Francis for theft of trade secrets. The company alleged that the ex-employee took manuals and other technical information that he knew to be proprietary. Francis claimed that the company routinely had left such information with customers and that he only was using knowledge about the industry. MAI ultimately got a temporary restraining order to stop him from selling to its clients, but only after losing 80 customers and spending thousands of dollars in legal fees. "This was clearly a violation that cost us," says Elliott Stein, associated general counsel for MAI.

The plight of MAI isn't an isolated incident—nor is it one confined to the computer

business or other high-tech industries. In today's hyper-competitive, copycat global economy, protecting such *trade secrets* as formulas, processes, customer lists, ideas developed at work and other intellectual property (see glossary of terms, page 465) has become a major concern for employers.

There are many reasons why. For one, today's work force is mobile. On top of that, U.S. firms face increasingly competitive pressures as the recession lingers and budgets remain tight. At the same time, corporate downsizing and cutbacks of the past three years have unleashed a flock of professionals back into the job market. In many cases, experienced employees have had little choice but to go to work for a competitor or begin consulting in their field. If they haven't been educated about what are protected trade secrets (and sometimes even if they have), it isn't unusual to find them using proprietary knowledge or information from their former jobs. It's hard to put something as intangible as a formula in someone's head under lock and key. "The question is, what do you do with people who don't spend an entire career with your company?" says Toni Simonetti, a communications manager for Detroit-based General Motors Co., a victim of the trade-secrets war. "How much of what they know is proprietary? How much of what's in a person's head belongs to them? I don't think you'll find an easy answer."

Despite the difficulty, a growing number of employers from hairstyling salons to manufacturing firms, stock brokerages to bakeries—are looking for new ways to protect what gives them an advantage, which is the possession and use of knowledge. Traditionally, this responsibility has fallen to corporate legal departments or outside attorneys. However, a handful of organizations have realized that safeguarding trade secrets goes beyond stopgap legal measures.

"It's starting to be recognized as a classic HR problem," says Mike Garelick, head of the compensation and human resources practice at consulting firm Towers Perrin in Chicago. He believes that HR managers can play a significant role in the protection of intellectual property. Why? The issue of safeguarding trade secrets is, at heart, a personnel issue, he maintains. "Competitive advantage is built around knowledge, and knowledge is generated by people. It's important to manage not only the knowledge, but also the people who are creating it," he says.

In many ways the role HR departments can play in a corporate campaign to eliminate trade-secret theft is similar to HR's involvement with wrongful termination cases. Where the legal department handles an employee lawsuit and may explain the fine points of the law, HR personnel are responsible for making sure that an employer documented the reasons for firing an individual and handled the termination according to company policy.

The HR department also attempts to help create an environment in which employees feel that their work is valued and that they're treated fairly. In the same vein, says Garelick, HR can ensure that employees are educated about what information is proprietary and that security measures are followed. HR staff also can follow up with employees who are departing to remind them of responsibilities and ensure that they aren't taking information or property with them. Finally, HR can help set up the reward and compensation systems to give valuable employees the recognition for their achievements, reducing their need to look for this elsewhere.

Security begins with awareness. First and foremost, HR personnel must familiarize themselves with their companies' trade secrets: It's hard to protect something if nobody knows it needs protecting. That sounds like a simple concept, but when it comes to trade secrets, it's one many corporate managers don't understand, says Alan Unikel, an employment attorney in Chicago and editor of the *Intellectual Property Newsletter.* "As a general rule, many companies don't have a good idea of what their trade secrets are, and they don't really recognize them,"

he says. As a result, the security measures to make sure this sensitive information doesn't fall into competitive hands are typically lax if they exist at all.

It doesn't help that the law surrounding trade secrets is murky. Definitions of what constitutes a trade secret, or what an organization should be protecting, can vary by industry and company. Examples of trade secrets include everything from notes in the margin of an employee manual to a procedure for tying a fishing lure. As technology has raced ahead and the nature of production has changed, the law has been slow to catch up. Although as many as 39 states have adopted some form of the proposed Uniform Trade Secrets Act, there's no federal law regulating what is and what isn't protected. There are only general guidelines.

For instance, for something to be considered a trade secret, a company has to show that the information isn't known in the industry, that the company has made efforts to keep it confidential and that the information provides the company some sort of competitive edge. "Many companies think something is a trade secret just because it's confidential," says Unikel. "It takes more than that."

Once the human resources department has learned what formulas, customer lists, product specification or processes give it an edge, security measures often are obvious. Robert Naeve, an employment attorney who has worked on both sides of trade secret cases, recommends to his clients that they limit access to proprietary material on a need-to-know basis. Customer lists or employee phone books can include dummy entries so that if they're stolen they'll be identifiable. Human resources personnel and other managers should set up access codes to computers and other data-storage areas so that only authorized persons can get into proprietary files. At Mead Data Corp., an information retrieval company in Dayton, Ohio, for example, employees are required to swipe badges to get into re-

The Lingo of Trade Secrets

Some HR managers may shy away from helping companies protect trade secrets because they dislike all the legal mumbo jumbo. The truth is, the area isn't as complex as it seems. Here's a primer to help the uninitiated unravel the jargon of proprietary property.

Confidential: Items or information that are secret and for which access is limited to certain people within an organization. Company documents often are marked confidential to denote that they're proprietary. However, confidential information isn't necessarily a trade secret. To be a trade secret, it also must have value to the company's competitors. A confidential customer list, for example, wouldn't be protected if the company's clients were obvious to everyone else in the industry.

Copyright: An exclusive legal right to reproduce, publish and sell the matter and form of a literary, musical or artistic work. Some companies copyright instruction manuals and training videos.

Intellectual Property: Ideas, processes, slogans or other intangible property that are created at an organization and give it added value or an edge over competitors. In recent years, this area has stretched. When David Letterman went to CBS from NBC, for example, NBC claimed that his "Top 10 List" and "Stupid Pet Tricks" were its intellectual property because Letterman originated the ideas while working for the network. Showing how hard these types of arrangements can be to enforce, Letterman did a Top 10 List on his first CBS broadcast.

Non-compete Agreements: A written agreement in which an employee agrees not to compete with his or her employer by working for a competitor or becoming a competitor, usually for a specified period. These agreements often are tied to pay or severance packages.

Non-disclosure Agreement: A written agreement in which an employee agrees to keep specific information confidential during and after his or her employment, or suffer damages as specified.

Patent: A legal right or privilege that gives an inventor the exclusive right to make, use or sell an invention for a specified period of time. Patents can be obtained on products, but often on processes as well, such as a patented process to manufacture a new drug or a toaster.

Trade Secret: Any formulas, ideas, customer lists, documents or knowledge that are proprietary to an organization and generally not known in the industry. A company generally must make efforts to keep this information confidential and prove that the information gives it a competitive edge.

Trademark: A registered word or device (logo) that points to origin or ownership of merchandise to which it's applied and gives the owner the legal right to proceeds from making or selling it. In recent years, the use of trademarks has been extended to include such things as ex-Los Angeles Lakers Coach Pat Riley's phrase "three-peat" to denote a team winning a championship three times in a row, and the decor of a Mexican restaurant, termed "trade dress" by a court that ordered it not be copied by another chain.

stricted areas. The HR department also has stringent polices about how to mark and distribute documents.

In some companies, formulas often are locked up, limited to one or two people and revealed on a need-to-know basis only. An example is Park City, Utah-based Mrs. Fields, Inc., at which the purchasing of ingredients for the company's cookies is handled separately and a special ingredients packet is sent mixed to stores so that no one can take the recipe.

Human resources professionals also should create policies about removing company property from the office. Upon termination, employees should be required to return all proprietary information and computer systems. Unikel recommends that a supervisor make up a list of what an employee has and then have the employee sign it indicating that he or she has returned everything.

Although these concepts sound basic, a surprising number of companies take chances in the security area, say attorneys. At MAI, for example, customer-service representatives did leave repair manuals with customers, so it was harder for the company to argue that this information was a trade secret. Naeve says that he advises many clients to make written manuals proprietary by marking them as such. "It's a simple idea," he says. "But you'd be amazed at the stuff that's published that companies don't label as confidential."

Human nature also can have a way of working against security measures. As people get to know one another, for example, they may trade computer passwords, or let unauthorized persons have access to restricted areas. "The problem is that individual workers are just careless," says James Lamont, a security consultant in Chicago. At one U.S. government agency in Washington, D.C., Lamont was able to get into an unauthorized room simply by fumbling around in his wallet, as if he were looking for an access card to open the door. An employee who saw him looking helpless unlocked the door with her card and motioned him in. "She obviously thought that I belonged there," he says. "But I might have been there to steal something."

As important as security is, it's also important to strike a balance between security and getting the job done. Some companies that have the best intentions have defeated the purpose by having so much security that it hinders production, says Garelick. "Sometimes what companies do to handle trade secrets interferes with innovation and creativity," he says.

This is precisely what happened at one large East Coast computer company with which Garelick worked. The company had extensive policies and procedures regarding trade secrets. Projects generally were broken up so that only one group knew one piece and another group knew another. By policy, communication between the groups was restricted. The result: The company was slow to develop products and slow to adapt and respond to changes in the market. Its financial performance suffered. "My suspicion is that this company had better breaks between organizational units than the CIA," says Garelick. "Except it wasn't as creative as it had been, and it was losing flexibility. They'd done such a good job at protecting their secrets that the secrets weren't worth that much anymore."

HR personnel can control use of legal agreements. One security measure that's becoming increasingly common doesn't limit an employee's access to information until he or she leaves the company. These are the legal agreements that some employers now are requiring new hires to sign. Typically called *non-compete agreements* or *non-disclosure agreements,* they're essentially a written promise that an employee won't use any proprietary information. "These are pretty standard," says Bob Romanchek, a compensation consultant with Hewitt Associates in Lincolnshire, Illinois. "No matter how much communication and education you have [about trade secrets], having something in writing is important."

General Motors began requiring its senior-level executives to sign these agreements shortly after the well-publicized case last June against the company's former purchasing executive, J. Ignacio Lopez de Arriortua (aka Inaki Lopez). GM accused Lopez of taking millions of dollars worth of proprietary information—including cartons of confidential data about pricing and new product designs—to his new employer, German-based Volkswagen AG. GM also accused him of pushing up strategy meetings before he left so that he could gather even more data for the competitor. Lopez, who had been instrumental in repositioning the automaker, has denied the charges.

However the case eventually is resolved, attorneys say it could end up costing both companies a great deal of money. GM's top managers and HR officials hope that the use of non-compete agreements will help prevent a recurrence of this kind of expensive headache.

The advantage of such agreements is that they provide a record that an employee has been told that information is a trade secret. Mead has been requiring certain employees to sign non-compete/non-disclosure agreements for almost a decade. The basic agreements stipulate that the employee has a duty to the employer not to disclose trade secrets or something he or she learned at the company. The employee also is barred from doing work for a competitor while employed at the company, and sometimes for a period of years afterwards, according to Nancy Nash, legal counsel in human resources at Mead. The damage this would cause the firm and penalties for violating the agreement are included. Sometimes, for research-and-development staffers in particular, the company adds a third provision to the agreement, which bars an employee from taking and using any invention he or she created at the company for six months after the person leaves Mead for a competitor.

There are several drawbacks to agreements, however, as Nash and other attorneys readily acknowledge. First, courts in many states have found these agreements unenforceable. In some cases, it's been determined that they can limit future employment of the worker. Often employees forget signing them, or don't want to sign them because that may hurt their chances of getting another job in the industry.

Still, Naeve and other human resources experts agree that these agreements can act as a first line of defense. "They're more of a threat than they are anything else," he says.

Companies that require employees to sign non-compete agreements should be ready to explain the agreement to new hires. At Mead, new technical employees, engineers and other workers in development areas are given an orientation and educational program about trade secrets. The company also holds periodic legal forums to remind employees of the necessity to protect proprietary information.

Some organizations, such as Fluor Daniel Inc., an engineering and construction firm in Irvine, California, require employees to recertify and review the agreements on an annual basis as a reminder. Experts say that human resources also should follow up with employees at the time of termination to ensure that they remember signing the agreements. Talent Tree Professionals, for example, which like many temporary-help firms has been in trade-secret battles with former sales people who take customer lists with them, sends a letter to employees when they leave, reminding them of their obligations, says David Seaver, vice president of human resources at the Houston-based agency.

Mead's HR staff gives employees copies of their agreements at the exit interviews and also makes sure that they understand their obligations regarding trade secrets. The departing workers also are asked to sign acknowledgement forms that state that they understand the terms of the original agreement and will be bound by it.

According to Nash, Mead only has had to pursue legal action and enforce a non-compete agreement once. That happened two years ago when someone attempted to use proprietary information about customers after he left. Because they had the documentation showing that the employee knew what information was protected, the company was able to get a temporary restraining order and a preliminary injunction to keep the ex-employee from using the trade secret at his new job. "I think most people believe [the company] when they sign these agreements, and they don't challenge them," says Nash.

At the same time, Nash emphasizes that merely having an employee sign these agreements isn't fail-safe. As MAI learned, a former employee still can do plenty of damage before any legal action can be taken.

Training provides understanding of trade secrets and protection devices. The best insurance against trade-secret theft is to combine these agreements with a strong training and awareness program. Too often, says Unikel, this isn't done. Most workers who take proprietary information do so inadvertently—the employees

Integrity Requires Protecting the Trade Secrets of Others

In the zeal to protect their trade secrets, companies often neglect the other half of the equation: How to prevent their own employees from using proprietary data from other companies.

As the battle between Detroit-based General Motors Co. and Germany-based Volkswagen AG demonstrates, this too can be a costly issue. GM is accusing former executive Inaki Lopez of taking reams of proprietary documents and information to his new job at Volkswagen. GM claims it stands to lose millions of dollars. The competitor is allowed to benefit from this information. But Volkswagen may lose as well. If the courts determine he had knowledge that the information was proprietary, it could be fined millions of dollars.

In another case, Diametrics Medical Inc., a Minneapolis based medical-equipment manufacturer, was forced to abort a $30 million initial public offering after Pittsburgh-based PPG Industries Inc. filed a lawsuit alleging theft of trade secrets and patent infringement. The suit accused Diametrics two founders, who formerly worked as a researcher and consultant to PPG of using proprietary information to develop a new blood gas analyzer. Diametrics denied the charges, but said the accusation tainted the deal.

Alan Unikel, a Chicago-based attorney and editor of *The Intellectual Property Newsletter,* says that companies need to realize that misappropriating trade secrets can come back to haunt them, as they have for these companies. The best approach is for HR to deal with the issue while interviewing new employees. "You've got to nip it in the bud at the outset," he says.

Typically, Unikel advises HR personnel to ask potential employees if they have any restrictive covenants barring them from competing against their current or former employer. If an employee has a copy of any such document, the recruiter should make a copy of it and pass it on quickly to the legal department before any hiring decision is made.

That's the procedure followed by Mead Data Corp., an information retrieval company in Dayton, Ohio. At times the agreement is an issue, but it doesn't always affect the work an employee will be doing at Mead. "You've got to be even-handed," says Nancy Nash, legal counsel for the information firm's HR department. "That way people expect you'll do the same things to protect your own secrets."

Talent Tree Professionals, which runs 130 temporary placement offices throughout the United States, won't hire anyone for a full-time position who has signed a restrictive covenant or agreement. However, David Seaver, Talent Tree's vice president of HR, notes that occasionally, rival firms will contact the company to get the agreement waived. Sometimes, a compromise can be worked out.

At Pioneer Hi-Bred International, a seedmaker in Des Moines, Iowa, a human resources representative talks with newly hired scientists to make sure that the organization isn't inadvertently getting any proprietary information from them. "If they've been in academia, they may not be thinking that things need to be protected," says Pat Sweeney, patent counsel for Pioneer. "Whoever is doing the hiring has to be aware of this kind of thing."

Where problems often arise is when an organization is strict about its own trade secrets, but acquisitive when it comes to getting at others' proprietary information. "A company may have a trade secret policy and then they'll hire someone away [from a competitor] and do exactly the thing they tell their employees not to respond to," says Mike Garelick, head of the compensation and human resources practice at consulting firm Towers Perrin in Chicago.

Indeed, this is what hurt MAI Systems in Irvine, California when it sued an employee for stealing trade secrets. The company said an ex-employee used knowledge of proprietary customer lists and service manuals to go after MAI customers. The employee countered that when he had come on board at MAI, management encouraged him to get customer lists from new employees.

This do-as-I-say-not-as-I-do approach sets up a "double bind for people in the organization," Garelick says. "It requires companies to take a delicate look at the ethical considerations of how they want to operate."

simply don't understand that the information is protected. "Many times, we recommend that companies adopt policies, but they seem to get a low priority until the companies have a big suit like General Motors," says Unikel.

Garelick agrees that this is an area in which too many organizations fall short. "What's often clear when I go into companies is that some information may be important from a managerial point of view, but the organization hasn't done a good job of communicating that to employees," he says.

At one software company, for example, an employee who worked on updating products went to a trade association meeting and told extensive war stories to competitors and the press about the development process. He talked about what didn't work and what did. "If you had wanted a detailed case study on [the company's] process, you couldn't have done any better," Garelick says.

Later, the employee was reprimanded for his indiscretion. Because the company improperly explained to him about the importance of keeping trade secrets secret, however, he walked away thinking he had gotten in trouble simply for talking to the press. He had no idea that the information was part of what gave the company a competitive advantage.

For this reason, managers at Mead explain to their employees that talking about their work at seminars is dangerous. The company also maintains strict control over what employees are allowed to publish. This often is an issue because many of the organization's researchers come from academia and are used to writing about their work. "We have to let them know that they can't tell the world about their latest gee-whiz discovery because it's a trade secret," Nash says.

Conveying why trade secrets are important to the firm may be the single most important step an HR department can take, says Pat Sweeney, patent counsel for Pioneer Hi-Bred International, a Des Moines, Iowa-based biotechnology firm at which engineers seed for such plants as

sorghum, sunflowers, wheat and soybeans. "If I were going to tell an HR manager what his or her role was, I would say it's to help make employees keenly aware of the great value in trade secrets," Sweeney says.

She should know. Two years ago, a competitor got hold of some of the company's proprietary seed. And, although it won a $46 million settlement against the competitor, these days the organization doesn't take any chances. Human resources managers explain to employees that their jobs are dependent on certain information remaining within the company and require them to sign non-disclosure agreements.

Also, Pioneer recently held a session for its receptionists reminding them of the importance of protecting trade secrets. The seminar, given by the company's legal and human resources departments, covered what intellectual property is and why it's important to the company. The reason that the company chose these employees to participate was because receptionists control the flow of people and some material in and out of the company, says Sweeney. "They could allow a non-employee into part of the system that's sensitive, and that person could wander around at will," she says.

According to Sweeney, the employees responded well to the seminar. One of the questions they were most curious about was how someone who was trying to appropriate information would try to do it. Pioneer was careful to be realistic in its expectations, recognizing that it was asking receptionists to be friendly and helpful and yet act as security. "That's kind of a hard cross," said Sweeney.

Create loyalty and retention through rewards and recognition. Asking employees to protect a company's trade secrets requires a payoff for them. Companies must look hard at their reward and compensation systems to see that they're properly recognizing employees for holding up their part of the bargain. Increasingly, Garelick says, human resources personnel consult with him about such issues as how to treat, reward and retain employees—specifically because a departing worker has taken trade secrets to a new employer. "Some of the main issues surrounding trade secrets have to do with management style and management process," he says.

Questions HR should be asking include: Are we rewarding people in a way that's meaningful to them? Are we recognizing individual achievements? "Sometimes all it takes is a letter from the company president commending someone for a job well done to make someone feel loyalty to the company," says John Hermann, an Irvine, California-based human resources consultant.

Often, however, it takes more than that. At Fluor, where engineers design projects, management realizes that rewarding performance goes beyond simply paying high salaries, says Mark Krause, director of human resources. "You have to build an environment in which employees clearly can see that they can have their innovativeness recognized." For this reason, Fluor managers have instituted such forums for recognition as monthly recognition days, at which employees are verbally thanked during a department meeting; company-paid lunches; and spot-bonus programs, at which a producer is given a cash award for a particular achievement. The company also has adopted a worker-friendly atmosphere of flexible hours and generous benefits.

Creating the right environment may go beyond blanket policies for the entire company. One high-technology company with which Garelick works had one particular employee who, in addition to doing his job, was proficient with software and computers and tinkered with developing new approaches. At one point, he invented a modification to some equipment that increased productivity. To reward him, management restructured his job so that he could work on his regular duties 20 hours a week, and then they gave him a budget of $5,000 a month and told him he could spend the other 20 hours each

week inventing and troubleshooting. "The company got tremendous mileage out of that," Garelikc says. "The person was motivated and did even more for the firm."

Minnesota Mining and Manufacturing Co. (3M) is another firm that has accrued benefits from setting up alternative programs to reward and encourage innovation. At the Minneapolis-based company, known for such products as Scotch Tape™ and Post-it™ Notes, research and development employees who have ideas for new products or applications are invited to present their plans to a management committee and apply for a grant. If the projects are approved, the company gives the employees a budget and the time to work on them.

Another alternative is to give employees who work on new products stock in the company so that they may realize any gains the product brings. Employers also should look at how compensation and bonuses are structured to see that they act both as a retention device for top talent and encourage the protection of trade secrets. Romanchek of Hewitt Associates has helped several companies set up reward systems that recognize performance. Options he suggests include:

- Offering supplemental retirement agreements that condition the payment of benefits on not competing or not revealing trade secrets. The same thing can be done with severance agreements in the event of a layoff. If an employee doesn't comply, he or she risks forfeiting his or her benefits. Stock-option plans also can be set up this way. "Restricted stock is the traditional retention device," says Romanchek
- Rewards or bonuses for performance or innovation can be spread out during a longer period to give employees an incentive for staying with the company. GM, for example, spreads out bonuses over a three- to five-year period. If an executive leaves before the time is up, he or she may lose part of his or her

compensation. The GM plan also is linked to stock so that the employee has a financial stake in the company's performance. Bonuses can be linked to the protection of trade secrets just as they're linked to management-by-objectives goals

- Compensation need not be based solely on output. HR might set up bonus plans to recognize the fact that someone came up with 10 new ideas. Or the company might provide a researcher with additional staff to determine whether a potential product has value. "Rewards don't have to be focused on the success of a product," Romanchek says. "I see no reason why you couldn't build rewards for creativity into the process. If employees are happy somewhere, they're less likely to be lured away solely by more money."

Programs designed to manage careers indirectly affect trade-secret spreading. It's just as important for employers to pay attention to career development and show employees where they can go within the company as it is to compensate them fairly. Micron Technology Inc. in Boise, Idaho, began developing a career-development program in 1991 to better retain employees in a competitive market. The company wasn't only concerned with losing trade secrets, but also the intellectual capital its employees had built up.

The program that HR and management developed is called "Reaching High Performance." It helps orient new hires to the company's corporate culture. It starts with a one-day course during which the company mission is conveyed, and new employees are encouraged to contribute immediately. Subsequent installments of the 15-hour course deal with career development and help employees map out a five-year plan. It also shows them what skills they will need to reach their goals.

The response? "People love it," says Karen Bridges, coordinator of instructional services.

"I've had people come up to me in the hallway and say, 'I got this promotion because of the RHP class.'"

Although protecting trade secrets wasn't a primary goal of the program, it did increase retention, and the firm hasn't been involved in any trade-secret disputes.

Therein lies the challenge in defining HR's role in protecting trade secrets. It's difficult—if not nearly impossible—to pinpoint what programs are preventing trade secrets from getting out. Fairfield, Connecticut-based General Electric Co., for example, which had a competitor steal its diamond formula, says it's hard to isolate programs that are specifically designed to help safeguard trade secrets. "We have ethical standards and company policies that are reviewed regularly with employees," says GE communications director Bruce Bunch. "But we don't have a lot of new and innovative things aimed at this particular part of behavior."

GE does have programs that allow individuals to design their own jobs and have more responsibility in decision making. The company also offers cash and other incentives for productivity. Yet, notes Bunch, if employees want to steal, it's hard to set up any policy to prevent that.

Other HR professionals agree. However, they also emphasize that this fact shouldn't stop employers from learning how to manage the "knowledge workers." Although the law on what is and isn't a trade secret still is evolving, the fact that people and the knowledge they possess are a company's most important resource isn't. Managers need to be taught how to handle people in flatter, leaner, more knowledge-powered organizations. And everyone is going to have to start to value intellectual capital, even if it can't be seen on a balance sheet. That means more career development, more recognition and emphasis on what truly gives value. Happy employees are less likely to want to do a company damage.

This was illustrated in the blockbuster *Jurassic Park*. In the movie, a computer programmer feels he isn't paid enough or recognized for the system he set up. So he steals the park's trade secrets—dinosaur embryos—and sells them to a competitor. This act leads to the end of Jurassic Park and devastates the seller's employer.

To professionals on the frontline like Pioneer's Sweeney, it's an apt reminder. "What's important to remember," she says, "is that it only takes one desensitized employee to lose a trade secret."

READING 10.2

Comment: Toward a Clearer Standard of Protectable Information: Trade Secrets and the Employment Relationship

Miles J. Feldman

I. INTRODUCTION

The business of innovation is increasingly competitive, as products quickly become obsolete in the face of rapidly evolving technology. Essential to the success of the technology-based firm are skilled employees with the knowledge and experience necessary to convert information into marketable products. The fast pace of development in the computer industry causes a high rate of employee turnover because companies need to compete for workers proficient in the latest technology. While this increase in employee mobility promotes competition, it also means that employers lose valuable information to their competitors. This problem is particularly acute in the computer industry.

Source: Miles J. Feldman, *High Technology Law Journal 9* (1) (1994). Copyright © Miles J. Feldman.

The law of trade secrets protects certain types of confidential information from wrongful disclosure or use. Applied to the employment relationship, the employer's interest in proprietary confidential information must be balanced against an employee's right to use his or her skills to earn a living. Trade secret law attempts to strike a balance between these competing concerns. However, trade secret law turns upon an uncertain distinction between trade secrets, which are protectable, and an employee's own knowledge and skill, which the employee may take to a new job. This uncertainty frustrates the goals of promoting innovation by employers through protection of legitimate trade secrets and allowing employees mobility in their chosen field.

The task of this Comment is to: (1) outline the uncertainties in the law of trade secrets, (2) identify the guidelines courts have used to distinguish protected trade secrets from unprotected employee knowledge and experience, and (3) propose a revision in the Uniform Trade Secrets Act[1] that reformulates the standard for defining a trade secret by including a specific balancing test to distinguish an employer's protectable "know how" from the employee's unprotectable "general knowledge and skill." This revision will make the law more certain and allow courts reasonable discretion in deciding each case on its specific facts.

II. THE TRADE SECRET LAW IN THE EMPLOYMENT CONTEXT CREATES TENSIONS BETWEEN COMPETING INTERESTS

The trade secret law protects an employer's confidential information from misappropriation by an employee. Yet an employee has the right to market his or her general knowledge and experience to new employers. A conflict arises where the employee's knowledge and experience is inextricably tied to the trade secrets that belong to a former employer.

A. Definition of a Trade Secret

The Restatement (First) of Torts[2] served as the pattern for state trade secret law until 1979, when the National Conference of Commissioners on Uniform Laws approved the Uniform Trade Secrets Act[3] (UTSA). To date, thirty-six states and the District of Columbia have adopted the UTSA with different variations.[4] In addition to the Restatement (First) of Torts and the UTSA, the recently drafted Restatement of Unfair Competition[5] covers trade secret law.

The Restatement (First) of Torts (Restatement (First)) defines a trade secret as: "any formula, pattern, device or compilation of information which is used in one's business, and which gives him an opportunity to obtain an advantage over competitors who do not know or use it."[6] The information must be secret: "Matters of public knowledge or of general knowledge in an industry cannot be appropriated by one as his secret." The UTSA defines a trade secret as:

> information, including a formula, pattern, compilation, program, device, methods, technique, or process, that: (i) derives independent economic value, actual or potential, from not being generally known to, and not being readily ascertainable by proper means by, other persons who can obtain economic value from its disclosure or use, and (ii) is the subject of efforts that are reasonable under the circumstances to maintain its secrecy.[7]

Unlike the Restatement (First) definition, which emphasizes the use of information, the UTSA focuses on the information and expands the definition of a trade secret to include programs, methods, techniques, and processes.[8] The UTSA also protects information that has either potential or actual value, and eliminates the requirement that a trade secret be used continuously in the holder's business. Therefore, the UTSA has expanded the definition of what constitutes a trade secret.

The proposed Restatement of Unfair Competition, which is currently being circulated in draft form, takes the more expansive approach of the UTSA. It defines a trade secret as "*any* information that can be used in the operation of a business or other enterprise and that is sufficiently valuable and secret to afford an actual or potential economic advantage over others."[9]

B. Secrecy

Secrecy, or confidentiality, has emerged as one of the core concepts in trade secret law. It is well-recognized that an employee in the computer industry is entitled to use experience gained while working for a company in subsequent employment. If, however, an employee possesses confidential information or knowledge gained at the employer's expense, the employee has a duty to maintain its secrecy. This principle was applied in one case to prohibit the employee from using technical knowledge of a computer system gained through an employer's training course, or from taking a competitive position that inevitably required the employee to use the protected knowledge.[10] The employee was free to apply his knowledge of the computer industry, as long as he did not service the employer's system.

Where the employer fails to take reasonable precautions to protect the secrecy of its computer operations, an employee has no duty to maintain confidentiality. Further, absent reasonable precautions, an employee's knowledge of the company's computer system may be considered unprotected general knowledge and experience.[11] In one frequently-cited case, the Supreme Court of Minnesota held that the absence of an understanding not to disclose particular information about the employer's computer system rendered that information part of the employee's general skill and experience.[12] The court reasoned that the employer's failure to take reasonable precautions to protect the confidentiality of its alleged trade secret was such that "the defendant employees could not be expected to have known what was confidential and what was not, what was unfair to disclose and what was not."[13] To assert trade secret rights in information, the firm or individual must maintain the information at some minimal level of confidentiality or secrecy.

C. The Problem of Concurrent Interests

The central policy conflict in employment trade secret cases is between the employer's interest in protecting its proprietary information and the employee's right to use his or her knowledge and skill to earn a living.[14]

This problem can be characterized as "concurrent interests." The concurrent interests in information potentially covered by trade secret law are best illustrated by cases in which, during the term of employment, an employee acquires skills, information, and knowledge that become unavoidably integrated into her professional identity. The same skills, information, and knowledge can be characterized as the employer's, because the employer has made investments by training the employee and developing the information. When the employee uses her skills in new employment, some of those skills may be unalterably tied to the trade secret information of the former employer. An employee who changes jobs, but remains in the same profession, may find it impossible to avoid drawing upon the skills and the experience developed at the previous job. Both parties' interests include private ethical and legal conceptions of ownership, investment, and the freedom to pursue one's profession.

Public policy considerations such as fostering innovation, advancing science and technology, and promoting free competition serve as the basis for trade secret law. Because of its broad reach, trade secret law's impact on technological innovation is great. Trade secret protection may, however, limit or discourage innovation. Broad legal protection for confidential information benefits an employer and encourages innovation and investment in new technology, because the firm that invests in the research and development of new ideas is protected from "free riders" who can exploit its investment.[15] At the same time, limited protection frees tech-

nical workers to use their knowledge and skill in various competing employment opportunities.[16]

Trade secret jurisprudence should enable both employer and employee to pursue their innovative goals by offering clear legal standards that enable the parties to distinguish between protectable and unprotectable skills, information, and knowledge.

D. The Conflict Between the Rights of the Employer and the Rights of the Employee Is Particularly Acute in Technology Industries

The concurrent interest problem is particularly acute in technology-based industries. The computer industry is an archetypal environment for trade secret disputes and concurrent interest problems for two reasons: high employee mobility, and the computer industry's heavy reliance on research and development, which is in turn dependent on information. The highly specialized skills involved and the volatile computer product market combine to cause a great deal of mobility among workers in the computer industry. There is intense competition for employees proficient in the latest technology.

Because the pace of change in the computer business and computer applications is so rapid, members of the industry change jobs very quickly. According to a 1989 *Computer Weekly* survey, only catering staff change jobs more often than those working in the computer industry.[17] The instability is caused by several factors. Voluntary and involuntary departure programs, such as the one IBM used in 1991, are becoming widespread in high-tech firms needing to downsize to stay competitive. In addition many computer firms have had no opportunity to develop employee loyalty due to their relative youth. Finally, a growing pool of independent contractors in the computer work force has made long-term employment with a single firm more unusual.

Hiring employees in high-technology firms often places the employer in a difficult predicament. The scientists and engineers who come to a high-technology company do so with considerable experience and knowledge of their own. In the computer industry, most firms hire these employees because they have knowledge of and experience with particular processes. These processes are, however, often considered proprietary by the employee's prior firm. This exposes firms to potential liability each time it hires a new employee.

In a computer firm, ideas and methodologies are viewed by management as property. Often, knowledge is evaluated solely in terms of market access. More simply, ideas are the primary assets of a computer firm.

In contrast, computer industry employees view information in terms of idea development and career advancement.[18] Most employees within the computer industry view ideas and methodologies not as property, but as means towards discoveries. The scientific community that produces most high-tech workers is process oriented, and emphasizes the disclosure of discoveries through publication or lecture so that discoveries may be duplicated and verified by others. For scientists and engineers, success is measured by progress and development, rather than in market terms. Thus, employees of computer firms with scientific backgrounds are not accustomed to maintaining the secrecy of scientific discoveries. Further, they may be disinclined to stop publishing or otherwise disclosing their inventions for fear of foreclosing the possibility of an academic career.[19]

A recent Federal Bureau of Investigation probe presents an extreme example of industry employees' devotion to the information itself. The Bureau recently investigated a former Apple Computer Corporation engineer for software theft in connection with the Nu Prometheus League.[20] The group is named after the Greek god who stole fire from the gods and gave it to man.[21] The former Apple engineer was served with a grand jury subpoena as a suspect in the on-going investigation of the League's unauthorized mailing of Apple software to other software developers.[22] The group's goal, that "the genius of a few Apple employees benefit the entire world," is apparently motivated by a desire to share philosophical information.[23] The attitudes of the Nu Prometheus League highlight the opposing views of information taken by employees and management. These divergent views exacerbate the concurrent interests problem.

E. Trade Secret Law Offers Potentially Much Broader Protection than Copyright or Patent Law

Trade secret law is rooted in state common law. Unlike patents, copyrights, and trademarks,[24] it is not preempted from state regulation under the mandate of the Constitution's intellectual property clause.

In *Kewanee Oil Co. v. Bicron Corp.*,[25] the United States Supreme Court held that state trade secret law is not preempted by federal patent law, although protection might overlap. The *Kewanee* Court reasoned that trade secret law does not interfere with the federal policies behind patent law because it deals with a limited subject matter, offers less protection, and focuses on conduct rather than on technology.[26]

Nor is trade secret law preempted by federal copyright law. In 1992, the United States Court of Appeals for the Second Circuit held in *Computer Associates International v. Altai*[27] that state law trade secret claims that arise in connection with copyright infringement are not preempted by federal copyright law.[28] The *Computer Associates* court reasoned that state trade secret law is not preempted by the federal Copyright Act because trade secret claims require proof of an element not included in a copyright infringement claim.[29]

The independence of state trade secret law from the Copyright and Patent Acts is significant for several reasons: (1) trade secret law creates de facto monopolies over information that are potentially infinite, while copyright and patent law provide monopolies for only a limited duration;[30] (2) trade secrets can exist without fixation, novelty, or originality;[31] and (3) trade secret law has emerged from a conflicting

body of common law and through relatively in-
sulated state legislative efforts,[32] while the
Patent and Copyright Acts were subjected to rigorous congressional debates before becoming
federal law.

F. Emergence of Trade Secret Law in the Computer Industry

Trade secret protection for computer programs
is fast emerging as one of the preeminent
grounds for asserting legal rights in software.[33]
One of the primary protections for computer
software is the federal Copyright Act.[34] The application of the Copyright Act to computer software has, however, come under severe criticism
from commentators and practitioners, who now
describe state trade secret law as new and valuable protection for computer software.[35] The
perception that the Copyright Act alone does not
provide adequate protection from computer software is partly due to the differences between
computer software and other forms of expression covered by the Copyright Act. In the context of the computer industry, establishing protectable expression can be difficult.[36]

Trade secret law, in contrast to copyright
law,[37] protects ideas that have not been fixed in
a tangible medium. The most common trade secret claim in the computer industry deals with
the alleged misappropriation of the computer
software.[38] Computer programs have qualified
as trade secrets under both the common law definition of a trade secret[39] and the UTSA definition.[40] The UTSA includes the word "program"
in its definition of a trade secret.[41] Some states
have gone further and amended the definition to
specifically cover computer programs. For example, the Idaho statute adds "computer program"[42] to the definition, Montana added "computer software,"[43] Alabama omitted "program"[44]
but added "computer software," and Nebraska
added "code."[45]

For a computer program to be granted trade
secret protection, it must be "secret," or not generally known in the industry. Several courts

have, however, held that a "unique combination"
of programs that are individually generic and
publicly known may be protected as a trade secret. In *Computer Associates International v.
Bryan,* the Eastern District of New York held
that a trade secret may consist of an accumula-
tion of generic computer programs in the public
domain which are linked together in a way not
generally known outside the firm.[46] The court
reasoned that a trade secret can exist in a combination of characteristics and components, each
of which, by itself, is in the public domain, but
the unified process and operation of which, in
unique combination, affords a competitive advantage.[47] Trade secret law can thus protect an
enormous amount of information that is not protectable by other means.[48]

In *Computer Associates v. Altai,* the Second
Circuit noted: "Precisely because [the] trade secret doctrine protects the discovery of ideas,
processes, and systems which are explicitly pre-
cluded from coverage under copyright law,
courts and commentators alike consider it a necessary and integral part of the intellectual property protection extended to computer programs."[49] The *Computer Associates* court
echoed Milgrim, who stated "[t]rade secret protection remains a 'uniquely valuable' weapon in
the defensive arsenal of computer programmers."[50] Therefore, trade secret law can provide
perpetual monopolies over computer programs
and surrounding information wholly apart from
the heavily legislated copyright and patent laws.
Such protection can have a direct impact on
technological innovation in this country.

III. THE CURRENT STATE OF TRADE SECRET LAW GENERATES UNCERTAINTY

The concurrent interest problem and the potential for unrestricted liability, which was created
without the extensive policy debates that characterized federal intellectual property legislation,[51]
are exacerbated by a legal doctrine steeped in

uncertainty and imprecision. The lack of a definitive rule in this area has led the courts to engage in fact-specific, case-by-case analysis, resulting in little uniformity among the computer trade secret decisions. This leaves firms and industry professionals with little or no guidance on how to assess trade secret protection or liability.

The origins, the conflicting theories of liability from which the law developed, and the ill-defined distinction between what is protectable and unprotectable frustrate the legal and social policies that serve as the basis for trade secret law. Knowledge and information are divided between the vague categories of general knowledge and skill, which an employee may freely use in subsequent employment, and know how, which an employer may protect as a trade secret. These categories neither further predictability of trade secret law nor help to establish what is or is not protectable information.

A. Origins of Trade Secret Law: Property or Relationships?

The overall lack of clarity in trade secret jurisprudence can be traced, in part, to the concepts from which the law evolved. Trade secret law is rooted in two distinct legal theories, property and tort, that each raise duties based on special relationships. The emerging view among many state courts is that trade secrets involve rights in property.[52] In 1984, the Supreme Court in *Ruckelshaus v. Monsanto*[53] recognized that trade secrets, although intangible, qualify as property rights and may be protected by the takings clause of the fifth amendment. The *Ruckelshaus* court noted that trade secrets share many of the characteristics of tangible forms of property, such as assignability, the ability to form the res of a trust, and the ability to be passed to a trustee in bankruptcy.[54]

Earlier courts took an entirely different view of the legal foundations of trade secret protection, finding that trade secret protection is based on the existence of a confidential relationship between the parties.[55] An example of the rela-

tionship-based conception of trade secret law is Justice Holmes's opinion in *E.I. DuPont de Nemours Powder Co. v. Masland.*[56] In *Masland*, Justice Holmes expressed the view that property is not the starting point in trade secret analysis. Rather, Justice Holmes stated:

> The word property as applied to trademarks and trade secrets is an unanalyzed expression of certain secondary consequences of the primary fact that the law makes some rudimentary requirements of good faith. Whether the plaintiffs have any valuable secret or not, the defendant knows the facts, whatever they are, through a special confidence he accepted. The property may be denied but the confidence cannot be. Therefore the starting point for the present matter is not property or due process of law, but that the defendant stood in confidential relations with the plaintiffs, or one of them.[57]

Significantly, some state courts still agree with this view, and have adopted the principle that trade secret protection is based on a confidential relationship.[58] The relationship between employer and employee is a quintessential example of a confidential agency relationship, in which the employee has a duty to refrain from disclosing the employer's confidential information in a way which would harm the employer.[59]

There are thus two opposing theories of trade secret protection—one emphasizing the nature of the plaintiff's property rights in secret information and the other emphasizing the tort of a defendant's misconduct. The view of trade secrets as property focuses on the status of the information itself, because the party who asserts trade secret rights must establish that the information at issue has been preserved as a protectable trade secret. In contrast, the view of trade secret misappropriation as a tort stresses the conduct of the defendant in breaching a duty to maintain the confidentiality of the trade secret.

Commentators have long complained that courts do not agree on the proper legal rationale for granting trade secret protection.[60] It could be argued that both theories are reflected in the law because the law requires that a plaintiff prove the existence of a trade secret as well as misappropriation by the defendant.[61] However, the divergent views on the legal rationales have created jurisprudential difficulties and fostered the uncertainties that exist within trade secret law.[62]

B. Liability for Misappropriation of a Trade Secret

Although the law is not settled, the trend regarding misappropriation is to impose liability, not only for the wrongful use or disclosure of another's trade secret, but also for improper acquisition of another's trade secret. The common law approach imposes liability upon one who discloses or uses another's trade secret if the secret was discovered by improper means.[63] This approach is based on the tort theory of trade secret protection and focuses on acquisition by "improper means," which is equivalent to breach of a confidential relationship.[64]

In contrast, the UTSA imposes liability for misappropriation based on the acquisition of another's trade secret by a person who knows or has reason to know that the trade secret was acquired by improper means.[65] This is broader than the common law approach, which required an actual use of the trade secret.[66] The UTSA also imposes liability for misappropriation based on the disclosure or use of another's trade secret without express or implied consent.[67] This type of misappropriation is entirely consistent with the prior common law. In addition, the UTSA imposes liability when, at the time of disclosure or use, the person knew or had reason to know that his knowledge of the trade secret was either derived from someone who used improper means to acquire it, acquired under circumstances giving rise to a duty to maintain its secrecy or limit its use, or derived from someone who owed a duty to the plaintiff to maintain its secrecy or limit its use.[68] These provisions, which are based on a duty of confidentiality, are readily applicable to cases involving former employees. Finally, the UTSA imposes liability for misappropriation for disclosure or use of a trade secret where, before a material change of his position, the person disclosing or using the trade secret knew or had reason to know that the information was a trade secret and that knowledge of it had been acquired by accident or mistake.[69]

Thus, the common law and the UTSA differ on whether mere acquisition of trade secret, without actual use, is enough to trigger liability. This is crucial to cases involving employment in the computer industry, because employees will inevitably bring potential trade secret information into their new firms. As a result, under the common law approach, liability may exist even absent any malicious act of misappropriation. The draft Restatement of Unfair Competition essentially follows the UTSA with respect to liability for appropriation of a trade secret. Both impose liability for the simple acquisition of another's trade secret by improper means.[70]

C. The Tension Between Protectable "Know How" and Unprotectable "General Knowledge and Skill"

Traditionally, courts have separated protectable and unprotectable information by using the term "know how" to denote protectable information and "general knowledge and skill" to denote non-protectable information. However, these terms do little to clarify or delineate the boundaries of trade secret protection. One commentator defines "know how" as referring to information that enables one to accomplish a particular task or to operate a particular device or process.[71] Others define "general skill" as personal knowledge based on an employee's education, ability, and experience, and general to the trade as a whole, as opposed to knowledge peculiar to the employer.[72]

Courts recognize that the meaning of "know how" is unclear and sometimes overlaps the unprotectable general knowledge of an employee.[73] In 1985, the Third Circuit commented that: "the concept of 'know how' is . . . a very fuzzily defined area, used primarily as a shorthand device for stating the conclusion that a process is protectable. It covers a multitude of matters, however, which in the broad sense are not protectable, e.g., an employee's general knowledge and skill."[74]

The line between an employer's protectable "know how" and an employee's personal knowledge and skill is especially unclear in the case of an employee who holds a technical or engineering position for a long period of time. In this situation, the employee has usually enhanced his knowledge and skill through exposure to the employer's trade secrets and through his own contribution to its development: "it is just such exposure and activities which are part of the experience that enters into the knowledge and skill which define a scientist or engineer."[75] Distinguishing know how and general skill is particularly difficult in the high technology area.

For example, in a recently filed trade secret dispute between manufacturers of ultrasound diagnostic equipment, Advanced Technology sued Siemens Medical Systems, who hired an engineer away from Advanced Technology. The engineer designed ultrasound probes, the crucial component that emits and receives the impulses from an unborn child that make ultrasound technology useful.[76] Advanced Technology was successful in gaining a temporary restraining order to entirely prevent the engineer from working on such probes at his new employer, despite the fact that the design of them was his field of expertise.[77] This ruling effectively prevented the engineer from engaging in his area of specialization-ultrasound probes.

1. The Restatement of Torts and the UTSA
The Restatement of Torts, which is still followed by many jurisdictions, offers no clear rule regarding what constitutes "general knowledge."[78] The Restatement comes closest to addressing this issue, albeit indirectly, through its articulation of one of the factors that compose the test

for whether information constitutes a trade secret: "the extent the information is known outside of the business."[79]

The present formulation of the UTSA also does not adequately confront the problem of defining the terms "general knowledge and skill" or "know how." The UTSA expanded the definition of a trade secret to expressly include "programs" and "know how." Nevertheless, the definition is circular; the designation "know how" merely denotes protectable information.[80] The UTSA does not specifically define "know how," and, like the Restatement of Torts, the UTSA is silent as to what constitutes unprotectable "general knowledge" and skill. This absence of an express definition has led to an inconsistent and often unfair application of trade secret law in the courts.

2. Inconsistency in Trade Secret Decisions
Structural Dynamics Research Corp. v. Engineering Mechanics Research Corp.[81] was a trade secret action in which Engineering Mechanics employed a former Structural Dynamics employee. The dispute centered around computer software that Structural Dynamics developed to implement isoparametric elements in structural analysis.[82] The Eastern District of Michigan stated in dictum that no duty to refrain from using or disclosing information arises where the trade secret is created through the employee's initiative. In such a case, the employee has an interest in the information that is at least equal to that of the employer; the knowledge is part of his skill and experience.[83] The court held, however, that the employees were liable for subsequent use or disclosure of the technology because they had signed an express "Employee Patent and Confidential Information Agreement."[84]

The Fifth Circuit followed this reasoning in *Plains Cotton Co-op v. Goodpasture Computer Services,*[85] where the defendant employee[s] developed particular ways to use the software. The software, Telcot, was designed to provide information regarding cotton prices and availability to the members of a cotton growing trade association.[86] The *Plains Cotton* court found that the defendant[s] had brought significant expertise in software development to the plaintiff firm.[87] Based on this finding, the court denied the plaintiff's motion for a preliminary injunction to prevent the defendant[s] from using the software functions in other applications.[88] Although the court acknowledged that the defendant employees had access to Telcot's object and source code,[89] the court found no evidence of copying, because the defendants used their expertise to develop the new software at the defendant firm.[90]

The same reasoning appeared again in *Universal Analytics v. MacNeal-Schwendler Corporation,*[91] which involved a trade secret claim brought pendant to an antitrust claim under the Sherman Act.[92] In *Universal Analytics,* both parties employed some of the same employees simultaneously. The federal district court reasoned that "[s]ecrets acquired and developed as a result of a long employment in the particular trade may be carried over and put to use by the new employer."[93]

The line of authority established in *Structural Dynamics, Universal Analytics,* and *Plains Cotton* allows employees who substantially participate in the development of computer software to continue using the experience gained in their previous firm, even where the new firm's software is similar in application to the previous firm's software. This line of cases is not, however, the only approach.

The Court of Appeals for North Carolina recently upheld a preliminary injunction in *Barr-Mullin, Inc. v. Browning.*[94] The *Barr-Mullin* court found that a prima facie case of misappropriation existed where the defendant helped to develop and service computer software during his employment with plaintiff, then subsequently developed similar software after leaving the plaintiff employer's firm.[95] The software was developed for the woodworking industry to optimize the way lumber is cut.[96] The employee,

a former vice president of engineering at the plaintiff firm, claimed that he had independently derived the subsequently developed software.[97] The court reasoned that the employee's contribution to the defendant's software development demonstrated his knowledge of the alleged trade secret and proved that he had access to copies of the source code prior to his resignation.[98] Contrary to *Plains Cotton,* the *Barr-Mullin* court made no mention of the employee's rights to his knowledge and skills in its reasoning. Further, the *Barr-Mullin* court held that access to the original software prevented the defendant employee's assertion of independent development.[99]

Other cases challenge the logic of *Structural Dynamics, Universal Analytics,* and *Plains Cotton.* In the recent case of *Avtec Systems, Inc. v. Peiffer,*[100] Avtec asserted trade secret rights in a computer program that the defendant developed as a marketing tool while employed by Avtec.[101] The employee used the program as a demonstration and marketing device several times on plaintiff's behalf.[102] The Eastern District of Virginia found that the plaintiff acquired a trade secret in the program's use for demonstrations and marketing in a manner similar to an employer's possession of "shop rights" in an employee's invention.[103] The court held that the use of the program by the defendant was a misappropriation of his former employer's trade secret.[104] Like the *Barr-Mullin* court, the *Avtec Systems* court made no mention of an employee interest in the information used to create the software, even though the employee substantially assisted in developing it.[105] These cases demonstrate the pattern of inconsistency present in trade secret decisions involving computer software.

There is so much confusion in this area that nearly identical facts can produce different conclusions. Compare two cases that arose in the chemical industry: *Wexler v. Greenberg*[106] and *Basic Chemicals v. Benson.*[107] In *Wexler,* defendant Greenberg was head chemist at plaintiff's chemical company, where he developed various formulas for plaintiff in the course of his duties.

Greenberg came to know all of the plaintiff's formulas, as well as their methods and costs of production. Greenberg left his job with the plaintiff to work for one of plaintiff's distributors, which soon began to manufacture the same products it had formerly bought from plaintiff.[108] The Pennsylvania Supreme Court held that Greenberg did not violate any confidential relationship "in disclosing or using formulas which he developed or were developed subject to his supervision . . . this information forms part of the technical knowledge and skill he has acquired by virtue of his employment with [the plaintiff] and which he has an unqualified privilege to use."[109]

Faced with an almost identical set of facts, the Supreme Court of Iowa reached the opposite result in *Basic Chemicals v. Benson.* In *Basic Chemicals,* the court held that the employee-developed formulas used by plaintiff were trade secrets.[110] The *Basic Chemicals* court found that the protectability of the information was not affected by the fact that Benson, the employee and defendant, developed the formulas; Benson's right to use the secrets in competition with Basic Chemicals was no greater than any other employee's.[111] The court's reasoning rested on the fact that Benson had previously referred to the formula as his employer's "know how."[112] Consequently, the court barred Benson from using the formulas in later employment.

Another example of different results being based on similar facts is evident when *AMP Inc. v. Fleischhacker*[113] is compared with *Air Products & Chemicals v. Johnson.*[114] Each case involved a high-level managerial employee who used knowledge of marketing and business operations gained while employed by the plaintiff in a subsequent position with the plaintiff's competitor. In *AMP,* the Seventh Circuit, following Illinois law, held that the former employer was not entitled to injunctive relief because the business and technical information at issue was general knowledge, widely known in the industry.[115] *AMP* found that, although an employee derives some benefits from his access to the collective experience of his or her employer, "[s]uch information comprises general skills and knowledge acquired in the course of employment. Those are things an employee is free to take and use in later pursuits."[116] In contrast, the *AIR Products* court ruled that information known to the employee, including knowledge of market opportunities, research and development projects, and pricing methods, was not "generally known in the industry" and was thus protectable as a trade secret. The *Air Products* court enjoined the employee from working for the plaintiff's competitor.[117] Although both courts applied the same common law definition of a trade secret, the end results were diametrically opposed.

The uneven application of trade secret law in the context of employment in the computer software and technical fields, illustrated by the above cases, can frustrate both an employee's ability to obtain new employment[118] and an employer's right to hire skilled employees. When an employee changes jobs within the same profession or trade, it is often impossible for him or her to avoid using skills and experience gained in previous positions.[119] The exception from trade secret protection for employee skill and knowledge is essential to fostering employee mobility and the competitive basis of our free market economy: "[a]ny other rule would force a departing employee to perform a prefrontal lobotomy on himself or herself."[120] The current state of the law leaves firms and employees with little guidance as to what a new employee may bring to a new position at a competing firm.

D. Lack of Clarity in the Law of Trade Secrets Hinders Innovation and Frustrates the Purpose of the Law

The uncertain state of trade secret law has a very real impact on computer and other technology-based firms that cannot readily distinguish protectable information from non-protectable information. As a consequence, the engagement or disengagement of employees subjects firms to unknowable risks and does not allow for proper risk allocation and decision-making. The uncertainty in trade secret law creates societal costs as well, because high litigation expenses reduce resources available for the development of new technology.

Litigating intellectual property disputes is expensive. For example, in the recent patent and trade secrets litigation over data-compression software between Microsoft and Stac Electronics, Stac spent approximately $500,000 per month—nearly $7 million for the entire trial.[121] Gary Clow, Stac's chief executive officer, stated, "I've got the most expensive legal education in the United States."[122] The case "transformed Stac from a company banking on its technology to a company praying for its lawyers."[123] Another trade secret dispute occurred between Titan Linkabit Corporation and Conquest Technologies after Conquest hired former Titan employees.[124] According to Conquest's founder, Titan's suit was merely an attempt to put his start-up out of business before it got off the ground by burying it in litigation costs.[125] Litigation thus drains valuable capital. The uncertainty in the area of trade secret law further aggravates the situation because companies do not know where they stand with respect to potential liability.

The uncertain status of what constitutes unprotectable employee knowledge and skill is inefficient because it results in both over-deterrence and under-deterrence. The deterrent effect arises from the remedies under trade secret law, which sanction an employee's improper use or acquisition of information, and deter the employee, as well as a prospective employer, from appropriations that trigger a cause of action. The ambiguity in the law frustrates this deterrent effect because the uneven application of an ambiguous doctrine creates rules which either permit too much misappropriation, or overly restrict employee mobility. Under-deterrence allows the employee to unfairly exploit confidential information gained in a former position for the benefit of himself or a new employer. Over-

deterrence impedes the employee who has a legitimate right to use knowledge gained through employment. A more certain rule would help to adjust the risks of litigation so that neither misappropriating employees nor over-protective employers may take advantage of the rule's lack of clarity.

Over-deterrence occurs in a situation when the parties lack an understanding of what constitutes a trade secret. For example, the possibility of litigation may discourage an employee from using his or her skills and experience to pursue a position at another firm. This creates over-deterrence because it inhibits an employee's ability to change jobs, which creates an economic inefficiency. The fear of a potential trade secret suit may also over-deter potential employers from hiring a competitor's former employees, even in industries with high employee mobility.[126]

Ambiguity in the law also creates under-deterrence. The absence of a distinct legal rule gives both employees and their prospective employers an incentive to capitalize on information that is not rightfully theirs. The employer may not be able to assess whether the information is protectable as a trade secret. Moreover, the parties will be uncertain as to who will ultimately prevail in litigation. The uncertainty of prevailing combined with the high costs of litigation reduces the risk of loss to the employee who then has a greater incentive to misappropriate. A more certain rule would help to adjust the risks of litigation so that neither party will take advantage of an unclear rule.

Finally, greater clarity is necessary because the number of trade secrets suits being brought by employers is rapidly growing.[127] The lack of clear rules prevents quick resolution of trade secret disputes, which can be very costly and have a significant impact on the reputation and viability of a firm.[128] The time consumed and prestige lost in such suits drain computer firms' resources as much as the monetary costs of the litigation.

The well-publicized dispute between Symantec, a Silicon Valley software producer, and Borland International is a good illustration. Symantec now faces both civil and criminal suits for trade secret misappropriation because it hired Eugene Wang, a senior executive at Borland, who is accused of misappropriating trade secrets.[129] Symantec's stock plunged on news of the dispute and its chief executive officer, Gordon Eubanks, claimed that he spends about one hour per day on the dispute.[130] This time would have been spent more efficiently on the company's business.

IV. STRATEGIES FOR GENERATING MORE CERTAINTY IN THE LAW OF TRADE SECRETS IN THE HIGH TECHNOLOGY EMPLOYMENT CONTEXT

A. The UTSA Should Be Revised to Deal More Directly with the Issue of Concurrent Interests

Federal regulation of trade secrets is not the answer. Congress has failed to respond to the continued judicial confusion in the area of trade secret law with respect to the problem of concurrent interests in the employment context.[131] National legislation would likely be politically difficult.[132] A more realistic strategy is that of the UTSA, which was formulated by the American Bar Association. The UTSA has helped to bring some uniformity to the law, but it has not been adopted by all states. The main problem with the UTSA is that it merely codifies the Restatement (First) of Torts when identifying trade secrets and resolving the problem of concurrent interests. The UTSA should be revised to meet the needs of the modern employment relationship. Once the revisions have been implemented, all of the fifty states should adopt the UTSA.

Resolving uncertainty in trade secret law presents a significant challenge to policy makers. An effective approach must evenly apply trade secret protection to increase certainty in the employment relationship in high technology areas. To ensure even application and consideration of the concurrent interest problem, the current standards articulated by the UTSA should be changed to incorporate a secondary test that balances employer and employee interests. While such an approach is not novel, it would acknowledge the tension between an employer's right to protect its investments and an employee's right to practice her profession.

It would be difficult—if not impossible—to construct a single definition of "general knowledge" or "know how" that would apply in all cases. Thus, trade secret analysis in the employment context must balance relevant considerations. A few courts have employed balancing tests in the past;[133] but to promote consistency and fairness, the courts should look at the facts of a case within an established, uniformly applied framework.

1. Basis for the Test The newly-drafted Restatement of Unfair Competition significantly advances the development of the trade secret law because it sets forth several relevant considerations and expressly addresses the issue of whether information comprises an employer's protectable trade secret or an employee's general skill, knowledge, training, and experience. Yet the proposed Restatement falls short of resolving the outstanding issues; it only discusses the factors to be considered in delineating employer/employee interests in information in comment d to section 42, which covers employee liability.[134] Thus, the proposed draft only tacitly addresses the problem of identifying general knowledge and know how as metaphors for employee and employer interests.

The factors outlined in the proposed Restatement include: (1) whether the information at issue is specialized and unique to the employer's business or is "widely known in the industry or derived from skills generally possessed by persons employed in the industry"; (2) the "relative contribution of the employer and the employee to the development of the information"; (3) whether "other competitors have been unsuccessful in independent attempts to develop the information"; (4) whether the employee, upon termination of the employment, appropriates some "physical embodiment" of the information; and (5) whether the information is "so closely integrated with the employee's overall employment experience that protection would deny the employee the ability to obtain employment commensurate with the employee's general qualifications."[135]

This analysis functions as a valuable default rule, which comes into play when there is no confidentiality agreement between the parties. These factors help to articulate and identify the concurrent interests of employers and employees and take into account the highly fact-specific nature of trade secret disputes involving former employees. By focusing on the nature of the information itself, as well as on the conduct of both the employer and the employee, the test acknowledges the competing goals of protection of confidential information and promotion of employee mobility. Courts should use these factors to guide their determinations, allowing parties to anticipate their trade secret rights and duties and to plan accordingly.

The balancing test should not be part of the plaintiff's prima facie case, but becomes relevant only after the plaintiff alleges the existence of a trade secret and the employee raises the defense that the information forms part of his general knowledge and skill. The plaintiff must prove some basic level of secrecy or confidentiality before the court addresses the concurrent interest problem; absent confidential information, there is no need to balance. In addition, the plaintiff must show misappropriation of the confidential information. Only after the plaintiff has shown the existence of a protectable trade secret should the court seek to identify the concurrent interests by addressing the issue of general knowledge versus know how.

2. Test for Delineating "General Knowledge and Skill" from "Know How" Under this test, a court should determine whether information is a protectable trade secret or part of the employee's general knowledge and skill by weighing the following factors:

1. Did the employee develop the disputed information? This factor incorporates the Wexler line of cases, which recognize an employee's interest in information or a process which he or she originated. If, however, the employee signed an agreement assigning all rights in any inventions to the employer, the fact that the employee developed the information will not support a finding that the information is part of the employee's own general skill and knowledge.
2. Is the information unique to the employer's business? This factor helps to determine whether the information is part of the collective knowledge of individuals employed in the industry.
3. Have competitors been unsuccessful in independent attempts to develop the disputed information? This factor helps to clarify the second factor because a competitor's failure to develop or produce the information indicates that it is particular to the employer and may thus qualify as a trade secret.
4. Has the employee, upon termination of the employment, appropriated some physical embodiment of the information, such as a written formula, blueprint, plan, or list? If so, this points toward a finding that the information is a trade secret. When, to the contrary, an employee draws on information in his memory, the information is more likely part of the employee's general knowledge and experience.[136] A defendant's reliance on memory should not, however, preclude trade secret protection in every case.[137] A protectable trade secret is not always written down or otherwise recorded. In contrast to copyright law, the distinction between knowledge of a concept or idea and a fixed expression of information is

unimportant because trade secret law expressly protects intangible information such as methods, techniques, and processes that an employee may have memorized.[138]

5. Is the information so closely integrated with the employee's overall experience that granting trade secret protection would deny the employee the ability to obtain employment commensurate with his or her general qualifications? This last factor addresses the public interest in employee mobility.

The balancing test should be flexibly applied, with no one factor being determinative. All factors should be given relative weight by the court. This is necessary because the variety of factual scenarios which trade secret litigation presents requires flexibility.

The suggestion that courts should engage in a balancing test in cases involving employee knowledge may be disquieting to some. After all, it only adds to an already extensive list of elements that must be established to prevail on a claim for misappropriation of trade secrets. Such a balancing test, it may be argued, does not help to clarify the law but instead makes the law more complex. The answer to such an argument is that the balancing test clarifies the existing factors and gives notice to potential litigants of the application of the factors. As a result, the balancing approach, which is based on the UTSA and the Restatement of Unfair Competition, would streamline trade secret law by adding clarification and specificity and by fostering more fair and efficient results.[139]

The parties may contract around these factors, if they so desire. The balancing test operates as a default rule, providing direction when there is no agreement between the parties.

The nature of the conflict between employers and employees suggests this solution. The tension between employee mobility and the protection of rights in confidential information cannot be reconciled with a single bright-line rule because it is impossible to satisfy both interests at

the same time. Surely, an employee is not free to take a job in his field of expertise if his former employer is able to enjoin him from using knowledge and experience gained while working for the former employer. Conversely, an employer's rights in confidential information lose much of their value if that same information is being used by a former employee who is now working for a competitor.

The balancing test proposed in this Comment would provide better guidance to employers and employees as to their respective rights, and would assist courts deciding trade secret cases in reaching fair and consistent results. Further, the balancing test will help minimize trade secret misappropriation and groundless trade secret cases while promoting employee mobility and employer development.

B. The Dissolution Theory Is Problematic Because the Main Remedy in Trade Secret Law Is Injunctive Relief

Various commentators have suggested solutions to the underlying policy dilemma present in current trade secret law. In 1988, Suellen Lowry presented a compelling argument in which she characterized the problem of the competing interests in trade secret law as cases of "inevitable disclosure."[140]

These are the hard cases where employees acquire skills and knowledge directly related to an employer's trade secrets then seek employment at another firm.[141] Lowry asserted that in these situations, the information will inevitably be disclosed. Lowry argued that in "inevitable disclosure" trade secret cases, the problem should be seen as involving a dissolution of concurrent property interests, such as in the law of tenancies in common and community property.[142] She argued for a new regime patterned on marital dissolutions.[143] Under Lowry's proposal, courts would engage in a valuation of the trade secret, and then would allocate the value between the parties.[144] The court would, in effect, create a licensing scheme.[145]

There are three problems with this approach. First, the primary remedy sought in trade secret cases is injunctive relief. Any type of an enforced license frustrates the purpose of an injunction which is to completely restrict the employee or the new firm from using the protected information. An injunction is an important remedy because the original firm could be ruined by the mere disclosure of the confidential information to its competitors. Second, Lowry's proposal could be abused by a firm that first sought a license but was refused, then sued for one under dissolution theory. Third, arriving at appropriate valuations of concurrent trade secret interests will be difficult. Judicial valuations that use market values of information may not be accurate, because the plaintiff firm may not have made a profit before the misappropriation. Because of the difficulty in making valuations, Lowry's approach does not further predictability before litigation.

C. The Criminal Approach Is Not Practical and Shifts the Enforcement from the Parties

In some states, criminal sanctions, in addition to civil liability, are available against a former employee who steals scientific or technical information.[146] While several recent appellate cases have upheld convictions under these statutes,[147] criminal trade secret cases are much less common than civil suits; the law concerning what constitutes a trade secret under various penal codes is still developing. As discussed above, both criminal and civil cases involving the use of electronic mail by two top executives at Symantec Corporation, a Silicon Valley software firm, are pending.[148] The computer industry is closely following the Symantec case due to its possible impact on the definition of a trade secret under criminal law.[149]

While increased criminalization of trade secret law would function as a potent deterrent to

misappropriation, it may create more problems than it resolves. For example, it would further deter employee mobility in the computer industry. At the same time, it does not adequately address the problem of securing enforceable rights for employers engaged in technological innovation.

The competing concurrent interests in information also make it difficult to assess criminal culpability, because ownership in the information is subject to uncertainty. Moreover, the limited resources of most prosecutors' offices makes criminal enforcement possible only in the clearest cases. Donald Ingraham, Assistant District Attorney for Alameda County, has commented that if a company believes they have a trade secret dispute, "the first step is not to call the local district attorney's office." His office turns away over half of the trade secret cases reported on the initial call.

D. Employment Contracts and Nondisclosure Agreements

One way a firm can achieve certainty about what is a protected trade secret is to draft noncompetition and nondisclosure agreements. A majority of courts will enforce a covenant restricting an employee from competing with a former employer so long as it is reasonable in scope, territory, and duration, and is necessary for the protection of the employer.[150] Some jurisdictions, however, take a more strict view and ban all restrictions on an individual's ability to engage in a profession.[151]

Covenants not to compete are distinct from non-disclosure or confidentiality agreements, which prohibit only an employee's unauthorized disclosure of an employer's confidential information, and which are generally upheld.[152]

Contractual agreements regarding confidentiality and ownership of technological information can be critical to the determination of liability in computer industry trade secrets cases.[153] Besides helping to define exactly what it is that an employer considers to be its trade secret, a written nondisclosure agreement serves notice to an employee of the confidential nature of the employer's proprietary information. While the mere existence of such a contract will not be determinative, it greatly increases the probability that an employer will obtain relief for breach of contract, even where the confidential information or technology does not qualify as a trade secret.[154]

In most computer trade secret cases in which the employee signs a nondisclosure agreement, the computer programs at issue are found to be trade secrets and the courts rule in favor of the employer.[155] For example in *Healthcare Affiliated v. Lippany,*[156] Healthcare Affiliated hired Lippany to develop computer programs for hospital management systems. Lippany signed a contract agreeing that any processes or methodologies developed by him during his employment with the plaintiff were the property of the plaintiff and agreeing to preserve the confidentiality of plaintiff's methodologies (which included a computer system defendant developed). The Western District of Pennsylvania granted a preliminary injunction in favor of the plaintiff, based on the defendant's having agreed that his efforts toward developing and enhancing the plaintiff's computer systems would inure to the plaintiff's benefit: "Equity will not permit him to appropriate plaintiff's systems, methodologies and programs for his own personal benefit."[157]

Having key employees sign a confidentiality agreement which states that any computer system, methodology, or product information now in existence, or that may be developed by an employee, is confidential and not to be disclosed to anyone outside of the company without appropriate controls to insure its confidentiality, is vital to a high-technology company's success in maintaining trade secret protection for its computer operations. Courts have tended to uphold such agreements, which provide a basis for contractual remedies; moreover, a valid nondisclosure agreement can facilitate proving the confidential relationship necessary

for trade secret protection of the information at issue.

1. Problems with Confidentiality Agreements
The problem with confidentiality agreements is that they are not always available to new or smaller firms, which have only limited access to legal counseling. Disputes usually arise after the employment relationship has ended, whereas confidentiality agreements must be secured at the outset of the employment relationship when its termination is often not contemplated by either party. Additionally, employees generally do not anticipate changing firms when they are signing nondisclosure agreements. There is also the problem of trying to protect the unknown— it may be impossible to define the trade secret at the outset of the employment relationship, because the underlying research and development has not yet been done.

Scientists and engineers who understand the mercurial nature of the technology industry are reluctant to sign confidentiality agreements because they do not want to sacrifice their future mobility. This can cause problems for emerging firms who need to attract top technical workers. In larger firms, technical workers do not have the leverage to abstain from executing an agreement because they have less bargaining power. In these situations, employees are generally not compensated for their decreased mobility.

Employees who have signed confidentiality contracts may discover that potential new employers are skittish about hiring them because they fear litigation.[158] For example, an employee with a confidentiality agreement with Microsoft will not be an attractive hire to a company with a small litigation budget because Microsoft has a legal department of over 50 lawyers and has a reputation for aggressive litigation.[159]

2. Recommendations for Drafting Employment Nondisclosure Agreements
To provide protection for confidential proprietary informa-

tion, a firm should use an employment nondisclosure agreement which includes the following provisions:

1. All aspects of information not published or generally known in the industry are to be treated as the employer's confidential or proprietary information until they become publicly available.
2. Employees agree that they will not discuss confidential information outside of the workplace. All publications or presentations dealing directly or indirectly with the confidential information must be cleared by the employer in advance.
3. All documents containing confidential information must be stamped "Proprietary Information" or "Company Confidential," and may be distributed only to those who have a need for the information in their work. Documents should not be reproduced unnecessarily, and should be disposed of in a manner which ensures that they will not be available to unauthorized persons. Employees agree to return all tangible forms of confidential information to the firm upon termination or at the firm's request.
4. Employees agree to disclose and assign to the employer all rights in all inventions or ideas relating to their work at the firm or that are aided by the use of the firm's equipment, facilities, or supplies.
5. Employees agree to hold in confidence, and not use or disclose without the firm's written authorization, any information obtained or created during the period of employment, which pertains to any aspect of the firm's business and is unknown to actual or potential customers.
6. Employees represent that they have not brought and will not bring or use in the performance of their duties any proprietary or confidential information, whether or not in writing, of a former employer without that employer's written authorization.
7. The agreement survives the employee's employment at the firm.

V. CONCLUSION

In the context of the employment relationship, trade secret law has become one of the primary tools for protecting computer software and other high-technology information. Protecting an employer's exclusive trade secret rights in properly guarded confidential information is critical to technological development and economic growth, especially in computer and technology based firms. Yet trade secret protection must not be used as a weapon by employers to restrain employee mobility or the development of new technologies.

Trade secret law remains uncertain and subject to uneven application. Such uncertainty creates difficulties for firms because they cannot readily distinguish between protectable and nonprotectable information.

In response, the UTSA should be revised to include a specific test to determine whether information is part of an employee's general knowledge and experience or an employer's protectable trade secret. Such a test will balance competing social policies using the specific considerations articulated in the proposed Restatement of Unfair Competition. This approach will inject more certainty into the law and promote fair competition in those cases where the parties have not clarified their respective rights by contract.

NOTES

1. UNIFORM TRADE SECRETS ACT §§ 1–12, 14 U. L. A. 437–467 (1990 & Supp. 1993) [hereinafter UTSA].
2. RESTATEMENT (FIRST) OF TORTS § 757 (1939).
3. UTSA, *supra* note 1.
4. The following states have adopted the UTSA: Alabama; Alaska; Arizona; Arkansas; California; Colorado; Connecticut; Delaware; District of Columbia; Florida; Hawaii; Idaho; Illinois;

Indiana; Iowa; Kansas; Kentucky; Louisiana; Maine; Maryland; Minnesota; Mississippi; Montana; Nebraska; Nevada; New Hampshire; New Mexico; North Dakota; Oklahoma; Oregon; Rhode Island; South Dakota; Utah; Virginia; Washington; West Virginia; Wisconsin. ARIZ. REV. STAT. ANN. § 44, ch. 4, art. 1 (1993).

5. RESTATEMENT OF THE LAW OF UNFAIR COMPETITION (Tentative Draft No. 4, 1993) [hereinafter RESTATEMENT OF UNFAIR COMPETITION].

6. RESTATEMENT OF TORTS, *supra* note 2, cmt. b.

7. UTSA, *supra* note 1, § 1.

8. Thus, trade secret law protects information and expression that is specifically not protected by the Copyright Act. 17 U.S.C. § 102(b) ("In no case does copyright protection for an original work of authorship extend to any idea, procedure, process, system, method of operation, concept, principle, or discovery, regardless of the form in which it is described, explained, illustrated, or embodied in such work.").

9. RESTATEMENT OF UNFAIR COMPETITION, *supra* note 5, § 39 (emphasis added).

10. ISC-Bunker Ramo v. Altech, 765 F. Supp. 1310, 1338 (N.D. Ill. 1990) (granting preliminary injunction against the use of trade secrets by a competitor that hired former employees of plaintiff).

11. *See* Fishing Concepts v. Ross, 226 U.S.P.Q. (BNA) 692, 695 (D. Minn. 1985) (commenting that the law of trade secrets only protects secret information, where the employer voluntarily reveals information about its computer system, there is no trade secret).

12. Josten's Inc. v. National Computer Systems, 318 N.W.2d 691 (Minn. 1982).

13. *Id.* at 702.

14. *See generally* MELVIN F. JAGER, TRADE SECRETS LAW § 8.01[3] (rev. 1992); ROGER MILGRIM, MILGRIM ON TRADE SECRETS § 5.02 (rev. 1990).

15. Kewanee Oil Co. v. Bicron Corp., 416 U.S. 470, 481 (1974) (the "encouragement of invention" is one of the policies behind trade secret law); E.I. duPont de Nemours & Co. v. American Potash & Chem. Corp., 200 A.2d 428, 437 (Del. Ch. 1964) (trade secret protection tends to encourage "substantial expenditures to find or improve ways and means of accomplishing commercial and industrial goals").

16. This dilemma represents the basic conundrum in all of intellectual property law: the tension between securing rights for innovators by granting them monopolies and the need for the open exchange of information. *Cf.* Stephen Breyer, *The Uneasy Case for Copyright,* 84 HARV. L. REV. 281 (1970); Zechariah Chaffee, *Reflections on the Law of Copyright,* 45 COLUM. L. REV. 503, 506–511 (1945); *see also,* Sony Corp. of Am. v. Universal City Studios, 464 U.S. 417, 429 (1984) (stating that congressional interpretation of the intellectual property clause of the Constitution "involves a difficult balance between the interests of authors and inventors in the control and exploitation of their writings and discoveries on the one hand, and society's competing interests in the free flow of ideas, information and commerce on the other").

17. Jonathan Greer-Armytage, *Survey: Staff Mobility,* COMPUTER WEEKLY, July 27, 1989, at 86.

18. *Cf.,* MICHAEL EPSTEIN, MODERN INTELLECTUAL PROPERTY, Chapter 11, § II(B)(1) (2d ed. 1991) (discussing employee backgrounds and conceptions of dissemination in biotechnology firms).

19. *Id.*

20. John Markoff, *U.S. Inquiry Into Theft from Apple,* N.Y. TIMES, Nov. 20, 1989, at D1.

21. *Id.*

22. *Id.*

23. *Id.*

24. The Constitution grants Congress the power to "promote the Progress of Science and useful Arts, by securing for limited Times to Authors and Inventors the exclusive Right to their respective Writings and Discoveries." U.S. CONST. art I, § 8, cl. 8. Federal law controls patent and copyright protection. *See* Patent Act of 1952, 66 Stat. 792 (1952), *codified at* 35 U.S.C. §§ 1–376 (1988); Copyright Act of 1976, Pub. L. No. 94–553, 90 Stat. 2541 (1976), *codified at* 17 U.S.C. §§ 1–810 (1988).

25. 416 U.S. 470 (1974).

26. *Id.* at 490–93.

27. 982 F.2d 693 (2d Cir. 1992) [hereinafter *Computer Associates*].

28. *Id.*

29. *Id.* at 717.

30. *See* 35 U.S.C. § 154; *see also supra* notes 1–15.

31. *See Computer Associates,* 982 F.2d at 717; *see also supra* notes 1–15.

32. *See supra* notes 2–9.

33. *See, e.g.,* Victoria Slind-Flor, *More Trade Secret Wars,* NAT'L L.J., Mar. 22, 1993, at 1, 34; Michael Greenberger & Robert Wasserman, *Keeping Secrets,* TEXAS LAWYER, June 14, 1993 at 24 (arguing that recent developments in copyright law suggest that software developers should not rely on copyright protection alone, but should protect valuable software as trade secrets) [hereinafter *Keeping Secrets*].

34. 17 U.S.C. §§ 1–810 (1988).

35. *See Keeping Secrets, supra* note 33, at 1, 34.

36. Several recent cases illustrate the complexity and difficulty of establishing protectable expression. *See* Atari Games Corp. v. Nintendo of Am., 975 F.2d 832 (Fed. Cir. 1992); Sega v. Accolade, 785 F. Supp. 1392 (N.D. Cal. 1992).

37. 17 U.S.C. § 102(a) (1973).

38. Trade secret issues also arise with respect to computer hardware, and "shrinkwrap" licenses for widely-distributed software. JAGER, *supra* note 14, § 9.02[1]–[3].

39. Integrated Cash Management Serv. v. Digital Transactions, 920 F.2d 171, 174 (2d Cir. 1990) (the architecture of plaintiff's utility programs was a trade secret under Restatement of Torts § 757); Trandes Corp. v. Guy F. Atkinson Co., 798 F. Supp. 284, 288 (D. Md. 1992) (computer program consisting of six modules written in object code qualified for trade secret protection under Maryland common law).

40. Avtec Sys. v. Peiffer, 805 F. Supp. 1312, 1319–20 (E.D. Va. 1992) (finding that plaintiff's use of a computer program as a demonstration and marketing device qualified the program as a trade secret under the Virginia Code); ISC-Bunker Ramo v. Altech, 765 F. Supp. 1310 (N.D. Ill. 1990) (holding that plaintiff's computer systems were trade secrets under Illinois trade secrets act); Aries Info. Sys. v. Pacific Management Sys. Corp., 366 N.W.2d 366, 369 (Ct. App. Minn. 1985) (plaintiff's financial accounting computer program was a trade secret under the Minnesota Trade Secrets Act).

41. UTSA, *supra* note 1, § 1.

42. IDAHO CODE § 48–801 (1993).

43. MONT. CODE ANN. § 30–14–402 (1985).

44. ALA. CODE § 8–27–1 (1987).

45. NEB. REV. STAT. § 87–502 (1988).

46. 784 F. Supp. 982, 988 (E.D.N.Y. 1992).

47. *Id.*

48. *See, e.g.,* Integrated Cash Management Servs. v. Digital Transactions, 920 F.2d 171, 173–74 (2d Cir. 1990) (sustaining relief for misappropriation of trade secrets, after plaintiff withdrew copyright infringement claim); Avtec Sys. v. Peiffer, 805 F. Supp. 1312, 1319–20 (E.D. Va. 1992) (court granted relief for trade secret claim, but rejected copyright claim); Cybertek Computer Prods. v. Whitefield, 203 U.S.P.Q. (BNA) 1020, 1024 (Cal. Super. Ct. 1977) (holding that the entire bundle or combination of general concepts not subject to protection, as utilized by the plaintiff in its computer system, constituted protectable trade secrets).

49. Computer Assoc. Int'l. v. Altai, Inc., 983 F.2d 693, 717 (2d Cir. 1992).

50. MILGRIM, BUSINESS ORGANIZATIONS, § 2.06A[5] [c] (1982).

51. Patent Act of 1952, 66 Stat. 792 (1952), *codified at* 35 U.S.C. §§ 1–376 (1988); Copyright Act of 1976, Pub. L. No. 94–553, 90 Stat. 2541 (1976), *codified at* 17 U.S.C. §§ 1–810 (1988).

52. MILGRIM, *supra* note 14, § 1.01 ("[C]ourts have overwhelmingly supported the property view.").

53. 467 U.S. 986 (1984).

54. *Id.* at 1002.

55. *See, e.g.,* Peabody v. Norfolk, 98 Mass. 452, 461 (1868).

56. 244 U.S. 100 (1917).

57. *Id.* at 102.

58. *See, e.g.,* Wiebold Studio v. Old World Restorations, 484 N.E.2d 280, 284 (Ohio App. 1985) ("The employer who has discovered or developed trade secrets is protected against unauthorized disclosure or use, not because he has a property interest in the trade secrets, but because the trade secrets were made known to the employee in a confidential relationship.").

59. *See* Ungar Elec. Tools v. Sid Ungar Co., 192 Cal. App. 2d 398, 403 (1961) (noting that courts protect the use of confidential information acquired by an employee in the course of his employment).

60. Laura Wheeler, *Trade Secrets and the Skilled Employee in the Computer Industry,* 61 WASH.

U.L.Q. 823, 826–27 (1982); *see* MILGRIM, *supra* note 14, at 1–6 to 1–7 n.15.

61. *See* UTSA, *supra* note 1.

62. *See supra* note 60.

63. RESTATEMENT (FIRST) OF TORTS, *supra* note 2. The Restatement also imposes liability when: "(2) the disclosure/use constitutes a breach of confidence which arose as a result of the other's disclosure of the trade secret; or (3) the trade secret was learned from a third person with notice of its secrecy and of the third person's having discovered it through improper means, or that the third person's disclosure was otherwise a breach of duty to the other; or (4) the secret was learned with notice of its secrecy and that it was disclosed by mistake." *Id.*

64. This concept was articulated by Justice Pitney in the seminal case of International News Serv. v. Associated Press, 248 U.S. 215, 235–45 (1918).

65. Under the UTSA, misappropriation is also centered around breach of a duty of confidence and the use of "improper means," yet with some crucial differences from the Restatement of Torts standard. The UTSA defines "improper means" to include theft, bribery, misrepresentation, breach or inducement of a breach of duty to maintain secrecy, or espionage through electronic or other means. Reverse engineering or independent derivation alone do *not* constitute improper means. UTSA, *supra* note 1, §§ 1(1)–(2).

66. Droeger v. Welsh Sporting Goods Corp., 541 F.2d 790, 792–93 (9th Cir. 1976) (holding that it is the defendant's wrongful use of the plaintiff's trade secret which gives rise to liability for damages).

67. UTSA, *supra* note 1, § 1(2)(ii)(A).

68. *Id.* § 1(2)(ii)(B).

69. *Id.* § (2)(ii)(C).

70. RESTATEMENT OF UNFAIR COMPETITION, *supra* note 5, § 40.

71. J. THOMAS MCCARTHY, MCCARTHY'S DESK ENCYCLOPEDIA OF INTELLECTUAL PROPERTY 180 (1991).

72. JAGER, *supra* note 14, § 8.01[3], at 8–13.

73. SI Handling Sys. v. Heisley, 753 F.2d 1244, 1261 (3d Cir. 1985) (quoting Van Prods. Co. v. General Welding & Fabricating Co., 213 A.2d 769, 777 (Pa. 1965)).

74. *Id.*

75. Dynamics Research Corp. v. Analytic Sciences Corp., 400 N.E.2d 1274, 1286–87 (Mass. App. 1980) (holding that plaintiff employer was not entitled to restrain the defendant's use of knowledge gained while working on the plaintiff's system, as plaintiff failed to keep the system sufficiently secret).

76. Rami Grunbaum, *Advanced Tech Takes Siemens to Court,* PUGET SOUND BUSINESS JOURNAL, Dec. 17, 1993, at 1–4 [hereinafter *Advanced Tech*].

77. *Id.*

78. RESTATEMENT OF TORTS, *supra* note 2.

79. *Id.*

80. UTSA, *supra* note 1, § cmt.

81. 401 F. Supp. 1102, 1111 (E.D. Mich. 1975).

82. *Id.*

83. *Id.* at 1114–1116.

84. *Id.*

85. 807 F.2d 1256, 1263 (5th Cir. 1987).

86. *Id.* at 1258.

87. *Id.*

88. *Id.*

89. *Id.*

90. *Id.*

91. 707 F. Supp. 1170, 1178 (C.D. Cal. 1989).

92. *Id.* at 1177.

93. *Id.* at 1178; *see also* Sarkes Tarian, Inc. v. Audio Devices, Inc., 166 F. Supp. 250 (S.D. Cal. 1958); Josten's, Inc. v. National Computer Sys., Inc., 318 N.W.2d 691, 701, 702 (Minn. 1982).

94. 424 S.E.2d 226, 230 (N.C. App. 1993).

95. *Id.* at 228.

96. *Id.*

97. *Id.*

98. *Id.* at 230.

99. *Id.*

100. 805 F. Supp. 1312, 1320 (E.D. Va. 1992).

101. *Id.* at 1320.

102. *Id.*

103. The doctrine of shop rights permits an employer to use an idea submitted by an employee, without compensation to the employee, to the extent that the idea pertains to the employer's business and was generated on company time using company materials and personnel. JAGER, *supra* note 14, § 8.02. The issue of employers' and employees' respective rights regarding employee inven-

tions also arises in patent and copyright law, and is regulated by statute in some states *See, e.g.,* CAL. LAB. CODE § 2870; ILL. REV. STAT. ch. 140, § 301; MINN. STAT. ANN. §181.78; N.C. GEN. STAT. 66–57.1; WASH. REV. CODE ANN. § 49.44.140.

104. 805 F. Supp. at 1320. In one closely watched case currently being litigated, IBM is seeking an injunction barring a former employee specially skilled in the field of magnetic resonance heads for computer disk drives from working for a competitor in a position involving development of magnetic resonance disk drive heads, as he would inevitably disclose IBM's trade secrets in this technology. Seagate Technology v. IBM Corp., 962 F.2d 12 (8th Cir. 1992).

105. *Id.*

106. 160 A.2d 430 (Pa. 1960).

107. 251 N.W.2d 220 (Iowa 1977).

108. 160 A.2d at 433–436.

109. *Id.* at 437.

110. 251 N.W.2d at 230.

111. *Id.* at 229–30.

112. *Id.*

113. 823 F.2d 1199 (7th Cir. 1987).

114. 442 A.2d 1114 (Pa. Super. 1982).

115. 823 F.2d at 1205–06.

116. *Id.*

117. 442 A.2d at 1122.

118. *Cf.* Maloney v. E.I. DuPont de Nemours & Co., 352 F.2d 936, 939 (D.C. Cir. 1965) (stating in the context of employment contracts that employers "will wish to avoid even the threat of [trade secret] litigation").

119. *See, e.g.,* E.I. Du Pont de Nemours & Co. v. American Potash & Chem. Corp., 200 A.2d 428, 437 (Del. Ch. 1964) (acknowledging the inherent conflict created when an employee is asked "to work in a trade secret area and thereby circumscribe his possible future liberty of action and the use of the knowledge and skills which are inextricably interwoven with his knowledge of the trade secrets").

120. AMP v. Fleischhacker, 823 F.2d at 1205 (quoting Fleming Sales Co. v. Bailey, 611 F. Supp. 507, 514 (N.D. Ill. 1985)).

121. Craig Rose, *Microsoft May Gain From Stac's Win,* SAN DIEGO UNION-TRIBUNE, Mar. 1, 1994, at C1 [hereinafter *Microsoft May Gain*].

122. *Id.*

123. *Id.*

124. Pamela Wilson, *Titan Linkabit Sues Former Exec,* SAN DIEGO DAILY TRANSCRIPT, June 11, 1991, at A1.

125. *Id.*

126. *AMP,* 823 F.2d at 1205 (quoting Harley & Lund Corp. v. Murray Rubber Co., 31 F.2d 932, 934 (2d Cir. 1929): "[I]t has never been thought actionable to take away another's employee, when the defendant wants to use him in his own business, however much the plaintiff may suffer. It is difficult to see how servants could get the full value of their services on any other terms. . . .").

127. Slind-Flor, *supra* note 33, at 1.

128. *See Advanced Tech, supra* note 76, at 1–4; *Microsoft May Gain, supra* note 121, at C1.

129. Jonathan Weber, *Software's Symantec Weathers Stormy Seas,* L.A. TIMES, Oct. 5, 1992, at D2.

130. *Id.*

131. Wheeler, *supra* note 60, at 843.

132. *See* Wheeler, *supra* note 60, at 843, 846 (proposing that statutes be expanded to encompass a definition of parties' ownership rights in trade secrets, and noting that a federal statute is warranted though not likely).

133. *See, e.g., In re* Innovation Constr. Sys., 793 F.2d 875, 879 (7th Cir. 1986) (supporting a balance between the competing interests of employers in precluding employees from exploiting specialized knowledge gained through their employment and employees in the general use of their skills and training); Amoco Prod. Co. v. Lindley, 609 P.2d 733, 745 (Okla. 1980) (noting that courts balance the equities between the right of the company to use its employees and resources to its advantage against the right of the highly developed mind and skill of the employee).

The *Amoco* court also set forth several factors to be considered:

how many of the innovative elements in the newly developed process are available in the prior art; how closely tied is the development to intrinsic knowledge of the innovator . . . is it possible to sort out the process from the inner workings of a man's knowledge; did the company treat the innovation with the requisite secrecy to place others on notice of its claim . . . [o]ther considerations are time and money and company facilities used in its production, and the employer's own knowledge thereof.

Id.

134. Section 42 of the Restatement of Unfair Competition provides, "An employee or former employee who discloses or uses a trade secret owned by the employer or former employer in breach of a duty of confidence is subject to liability for appropriation of the trade secret. . . ." RESTATEMENT OF UNFAIR COMPETITION, *supra* note 5, § 42.

135. *Id.* at cmt. d., p. 95.

136. AMP Inc. v. Fleischhacker, 823 F.2d 1199, 1204–05 (7th Cir. 1987) (refusing to grant an injunction for the employer in the absence of any evidence that the defendant employee "ever systematically recorded, copied, compiled, or even purposefully memorized any of AMP's confidential business information. . . .").

137. *See, e.g.,* Allen v. Johar Inc., 823 S.W.2d 824, 827 (Ark. 1992) (finding that whether the information used was written down or memorized is immaterial; the proper issue is whether it is protectable as a trade secret).

138. The Copyright Act of 1976 states that: "In no case does copyright protection for an original work of authorship extend to any idea, procedure, process, system, method of operation, concept, principle, or discovery. . . ." 17 U.S.C. §102(b) (1988).

139. A similar factor-based approach is used by the Ninth circuit in trademark infringement cases brought under the Lanham Act for determining likelihood of confusion. *See, e.g.,* AMF Corp. v. Sleekcraft Boats, 599 F.2d 341, 348–49 (9th Cir. 1979).

140. Suellen Lowry, *Inevitable Disclosure Trade Secret Disputes: Dissolutions of Concurrent Property Interests,* 40 STAN. L. REV. 519, 539–44. (1988).

141. *Id.*

142. *Id.; see also* Bruce Alan Kugler, *Limiting Trade Secret Protection,* 22 VAL. U. L. REV. 725, 757 (1988) (proposing that trade secrets should be categorized as either "property quality" or "nonproperty quality" using a quasi-patent analysis, and that "property quality" trade secrets would require only implied notice to the employee and be protected for an unlimited amount of time, while "nonproperty quality" trade secrets would require actual notice to the employee and have a restricted period of protection).

143. *Id.*

144. *Id.*

145. *Id.*

146. *See, e.g.,* CAL. PENAL CODE § 499c (b) (West 1988); TEX. PENAL CODE ANN. § 31.05 (West 1989).

147. Schalk v. State, 823 S.W.2d 633 (Tex. Ct. Crim. App. 1991) (en banc); Leonard v. State, 767 S.W.2d 171 (Tex. 1988); People v. Gopal, 171 Cal. App. 3d 524 (1985).

148. Tom Abate, *Symantec Chief Charged in Trade Secrets Case,* S.F. EXAMINER, Mar. 5, 1993, at A-1 [hereinafter *Chief Charged*].

149. Ken Siegmann, *2 Symantec Execs Indicted in Secrets Case,* S.F. CHRONICLE, Mar. 5, 1993, at D1; *Chief Charged, supra* note 148, at A-1.

150. JAGER, *supra* note 14, § 13.01[2].

151. *See, e.g.,* CAL. BUS. & PROF. CODE § 16600 (West 1987) ("every contract by which anyone is restrained from engaging in a lawful profession, trade or business of any kind is to that extent void").

152. JAGER, *supra* note 14, § 13.01[1].

153. *See, e.g.,* Cybertek Computer Prods. v. Whitfield, 203 U.S.P.Q. (BNA) 1020, 1023 (Cal. Super. Ct. 1977) (Employee Nondisclosure Agreement executed by former employee which provided that all techniques and methods relating to plaintiff employer's computer system were trade secrets and confidential was given "considerable weight" in the court's finding that defendant was liable for disclosing and utilizing substantial aspects of plaintiff's system in the development of a similar system for a competitor).

154. *See, e.g.,* Structural Dynamics Research Corp. v. Engineering Mechanics Research Corp., 401 F. Supp. 1102, 1114 (E.D. Mich. 1975).

155. Cases holding that computer program information covered by a confidentiality agreement was a protectable trade secret include: Integrated Cash Management Serv. v. Digital Transactions, 920 F.2d 171, 174 (2d Cir. 1990); ISC-Bunker Ramo Corp. v. Altech, Inc., 765 F. Supp. 1310, 1323 (N.D. Ill. 1990); Healthcare Affiliated v. Lippany, 701 F. Supp. 1142, 1146 (W.D. Pa.

1988); Aries Info. Sys. v. Pacific Management Sys. Corp., 366 N.W.2d 366, 367 (Ct. App. Minn. 1985); J & K Computer Sys. v. Parrish, 642 P.2d 732, 734 (Utah 1982); and Cybertek Computer Prods., v. Whitfield, 203 U.S.P.Q. (BNA) 1020 (Cal. Super. Ct. 1977). *But see* Amoco Production Co. v. Lindley, 609 P.2d 733, 745 (Okla. 1980) (no trade secret protection available where the program at issue was not an "invention" within the meaning of the parties' contract).

156. 701 F. Supp. 1142 (W.D. Pa. 1988).
157. *Id.* at 1155–56.
158. Magee Harett, *Wait! Don't Sign That Employment Contract,* EDN, Nov. 14, 1991, at 57.
159. *Microsoft May Gain, supra* note 121, at C1.

<hr>

READING 10.3

Justifying Intellectual Property

Edwin C. Hettinger

Property institutions fundamentally shape a society. These legal relationships between individuals, different sorts of objects, and the state are not easy to justify. This is especially true of intellectual property. It is difficult enough to determine the appropriate kinds of ownership of corporeal objects (consider water or mineral rights); it is even more difficult to determine what types of ownership we should allow for noncorporeal, intellectual objects, such as writings, inventions, and secret business information. The complexity of copyright, patent, and trade secret law reflects this problem.

According to one writer "patents are the heart and core of property rights, and once they are destroyed, the destruction of all other property

Source: Hettinger, Edwin; *Justifying Intellectual Property.* Copyright © 1989 by Princeton University Press. Reprinted by permission of Princeton University Press.

rights will follow automatically, as a brief postscript."[1] Though extreme, this remark rightly stresses the importance of patents to private competitive enterprise. Intellectual property is an increasingly significant and widespread form of ownership. Many have noted the arrival of the "post-Industrial society"[2] in which the manufacture and manipulation of physical goods is giving way to the production and use of information. The result is an ever-increasing strain on our laws and customs protecting intellectual property.[3] Now, more than ever, there is a need to carefully scrutinize these institutions.

As a result of both vastly improved information-handling technologies and the larger role information is playing in our society, owners of intellectual property are more frequently faced with what they call "piracy" or information theft (that is, unauthorized access to their intellectual property). Most readers of this article have undoubtedly done something considered piracy by owners of intellectual property. Making a cassette tape of a friend's record, videotaping television broadcasts for a movie library, copying computer programs or using them on more than one machine, photocopying more than one chapter of a book, or two or more articles by the same author—all are examples of alleged infringing activities. Copyright, patent, and trade secret violation suits abound in industry, and in academia, the use of another person's ideas often goes unacknowledged. These phenomena indicate widespread public disagreement over the nature and legitimacy of our intellectual property institutions. This article examines the justifiability of those institutions.

COPYRIGHTS, PATENTS, AND TRADE SECRETS

It is commonly said that one cannot patent or copyright ideas. One copyrights "original works of authorship," including writings, music, drawings, dances, computer programs, and movies; one may not copyright ideas, concepts, principles, facts, or knowledge. Expressions of ideas are copyrightable; ideas themselves are not.[4] While useful, this notion of separating the content of an idea from its style of presentation is not unproblematic.[5] Difficulty in distinguishing the two is most apparent in the more artistic forms of authorship (such as fiction or poetry), where style and content interpenetrate. In these mediums, more so than in others, *how* something is said is very much part of *what* is said (and vice versa).

A related distinction holds for patents. Laws of nature, mathematical formulas, and methods of doing business, for example, cannot be patented. What one patents are inventions—that is, processes, machines, manufactures, or compositions of matter. These must be novel (not previously patented); they must constitute nonobvious improvements over past inventions; and they must be useful (inventions that do not work cannot be patented). Specifying what sorts of "technological recipes for production"[6] constitute patentable subject matter involves distinguishing specific applications and utilizations from the underlying unpatentable general principles.[7] One cannot patent the scientific principle that water boils at 212 degrees, but one can patent a machine (for example, a steam engine) which uses this principle in a specific way and for a specific purpose.[8]

Trade secrets include a variety of confidential and valuable business information, such as sales, marketing, pricing, and advertising data, lists of customers and suppliers, and such things as plant layout and manufacturing techniques. Trade secrets must not be generally known in the industry, their nondisclosure must give some advantage over competitors, and attempts to prevent leakage of the information must be made (such as pledges of secrecy in employment contracts or other company security policies). The formula for Coca-Cola and bids on government contracts are examples of trade secrets.

Trade secret subject matter includes that of copyrights and patents: anything which can be copyrighted or patented can be held as a trade secret, though the converse is not true. Typically a business must choose between patenting an invention and holding it as a trade secret. Some advantages of trade secrets are (1) they do not require disclosure (in fact they require secrecy), whereas a condition for granting patents (and copyrights) is public disclosure of the invention (or writing); (2) they are protected for as long as they are kept secret, while most patents lapse after seventeen years; and (3) they involve less cost than acquiring and defending a patent. Advantages of patents include protection against reverse engineering (competitors figuring out the invention by examining the product which embodies it) and against independent invention. Patents give their owners the *exclusive* right to make, use, and sell the invention no matter how anyone else comes up with it, while trade secrets prevent only improper acquisition (breaches of security).

Copyrights give their owners the right to reproduce, to prepare derivative works from, to distribute copies of, and to publicly perform or display the "original work of authorship." Their duration is the author's life plus fifty years. These rights are not universally applicable, however. The most notable exception is the "fair use" clause of the copyright statute, which gives researchers, educators, and libraries special privileges to use copyrighted material.[9]

INTELLECTUAL OBJECTS AS NONEXCLUSIVE

Let us call the subject matter of copyrights, patents, and trade secrets 'intellectual objects.'[10] These objects are nonexclusive: they can be at many places at once and are not consumed by their use. The marginal cost of providing an intellectual object to an additional user is zero, and though there are communications costs, modern technologies can easily make an intellectual object unlimitedly available at a very low cost.

The possession or use of an intellectual object by one person does not preclude others from possessing or using it as well.[11] If someone borrows your lawn mower, you cannot use it, nor can anyone else. But if someone borrows your recipe for guacamole, that in no way precludes you, or anyone else, from using it. This feature is shared by all sorts of intellectual objects, including novels, computer programs, songs, machine designs, dances, recipes for Coca-Cola, lists of customers and suppliers, management techniques, and formulas for genetically engineered bacteria which digest crude oil. Of course, sharing intellectual objects does prevent the original possessor from selling the intellectual object to others, and so this sort of use is prevented. But sharing in no way hinders *personal* use.

This characteristic of intellectual objects grounds a strong prima facie case against the wisdom of private and exclusive intellectual property rights. Why should one person have the exclusive right to possess and use something which all people could possess and use concurrently? The burden of justification is very much on those who would restrict the maximal use of intellectual objects. A person's right to exclude others from possessing and using a physical object can be justified when such exclusion is necessary for this person's own possession and unhindered use. No such justification is available for exclusive possession and use of intellectual property.

One reason for the widespread piracy of intellectual property is that many people think it is unjustified to exclude others from intellectual objects.[12] Also, the unauthorized taking of an intellectual object does not feel like theft. Stealing a physical object involves depriving someone of the object taken, whereas taking an intellectual object deprives the owner of neither possession nor personal use of that object—though the owner is deprived of potential profit. This nonexclusive feature of intellectual objects should be kept firmly in mind when assessing the justifiability of intellectual property.

OWNING IDEAS AND RESTRICTIONS ON THE FREE FLOW OF INFORMATION

The fundamental value our society places on freedom of thought and expression creates another difficulty for the justification of intellectual property. Private property enhances one person's freedom at the expense of everyone else's. Private intellectual property restricts methods of acquiring ideas (as do trade secrets), it restricts the use of ideas (as do patents), and it restricts the expression of ideas (as do copyrights)—restrictions undesirable for a number of reasons. John Stuart Mill argued that free thought and speech are important for the acquisition of true beliefs and for individual growth and development.[13] Restrictions on the free flow and use of ideas not only stifle individual growth, but impede the advancement of technological innovation and human knowledge generally.[14] Insofar as copyrights, patents, and trade secrets have these negative effects, they are hard to justify.

Since a condition for granting patents and copyrights is public disclosure of the writing or invention, these forms of intellectual ownership do not involve the exclusive right to possess the knowledge or ideas they protect. Our society gives its inventors and writers a legal right to exclude others from certain uses of their intellectual works in return for public disclosure of these works. Disclosure is necessary if people are to learn from and build on the ideas of others. When they bring about disclosure of ideas which would have otherwise remained secret, patents and copyrights enhance rather than restrict the free flow of ideas (though they still restrict the idea's widespread use and dissemination). Trade secrets do not have this virtue. Regrettably, the common law tradition which offers protection for trade secrets encourages secrecy. This makes trade secrets undesirable in a way in which copyrights or patents are not.[15]

LABOR, NATURAL INTELLECTUAL PROPERTY RIGHTS, AND MARKET VALUE

Perhaps the most powerful intuition supporting property rights is that people are entitled to the fruits of their labor. What a person produces with her own intelligence, effort, and perseverance ought to belong to her and to no one else. "Why is it mine? Well, it's mine because I made it, that's why. It wouldn't have existed but for me."

John Locke's version of this labor justification for property derives property rights in the product of labor from prior property rights in one's body.[16] A person owns her body and hence she owns what it does, namely, its labor. A person's labor and its product are inseparable, and so ownership of one can be secured only by owning the other. Hence, if a person is to own her body and thus its labor, she must also own what she joins her labor with—namely, the product of her labor.

This formulation is not without problems. For example, Robert Nozick wonders why a person should gain what she mixes her labor with instead of losing her labor. (He imagines pouring a can of tomato juice into the ocean and asks whether he thereby ought to gain the ocean or lose his tomato juice.)[17] More importantly, assuming that labor's fruits are valuable, and that laboring gives the laborer a property right in this value, this would entitle the laborer only to the value she added, and not to the *total* value of the resulting product. Though exceedingly difficult to measure, these two components of value (that attributable to the object labored on and that attributable to the labor) need to be distinguished.

Locke thinks that until labored on, objects have little human value, at one point suggesting that labor creates 99 percent of their value.[18]

This is not plausible when labor is mixed with land and other natural resources. One does not create 99 percent of the value of an apple by picking it off a tree, though some human effort is necessary for an object to have value for us.

What portion of the value of writings, inventions, and business information is attributable to the intellectual laborer? Clearly authorship, discovery, or development is necessary if intellectual products are to have value for us: we could not use or appreciate them without this labor. But it does not follow from this that all of their value is attributable to that labor. Consider, for example, the wheel, the entire human value of which is not appropriately attributable to its original inventor.[19]

The value added by the laborer and any value the object has on its own are by no means the only components of the value of an intellectual object. Invention, writing, and thought in general do not operate in a vacuum; intellectual activity is not creation *ex nihilo*. Given this vital dependence of a person's thoughts on the ideas of those who came before her, intellectual products are fundamentally social products. Thus even if one assumes that the value of these products is entirely the result of human labor, this value is not entirely attributable to *any particular laborer* (or small group of laborers).

Separating out the individual contribution of the inventor, writer, or manager from this historical/social component is no easy task. Simply identifying the value a laborer's labor adds to the world with the market value of the resulting product ignores the vast contributions of others. A person who relies on human intellectual history and makes a small modification to produce something of great value should no more receive what the market will bear than should the last person needed to lift a car receive full credit for lifting it. If laboring gives the laborer the right to receive the market value of the resulting product, this market value should be shared by all those whose ideas contributed to the origin of the product. The fact that most of these contributors are no longer present to receive their fair share is not a reason to give the entire market value to the last contributor.[20]

Thus an appeal to the market value of a laborer's product cannot help us here. Markets work only after property rights have been established and enforced, and our question is what sorts of property rights an inventor, writer, or manager should have, given that the result of her labor is a joint product of human intellectual history.

Even if one could separate out the laborer's own contribution and determine its market value, it is still not clear that the laborer's right to the fruits of her labor naturally entitles her to receive this. Market value is a socially created phenomenon, depending on the activity (or non-activity) of other producers, the monetary demand of purchasers, and the kinds of property rights, contracts, and markets the state has established and enforced. The market value of the same fruits of labor will differ greatly with variations in these social factors.

Consider the market value of a new drug formula. This depends on the length and the extent of the patent monopoly the state grants and enforces, on the level of affluence of those who need the drug, and on the availability and price of substitutes. The laborer did not produce these. The intuitive appeal behind the labor argument—"I made it, hence it's mine"—loses its force when it is used to try to justify owning something others are responsible for (namely, the market value). The claim that a laborer, in virtue of her labor, has a "natural right" to this socially created phenomenon is problematic at best.

Thus, there are two different reasons why the market value of the product of labor is not what a laborer's labor naturally entitles her to. First, market value is not something that is produced by those who produce a product, and the labor argument entitles laborers only to the products of their labor. Second, even if we ignore this point and equate the fruits of labor with the market value of those fruits, intellectual products result from the labor of many people besides the latest contributor, and they have claims on the market value as well.

So even if the labor theory shows that the laborer has a natural right to the fruits of labor, this does not establish a natural right to receive the full market value of the resulting product. The notion that a laborer is naturally entitled as a matter of right to receive the market value of her product is a myth. To what extent individual laborers should be allowed to receive the market value of their products is a question of social policy; it is not solved by simply insisting on a moral right to the fruits of one's labor.[21]

Having a moral right to the fruits of one's labor might also mean having a right to possess and personally use what one develops. This version of the labor theory has some force. On this interpretation, creating something through labor gives the laborer a prima facie right to possess and personally use it for her own benefit. The value of protecting individual freedom guarantees this right as long as the creative labor, and the possession and use of its product, does not harm others.

But the freedom to exchange a product in a market and receive its full market value is again something quite different. To show that people have a right to this, one must argue about how best to balance the conflicts in freedoms which arise when people interact. One must determine what sorts of property rights and markets are morally legitimate. One must also decide when society should enforce the results of market interaction and when it should alter those results (for example, with tax policy). There is a gap—requiring extensive argumentative filler—between the claim that one has a natural right to possess and personally use the fruits of one's labor and the claim that one ought to receive for one's product whatever the market will bear.

Such a gap exists as well between the natural right to possess and personally use one's intellectual creations and the rights protected by copyrights, patents, and trade secrets. The natural right of an author to personally use her writings is distinct from the right, protected by copyright, to make her work public, sell it in a market, and then prevent others from making copies. An inventor's natural right to use the invention for her own benefit is not the same as the right, protected by patent, to sell this invention in a market and exclude others (including independent inventors) from using it. An entrepreneur's natural right to use valuable business information or techniques that she develops is not the same as the right, protected by trade secret, to prevent her employees from using these techniques in another job.

In short, a laborer has a prima facie natural right to possess and personally use the fruits of her labor. But a right to profit by selling a product in the market is something quite different. This liberty is largely a socially created phenomenon. The "right" to receive what the market will bear is a socially created privilege, and not a natural right at all. The natural right to possess and personally use what one has produced is relevant to the justifiability of such a privilege, but by itself it is hardly sufficient to justify that privilege.

DESERVING PROPERTY RIGHTS BECAUSE OF LABOR

The above argument that people are naturally entitled to the fruits of their labor is distinct from the argument that a person has a claim to labor's fruits based on desert. If a person has a natural right to something—say her athletic ability—and someone takes it from her, the return of it is something she is *owed* and can rightfully demand. Whether or not she deserves this athletic ability is a separate issue. Similarly, insofar as people have natural property rights in the fruits of their labor, these rights are something they are *owed,* and not something they necessarily deserve.[22]

The desert argument suggests that the laborer deserves to benefit from her labor, at least if it is an attempt to do something worthwhile. This proposal is convincing, but does not show that what the laborer deserves is property rights in the object labored on. The mistake is to conflate the created object which makes a person deserving of a reward with what that reward should be. Property rights in the created object are not the only possible reward. Alternatives include fees, awards, acknowledgment, gratitude, praise, security, power, status, and public financial support.

Many considerations affect whether property rights in the created object are what the laborer deserves. This may depend, for example, on what is created by labor. If property rights in the very things created were always an appropriate reward for labor, then as Lawrence Becker notes, parents would deserve property rights in their children.[23] Many intellectual objects (scientific laws, religious and ethical insights, and so on) are also the sort of thing that should not be owned by anyone.

Furthermore, as Becker also correctly points out, we need to consider the purpose for which the laborer labored. Property rights in the object produced are not a fitting reward if the laborer does not want them. Many intellectual laborers produce beautiful things and discover truths as ends in themselves.[24] The appropriate reward in such cases is recognition, gratitude, and perhaps public financial support, not full-fledged property rights, for these laborers do not want to exclude others from their creations.

Property rights in the thing produced are also not a fitting reward if the value of these rights is disproportional to the effort expended by the laborer. 'Effort' includes (1) how hard someone tries to achieve a result, (2) the amount of risk voluntarily incurred in seeking this result, and (3) the degree to which moral considerations played a role in choosing the result intended. The harder one tries, the more one is willing to sacrifice, and the worthier the goal, the greater are one's deserts.

Becker's claim that the amount deserved is proportional to the value one's labor produces is mistaken.[25] The value of labor's results is often significantly affected by factors outside a person's control, and no one deserves to be rewarded for being lucky. Voluntary past action is the only valid basis for determining desert.[26] Here only a person's effort (in the sense defined) is relevant. Her knowledge, skills, and achievements insofar as they are based on natural talent and luck, rather than effort expended, are not. A person who is born with extraordinary natural talents, or who is extremely lucky, *deserves* nothing on the basis of these characteristics. If such a person puts forward no greater effort than another, she deserves no greater reward. Thus, two laborers who expend equal amounts of effort deserve the same reward, even when the value of the resulting products is vastly different.[27] Giving more to workers whose products have greater social value might be justified if it is needed as an incentive. But this has nothing to do with giving the laborer what she deserves.

John Rawls considers even the ability to expend effort to be determined by factors outside a person's control and hence a morally impermissible criterion for distribution.[28] How hard one tries, how willing one is to sacrifice and incur risk, and how much one cares about morality are *to some extent* affected by natural endowments and social circumstances. But if the ability to expend effort is taken to be entirely determined by factors outside a person's control, the result is a determinism which makes meaningful moral evaluation impossible. If people are responsible for anything, they are responsible for how hard they try, what sacrifices they make, and how moral they are. Because the effort a person expends is much more under

her control than her innate intelligence, skills, and talents, effort is a far superior basis for determining desert. To the extent that a person's expenditure of effort is under her control, effort is the proper criterion for desert.[29]

Giving an inventor exclusive rights to make and sell her invention (for seventeen years) may provide either a greater or a lesser reward than she deserves. Some inventions of extraordinary market value result from flashes of genius, while others with little market value (and yet great social value) require significant efforts.

The proportionality requirement may also be frequently violated by granting copyright. Consider a five-hundred-dollar computer program. Granted, its initial development costs (read "efforts") were high. But once it has been developed, the cost of each additional program is the cost of the disk it is on—approximately a dollar. After the program has been on the market several years and the price remains at three or four hundred dollars, one begins to suspect that the company is receiving far more than it deserves. Perhaps this is another reason so much illegal copying of software goes on: the proportionality requirement is not being met, and people sense the unfairness of the price. Frequently, trade secrets (which are held indefinitely) also provide their owners with benefits disproportional to the effort expended in developing them.

THE LOCKEAN PROVISOS

We have examined two versions of the labor argument for intellectual property, one based on desert, the other based on a natural entitlement to the fruits of one's labor. Locke himself put limits on the conditions under which labor can justify a property right in the thing produced. One is that after the appropriation there must be "enough and as good left in common for others."[30] This proviso is often reformulated as a "no loss to others" precondition for property acquisition.[31] As long as one does not worsen another's position by appropriating an object, no objection can be raised to owning that with which one mixes one's labor.

Under current law, patents clearly run afoul of this proviso by giving the original inventor an exclusive right to make, use, and sell the invention. Subsequent inventors who independently come up with an already patented invention cannot even personally use their invention, much less patent or sell it. They clearly suffer a great and unfair loss because of the original patent grant. Independent inventors should not be prohibited from using or selling their inventions. Proving independent discovery of a publicly available patented invention would be difficult, however. Nozick's suggestion that the length of patents be restricted to the time it would take for independent invention may be the most reasonable administrative solution.[32] In the modern world of highly competitive research and development, this time is often much shorter than the seventeen years for which most patents are currently granted.

Copyrights and trade secrets are not subject to the same objection (though they may constitute a loss to others in different ways). If someone independently comes up with a copyrighted expression or a competitor's business technique, she is not prohibited from using it. Copyrights and trade secrets prevent only mimicking of other people's expressions and ideas.

Locke's second condition on the legitimate acquisition of property rights prohibits spoilage. Not only must one leave enough and as good for others, but one must not take more than one can use.[33] So in addition to leaving enough apples in the orchard for others, one must not take home a truckload and let them spoil. Though Locke does not specifically mention prohibiting waste, it is the concern to avoid waste which underlies his proviso prohibiting spoilage. Taking more than one can use is wrong because it is wasteful. Thus Locke's concern here is with appropriations of property which are wasteful.

Since writings, inventions, and business techniques are nonexclusive, this requirement prohibiting waste can never be completely met by intellectual property. When owners of intellectual property charge fees for the use of their expressions or inventions, or conceal their business techniques from others, certain beneficial uses of these intellectual products are prevented. This is clearly wasteful, since everyone could use and benefit from intellectual objects concurrently. How wasteful private ownership of intellectual property is depends on how beneficial those products would be to those who are excluded from their use as a result.

SOVEREIGNTY, SECURITY, AND PRIVACY

Private property can be justified as a means to sovereignty. Dominion over certain objects is important for individual autonomy. Ronald Dworkin's liberal is right in saying that "some sovereignty over a range of personal possessions is essential to dignity."[34] Not having to share one's personal possessions or borrow them from others is essential to the kind of autonomy our society values. Using or consuming certain objects is also necessary for survival. Allowing ownership of these things places control of the means of survival in the hands of individuals, and this promotes independence and security (at least for those who own enough of them). Private ownership of life's necessities lessens dependence between individuals, and takes power from the group and gives it to the individual. Private property also promotes privacy. It constitutes a sphere of privacy within which the individual is sovereign and less accountable for her actions. Owning one's own home is an example of all of these: it provides privacy, security, and a limited range of autonomy.

But copyrights and patents are neither necessary nor important for achieving these goals. The right to exclude others from using one's invention or copying one's work of authorship is not essential to one's sovereignty. Preventing a person from personally using her own invention or writing, on the other hand, would seriously threaten her sovereignty. An author's or inventor's sense of worth and dignity requires public acknowledgment by those who use the writing or discovery, but here again, giving the author or inventor the exclusive right to copy or use her intellectual product is not necessary to protect this.

Though patents and copyrights are not directly necessary for survival (as are food and shelter), one could argue that they are indirectly necessary for an individual's security and survival when selling her inventions or writings is a person's sole means of income. In our society, however, most patents and copyrights are owned by institutions (businesses, universities, or governments). Except in unusual cases where individuals have extraordinary bargaining power, prospective employees are required to give the rights to their inventions and works of authorship to their employers as a condition of employment. Independent authors or inventors who earn their living by selling their writings or inventions to others are increasingly rare.[35] Thus arguing that intellectual property promotes individual security makes sense only in a minority of cases. Additionally, there are other ways to ensure the independent intellectual laborer's security and survival besides copyrights and patents (such as public funding of intellectual workers and public domain property status for the results).

Controlling who uses one's invention or writing is not important to one's privacy. As long as there is no requirement to divulge privately created intellectual products (and as long as laws exist to protect people from others taking information they choose not to divulge—as with trade secret laws), the creator's privacy will not be infringed. Trying to justify copyrights and patents on grounds of privacy is highly implausible given that these property rights give the au-

thor or inventor control over certain uses of writings and inventions only after they have been publicly disclosed.

Trade secrets are not defensible on grounds of privacy either. A corporation is not an individual and hence does not have the personal features privacy is intended to protect.[36] Concern for sovereignty counts against trade secrets, for they often directly limit individual autonomy by preventing employees from changing jobs. Through employment contracts, by means of gentlemen's agreements among firms to respect trade secrets by refusing to hire competitors' employees, or simply because of the threat of lawsuits, trade secrets often prevent employees from using their skills and knowledge with other companies in the industry.

Some trade secrets, however, are important to a company's security and survival. If competitors could legally obtain the secret formula for Coke, for example, the Coca-Cola Company would be severely threatened. Similar points hold for copyrights and patents. Without some copyright protection, companies in the publishing, record, and movie industries would be severely threatened by competitors who copy and sell their works at lower prices (which need not reflect development costs). Without patent protection, companies with high research and development costs could be underpriced and driven out of business by competitors who simply mimicked the already developed products. This unfair competition could significantly weaken incentives to invest in innovative techniques and to develop new products.

The next section considers this argument that intellectual property is a necessary incentive for innovation and a requirement for healthy and fair competition. Notice, however, that the concern here is with the security and survival of private companies, not of individuals. Thus one needs to determine whether, and to what extent, the security and survival of privately held companies is a goal worth promoting. That issue turns on the difficult question of what type of economy is most desirable. Given a commitment to capitalism, however, this argument does have some force.

THE UTILITARIAN JUSTIFICATION

The strongest and most widely appealed to justification for intellectual property is a utilitarian argument based on providing incentives. The constitutional justification for patents and copyrights—"to promote the progress of science and the useful arts"[37]—is itself utilitarian. Given the shortcomings of the other arguments for intellectual property, the justifiability of copyrights, patents, and trade secrets depends, in the final analysis, on this utilitarian defense.

According to this argument, promoting the creation of valuable intellectual works requires that intellectual laborers be granted property rights in those works. Without the copyright, patent, and trade secret property protections, adequate incentives for the creation of a socially optimal output of intellectual products would not exist. If competitors could simply copy books, movies, and records, and take one another's inventions and business techniques, there would be no incentive to spend the vast amounts of time, energy, and money necessary to develop these products and techniques. It would be in each firm's self-interest to let others develop products, and then mimic the result. No one would engage in original development, and consequently no new writings, inventions, or business techniques would be developed. To avoid this disastrous result, the argument claims, we must continue to grant intellectual property rights.

Notice that this argument focuses on the users of intellectual products, rather than on the producers. Granting property rights to producers is here seen as necessary to ensure that enough intellectual products (and the countless other goods based on these products) are available to users. The grant of property rights to the producers is a mere means to this end.

This approach is paradoxical. It establishes a right to restrict the current availability and use of intellectual products for the purpose of increasing the production and thus future availability and use of new intellectual products. As economist Joan Robinson says of patents: "A patent is a device to prevent the diffusion of new methods before the original investor has recovered profit adequate to induce the requisite investment. The justification of the patent system is that by slowing down the diffusion of technical progress it ensures that there will be more progress to diffuse. . . . Since it is rooted in a contradiction, there can be no such thing as an ideally beneficial patent system, and it is bound to produce negative results in particular instances, impeding progress unnecessarily even if its general effect is favorable on balance."[38] Although this strategy may work, it is to a certain extent self-defeating. If the justification for intellectual property is utilitarian in this sense, then the search for alternative incentives for the production of intellectual products takes on a good deal of importance. It would be better to employ equally powerful ways to stimulate the production and thus use of intellectual products which did not also restrict their use and availability.

Government support of intellectual work and public ownership of the result may be one such alternative. Governments already fund a great deal of basic research and development, and the results of this research often become public property. Unlike private property rights in the results of intellectual labor, government funding of this labor and public ownership of the result stimulate new inventions and writings without restricting their dissemination and use. Increased government funding of intellectual labor should thus be seriously considered.

This proposal need not involve government control over which research products are to be pursued. Government funding of intellectual labor can be divorced from government control over what is funded. University research is an example. Most of this is supported by public funds, but government control over its content is minor and indirect. Agencies at different governmental levels could distribute funding for intellectual labor with only the most general guidance over content, leaving businesses, universities, and private individuals to decide which projects to pursue.

If the goal of private intellectual property institutions is to maximize the dissemination and use of information, to the extent that they do not achieve this result, these institutions should be modified. The question is not whether copyrights, patents, and trade secrets provide incentives for the production of original works of authorship, inventions, and innovative business techniques. Of course they do. Rather, we should ask the following questions: Do copyrights, patents, and trade secrets increase the availability and use of intellectual products more than they restrict this availability and use? If they do, we must then ask whether they increase the availability and use of intellectual products more than any alternative mechanism would. For example, could better overall results be achieved by shortening the length of copyright and patent grants, or by putting a time limit on trade secrets (and on the restrictions on future employment employers are allowed to demand of employees)? Would eliminating most types of trade secrets entirely and letting patents carry a heavier load produce improved results? Additionally, we must determine whether and to what extent public funding and ownership of intellectual products might be a more efficient means to these results.[39]

We should not expect an across-the-board answer to these questions. For example, the production of movies is more dependent on copyright than is academic writing. Also, patent protection for individual inventors and small beginning firms makes more sense than patent protection for large corporations (which own the majority of patents). It has been argued that patents are not important incentives for the research and innovative activity of large corporations in competitive markets.[40] The short-term advantage a company gets from developing a new product and being the first to put it on the market may be incentive enough.

That patents are conducive to a strong competitive economy is also open to question. Our patent system, originally designed to reward the individual inventor and thereby stimulate invention, may today be used as a device to monopolize industries. It has been suggested that in some cases "the patent position of the big firms makes it almost impossible for new firms to enter the industry"[41] and that patents are frequently bought up in order to suppress competition.[42]

Trade secrets as well can stifle competition, rather than encourage it. If a company can rely on a secret advantage over a competitor, it has no need to develop new technologies to stay ahead. Greater disclosure of certain trade secrets—such as costs and profits of particular product lines—would actually increase competition, rather than decrease it, since with this knowledge firms would then concentrate on one another's most profitable products.[43] Furthermore, as one critic notes, trade secret laws often prevent a former employee "from doing work in just that field for which his training and experience have best prepared him. Indeed, the mobility of engineers and scientists is often severely limited by the reluctance of new firms to hire them for fear of exposing themselves to a lawsuit."[44] Since the movement of skilled workers between companies is a vital mechanism in the growth and spread of technology, in this important respect trade secrets actually slow the dissemination and use of innovative techniques.

These remarks suggest that the justifiability of our intellectual property institutions is not settled by the facile assertion that our system of patents, copyrights, and trade secrets provides necessary incentives for innovation and ensures maximally healthy competitive enterprise. This argument is not as easy to construct as one might at first think; substantial empirical evidence is needed. The above considerations suggest that the evidence might not support this position.

CONCLUSION

Justifying intellectual property is a formidable task. The inadequacies of the traditional justifications for property become more severe when applied to intellectual property. Both the nonexclusive nature of intellectual objects and the presumption against allowing restrictions on the free flow of ideas create special burdens in justifying such property.

We have seen significant shortcomings in the justifications for intellectual property. Natural rights to the fruits of one's labor are not by themselves sufficient to justify copyrights, patents, and trade secrets, though they are relevant to the social decision to create and sustain intellectual property institutions. Although intellectual laborers often deserve rewards for their labor, copyrights, patents, and trade secrets may give the laborer much more or much less than is deserved. Where property rights are not what is desired, they may be wholly inappropriate. The Lockean labor arguments for intellectual property also run afoul of one of Locke's provisos—the prohibition against spoilage or waste. Considerations of sovereignty, security, and privacy are inconclusive justifications for intellectual property as well.

This analysis suggests that the issue turns on considerations of social utility. We must determine whether our current copyright, patent, and trade secret statutes provide the best possible mechanisms for ensuring the availability and widespread dissemination of intellectual works and their resulting products. Public financial support for intellectual laborers and public ownership of intellectual products is an alternative which demands serious consideration. More modest alternatives needing consideration include modifications in the length of intellectual property grants or in the strength and scope of the restrictive rights granted. What the most efficient mechanism for achieving these goals is remains an unresolved empirical question.

This discussion also suggests that copyrights are easier to justify than patents or trade secrets. Patents restrict the actual usage of an idea (in making a physical object), while copyrights restrict only copying an expression of an idea. One can freely use the ideas in a copyrighted book in one's own writing, provided one acknowledges their origin. One cannot freely use the ideas a patented invention represents when developing one's own product. Furthermore, since inventions and business techniques are instruments of production in a way in which expressions of ideas are not, socialist objections to private ownership of the means of production apply to patents and trade secrets far more readily than they do to copyrights. Trade secrets are suspect also because they do not involve the socially beneficial public disclosure which is part of the patent and copyright process. They are additionally problematic to the extent that they involve unacceptable restrictions on employee mobility and technology transfer.

Focusing on the problems of justifying intellectual property is important not because these institutions lack any sort of justification, but because they are not so obviously or easily justified as many people think. We must begin to think more openly and imaginatively about the alternative choices available to us for stimulating and rewarding intellectual labor.

NOTES

1. Ayn Rand, *Capitalism: The Unknown Ideal* (New York: New American Library, 1966), p. 128.
2. See, for example, John Naisbitt's *Megatrends* (New York: Warner Books, 1982), chap 1.

3. See R. Salaman and E. Hettinger, *Policy Implications of Information Technology,* NTIA Report 84–144, U.S. Department of Commerce, 1984, pp. 28–29.

4. For an elaboration of this distinction see Michael Brittin, "Constitutional Fair Use," in *Copyright Law Symposium,* no. 28 (New York: Columbia University Press, 1982), pp. 142ff.

5. For an illuminating discussion of the relationships between style and subject, see Nelson Goodman's *Ways of Worldmaking* (Indianapolis: Hackett, 1978), chap. 11, esp. sec. 2.

6. This is Fritz Machlup's phrase. See his *Production and Distribution of Knowledge in the United States* (Princeton: Princeton University Press, 1962), p. 163.

7. For one discussion of this distinction, see Deborah Johnson, *Computer Ethics* (Englewood Cliffs, N.J.: Prentice-Hall, 1985), pp. 100–101.

8. What can be patented is highly controversial. Consider the recent furor over patenting genetically manipulated animals or patenting computer programs.

9. What constitutes fair use is notoriously bewildering. I doubt that many teachers who sign copyright waivers at local copy shops know whether the packets they make available for their students constitute fair use of copyrighted material.

10. 'Intellectual objects', 'information', and 'ideas' are terms I use to characterize the "objects" of this kind of ownership. Institutions which protect such "objects" include copyright, patent, trade secret, and trademark laws, as well as socially enforced customs (such as sanctions against plagiarism) demanding acknowledgment of the use of another's ideas. What is owned here are objects only in a very abstract sense.

11. There are intellectual objects of which this is not true, namely, information whose usefulness depends precisely on its being known only to a limited group of people. Stock tips and insider trading information are examples.

12. Ease of access is another reason for the widespread piracy of intellectual property. Modern information technologies (such as audio and video recorders, satellite dishes, photocopiers, and computers) make unauthorized taking of intellectual objects far easier than ever before. But it is cynical to submit that this is the major (or the only) reason piracy of information is widespread. It suggests that if people steal physical objects as easily as they can take intellectual ones, they would do so to the same extent. That seems incorrect.

13. For an useful interpretation of Mill's argument, see Robert Ladenson, "Free Expression in the Corporate Workplace," in *Ethical Theory and Business,* 2d ed., ed. T. Beauchamp and N. Bowie (Englewood Cliffs, N.J.: Prentice-Hall, 1983), pp. 162–69.

14. This is one reason the recent dramatic increase in relationships between universities and businesses is so disturbing: it hampers the disclosure of research results.

15. John Snapper makes this point in "Ownership of Computer Programs," available from the Center for the Study of Ethics in the Professions at the Illinois Institute of Technology. See also Sissela Bok, "Trade and Corporate Secrecy," in *Ethical Theory and Business,* p. 176.

16. John Locke, *Second Treatise of Government,* chap. 5. There are several strands to the Lockean argument. See Lawrence Becker, *Property Rights* (London: Routledge and Kegan Paul, 1977), chap. 4, for a detailed analysis of these various versions.

17. Robert Nozick, *Anarchy, State, and Utopia* (New York: Basic Books, 1974), p. 175.

18. Locke, *Second Treatise,* chap. 5, sec. 40.

19. Whether ideas are discovered or created affects the plausibility of the labor argument for intellectual property. "I discovered it, hence it's mine" is much less persuasive than "I made it, hence it's mine." This issue also affects the cogency of the notion that intellectual objects have a value of their own not attributable to intellectual labor. The notion of mixing one's labor with something and thereby adding value to it makes much more sense if the object preexists.

20. I thank the Editors of *Philosophy & Public Affairs* for this way of making the point.

21. A libertarian might respond that although a natural right to the fruits of labor will not by itself justify a right to receive the market value of the resulting product, that right plus the rights of free association and trade would justify it. But mar-

ketplace interaction presupposes a set of social relations, and parties to these relations must jointly agree on their nature. Additionally, market interaction is possible only when property rights have been specified and enforced, and there is no "natural way" to do this (that is, no way independent of complex social judgments concerning the rewards the laborer deserves and the social utilities that will result from granting property rights). The sorts of freedoms one may have in a marketplace are thus socially agreed-upon privileges rather than natural rights.

22. For a discussion of this point, see Joel Feinberg, *Social Philosophy* (Englewood Cliffs, N.J.: Prentice-Hall, 1973), p. 116.
23. Becker, *Property Rights,* p. 46.
24. This is becoming less and less true as the results of intellectual labor are increasingly treated as commodities. University research in biological and computer technologies is an example of this trend.
25. Becker, *Property Rights,* p. 52. In practice, it would be easier to reward laborers as Becker suggests, since the value of the results of labor is easier to determine than the degree of effort expended.
26. This point is made nicely by James Rachels in "What People Deserve," in *Justice and Economic Distribution,* ed. J. Arthur and W. Shaw (Englewood Cliffs, N.J.: Prentice-Hall, 1978), pp. 150–63.
27. Completely ineffectual efforts deserve a reward provided that there were good reasons beforehand for thinking the efforts would pay off. Those whose well-intentioned efforts are silly or stupid should be rewarded the first time only and then counseled to seek advice about the value of their efforts.
28. See John Rawls, *A Theory of Justice* (Cambridge: Harvard University Press, 1971), p. 104: "The assertion that a man deserves the superior character that enables him to make the effort to cultivate his abilities is equally problematic; for his character depends in large part upon fortunate family and social circumstances for which he can claim no credit." See also p. 312: "the effort a person is willing to make is influenced by his natural abilities and skills and the alternatives open to him.

The better endowed are more likely, other things equal, to strive conscientiously."
29. See Rachels, "What People Deserve," pp. 157–58, for a similar resistance to Rawls's determinism.
30. Locke, *Second Treatise,* chap. 5, sec. 27.
31. See Nozick, *Anarchy,* pp. 175–82, and Becker, *Property Rights,* pp. 42–43.
32. Nozick, *Anarchy,* p. 182.
33. Locke, *Second Treatise,* chap. 5, sec. 31.
34. Ronald Dworkin, "Liberalism," in *Public and Private Morality,* ed. Stuart Hampshire (Cambridge: Cambridge University Press, 1978), p. 139.
35. "In the United States about 60 per cent of all patents are assigned to corporations" (Machlup, *Production,* p. 168). This was the case twenty-five years ago, and I assume the percentage is even higher today.
36. Very little (if any) of the sensitive information about individuals that corporations have is information held as a trade secret. For a critical discussion of the attempt to defend corporate society on the basis of privacy see Russell B. Stevenson, Jr., *Corporations and Information* (Baltimore: Johns Hopkins University Press, 1980), chap. 5.
37. U.S. Constitution, sec. 8, para. 8.
38. Quoted in Dorothy Nelkin, *Science as Intellectual Property* (New York: Macmillan, 1984), p. 15.
39. Even supposing our current copyright, patent, and trade secret laws did maximize the availability and use of intellectual products, a thorough utilitarian evaluation would have to weigh all the consequences of these legal rights. For example, the decrease in employee freedom resulting from trade secrets would have to be considered, as would the inequalities in income, wealth, opportunity, and power which result from these socially established and enforced property rights.
40. Machlup, *Production,* pp. 168–69.
41. Ibid., p. 170.
42. See David Noble, *America by Design* (New York: Knopf, 1982), chap. 6.
43. This is Stevenson's point in *Corporations,* p. 11.
44. Ibid., p. 23. More generally, see ibid., chap. 2, for a careful and skeptical treatment of the claim that trade secrets function as incentives.

READING 10.4

Trade Secrets and the Justification of Intellectual Property: A Comment on Hettinger

Lynn Sharp Paine

In a recent article Edwin Hettinger considers various rationales for recognizing intellectual property.[1] According to Hettinger, traditional justifications for property are especially problematic when applied to intellectual property because of its nonexclusive nature.[2] Since possessing and using intellectual objects does not preclude their use and possession by others, there is, he says, a "strong prima facie case against the wisdom of private and exclusive intellectual property rights" (p. 496). There is, moreover, a presumption against allowing restrictions on the free flow of ideas (p. 505).

After rejecting several rationales for intellectual property, Hettinger finds its justification in an instrumental, or "utilitarian,"[3] argument based on incentives (p. 504).[4] Respecting rights in ideas makes sense, he says, if we recognize that the purpose of our intellectual property institutions is to promote the dissemination and use of information (p. 503). To the extent that existing institutions do not achieve this result, they should be modified.[5] Skeptical about the effectiveness of current legal arrangements, Hettinger concludes that we must think more imaginatively about structuring our intellectual property institutions—in particular, patent, copyright, and trade secret law—so that they increase the availability and use of intellectual products. He ventures several possibilities for consideration: eliminating certain forms of trade secret protection, shortening the copyright and

patent protection periods, and public funding and ownership of intellectual objects (p. 503).

Hettinger's approach to justifying our intellectual property institutions rests on several problematic assumptions. It assumes that all of our intellectual property institutions rise or fall together—that the rationale for trade secret protection must be the same as that for patent and copyright protection.[6] This assumption, I will try to show, is unwarranted. While it may be true that these institutions all promote social utility or well-being, the web of rights and duties understood under the general heading of "intellectual property rights" reflects a variety of more specific rationales and objectives.[7]

Second, Hettinger assumes that the rights commonly referred to as "intellectual property rights" are best understood on the model of rights in tangible and real property. He accepts the idea, implicit in the terminology, that intellectual property is like tangible property, only less corporeal (p. 494). This assumption leads him to focus his search for the justification of intellectual property on the traditional arguments for private property. I will try to show the merits of an alternative approach to thinking about rights in ideas—one that does not depend on the analogy with tangible property and that recognizes the role of ideas in defining personality and social relationships.

The combined effect of these assumptions is that trade secret law comes in for particularly serious criticism. It restricts methods of acquiring ideas (p. 496); it encourages secrecy (p. 496); it places unacceptable restrictions on employee mobility and technology transfer (p. 505); it can stifle competition (p. 504); it is more vulnerable to socialist objections (p. 505). In light of these deficiencies, Hettinger recommends that we consider the possibility of "eliminating most types of trade secrets entirely and letting patents carry a heavier load" (p. 503). He believes that trade secrets are undesirable in ways that copyrights and patents are not (p. 497).

Without disagreeing with Hettinger's recommendation that we reevaluate and think more imaginatively about our intellectual property institutions, I believe we should have a clearer understanding of the various rationales for these institutions than is reflected in Hettinger's article. If we unbundle the notion of intellectual property into its constituent rights,[8] we find that different justifications are appropriate for different clusters of rights.[9] In particular, we find that the rights recognized by trade secret law are better understood as rooted in respect for individual liberty, confidential relationships, common morality, and fair competition than in the promotion of innovation and the dissemination of ideas. While trade secret law may serve some of the same ends as patent and copyright law, it has other foundations which are quite distinctive.[10]

In this article, I am primarily concerned with the foundations of trade secret principles. However, my general approach differs from Hettinger's in two fundamental ways. First, it focuses on persons and their relationships rather than property concepts. Second, it reverses the burden of justification, placing it on those who would argue for treating ideas as public goods rather than those who seek to justify private rights in ideas. Within this alternative framework, the central questions are how ideas may be legitimately acquired from others, how disclosure obligations arise, and how ideas become part of the common pool of knowledge. Before turning to Hettinger's criticisms of trade secret principles, it will be useful to think more broadly about the rights of individuals over their undisclosed ideas. This inquiry will illustrate my approach to thinking about rights in ideas and point toward some of the issues at stake in the trade secret area.

THE RIGHT TO CONTROL DISCLOSURE

If a person has any right with respect to her ideas, surely it is the right to control their initial disclosure.[11] A person may decide to keep her ideas to herself, to disclose them to a select few, or to publish them widely. Whether those ideas are best described as views and opinions, plans and intentions, facts and knowledge, or fantasies and inventions is immaterial. While it might in some cases be socially useful for a person to be generous with her ideas, and to share them with others without restraint, there is no general obligation to do so. The world at large has no right to the individual's ideas.[12]

Certainly, specific undertakings, relationships, and even the acquisition of specific information can give rise to disclosure obligations. Typically, these obligations relate to specific types of information pertinent to the relationship or the subject matter of the undertaking. A seller of goods must disclose to potential buyers latent defects and health and safety risks associated with the use of the goods. A person who undertakes to act as an agent for another is obliged to disclose to the principal information she acquires that relates to the subject matter of the agency. Disclosure obligations like these, however, are limited in scope and arise against a general background right to remain silent.

The right to control the initial disclosure of one's ideas is grounded in respect for the individual. Just as a person's sense of herself is intimately connected with the stream of ideas that constitutes consciousness, her public persona is determined in part by the ideas she expresses and the ways she expresses them. To require public disclosure of one's ideas and thoughts—whether about "personal" or other matters—would distort one's personality and, no doubt, alter the nature of one's thoughts.[13] It would seriously interfere with the liberty to live according to one's chosen life plans. This sort of thought control would be an invasion of privacy and personality of the most intrusive sort. If anything is private, one's undisclosed thoughts surely are.[14]

Respect for autonomy, respect for personality, and respect for privacy lie behind the right to control disclosure of one's ideas, but the right is also part of what we mean by freedom of thought and expression. Frequently equated with a right to speak, freedom of expression also implies a prima facie right not to express one's ideas or to share them only with those we love or trust or with whom we wish to share.[15] These observations explain the peculiarity of setting up the free flow of ideas and unrestricted access as an ideal. Rights in ideas are desirable insofar as they strengthen our sense of individuality and undergird our social relationships. This suggests a framework quite different from Hettinger's, one that begins with a strong presumption against requiring disclosure and is in favor of protecting people against unconsented-to acquisitions of their ideas.[16] This is the moral backdrop against which trade secrecy law is best understood.

CONSEQUENCES OF DISCLOSURE

Within this framework, a critical question is how people lose rights in their ideas. Are these rights forfeited when people express their ideas or communicate them to others? Surely this depends on the circumstances of disclosure. Writing down ideas in a daily journal to oneself or recording them on a cassette should not entail such a forfeiture. Considerations of individual autonomy, privacy, and personality require that such expressions not be deemed available for use by others who may gain access to them.[17]

Likewise, communicating an idea in confidence to another should not render it part of the common pool of knowledge. Respect for the individual's desire to limit the dissemination of the idea is at stake, but so is respect for the relationship of trust and confidence among the persons involved. If A confides in B under circumstances in which B gives A reason to believe she will respect the confidence, A should be able to trust that B will not reveal or misuse the confidence and that third parties who may intentionally or accidentally discover the confidence will respect it.[18]

The alternative possibility is that by revealing her ideas to B, A is deemed to forfeit any right to control their use or communication. This principle is objectionable for a couple of reasons. First, it would most certainly increase reluctance to share ideas since our disclosure decisions are strongly influenced by the audience we anticipate. If we could not select our audience, that is, if the choices were only between keeping ideas to ourselves and sharing them with the world at large, many ideas would remain unexpressed, to the detriment of individual health as well as the general good.

Second, the principle would pose an impediment to the formation and sustenance of various types of cooperative relationships—relationships of love and friendship, as well as relationships forged for specific purposes such as education, medical care, or business. It might be thought that only ideas of an intimate or personal nature are important in this regard. But it is not only "personal" relationships, but cooperative relationships of all types, that are at stake. Shared knowledge and information of varying types are central to work relationships and communities—academic departments and disciplines, firms, teams—as well as other organizations. The possession of common ideas and information, to the exclusion of those outside the relationship or group, contributes to the group's self-definition and to the individual's sense of belonging. By permitting and protecting the sharing of confidences, trade secret principles, among other institutions, permit "special communities of knowledge" which nurture the social bonds and cooperative efforts through which we express our individuality and pursue common purposes.[19]

Of course, by disclosing her idea to B, A runs the risk that B or anyone else who learns about the idea may use it or share it further. But if B has agreed to respect the confidence, either explicitly or by participating in a relationship in which confidence is normally expected, she has a prima facie obligation not to disclose the information to which she is privy.[20] Institutions that give A a remedy against third parties who appropriate ideas shared in confidence reduce the risk that A's ideas will become public resources if she shares them with B. Such institutions thereby support confidential relationships and the cooperative undertakings that depend on them.

Yet another situation in which disclosure should not be regarded as a license for general use is the case of disclosures made as a result of deceit or insincere promises. Suppose A is an entrepreneur who has created an unusual software program with substantial sales potential. Another party, B, pretending to be a potential customer, questions A at great length about the code and other details of her program. A's disclosures are not intended to be, and should not be deemed, a contribution to the general pool of knowledge, nor should B be permitted to use A's ideas.[21] Respect for A's right to disclose her ideas requires that involuntary disclosures—such as those based on deceit, coercion, and theft of documents containing expressions of those ideas—not be regarded as forfeitures to the common pool of knowledge and information. In recognition of A's right to control disclosure of her ideas and to discourage appropriation of her ideas against her wishes, we might expect our institutions to provide A with a remedy against these sorts of appropriation. Trade secret law provides such a remedy.

Competitive fairness is also at stake if B is in competition with A. Besides having violated standards of common morality in using deceit to gain access to A's ideas, B is in a position to exploit those ideas in the marketplace without having contributed to the cost of their development. B can sell her version of the software more cheaply since she enjoys a substantial cost advantage compared to A, who may have invested a great deal of time and money in developing the software. Fairness in a competitive economy requires some limitations on the rights of firms to use ideas developed by others. In a system based on effort, it is both unfair and ultimately self-defeating to permit firms to have a free ride on the efforts of their competitors.[22]

PROBLEMATIC ISSUES

Respect for personal control over the disclosure of ideas, respect for confidential relationships, common morality, and fair competition all point toward recognizing certain rights in ideas. Difficult questions will arise within this system of rights. If A is not an individual but an organization or group, should A have the same rights and remedies against B or third parties who use or communicate information shared with B in confidence? For example, suppose A is a corporation that hires an employee, B, to develop a marketing plan. If other employees of A reveal in confidence to B information they have created or assembled, should A be able to restrain B from using this information to benefit herself (at A's expense)? Does it matter if A is a two-person corporation or a corporation with 100,000 employees? What if A is a social club or a private school?

Hettinger seems to assume that corporate A's should not have such rights—on the grounds that they might restrict B's employment possibilities. It is certainly true that giving A a right against B if she reveals information communication to her in confidence could rule out certain jobs for B. However, the alternative rule—that corporate A's should have no rights in ideas they reveal in confidence to others—has problems as well.

One problem involves trust. If our institutions do not give corporate A's certain rights in ideas they reveal in confidence to employees, A's will seek other means of ensuring that competitively valuable ideas are protected. They may contract individually with employees for those rights, and if our legal institutions do not uphold those contracts, employers will seek to hire individuals in whom they have personal trust. Hiring would probably become more dependent on family and personal relationships and there would be fewer opportunities for the less well connected. Institutional rules giving corporate A's rights against employees who reveal or use information given to them in confidence are a substitute for personal bonds of trust. While such rules are not cost-free and may have some morally undesirable consequences, they help sustain cooperative efforts and contribute to more open hiring practices.

Contrary to Hettinger's suggestion, giving corporate A's rights in the ideas they reveal in confidence to others does not always benefit the strong at the expense of the weak, or the large corporation at the expense of the individual, although this is surely sometimes the case.[23] Imagine three entrepreneurs who wish to expand their highly successful cookie business. A venture capitalist interested in financing the expansion naturally wishes to know the details of the operation—including the prized cookie recipe—before putting up capital. After examining the recipe, however, he decides that it would be more profitable for him to sell the recipe to CookieCo, a multinational food company, and to invest his capital elsewhere. Without money and rights to prevent others from using the recipe, the corporate entrepreneurs are very likely out of business. CookieCo, which can manufacture and sell the cookies much more cheaply, will undoubtedly find that most of the entrepreneurs' customers are quite happy to buy the same cookies for less at their local supermarket.

NON-PROPERTY FOUNDATIONS OF TRADE SECRET LAW

To a large extent, the rights and remedies mentioned in the preceding discussion are those recognized by trade secret law. As this discussion showed, the concept of property is not necessary to justify these rights. Trade secret law protects against certain methods of appropriating the confidential and commercially valuable ideas of others. It affords a remedy to those whose commercially valuable secrets are acquired by misrepresentation, theft, bribery, breach or inducement of a breach of confidence, espionage, or other improper means.[24] Although the roots of trade secret principles have been variously located, respect for voluntary disclosure decisions and respect for confidential relationships provide the best account of the pattern of permitted and prohibited appropriations and use of ideas.[25] As Justice Oliver Wendell Holmes noted in a 1917 trade secret case, "The property may be denied but the confidence cannot be."[26] Trade secret law can also be seen as enforcing ordinary standards of morality in commercial relationships, thus ensuring some consistency with general social morality.[27]

It may well be true, as Hettinger and others have claimed, that the availability of trade secret protection provides an incentive for intellectual labor and the development of ideas. The knowledge that they have legal rights against those who "misappropriate" their ideas may encourage people to invest large amounts of time and money in exploring and developing ideas. However, the claim that trade secret protection promotes invention is quite different from the claim that it is grounded in or justified by this tendency. Even if common law trade secret rights did not promote intellectual labor or increase the dissemination and use of information, there would still be reasons to recognize those rights. Respect for people's voluntary disclosure decisions, respect for confidential relationships, standards of common morality, and fair competition would still point in that direction.

Moreover, promoting the development of ideas cannot be the whole story behind trade secret principles, since protection is often accorded to information such as customer data or cost and pricing information kept in the ordinary course of doing business. While businesses may need incentives to engage in costly research and development, they would certainly keep track of their customers and costs in any event. The rationale for giving protection to such information must be other than promoting the invention, dissemination, and use of ideas. By the same token, trade secret principles do not prohibit the use of ideas acquired by studying products available in the marketplace. If the central policy behind trade secret protection were the promotion of invention, one might expect that trade secret law, like patent law, which was explicitly fashioned to encourage invention, would protect innovators from imitators.

The fact that Congress has enacted patent laws giving inventors a limited monopoly in exchange for disclosure of their ideas without at the same time eliminating state trade secret law may be a further indication that trade secret and patent protection rest on different grounds.[28] By offering a limited monopoly in exchange for disclosure, the patent laws implicitly recognize the more fundamental right not to disclose one's ideas at all or to disclose them in confidence to others.[29]

REASSESSING HETTINGER'S CRITICISMS OF TRADE SECRET LAW

If we see trade secret law as grounded in respect for voluntary disclosure, confidential relationships, common morality, and fair competition, the force of Hettinger's criticisms diminishes somewhat. The problems he cites appear not merely in their negative light as detracting from an ideal "free flow of ideas," but in their positive role as promoting other important values.

a. Restrictions on Acquiring Ideas Hettinger is critical, for example, of the fact that trade secret law restricts methods of acquiring ideas. But the prohibited means of acquisition—misrepresentation, theft, bribery, breach of confidence, and espionage—all reflect general social morality. Lifting these restrictions would undoubtedly contribute to the erosion of important values outside the commercial context.

How much trade secrecy laws inhibit the development and spread of ideas is also open to debate. Hettinger and others have claimed that trade secrecy is a serious impediment to innovation and dissemination because the period of permitted secrecy is unlimited. Yet, given the fact that trade secret law offers no protection for ideas acquired by examining or reverse-engineering products in the marketplace, it would appear rather difficult to maintain technical secrets embodied in those products while still exploiting their market potential. A standard example used to illustrate the problem of perpetual secrecy, the Coke formula, seems insufficient to establish that this is a serious problem. Despite the complexity of modern technology, successful reverse-engineering is common. Moreover, similar technical advances are frequently made by researchers working independently. Trade secret law poses no impediment in either case. Independent discoverers are free to exploit their ideas even if they are similar to those of others.

As for nontechnical information such as marketing plans and business strategies, the period of secrecy is necessarily rather short since implementation entails disclosure. Competitor intelligence specialists claim that most of the information needed to understand what competitors are doing is publicly available.[30] All of these considerations suggest that trade secret principles are not such a serious impediment to the dissemination of information.

b. Competitive Effects Hettinger complains that trade secret principles stifle competition. Assessing this claim is very difficult. On one hand, it may seem that prices would be lower if firms were permitted to obtain cost or other market advantages by using prohibited means to acquire protected ideas from others. Competitor access to the Coke formula would most likely put downward pressure on the price of "the real thing." Yet, it is also reasonable to assume that the law keeps prices down by reducing the cost of self-protection. By giving some assurance that commercially valuable secrets will be protected, the law shields firms from having to bear the full costs of protection. It is very hard to predict what would happen to prices if trade secret protection were eliminated. Self-protection would be more costly and would tend to drive prices up, while increased competition would work in the opposite direction. There would surely be important differences in morale and productivity. Moreover, as noted, any price reductions for consumers would come at a cost to the basic moral standards of society if intelligence-gathering by bribery, misrepresentation, and espionage were permitted.

c. Restrictions on Employee Mobility

Among Hettinger's criticisms of trade secret law, the most serious relate to restrictions on employee mobility. In practice, employers often attempt to protect information by overrestricting the postemployment opportunities of employees. Three important factors contribute to this tendency: vagueness about which information is confidential; disagreement about the proper allocation of rights to ideas generated by employees using their employers' resources; and conceptual difficulties in distinguishing general knowledge and employer-specific knowledge acquired on the job. Courts, however, are already doing what Hettinger recommends, namely, limiting the restrictions that employers can place on future employment in the name of protecting ideas.[31] Although the balance between employer and employee interests is a delicate one not always equitably struck, the solution of eliminating trade secret protection altogether is overboard and undesirable, considering the other objectives at stake.

d. Hypothetical Alternatives

Hettinger's discussion of our intellectual property institutions reflects an assumption that greater openness and sharing would occur if we eliminated trade secret protection. He argues that trade secret principles encourage secrecy. He speaks of the "free flow of ideas" as the ideal that would obtain in the absence of our intellectual property institutions. This supposition strikes me as highly unlikely. People keep secrets and establish confidential relationships for a variety of reasons that are quite independent of any legal protection these secrets might have. The psychology and sociology of secrets have been explored by others. Although much economic theory is premised on complete information, secrecy and private information are at the heart of day-to-day competition in the marketplace.

In the absence of something like trade secret principles, I would expect not a free flow of ideas but greater efforts to protect information through contracts, management systems designed to limit information access, security equipment, and electronic counterintelligence devices. I would also expect stepped-up efforts to acquire intelligence from others through espionage, bribery, misrepresentation, and other unsavory means. By providing some assurance that information can be shared in confidence and by protecting against unethical methods of extracting information and undermining confidentiality, trade secret principles promote cooperation and security, two important conditions for intellectual endeavor. In this way, trade secret principles may ultimately promote intellectual effort by limiting information flow.

THE BURDEN OF JUSTIFICATION

We may begin thinking about information rights, as Hettinger does, by treating all ideas as part of a common pool and then deciding whether and how to allocate to individuals rights to items in the pool. Within this framework, ideas are conceived on the model of tangible property.[32] Just as, in the absence of social institutions, we enter the world with no particular relationship to its tangible assets or natural resources, we have no particular claim on the world's ideas. In this scheme, as Hettinger asserts, the "burden of justification is very much on those who would restrict the maximal use of intellectual objects" (p. 496).

Alternatively, we may begin, as I do, by thinking of ideas in relation to their originators, who may or may not share their ideas with specific others or contribute then to the common pool. This approach treats ideas as central to personality and the social world individuals construct for themselves. Ideas are not, in the first instance, freely available natural resources. They originate with people, and it is the connections among people, their ideas, and their relationships with others that provides a baseline for discussing rights in ideas. Within this conception, the burden of justification is on those who would argue for disclosure obligations and general access to ideas.

The structure of specific rights that emerges from these different frameworks depends not only on where the burden of justification is located, but also on how easily it can be discharged.[33] It is unclear how compelling a case is required to overcome the burden Hettinger sets up and, consequently, difficult to gauge the depth of my disagreement with him.[34] Since Hettinger does not consider the rationales for trade secret principles discussed here, it is not clear whether he would dismiss them altogether, find them insufficiently weighty to override the presumption he sets up, or agree that they satisfy the burden of justification.

One might suspect, however, from the absence of discussion of the personal and social dimension of rights in ideas that Hettinger does not think them terribly important, and that his decision to put the burden of justification on those who argue for rights in ideas reflects a fairly strong commitment to openness. On the assumption that our alternative starting points reflect seriously held substantive views (they are not just procedural devices to get the argument started) and that both frameworks require strong reasons to overcome the initial presumption, the resulting rights and obligations are likely to be quite different in areas where neither confiden-

tiality nor openness is critical to immediate human needs. Indeed, trade secrecy law is an area where these different starting points would be likely to surface.

The key question to ask about these competing frameworks is which is backed by stronger reasons. My opposition to Hettinger's allocation of the burden of justification rests on my rejection of his conception of ideas as natural resources and on different views of how the world would look in the absence of our intellectual property institutions. In contrast, my starting point acknowledges the importance of ideas to our sense of ourselves and the communities (including work communities) of which we are a part. It is also more compatible with the way we commonly talk about ideas. Our talk about disclosure obligations presupposes a general background right not to reveal ideas. If it were otherwise, we would speak of concealment rights. To use the logically interesting feature of nonexclusiveness as a starting point for moral reasoning about rights in ideas seem wholly arbitrary.

CONCLUSION

Knives, forks, and spoons are all designed to help us eat. In a sense, however, the essential function of these tools is to help us cut, since without utensils, we could still consume most foods with our hands. One might be tempted to say that since cutting is the essential function of eating utensils, forks and spoons should be designed to facilitate cutting. One might even say that insofar as forks and spoons do not facilitate cutting, they should be redesigned. Such a modification, however, would rob us of valuable specialized eating instruments.

Hettinger's train of thought strikes me as very similar. He purports to examine the justification of our various intellectual property institutions. However, he settles on a justification that really only fits patent and, arguably, copyright institutions. He then suggests that other intellectual property rights be assessed against the justification he proposes and redesigned insofar as they are found wanting. In particular, he suggests that trade secret principles be modified to look more like patent principles. Hettinger fails to appreciate the various rationales behind the rights and duties understood under the heading "intellectual property," especially those recognized by trade secret law.

I agree with Hettinger that our intellectual property institutions need a fresh look from a utilitarian perspective.[35] The seventeen-year monopoly granted through patents is anachronistic given the pace of technological development today. We need to think about the appropriate balance between employer and employee rights in ideas developed jointly. Solutions to the problem of the unauthorized copying of software may be found in alternative pricing structures rather than in fundamental modifications of our institutions. Public interest considerations could be advanced for opening access to privately held information in a variety of areas. As we consider these specific questions, however, I would urge that we keep firmly in mind the variety of objectives that intellectual property institutions have traditionally served.[36] If, following Hettinger's advice, we single-mindedly reshape these institutions to maximize the short-term dissemination and use of ideas, we run the risk of subverting the other ends these institutions serve.

NOTES

1. Edwin C. Hettinger, "Justifying Intellectual Property," *Philosophy & Public Affairs* 18, no. 1 (Winter 1989): 31–52. Subsequent page references to this article appear in parentheses in the text.
2. Thomas Jefferson agrees. See Jefferson's letter to Isaac McPherson, 13 August 1813, in *The Founders' Constitution,* ed. Philip B. Kurland and Ralph Lerner (Chicago: University of Chicago Press, 1987), 3:42.
3. Hettinger uses the term *utilitarian* in a very narrow sense to refer to a justification in terms of

maximizing the use and dissemination of information. Some utilitarians might see intellectual property institutions as promoting objectives other than information dissemination. My discussion of the roots of trade secret principles is perfectly consistent with a utilitarian justification of those principles. Indeed, a utilitarian could argue (as many economists do) that giving people certain rights in ideas they generate through their own labor advances social well-being by promoting innovation. See, e.g., Robert U. Ayres, "Technological Protection and Piracy: Some Implications for Policy," *Technological Forecasting and Social Change* 30 (1986): 5–18.

4. In Hettinger's paper and in mine, the terms *justification, goal, purpose, rationale,* and *objective* are used loosely and somewhat interchangeably. But, of course, identifying the purpose or goal of our intellectual property institutions does not automatically justify them. Some further legitimating idea or ultimate good, such as the general welfare or individual liberty, must be invoked. A difficulty with Hettinger's argument is that he identifies an objective for our intellectual property institutions—promoting the use and dissemination of ideas—and concludes that he has justified them. However, unless maximizing the use and dissemination of ideas is an intrinsic good, we would expect a further step in the argument linking this objective to an ultimate good. Hettinger may think this step can be made or is self-evident from his terminology. However, it is not clear whether he calls his justification "utilitarian" because of its consequentialist form or because he means to appeal to social well-being or some particular good he associates with utilitarianism.

5. Hettinger seems to think that he has provided a clear-cut objective against which to measure the effectiveness of our intellectual property institutions. Yet, a set of institutions that maximized the "dissemination and use of information" (p. 503) would not necessarily be most effective at "promoting the creation of valuable intellectual works" or promoting "'the progress of science and the useful arts'" (p. 502). A society might be quite successful at disseminating information, but rather mediocre at creating valuable intellectual works.

There is an inevitable tension between the objectives of innovation and dissemination. The same tension is present in other areas of law concerned with rights in information—insider trading, for example. For discussion of this tension, see Frank H. Easterbrook, "Insider Trading, Secret Agents, Evidentiary Privileges, and the Production of Information," *1981 Supreme Court Review,* p. 309. While we struggle to piece together a system of information rights that gives due consideration to both objectives, we must be wary of the notion that there is a single optimal allocation of rights.

Indeed, the very idea of a "socially optimal output of intellectual products" (p. 502) is embarrassingly imprecise. What is a socially optimal output of poems, novels, computer programs, movies, cassette recordings, production processes, formulations of matter, stock tips, business strategies, etc.? How we allocate rights in ideas may affect the quality and kinds of intellectual products that are produced as well as their quantity and dissemination. Hettinger seems concerned primarily with quantity (p. 502). The use of general terms like *intellectual product* and *socially optimal output* obscures the complexity of the empirical assessment that Hettinger proposes.

6. Hettinger mentions trademark as another of our intellectual property institutions, along with our social sanction on plagiarism, but his central discussion focuses on copyright, patent, and trade secret concepts. Neither trademark principles nor the prohibition on plagiarism fits comfortably with his justification in terms of increasing the dissemination and use of ideas. Both are more closely related to giving recognition to the source or originator of ideas and products.

7. It may be helpful to think of two levels of justification: (1) an intermediate level consisting of objectives, purposes, reasons, and explanations for an institution or practice; and (2) an ultimate level linking those objectives and purposes to our most basic legitimating ideas such as the general good or individual liberty. Philosophers generally tend to be concerned with the ultimate level of justification while policymakers and judges more frequently operate at the intermediate level. Hettinger has, I think, mistaken an intermediate-level justification of patents and copyrights (pro-

moting the dissemination and use of ideas) for an ultimate justification of intellectual property institutions.

8. Hettinger, of course, recognizes that various rights are involved. He speaks of rights to possess, to personally use, to prevent others from using, to publish, and to receive the market value of one's ideas. And he notes that one might have a natural right to possess and personally use one's ideas even if one might not have a natural right to prevent others from copying them (p. 499). But he does not consider the possibility that the different rights involved in our concept of intellectual property may rest on quite varied foundations, some firmer than others.

9. It is generally accepted that the concept of property is best understood as a "bundle of rights." Just as the bundle of rights involved in home ownership differs substantially from the bundle of rights associated with stock ownership, the bundle of rights involved in patent protection differs from the bundle of rights involved in trade secret protection.

10. Today we commonly speak of copyright protection as providing incentives for intellectual effort, while at the same time ensuring widespread dissemination of ideas. As Hettinger notes, the effectiveness of copyright protection in achieving these aims may depend partly on the period of the copyright grant. Historically, at least before the first English copyright act, the famous 1710 Act of Anne, it appears that the dissemination of ideas was not so central. The common law gave the author an exclusive first right of printing or publishing her manuscript on the grounds that she was entitled to the product of her labor. The common law's position on the author's right to prohibit subsequent publication was less clear. See generally Wheaton v. Peters, 8 Pet. 591 (1834), reprinted in *The Founders' Constitution* 3:44–60.

11. Hettinger recognizes a right not to divulge privately created intellectual products (p. 502), but he does not fit this right into his discussion. If the right is taken seriously, however, it will, I believe, undermine Hettinger's own conclusions.

12. We would hope that the right to control disclosure would be exercised in a morally responsible way and that, for example, people with socially

useful ideas would share them and that some types of harmful ideas would be withheld. But the potential social benefits of certain disclosures cannot justify a general requirement that ideas be disclosed.

13. Here, I am using the term *personal* to refer to ideas about intimate matters, such as sexual behavior.

14. The right to control disclosure of one's thoughts might be thought to be no more than a reflection of technical limitations. Enforcing a general disclosure requirement presupposes some way of identifying the undisclosed thoughts of others. Currently, we do not have the technology to do this. But even if we did—or especially if we did—respect for the individual would preclude any form of monitoring people's thoughts.

15. On the relation between privacy and intimate relationships, see Charles Fried, "Privacy," *Yale Law Journal 77* (1968): 475–93. Below, I will argue that confidentiality is central to other types of cooperative relationships as well.

16. Whether the presumption is overcome will depend on the importance of the objectives served by disclosure, and the degree of violence done to the individual or the relationship at stake.

17. Technically, of course, others have access to ideas that have been expressed whereas they do not have access to undisclosed thoughts. But ease of access is not the criterion for propriety of access.

18. This is the fundamental principle behind the prohibition on insider trading.

19. The phrase "special communities of knowledge" comes from Kim Lane Scheppele, *Legal Secrets* (Chicago: University of Chicago Press, 1988), p. 14.

20. In practice, this prima facie obligation may sometimes be overriden when it conflicts with other obligations, e.g., the obligation to prevent harm to a third party.

21. An actual case similar to this was litigated in Pennsylvania. See Continental Data Systems, Inc. v. Exxon Corporation, 638 F. Supp. 432 (D.C.E.D. Pa. 1986).

22. For the view that fair and honest business competition is the central policy underlying trade secret protection, see Ramon A. Klitzke, "Trade Secrets: Important Quasi-Property Rights," *Business Lawyer* 41 (1986): 557–70.

23. It appears that Hettinger is using the term *private company* in contrast to individuals rather than to public companies—those whose shares are sold to the public on national stock exchanges. If one wishes to protect individuals, however, it might be more important to distinguish small, privately held companies from large, publicly held ones than to distinguish individuals from companies. Many individuals, however, are dependent on large, publicly held companies for their livelihood.

24. *Uniform Trade Secrets Act with 1985 Amendments,* sec. 1, in *Uniform Laws Annotated,* vol. 14 (1980 with 1988 Pocket Part). The Uniform Trade Secrets Act seeks to codify and standardize the common law principles of trade secret law as they have developed in different jurisdictions.

25. See Klitzke, "Trade Secrets." Different theories of justification are discussed in Ridsdale Ellis, *Trade Secrets* (New York: Baker, Voorhis, 1953). Kim Lane Scheppele is another commentator favoring the view that breach of confidence is what trade secret cases are all about. See *Legal Secrets,* p. 241. In their famous article on privacy, Warren and Brandeis find the roots of trade secret principles in the right to privacy. Samuel D. Warren and Louis D. Brandeis, *Harvard Law Review* 4 (1890): 212.

26. E. I. DuPont de Nemours Powder Co. v. Masland, 244 U.S. 100 (1917).

27. One commentator has said, "The desire to reinforce 'good faith and honest, fair dealing' in business is the mother of the law of trade secrets." Russell B. Stevenson, Jr., *Corporations and Information* (Baltimore: Johns Hopkins University Press, 1980), p. 19.

28. Support for this interpretation is found in Justice Thurgood Marshall's concurring opinion in Kewanee Oil Co. v. Bicron Corp., 416 U.S. 470, 494 (1974). The court held that the federal patent laws do not preempt state trade secret laws.

29. Congress may have realized that trying to bring about more openness by eliminating trade secret protection, even with the added attraction of a limited monopoly for inventions that qualify for patent protection, would be inconsistent with fundamental moral notions such as respect for confidential relationships, and would probably not have worked anyway.

30. See, e.g., the statement of a manager of a competitor surveillance group quoted in Jerry L. Wall, "What the Competition Is Doing: Your Need to Know," *Harvard Business Review* 52 (November-December 1974): 34. See generally Leonard M. Fuld, *Competitor Intelligence: How to Get It—How to Use It* (New York: John Wiley and Sons, 1985).

31. See, e.g., John Burgess, "Unlocking Corporate Shackles," *Washington Business,* 11 December 1989, p. 1.

32. Hettinger speaks of ideas as objects, and of rights in ideas as comparable to water or mineral rights. Indeed, according to Hettinger, the difficulty in justifying intellectual property rights arises because ideas are not in all respects like tangible property, which he thinks is more easily justified.

33. The Editors of *Philosophy & Public Affairs* encouraged me to address this point.

34. His argument from maximizing the production and dissemination of ideas suggests that the presumption in favor of free ideas is not terribly strong: it can be overridden by identifying some reasonable objective likely to be served by assigning exclusive rights.

35. That is, we should look at the effects of these institutions on social well-being in general and select the institutions that are best on the whole.

36. A utilitarian assessment will also include consideration of the various interests that would be affected by alternative allocations of intellectual property rights. For example, denying authors copyright in their works may increase the power and profit of publishers and further impair the ability of lesser-known writers to find publication outlets. One scholar has concluded that America's failure to recognize the copyrights of aliens before 1891 stunted the development of native literature. For fifty years before the passage of the Platt-Simmonds Act, publishing interests vigorously and successfully opposed recognition of international copyright. This is understandable since the works of well-known British authors were available to publishers free of charge. Publishers were not terribly concerned with the artistic integrity of these works. They sometimes substituted alternative endings, mixed the works of different authors, and edited as economically necessary. There were few reasons to take the risks involved in publishing the works of unknown and untested American writers who might insist on artistic integrity. See generally Aubert J. Clark, *The Movement for International Copyright in Nineteenth Century America* (Westport, Conn.: Greenwood Press, 1973).